the
UNIVERSITY
of
GREENWICH

PESTICIDES AND ALTERNATIVES:
Innovative chemical and biological approaches to pest control

In the conference logo on the front cover the two hornets arranged about a honeycomb are a gold pendant from Mallia 1700–1550 B.C. (Heraklion Museum)

PESTICIDES AND ALTERNATIVES:

Innovative Chemical and Biological Approaches to Pest Control

Proceedings of an International Conference
Orthodox Academy of Crete Kolymbari, Crete, Greece
4–8 September 1989

Edited by

JOHN E. CASIDA

Pesticide Chemistry and Toxicology Laboratory
Department of Entomological Sciences
University of California, Berkeley, CA USA

1990

ELSEVIER SCIENCE PUBLISHERS
Amsterdam / Oxford / New York

ISBN 0 444 81355 1

This book is printed on acid-free paper.

Published by:
Elsevier Science Publishers B.V.
(Biomedical Division)
P.O. Box 211
1000 AE Amsterdam
The Netherlands

Sole distributors for the USA and Canada:
Elsevier Science Publishing Company Inc.
655 Avenue of the Americas
New York, NY 10010
USA

Library of Congress Cataloging-in-Publication Data

Pesticides and alternatives : innovative chemical and biological
   approaches to pest control : proceedings of an international
   conference, Orthodox Academy of Crete, Kolymbari, Crete, Greece,
   Sept. 4-8, 1989 / edited by John E. Casida.
       p.   cm.
   ISBN 0-444-81355-1 (alk. paper)
   1. Pesticides--Congresses. 2. Natural pesticides--Congresses.
   3. Pests--Biological control--Congresses.   I. Casida, John E.,
   1929-   .
   SB950.93.P468   1990
   632'.95--dc20   90-33541
                                                              CIP

Printed in The Netherlands

PREFACE

'Innovative Chemical and Biological Approaches to Pest Control' served as the theme for an international conference at the Orthodox Academy of Crete in Kolymbari, Crete, Greece for the period of September 4 to 8, 1989. About 120 scientists from 25 countries contributed lectures, posters and fruitful discussions in the format of position statements and current reviews of the progress and prospects and the risks and benefits in using 'Pesticides and Alternatives' for pest control. One goal of the meeting was to promote dialogue and understanding between biologists and chemists relative to pest problems involving insects, plant pathogens, and weeds. Another was to update each participant on progress in the science and technology of pest control. The problems and solutions are multidisciplinary and complex as clearly illustrated by the lectures and posters presented at the Kolymbari Conference.

Nickos Psylakis, the Secretary General of the Greek Ministry of Agriculture, opened the Symposium. As a scientist and administrator, he has had a profound influence on enhancing agricultural production in the area of Chania, of Crete as a whole, and more recently for all of Greece.

Alexandros Papaderos, the Director of the Orthodox Academy of Crete, addressed the Conference on the topic 'Dissemination of Knowledge: a Main Objective of the Orthodox Academy of Crete'. He pointed out that special priority in the activities for this institution is given to issues related to development, technology and scientific fields such as biology and genetics. He also noted the environmental concerns of the Orthodox Academy of Crete by quoting from the European Ecumenical Assembly report *Peace With Justice* (May 1989, Basel, Switzerland): 'It is already clear that irreparable damage has been inflicted on nature by humanity.' 'Environmental problems cannot be solved by governments on a national level. An international ecological order is required.' Thus, the goal of this conference was to encourage the growing spirit of cooperation, mutual respect and solidarity among scientists from all over the world.

Fifty-five contributions from the Symposium on 'Pesticides and Alternatives' are included in this volume. They are organized into an introductory section on pesticide chemistry and toxicology for papers spanning several areas of pest control followed by individual treatments of control strategies for insects, plant pathogens and weeds. More emphasis is given to insects than to other pests in part because more approaches have been used experimentally or practically in their control.

From a personal standpoint, it was a great pleasure to serve as chairman of the organizing committee and editor of the proceedings. Friends and colleagues came together to discuss topics of mutual interest and international importance.

Cooperative programs and personal friendships were reaffirmed and expanded. We met with a common goal of improving the effectiveness and safety of pest control procedures. Considerable progress has been made in 'Innovative Chemical and Biological Approaches to Pest Control'. Judge for yourself from the contributions in this volume.

John E. Casida, Editor

Kolymbari, Crete, September 1989
Berkeley, California, January 1990

ACKNOWLEDGEMENTS

The Organizing Committee for the Conference consisted of ten scientists from five different countries as follows:

Professor John E. Casida (Chairman)
Pesticide Chemistry and Toxicology Laboratory, Department of Entomological Sciences, University of California, Berkeley, California 94720, U.S.A.
Dr. Aristides P. Economopoulos
Entomology Unit, International Atomic Energy Agency Laboratories, A-2444, Seibersdorf, Austria.
Professor Spyros G. Georgopoulos
Agricultural Department, Lapapharm Inc., 73 Menandrou Street, 10437 Athens, Greece.
Professor Fotis C. Kafatos
Department of Biology, University of Crete, Heraklion, Crete, Greece, and Department of Cellular and Developmental Biology, Harvard University, Cambridge, Massachusetts, 02138, U.S.A.
Professor Michael Loukas
Department of Genetics, Agricultural University of Athens, Iera odos 75, Votanikos, Athens, Greece.
Professor Sooichi Matsunaka
Pesticide Science Laboratory, Faculty of Agriculture, Kobe University, Kobe 657, Japan.
Dr. Alan S. Robinson
Institute of Molecular Biology and Biotechnology, Heraklion 71110, Crete, Greece.
Dr. Robert F. Toia
Pesticide Chemistry and Toxicology Laboratory, Department of Entomological Sciences, University of California, Berkeley, California 94720, U.S.A.
Professor Minos E. Tzanakakis
Laboratory of Applied Zoology and Parasitology, Faculty of Agriculture, University of Thessaloniki, 54006 Thessaloniki, Greece.
Dr. Günther Voss
Agricultural Division, CIBA-GEIGY, Limited, CH-4002 Basle, Switzerland.

The success of this conference was due to the consistent efforts and continuous optimism of each of these individuals, and particularly Dr. Economopoulos.
The International Conference on Pesticides and Alternatives and the publication of the proceedings were sponsored and supported by the following organizations:

Ministry of Agriculture of Greece
Ministry of Culture and Science of Greece
Agricultural Bank of Greece

viii

Geotechnical Chamber of Greece
Dr. R. Maag AG, Dielsdorf, Switzerland
Sumitomo Chemical Company Ltd., Osaka, Japan, with personal gratitude to Dr.
Yoshihiko Nishizawa
International Atomic Energy Agency, Joint FAO/IAEA Division of Nuclear
Techniques in Food and Agriculture, Vienna, Austria
World Health Organization, Division of Vector Biology and Control, Geneva,
Switzerland, with gratitude to Drs. Rudolf Sloof and G. Quélennec
University of California at Berkeley, College of Natural Resources
Orthodox Academy of Crete

The FAO/IAEA research coordination meeting on 'Development of Controlled-Release Formulations of Pesticides Using Nuclear Techniques' under the coordination of Dr. Manzoor Hussain was held in conjunction with the Conference on Pesticides and Alternatives. The development and use of controlled-release pesticide formulations has the potential to reduce environmental contamination due to pesticides, to improve their safety, and to make them work more effectively and at lower cost. We are indebted to Dr. Hussain and his collleagues for their productive interactions.

Publication of this Conference proceedings involved close cooperation with Jan Geelen, Sidhu Patel and Karena Beerse of the Biomedical Division of Elsevier Science Publishers, Amsterdam, The Netherlands. Their encouragement, devotion and patience are gratefully acknowledged. Deborah Gibson of the Pesticide Chemistry and Toxicology Laboratory at Berkeley skillfully coordinated the correspondence and organizational aspects of the Conference.

The Orthodox Academy of Crete provided an excellent environment and facility for this conference. Special thanks are extended to Alexandros and Anna Papaderos, Vickie Diakoupolou, Alexander Spangler, Lilika Christodovlaki and their colleagues at the Academy for their help and friendship during the conference and for a wondeful introduction to the life and culture of Crete.

This book is dedicated to Grecophile Kati Casida.

CONTENTS

Hormones and neuropeptides

Natural products

Insecticides and acaricides

xii

Resistance mechanisms

PLANT PATHOGENS

WEEDS

PESTICIDE CHEMISTRY AND TOXICOLOGY

© 1990 Elsevier Science Publishers B.V. (Biomedical Division)
Pesticides and alternatives, editor J.E. Casida

INNOVATION IN THE PLANT PROTECTION INDUSTRY: REQUIREMENTS AND CONSTRAINTS

GÜNTHER VOSS and HANS GEISSBÜHLER
Agricultural Division, CIBA-GEIGY Ltd., 4002 Basel, Switzerland

INTRODUCTION

In 1939, exactly 50 years ago, Paul Müller detected the insecticidal activity of DDT at the Geigy laboratories in Basel, Switzerland. His Nobel prize awarded pioneer invention contributed to a worldwide search for new types of useful and highly active plant protection chemicals. Although hundreds of compounds representing dozens of chemical classes have now been identified and developed, the users of these products and society continue to call for more innovation in chemical and biological plant protection, especially in terms of environmental acceptability.

The factors influencing innovation have changed dramatically since 1939 when industry began to introduce a rapidly developing technology into wide open and far less regulated markets. A modern conference directed to innovative approaches in insect, weed, and disease control cannot ignore to take note of these changes. It must reflect on today's requirements and constraints, since both determine the future rates of success and failure within our industry.

OPPORTUNITIES

Before we define these requirements and constraints in more detail, we like to address some problems and expected developments in agriculture and our society, and the short- and long-term opportunities arising for R&D plant protection:
- The continuing task of improving and economizing crop production technologies and the need for preserving natural resources requires a permanent adjustment of plant protection measures. Well-known examples are reduced tillage aiming at soil conservation, improved water management, or integrated pest control.
- When populations of insect pests, weeds and plant pathogens are exposed to the selecting force of plant protection chemicals, they can become resistant, or previously secondary pest problems can turn into primary ones, as experienced in many cotton growing areas with the acceleration of sucking insects and mites. In both cases the new pest situation requires new solutions.
- Many plant protection chemicals suffer from real or perceived safety problems in terms of handling, disposal or environmental behavior. These disadvantages must be solved by creating better formulations, packaging or application systems, and especially by identifying and developing new and safer active ingredients.

4

- Last but not least, it is the rapid advancement of science which offers industry
  a wide spectrum of new opportunities for innovation in crop production and plant
  protection. Computer assisted molecular modeling and biochemical mode of action
  studies can allow for a more rational design of new pesticides, natural products
  provide chemists with fascinating leads, economic large-scale production of biological products is becoming a challenge, and biotechnology continues to offer
  the promise that non-chemical solutions in agriculture might become reality.

DEFINITION

Product innovation occurs in two distinctly different steps. The first one is
conceptual in nature and based on the intuition and imagination of motivated,
creative, knowledgable and experienced scientists. If their reflections lead to
new ideas and inventions, the second step will have to follow: the organized and
planned realization which does not only require technical competence, discipline,
and the ability to cooperate and communicate, but also a keen sense for customer
needs in highly competitive markets, cost and time awareness, as well as a high
degree of social and ecological responsibility. Unfortunately, only very few
inventions survive the long and often painful process of development to give rise
to new marketable products or services.

REQUIREMENTS

Innovations result from quality in R&D, from interdisciplinary cooperation, and
from work efficiency (Fig. 1). Quality is achieved by competent people who know
their objectives as defined in R&D plans, cooperation and communication are facilitated in organisations meeting the needs of people, and efficiency is created by
implementing R&D plans in properly designed organisations.

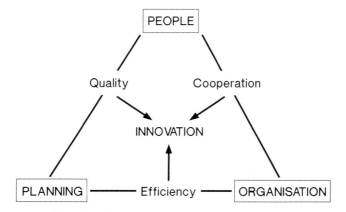

Fig. 1. The main requirements to innovation

People and Resources

The first and by far the most important requirement for being innovative in industrial plant protection R&D are people
- who have and maintain a high scientific/technical competence and willingness to share their knowledge with others,
- who enjoy experimenting and exploring the unknown more than merely building on previous experience,
- who are achievement-minded, ready for job rotations, and enjoy fair competition,
- who show a continuing interest and willingness to learn,
- who demonstrate perseverance and patience in their work, especially under conditions of stress,
- who communicate easily, effectively, and clearly with each other, and
- who accept a collective commitment to predefined R&D objectives.

In order to maintain or improve the qualification of personnel in all areas relevant to industrial innovation, R&D managers have to
- select staff members with scientific depth and latitude, team spirit, commitment, and leadership potential,
- motivate people by providing challenging objectives, by delegating responsibilities, by creating a climate of open communication, and by recognizing individual aspirations,
- appraise their coworkers' achievements regularly, assess their strengths and weaknesses, improve their future performance and discuss career expectations and potentials,
- train their R&D staff in a systematic way through appropriate courses, company internal job rotations, and international transfers within the company or to external research institutions.

When we at CIBA-GEIGY look at the evolution of our main categories of R&D personnel over time, we find evidence for a steady increase of academic staff at the expense of untrained technicians. Among the university graduates, the classical fraction of synthesis chemists and screening biologists has grown less rapidly than that of other scientists representing basic and speculative research, biochemistry, chemodynamics, safety assessments, biological and integrated control, computer applications, and other activities. These developments reflect the more demanding and complex tasks of a modern industrial R&D operation, and point to its growing multidisciplinary character.

According to the Stanford Research Institute, most agrochemical companies do now spend 8-12% of sales for R&D. Taking into account a 10% average and a worldwide turnover of 22 Bio US$, we have to assume that the expenses for all industrial R&D

have reached an impressive 2200 Mio US$ level annually with a definite trend upwards. Within the industry it is widely accepted, that only those companies will continue to remain competitive in the long-term, which can afford an annual R&D budget of at least 100 Mio US$ each.

Although the development of CIBA-GEIGY's annual and worldwide R&D costs may not be representative for the entire industry, it points to an increase of R&D expenses over time in both absolute terms and in percentage of sales. Furthermore, the cost fraction devoted to the maintenance of existing products in the market has grown faster than, and at the expense of, work aiming at the search and development of new products.

Planning

Although scientists do often feel that planning can be detrimental to creative research, a modern R&D management cannot do without it. Planning is a necessary tool to

- define objectives, priorities, and time requirements for R&D work,
- secure organisational and operational efficiency,
- improve the quality of cooperation and to make progress controllable,
- analyze the technical value and the commercial potential of projects,
- identify attractive long-term business opportunities and the corresponding research areas.

The scope and complexity of planning in R&D can easily be explained by listing the consequences of simply defining the objectives of R&D in insect control: "Continue to invent/develop safe and competitive products/methods against important pest species worldwide". This one sentence embraces the attention of R&D Management to such diverse activities as

- long-range planning and the search for new business opportunities,
- resource and investment planning which also includes the acquisition of third-party products,
- a sophisticated planning procedure securing the timely availability of safety data needed for product registration,
- a quality concept which provides competitive advantage,
- a well-balanced research portfolio considering both conventional and speculative R&D projects in the right proportion,
- a market oriented selection system for research projects which allows priority setting and productivity control,
- sophisticated R&D efforts in the area of Integrated Pest Management, which favors selective products, and
- an efficient international R&D operation.

Organisation

The third pillar in industrial innovation management is organisation. Ideally it
- reflects business orientation to ensure continuity in product development from
  early research to marketing,
- is transparent with regard to tasks and accountability, and flexible enough to
  allow for swift adjustments,
- is capable of coping with unavoidable matrixes through solid terms of reference,
- enables effective communication within a decentralized international company.

Among the numerous disciplines, activities, problems and aspects to be managed
within R&D plant protection are chemical synthesis, formulation and process development, chemodynamics, patent applications, resistance monitoring, mode of action
studies, biochemistry, laboratory and greenhouse screening, basic and speculative
research, product and residue analysis, biological profiling, toxicological and
ecological studies of a growing number and complexity, field trials in many countries all over the globe, registration, safe application, product economics and
positioning, knowledge of competitive products, extramural research, and many
others. This set of interrelated activities requires an effective organisation
capable of linking the R&D line function to an appropriate matrix structure. The
result can be a three-dimensional organisation (Fig. 2), in which the first functional dimension, comprises most of the areas related to experimental R&D, whereas
the second one, the interfunctional dimension, defines strategic business concepts
and coordinates the work of all units involved in product development, registration, production and marketing. The third, geographical dimension initiates, controls and coordinates worldwide field trials and product registrations, joint
research projects with universities in many countries of the world, third-party
product acquisitions, and cooperation among companies at various levels.

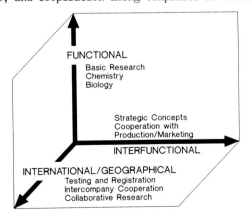

Fig. 2. Innovation in plant protection: a three-dimensional task

8

CONSTRAINTS

In spite of creative scientists, a satisfactory resource situation, sound R&D
plans and effective organisations, the rate of innovation has come to a slow-down.
The main reasons for the apparent decline in innovation are technological/economic
and regulatory constraints.

Technology and Economy

If one regards the annual number of product introductions over time to be an
appropriate measure of innovation rates, the conclusion is clear: Innovation in
chemical plant protection has been declining since the early seventies (Fig. 3).

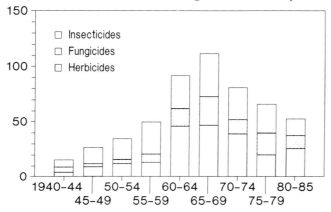

Fig. 3. Number of pesticides introduced 1940-1985

This is not only true for all compounds listed in the Pesticide Manual (1), but
also for those 10% of products which, according to our own inhouse analysis by
marketing, rank highest with regard to their annual sales volumes. Particularly
for insecticides this development is obvious: New and commercially "big" products
have become rare in a market dominated by cost-effective and well-performing chemicals which have now reached or approach their commodity status.

The present gap between conventional solutions and new opportunities, however,
has a more economical than a technical background. Firstly, new and patentable
chemical structures are becoming more and more complex and expensive to compete
with cheaper commodities. This can be demonstrated by calculating the average
number of steps required to synthesise an active compound of a defined quality.
While only 3 and 4.1 steps were necessary in 1973 and 1983, respectively, we have
now reached 6.3 steps for each of our products promoted to the internal development stage. Secondly, many potentially valuable new compounds are too selective to
justify a 100 Mio US$ investment for their production and development into small
or even unprofitable markets.

Legislation/Regulation

Industry recognizes and accepts its responsibility for product safety vis-à-vis users, consumers and the environment, and now devotes up to one third of its R&D budget to safety assessments. This resource commitment is a heavy constraint, because it competes with that urgently needed for the more innovative part of industrial research.

The main constraints associated with pesticide legislation and regulation can be grouped into three categories:

- Administrative procedures established by registration authorities differ from country to country and require the compliance with many different forms and questionnaires, languages, data presentations, summaries, or expert opinions. This does not only relate to new chemicals but also to the re-registration of older commercial products. While industry actively supports all efforts to close significant data gaps, it suffers from the costly and time-consuming repetition of scientifically valid older studies requested with little more justification than merely the formal compliance with the latest regulatory guidelines. At the same time the review of older products also ties up a great deal of resources of regulatory authorities, which in turn causes progressive delays for new submissions and a further shortening of a products patent protected commercial life.

- Lack of harmonisation, however, is not only confined to the purely administrative aspects of registration. It also extends to the type of data requested by governments and their interpretation. While most countries now accept OECD guidelines, some do not and have developed their own systems. One agency requests subchronic toxicity data on formulated products, others require extensive investigations on several local soil types. Why do some countries rely on fish toxicity studies on active ingredients carried out in a glass aquarium, but others on formulated products tested in the field? What is the rationale behind the decision of some governments, not to register product combinations, while others are convinced, that mixtures are useful tools in combating insecticide and fungicide resistance?

- The qualitative and quantitative extension of safety data is a phenomenon known to all companies experienced in registration of plant protection chemicals. Ten years ago, a standard chronic toxicity report carried approximately 500 pages, while 6000 are normal today. In 1972 EPA required a total of 81 studies to register our insecticide methidathion on food crops. A non-food registration of the fungicide metalaxyl had to be based on 102 experiments eight years later, and in 1987 no less than 184 studies had to be delivered for a food crop label of propiconazole, another fungicide. Our recent experience also indicates that the numbers of environmental and metabolism studies have grown more rapidly than

10

those devoted to toxicity and residues, which is partly a result of an increased
and justified environmental awareness, but also due to some exaggerated and sen-
sational reports in the media.

CONCLUSION

Innovation in the plant protection industry - requirements and constraints:
Those of us who devote their professional lives to chemical synthesis, biological
research and the development of plant protection products know, that creative and
motivated R&D people will continue to be the most important asset for any innovative company, that planning will have to assist in finding the way into areas
still unexploited, and that organisational structures may require frequent changes
in order to facilitate the growing need for complex interdisciplinary research. We
also assume, that even more economic and regulatory constraints may have to be
accepted during the 90´s, but hope that society as a whole will eventually acknowledge our achievements for the benefit of world agriculture. We in industry recognize that even precise and reliable scientific findings cannot eliminate subjec-
tive feelings and judgements on risks and benefits. Common sense, competence and
the cognizance of responsibility, however, should form a common base for all plant
protection scientists to mutually define, analyse, and solve those problems which
continue to exist. Being committed to scientific truth, all of us in academia and
industry should speak up whenever established facts are being misused by those who
try to capitalize on the "fear of the unknown" or who claim that new miracle solutions are just around the corner. Let us try to cope with these unjustified fears
and hopes and focus on improvements that can and must be achieved in R&D plant
protection.

REFERENCE

1. Worthing CR, Walker SB (1987): The Pesticide Manual (8th ed.). British Crop
   Protection Council

© 1990 Elsevier Science Publishers B.V. (Biomedical Division)
Pesticides and alternatives, editor J.E. Casida

PESTICIDE MODE OF ACTION: EVIDENCE FOR AND IMPLICATIONS OF
A FINITE NUMBER OF BIOCHEMICAL TARGETS

JOHN E. CASIDA

Pesticide Chemistry and Toxicology Laboratory, Department of Entomological Sciences,
University of California, Berkeley, CA 94720 (USA)

INTRODUCTION

Fifty years have passed since the introduction of highly effective pest control
chemicals greatly changed the productivity of agriculture and the effectiveness
of public health programs. This half century was a highly successful and fascinating era of agrochemical discovery and development. In looking to the future
there is growing evidence that introduction of compounds with totally new modes
of action will be less frequent than in the past. This review considers the
evidence for and implications of a potentially finite number of biochemical
targets useful on a practical basis in pest control.

The current pesticides, about 1,000 of major importance, include a wide diversity
of chemical types. They came from two sources. Natural products were used directly
or as prototypes to prepare improved synthetic analogs. Synthesis and testing
programs sought totally new classes of pesticides either by chance on screening
hundreds of thousands of chemicals or by rational design in biochemical projects.
Both approaches involve structure optimization and major investments to achieve
the desired properties and proprietary position.

The discovery and development of new agrochemicals are important in keeping pace
with an expanding demand for pest control to increase food and fiber production
and to protect man and livestock from disease. Most of the present pesticides
are quite effective and reasonably safe. Attempts to improve them are somewhat
different than in the past with greater focus on specific major pests, closer
coordination between chemists, biochemists and toxicologists, and fewer and
larger programs to match the required resources with the scope of the problems.
The goals are effective, selective and profitable chemicals. The constraints are
regulations, resistance and the magnitude of economic investment.

BIOCHEMICAL TARGETS

Pesticides are inhibitors, blockers, modulators or inducers of specific sites
on enzymes, receptors, channels or membranes. The most important biochemical
targets are so physiologically significant they are critical to the survival of
a broad range of pests. They are ideally less important or less sensitive in
crops and beneficial organisms than in the pests. The site of action may already
be known when the pesticide is based on or modified from an identified biochemical
inhibitor or blocking agent. Often the agent is of unknown mode of action.

This was the case for most pesticides, at least until recently.

Research to understand life processes is often facilitated by and is sometimes dependent on a suitable biochemical probe to disrupt a specific site or function. The pesticide industry provides biochemical probes of great benefit in agriculture and medicine. Pesticides are designed for high biological activity of diverse types. In sifting hundreds of thousands of compounds for pesticidal activity, the end result is the selection of a potential plethora of biochemical probes for use in dissecting normal metabolic functions. The structure optimization of a new class of pesticides often takes place without knowledge of the biochemical target but in turn provides a structure-activity pattern critical to establishing the relevance of that target and to mapping the topology of the active site. When a new target is established in industry, the reporting of the discovery is sometimes delayed many years until a product either is commercialized or is no longer of interest for development. New chemical classes more frequently act on known biochemical mechanisms than on totally new targets.

In theory there are an apparently inexhaustible and almost infinite number of potential biochemical targets for pesticide action. In practice, however, only a few hundred targets are known. Most of these utilize specific sites but some involve "non-specific" action. In economic use, in contrast, most pesticides act on a surprisingly few biochemical targets. These are the targets allowing the required cost-effectiveness, selectivity and safety. Several analogs are normally commercialized for each major biochemical target. Often one or more unrelated classes of compounds also work at this same target. The rapidly expanding number of classes of pesticide chemicals far exceeds the number of biochemical targets.

Some sites of pesticide action are overworked targets. Several companies may have one or more analogs or additional classes of chemicals with the same mode of action. This situation may result in a high selection pressure on the target and eventually to cross resistance to each of the relevant classes of pesticides. Cross resistance is sometimes due to metabolic detoxification but often results from insensitivity of the target site.

There are certain preferred biochemical targets for each type of pesticide. Most insecticides are liposoluble nerve poisons. Neurotoxicants have dominated the field for 50 years. They are the most cost effective chemicals to control insect pests and considerable reeducation would be required to shift to other approaches. A major portion of the herbicides and fungicides are inhibitors of biosynthetic and energetic pathways with many of the targets not present in mammals, providing important selectivity. Growth regulators (both insect and plant) are generally less important. Established compounds and agricultural practices will continue to be used until improvements are clearly demonstrated.

There may be a finite number of biochemical targets useful on a practical basis for pesticide action. This possibility is applicable to insecticides, herbicides and fungicides (just as it also applies to various types of antibiotics and pharmaceuticals). Two types of evidence support this proposal. The first is cross-resistance sometimes reaching the point that few sensitive targets remain within some important pest organisms. Cross resistance due to target site insensitivity is one of the best ways to establish a common mode of action. The second is the logistics of finding new targets. When new classes of compounds are found they often work not on new targets but at the same old sites. Alternatively, when the mode of action is determined for an established group of compounds this new target is soon found to encompass several old or new classes of pesticides.

INSECTICIDES

Insecticides act at three principal targets which are all sites in the nervous system. Two of these targets are channels [the voltage-dependent sodium channel and the γ-aminobutyric acid (GABA)-gated chloride channel] and one is an enzyme (acetylcholinesterase or AChE). A potent natural product disrupts each of these target sites and dozens of synthetic compounds of diverse types also work in the same way.

VOLTAGE–DEPENDENT SODIUM CHANNEL

DDT
(diphenylethane)

pyrethrins   (R = CH$_3$ or CO$_2$CH$_3$;
R′ = CH$_3$ or CH$_2$CH$_3$ or CH=CH$_2$)
(botanical–pyrethrum)

fenvalerate
(ester pyrethroid)

The voltage-dependent sodium channel is the target for two major and very different classes of insecticides, i.e., the pyrethroids and the DDT-type. Pyrethrins, the active ingredients of pyrethrum flowers, have been used for more than 200 years and served as the prototype for the very important synthetic pyrethroids. It is not surprising that pyrethroids closely related to the pyrethrins act in the same way and even that an ester such as fenvalerate that appears superficially very different still acts at the same site since it has many structural and stereochemical features in common with the natural materials. Further developments replacing almost every portion within the molecular structure of the pyrethrins by an isosteric equivalent (e.g., ester group by ether or alkane functionality) make it very surprising that the same mode of action is maintained. More amazing is the fact that DDT and its analogs work the same way. These synthetic compounds, used extensively for 50 years and with almost no structural features in common with the pyrethroids, act at the same site and show an appropriate cross-resistance pattern resulting from the common target. Thus, the first highly effective insecticides (the pyrethrins and DDT) and the latest major "class" of insecticides (the synthetic pyrethroids) all work in essentially the same way.

<u>GABA–GATED CHLORIDE CHANNEL</u>

picrotoxinin
(botanical–fishberry)

polychloro-
cycloalkanes

lindane

trioxabicyclooctane
(synthetic prototype)

toxaphene
(9–Cl–B)

α–endosulfan
(cyclodiene)

The GABA-gated chloride channel is the site of action for a natural toxicant (picrotoxinin) and three major classes of synthetic insecticides (collectively referred to as the polychlorocycloalkanes used to the extent of three billion pounds). The polychlorocycloalkanes include a half dozen cyclodienes and the most active isomers of the toxaphene (polychlorobornane) and hexachlorocyclohexane (including lindane) components. They originated from an era when many cyclic hydrocarbons were chlorinated as candidate insecticides. The recent discovery of their mode of action came about by comparing their effects on nerve preparations with those of the natural epoxylactone picrotoxinin (once used as an insecticide). The trioxabicyclooctanes, some with exceptional insecticidal potency, also disrupt the same target. The GABA-gated chloride channel was an overworked target with some resistance before the cyclodienes, toxaphene and hexachlorocyclohexane were in the most part phased out for reasons of adverse toxicology and/or persistence. It is for now an underutilized target and the subject of current research.

ACETYLCHOLINESTERASE

methylcarbamates

organophosphates

physostigmine
(botanical prototype)

TEPP
(pyrophosphate)

carbaryl
(methylcarbamate)

profenofos
(S –alkyl phosphorothiolate)

The recognition of AChE as a critical enzyme for nerve function was due in part to studies using the natural methylcarbamate physostigmine as a probe. Organophosphorus compounds were the first insecticides acting at this target and their discovery was made without knowledge of their mode of action. Methylcarbamate insecticides such as carbaryl, a later development, came from research on physostigmine-type compounds. However, the first carbamate insecticide, the dimethyl-carbamate dimetan, was a serendipitous discovery from research on insect repellents. Thus both important classes of insecticidal AChE inhibitors, the organophosphorus compounds and methylcarbamates, were discovered in synthesis and testing programs without knowledge of their mode of action, yet they each work at the same target emphasizing the importance of AChE in insect control. The majority of the current insecticides act by inhibiting AChE so cross resistance from a modified target is potentially very serious. Some of the inhibitors (such as profenofos) are less prone to resistance providing an incentive to continue research on AChE inhibitors as insecticides.

There are a variety of other classes of insecticides and many more than three targets for insecticide action. The sodium channel is also the target for the iso-butylamides (based on natural prototypes) and the dihydropyrazoles (and related synthetic compounds) which have sufficient potency to be of considerable interest for development. The GABA-gated chloride channel is the target for the avermectins which act at a site different than that discussed above. The octopamine receptor is blocked by the formamidine chlordimeform and many related compounds of former or potential importance as neurotoxic insecticides and miticides. Development is inhibited by insect growth regulators including juvenoids that mimic the action of the insect's juvenile hormone and by benzoylarylureas that block chitin synthesis. Although of only minor significance, there are potent natural product insecticides that act by inhibiting NADH oxidase (i.e., rotenone and piericidins) and a calcium-activated calcium channel (i.e., ryanodine). However, despite extensive efforts the major current compounds for insect control continue to be neurotoxicants acting at only three targets.

HERBICIDES

There are larger numbers of important biochemical targets for herbicide action than for insecticide action. In contrast to insecticides, the major synthetic herbicides are not based on or closely related to natural products with herbicidal activity. Resistance is much less of a problem for herbicides than for insecticides. Six targets for herbicides or herbicide safeners are of special interest in the present context. Much of the relevant information was generated in the last few years and some is of very recent origin relative to diverse classes of commercial compounds found to act at the same site thereby indicating a possible finite number of practical herbicide targets.

PLASTOQUINONE / HERBICIDE
BINDING PROTEIN OF PHOTOSYSTEM II
(selected examples)

diuron
(dimethylurea)

atrazine
(s –triazine)

metribuzin
(triazinone)

The plastoquinone/herbicide binding protein of photosystem II is the target for more herbicides than any other site. Three of many chemical classes working at this target are the ureas, s-triazines and triazinones. Most of these compounds were discovered in synthesis and screening programs without utilizing target site assays which have nevertheless had an important impact in recent years. Resistance is sometimes a problem and cross-resistance must be considered on a compound-by-compound and weed-by-weed basis. The binding protein is well defined from the standpoint of structure, conformation, genetic coding, and modifications conferring tolerance or resistance. From the standpoint of herbicide use, it is clearly one of the most important targets and possibly one that has been "overworked or overutilized".

17

ACETOHYDROXYACID SYNTHASE
(selected examples)

chlorsulfuron
(sulfonylurea)

imazaquin
(imidazolinone)

Acetohydroxyacid synthase is the target of two major but very different classes of herbicides, the sulfonylureas and imidazolinones. The two classes were discovered and optimized independently and in the most part without knowledge of their target. With the target now known the enzyme assay has revealed new classes of inhibitors and increased the ease of finding new herbicides acting at this site. Genetic engineering of crop tolerance to herbicides has been particularly successful with this target.

ACETYL–CoA CARBOXYLASE
(selected examples)

fluazifop–butyl
(oxyphenoxypropionate)

sethoxydim
(cyclohexendione)

PP600
(triazinedione prototype)

Acetyl-CoA carboxylase is the target of the oxyphenoxypropionates such as fluazifop-butyl, the cyclohexendiones such as sethoxydim, and a triazinedione, three classes of herbicides of very different structures. Many other commercial compounds of the former two classes work at the same target. They were optimized and extensively developed before their common mode of action was established, thereby adding acetyl-CoA carboxylase to the relatively small list of practical herbicide targets.

PROTOPORPHYRINOGEN IX OXIDASE
(selected examples)

acifluorfen
(nitrodiphenyl ether)

S-23142
(N –phenylimide prototype)

oxadiazon
(oxadiazolone)

phenopylate
(carbamate prototype)

Protoporphyrinogen IX oxidase is inhibited by many herbicides of widely diverse types including nitrodiphenyl ethers, oxadiazolones and prototype N-phenylimides and carbamates. The oxidase block leads to tetrapyrrole accumulation and singlet oxygen damage. Each class of compound was optimized without knowledge of its mode of action. The impression of diversity in herbicide action was lost on realizing that all these types of compounds act at the same target.

PHYTOENE DESATURASE
AND LATER DESATURATION REACTIONS
(selected examples)

norflurazon
(phenylpyridazinone)

fluoridone
(pyrrolidinone)

flurochloridone
(phenylpyrrolidone)

diflufenican
(phenoxynicotinamide)

Phytoene desaturase or later desaturation reactions in carotenoid biosynthesis are inhibited by various pyridazinones, pyrrolidones, pyrrolidinones and nicotinamides, among other chemical classes. Although they may not all disrupt the same site in the same way, they clearly act within a small sequence of reactions in carotenoid biosynthesis. Most of these bleachers were optimized without knowledge that the ultimate target was similar to or the same as that of such a diversity of other compounds.

INDUCERS OF INCREASED GSH LEVEL
AND GST ACTIVITY
(selected examples)

dichlormid   flurazole   oxabetrinil

The limited number of targets is also evident with herbicide safeners or antidotes. These compounds facilitate herbicide detoxification by inducing increased glutathione (GSH) levels and glutathione S-transferase (GST) activity, a mode of action first noted with dichlormid in corn which is also applicable to oxabetrinil and flurazole. No other major mechanism of herbicide safener action has come forth despite the testing of thousands of compounds.

There are many targets of herbicide action other than those indicated above but they are either less well understood or there are not a variety of blocking agents. Of these targets 5-enolpyruvyl-shikimate-3-phosphate synthase is most important as the target of glyphosate (but no other major compound). Glutamine synthetase is the target for another phosphonate, glufosinate. Other targets are modified auxin transport, inhibition of gibberellin biosynthesis, and diversion of photosynthetic electron transport leading to toxic oxygen species.

FUNGICIDES

Fungicides act on a great variety of targets and are plagued with problems of resistance. As with insecticides and herbicides, diverse classes of fungicides, discovered independently, were subsequently found to work at the same target. Three examples are given below for this type of indication for a finite number of practical fungicide targets.

STEROL C-14 DEMETHYLASE
(selected examples)

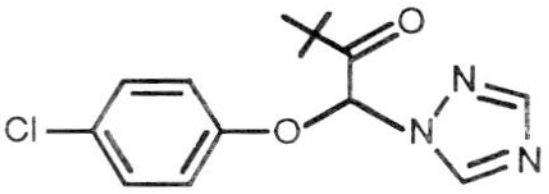

triadimefon
(triazole)

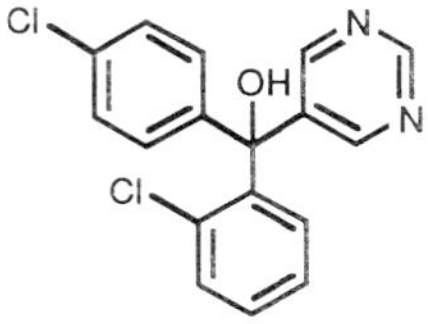

fenarimol
(pyrimidine)

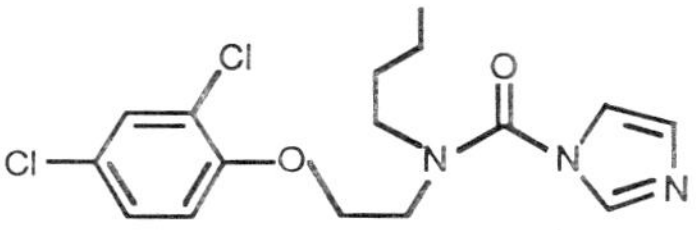

prochloraz
(imidazole)

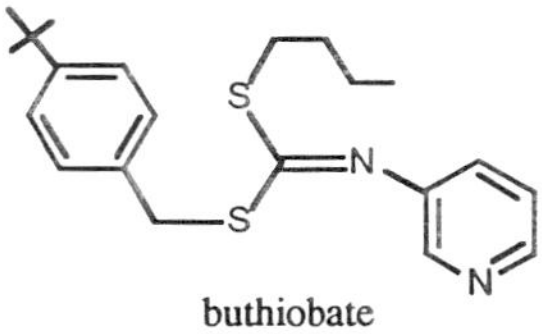

buthiobate
(pyridine)

The sterol C-14 demethylase inhibitors (now about 20 commercial fungicides) include triazoles, pyrimidines, imidazoles and pyridines as well as many other types discovered without knowledge of their target site. Some of these developments were based on completely independent discoveries followed by structure optimization. Several series were developed later based on the target site model.

MICROTUBULE SUBUNIT POLYMERIZATION

thiophanate–methyl

benomyl

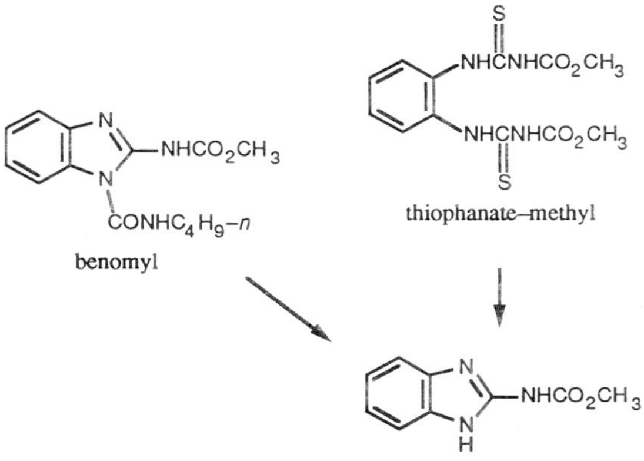

carbendazim

Microtubule subunit polymerization is inhibited by benomyl and thiophanate-methyl which were completely independent discoveries as fungicides, yet they both work at the same site in the same way by forming carbendazim as the ultimate active fungicide.

RNA POLYMERASE II

metalaxyl   cyprofuram

The RNA polymerase II inhibitors include not only metalaxyl and many analogs but also the anilide cyprofuram which was discovered independently but still acts at the same target site.

Clearly the selection of commercial fungicides from screening programs is focused and refocused on a very few targets as the most cost effective. Many other fungicide targets have multiple agents for disruption, often with intriguing negatively-correlated cross resistance.

SUMMARY

Current commercial and candidate pesticides are the end products of sifting hundreds of thousands of synthetic compounds and natural products for potency, selectivity and cost effectiveness. They are characterized by widely diverse chemical structures and functional groups. In most cases they were discovered and optimized without any knowledge of their biochemical targets. Mode of action studies are beginning to fill this gap. In a surprising number of cases the newly-defined target site for one type of pesticide is soon found to also be the target for other types or often even diverse classes of previously-known pesticides. It is becoming increasingly apparent that there are many chemical classes of potentially useful pesticides but there are surprisingly few modes of action or target sites represented. Thus, the frequency that very different chemical classes discovered and developed independently are later found to work at the same site, many of which are illustrated in this review, clearly indicates the possibility that there are relatively few modes of action useful in pest control as currently practiced and that there may be a finite number of relevant biochemical targets.

There are four important implications of a finite number of target sites suitable for practical pesticide action. The first is very favorable. Each target can be more thoroughly understood than in the past. The enzyme or receptor can be isolated and its structural components identified. The conformation of the binding site can be mapped and the critical interactions established. The genetic coding can be elucidated and modified to favorably alter organismal specificity. Safe and efficient use of these pesticides can be based on thorough fundamental scientific knowledge of the target site. The second implication is of concern. The development of resistance to one class of pesticide may lead to cross resistance to some or all other pesticides acting at that target. On the same basis, genetic engineering to modify the target in the crop or predator or parasite can lead to altered sensitivity to all other pesticides acting in the same way at that target. In this context, the policies and products of one pesticide manufacturer may have a direct impact on those of competitive companies and the public as a whole. The third implication is that each target of pesticide action becomes a critical and irreplaceable resource. To achieve pest management on a long term basis, it therefore becomes necessary to practice pesticide management to preserve the potentially finite and dwindling number of biochemical targets. Fourth and finally, sustained programs and increased efforts are required to discover new and unique targets for pesticide action. Clearly this is becoming progressively more difficult as it becomes increasingly more important. Innovative new biology and chemistry are needed. We cannot rely on merely continuing our current discovery and development procedures to provide adequate pest control agents for the future. New and innovative approaches are essential in the development of agrochemicals and their integration with other methods of pest management.

RELATED REFERENCES

Böger, P. and Sandmann, G., Eds. (1989) Target Sites of Herbicide Action. CRC Press, Boca Rotan, Fla., 295 pp.

Corbett, J.R., Wright, K. and Baillie, A.C. (1984) The Biochemical Mode of Action of Pesticides. 2nd Ed. Academic Press, London, 382 pp.

Greenhalgh, R. and Roberts, T.R. (1987) Pesticide Science and Biotechnology: Proceedings of the Sixth International Congress of Pesticide Chemistry held in Ottawa, Canada, 10-15 August, 1986. Blackwell, Oxford, 604 pp.

Lyr, H., Ed. (1987) Modern Selective Fungicides: Properties, Applications, and Mechanisms of Action. Longman Scientific & Technical, Harlow, England, 383 pp.

Matsumura, F. (1985) Toxicology of Insecticides. 2nd Ed. Plenum Press, New York, 598 pp.

Ware, G.W. (1989) The Pesticide Book. Thomson Publications, Fresno, California, 340 pp.

Worthing, C.R., Ed. (1987) The Pesticide Manual: A World Compendium. 8th Ed. British Crop Protection Council, Lavenham Press, Lavenham, Suffold, England, 1081 pp.

ACKNOWLEDGMENTS

Preparation of this review was supported in part by National Institutes of Health Grant P01 ES00049. Useful comments were provided by Robert Toia of this laboratory, Donald James and Stuart Ridley of ICI Agrochemicals (Richmond, CA) and Wolfram Koeller of Cornell University (Ithaca, NY).

© 1990 Elsevier Science Publishers B.V. (Biomedical Division)
Pesticides and alternatives, editor J.E. Casida

EXTRACELLULAR BIOPOLYMERS AS TARGETS FOR PEST CONTROL

EPHRAIM COHEN
Department of Entomology, Faculty of Agriculture, Rehovot 76 100,
Israel

INTRODUCTION

   A variety of polymers which are deposited on the outside of plasma
membranes serve primarily as support elements and as a protective barriers from mechanical damage or osmotic pressure. These polymers like
cellulose, massively produced by plants and algae, or chitin, deposited by zooplankton, various fungi, and aquatic and terrestrial arthropods, consist the bulk of the global organic material synthesized by
living organisms.

   The organic polymers in nature are largely various types of polysaccharides and proteins which in conjunction with minor components such
as lipids, pigments or minerals are present in invertebrates as well
as in vertebrates. In most cases, the polymer chains coalesce to form
microfibrils which are reflected by the typical fibrous texture of the
extracellular structures. The constraints, often imposed by the rigid
structural polymers, has to be partially or fully removed to enable
growth of organisms such as arthropopds or hyphal extention and branching as in filamentous fungi. The periodically or continuously removal
of the constraints is accomplished by the action of hydrolytic enzymes
which degrade the polymers.

   Since extracellular biopolymers are essential components of living
organisms, any interference with their formation or untimely degradation is likely to be detrimental. Integumental structures of arthropods
and cell walls of many fungi contain large deposits of polymers. These
polymers has been considered as a target for controlling arthropod
pests and phytopathogens. The complexity of prokaryotic extracellular
polymers or their possible disruption, are not addressed in this article.

POLYMERS

   The presence of various extracellular polymers in organisms is summarized in Table I. Cellulose and glucan, which are polymers of glucose, can be found in plants, algae and fungi. Chitin, and to a lesser
extent chitosan (the deacetylated form of chitin) (see Figure 1), are
components of fungal cell walls (1). Chitin is prevalent in arthropod
cuticles (2,3), insect peritrophic membranes (4), nematode eggs (5) as
well as in certain species of diatom algae (6,7). Complex polysaccharides such as chondroitin sulfate and heparan sulfate are formed in

vertebrates. Extracellular proteins are major structural components of arthropod cuticle and peritrophic membranes (1,4). Collagens and keratins are well defined proteins deposited by vertebrates. In general, composite polymers of polysaccharides or polysaccharides in conjunction with various proteins were observed. In the fungal cell wall, a combination of chitin (or chitosan), glucan and mannoproteins was detected (8), and in arthropods, the cuticle and the peritrophic membranes are essentially chitinoprotein structures. An unusual combination of keratin and chitin was observed in a brachipod species (9). Very seldom one type of polymer is soley deposited as observed in certain unicellular organisms (6,10), which secrete pure chitin polymers.

TABLE I.
DISTRIBUTION OF MAJOR EXTRACELLULAR POLYMERS

Polymer	Organisms
Cellulose	Plants, algae, fungi (Phycomycetes)
Glucan	Plants, algae, fungi
Hemicellulose	Plants
Lignin, pectin	Plants
Melanins	Fungi, vertebrates, invertebrates
Chitin (chitosan)	Fungi, invertebrates (arthropods)
Collagens, keratins	Vertebrates
Proteoglycans (chondroitin, heparin)	Vertebrates

One desirable attribute of a target for pest control is related to its selectivity. Obviously, the aminopolysaccharide chitin, being formed by arthropod pests, nematodes and phytopathogens but not by vertebrates and plants, emerges as a highly selective target.

CHITIN

Chitin is a straight-chain polymer of the amino sugar N-acetyl-D-glucosamine (GlcNAc) synthesized by clusters of catalytic units (chitin synthetase) integrated in the cell membrane. The above arrangement ensures close proximity of the deposited nascent chitin polymers which are ready to coalesce by hydrogen bondings and form microfibrils (11).

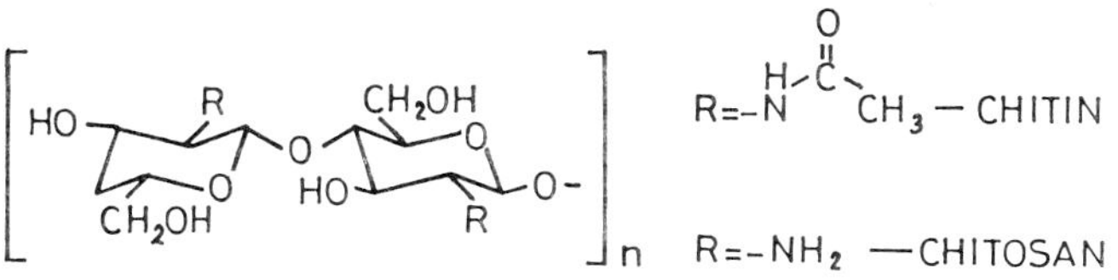

Fig. 1. Basic units of chitin and chitosan

The polymerase units, at least in arthropods, undergo cycles of synthesis and degradation which are apparently under hormonal control
(12,13). In yeasts and filamentous fungi, the chitin synthetase is
initially in a zymogenic state which subsequently undergoes activation
by endogenous proteolytic enzymes (14). Other regulatory mechanisms
involve the activation of the polymerase upon removal of inhibitory
proteins (15). The pathway of chitin synthesis has been studied in
insects (16) and fungi (8,17). It comprises a cascade of biotransformations starting from glucose (or the disaccharide trehalose) which
undedgoes phosphorylations, amination, and conjugation with UDP to
form UDP-N-acetyl-D-glucosamine (UDP-GlcNAc), the chitin synthetase
substrate. Evidence from the microorganisms *Saccharomyces cerevisiae*
(18), *Candida albicans* (19) and *Mucor rouxii* (20) suggests that the
chitin synthetase faces the cytoplasm. This imply a mechanism whereby
the nascent chitin polymer is translocated outside the plasma membrane. Once outside the plasma membrane, the chitin chains form crystal-
lites by hydrogen bonds. This process can be disrupted by compounds
such as Calcofluor White or Congo Red known to interfere with hydrogen
bondings (21).

Chitin microfibrils can be degraded by a dual action of chitinase
(endoenzyme) and chitobiase (exoenzyme) (1,23). These hydrolytic enzymes are active in the chitin producing organisms and are vital for
molting of arthropods (23) and cell growth, cell separation and branching of fungi (14). The hydrolytic enzymes are active also in plants
as a defence mechanism against invading pathogens (24,25), in entomop-
athgogens (26), mycoparasites (27), and in chitinolytic microflora
scavenging chitin residues (28).

INHIBITORS AND PESTICIDES
Chitin synthesis and degradation as targets for possible pest control agents have a number of sites for interference (29). Only one
site, i.e. the polymerization step, yielded commercial pesticides. In
vitro inhibition of the amination step by tetaine (bacilysin) was

shown in *C. albicans* (30). Colchicine and vinblastine which disrupt
the synthesis of cytoskeletal elements inhibited chitin deposition in
imaginal disks of the Indian meal moth *Plodia interpunctella* (22);
Calcofluor White and Congo Red block chitin fibrillogenesis (21); compounds like captan (31) or certain terpenoyl benzimidazoles (32) exhibit moderate potency as chitin synthetase inhibitors. Recently, a specific inhibitor of invertebrate chitinase was extracted from a
Streptomyces species (33,34). Allosamidin (see Figure 2), which is a
combination of an epimer of chitobiose and the alloxan moiety, did not
inhibit plant and fungal chitinases. Due to its insecticidal properties, allosamidin (or its derivatives) may have commercial potential.

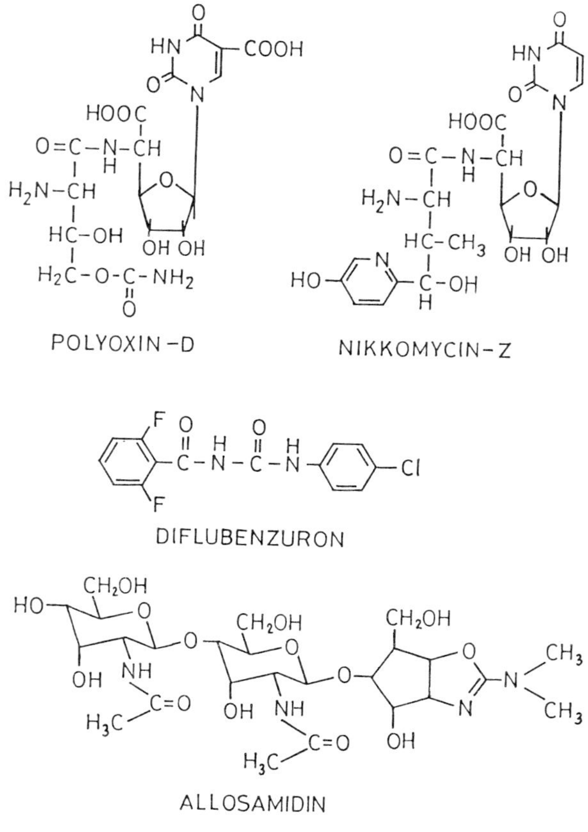

POLYOXIN-D

NIKKOMYCIN-Z

DIFLUBENZURON

ALLOSAMIDIN

Fig. 2. Inhibitors of chitin synthesis and hydrolysis

Currently, compounds belonging to two groups of chemicals which act
by disrupting chitin formation have been registered for pest control.
The fungicidal activity of polyoxins has been discovered by Japanese

scientists in the mid 60s' (35,36). Polyoxins, which are nucleoside peptide antibiotics extracted from *Streptomyces cacaoi,* resemble the structure of UDP-GlcNAc and act as competitive inhibitors of chitin synthetase. Their commercial application is restricted to Japan where they have been used for controlling various vegetable and fruit diseases (37-39). The potenial of polyoxin-D added to the soil to effectively protect melon, bean and chickpea plants from the soil-borne phytopathogen *Sclerotium rolfsii* is illustrated in Figure 3.

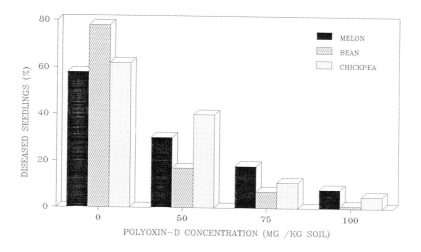

Fig. 3. Protection of plants from the phytopathogen *Sclerotium rolfsii* by polyoxin-D added to the soil.

Levels as low as 5mg per kg of soil gave appreciable reduction in the incidence of the disease. Also seed treatment with the chitin synthesis inhibitor was very effective (27). Nikkomycins extracted from *Streptomyces tendai* are also peptide antibiotics similar in structure to polyoxins and share the same mode of action (40,41). Their development by Bayer as fungicides has been discontinued due in part to cost and toxicological problems. Although the peptide antibiotics are powerful inhibitors of insect chitin synthetase, they lack insecticidal properties due to their hydrophilic nature or the absence of dipeptide transport systems in insect midgut cells.

The insecticidal effects of acylureas were observed incidently when screened with larvae of the large cabbage white, *Pieris brassicae* (42). Insects failed to molt and died because of desiccation, and histological and biochemical studies have indicated that chitin synthesis was disrupted. The exact mechanism of action of the insecticidal acylureas is unknown. Since chitin synthetase is not inhibited (31) and no effect is observed prior to polymerization (42), it has been recently postulated that sensitive membrane components within the complex of chitin polymerization-translocation are involved (43).

The first acylurea compound to be registered as an insecticide for controlling lepidopteran and dipteran larvae was diflubenzuron (Dimilin) (42). Other compounds like triflumuron (BAY SIR 8514) (44) were later introduced followed by more potent benzoylaryl ureas such as chlorfluazuron (IKI-7899) (45).

BIOPOLYMERS AND PLANT-PARASITE INTERACTIONS

It has been demonstrated that addition of chitin to soil will alleviate problems inflicted by soil-borne phytopathogens (46). This effect was considered the result of a change in microflora favoring chitinolytic microorganisms. Glucan, chitin or its deacetylated polycationic form and their respective oligomers are presumably used as signals for the induction of defensive mechanisms in plants (47). Such mechanisms include enhanced lignification (48), callose formation (49), synthesis of various allelochemicals (50,51) and hydrolytic enzymes such as chitinase and glucanase (52,53). It has been suggested that chitosan may be a transducing signal in the interaction between plant and a gall-forming mite (54). Since plants have no chitin, it is assumed that chitinase serves as one line of defence against pathogen penetration and cell invasion. Although chitinase is clearly induced, there is no direct evidence that the enzyme prevent pathogen growth by degrading the chitin component in fungal hyphae. A strong indication that oligosaccharides act at the genomic level emerges from the evidence that radioactive chitosan oligomers applied externally were found inside the plant nuclei (55).

The scheme in Figure 4 depicts various chemical and biological measures which play a significant role in controlling chitin-producing pests. In addition to chemicals which inhibit chitin synthesis or chitin degradation, the polymer per se, when added to phytopathogen-infested soils, stimulate chitinolytic microflora. Plant defensive mechanisms against phytopathogens, which include enhanced production of chitinase, are induced by chitin, chitosan and their respective oligomers. It appears that chitin in fungi and arthropod pests has been used during co-evolutionary processes influenced by close interactions between plants and pathogens, as a transducing signal for plant defensive mechanism.

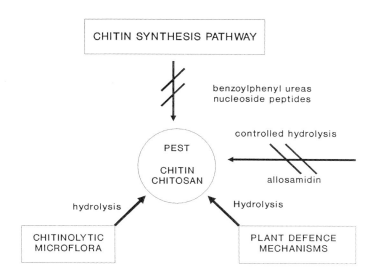

Fig. 4. A schematic representation of the possible control of chitin-producing pests by chemical means and by biological systems

PROSPECTS

1. Due to development of resistance to various fungicides, nucleoside peptide antibiotics acting as chitin synthesis inhibitors might offer alternative pesticides with adifferent mode of action. Soil and seed treatments with these compounds are expected to yield favorable results against soil-borne phytopathogens.

2. Medical use of polyoxins, nikkomycins and more effective derivatives against various mycoses.

3. Development of more potent benzoylaryl ureas for controllig insect and mite pests.

4. Recombinandt DNA technology can be used to incorporate genes encoding for hydrolytic enzymes into sensitive plants. These enzymes being induced by fungal chitin or chitosan will help plants to generate adequate levels of degrading enzymes for protection against phytopathogens. Also preventive measures can be excercised by inducing plant protective enzymes with prior applications of suitable polysaccharides.

ACKNOWLEDGEMENTS

The help of Avraham Gamliel (Department of Phytopathology) and Ariela Barak (Computer Center) in preparing the manuscript is greatly appreciated.

REFERENCES
1. Muzzarelli RAA (1977) Chitin, Pergamon, Oxford

2. Andersen SO (1979) Ann Rev Entomol 24: 24-61

3. Neville AC (1975) Biology of Arthropod Cuticle. Springer-Verlag, New York

4. Peters W (1976) In: Hepburn HR (ed) The Insect Integument. Elsevier, Amsterdam, pp 515-543

5. Brydon LJ Gooday GW, Chappell LH, King TP (1987) Molec Biochem Parasitol 25: 267-272

6. Herth W, Zugenmaier P (1977) J Ultrastruct Res 61: 230-239

7. Blackwell J, Parker, KD, Rudall KM (1967) J Mol Biol 28: 383-385

8. Gooday GW, Trinci APJ (1980) Eukaryotic Microbial Cell. Soc Gen Microbiol. Symp. Cambridge 30: 207-252

9. Tanaka K, Katsura N, Saku T, Kasuga S (1988) Polymer J 20: 119-123

10. Herth W, Mulisch M, Zugenmaier P (1986) In: Muzzarelli R, Jeuniaux C, Gooday, GW (eds) Chitin in Nature and Technology. Plenum, New York, pp 107-120

11. Cohen E (1987) Ann Rev Entomol 32: 71-93

12. Locke M, Huie P (1979) Tissue Cell 11: 277-291

13. Locke M (1985) In: Kerkut GA, Gilbert LI (eds) Comprehensive Insect Physiology, Biochemistry and Pharmacology. Pergamon, Oxford, Vol 2: 87-149

14. Cabib E (1987) In: Meister A (ed) Advances in Enzymology and Related Areas of Molecular Biology. John Wiley, New York, pp 59-101

15. Ulane RE, Cabib E (1974) J Biol Chem 249: 3418-3422

16. Candy DJ, Kilby BA (1962) J Exp Biol 39: 129-140

17. Cabib E (1981) In: Tanner W, Loewus FA (eds) Encyclopedia of Plant Physiology, Vol 13, Plant Carbohydrates. II. Extracellular Carbohydrates. Springer-Verlag, Berlin, pp 395-415

18. Duran A, Bowers B, Cabib E (1975) Proc Natl Acad Sci USA 72: 3952-3955

19. Braun PC, Calderone RA (1978) J Bacteriol 140: 666-670

20. Sentandreu R, Martinez-Ramon A, Ruiz-Herrera J (1984) J Gen Microbiol 130: 1193-1199

21. Herth W (1980) J Cell Biol 87: 442-450

22. Oberlander H, Lynn DE, Leach CE (1983) J Insect Physiol 29: 47-53

23. Kramer KJ, Koga D (1986) Insect Biochem 16: 851-877

24. Abeles FB, Bosshart RP, Forrence, LE, Habig WH (1970) Plant Physiol 47: 129-134

25. Boller T, Gehri A, Mauch F, Vogeli U (1983) Planta 157: 22-31

26. St. Leger RJ, Cooper RM, Charnley AK (1987) J Gen Microbiol 132: 1509-1517

27. Chet I, Cohen E, Elster I (1986) In: Muzzarelli A, Jeuniaux C, Gooday GW (eds) Chitin in Nature and Technology. Plenum, New York, 237-240

28. Sturz H, Robinson J (1986) In: Muzzarelli A, Jeuniaux C, Gooday GW (eds) Chitin in Nature and Technology. Plenum, New York, pp 531-538

29. Cohen E (1987) In: Wright JE, Retnakaran A (eds) Chitin and benzoylphenyl ureas. Junk, Dodrecht, pp 43-73

30. Milewski S, Chmara H, Borowski E (1986) Arch Microbiol 145: 234-240

31. Cohen E, Casida JE (1980) Pestic Biochem Physiol 13: 129-136

32. Cohen E, Kuwano E, Eto M (1984) Agric Biol Chem 48: 1617-1620

33. Koga D, Isogai A, Sakuda S, Matsumoto S, Suzuki A, Kimura S, Ide A (1987) Agric Biol Chem 51: 471-476

34. Sakuda S, Isogai A, Makita T, Matsumoto S, Koseki K, Kodama H, Suzuki A (1987) Agric Biol Chem 51: 3251-3259

35. Suzuki S, Isono K, Nagatsu J, Mizutani T, Kawashima Y, Mizuno T (1965) J Antibiot Ser A 18: 131

36. Isono K, Suzuki S (1968) Tetrahedron Lett No 9: 1133-1137

37. Misato T (1982) J Pestic Sci 7: 301-305

38. Misato T, Kakiki K, Hori M (1979) In: Geissbühler H, Brooks GT, Kearney PC (eds) Advances in Pesticide Science. Pergamon, Oxford, pp 458-464

39. Hori M, Eguchi J, Kakiki K, Misato M (1974) J. Antibiot 27: 260-266

40. Dähn U, Hagenmaier H, Höhne H, Konig WA, Wolf GA, Zähner H (1976) Arch Microbiol 107: 143-160

41. Kobinata K, Uramoto M, Nishii M, Kusakabe H, Nakamura G, Isono K (1980) Agric Biol Chem 44: 1709-1711

42. Verloop A, Ferrell CD (1977) In: Plimmer JR (ed) Pesticide Chemistry in the 20th Century. ACS Symp Ser, Am Chem Soc, Washington DC, pp 237-270

43. Cohen E (1990) In: Retnakaran A, Binnington KC (eds) The Physiology of the Insect Epidermis. Inkata, North Layton, In press

44. Zoebelein G, Hamman I, Sirrenberg W (1980) Z Angew Entomol 89: 289-297

45. Haga T, Toki T, Koyanaki T, Nishiyama R (1985) J Pestic Sci 10: 17-223

46. Mithcell R, Alexander M (1961) Nature 190: 109-110

47. Lamb CJ, Lawton MA, Dron M, Dixon RA (1989) Cell 56: 215-224

48. Barber MS, Bertram RE, Ride JP (1989) Physiol Molec Plant Pathol 34: 3-12

49. Kauss H, Jeblick W, Domard A (1989) Planta 178: 385-392

50. Kendra DF, Hadwiger LA (1984) Exp. Mycol 8: 276-281

51. Sharp JK, Valent B, Albersheim P (1984) J Biol Chem 259: 11312-11320

52. Mauch F, Hadwiger LA, Boller T (1984) Plant physiol 76: 607-611

53. Boller T (1986) In: Muzzarelli R, Jeuniaux C, Gooday GW (eds) Chitin in Nature and Technology. Plenum, New York, pp 223-230

54. Bronner R, Westphal E, Dreger F (1989) Physiol Molec Plant Pathol 34: 117-130

55. Hadwiger LA, Kendra DF, Fristensky BW, Wagoner W (1986) In: Muzzarelli R, Jeuniaux C, Gooday GW (eds) Chitin in Nature and Technology. Plenum, New York, pp 209-214

© 1990 Elsevier Science Publishers B.V. (Biomedical Division)
Pesticides and alternatives, editor J.E. Casida

ORGANOPHOSPHORUS AGROCHEMICALS: PROGRESS AND PROSPECTS

MORIFUSA ETO

Department of Agricultural Chemistry, Kyushu University, Fukuoka 812, Japan

INTRODUCTION

A number of organophosphorus (OP) compounds are utilized as agrochemicals all over the world (1). Although insecticides including acaricides are main OP agrochemicals, fungicides, herbicides, and plant growth regulators have also been developed. Moreover, nematicides, rodenticides, insect chemosterilants, and insecticide synergists are known. The majority of them are neutral ester or amide derivatives of P(V) oxyacids carrying a phosphoryl (P=O) or thiophosphoryl (P=S) group. Some acids, phosphonium salts, and trivalent phosphorus compounds are also utilized. It is noteworthy that the chemical, physical, and biological properties of OP compounds are remarkably variable by combination of four groups or atoms attached to the phosphorus atom.

The reactivity of OP esters is basically due to the positive charge on the phosphorus atom. Nucleophiles attack not only the phosphorus atom (phosphorylation), but also the α-carbon atom of the ester alkyl group (alkylation)(Scheme 1). The serine hydroxyl group at the active center of acetylcholinesterase (AChE) as well as hydroxide ion prefers the phosphoryl P atom, whereas the SH group prefers the tetrahedral C atom.

Schrader's acyl rule and the P-X-Y=Z system (Scheme 2) proposed by Clark are useful to predict the insecticidal, anti-AChE, or phosphorylating activity of OP compounds. There are some exceptions, however, and the activities of OP fungicides, herbicides, and plant growth regulators are due to other properties of OP compounds.

STRUCTURE AND ACTION OF ORGANOPHOSPHORUS INSECTICIDES

Phosphorothioates

Except a small number of enol phosphates such as dichlorvos, almost all OP insecticides are of thiono (P=S) type, which are generally more stable, lipophilic, and penetrable through insect integument than the corresponding oxon

(P=O). Since the P=S bond does not so polarize as the P=O bond, the thiono type insecticides are not able to phosphorylate AChE, unless they are transformed into the oxons. Mixed function oxidase (mfo) is responsible for the biotransformation, which proceeds in a stereospecific manner with retention at phosphorus configuration (2). Mfo catalyzes a variety of oxidative activation of OP insecticides, including oxidation of the sulfide group into the sulfoxide and then sulfone. The first step appears to be stereoselective (3).

Phosphorothiolate esters are, in general, more potent as anti-AChE agents than the corresponding phosphate esters (thiolo effect). For example, diethyl *S-p*-tolyl phosphorothiolate is 50,000 times as active as the corresponding phosphate. This is much more than expected from the acidity of phenol and thiophenol. The thiolo effect may be attributed, at least in part, to little contribution of $d\pi$-$p\pi$ bonding to the P-S linkage because of poor overlap between the 3d orbital of P and the 3p orbital of S in a long bond length and of antibonding overlap between the d orbital and the 2p orbital of S.

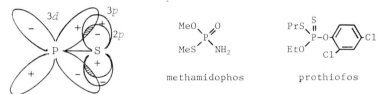

methamidophos   prothiofos

The thiolo effect is, however, not always enough in *S*-alkyl esters and amides to inhibit AChE effectively. Nevertheless some of them are much more insecticidal than expected from their anti-AChE activity. Chemical or biochemical oxidation enhances the anti-AChE activity of methamidophos (4) and some others, suggesting their transformation into the sulfoxides. Some asymmetric *S*-propyl *O*-alkyl *O*-aryl phosphorothiolates and thiolothionates such as profenofos and prothiofos have been found to be effective against some OP-resistant insects. The substituted aryloxy groups of these OP insecticides are Schrader's "acyl", whereas the *S*-propyl group can be converted into a better leaving group by biooxidation. (*R*)(-)-profenofos is less potent *in vitro* as an AChE inhibitor, but is converted into a more potent inhibitor by mfo oxidation than the (*S*)-isomer. AChE reacts well with the oxidized (*R*)(-)-profenofos but less with the oxidized (*S*)-isomer, which is converted into an inactive form (Fig. 1)(5).

Cyclic Phosphorus Compounds

In spite of absence of any special electron-withdrawing group, the cyclic OP compound salithion has a high insecticidal activity and its active form salioxon is a potent AChE inhibitor (6). Although six-membered cyclic phosphates are only several times as active as acyclic esters, ring fusion causes the cyclic phosphates to be considerably active. On the other hand, five-membered cyclic

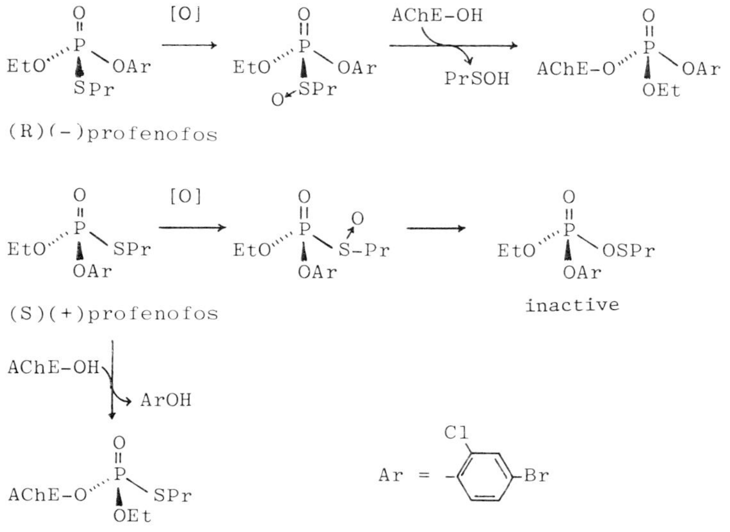

Fig. 1. Stereospecificity of profenofos as anti-AChE (5)

phosphates are too reactive to be effective as insecticides. The extremely high reactivity is attributed to ring strain which results in lowered $d\pi$-$p\pi$ contribution to the P-O bonds. Introduction of an electron-donative amide nitrogen atom into the ring system may give appropriate stability.

Finding L-leucine as neuroactive substance in blood of silkworm larvae poisoned with DDT, we prepared five-membered cyclic phosphoramidates from various amino acids. Thus, some insecticidal 2-methoxy-1,3,2-oxazaphospholidine 2-sulfides were obtained. The most active ones were derived from leucine (BMOS) or valine (7). For the high insecticidal activity, the C_4-configuration should be (S) as the natural amino acids, whereas (R) was preferable for the phosphorus configuration (8). On the other hand, tyramine was found another neuroactive substance in insects. Since it is the precursor of octopamine, we took interest to prepare octopamine related cyclic phosphoramidates and got the insecticidal 5-phenyl-oxazaphospholidine (5-PMOS). The highest insecticidal stereomer has the same configuration (R) at the C_5-position as natural octopamine and (R) configuration at the phosphorus atom (9).

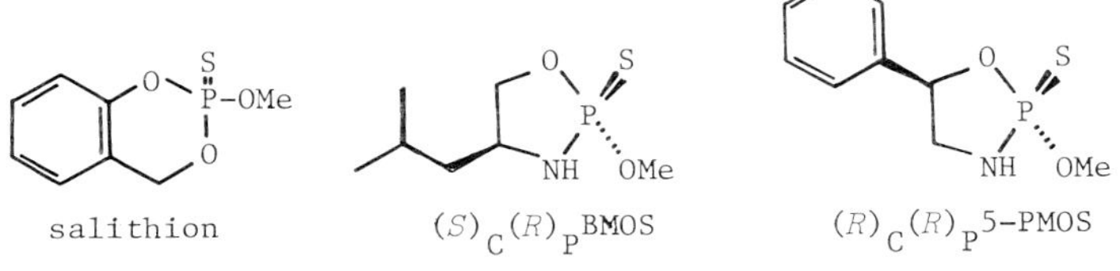

salithion $(S)_C (R)_P$BMOS $(R)_C (R)_P$5-PMOS

Some insecticidal cyclic phosphorus compounds

Molecular Recognition of AChE for OP Insecticides

In the inhibitory process of OP compounds against AChE the affinity of the
inhibitor with the enzyme is important as well as the phosphorylating activity.
Some examples of OP insecticides whose structures are complementary with the
active zone of AChE are shown in Fig. 2. Distance between the P atom and the
most positive or hydrophobic center in the molecule is always about 5Å, corresponding to that between the carbonyl C and the tertiary ammonium N in the acetylcholine molecule. Since the binding site of AChE is located in the hydrophobic
region, the enzyme-inhibitor binding is due to hydrophobic interaction as well as
electrostatic one.

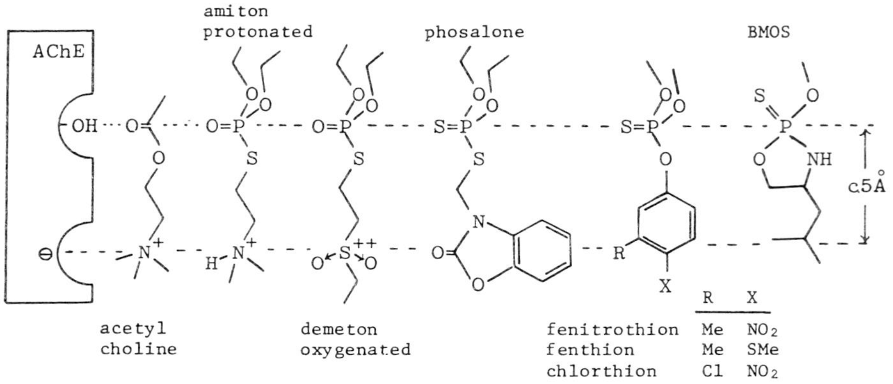

Fig. 2. Complementarity of OP insecticides with AChE active zone

Difference in the feature of AChE among animal species is evident. Dimethyl
phenyl phosphates having a methyl group or a Cl atom at the m-position show less
affinity to mammalian AChE whereas more affinity to insect AChE than the corresponding nonsubstituted esters. This selectivity was attributed to difference
between mammalian and insect AChEs in the distance between the binding and the
esteratic sites (10).

AChE recognizes the chirality of OP-inhibitors. The structures of more potent
enantiomers are shown in Fig. 3 by placing the leaving groups to point toward the
observer and the P=O or P=S group vertically with P at lower position. All these
compounds including both profenofos and its activated sulfoxide have a smaller
substituent at the left side and a larger one at the opposite side, suggesting
a steric room size allowable for the inhibitors to bind at the target site. This
is also the case for the steric structure-insecticidal activity relationship of
P=S compounds, being consistent with the stereochemistry of oxidative desulfuration.

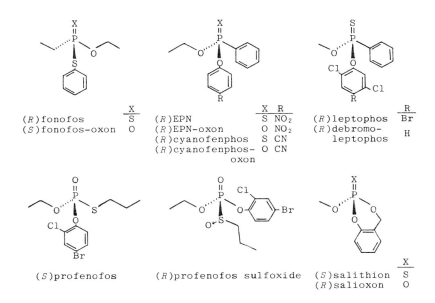

Fig. 3. Biologically more active enantiomers of chiral OP insecticides

Mutant AChE of the OP-resistant housefly strain 3Y was insensitive to feni-
troxon, its K_d value being 44 times that of the susceptible strain, whereas it
was less insensitive to salioxon whose K_d value was 7 times that of the susceptible one (11). Considerable difference in amino acid composition between wild
and resistant insect strains is known. The *ace* gene encoding AChE of susceptible
and resistant *Drosophilla melanogaster* strains indicates significant mutation
involving the replacement of phenylalanine by tyrosine in the resistant strain
DNA (12).

OP-compounds inhibit not only AChE but also other serine enzymes. The selectivity of OP compounds in enzyme inhibition is greatly due to the structure of
non-leaving groups and the steric configuration of phosphorus. For example, (+)-
p-nitrophenyl ethyl(phenyl)phosphinate is 84 times as active as the (-)-enantio-
mer to inhibit AChE, whereas the latter is 12 times the activity of the former
against chymotrypsin (13). Salioxon inhibits AChE 20 times as active as its
phenyl ester analog (K-2), which inhibits preferably aliesterase than AChE with
some 100 times of selectivity ratio (6).

K-2   TPEP metabolite

Delayed Neurotoxicity and Esterase Inhibition

Although salithion shows no delayed neurotoxicity, K-2 is highly neurotoxic but
little insecticidal. Similar phenomena were observed in chemical modification of
the active metabolite of tri-p-ethylphenyl phosphate (TPEP). The α-oxo-metabolite
showed the delayed neurotoxicity but no insecticidal activity, whereas alteration
of the aromatic non-leaving ester groups into methyl groups made the ester be
insecticidal without delayed neurotoxicity (6).

Biochemical sequences for the delayed neuropathy have been proposed as initial
phosphorylation of "neuropathy target esterase (NTE)" followed by subsequent
"aging", i.e. dealkylation, of the phosphorylated NTE (14). K-2 is a potent NTE
inhibitor. Some phenylphosphonate type insecticides including EPN and leptophos
(or its debrominated product) cause delayed neuropathy. Of these asymmetric
compounds, (R)(+)-isomers are more insecticidal and less delayed neurotoxic than
their optical antipodes. (R)(+)EPN-oxon is more active against AChE and less
against NTE as an inhibitor than the (S)-isomer (2).

Metabolism and Selective Toxicity

Proinsecticides which should be activated show higher selective toxicity than
direct AChE inhibitors. Biological activation should occur preferentially in
insects. Butonate and acephate are oxon type proinsecticides activatable via
hydrolase process. Metabolic activation is often a part of degradation process.
Mfo oxidation of thiophosphoryl group causes cleavage of ester bond as well as
desulfuration. Sulfide oxidation is also the case.

Presence of a biovulnerable group such as carboxy ester and amide in the molecule increases the selective toxicity as exemplified by malathion and dimethoate.
Dealkylation by glutathione transferase is also important for OP detoxication.
Saligenin cyclic phosphates show synergism with some OP insecticides. They
inhibit not only carboxyesterase but also glutathione transferase. The former
is inhibited by enzyme phosphorylation and the latter is by alkylation of the SH
group of glutathione. The product S-o-hydroxybenzylglutathione is a competitive
inhibitor for glutathione transferase (Scheme 3)(15).

| butonate | acephate | malathion | dimethoate |

esterase inhibition (aged form)   GSH transferase inhibitor Ki = 6.3 μM   (3)

Other Insecticidal Mechanisms than AChE Phosphorylation

The dithiolane sulfoxide and sulfone from phosfolan are of increased potency as AChE inhibitors. AChE inhibition by alkylation rather than phosphorylation has been suggested (Scheme 4)(16).

$$(EtO)_2\overset{O}{\underset{}{P}}-N\diagdown\diagup_S \quad \xrightarrow{[O]} \quad (EtO)_2\overset{O}{\underset{}{P}}-N\diagdown\diagup_S^{\overset{O_n}{S}} \quad \xrightarrow{Nu} \quad (EtO)_2\overset{O}{\underset{}{P}}-N\diagdown\diagup_S \diagdown SO_nH \qquad (4)$$

phosfolan   n= 1 or 2   Nu= MeOH, AChE

Some 2,6,7-trioxa-1-phosphabicyclo[2.2.2]octanes (BP) carrying particularly a bulky alkyl group at 4-position are highly toxic to mammals. They are not AChE inhibitors, but GABA$_A$ receptor antagonists. Propyl thiono-BP (II) is more toxic to insects than the t-butyl derivative (I) (17). Moreover, bicycloorthocarboxylates (III) suitably substituted are also GABA antagonists and selectively toxic to insects (18).

	I	II	III
LD$_{50}$ µg/g HF	>500	5.0	0.53
SR(LD$_{50}$ mouse/HF)	<0.0001	0.16	100

Selective toxicity of trioxabicyclo[2.2.2]octanes

OTHER ORGANOPHOSPHORUS AGROCHEMICALS THAN INSECTICIDES

Fungicides

Various thiolate type OP fungicides have been developed. The anti-rice blast agent IBP and related S-benzyl phosphorothiolates inhibit the N-methylation of phosphatidylethanolamine in the process of phosphatidylcholine biosynthesis (Scheme 5)(19). This is also the case for S,S-diphenyl phosphorodithiolate EDDP. Although IBP metabolites hydroxylated at o- or p-position are not found yet, they are potent alkylating agents and inhibit SH enzymes (20). EDDP gives the fungicidal p-hydroxy metabolite. Thioquinol phosphate esters are also SH inhibitors (21).

$$\begin{array}{ccc} RCOO\rceil & & RCOO\rceil \\ RCOO\mid & \text{methyl transferase} & RCOO\mid \\ \rfloor\ O-\overset{O}{\underset{O^-}{P}}-O\diagdown NH_2 & \xrightarrow{\;SAM \times 3\;} \longrightarrow \longrightarrow & \rfloor\ O-\overset{O}{\underset{O^-}{P}}-O\diagdown\overset{Me}{\underset{Me}{\overset{+}{N}}}-Me \end{array} \qquad (5)$$

phosphatidyl   (iPrO)$_2$$\overset{O}{P}SCH_2$⟨benzyl⟩   phosphatidyl
ethanolamine   IBP   choline

EtO$\overset{O}{P}$(S-⟨phenyl⟩)$_2$ EDDP

Some phosphorothionate fungicides such as tolclofos-methyl and pyrazophos have been developed. Since tolclofos-methyl oxon has little fungicidal activity and the introduction of an electron-withdrawing group to the benzene ring instead of the p-methyl group is not effective for fungicidal activity, the fungicidal action may not relate to phosphorylation (22). As amide type OP fungicides besides phosbutyl, nitrogen-containing heterocyclic derivatives such as triamiphos are known. It has insecticidal activity and high mammalian toxicity too. The phthalimide derivative ditalimfos, however, has a low mammalian toxicity. Its non-phosphorus analog folpet shows also similar fungicidal activity, suggesting the fungicidal activity is not due to phosphorylation but probably to acylation.

tolclofos-methyl   pyrazophos   fosetyl

phosbutyl   triamiphos   phosphonoformate

ditalimfos R= P(S)(OEt)$_2$
folpet   R= SCCl$_3$ IV   V   AX
                                                       flusilazol   Si-Me

Some examples of organophosphorus fungicides

Azole type systemic fungicides such as diclobutrazole inhibit the biosynthesis of fungus ergosterol by competing with lanosterol on cytochrome P450. The similar activity was found in *threo* ethyl[hydroxy-(pyrid-3-yl)-methyl]-4-fluorophenyl-phosphinate (IV) and triazolylmethyldiphenylphosphine sulfides (V)(23,24). Their structure similarity is noteworthy. Replacement of the P=S group of V by an SiMe group gives the fungicide flusilazol.

Aluminum ethyl phosphonate (fosetyl) is a systemic fungicide, which can not be converted into phosphate by susceptible fungi (25). The anti-virus agent phosphonoformate inhibits DNA-polymerase by competing with pyrophosphate. The anti-bacterial agent alaphosphin inhibits the biosynthesis of cell wall peptidoglycan by competing with L-alanine. Phosphonomycin inhibits UDP-N-acetylglucosamine-pyruvate transferase by competing with phosphoenolpyruvate, blocking bacterial cell wall formation.

alaphosphin

phosphonomycin

Herbicides and Plant Growth Regulators

Phosphorothiolothionate type herbicides anilifos and piperophos, similar to dimethoate in structure, have recently been developed after bensulide. Although acetylcholine and AChE-like enzymes are present in plants, no relationship between them and the mode of action of these OP herbicides is known. Some phosphoramidate type herbicides like amiprofos-methyl and butamifos are again similar to some OP insecticides in structure. The herbicides, however, suppress mitosis by inhibiting microtuble biosynthesis (26).

bensulide

anilofos

piperophos

amiprofos-methyl

butamifos

bialaphos

$$\text{L-glutamate} + NH_3 \xrightarrow[\text{ATP}]{\text{glutamine synthase}} \text{L-}\gamma\text{-glutamyl phosphate – ammonia complex} \rightarrow \text{L-glutamine} \quad (6)$$

K_m= 2mM

phosphinothricin
K_i= 6 µM

There are some important OP herbicides related to amino acids. The herbicide bialaphos gives the active metabolite phosphinothricin which inhibits glutamine synthase. At the enzyme active site, glutamic acid and ammonia are activated in the presence of ATP to form a tetrahedral transition state, i.e. L-γ-glutamyl phosphate-ammonia complex. Phosphinothricin (K_i = 6 µM) is bound to the enzyme more tightly than glutamic acid (K_m = 2 mM), suggesting that phosphinothricin is a transition state analog rather than a simple substrate analog (Scheme 6)(27). Glyphosate blocks the shikimate pathway for aromatic amino acid biosynthesis by competing with phosphoenolpyruvate to inhibit 5-enolpyruvylshikimate-3-phosphate

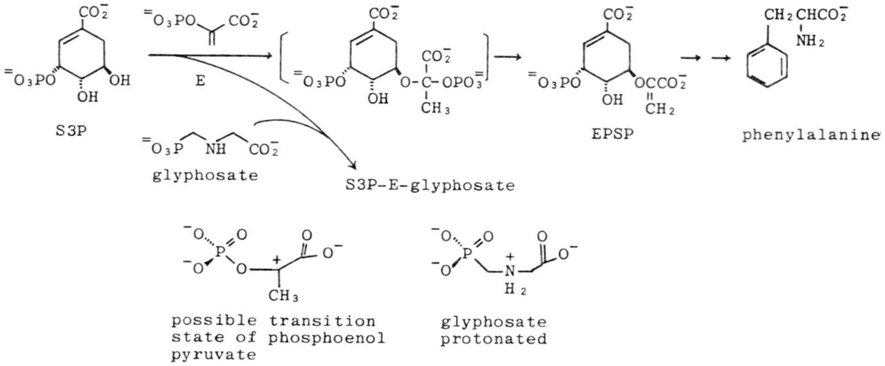

Fig. 4. Inhibition of aromatic amino acid biosynthesis by glyphosate
E= 5-enolpyruvylshikimate-3-phosphate (EPSP) synthase

synthase, forming the stable dead-end ternary complex with the enzyme and shikimate-3-phosphate (S3P)(Fig. 4)(28).

2,4-DEP is hydrolyzed in soil or plants, releasing 2,4-dichlorophenoxyethanol which is converted into the herbicidal principle 2,4-D by metabolic oxidation (Scheme 7). The plant growth regulator (PGR) ethephon is decomposed in plants releasing ethylene, that is a plant hormone for ripening (Scheme 8). The phosphorus moieties of these two examples are thus carriers or protective groups for active principles. The PGR chlorphonium retards the growth of plants. The phosphonium interfers with gibberellin biosynthesis as other onium type growth retardants, inhibiting the cyclization processes from geranylgeranyl pyrophosphate to kaurene (29).

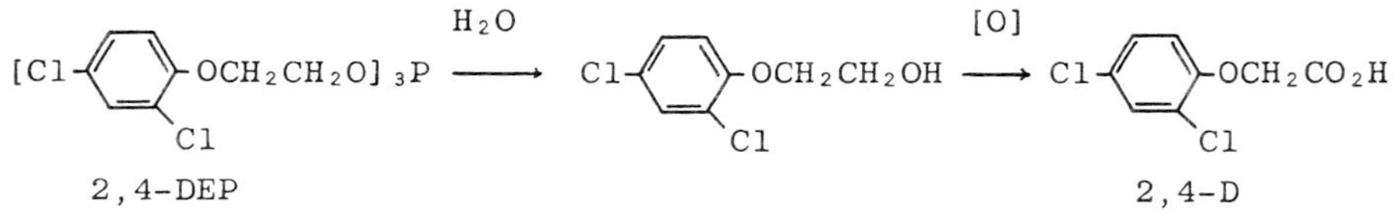

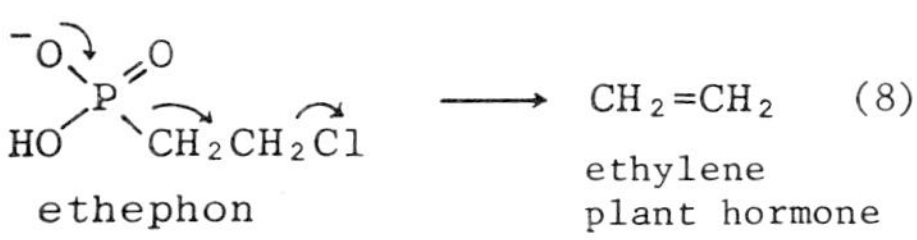

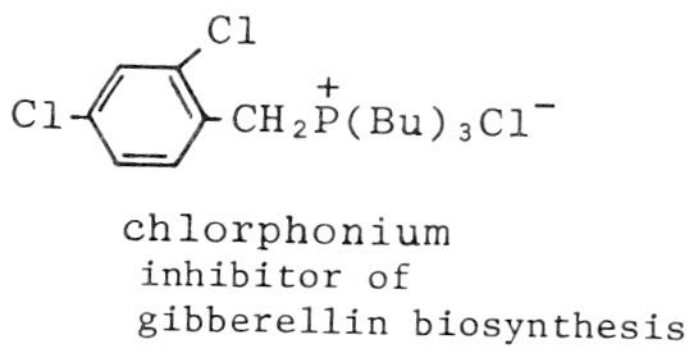

Some OP plant growth regulators

Miscellaneous

For the control of soil nematodes, vaporizable haloalkanes have been used. They are alkylating agents and can be used only before sowing or planting because of their phytotoxicity. Therefore, some less vaporizable OP nematicides with less phytotoxicity have been developed. They are anti-AChE agents anyhow.

The rodenticide Gophacide is so slowly activated *in vivo* into an AChE inhibitor that each individual in a rodent herd takes the poisoned bait without taking notice. Another phosphorus rodenticide phoszin (zink phosphide) is hydrolyzed by acid in the stomach to release phosphin which inhibits cytochrome oxidase. The fumigant phostoxin (aluminum phosphide) releases phosphin similarly by moisture.

The phosphorus aziridine derivatives such as tepa and apholate are biological alkylating agents effective as insect chemosterilants. The non-aziridine containing sterilant hempa is activated *in vivo* into a methylol intermediate which is responsible for sterilization.

CONCLUSION - ROLE OF PHOSPHORUS MOIETY IN AGROCHEMICAL MOLECULE

Phosphorus compounds show a great variety of agrochemical activities. The role of phosphorus moiety in OP agrochemicals is classified into several categories. 1) The principal in phosphorylation; the reactivity is greatly affected by the electronic properties including ring structure and metabolic activation. 2) The leaving group in alkylation as seen in dealkylation by glutathione transferase. 3) A carrier or protective group for the other active moiety as exemplified by ethephon. 4) An analog for the carboxyl group as seen in phosphinothricin, a glutamate analog. 5) Mimic for physiological phosphates; glyphosate appears an anti-metabolite of phosphoenolpyruvate. 6) A building block to keep suitably the shape or physical properties of a molecule; the phosphorus atom can be replaced by other atoms or group like that in bicyclooctanes and onium type PGR. 7) Unknown as some OP fungicides and herbicides.

Because of various functions of phosphorus and almost infinite combination of four groups attached to the phosphorus atom, a great variety of new compounds will be further found to be useful as agrochemicals in various aspects. Displacing a carboxyl group in a bioactive carboxylate characteristic to target organisms by a phosphoryl group may be very useful for seeking agrochemical lead compounds. Physiologically important phosphates can also serve for seeking leads. In order to exert a definite biological activity, the OP molecule should have a specified structure suitable for biokinetics and biodynamics in target organism. The degradability in biological systems and natural environment is the great advantage of OP compounds. Undesirabla impurities, however, should be carefully eliminated from the products.

44

REFERENCES

1. Eto M (1974) Organophosphorus Pesticides: Organic and Biological Chemistry. CRC, Cleveland, pp 1-387

2. Ohkawa H (1982) In: Coats CR (ed) Insecticide Mode of Action. Academic Press, New York, pp 163-185

3. Miyazaki M, Nakamura T, Marumo S (1989) Pestic Biochem Physiol 33:11-15

4. Eto M, Okabe S, Maekawa K (1977) Pestic Biochem Physiol 7:367-377

5. Wing KD, Glickman AH, Casida JH (1984) Pesitc Biochem Physiol 21:22-30

6. Eto M (1983) J Environ Sci Health B18:119-145

7. Eto M, Tawata S, Sakamoto K, Oshima K (1978) J Pestic Sci 3:161-163

8. Wu SY, Takeya R, Eto M, Tomizawa C (1987) J Pestic Sci 12:221-227

9. Wu SY, Hirashima A, Takeya R, Eto M (1989) Agric Biol Chem 53:165-174

10. Hollingworth RM, Fukuto TR, Metcalf RL (1967) J Agric Food Chem 15:235-241

11. Shiotsuki T, Eto M (1987) J Pestic Sci 12:17-21

12. Bergé JB (1988) Proceedings 18th Internat Cong Entomol p 461

13. Grothusen JR, Brown TM (1987) Pestic Biochem Physiol 26:100-106

14. Johnson MK (1982) Rev Biochem Toxicol 4:141-212

15. Shiotsuki T, Koiso A, Eto M (1989) J Pestic Sci 14:337-344

16. Gorder GW, Holden I, Ruzo LO, Casida JE (1985) Bioorg Chem 13:353-361

17. Ozoe Y (1987) In: Hollingworth RM, Green MB (eds) Sites of Action for Neurotoxic Pesticides. ACS Sympo Ser 356, pp 83-96

18. Palmer CJ, Casida JE (1987) In: Hollingworth RM, Green MB (eds) Sites of Action for Neurotoxic Pesticides. ACS Sympo Ser 356, pp 71-82

19. Akatsuka I, Kodama O (1984) J Pestic Sci 9:375-382

20. Manabe A, Eto M (1983) J Pestic Sci 8:363-366

21. Hashimoto Y, Eto M (1975) J Fac Agr Kyushu Univ 19:197-204

22. Sasaki M, Ooishi T, Kato T, Takayama C, Mukai K (1984) J Pestic Sci 9:737-744

23. Sasaki M, Kato T, Yamamoto S, Mukai K (1984) J Pestic Sci 9:717-723

24. Sasaki M, Takano H, Kato T (1987) Agric Biol Chem 51:1727-1728

25. Barchietto T, Saindrenan P, Bompeix G (1988) Pestic Sci 22:159-167

26. Collis PS, Weeks DP (1978) Science 202:440-442

27. Logusch EW, Walker DM, McDonald JF, Franz JE (1989) Biochem 28:3043-3051

28. Castellino S, Leo GC, Sammons RD, Sikorski JA (1989) Biochem 28:3856-3868

29. Jung J (1985) In: Hedin PA (ed) Bioregulators for Pest Control. ACS Sympo Ser 276, pp 95-107

© 1990 Elsevier Science Publishers B.V. (Biomedical Division)
Pesticides and alternatives, editor J.E. Casida

OXIDATIVE BIOMIMETIC ACTIVATION OF SULFUR-CONTAINING PESTICIDES

YOFFI SEGALL
Israel Institute for Biological Research, P.O. Box 19, Ness Ziona 70450, Israel

INTRODUCTION. Very few pesticides act directly at the target site. Their major part, particularly those containing sulfur, are bioactivated or detoxified by metabolic activation. Essential bioactivation transformations involve $\underline{S}$-oxidation, oxidative-desulfuration, $\underline{N}$-methylene oxidation, alkyl group and aryl hydroxylation and miscellaneous non-oxidative reactions (1). Although usually occurring to a small extent, oxidative bioactivation, carried out by P-450 dependent mixed function oxidases (MFO), is an important $\underline{in}$ $\underline{vivo}$ pathway that converts xenobiotics into reactive intermediates or products. Further reactions may involve hydrolysis, functional group transfer, rearrangement, reduction and conjugation, processes usually associated in part with degradation or detoxification.

Much information has been collected on pesticide metabolism ($\underline{e}$.$\underline{g}$., 2,3). The data identify ultimate products and conjugates, but may overlook transient intermediates, due to their instability or short-lived nature. Yet, intermediate studies are indispensable to understanding pesticide selectivity and their safe use in a nontarget organism environment. Biomimetic intermediate studies may often contribute significantly to clarify this gap (4-8). Peracids, such as meta-chloroperoxybenzoic acid (MCPBA) or monoperoxyphthalic acid (MPPA, as Mg salt), have been widely used as biomimetic models (4,5, 8-12). However, their relevance as suitable models has to be established in each experiment.

This manuscript considers studies on selected reactive intermediates formed on MCPBA oxidation of sulfur-containing pesticides, with emphasis on phosphorothiolates. Where appropriate, the biological relevance and toxicological significance are highlighted.

SULFOXIDATION OF HERBICIDAL CARBAMOTHIOATES - ACTIVATION TO POTENT MUTAGENS.

Results from a biomimetic experiment might be helpful in recognizing mechanisms and products involved in related research areas. Cancer studies revealed that the carbamothioate herbicide diallate, $\underline{1}$, is an active carcinogen in mice (13) and the carbamodithioate sulfallate, $\underline{2}$, in mice and rats (14).

1   **2**

Since other carbamothioate herbicides lack the 2-chloropropenyl moiety, the mutagenic activity was primarily attributed to the presence of that group in each.

It was revealed by spectroscopic methods that the thermally unstable sulfoxide, 3, from MCPBA oxidation of diallate at low temperature (15), is converted by a [2,3]sigmatropic rearrangement, followed by 1,2-elimination reaction to the ultimately highly mutagenic 2-chloropropenal (Eq. 1).

(eq. 1)

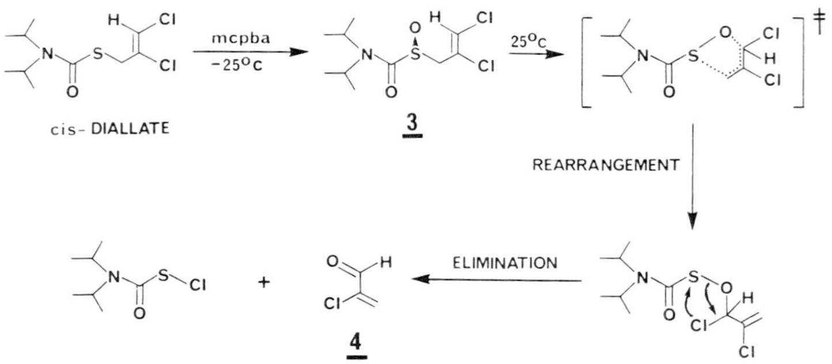

cis- DIALLATE   3

REARRANGEMENT

ELIMINATION

4

Sulfoxide, 3, in vivo undergoes either detoxification via GSH conjugation or activation through rearrangement-elimination reactions to liberate 2-chloropropenal, 4. Thus, 1 is not mutagenic without S-9 fraction. However, 3 is a direct mutagen.

These results led to the examination of a series of 2-halopropenals for their mutagenic activity, establishing 2-bromopropenal, but not 2-fluoro- or 2-iodo-propenal, as the most powerful direct mutagen in the 2-halopropenal series (16, 17).

The latter results led to the assumption that an identical ultimate mutagen is likely to be involved with the carcinogenic nematocide 2,3-dibromo-1-chloropropane, 5 (DBCP) and the flame retardant tris-[2,3-dibromopropyl] phosphate, 6 (tris-BP), as indicated in Eq. 2 (18, 19).

(eq. 2)

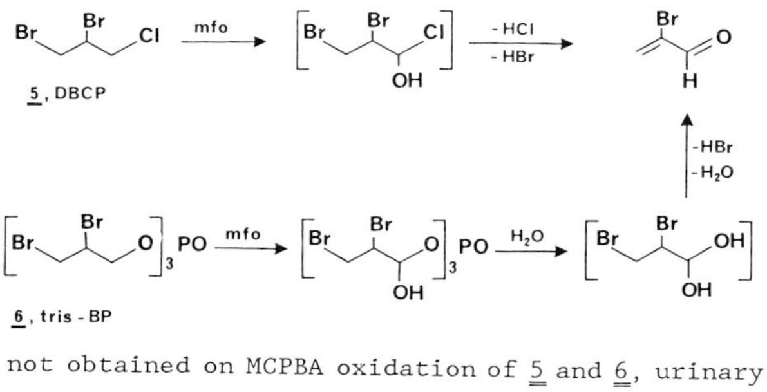

5, DBCP

6, tris - BP

Thus, although not obtained on MCPBA oxidation of 5 and 6, urinary bromopropenoic acids are excreted from rats treated with these carcinogens, presumably following hydroxylation at α-carbon. That supports the assumption that part of the metabolic pathway involves 2-bromopropenal, which is further oxidised to 2-bromopropenoic acid.

However, the MCPBA peracid system proved not a suitable model for the activation of sulfallate, 2 (20), as depicted in Eq. 3. NMR monitoring revealed that carbamodithioates, including 2, react quickly with one equivalent of MCPBA to form sulfine derivatives A (Eq. 3), but their attempted isolation led only to the unmodified carbamodithioate. Sulfoxidation is, therefore, preferred at the thion rather than the thiol sulfur. Sulfallate with excess MCPBA produces 2 major products

(eq. 3)

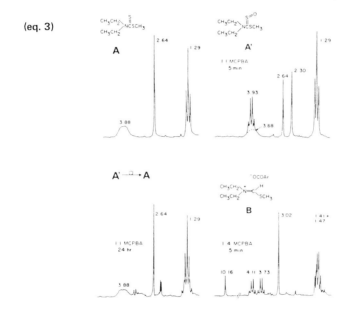

2-chloropropenyldisulfide and diethylformamide via the iminium ion intermediate B (Eq. 3). Thus, with monoequivalent MCPBA, the mutagenic activity of sulfallate, in the S-9 activated Salmonella typhimurium mutagenicity test, is retained as if 2 alone was introduced. However, with excess MCPBA the mutagenic activity is completely lost due to the extensive breakdown to non-active fragments.

An alternative highly efficient mechanism, by which 2-chloropropenal might be formed, involves α-hydroxylation of 2, followed by immediate decomposition to 4 as in Eq. 4 (21).

(eq. 4)

| sulfallate | α-hydroxy compound | 2-chloropropenal |
| promutagen | proximate mutagen | ultimate mutagen |

OXIDATION OF SULFUR IN MULTIFUNCTIONAL S-CONTAINING PESTICIDES

Phosphorothionates

Many thiophosphorus insecticides undergo oxidative bioactivation to form more reactive phosphorylating agents and more potent AChE inhibitors. Selected examples are the conversion, by oxidative desulfuration , of parathion, malathion and fonofos to their oxo-analogs, by both peracid and bioactivation, as depicted in Table I.

TABLE 1.   THIONOPHOSPHORUS INSECTICIDES KNOWN TO UNDERGO
BOTH MCPBA AND METABOLIC ACTIVATION

$$\begin{array}{c} RO \\ R' \end{array} P {\Large{\stackrel{\displaystyle S}{\diagdown}}} X \longrightarrow \begin{array}{c} RO \\ R' \end{array} P {\Large{\stackrel{\displaystyle O}{\diagdown}}} X$$

COMPOUND	R	R'	X	I_{50} (AChE , MOL.)		LD_{50} (RAT , mg/kg)	
				THIONO	OXO	THIONO	OXO
PARATHION	C_2H_5	C_2H_5O	$OC_6H_4NO_2$	1.10^{-4}	7.10^{-9}	3.3	1.4
MALATHION	CH_3	CH_3O	$SCH{<}^{CO_2C_2H_5}_{CH_2CO_2C_2H_5}$	3.10^{-3}	7.10^{-7}	2600	308
FONOFOS	C_2H_5	C_2H_5	SC_6H_5	2.10^{-5}	3.10^{-8}	14.7	2.8

Thus, the oxo analogs are far better AChE inhibitors and more toxic compared with the thio analogs. These insecticides are known to undergo a similar activation by MCPBA (22, 23).

Oxidation of a sulfur atom remote from phosphorus

Phosfolan insecticide, $\underline{7}$, is a poor _in vitro_ AChE inhibitor, yet acts as a potent inhibitor _in vivo_. A coupled MFO activation-AChE inhibition assay verified that pholan undergoes a bioactivation process prior to its AChE inhibition (24). Likewise, products from MCPBA oxidation are of increased potency (5400 fold relative to $\underline{7}$) as AChE inhibitors (Eq. 5). Surprisingly, the sulfone from $\underline{7}$, reacts with methanol by nucleophilic attack at the imino carbon rather than the phosphorus center. Thus, phospholan may ultimately function as an iminoalkylating rather than a phosphorylating agent (7). A common ultimate product,

(eq. 5)

$\underline{7}$

n = I or 2

diethyl phosphoroamidate is found in both MFO and MCPBA oxidation systems.

Biomimetic system makes it possible to evaluate the order of S-oxidation in a multifunctional sulfur-containing insecticide such as sulprofos, 8 (Eq. 6).

(eq. 6)

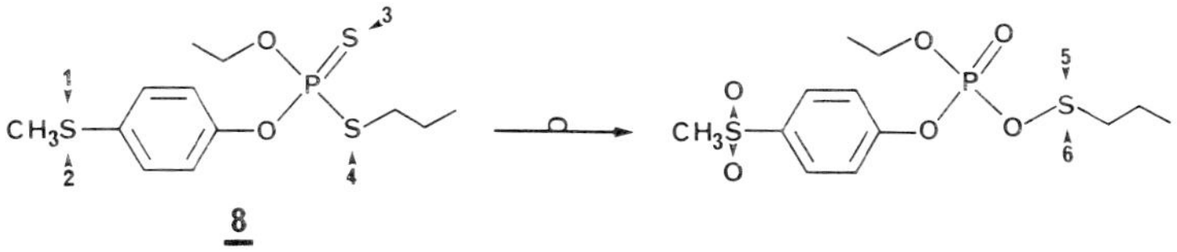

8

As monitored by ^{31}P NMR, MCPBA oxidation of 8 gives in sequence the reaction rate preferences illustrated in Eq. 6 (25). This insecticide is an AChE inhibitor only after conversion of the P=S and 4-methylthiophenyl to P=O and 4-methylphenyl-sulfonyl, respectively. Thus, oxidation rates are consistent with

thioester > thion >> thiol

Oxidation of the remote sulfur has a significance influence on the activity, but to a lesser extent as obtained from oxidative desulfuration (Table I) such as of disulfoton and fensulfothion (1).

OXIDATION STUDIES WITH S-ALKYL PHOSPHOROTHIOLATES   The oxidatian rate of the sulfur atom directly bonded to phosphorus (step 4 in Eq. 6) is much slower compared with that of a remote sulfur and is accompanied by further rearrangement and oxidation as depicted in Eq. 7(25).

(eq. 7)

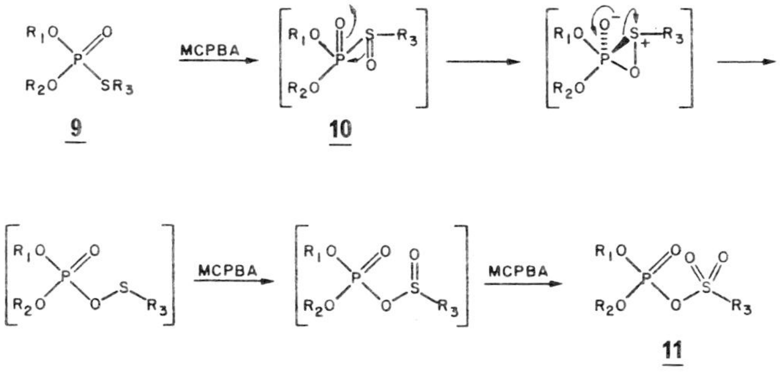

9   10

11

MCPBA oxidation of S-alkylphosphorothiolates 9, presumably leads to extremely reactive, very short lived S-oxide intermediates 10 (not observed by ^{31}P NMR), that, unless formed in the presence of nucleophiles, ultimately rearrange, via a phosphoraneoxide intermediate, to phosphinyloxysulfonates 11, after further extensive oxidations (Eq. 7). Oxysulfonates 11 lack any phosphorylation properties (25-27).

The potent phosphorylation properties of intermediates 10 was observed serendipitiously when the oxidative reaction of profenofos insecticide, 12, was carried out in CHCl$_3$ (Eq. 8) (7,8).

(eq. 8)

*stabilized with 0.75% EtOH

The unexpected diethyl ester 13, obtained as a major product, by replacement of the PrS-moiety with EtO, was a result of phosphorylation of 0.75% ethanol, normally added to CHCl$_3$ as a stabilizer, by the apporopriate S-oxide intermediate 10 (Eq. 7, R$_1$=Et, R$_2$=2-Cl-4-Br-C$_6$H$_3$, R$_3$=Pr). In ethanol free CHCl$_3$, only oxysulfonate derivatives are obtained (8). It appears that the R$_3$S(O) group attached to phosphorus in intermediate 10 is one of the best known leaving groups. That intermediate is so reactive, that its phosphorylation rate vs. rearrangement to 11 is almost independent of the other substituents attached to phosphorus, but is rather sterically controlled by the nucleophile (27). Thus, phosphorylation is the exclusive route for 10 in primary alcohols, as opposed to the rearrangement reaction in tertiary alcohol, while both routes are almost equally expressed in secondary alcohols (Eq. 9).

(eq. 9)

With optically active phosphorothiolate S-oxide, racemization does not occur prior to phosphorylation, which is assumed to proceed with inversion of the configuration about the phosphorus (23).

These results tentatively led to assume the biological relevance as proposed in Eq. 10.

(eq. 10) phosphorothiolate —[mfo [O] / activation]→ [phosphorothiolate S-oxide] —AChE→ phosphorylated enzyme

deactivation ↓

phosphinyloxy-sulfenate —H₂O→ hydrolysis products

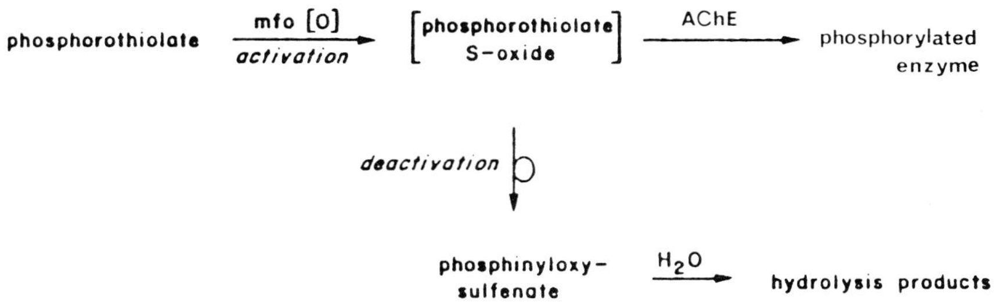

Thus, if the S-oxide intermediate is formed on MFO activation within the cell, it may immediately phosphorylate sensitive sites, such as hydrolases, including AChE. However, its formation in an environment where rearrangement occurs faster than phosphorylation, the overall result is a deactivation process of hydrolysis (26).

This assumption, primarily based on the MCPBA biomimetic system, was verified by examining behavioral differences in the chiral isomers of profenofos, 12 (28, 29). Using a system containing liver microsomes ± NADPH for metabolism and control, combined with AChE, it was established that the bioactivation reaction is stereo-specific for the chiral isomers of profenofos (Eq. 11). The more toxic, (-)-12, becomes a 34-fold better inhibitor of AChE in vitro, whereas the less toxic, (+)-12 isomer, is detoxified by a factor of 2.

(eq. 11)

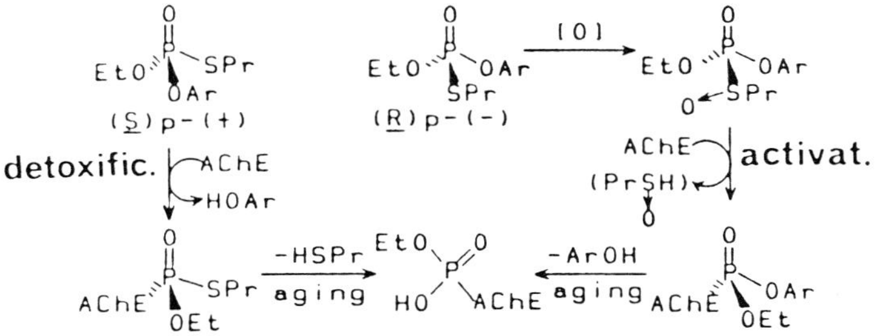

Ar = 2-chloro-4-bromophenyl

This observation led to the proposal that (-)-profenofos sulfoxide is formed with retention of the configuration and this product is the effective AChE inhibitor. In contrast, (+)-profenofos acts directly with the aryloxide as the leaving group (Eq. 11).

Loss of a second substituent (either PrSH or AroH) from the phosphorylated enzyme, gives aged AChE. These models are also consistent with the toxicity of (+)- and (-)-profenofos.

Probicyclophosphates (pro-BP). The behavior found for the individual stereoisomers of monocyclophosphorothiolates 13 and 14 (Eq. 12), on oxidation with MCPBA, is solvent dependent. If either isomer is oxidixed in ethanol-free chloroform, the corresponding bicyclophosphate 15 is obtained in quantitative yields and thus 13 and 14 are pro-BPs (30). However, in methanol, only the axial pro-BP isomer yields quantitatively BP 15, whereas, the equatorial isomer quantitatively phosphorylates the solvent (Eq. 12), a reaction proceeding with inversion of the configuration at phosphorus.

(eq. 12)

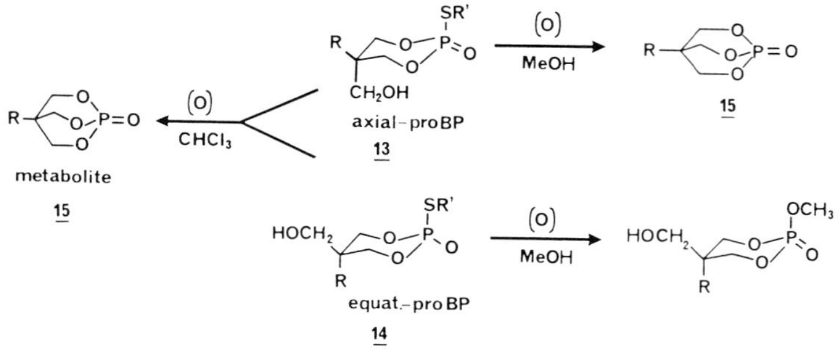

This unimolecular internal cyclization is consistent with the results obtained with oxidation of S-alkyl phosphorothiolates in the presence of alcohols (8). Direct formation of these BP GABA antagonists was observed by ^{31}P NMR spectroscopy, by monitoring the fate of the Pro-BP with liver microsomes, in vitro.

Phosphorothioic acids. Many phosphorothiolate pesticides, such as Kitazin and demeton-S are prepared by reacting an alkyl halide with a phosphorothioic acid salt. Hydrolysis (1) and metabolism (31) are two other sources by which phosphorothioic acids might be produced. Selected examples are given by Eq. 13.

(eq. 13)

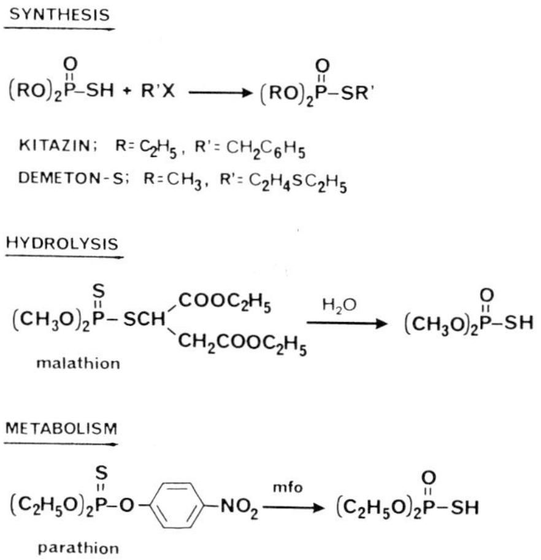

The further fate of phosphorothioic acids, under metaboic and environmental conditions, is therefore of considerable interest.

MCPBA oxidation of phosphorothioic acid 16 in ethanol (Scheme), initially gives only one major intermediate, identified as phosphoro(thioperoxoic) acid 17, which, unlike S-oxide intermediates from S-alkyl phosphorothiolates (8), is detectable by ^{31}P NMR. The time course of further product formation suggests the reaction sequence shown in the Scheme.

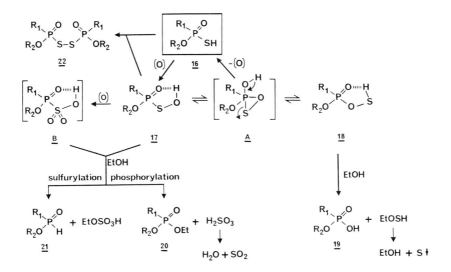

Intermediate 17, in ethanol, reacts by four different routes. Rearrangement via hydroxyphosphorane A may lead either to the starting material 16 or to oxysulfenate 18. Being a sulfurylating rather than a phosphorylating agent, intermediate 18 further reacts with ethanol to yield phosphoric acid 19 and elemental sulfur. Two other routes by which 17 reacts, are phosphorylation to give ethyl ester 20, and sulfurylation which, unexpectedly, yields phosphite 21 (32).

The reaction of intermediate 17 with the starting material 16 yielding the symmetrical disulfide 22, suggests an analogous metabolic route by which activated intermediate 17 may be detoxified on reaction with GSH.

Preliminary results, obtained by administration of various intermediates 17 to mice, indicate that phosphorothioic acids 16 are activated by 1:1 oxidation with MCPBA. The applicability of the MCPBA model system will only be determined after identifying the target site.

SUMMARY REMARKS   As indicated by the selected examples in this manuscript, biomimetic models have several advantages: a) isolation of intermediates and ultimate products in relatively large quantities; b) monitoring of the progress of reactions using multiple spectroscopic methods; c) performing reactions also in non-aqueous media, at low or high temperatures, with appropriate reagent stoichiometry; d) determination of the order or reactivity of functional groups in pesticides with many types of substituents; e) focus on candidate reactive intermediates in pesticide action.

REFERENCES

1. Eto M (1974) Organophosphorus pesticides: organic and biological chemistry. CRC Press. Cleveland, OH.

2. Aizawa H (1982) Metabolic maps of pesticiees. Academic Press, New York.

3. Dagley S, Nicholson DE (1970). An introduction to metabolic pathways. John Wiley, New York.

4. Segall Y (1989) In: Damani LA (ed) Sulphur-containing drugs and related organic compounds. Ellis Horwood, England, Vol I B, pp 91-132.

5. Casida, JE, Ruzo LO (1986) Xenobiotica 16:1003-1015.

6. Casida JE (1984) In: Brzin M, Barnard EA, Sket DS (eds) Cholinesterases: Fundamental and Applied Aspects de Gruyter, New York, pp 427-440.

7. Casida JE (1987) In: Eto M (ed) A new turn in pesticide sciences. Soft Science publications, Tokyo, Japan, pp. 115-144.

8. Segall Y, Casida JE (1981) In: Quin LD, Verkade J (eds) Phosporus Chemistry. ACS Symposium Series 171, Washington, DC, pp. 337-340.

9. Holden I, Segall Y, Kimmel EC, Casida JE (1982) Tetrahedron Letters 23:5107-5110.

10. Schuphan I, Rosen JD, Casida JE (1979) Science 205:1013-1015.

11. Bleck MS, Smith, MT, Casida JE (1985) Pest. Biochem. Physiol. 23: 123-130.

12. Kimmel EC, Holden I, Segall Y, Casida JE (1983) Tetrahedron Letters 24:2819-1820.

13. Innes JRM, Ulland BM, Valerio MG, Petrucelli L, Fishbein L, Hart E, Pallotta AJ, Bates RR, Falk HL, Gart JJ, Klein M, Mitchel I, Peters JJ (1969) J. Nat. Cancer Inst. 42: 1101-1114.

14. National Cancer Institute (1978) In: Carcinogens, Technical reports series 115. DHEW NIH 78-1370.

15. Schuphan I, Casida JE (1979) Tetrahedron Letters 10: 841-844.

16. Segall Y, Kimmel EC, Dohn DR, Casida JE (1985) Mutation Res. 158:61-68.

17. Rosen JD, Segall Y, Casida JE (1980) Mutation Res. 78: 13-119.

18. Marsden PJ, Casida JE (1982) J. Agric. Food Chem. 30:627-631.

19. Dohn DR, Graziano MJ, Casida JE (1988) Biochem. Pharmacol. 37: 3485-3495.

20. Segall Y, Casida JE (1983) J. Agr. Food Chem. 31: 242-246.

21. Rosen JD, Schuphan I, Segall Y, Casida JE (1980) J. Agr. Food Chem. 28:880-881.

22. Neal RA (1981) In: Rosen JD, Magee PS, Casida JE (eds) Sulfur in pesticide action and metabolism. ACS Symposium Series 158, pp 19-43.

23. McBain JB, Yamamoto I, Casida JE (1971) Life Sci. 10: 1311-1315.

24. Gorder GW, Holden I, Ruzo LO, Casida JE (1985) Bioorg. Chem. 13:344-352.

55

25.   Segall Y, Casida JE (1982) Tetahedron Letters 23: 139-142.

26.   Segall Y, Casida JE (1981) In: Quin L D, Verkade J (eds) Phosphorus cohemistry. ACS Symposium Series 171. Washington, DC, pp 337-340.

27.   Segall Y, Casida JE (1982) Phosphorus and sulphur 18:209-212.

28.   Wing KD, Glickman AH, Casida JE (1983) Science 219:63-65.

29.   Wing KD, Glickman AH, Casida JE (1984) Pestic. Biochem. Physiol. 21: 22-30.

30.   Toia RF, Casida JE (1985) Toxicol. Appl. Pharmacol. 81: 50-57.

31.   Neal RA (1967) Biochem. J. 103:183-187.

32.   Segall Y, Wu SY, Toia RF, Casida JE (1989) Tetrahedron Letters, submitted.

© 1990 Elsevier Science Publishers B.V. (Biomedical Division)
Pesticides and alternatives, editor J.E. Casida

THE DEATH OF DAMINOZIDE

JOSEPH D. ROSEN
Department of Food Science, Cook College, Rutgers University, New Brunswick,
NJ 08903 USA

On June 2, 1989 the Uniroyal Chemical Company "voluntarily" cancelled
United States sales of daminozide, a plant growth regulator sold under
the tradename Alar . The events leading up to this decision are recounted
here in order to educate the reader about the current pesticide situation
in the United States, a situation that is the result of confusing and
paradoxical laws, a regulatory policy that not only is based on unproven
scientific theories but also lacks common sense, ignorant environmental
activists, gullible journalists and a chemophobic citizenry.

Agrochemicals are regulated by the United States under authority
of the Federal Insecticide Fungicide and Rodenticide Act (FIFRA). The
act permits the U.S. Environmental Protection Agency (EPA) to set tolerances
(permissible residues) for individual pesticides on a variety of agricultural
commodities. These tolerances are designed in such a way that even under
worst-case weather conditions the total residues on all the commodities
on which the pesticide will be used will not exceed the acceptable daily
intake (ADI) for a human. The ADI is calculated by determining the dose
that is non-toxic to laboratory animals and dividing it by a 100:1 safety
factor to account for the possibility that humans might be more susceptible.
Should the pesticide have tumorigenic properties, the EPA is required
by law to perform a risk/benefit analysis before deciding whether or
not to permit registration. An important benefit consideration would
be that no other effective pesticide exists for control of an insect
that is causing severe economic loss. Tumor risk is considered unacceptable
if it is greater than one excess cancer per million people over a 70
year lifetime as determined from animal tumor data, the proposed tolerance
level and estimates of how much food on which the pesticide will be permitted
is consumed. The risk assessments and exposure estimates are mainly
guesses and there is considerable disagreement as to their accuracy.
For a new pesticide, the burden of proof for its safety rests with the
manufacturer and a pesticide with tumorigenic properties is very difficult
to register.

Once a pesticide is granted a tolerance, its registration can be
revoked if subsequent research determines that the material poses a risk
to human health. However, the burden of proof now rests with the government.

Should EPA determine that the pesticide causes an unreasonable risk (more than 1 excess cancer per 1,000,000 people over a 70-year lifetime), the agency acts to cancel the pesticide's registration. Use of the pesticide may continue, however, until the final outcome of the cancellation proceedings and associated appeals. This process may take several years. If an imminent danger exists, i.e., more than one additional cancer per 1,000,000 people over the next 1.5-2 years, EPA suspends registration, and the pesticide may not be used during the cancellation process. Not surprisingly, the average person finds it difficult to understand why some cancer-causing pesticides are permitted while others are not and why it takes so long for removal of these chemicals from the food supply.

Even more difficult to understand is the so-called "Delaney Paradox". Under Section 408 of the Food, Drug and Cosmetic Act, tumorigenic pesticides are permitted on raw agricultural commodities provided that they do not constitute an unreasonable risk or if their benefits outweigh their risks. EPA has identified over 50 potentially such pesticides and has published Q^* values (tumor animal incidence per mg pesticide per kg body weight per day) for 29 of them. Should the raw agricultural commodity be used in a processed food, Section 409 is applicable and the food may now be legally adulterated. Section 409 contains the Delaney Clause, which forbids the addition of any cancer causing agent to food. Thus, a tumorigenic pesticide is permitted on tomatoes but is illegal if the tomatoes are used to make tomato paste, should the pesticide residue increase in concentration.

Consumer groups do not draw the fine line between unreasonable and imminent risks or between tomatoes and tomato paste and have been active, through lobbying, judicial and public relations efforts, in demanding immediate deregistration of all those pesticides for which tumorigenic activity has been demonstrated. During the early part of 1989, these differences were the background for a public furor about the safety of the US food supply. Particular attention was focused on daminozide and its alleged effect on the health of America's children.

Daminozide is a plant growth regulator which prevents pre-harvest fruit drop, increases storage life and promotes color development in some agricultural commodities. It was first registered on ornamental crops in 1963 and received a tolerance for use on apples in 1968. It is also registered for use on peanuts, grapes and cherries. Daminozide is synthesized from a derivative of succinic acid and 1,1-dimethylhydrazine (unsymetrical dimethylhydrazine, UDMH); technical daminozide probably contains small amounts of UDMH. UDMH is an animal metabolite of daminozide (the EPA estimates that approximately 1% ingested daminozide is converted to UDMH by humans). In addition, heat accelerates the hydrolysis of daminozide to UDMH and significant quantities of UDMH (approximately 5% conversion) are found in applesauce and apple juice as a result of the processing conditions used. In 1973, Bela Toth at the Eppley Institute for Research in Cancer in Omaha found that UDMH was responsible for the appearance of blood vessel, lung, kidney and liver tumors in mice. A subsequent study in 1977 also revealed high tumor incidence in mice that had been dosed with daminozide. These data led EPA to initiate a "Special Review" of daminozide in 1980. This is an intensified review of a pesticide's risk based on new data not considered at the time of the pesticide's original registration. The review was cancelled after private discussions with Uniroyal but reimposed after judicial action was initiated by the Natural Resources Defense Council (NRDC), a private organization whose aims are to protect the public from environmental dangers. As part of this review, the FIFRA Scientific Advisory Panel (a group of academic consultants) were asked to examine Toth's results and procedures and to determine if they were good enough to withstand the legal challenges that Uniroyal would almost surely bring should EPA revoke daminozide tolerances. The panel concluded (in September 1985) that Toth's data were inadequate to serve as a basis for a quantitative risk assessment and further, that the studies were so unreliable that they failed to provide EPA with the burden of proof needed to cancel registration. The major problem cited by the panel was that Toth treated the animals with doses above the maximum tolerated dose (MTD) and the resulting high toxicity caused biochemical changes which may have produced the observed tumors. Other deficiencies with the Toth studies were use of inadequate controls (the cancer incidence data for untreated mice were from studies conducted at the University of Chicago in the late sixties), and that there had been no chemical analyses of the test substances. Given the high doses of daminozide used by Toth, a 0.2-1% impurity of UDMH in the test substance would have resulted in the carcinogenic evaluation of the UDMH and not daminozide. Furthermore, UDMH has a half-life of 14 hours in water and Toth only provided fresh water every 48-72 hrs, so it was not at all clear just what chemical was being tested. Other procedural deficiencies included poor weight gain by the mice (due to high toxicity) in both studies and dehydration of the mice during most of the daminozide assay. Given the inadequacy of the Toth data, EPA announced in January 1986 that it would permit continued use of daminozide but ordered Uniroyal to provide chronic toxicity and residue data. The residue data (shown

in Table 1) for 12 commodities and processed foods indicate average values
of 0.37-1.45 µg/g (ppm) for daminozide and much lower values, 1.52-108
ng/kg (ppb) for UDMH. Limits of detection in these assays were 0.01
ppm and 0.001 ppm for daminozide and UDMH, respectively. The new toxicology
data performed by the International Research and Development Corporation
(IRDC) under contract to Uniroyal demonstrated that daminozide did not
cause increased cancer incidence in either mice or rats when fed at doses
as high as 10,000 ppm/day in drinking water. UDMH was negative at all
doses in rats. In mice, no tumors were observed at either 10 or 20 ppm/day
after 1 year.   One mouse of a group of 45 that had been given UDMH for
one year at 40 ppm/day had a lung tumor while blood vessel (both benign
and malignant) and lung (benign only) tumors were observed in eleven
of fifty-two animals that had received 80 ppm UDMH/day. Eighty per cent
of the male mice died prematurely because of extreme toxicity strongly
suggesting that the MTD had again been surpassed. Indeed, the results
of a 90-day UDMH feeding study several years earlier had demonstrated
an MTD of 20 ppm/day but EPA forced Uniroyal to conduct the cancer studies
at the higher feeding levels. By extrapolation of just one data point
(80 ppm), EPA determined that continued use of daminozide would result
in an increased lifetime cancer risk of 4.5 per 100,000 (upper bound
of the 95% confidence limit) exposed individuals, a risk 45 times greater
than the "socially acceptable" risk of one in a million. Since this
did not constitute an imminent risk, EPA announced it would continue
the daminozide tolerance in effect on apples until July 31, 1990, but
intended to cancel all registrations after that date. In a February
1, 1989 press release, EPA noted that the mice fed 80 ppm UDMH/day were
dying early but insisted that these deaths were due to the tumors. Strangely,
the EPA press release went on to say that "it may be argued that the
deaths are the result of excessive toxicity, which may compromise the
outcome of the study". Dr. Christine Chaisson, a cell biologist employed
by Technical Assessment Systems, argues that the observed mouse tumors
are due to an excessive buildup of hormones brought about by an interference
with steroid metabolism in the liver as a result of the highly toxic
doses of UDMH administered. In humans, blood vessel tumors are very
rare (only 80 cases per year in the United States) and are found mainly
in women who are undergoing estrogen therapy. In fact, children who
are supposed to be at the highest risk are in reality at the lowest risk
because they have much lower steroid levels than adults. By February
1, NRDC had completed its own risk assessments of daminozide and several
other agrochemicals. They scheduled release of their report, "Intolerable

Risk: Pesticides in our Children's Food", for February 27, one day after
a scheduled story about daminozide on **60 Minutes**, an extremely popular
television program with an estimated audience of approximately 30,000,000
viewers. A public relations firm, Fenton Communications, was hired to
publicize the report. The public relations thrust was clearly aimed
at connecting pesticides with cancer in children. Lost in the media
blitz was that the risks were to children who were going to be exposed
for 70 years. "We deliberately chose **60 Minutes** because we wanted to
reach the parents of young children", said NRDC spokeswoman Jeanne Whalen.
"We talked to them, and they said they would do the story if they got
an exclusive".

The NRDC lifetime risk estimates were quite disturbing - 240 per
1,000,000 for children who were average consumers of daminozide-treated
foods and a whopping 910 per 1,000,000 ("an additional cancer case for
every 1,100 children exposed") for heavy consumers (95th percentile).
These risk assessments were much higher than that of the EPA for several
reasons. First, NRDC used the Toth cancer incidence data while EPA relied
on the more recent studies. The Q^* value from the new study was ten
times less than the Q^* value from the Toth study. Second, NRDC chose
to make its risk estimate using a time-dependent mathematical model instead
of the time-independent model used by EPA. The time-dependent model
assumes that exposure to a genotoxin (a material that initiates cancer
by changing the genetic material in normal cells) early in life is much
more serious than subsequent exposures because the cells initiated by
the genotoxin have much more time to multiply (probably true) and that
children are more sensitive than adults (sometimes true, depending on
the chemistry and metabolism of the genotoxin in question). Although
it is reasonable to assume that tumors initiated early in life are more
dangerous, this assumption has absolutely nothing to do with either daminozide
or UDMH, neither of which are genotoxins. Both of these materials have
repeatedly been tested for genotoxicity and every result has been negative,
or at best, equivocal. The genotoxicity data was known to NRDC at the
time it published its report. Third, NRDC and EPA also differed on their
estimates of the amount of apples and apple products ingested. EPA used
data from a 1977-1978 consumption survey of about 30,000 people made
by the U.S. Department of Agriculture (USDA), while NRDC relied on a
1985-6 USDA study of just 2,000 persons, a study that suggested that
fruit and vegetable consumption had increased 30% during the interval
between surveys. Both EPA and NRDC agreed that children aged 0-5 consumed
more fruits than adults, and both claimed that they used the average

TABLE I

AVERAGE CONCENTRATIONS OF DAMINOZIDE AND UDMH FOUND IN UNIROYAL
MARKET BASKET SURVEY 1986-1987.

Product	No. Samples	Daminozide (μg/g)	UDMH (μg/kg)
Red Delicious	70	1.04	1.65
Golden Delicious	70	0.70	1.57
McIntosh	44	1.08	1.79
Apples (Other)	48	1.33	2.78
Adult Apple Juice	70	0.37	14.16
Adult Apple Sauce	70	0.38	23.90
Cherry Filling	70	1.45	107.76
Peanuts	71	0.87	24.86
Peanut Butter	71	0.50	10.65
Grape Juice	48	0.03	1.52
Baby Apple Juice	40	0.47	35.44
Baby Apple Sauce	40	0.49	44.05

TABLE II

VARIOUS RISK ASSESSMENTS FOR DAMINOZIDE.*

Group/ Agency	Animal Data	Exposure Data	Mathematical Model	Risk($\times 10^{-6}$) (Upper Bound)
EPA	Uniroyal (80 ppm only)	1978 USDA	Time-Independent	45
NRDC	Toth (1973 and 1977)	1986 USDA	Time-Dependent (Exponent of 5 for Ages 0-5)	910
CDFA	Uniroyal (All Doses)	1978 USDA	Time-Dependent (Exponent of 3 for Ages 0-5)	2.6

*All risk estimates made from either all or some of residue data in
Table I.

residue data provided by Uniroyal. A subsequent risk analysis made by
the California Department of Food and Agriculture used the 1977-8 USDA
exposure data and, differing from EPA, determined cancer incidence in
mice by including the negative results from the 40 and 20 ppm/day feeding
regimens. An exponent of 3 (NRDC used an exponent of 5) was used to
give a higher risk factor for childhood exposures. CDFA's risk estimate
was 2.6 excess cancers per million people, a risk still above "socially
acceptable", but one that could be managed by revoking some tolerances
(such as cherries or peanuts) or by imposing a zero tolerance on apple
juice. The three studies are summarized in Table 2.

The CDFA risk estimate was not available to NRDC or the producers
of **60 Minutes** on the night of February 26, although the new carcinogenicity
data and the EPA risk analysis had been available to them since the beginning
of that month. The FIFRA Science Advisory Panel's analysis of the Toth
data and the genotoxicity data had been available much longer. The **60
Minutes** telecast started with the narrator, Ed Bradley, seated in front
of a backdrop which pictured a skull and crossbones superimposed on an
apple. An interview with Dr. Jack Moore, EPA Assistant Administrator
for Pesticides and Toxic Substances, revealed that a tolerance application
for daminozide would be denied under current regulations. However, the
law prevented him from immediately cancelling the existing tolerance
because Uniroyal could sue in court. "Let them sue...." says the next
interviewee, Congressman Jerry Sikorsky, "....go to a cancer ward in
any children's hospital in this country and see the bald, wasting away
kids and then make a decision whether the risks balance over the benefits".
This is followed by pictures of toddlers drinking apple juice and a voiceover
by Ed Bradley explaining that kids are at high risk because they drink
eighteen times more apple juice than their mothers. Cut to Janet Hathaway
who claims that daminozide is "a cancer-causing agent used on food that
the EPA **knows** will cause cancer in thousands of children over their lifetime".
And so on. Dr. Edward Groth of Consumer's Union (CU), reveals that 23
of 31 samples of apple juice purchased by CU in New York City supermarkets
contained daminozide. He does not mention that the average amount of
daminozide detected in these 31 samples was only 0.23 ppm and that only
about 5% of the daminozide is converted to UDMH during processing. In
an utter disregard for objective reporting, there is not one hint that
there is another side to the story. During the following week, parents
throughout the country send their children to school with notes demanding
that apple juice not be provided at recess, and several school systems
remove apples and apple products from lunch menus. Meryl Streep testifies

before Congress about the pesticide peril and the event is covered on
every news telecast that evening. Testimony to the safety of the food
supply by Jack Moore, by the Surgeon General and by the Food and Drug
Administration Director are largely ignored. "Newsweek" and "Time" devote
full stories to the issue. Newspapers across the country warn of the
dangers of giving apples to children. Ordinary citizens become involved.
A New Jersey housewife forms a citizens action group, "Parents Against
Pesticide Abuse", after her 6-year old son sees a television program
on daminozide and asks if he was "going to get cancer and die?". Consumers
stop buying apples. Within two months of the **60 Minutes** telecast, apple
growers report losses of $100,000,000 and demand that EPA remove daminozide
from the market. Legislation to immediately revoke daminozide tolerances
is introduced in the United States Senate. Finally, besieged on all
sides, Uniroyal announces that it is suspending sales of daminozide in
the United States until a final EPA decision can be made.

During this period of paranoia and misinformation, viewers of **Donahue**,
a popular daytime television talk show, were given some chilling news
about the dangers of cancer-causing pesticides in fruits and vegetables.
Donahue's guests were Meryl Streep; Robin Whyatt, an NRDC staff member
and co-author of their report; Janet Hathaway, an attorney and senior
lobbyist for NRDC; and Stephen Markowitz, MD, Assistant Director of Environmental
and Occupational Medicine at Mt. Sinai Hospital in New York. Other than
providing an outdated view of the relationship between cancer and the
environment, Dr. Markowitz sat by silently while the three others advised
the studio audience and approximately 10,000,000 viewers how to protect
themselves, and particularly their children, from cancer. This advice
consisted of either peeling the produce or washing it in detergent; avoiding
produce that looked too good, was out of season or was imported; getting
to know their supermarket produce manager (who was almost as important
to their child's health as their pediatrician), insisting that organic
produce be made available and demanding that their legislators do a better
job in assuring a safer food supply. Several facts were omitted: Doll
and Peto, two of the world's leading epidemiologists believe that "the
occurrence of pesticides as dietary contaminants seems unimportant",
a view shared by most scientists; after 40 years of widespread pesticide
use, only smoking-related cancer incidence had increased; the daily dose
of UDMH that caused tumors in mice was over 266,000 times higher than
the amount ingested every day by those humans (pre-school children) alleged
to be most at risk. The panelists did not inform the audience that some
detergent chemicals had never been adequately tested for cancer; most

of the pesticides of concern could not be washed off because they were
inside the food; fiber and nutrients, considered by the National Cancer
Institute to be anti-carcinogens, would be lost by peeling fruit; Food
and Drug Administration analysts have determined that out of season,
good-looking, or imported produce do not necessarily contain higher levels
of pesticides than in-season, damaged or domestic produce; avoidance
of such fruits and vegetables (with or without pesticide) would probably
increase cancer risk; many of the naturally-occurring chemicals found
in food are themselves carcinogens and are present at levels 100-1000
times higher than even the most-heavily applied pesticides; organically-grown
produce may contain high levels of carcinogenic mycotoxins (toxins produced
by fungi) because fungicides cannot be used; organic produce costs 10-50%
more than pesticide-treated produce because of insect, weed and fungus
damage; some organic farmers use natural pesticides whose carcinogenicity
has never been tested and for which there are no adequate analytical
methods.

The death of daminozide illustrates the current sad state of pesticide
regulation in the United States. Policies that are supposed to protect
the health of the American people while at the same time assuring an
ample and low cost food supply are now at the mercy of self-appointed
guardians of public health and irresponsible, sensation-seeking journalists.
Many Americans have lost faith in their government's ability to protect
them and have, instead, turned for advice to people who are unqualified
to give advice.

How did we get into this situation?

Some of our problems stem from the government's goal of preventing
exposure to chemicals whose use would constitute a cancer risk greater
than 1 in a million. While this is a laudable goal, it allows people
who have mastered simple arithmetic and have access to a microphone to
tell vast television audiences that daminozide is 240 times more dangerous
than EPA finds acceptable. An even more bizzare bastardization of EPA's
utopian goal was made by **Consumer Reports,** warning that UDMH cancer incidence
in mice (22% at 80 ppm/day) was "220,000 times greater than the 1 in
1 million risk (projected from animal studies of this type) that the
government considers a public health concern". Then there is the manner
in which EPA calculates and communicates risk. Risk is determined from
the **total** number of benign and malignant tumors at the target site
in the **most sensitive** species fed the **highest dose possible,** usually thousands
of times higher than the actual human dose. Extremely conservative
mathematical models designed to maximize risk are used. Negative

data (such as the absence of UDMH-caused tumors in rats) is ignored and all chemicals tested are treated as genotoxins even if there is data to the contrary. The determined risk is, in reality, a **worst case scenario** value and has very little to do with actual risk, which may well be zero. This important fact is not communicated in language that the layman can understand.

Although EPA administrators are well aware that the risk assessment values they calculate are highly speculative, they ignore other data that could be used to ascertain whether or not the risk assessment values have any validity. If they had used such a common sense approach for daminozide/UDMH they could have told worried parents throughout America that:

1. The most sensitive species of animal tested (the mouse) showed no evidence of any cancers at an exposure rate of 2.89 mg UDMH per kg body weight per day. This dose is more than 35,000 times higher than the dose calculated by NRDC for the group with the highest exposure, pre-schoolers.

2. Based on the highest average values of daminozide and UDMH determined in apples (1.33 ppm and 2.78 ppb, respectively), a person would have to eat 150 pounds of apples every day for 70 years in order to ingest just one ounce of UDMH.

3. A person whose diet consisted of nothing else except applesauce (4.4 lbs of applesauce every day) would ingest, in one year, an amount of UDMH (about 20 milligrams) equal in weight to the tar contained in two filtered cigarettes! (This calculation is based on the food found to contain the most UDMH [Table 1] and includes 1% metabolic conversion of daminozide to UDMH).

4. The blood vessel tumors observed in the treated mice are extremely rare (only 80 cases per year) in humans and appear to be causally related to estrogen therapy, not apples.

In summary, the events leading up to and culminating with the death of daminozide present a serious challenge to American agriculture, the agrochemicals industry, the way the United States regulates toxic chemicals in food and the manner in which risk is communicated to the consumer. Unless better efforts are made to stem the tide of ignorance and the public hysteria manufactured by special interest groups, we face some trying times ahead.

This is NJ Agricultural Experiment Station Publication No. F-10119-1-89.

INSECTS
Genetic control

© 1990 Elsevier Science Publishers B.V. (Biomedical Division)
Pesticides and alternatives, editor J.E. Casida

CURRENT STATUS AND FUTURE PROSPECTS FOR GENETIC METHODS OF INSECT CONTROL OR
ERADICATION

D.A. LINDQUIST, B. BUTT, U. FELDMANN, R.E. GINGRICH & A. ECONOMOPOULOS
Joint FAO/IAEA Division, P.O. Box 100, Vienna, Austria and IAEA Seibersdorf
Laboratory, Austria

INTRODUCTION

The control of insects is necessary for successful agricultural
production and to protect humans and animals from vector-borne diseases.
Insecticides are the primary method of controlling insects and will remain so
in the foreseeable future. However, these chemicals continue to cause
environmental concerns and insects continue to become resistant to them. The
very high cost of developing new insecticides, primarily resulting from
acknowledgement that these chemicals may pose health problems, is a limiting
factor in the rapid development of new insecticides. Insect control
specialists would like to have narrow spectrum, more species-specific
insecticides. However, industry cannot supply these because profits are
insufficient to pay for development costs. These factors have led to
increased research for alternative methods of controlling insects.

Ecological research on insect movement, overwintering, population changes
and migration, as well as alternate host availability, have led scientists to
propose that in some cases insect control can be effectively and economically
applied at a site different from the crop to be protected, or at a time other
than normal. This approach to insect control, commonly called area-wide
control, differs considerably from the more usual field by field approach to
insect control. Area-wide control is routinely used against mosquitoes,
tsetse flies, most forest insects, locusts and for all eradication
programmes. All genetic methods of insect control, inundative release of
parasites, male annihilation, mass trapping, and use of pheromones as mating
deterrents are effective only when applied on an area-wide basis. In most
cases area-wide control is currently applied where it is the only approach to
solving the problem. Occasionally it will be used against key insect species,
i.e. species which if controlled are of direct economic benefit to the
producer, are a major pest, or normal control procedures result in a minor

insect pest becoming very important.

For the purpose of this paper, genetic methods of insect control are defined as autocidal in which genetic change is transmitted to the next generation.

Large insect control and eradication programmes using genetic methods have serious potential problems. In nearly all cases mass-rearing and use of the sterile or genetically altered insects are done by the same organization under the same management. This dual responsibility, manufacturing and use, can lead to difficulties. Even though most technical people are not experienced managers, most large eradication programmes are managed by technical people. This arrangement frequently leads to good science but poor management. Trained managers should have overall responsibility with a solid technical support staff.

The requirement for a continuous supply of a predetermined number of high quality insects for the programme should not be underestimated. Mass-rearing of insects on a continuous basis requires ingenuity, a 7-day week work-force and a good bit of luck. Labour unrest, particularly of the workers in the unpleasant conditions in mass-rearing facilities, can cause difficulties. All mass-rearing operations suffer from fluctuations in insect quality and production, often from unknown reasons. These programmes operate in large areas, involving many people and frequently using airplanes for release of the biological material and insecticides. Thus the programme is very visible to the public. Therefore, an effective programme to inform the public about the project is essential. Most programmes are run by government organizations and therefore susceptible to political whims. Large programmes require strong political support and are sometimes drastically affected by changes in government leadership and policies. Releasing the damaging stage of an insect may cause damage that must be tolerated before eradication is achieved. Despite these problems there is an increasing number of large programmes utilizing genetic methods of insect control.

PRESENT STATUS

Sterile Insect Technique (SIT)

The Sterile Insect Technique (SIT), the oldest of the genetic methods of insect control, is essentially birth control of insects. Large numbers of the target insect are reared in factories, sterilized with gamma radiation and released in the field in isolated or very large areas. The sterile males compete with the native males for mating. Matings involving sterile insects do not produce progeny. If sufficient numbers of sterile insects are released the native population in the next generation will decrease. Continued releases of sufficient numbers of sterile insects in an area over several generations without invasion of mated wild females will result in eradication.

In most programmes both sterile males and sterile females are released since the sexes cannot be easily separated in large numbers. When only sterile males are released, there is usually an increased efficiency of the sterile males since there are no sterile sisters to compete with the native females. By eliminating females during the egg or young larval stage a cost savings in rearing is achieved. Research on genetic methods of separating insects by sex or producing males only for SIT programmes is of high priority.

If the target species mates more than once, the sperm from the sterile male must effectively compete with the sperm from the native male.

The quality of the released insects must be very high. These sterile insects must compete effectively with the native insects in flight ability, longevity, mating competitiveness, time and location of mating and distribution. Standard tests to determine quality have been developed for a number of species.

Diptera

(1) Screwworm (Cochliomyia hominivorax). Screwworm larvae are an important parasite of livestock and other warm-blooded animals. It is the insect model for the SIT (1). The SIT was proven successful against the screwworm in 1954 when it was eradicated from Curacao. Eradication was initiated in Florida in 1958 and completed in 1959, then initiated in the south-west U.S.A. in 1962 and completed in 1982. The initial objective was to eradicate the pest from the U.S.A. Later the objective included eradication from Mexico, not only because of the extensive damage it caused in Mexico, but also because it proved impossible to prevent reintroduction of the pest into the U.S.A. An eradication programme was initiated in Mexico in 1977 and is now essentially complete. The programme is now

releasing sterile flies in Guatemala and Belize and is planned to go through Panama (1).

The cost/benefit of the screwworm programme is very favourable; estimated savings (benefits) through 1987 were US$ 4,000 million (2).

The present mass-rearing factory at Tuxtla Gutierrez, Mexico is producing 250 million flies per week. A maximum of 500 million per week can be produced.

The flies are treated with 55 Gy (5.5 Krads) gamma radiation and released in boxes containing 1,500 flies each by aircraft flying a 3 km swath width twice weekly for a total release of 700 to 3,000 flies per km^2 per week.

The primary problems that had to be solved during the programme included obtaining sufficient funds, maintaining a strong research support effort in the face of success, maintaining high quality sterile flies, the necessity of developing solutions to problems that were unique to this first large SIT programme, and the political problems which resulted partially from articles in scientific journals stating that the programme would not succeed for a number of reasons, primarily genetic. Fortunately none of these genetic problems proved real (1).

(2) Mediterranean Fruit Fly (Ceratitis capitata). The Mediterranean fruit fly (medfly) has been the subject of intensive research and development as well as eradication programmes utilizing the SIT. The practical use of the SIT for medfly eradication was initiated when the pest moved into Mexico from Guatemala in 1977. The Ministries of Agriculture of Mexico, Guatemala and the U.S.A. formed the Moscamed programme to combat this pest (3). The objective was to eradicate the medfly from Mexico and subsequently from Guatemala, and eventually from all of Central America and Panama.

The mass-rearing facility for the programme was constructed at Metapa, Mexico, very close to the Guatemalan border. The construction of the facility was completed in 1979 and 100 million insects per week were being reared by the end of the year. By combining the discreet use of malathion bait spray with release of sterile medflies, eradication of the pest from the infested area of Mexico (8,000 km^2) was completed in 1982. During the peak of this eradication campaign, more than 500 million medflies per week were being reared at the Metapa facility. The total cost of the Mexican programme exceeded US$ 100 million. The economic benefits have been estimated at more than US$ 1,000 million per year (4).

The programme is continuing in Guatemala where most of the sterile insects from the Metapa facility are being released. In addition, a mass-rearing facility has been constructed near Guatemala City which is currently producing about 200 million sterile flies per week. About 7,000 km^2 are now free of the medfly. The long-term objective remains to eradicate this pest from all of Central America and Panama (5)(6).

The SIT has also been utilized in the U.S.A. to eradicate accidental introductions in Florida and California.

All insects to be released are marked with a fluorescent dye immediately before irradiation. Medfly pupae are irradiated with 145 Gy (14.5 Krads) under anoxia 48 hours prior to adult emergence. Anoxia is induced by placing cooled pupae (18-19°C) in sealed containers one hour before irradiation.

The sterile flies are marked to distinguish them from wild flies caught in traps to determine the ratio of sterile to wild flies and for programme evaluation. Irradiating medfly pupae under anoxia results in a better quality sterile fly than irradiation in air.

After radiation, the pupae are placed in paper bags, 20,000 per bag, with sugar as a food source. When approximately 80% of the adults have emerged, the paper bags are released by single engine aircraft on a grid pattern over the target area. The grid pattern is supplemented by additional releases over known areas of potential high medfly populations, based on ecological data. Programme progress is measured by fruit infestation and adult trapping.

The primary problems encountered were large fluctuations in numbers of sterile flies available and the associated problems of low quality flies.

(3) Melon Fly (Dacus cucurbitae). The larvae of the melon fly are a
     serious pest of fruit and vegetables. This pest causes quarantine
     restrictions of its hosts in the southern islands of Japan. The
     Japanese Government decided to eradicate the fly by the SIT. The
     adult population was suppressed with one or more treatments of a
     lure/toxicant (cue-lure/nalad) prior to releases of sterile flies.
     An eradication programme was begun in 1972 to eradicate the melon
     fly from Kume Island (6,247 ha.) with releases of 6 to 20 million
     sterile flies per month and in adjacent islands (4,764 ha.) of 6 to
     15 million sterile flies per month. Eradication was achieved in
     1976. Releases began on Miykao Islands and adjacent islands
     (23,000 ha.) in 1984 and eradication was achieved in 1987.

     An eradication programme was started in the Okinawa Islands
     (144,000 ha.) in 1986 and completed in the northern section in
     1987. Eradication in the remaining sections will be complete in the
     near future. The eradication of the melon fly from the last area of
     the Okinawa prefecture, Yaeyama Island (58,000 ha.) was begun in
     1989.

     The Naha city rearing plant can produce 200 million insects per
     week. Pupae are sterilized at 70 Gy (7 Krads) 3 days before
     emergence and the adults are released in bags or in a free-release
     system from a helicopter.

     The facility is 6,367.85 m^2 and costs about 3.6 million yen.
     Benefits from eradication should be over 10 billion yen per year (7).

     There were problems with flies moving in from other areas and also
     "hot-spots" in the release area. (Kuba, A. and Kakinohana, H.,
     Okinawa Prefectural Fruit Fly Eradication Project Office, pers.
     commun.)

(4) Mexican Fruit Fly (Anastrepha ludens). Sterile Mexican fruit flies
     are released in a quarantine effort along the U.S.-Mexican border to
     protect U.S. citrus from establishment of this serious pest. From
     25 to 30 million flies are reared per week at Mission, Texas and 20
     million are released each week in the Lower Rio Grande Valley of
     Texas to protect over 15,900 ha. of citrus. An additional 2 million
     flies per week are released in Mexico. Flies are also released

along the Californian-Mexican border to prevent the movement of
Mexican fruit flies into California (3 million flies per week).

The flies are irradiated in the late pupal stage with 70 Gy
(7 Krads) and released as adults by ground in Mexico and by air in
the U.S.A. using a free-release system.

No flies are trapped in south Texas from June to September. It is
unknown if the fly remains at an undetectable level or if it moves
in from Mexico each year. (John Worley, USDA-APHIS, pers. commun.)

(5) Onion Fly (Delia antiqua). For the past 9 years the onion fly has
been controlled in the Netherlands by a private company, De Groene
Vlieg, using the SIT.

Contracts are made with individual growers at a cost lower than the
cost of chemical control. In 9 months each year 170 million flies
are produced and released 10 times in 1,350 ha. of onions. The
flies are sterilized with 30 Gy (3 Krads).

The onion fly is controlled by the SIT in one-half of the onion
fields in the Netherlands by the private company and the other half
by insecticides applied by individual producers. The chemical and
SIT controlled fields are inter-mixed. This creates a problem
because some farmers get poor control by chemicals and therefore the
fly population increases. Also, the inter-mixing means a greater
distance between the release fields and therefore greater travel
distance and costs for releases. (M. Loosjes, De Groene Vlieg,
pers. commun.)

(6) Tsetse Fly (Glossina spp.). The tsetse fly is the vector of
Trypanosoma spp., parasites causing nagana in livestock and human
sleeping sickness. Thus in 28 countries of tropical Africa 20,000
victims of human sleeping sickness are registered and about 1.5
million tons of beef are lost per year.

The first field experiment on tsetse flies using the SIT was
conducted for 15 months on a small island in Lake Kariba, Zimbabwe
(8). G. morsitans puparia were field collected, treated with
chemosterilants (9), and transported to the release sites before

adult emergence. The original wild population of 300 – 600 females
was reduced to below a detectable level within 20 months.

A larger field test to control G. morsitans morsitans was conducted
in Tanzania. A control area of 195 km^2 was sprayed twice within
28 days by air with endosulfan (10). Then G. m. morsitans pupae
from a colony of up to 60,000 females, fed on goats, were sterilized
by 120 Gy (12 Krads) of gamma irradiation under nitrogen and
transported to the release area before adult emergence (11)(12). A
brush-free barrier 1 km wide around the test area was insufficient
to prevent flies from immigrating (13)(14). The G. m. morsitans
population in the test area was reduced 81%.

In 1981 an integrated tsetse fly eradication project was initiated
in Burkina Faso by the Deutsche Gesellschaft für Technische
Zusammenarbeit GmbH and the Institut d'Elevage et de Médecine
Vétérinaire des Pays Tropicaux. Two gallery forest species,
G. palpalis gambiensis and G. tachinoides, and one savannah species
(G. morsitans submorsitans) were to be eradicated from 3,000 km^2,
containing 500 – 600 linear kilometres of riverine forest.
Depending on the season, between 40,000 and 75,000 cattle were at
risk of nagana in the area (15). Prior to release, the tsetse fly
population was reduced 94% by traps and deltamethrin impregnated
cloth screens (16). The sterile male releases began in the rainy
season on a weekly basis and later every fortnight. Adult males
were treated with 110 – 130 Gy (11 – 13 Krads) and released at 35
per linear kilometre of riverine forest. The fly colonies, i.e. up
to 150,000 G. p. gambiensis, 85,000 G. tachinoides and 65,000 G. m.
submorsitans, provided one million sexually sterile males for
release (15)(17). The wild populations constantly decreased 4
months after the initial releases and subsequently disappeared. Use
of insecticide impregnated screens reduced the fly population but
did not achieve eradication even when used over an extensive period
of time. Using the screens to reduce the wild population and then
releasing sterile flies quickly eradicated the species from the
narrow riverine forests.

Another tsetse fly eradication project was initiated in central
Nigeria in 1979. The eradication of G. palpalis palpalis from
1,500 km^2 of agro-pastoral land containing 40,000 – 50,000 cattle

and 450 km of riverine forest of up to 300 m in width was carried out by the combined use of traps, insecticide impregnated screens and the SIT. The project was supported by IAEA/FAO, the host country and a donor country.

The sequence of control and eradication was similar to those in Burkina Faso (18)(19)(20)(21) and eradication was achieved (22)(23). To produce 200 - 500 non-teneral irradiated (120 Gy or 12 Krads) males per release point per week, a colony of up to 180,000 G. p. palpalis females had to be maintained, which in total provided 1.5 million males. During the last 18 months of the project weekly releases averaged more than 10,500 sterile males.

In any eradication programme, reinfestation must be prevented. With some species of tsetse flies insecticide impregnated screens prevent fly reinvasion. At present the expenses involved when applying the SIT for tsetse fly control is comparable to the costs for air-spraying operations. The placement of traps and screens with odour attractants appears to be cheaper than chemical control, at least in the savannah and thin riverine forest systems. In inaccessible terrain or if different Glossina spp. with different requirements for visual or olfactory attractants have to be controlled, the costs for the placement and reimpregnation of screens multiply.

In order to make the SIT more economical, labour requirements for mass-rearing need to be reduced. Regional rearing facilities for supplying biological material to several SIT programmes should be encouraged. Application of the SIT for tsetse fly control is likely to increase in the near future.

Lepidoptera

(1) Codling Moth (Cydia pomonella). The codling moth is a key pest of pome fruits in most of the world. Control of the pest by chemicals often creates other pest problems, including spider mite and leaf roller outbreaks. Codling moth control by the SIT has been demonstrated in Canada, U.S.A., Switzerland and the U.S.S.R. These are reviewed by Proverbs (24).

An eradication programme, planned in British Columbia (BC), Canada, will be financed by the BC Fruit Growers Association and the BC and Canadian governments. The release area containing 9,117 ha. apples and 867 ha. pears will be divided into two parts. The first part will have a pre-release period of two years for population reduction by sanitation and insecticides followed by three years of releases. The second part will lag the first by three years (25).

To pay for the eradication programme there will be a nominal property tax for eight years. The federal and provincial governments will contribute CAN$ 1.5 million. The growers will be taxed CAN$ 100 per hectare when the release starts in their area, then drop to CAN$ 40.18 per hectare, and eventually to CAN$ 19.98 per hectare. Cost of present guthion sprays is CAN$ 126 per hectare. Monitoring for codling moth reinfestation will continue as long as there is a threat of reinfestation.

Rearing capacity will be 5.2 million moths per week with a planned release of 3.5 million per week. Ten percent will be returned to rearing and the remaining will be used for insurance against rearing problems. Release will be by special ground equipment at 300 moths per hectare twice a week. A minimal ratio of 40:1 will be maintained. Adults will probably be irradiated at 300 - 400 Gy (30 - 40 Krads).

Disadvantages of the programme are the large initial capital expense and that the programme takes away some of the growers' freedom.

Advantages of SIT are that it is cheaper than insecticides, it avoids the possibility of the codling moth developing resistance to the insecticide (guthion), the price of the insecticide may rise faster than apple and pear prices, and future use of the insecticide may be restricted.

(2) Pink Bollworm (Pectinophora gossypiella). The pink bollworm is a serious cotton pest in many parts of the world.

Sterile adults have been released annually since 1968 in 6,000 to 145,000 ha. of cotton in the San Joaquin Valley of California, U.S.A. This programme is to prevent the pest from becoming

established in the San Joaquin Valley where 400,000 ha of cotton are
grown.

Approximately 35 million pink bollworm per week are reared in a USDA
Animal and Plant Health Inspection Service facility in Phoenix,
Arizona. The adults are irradiated at 200 Gy (20 Krads) of gamma
radiation and flown to California where most are released by air.
When the ratio of sterile to native insects is low, pheromone
applications to inhibit mating are used to augment the effort.
Cotton plant destruction and crop plough-down to maintain a 90-day
host-free period are also part of the programme.

The pink bollworm has not become established in the San Joaquin
Valley, thus it appears that the release of sterile moths at a
sterile to native ratio of more than 200:1 throughout the season has
been successful (26). (Henneberry, T.J., USDA-ARS, pers. commun.)

F-1 or Inherited Sterility

Lepidoptera require a high dose of radiation to induce complete sexual
sterility, and consequently, often suffer excessive damage which reduces their
competitiveness. At lower doses the more competitive treated insects are not
completely sterile, but their offspring are sterile with a sexual ratio in
favour of the males. F-1 sterility release programmes can reduce, or even
eradicate populations of Lepidoptera in fewer generations than the SIT. In
general, the requirements of F-1 sterility are the same as the SIT. Doses of
100 - 200 Gy (10 to 20 Krads) are normally required for F-1 sterility
eradication programmes, but if the goal is only population suppression,
50 - 100 Gy (5 to 10 Krads) may be more effective.

Treated insects or their F-1 generation may be released. The advantages
differ with the species and situation. Excessive numbers of treated or F-1
insects should not be released because the larvae may cause feeding damage.

Gypsy Moth (Lymantria dispar). The gypsy moth is an established major
pest of hardwood trees in some areas of North America. Present efforts
are to prevent infestations from expanding and to eradicate new isolated
infestations. The moth is established in north-eastern U.S.A., as far
south as Virginia and as far west as Ohio. From 10 to 20 isolated outbreaks are eradicated each year by use of insecticides or F-1 sterility.

The F-1 sterility eradication programme utilizes pupae sterilized with
150 Gy (15 Krads) of irradiation. More recently, male pupae are treated
at 100 Gy (10 Krads) and mated with normal females. The resulting egg
masses are held in diapause and stockpiled until needed. The egg masses
are released in the spring and thus hatch is synchronized with that of
the native insects. The F-1 adults are sterile and mating with native
produces no progeny. This programme was successful in eradicating
isolated outbreaks of the gypsy moth from Bellingham, Washington, U.S.A.
and Darke County, Ohio, U.S.A. If suppression rather than eradication is
a goal, the dose can be reduced to 60 Gy (6 Krads) (27).

Rearing continues to be a major problem. Since F-1 larvae could cause
some damage, the release rate should not exceed the number required for
eradication. (Mastro, V.C., USDA-APHIS, pers. commun.)

Hybrid Sterility

Crosses between species often result in sterile hybrid progeny. In some
cases, when these hybrids mate with wild insects, no progeny are produced.
This has been demonstrated in the mosquitoes of the Anopheles gambiae complex
(28), in cricket crosses of Teleogrylus oceanicus and T. comodus (29), in
laboratory strains of the spider mite, Tetranychus urticae (30)(31), in ticks
in crosses of Boophilus annulatus and B. microplus (32), in Glossina morsitans
complex (33), and other arthropods.

To date, no practical insect control/eradication programmes have been
based on hybrid sterility.

Backcross Sterility

In backcross (BC) sterility two species or sub-species are hybridized and
the hybrid male or female then backcrossed to one of the parental lines. In
some cases these BC insects possess inherited sterility factors which, when
the insects are released into field populations, is infused into the native
population. BC sterility in Heliothis virescens and H. subflexa has been
studied in detail. H. virescens males are crossed with H. subflexa females
producing partially fertile females and sterile males (34). Continual
backcrosses of hybrid or BC females to H. virescens males perpetuate a line
that restores full fertility to females but continues to produce sterile
males. Martin et al. (35) reported that this male sterility, inherited

through the BC female, has persisted through at least 90 generations.

Models (36) suggest that a single release of BC insects could eventually lead to eradication if the BC to native ratio was sufficient and the population isolated.

Four releases of BC insects were made in 1979-1980 on St. Croix, U.S. Virgin Islands (218 km^2) to control H. virescens. Hatch of eggs laid by native females dropped from 89.0% to 33.1% and those laid by BC females from 82.9% to 25.8% (37).

The advantage of BC sterility is that it exerts a greater suppression with fewer releases for a longer period of time than SIT or F-1 sterility. The disadvantages are that two insect strains must be reared and that each generation of BC females must be outcrossed with males to perpetuate the line. The lines must be kept pure. No practical use has yet been made of backcross sterility.

Chromosome Rearrangements and Deleterious Mutations

Insect damage may be controlled by introducing genotypes that reduce the pest population by carrying a conditional lethal gene or by reducing the insect to a non-damaging status (38)(39). Examples of the first type would be sensitivity to high or low temperatures, susceptibility to insecticides, sex-linked translocations, eye defects, etc. Examples of the second type would be interruption of disease transmission by replacing vectors with non-vectors. These approaches are reviewed by Foster et al. (40) and Whitten (41)(42). Computer models comparing SIT and sex-linked translocation strains show that at a high release rate, sterile males cause more rapid suppression and eradication, but if the programme is interrupted before eradication, recovery is more rapid in the case of SIT. At lower release rates sex-linked translocation strains can be more effective than sterile males (43).

Sheep Blowfly (Lucilia cuprina). The sheep blowfly is the most important myiasis pest of sheep in Australia, causing losses estimated at AUS$ 149 million per year. Also the pest is now becoming resistant to insecticides.

After evaluating the potential of several approaches to genetic control, Commonwealth Scientific and Industrial Research Organization decided to

82

FIG. 1

PROBABLE PATH TO IMPROVED GENETIC METHODS OF INSECT CONTROL

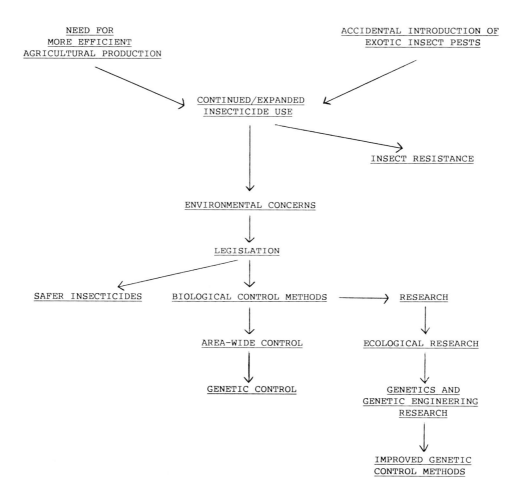

conduct field trials using female-killing systems constructed from sex-linked translocations and deleterious genes, such as eye colour mutations. The first trial was in the southern Shoalhaven River valley of N.S.W. (240 km^2) during 1984-1985. Weekly releases of 400 males per km^2 achieved a 9:1 release:wild male ratio resulting in a genetic death rate of 50% per generation. Since there was immigration of wild flies into the test area, a second test was conducted in an isolated area (Flinders Is., 40 km^2) located 27 km off the coast of Eyre Peninsula in South Australia. In 1985-1986 weekly releases of 3,000 - 4,000 males per km^2 resulted in a peak genetic death rate of 87% after 6 months, and a decline in population from a peak of 345 males per hectare in October 1985 to less than 1 female per hectare in May 1986. Because of the continuing genetic death from translocation semi-sterility and homozygosis of mutations, populations did not recover to 4 females per hectare until March 1987.

The next field trial will be in the Furneaux Is. group (1,992 km^2) in Bass Strait in co-operation with the Tasmanian Department of Agriculture. Studies began in 1987 and releases are scheduled to begin in September 1989. Problems are similar to those of SIT including isolation, insect production, and how to finance and implement area-wide programmes. (Foster, G.G., CSIRO, pers. commun.)

FUTURE PROSPECTS

When attempting to look into the future, certain assumptions must be made. In the case of genetic methods for insect control and eradication, the assumptions are summarized in Fig. 1.

There will be a continuous need for more efficient agricultural production and improved human and animal health which will require insect control, most commonly achieved by the use of insecticides. Therefore, insecticide use will remain high and possibly increase. Another factor will be the more frequent introduction of exotic insect pests, such as the screwworm in North Africa (44), which should be eradicated to prevent increased losses in agricultural production and simultaneously increased use of insecticides. Insects will continue to become resistant to insecticides. Pesticide residues on agricultural commodities will become more tightly regulated which will conflict with the continued or increased use of insecticide.

The major assumption, however, is that there will be an increase in overall environmental concerns, including concerns about insecticides. These concerns will very likely result in legislation which will directly impact on the use of insecticides. It is conceivable that legislation will make it mandatory for producers to control insects on their land below a certain level to prevent them from infesting their neighbour's crops. This legislation will apply to relatively few insect species, but these will be of major national importance and will most likely be key pest species. Legislation also may be enacted that will require producers to maintain a certain population of specific beneficial insects on their land.

More rapid development of biological control methods will result from legislation dealing with the environment. Many biological control methods, including genetic methods, are not applicable on a field by field basis, but can only be used on an area-wide basis. It is in this arena that genetic control methods will be used. Genetic engineering research will provide many of the tools to obtain the genetically manipulated insects which can be used for new and improved genetic control methods (45).

An increase in area-wide control will come about because some insect control technologies can only be applied on an area-wide basis. Further, the cost of controlling some of the more important insect species by insecticides can be reduced considerably if an area-wide approach is used.

Area-wide insect control will require a shift in the type of ecological research conducted. More knowledge about total insect populations, movement, reproductive rates and alternate hosts will be needed. This is difficult and expensive research.

In effect, area-wide insect control must be preventive. Preventive insect control is not common, except against some soil insects and by using host plant resistance. The use of insecticides as a preventive insect control technology, when applied on a field by field basis, is not acceptable to most insect control specialists. This procedure, frequently applied by calendar date, often leads to excessive use of insecticides, minor pests becoming major pests, and increased risk of resistance to the insecticides. Preventive insect control should be viewed on an area-wide basis utilizing as little insecticide as possible.

With increased travel and agricultural trade, there will be an increase in the introduction of exotic pests. If one assumes that there will be increased detection capability, then it is likely that these introductions will be discovered before they become well established. Under these conditions, eradication of these accidental introductions will become common practice. Again, however, environmental concerns about insecticide application will limit the use of these chemicals and encourage the development of genetic and other biological methods for eradication. This will require facilities of sufficient size to rear enough genetically altered insects for these campaigns. Regional facilities with highly automated insect rearing technologies and new concepts for mass-rearing, handling and shipping probably will be developed.

One of the most important limiting factors for the increased development of genetic methods of insect control is the lack of a shelf life. This also is a problem with parasites and predators to be used for inundative releases. If insects could be stored for a year or more at a reasonable cost in the stage that they will be released, the development of these control technologies would be much more rapid. Smaller rearing facilities would be required to meet the demands and the impact of rearing failures would be reduced. Commercialization would undoubtedly take place. Research support would increase as the technologies prove successful. The development of insect storage methods should be a high priority research objective.

During the past 20 years there has been much written on the potential for autocidal or genetic methods of insect control (45). Included have been the use of meiotic drive, synthetic translocations, conditional lethals, and a whole array of other types of genetic changes which, if introduced into a population, would result in control or eradication. As shown in the previous section of this paper, the use of the SIT remains the most commonly used method of genetic control. The recent success of the Australian sheep blowfly programme using sex-linked translocations and deleterious genes should encourage research on this approach for use against other species.

The ability to transfer genetic material from one species of insect to another through genetic engineering offers enormous potential (45). To date this potential has not been realized. This road-block will probably be overcome within a few years. When this occurs, there will be an explosion of new opportunities for the development of genetic methods for insect control and eradication.

REFERENCES

1. Graham, O.H. (ed.) (1985) Miscellaneous Publications of the Entomol. Soc.
    Amer. No. 62, 68 pp

2. Snow, J.W. (1988) in Proceedings of an International Symposium on Modern
    Insect Control: Nuclear Techniques and Biotechnology. Jointly organized
    by the International Atomic Energy Agency and the Food and Agriculture
    Organization of the United Nations, Vienna, 16 - 20 November 1987,
    pp 3-13

3. Reyes, J., Villaseñor, A., Schwarz, A. and Hendrichs, J. (1988) in
    Proceedings of an International Symposium on Modern Insect Control:
    Nuclear Techniques and Biotechnology. Jointly organized by the
    International Atomic Energy Agency and the Food and Agriculture
    Organization of the United Nations, Vienna, 16 - 20 November 1987,
    pp 107-116

4. Hendrichs, J., Ortiz, G., Liedo, P. and Schwarz, A. (1982) in Cavalloro
    (ed.) Proceedings of the CEC/IOB International Symposium on Fruit Flies
    of Economic Importance, Athens, Greece, 16 - 19 November 1982, pp 353-365

5. Hentze, F. and Mata, R. (1987) in Fruit Flies. Proc. of the Second
    International Symposium, 16 - 21 September 1986, Colymbari, Crete,
    Greece, pp 533-539

6. Ortiz, G., Liedo, P., Schwarz, A., Villaseñor, A., Reyes, J. and Mata, R.
    (1987) in Fruit Flies. Proc. of the Second International Symposium,
    16 - 21 September 1986, Colymbari, Crete, Greece, pp 523-532

7. Okinawa Prefectural Fruit Fly Eradication Project Office (1987) Melon Fly
    Eradication Project in Okinawa Prefecture, 29 pp

8. Dame, D.A. and Schmidt, C.H. (1970) Bull. Ent. Soc. Amer. 16:24-30

9. Dame, D.A. and Ford, H.R. (1966) Bull. Ent. Res. 56:649-658

10. Williamson, D.L., Dame, D.A., Lee, C.W., Gates, D.B. and Cobb, P.E.
    (1983) Bull. Ent. Res. 73:383-389

11. Williamson, D.L., Baumgartner, H.H., Mtuya, A.G., Warner, P.V.,
    Tarimo, S.A. and Dame, D.A. (1983) Bull. Ent. Res. 73:259-265

12. Williamson, D.L., Baumgartner, H.H., Mtuya, A.G., Gates, D.B., Cobb, P.E.
    and Dame, D.A. (1983) Bull. Ent. Res. 73:267-273

13. Gates, D.B., Cobb, P.E., Williamson, D.L., Bakuli, B., Dame, D.A. and
    Blaser, E. (1983) Bull. Ent. Res. 73:373-381

14. Williamson, D.L., Dame, D.A., Gates, D.B., Cobb, P.E., Bakuli, B. and
    Warner, P.V. (1983) Bull. Ent. Res. 73:391-404

15. Cuisance, D., Politzar, H., Merot, P., Tamboura, I., Bauer, B.,
    Kabore, I. and Fidellier, J. (1986) in Proc. 18th Meet. OAU/STRC
    (ISCTRC), Harare, Zimbabwe, Doc. No. 604, 334-343

16. Cuisance, D. and Politzar, H. (1983) Rev. Elev. Méd. Vét. Pays Trop.
    36:159-168

17. Politzar, H. and Cuisance, D. (1984) Insect Sci. Appl. 5:439-442

18. Tenabe, S.O., Feldmann, H.U., Hamann, H.J., Onah, J., Ndams, I.S., Dalhatu, A., Ejeh, J., Ajagbonna, B.O., Oladunmade, M.A. and Takken, W. (1986) in Proc. 18th Meet. OAU/STRC (ISCTRC), Harare, Zimbabwe, Doc. No. 317, 293-297

19. Oladunmade, M.A., Takken, W., Dengwat, L. and Ndams, I.S. (1985) Bull. Ent. Res. 75:275-281

20. Oladunmade, M.A., Takken, W., Dengwat, L., Tenabe, S.O., Feldmann, H.U. and Hamann, H.J. (1986) in Proc. 18th Meet. OAU/STRC (ISCTRC), Harare, Zimbabwe, Doc. No. 606, 351-363

21. Takken, W., Oladunmade, M.A., Dengwat, L., Feldmann, H.U., Onah, J.A., Tenabe, S.O. and Hamann, H.J. (1986) Bull. Ent. Res. 76:275-286

22. Lindquist, D.A. (1984) IAEA Bull. 26(2):22-25

23. IAEA (International Atomic Energy Agency) (1987) IAEA Newsbriefs 2(7), p 3

24. Proverbs, M.D. (1982) in Sterile Insect Technique and Radiation in Insect Control, Proceedings of a Symposium on the Use of Radiation in Genetic Insect Control. Jointly organized by the IAEA and FAO, Neuherberg, FRG, 29 June - 3 July 1981, pp 85-99

25. British Columbia Fruit Growers Association (1988) Codling Moth Sterile Insect Release Study, 130 pp

26. Henneberry, T.J. and Keaveny, D.E. III (1985) U.S. Dept. Agri., Agri. Res. Ser. ARS-32, 74 pp

27. Mastro, V.C. and Schwalbe, C.P. (1988) in Proceedings of an International Symposium on Modern Insect Control: Nuclear Techniques and Biotechnology. Jointly organized by the International Atomic Energy Agency and the Food and Agriculture Organization of the United Nations, Vienna, 16 - 20 November 1987, pp 15-40

28. Davidson, G., Odetoyinbo, J.A., Colussa, B. and Coz, J. (1970) Bull. Wld. Hlth. Org. 42:55-67

29. Hogan, T.W. (1974) in The Use of Genetics in Insect Control, Pal, R. and Whitten, M.J. (eds.), Elsevier/North Holland, pp 57-70

30. Overwieer, W.P.J. and Van Zon, A.Q. (1973) Entomol. Exp. & Appl. 16:389-394

31. DeBoer, R. (1982) Genetica 58:23-33

32. Osborn, R.L. and Knipling, E.F. (1982) J. Med. Entomol. 19:637-644

33. Rawlings, P. (1985) Bull. Entomol. Res. 75:689-699

34. Laster, M.L. (1972) Environ. Entomol. 1:682-687

35. Martin, D.F., Proshold, F.I. and Laster, M.L. (1981) Proc. Beltwide Cotton Prod. Res. Conf. 1981:150-151

36. Makela, M.E. and Huettel, M.D. (1979) Theor. Appl. Genet. 54:225-233

37. Proshold, F.I., Raulston, J.R., Martin, D.F. and Laster, M.L. (1983) J. Econ. Entomol. 76:626-631

38. Curtis, C. (1979) in Genetics in Relation to Insect Management. Working papers, The Rockefeller Foundation, pp.19-30

39. Pal, R. and Whitten, M.J. (ed.) (1974) The Use of Genetics in Insect Control, Elsevier, Amsterdam, 241 pp

40. Foster, G.G., Whitten, M.J., Prout, T. and Gill, R. (1972) Science 176:875-880

41. Whitten, M.J. (1971) Science 171:682-684

42. Whitten, M.J. (1988) in Proceedings of an International Symposium on Modern Insect Control: Nuclear Techniques and Biotechnology. Jointly organized by the International Atomic Energy Agency and the Food and Agriculture Organization of the United Nations, Vienna, 16 - 20 November 1987, pp 41-55

43. Foster, G.G., Vogt, W.G., Woodburly, T.L. and Smith, P.H. (1988) Ther. Appl. Genet. 76:870-879

44. Wyatt, N.P., Pont, A.C., Gabaj, M.M., Beesley, W.N., El-Azazy, O., Gusbi, A.M. and Awan, M.H.Q. (1989) Veterinary Record (in press).

45. Cockburn, A.F. and Seawright, J.A. (1989) Handbook of Natural Pesticides: Insects Vol. III (in press)

© 1990 Elsevier Science Publishers B.V. (Biomedical Division)
Pesticides and alternatives, editor J.E. Casida

PROGRESS IN THE STERILE INSECT TECHNIQUE AGAINST FRUIT FLIES

A.P. ECONOMOPOULOS

Entomology Unit, Joint FAO/IAEA Programme, Agency's Laboratories, A-2444, Seibersdorf, Austria.

INTRODUCTION

In the last four decades research and development has been concentrated on the control of several insect pests by genetic methods (1, 2). Most of this work involved the sterile insect technique (SIT) with considerable effort focused on fruit flies (Diptera: Tephritidae) (Table 1).

TABLE I

FRUIT FLIES AGAINST WHICH SIT HAS BEEN APPLIED IN THE FIELD

Species	Country(ies)	Results	Period *
Area-wide or routine application			
Mediter. fruit fly	Mexico/Guatemala**	Eradication	1977-82 (3)
Mediter. fruit fly	USA (Calif., Florida)	Eradication of new introductions	Several times since 1980 (Rohwer p.c.)
Melon fly	Japan (Okinawa Pref.)	Eradication	1972-87 (4,26)
Mexican fruit fly	Mexico/USA (border)	Immigration prevented	1983-present (Worley p.c.)
Onion fly	The Netherlands	Control***	1971-present (9, Loosjes p.c.)
Restricted application			
Caribbean fruit fly	USA (Florida)	Control***	1970-72 (6)
Cherry fly	Switzerland	Control***	1976-79 (7)
Olive fly	Greece	Not clear control	1973-74 (8)
Oriental fruit fly	Mariana Islands	Eradication	1962-65 (10)
Queensland fruit fly	Australia	Control***	1962-65 (11)

*   In parenthesis reference number.
**   In addition, several smaller successful programmes around the world, e.g. Italy, Peru, Australia.
***   Population suppression.

The SIT has been developed for area-wide, routine use for a few species of fruit flies: Mediterranean fruit fly, Ceratitis capitata (Wiedemann) (3, G. Rohwer USDA/APHIS personal communication); melon fly, Dacus cucurbitae Coquillett (4,26); Mexican fruit fly, Anastrepha ludens (Loew) (5, J. Worley USDA/APHIS personal communication); onion fly, Delia antiqua (Meigen) (9, M. Loosjes personal communication). In other fruit fly species, the technique has been developed for restricted field application or testing: Caribbean fruit fly, Anastrepha suspensa Loew (6); cherry fly, Rhagoletis cerasi L. (7); olive fly, Dacus oleae (Gmelin) (8); oriental fruit fly, Dacus dorsalis Hendel (10); Queensland fruit fly, Dacus tryoni (Froggatt) (11). The most spectacular successes were the eradications of the Mediterranean fruit fly from southern Mexico and of the melon fly from most of Okinawa and the prevention of Mexican fruit fly from invading California and Texas. With other fruit flies there were smaller successful control applications or testing, except the olive fly where no clear control was achieved in the field. Some flies are well-established in complex natural environments where they co-exist with other species, therefore their eradication will probably result in another species becoming major pest (5, 12). If so, the cost of eradicating one species is not practical, however, a multi-species programme may be cost effective. A four fruit-fly-species eradication programme, with SIT as its basic component, is a goal in Hawaii (13). There is a need for extensive basic information on the possibility of other species assuming major pest status in case a well-established species is eradicated.

The "quality" of mass-reared insects appears to be a major obstacle in fruit fly control by SIT. Procedures in mass production, sterilization and release operation, all exercise strong selection against the natural behaviour of the insect. Near-normal sexual behaviour of released flies is a prerequisite for a successful SIT application. This has been well documented and considerable research has been directed to solving the problem (14-18). It is very difficult to correct "quality" problems since they may be connected with genetic changes induced by specific artificial rearing components (19).

The initial enthusiasm for a relatively simple, environmentally clean, no resistance inducing control methodology which could be used against specific insect pests has often turned to disappointment. It is now clear that extensive information on the target species and its environment is required, the initial cost is often high, and ingenuity is required to insure that the released flies effectively compete sexually with their wild counterparts. Information on several fruit flies, acquired in SIT programmes, is very valuable in other control methods as well.

CURRENT STATUS

Private industry has shown little interest in SIT. The development of the method has been by national and international organizations. The latter was necessary, because of area-wide applications involving more than one country, and to facilitate the transfer of a sophisticated and expensive technology to less developed countries. Most small programmes have been abandoned, especially those involving species difficult to rear or with complex sexual behaviour which could be critically affected by the mass-rearing. The effort now concentrates on a small number of highly destructive species for which SIT proved very successful, e.g. the Mediterranean fruit fly and the melon fly. Research is aimed at finding simpler, cheaper and more effective technology which could appeal to private industry or could be supported by private organizations or farmer associations. Mass-rearing, quality control, genetic sexing, population studies and sexual behaviour in the field are subjects of research focus. The Mediterranean fruit fly is the model species, since it is the most important fruit fly world-wide. Much of the research is co-ordinated internationally by the Insect and Pest Control Section of the Joint FAO/IAEA Division of Nuclear Techniques in Food and Agriculture.

Mass-rearing. The use of standardized materials, even inert materials (to replace the bulk texture-material in the larval diet) and the reuse of spent larval diet are being investigated (20, 21, Economopoulos unpublished). Also, research is focused on using mass-rearing conditions with minimal impact on the natural behaviour of flies (22-24).

Quality of mass-reared flies. The quality of mass produced insects has been actively investigated and there are numerous publications on the subject, however this problem still remains largely unsolved. For many species, quality is probably the single most important factor for the success of SIT. Standard quality control tests have been developed and are applied routinely for the Mediterranean fruit fly (18, 25), the melon fly (26) and the Mexican fruit fly (Worley personal communication). Nevertheless, there is no simple, reliable method to evaluate the suitability of released flies under field conditions.

Genetic sexing. To reduce the cost of mass-producing and handling the flies, there have been recent attempts to separate the sexes and release only sterilized males. This will oblige the released males to mate with wild females. Most of this effort has been on the Mediterranean fruit fly (27). So far, only techniques involving strains with pupal colour sexual dimorphism have been developed to the stage of mass-rearing and field testing (28-32, Economopoulos unpublished, Nitzan et al. unpublished). Research aiming at sex separation at the egg or young-larval instar has not yet produced practical results but if successful, will result in substantial cost reduction for the

SIT operation.

   Population changes and field behaviour. In most of these studies, both the
artificially-reared and wild flies are studied under laboratory and field
conditions. Feeding, mating, oviposition, dispersal, survival and learning
studies have been undertaken with several fruit flies (33-46). Also,
population studies assessing the suppression of wild populations with different
SIT application techniques have been undertaken (47, 48). Such studies are a
prerequisite before major control applications. In spite of all the efforts,
there is no simple, practical test available to predict the performance of
sterile flies and consequently the outcome of the control or eradication
programme.

CONCLUSIONS

   The non-polluting SIT method is successful in area-wide programmes against
the Mediterranean fruit fly, the melon fly and the Mexican fruit fly. The SIT
has proven effective in smaller experiments with several other fruit fly
species. Research-wise the most difficult problems to be solved are: cost
reduction, pre-release population suppression, mass-producing and releasing
insects of acceptable field effectiveness (successful matings with wild
females), information on the insect's field behaviour, and developing a
practical method to monitor the field performance of released insects.

FUTURE PROSPECTS

   Environmental pollution will be a key global problem for many years to
come. Insecticides contribute to this problem. Resistance to insecticides
grows exponentially, intensifying pesticide application. From a single case
detected in 1905, 12 in the early 1940s, 490 species of insects and mites were
recorded as having developed resistance by the end of 1986 (49). The Diptera
contained the largest proportion (36%) of the above cases, apparently because
of the intensive use of chemicals against the pest species of that order. This
situation makes it very urgent that insect control moves to methods of no or
reduced pollution. In most pest species this is not an easy road. In several
cases non-polluting methods have been developed but their application is
costly, complex, and not always effective.

   The sterile insect technique has been applied successfully against a small
number of species because of the problems listed above. Future research could
solve most of these problems by concentrating on: less costly and less
selective mass-rearing technology, production of more efficient sterile
insects, and in depth study of the target species (both wild and artificially
reared), especially field behaviour and population changes. There is growing

optimism that the recent developments in molecular genetic technology (50) will solve some of the problems, making genetic control a more practical insect control methodology.

ACKNOWLEDGMENTS

Thanks are expressed to B. Butt for commenting on the manuscript. Ms. Clara Peruzzi is thanked for typing the manuscript.

REFERENCES

1. Snow JW (1988) Radiation, insects and eradication in North America: An overview from screwworm to bollworm, pp. 3–13. In Modern Insect Control: Nuclear Techniques and Biotechnology, Proceedings of an International Symposium organized by IAEA/FAO, November 1987, Vienna. IAEA STI/PUB/763

2. Whitten MJ (1988) A genetic perspective on pest control and the future of autocidal control, pp. 41–55. In Modern Insect Control: Nuclear Techniques and Biotechnology, Proceedings of an International Symposium organized by IAEA/FAO, November 1987, Vienna. IAEA STI/PUB/763

3. Hendrichs J, Ortiz G, Liedo P, Schwarz A (1983) Six years of successful medfly program in Mexico and Guatemala, pp. 353–365. In Fruit Flies of Economic Importance, Proceedings of an International Symposium organized by Greek Authorities/CEC/IOBC, November 1982, Athens. A.A. Balkema, Rotterdam

4. Iwahashi O (1977) Eradication of the melon fly, Dacus cucurbitae, from Kume Is., Okinawa, with the sterile insect release method. Res. Popul. Ecol. 19:87–98

5. Aluja MR, Liedo PF (1986) Perspective on future integrated management of fruit flies in Mexico, pp. 9–42. In Pest Control, Operations and Systems Analysis in Fruit Fly Management, Proceedings of an Advanced Workshop organized by NATO Scientific Affairs Division, August 1985, Bad Windscheim, West Germany. Springer–Verlag, Berlin

6. Burditt AKJr, Lopez-D F, Steiner LF, von Windeguth DL, Baranowski R., Anwar M (1975) Application of sterilization techniques to Anastrepha suspensa Loew in Florida, USA, pp. 93–101. In Sterility Principle for Insect Control, Proceedings of an International Symposium organized by IAEA/FAO, July 1974, Innsbruck. IAEA STI/PUB/377

7. Boller EF, Remund U (1983) Field feasibility study for the application of SIT in Rhagoletis cerasi L. in Northwest Switzerland (1976–1979), pp. 366–370. In Fruit Flies of Economic Importance, Proceedings of an International Symposium organized by Greek Authorities/CEC/IOBC, November 1982, Athens. A.A. Balkema, Rotterdam

8. Economopoulos AP, Avtzis N, Zervas G, Tsitsipis J, Haniotakis G, Tsiropoulos G, Manoukas A (1977) Experiments on the control of the olive fly, Dacus oleae (Gmel.), by the combined effect of insecticides and releases of gamma-ray sterilized insects. Z. ang. Ent. 83(2):201–215

9. Theunissen J, Loosjes M, Noordink JPhW, Norlander J, Ticheler J (1975)
    Small-scale field experiments on sterile-insect control of the onion fly,
    Hylemya antiqua (Meigen), pp. 83-91. In Controlling Fruit Flies by the
    Sterile Insect Technique, Proceedings of a Panel and Research Co-ordination
    Meeting organized by IAEA/FAO, November 1973, Vienna. IAEA STl/PUB/392

10. Steiner LF, Hart WG, Harris EJ, Cunningham RT, Ohinata K, Kamakahi DC (1970)
    Eradication of the oriental fruit fly from the Mariana Islands by the
    methods of male annihilation and sterile insect release. J. Econ. Entomol.
    63(1):131-135

11. Andrewartha HG, Monro J, Richardson NL (1967) The use of sterile males to
    control populations of Queensland fruit fly, Dacus tryoni (Frogg.)
    (Diptera: Tephritidae). II. Field Experiments in New South Wales. Aust. J.
    Zool. 15:475-499

12. Fletcher BS, Bateman MA (1983) Combating the fruit fly problems in
    Australia: The current situation and future prospects, pp. 555-563. In
    Fruit Flies of Economic Importance, Proceedings of an International
    Symposium organized by Greek Authorities/CEC/IOBC, November 1982, Athens.
    A.A. Balkema, Rotterdam

13. Gilmore JE (1987) Research on trifly eradication, pp. 567-574. In Fruit
    Flies, Proceedings of the Second International Symposium, September 1986,
    Colymbari, Crete. Elsevier, Amsterdam

14. Boller EF, Katsoyannos BI, Remund U, Chambers DL (1981) Measuring,
    monitoring and improving the quality of mass-reared Mediterranean fruit
    flies, Ceratitis capitata Wied. 1. The RAPID quality control system for
    early warning Z. ang. Ent. 92:67-83

15. Economopoulos AP, Zervas GA (1982) The quality problem in olive flies
    produced for SIT experiments, pp. 357-368. In Sterile Insect Technique and
    Radiation in Insect Control, Proceedings of an International Symposium
    organized by IAEA/FAO, June-July 1981, Neuherberg, West Germany. IAEA
    STI/PUB/595

16. Koyama J (1982) Quality problems in the mass-rearing for the melon fly,
    Dacus cucurbitae Coquillett. JARQ 16(3):181-187

17. Chambers DL, Calkins CO, Boller EF, Ito Y, Cunningham RT (1983) Measuring,
    monitoring and improving the quality of mass-reared Mediterranean fruit
    flies, Ceratitis capitata (Wied.). 2. Field tests for confirming and
    extending laboratory results. Z. ang. Ent. 95:285-303

18. Brazzel JR, Calkins C, Chambers DL, Gates DB (1986) Required quality
    control tests, quality specifications, and shipping procedures for
    laboratory produced Mediterranean fruit flies for sterile insect control
    programs. USDA/APHIS/PPQ, APHIS 81-51, 32 pp.

19. Economopoulos AP, Loukas M (1986) ADH allele frequency changes in olive
    fruit flies shift from olives to artificial larval food and vice versa,
    effect of temperature. Entomol. exp. appl. 40:215-221

20. Bruzzone ND (1987) Recycling larval media for mass-rearing the Mediterranean
    fruit fly, pp. 277-281. In Fruit Flies, Proceedings of the Second
    International Symposium, September 1986, Colymbari, Crete. Elsevier,
    Amsterdam

21. Fay HAC (1988) A starter diet for mass-rearing larvae of the Mediterranean
    fruit fly, Ceratitis capitata (Wied.). J. Appl. Ent. 105:496-501

22. Krainacker DA, Carey JR, Vargas RI (1989) Size-specific survival and fecundity for laboratory strains of two tephritid (Diptera-Tepritidae) species: implications for mass rearing. J. Econ. Entomol. 82(1):104-108

23. Economopoulos AP, Judt S (1989) Artificial rearing of the Mediterranean fruit fly (Diptera:Tephritidae): size of oviposition holes. J. Econ. Entomol. 82(2):668-674

24. Economopoulos AP, Bruzzone ND (1989) Mass rearing of the Mediterranean fruit fly (Diptera:Tephritidae): continous light in the adult stage. J. Econ. Entomol. 82(5):1482-1490

25. Calkins CO, Nguyen R, Corwin K, Brazzel JR (1988) Evaluations of quality of irradiated Mediterranean fruit fly, Ceratitis capitata (Wiedemann) (Diptera: Tephritidae), at the release site in Miami, Florida during an eradication program in 1985. Florida Entomologist 71(3):346-351

26. Anonymous (1987) Melon fly eradication project in Okinawa Prefecture, 26 pp. Okinawa Prefecture Fruit Fly Eradication Project Office, 123 Maji, Naha 902, Japan. Printed by Akatsuki Printing Ltd. (revised edition)

27. International Atomic Energy Agency (1989 in press) Genetic Sexing of the Mediterranean Fruit Fly. Proceedings of the Final Research Coordination Meeting organized by IAEA/FAO, September 1988, Colymbari, Crete. IAEA

28. Robinson AS, van Heemert C (1982) Ceratitis capitata, a suitable case for genetic sexing. Genetica 58:229-237

29. Hooper GHS, Robinson AS, Marchand RP (1987) Behaviour of a genetic sexing strain of Mediterranean fruit fly, Ceratitis capitata, during large scale rearing, pp. 349-362. In Fruit Flies, Proceedings of the Second International Symposium, September 1986, Colymbari, Crete. Elsevier, Amsterdam

30. Cirio U, Capparella M, Economopoulos AP (1987) Control of medfly (Ceratitis capitata Wiedemann) by releasing a mass-reared genetic sexing strain, pp. 515-522. In Fruit Flies, Proceedings of the Second International Symposium September 1986, Colymbari, Crete. Elsevier, Amsterdam

31. Bush-Petersen E, Ripfel J, Pyrek A, Kafu A (1988) Isolation and mass-rearing of a pupal genetic sexing strain of the Mediterranean fruit fly Ceratitis capitata (Wied.), pp. 211-219. In Modern Insect Control: Nuclear Techniques and Biotechnology, Proceedings of an International Symposium organized by IAEA/FAO, November 1987, Vienna. IAEA STI/PUB/763

32. Economopoulos AP (1989 in press) Evaluation of a white-female-pupa genetic sexing strain of Mediterranean fruit fly under selection procedures. In Genetic Sexing of the Mediterranean Fruit Fly, Proceedings of the Final Research Coordination Meeting organized by IAEA/FAO, September 1988, Colymbari, Crete. IAEA

33. Fletcher BS, Economopoulos AP (1976) Dispersal of normal and irradiated laboratory strains and wild strains of the olive fly Dacus oleae in an olive grove. Entom. Exp. Appl. 20:183-194

34. Nakagawa S, Steiner LF, Farias GJ (1981) Response of virgin female Mediterranean fruit flies to live mature normal males, sterile males and Trimedlure in plastic traps. J. Econ. Entomol. 74:566-567

35. Koyama J, Chigira Y, Iwahashi O, Kakinohana H, Kuba H, Teruya T (1982) An estimation of the adult population of the melon fly, Dacus cucurbitae Coquillett (Diptera: Tephritidae), in Okinawa Island, Japan. Appl. Ent. Zool. 17(4): 550-558

36. Kuba H, Koyama J (1982) Mating behaviour of the melon fly, Dacus cucurbitae Coquillett (Diptera: Tephritidae): Comparative studies of one wild and two laboratory strains. Appl. Ent. Zool. 17(4): 559-568

37. Wong TTY, Whitehand LC, Kobayashi RM, Ohinata K, Tanaka N, Harris EJ (1982) Mediterranean fruit fly: dispersal of wild and irradiated and untreated laboratory-reared males. Environ. Entomol. 11:339-343

38. Arita LH, Kaneshiro KY (1985) The dynamics of the lek system and mating success in males of the Mediterranean fruit fly, Ceratitis capitata (Wiedemann). Proceedings of the Hawaiian Entomological Society 25:39-48

39. Galun R, Gothilf S, Blondheim S, Sharp JL, Mazor M, Lacham A (1985) Comparison of aggregation and feeding responses by normal and irradiated fruit flies, Ceratitis capitata and Anastrepha suspensa (Diptera: Tephritidae). Environ. Entomol, 14:726-732

40. McDonald PT, McInnis DO (1985) Ceratitis capitata (Diptera: Tephritidae): Oviposition behaviour and fruit punctures by irradiated and untreated females in laboratory and field cages. J. Econ. Entomol. 78:790-793

41. Robacker DC, Hart WG (1985) Courtship and territoriality of laboratory-reared Mexican fruit flies, Anastrepha ludens (Diptera: Tephritidae), in cages containing host and nonhost trees. Ann. Entomol. Soc. Am. 78:488-494

42. Baker PS, Chan AST, Zavala MAJ (1986) Dispersal and orientation of sterile Ceratitis capitata and Anastrepha ludens (Tephritidae) in Chiapas, Mexico. Journal of Applied Ecology 23:27-38

43. Fay HAC, Meats A (1987a) Survival rates of the Queensland fruit fly, Dacus tryoni, in early spring: Field-cage studies with cold acclimated, laboratory flies. Aust. J. Zool. 35:187-195

44. Fay HAC, Meats A (1987b) The sterile insect release method and the importance of thermal conditioning before release: Field-cage experiments with Dacus tryoni in spring weather. Aust. J. Zool. 35:197-204

45. Papaj DR, Prokopy RJ, McDonald PT, Wong TTY (1987) Differences in learning between wild and laboratory Ceratitis capitata flies. Entomol. Exp. Appl. 45:65-72

46. Vargas RI, Carey JR (1989) Comparison of demographic parameters for wild and laboratory-adapted Mediterranean fruit fly (Diptera: Tephritidae). Ann. Entomol. Soc. Am. 82(1):55-59

47. McInnis DO, Wong TTY, Tam SYT (1986) Mediterranean fruit fly, (Diptera: Tephritidae): suppression efficiencies of unisexual and bisexual sterilized release populations in field cages. Ann. Entomol. Soc. Am. 79:931-937

48. Wong TTY, Kobayashi RM, McInnis DO (1986) Mediterranean fruit fly (Diptera: Tephritidae): methods of assessing the effectiveness of sterile insect releases. J. Econ. Entomol. 79:1501-1506

49. Georghiou GP (1987) Insecticides and pest resistance: The consequences of abuse. Faculty Research Lecture, Academic Senate, Univ. of Calif., Riverside, 27 pp.

50. Cockburn AF, Seawright JA (1989) Application of molecular genetics to insect control. Handbook of Natural Pesticides: Insects, Vol. III, in press

Microbial control

© 1990 Elsevier Science Publishers B.V. (Biomedical Division)
Pesticides and alternatives, editor J.E. Casida

BIOLOGICAL CONTROL PRODUCTS:

DEMANDS OF INDUSTRY FOR SUCCESSFUL DEVELOPMENT

PAUL REINECKE

Bayer AG, Agrochemicals Division, Research and Development,
Biological Research, Institute of Biotechnology,
Pflanzenschutzzentrum Monheim, 5090 Leverkusen-Bayerwerk, FRG.

SUMMARY

The possibility of biological control has been demonstrated since a very long time. This is not only true of predators and parasites, but also of microorganisms, which should be discussed here exclusively.

Bacteria, fungi, viruses and protozoa have been developed for a broad range of applications by numerous companies. In principle, weeds, fungi and bacteria causing plant diseases, and many insects and nematodes can be controlled biologically.

Despite the rapid progress made in fundamental research, only products on the basis of Bacillus thuringiensis and its different strains have reached a certain market share. Compared to chemical pesticides, only minor amounts of it are sold as yet.

There are numerous reasons for the slow introduction of biological control into large scale pest control practice which are outlined in detail:

Activity of biocontrol agents under practical conditions is often not sufficient, owing to numerous environmental (temperature, humidity), host (behaviour, susceptibility) or antagonist (shelf live, speed of action) conditions. Under the critical eyes of the grower, biological products have to compete with chemical pesticides. They are often slower in activity and the level of control achieved is relatively low and unpredictable.

Large scale production of microorganisms is absolutely necessary for commercialization. In nearly all cases, this means that the antagonist has to be produced in a fermenter in a liquid and cheap medium. To handle and distribute large amounts of living organisms, they have to stay alive for a certain time after they have been formulated, which is a problem in itself, and they have to be packed.

Natural microorganisms are not per se undangerous. So, it has to be made sure that no organisms being pathogenic or producing toxic metabolites for mammals, beneficial organisms or crop plants, are chosen for development.

In many countries there exist no detailed registration guidelines for biologicals. This makes it difficult for companies to estimate costs and time necessary for the development of biological pesticides. In addition, the estimation of potential markets is extremely difficult, because at the moment such markets in fact do not exist, except for B.t..

Introduction of biological pesticides into general practice requires considerable advisory capacities, because these products often need more knowledge about the life cycle and behaviour of pests and diseases compared to the use of chemicals.

INTRODUCTION

By his mere existence, especially when becoming a farmer, man has disturbed the natural balance of his environment. He favours plants being useful for nutrition, clothing or house-building of his own population. Automatically he also creates favourable conditions for a large number of pests, which feel comfortable in man's garden. Thus, paradise was lost, man had to start working, plant protection became a high priority job.

But nothing is new under the sun! What we call insecticides, fungicides or herbicides has been created by mother nature millions of years ago. Surprisingly she also used chemical synthesis for her products - at least partly - and the result of a long time evolution was a number of perfectly adopted microorganisms, which control outgrowing populations of animals, fungi or plants by direct parasitism or with antibiotics.

Besides plant breeding and agricultural management the onset of chemical pesticides has dominated plant protection in the last decades - and they will continue to be the most powerful tools for the foreseeable future.

Biological control has always been existing and man has often tried to use this approach to protect his crop - with more or less success. The pesticide industry was reluctant as far as great investments (research and money) were concerned. Even though there is a considerable number of biological products on the market, the market share of these products compared to chemicals is very low.

Nevertheless, efforts to develop biological pesticides are increasing and an increasing number of companies are getting interested in that special field of plant protection.

ANTAGONISTIC MICROORGANISMS OFTEN REFERRED TO IN LITERATURE
AND THEIR PRACTICAL APPLICATION FOR BIOLOGICAL PLANT PROTECTION

Microorganism	Target	Production	Trade Name	Country	Commercial success
1. Antagonists against plant diseases					
Trichoderma harzianum	soilborne diseases	lab	-	-	-
Gliocladium virens	soilborne diseases	lab	-	-	-
Pseudomonas fluorescens	soilborne diseases	industry	Dagger G	USA	start in 89/90
Bacillus subtilis	soilborne diseases	industry	Quantum 4000 GUS 4000	USA	small?
2. Antagonists against plant pests					
Metarhizium anisopliae	planthopper	farmer cooperatives	Metaquino	Brazil	unknown
Beauveria bassiana	colorado potato beetle	industry?	Beauverin	USSR	unknown
Verticillium lecanii	white fly aphids	industry	Mycotal Vertalec	UK	production stopped
Hirsutella thompsonii	citrus mite	industry	Mycar	USA	production stopped
Bacillus thuringiensis	lepidopterous larvae and others	industry	many products	world-wide	moderate
3. Antagonists against nematodes					
Arthrobotrys irregularis	gall nematodes	industry	Royal 350	F	production stopped
Verticillium chlamydosporium	cyst nematodes	lab	-	-	-
Paecilomyces lilacinus	gall nematodes and others	industry	Biocon	Philipp.	unknown
4. Antagonists against weeds					
Colletotrichum gloeosporioides f.sp.aeschynomene	northern joint vetch	industry	Collego	USA	small
Phytophthora palmivora	milkweed vine	industry (made-to-order basis)	DeVine	USA	minimal
Alternaria cassiae	sicklepod	industry	Sickle	USA	unknown

Reasons for failure in the past and need for future efforts
Biological control has been a well-known possibility of crop protection
since more than one hundred years.

As early as 1878, the Russian entomologist Elias Metschnikoff carried out
experiments to control beetles in cereals with the entomopathogenic fungus
Metarhizium anisopliae. He isolated this fungus from diseased insects,
propagated it and used it for trials to control the beetles. Although he
was not very successful, he fulfilled Koch's postulates for the indubitable
characterization of a pathogen by isolation, determination and reinfestation of a pathogenic microorganism. Robert Koch, by the way, was 35 years
old in 1878 and had just discovered the anthracis bacillus two years ago.

But it was by no means new at that time that fungi could kill insects.
Already in 1835 the Italian scientist Agostino Bassi discovered the cause
of the mysterious disease of the very valuable silkworms in the Mediterranean area. He identified a fungus, which today we call Beauveria bassiana.

But until now, biological control still plays a minor role in the game of
pest control. If somebody wants to alter this - and public and political
pressure is directed towards this change - one has to identify the reasons
for the failure.

The most critical points for the successful development of biopesticides
may be the following:
- Interdisciplinary Approach
- Activity under Practical Conditions
- Large Scale Production and Formulation
- Storage and Distribution
- Toxicology and Environment
- Registration
- Education, Advisory Service

1. Interdisciplinary Approach
For the development of chemical pesticides within the pesticide industry
there exists a well-going machinery for research, development and marketing
of new products. Besides the technical advantages of chemical pesticides,
this network of chemists, biologists, agronomists and scientists of many
other disciplines developed over the past decades, led to the success of
ever more sophisticated pesticides.

In case of biological pesticides there is hardly any cooperation between
different specialists even on the research level. But as in other multi-
discipline approaches, teamwork is absolutely necessary.

For the development of a bioinsecticide, for example, the following groups have to cooperate, including their technical equipment: entomologists, mycologists, microbiologists, toxicologists, formulation specialists, field researchers, advisory services and sales managers, only to name the most important ones. Thus, there is no chance for solitary fighters!

2. Activity under Practical Conditions

Thousands of isolates of fungal and bacterial microorganisms have been tested in the last decades and many of them have shown promising activities. But most of these tests have been carried out under laboratory or greenhouse conditions under the careful supervision of scientists. Agriculture, however, in its realistic sense takes place in the field and the main actor is the practical farmer, who has to produce agricultural products in the best way - economically and oecologically.

That means that a pesticide (chemical or biological) sold to and applied by the farmer has to fulfil its job in a predictable manner. Failures can not be tolerated, because they threaten the farmer's existence.

The activity of a pesticide under field conditions is influenced by numerous factors. The problem for biologicals is that they are often influenced much more than chemicals.

INFLUENCE OF CLIMATIC FACTORS ON THE EFFECT OF BIOLOGICAL PLANT PROTECTION

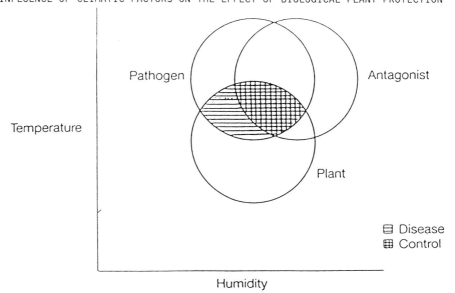

Temperature, for example, can have a certain influence on the activity of a chemical, for a biopesticide it is one of the limiting factors. The same is true for humidity. Fungal antagonists depend on moisture for the germination of their conidia. This makes it, for example, very difficult to control powdery mildew, which requires comparatively little water. So the control of powdery mildews of cereals and even those of vegetables in the greenhouse will remain the domain of chemical fungicides.

One of the advantages of biopesticides in many cases may be their long-lasting effect, especially when fungal conidia are concerned. Curative activity, however, to control fungal or insect pests may be limited or starts only very slowly. Crops, which tolerate only a very low level of a certain disease or pest, are therefore not very suitable for biological control. Bacillus thuringiensis, being active only for a few days, is not a very typical biopesticide in this respect. The same may be true for antagonistic entomopathogenic nematodes.

3. Large Scale Production and Formulation

Pesticide use in important crops is a question of tons rather than kilograms. Therefore, a sufficiently large scale production has to be guaranteed. The one and only way to produce these large amounts is using the liquid fermentation technique.

Also B.t., which today is by far the largest biopesticide, is produced in liquid culture.

This has consequences not only for the kind of microorganism, which can be chosen for a project, but also for the kind of "propagule", which will finally represent the bioproduct. Obligatory parasites, like e.g. some Entomophthora spp. or Bacillus penetrans, which occurs on nematodes, are not suitable for other than laboratory or small scale trials. This may be also true for viruses in general. Moreover, fungi usually do not produce conidia in liquid culture. So, another durable structure of the fungus has to be produced in the fermenter, if the use of the product should not be limited to sales at call.

Also the formulation of the "active ingredient", which means the living microorganism, is a critical point. On the one hand the bacterium or fungus has to stay alive in the formulation, on the other hand the formulation must meet the farmer's desire to apply the product in a way which he is used to. That means, he will spray a wettable powder or an emulsifiable concentrate or use a granulated product. To introduce a new technology, which must be adapted to the special needs for the biopesticide and which the farmer is not familiar with, makes the procedure a risky enterprise.

4. Storage and Distribution

Because large quantities of biopesticides have to be produced for a successful broad scale introduction into practice, the time for packaging and distribution will become an important factor.

The active ingredient of the biopesticide therefore has to stay alive as long as possible. A minimum shelf-life of about a year has to be required.

DURATION OF LIFE OF BIOLOGICAL STRUCTURES IN NATURAL HABITATS

Structure	Duration of life	Habitat	Example
Viruses	hours - days	Leaves	Nuclear-Polyhedrosis-Virus(NPV)
Fungal Blastospores	hours - days	Leaves	Beauveria
Bacterial Cells	days weeks - months years	Leaves Soil Soil	Pseudomonas Pseudomonas Bacillus
Fungal Hyphae	weeks - months	Soil	Trichoderma
Nematodes (Larvae)	weeks - months	Soil	Heterorhabditis
Fungal Spores (Conidia)	hours weeks months - years	Leaves Leaves Soil	Entomophthorales Aschersonia Metarhizium
Chlamydospores	more than 1 year	Soil	Fusarium
Sclerotia	more than 2 years	Soil	Sclerotinia

5. Toxicology and Environment

Some of the most powerful poisons are produced by microorganisms, e.g. botulism toxin or aflatoxin. On the other hand, fungi also produce penicillin or other useful antibiotics.

Also with regard to the use of living organisms assigned for biological control of plant pests and diseases, good and evil are close together. Numerous fungi and bacteria exist, which are restricted to their respective host which may be an insect pest (Metarhizium, Beauveria) or a weed (rust fungi).

On the other hand, fungal species like Paecilomyces lilacinus, which may be effective against nematodes, may include strains, which are pathogenic to humans, causing severe diseases of e.g. lung or eyes.

Thus, also in case of biopesticides a certain set of toxicological data has to be generated before they are used on a large scale. As structures of microbial products - like pollen grains - exist which have an allergenic potency, this particular effect has to be studied carefully in order to allow protecting people being involved in the production process and in application. Tests should also cover the environmental behaviour, e.g. the effects on honey bees and earthworms.

6. Registration

For chemical pesticides a clearly defined registration procedure exists in most countries of the world. It may be very expensive to develop the required data (roughly 100 Mill. $ development costs per compound; a large part of this is spent for toxicological and environmental safety tests), but the costs are predictable for the companies.

Such catalogues of exactly defined criteria often do not exist for biopesticides. This makes the development costs unpredictable for the companies.

In any case, the registration of biopesticides should be implemented in close dialogue between official registration authorities and the applicant. Many of the tests necessarily required for chemicals are either impossible or senseless to conduct with biologicals. For example, it is very difficult or even impossible to obtain a dust atmosphere of fungal spores for a toxicological inhalation trial.

The EPA, for example, is following a tier-system for the evaluation of microbial products. It demands a certain basic set of toxicological and environmental data. If some striking effects occur, continuing tests in the respective area - and only there! - are necessary to be carried out.

7. Education, Advisory Service

Despite the fact that a biopesticide should be developed in a way that the farmer can use it like a chemical which he can handle in a familiar way, biologicals will still have their special peculiarities. They require more knowledge of the growing conditions and behaviour of the crop and a detailed information about the life cycle or growing conditions of the pest or pathogen. This means the need for better scientific education also for the advisory service staff, who can transfer their experience to the farmer.

PROSPECTS FOR BIOLOGICAL CONTROL

a) from the point of indications

In the foreseeable future chemical pesticides will not be replaced by biological products. This is especially true for herbicides, which constitute

the major part of the worlds agrochemicals. Bioherbicides will be restricted to special circumstances, where weed populations exist with only one or
few predominant species. It is not likely to happen that a microorganism
will kill several weed species of various plant families without doing any
harm to the crop plant.

Biopesticides will gain certain importance as bioinsecticides or bio-
fungicides. Particularly in the soil, often one insect pest or one fungal
pathogen attacks the crop plant. Examples where biological control can be
successful may be the polyphagus beetle Otiorrhynchus sulcatus, whose
larvae feed on rootstocks of many ornamentals, or Rhizoctonia solani which
occurs on nearly all species of plants as damping-off fungus.

b) from the point of the environmental conditions of the crop
The use of biopesticides will be favoured by controlled environmental conditions, that means that temperature and humidity should be in a range
suitable for the growth of microorganisms. Moreover, intensive agricultural
practices will also promote their use.

Therefore, greenhouses cultures and intensive vegetable or ornamental
crops may be the target for biological control measures rather than huge
acreage field crops such as corn or wheat.

c) from the point of agricultural policy
Agrochemicals are and will be absolutely necessary to help to produce the
food basis of the rapidly increasing world population. This does not mean
that they are not under a strong public and political discussion and in
special cases their application may be restricted or even prohibited. In
some countries the limitation of agrochemicals and fertilizers will even be
used as a means to decrease the agricultural overproduction. In the industrial countries, biopesticides may therefore play an increasing role in
water preservation areas or in the home and garden sector.

Biopesticides will certainly not replace agrochemicals within the next
one or two decades. Also the perspectives of genetic engineering of plants
will not render chemical or biological crop protection measures unneces-
sary.

The step from research to practical agriculture, however, will be a difficult and stony way. In any case the development of biopesticides will be
a high-tech procedure, which will need much input of modern technology,
manpower and capital and - last not least - personal engagement of ide-
alists sometimes being given a condescending smile. According to recently
published market reports by Frost & Sullivan (New York), the world market
for pesticides amounts to $ 20 billion, 0.5 % (=$ 100 million) of which

account for biopesticides. The forecast, however, for the year 2000 is $ 8 billion for biologicals, which would mean 40% market share, if the total market stays unchanged within the next 10 years.

This prognosis seems rather optimistic, but several years ago, nobody would even have an imagination like that.

© 1990 Elsevier Science Publishers B.V. (Biomedical Division)
Pesticides and alternatives, editor J.E. Casida

INNOVATIVE APPROACHES TO THE INDUSTRIALIZATION OF MICROBIAL PESTICIDES

LOUIS A. FALCON

Department of Entomological Sciences, University of California, Berkeley, CA 94720, USA

INTRODUCTION

The so-called era of "Biotechnology and Genetic Engineering" has yet to provide any revolutionary products that can be sold for pest control purposes. Many of those on the drawing boards face difficult regulatory obstacles and may never be commercialized (1). Assuming a major breakthrough soon, it may take 10 or more years to complete registration, commercialize and provide general availability of a product. In the meantime, alternatives to chemical farming methods and products are needed so that farmers can produce the quantity and quality of foods and fibers the world needs. The potential for utilizing naturally-occurring insect pathogens as microbial pesticides has been before us for many years. While hundreds have been identified, only 14 insect pathogens used in about 100 microbial pesticide products have been registered by the US Environmental Protection Agency (EPA) as of 1987. Globally, the amounts of microbial pesticides used is minuscule. In the past 20 years more companies have given up development of microbial pesticides than are currently doing so. Although most insect pathogens are known only as a record in a diagnosis report, there are at least 25 which, in my opinion, have been sufficiently studied to demonstrate potential as useful microbial pesticides (2). The immediate potential lies not in the development of genetically-engineered insect pathogens, but in the elaboration of non-engineered, naturally-occurring insect pathogens as industrialized, commercial microbial pesticides. With the exception of the *Bacillus thuringiensis* (Bt) complex though, the pesticide industry continues to ignore, for the most part, this potential. In this paper, I use the term "industrialized" to mean "developed as a commercial, business enterprise".

There are times I feel there is a conspiracy at hand which, while not premeditated, is fostered by a desire to justify the errors of the past as regards R&D and registration of pesticides. This is obstructive and harmful to the development of microbial pesticides which can provide useful alternatives to the toxic chemical pesticides. On one side, all of the problems created by the development and use of hazardous toxic chemical pesticides has made the regulatory process more complex and difficult in an effort to prevent a reoccurrence of the mistakes of the past. On the other side, the fears created by the possibilities of developing genetically-engineered/-altered pesticides has lead to confusion and chaos in the regulatory process that may take years to sort out, or may never happen. Unfairly, the process of developing non-genetically-engineered/-altered microbial pesticides from naturally- occurring microbial agents has been negatively affected by both sides. Also, the EPA is deeply involved in the "reregistration" of some 25000 pesticides which must be completed by 1997. This activity is very demanding and draining of resources from an agency that is said to be underfinanced and overworked. The resource distribution favors reregistration at the expense of developing alternatives to replace the faltering problem-laden toxic chemical pesticides. Thus, microbial pesticides developed from nontoxic, naturally-occurring insect pathogens are far more difficult to register than need be the case. The reregistration process will significantly contribute to the demise of toxic chemical pesticides in the USA mainly because of economics. The 17-year patent protection period for many of the chemical pesticides up for reregistration has or will expire soon. The cost of reregistration along with lost product protection has already discouraged the reregistration of many chemical pesticide products. Thus, what I see happening is a great reduction in the farmer's pest control arsenal as old products are removed and new ones are prevented from coming to the marketplace. Of course, many of the problems stem from the political process as the chemical pesticide industry and supporting entities, can and do influence legislation that would otherwise facilitate the R&D and registration of alternatives to toxic hazardous chemical pesticides and the development of other low input farming methods. They are able to do this through a well financed, powerful political lobby network at the federal and state levels.

What are the virtues of microbial pesticides? "Specificity" is one that most possess. Some are genus specific while others may be specific to one or more families within an order. This type of specificity is unknown in the synthetic organic chemical arena and unfortunately, is not sought after by chemical pesticide firms for economic reasons. Specificity means that the microbial agent causes harm only to its host and is harmless to everything else. For example, the codling moth granulosis virus infects only the codling moth larva and the larvae of a few close relatives within the family Tortricidae, all of which are considered potential plant pests. *Autographa californica* NPV is termed "broad spectrum" by some insect pathologists, but only because it infects several genera within the Lepidoptera. The Bt "kurstaki" strain, the most widely used microbial pesticide, is specific for the larvae of moths and butterflies. While this group contains aesthetically important species, it is not known to include species of beneficial insects. On the other hand, the "israelensis" strain infects only mosquito and blackfly larvae and the "tenebrionis" strain is reportedly selective for beetles. The fungus, *Hirsutella thompsoni*, appears to be specific for mite species in the family Eriophyidae. Specificity is a great asset for farmers growing crops using ecologically-oriented, sustainable farming methods. Also, of great importance, specificity means the microbial agent is not hazardous for humans and other warm blooded animals.

There are many reasons for the existing situation which is not entirely recent (3). Briefly, as I see it, some of the most important obstacles to the development of microbial pesticides are: 1). The fact that naturally-occurring biological control agents cannot be patented because they occur naturally thus, royalties are not possible; 2). The fact that in the USA, and in many other countries, an insect pathogen or any other substance sold as a pesticide, must be shown to be non-hazardous before it can be registered with federal and state regulatory agencies. This is a costly, time consuming and complex process; 3). Due to their specificity, R&D costs of microbial pesticides may be relatively high in relation to market potential; 4). The mass production of insect pathogens as microbial pesticides may be difficult; 5). Microbial pesticides may not be as easy to use as toxic chemical pesticides, they do not behave in the same manner, and they are slower acting; 6). The potential of insect pathogens as microbial pesticides is not fully known because resources and funding allocated for this purpose have been insufficient. 7). The populace in general is fearful of microbial agents because they associate them with maladies such as the common cold, stomach flu, AIDS, etc.; and 8). There is a general lack of understanding by most people of what pest control is all about. This is evidenced by the many problems that have surfaced and continue to emerge due to the development and use of the post-World War II synthetic, toxic, organic chemical pesticides and, non-ecological, non-sustainable agriculture farming methods, which most farmers have been conditioned to believe is the "the only way to farm". The problems thus created (resistance, pest resurgence, environmental pollution, human health hazards, consumer fears, etc.) now have chemical companies and research scientists looking in every possible direction for alternatives. In my opinion though, much of their search continues to be misguided, because they continue to seek broad spectrum, fast acting "new" pesticides with little regard for the ecological consequences of their use beyond what government regulatory agencies may call for. This situation must and will change because of the increasing demand by all of us for a cleaner environment and a safe food supply.

In the USA there is a mounting demand by farmers for safe and effective pest control products and methods. This is being spurred by a growing consumer demand for safe food, water and air supplies. The situation is especially critical for the apple industry where a near death blow was struck by the "alar problem" in 1989. "Organic farming" is in and "chemical farming" is out! The situation though, is one of confusion and chaos. In the market place the food industry is trying very hard to assure the public that the food supply is safe and wholesome. The consumer is being confused by jargon such as "natural", "pesticide-free", "IPM Grown", "transition", "Organic", "Certified Organic", "wholesome", "we choose only the best", "our food is inspected", "our food has been tested", etc. The transition from chemical to organic farming will be slow because chemical farming methods have dominated for so long that there is little useful information available on non-chemical farming methods and, there are too few qualified specialists capable of providing the needed know-how. Out of fear and desperation, many farmers will follow almost any lead. As a result, "quacks and quackery" are rampant! The institutions that should be providing the information and leadership such as the federal and state departments of agriculture, experiment stations and extension services, seem to spend more time trying to justify the errors of the past rather than admitting to ignorance in the present! Fortunately, a few small, innovative, industrialized firms seem to be providing some of the products and much of the leadership for a growing number of farmers seeking to produce food employing non-hazardous methods (e.g. Evans BioControl, Inc.; Mycogen Corp.; Novo Laboratories, Inc.;).

INNOVATIVE APPROACHES

Product Protection

The nonpatentability of naturally-occurring biological control agents may really only be overcome with the development of genetically-engineered/-altered microbial pesticides. In the meantime, only such areas as production methods and formulations may be patentable. Currently, the US Department of Agriculture (USDA) is seeking a patent for a formulation developed by them for using the Indian meal moth granulosis virus to protect packaged nuts and dried fruits. In this manner, the USDA hopes to attract an industrial firm to buy the patent and produce and market the virus product (P. Vail, personal communication). In the USA, a registrant of a pesticide product is protected for a period of 10 years from other companies using its data without permission. The University of California, in collaboration with IR-4, is developing the registration of the codling moth granulosis virus, using public funds. Once issued, the University will be in a position to license the viral pesticide to industrial firms for the purposes of marketing and production. Another approach would be a "nonpatentable product licensing program" where, by paying a fee, private sector interests could acquire exclusive rights to the development and marketing of a microbial pesticide for a specified time and as long as significant development activity was sustained.

The Registration Process

While the cost of registering a microbial pesticide with the EPA (ca US$1M) is relatively low compared to a chemical pesticide (ca US$50M+), a small market potential (US$50M or less/annum for a microbial pesticide vs US$100M+ for a chemical pesticide) can magnify the cost of registration. In addition to the cost of registration, it may take several years to complete the process. Firstly, some of the required tests may necessitate special conditions that laboratories may not be setup to do (e.g. bioassay). Secondly, the regulatory agencies (e.g. EPA) are mostly staffed by toxicologists and lawyers who are accustomed to dealing with toxic chemical substances and little else. They are neither trained to handle microbial agents, nor are they sympathetic to the problems. Thirdly, the required tests are not always practical nor sensible (e.g. How can one measure the toxicity of a baculovirus when they are not toxic?). Finally, a clear separation is needed between the non-toxic and the toxic and, of the naturally-occurring from the the genetically-engineered/-altered. The regulatory agencys must make changes in order to facilitate the registration of microbial pesticides and other alternatives to toxic chemical pesticides. They can begin by hiring more microbiologists and other specialists knowledgeable and sympathetic to the registration of alternatives to toxic chemical pesticides. They can reorganize and create review groups to deal exclusively with alternatives to toxic chemical pesticides and who have the authority to register them. They can revise the rules governing the registration of alternatives to toxic chemical pesticides and make them more applicable to the situation. They can employ the "generic registration" concept whereby the registration of one representative of a group would simplify it for the rest of the members of the same group (e.g. granulosis viruses).

Those legislators who truly support clean environment issues need to be educated about the existence and value of microbial pesticides as alternatives to toxic chemical pesticides. This may be done through lobbying and other types of education programs directed at lawmakers and the general public as well. When referenda dealing with the toxic pesticide issues are brought before the voters, they should not just ban toxic chemical pesticides, they should also provide a mechanism to allow for the development of alternatives to replace what has been banned.

Market Size

The specificity of most microbial pesticides limits market size. Specificity, though, is needed for successful ecologically-based pest management programs. The chemical pesticide industry, however, is not excited about developing such pesticides. The fear of insufficient financial returns to cover R&D costs and produce profits is a major deterrent. An innovative way to provide R&D costs is to allow the users (farmer and forester) and benefactors of safer pesticides (all of us) to bear some of the R&D costs. This could be done by federal or state governments using tax payer funds to make available grants and low or no interest loans to private firms specifically earmarked for the development of alternatives to toxic chemical pesticides. Several models have been provided. The US Forest Service (USFS) provided a model which was financed by federal taxpayers and resulted in the R&D and registration of three microbial insecticides (Douglas fir tussock moth NPV; gypsy moth NPV; pine sawfly NPV). This was done to provide the USFS with ecologically safe pesticides to be used for suppression of forest pests in environmentally sensitive areas. By doing this, USFS benefits in many ways, including reducing the possibilities of legal actions brought against it when toxic chemical pesticides are used in the government controlled forest lands. Once registered, the USFS proceeded to farm out to private industry via contracts, production and formulation of the registered microbial pesticides. The USDA bore much of the R&D costs for the development and registration of the protozoan, *Nosema locustae*, for the control of rangeland grasshoppers. This pathogen is currently produced and further researched by private industrial firms (e.g. Evans Biological Control). Much of the money that went into the development and registration of *B.t.israelensis* was provided by the World Health Organization (WHO) because they needed it to combat disease-bearing mosquitos. *Heliothis zea* NPV was developed and registered as the microbial insecticide Elcar (TM), with funds from private industry, USDA, and grower organizations. In West Germany, the Federal Government and the F. Hoechst Co., have worked jointly for several years in an effort to develop insect viruses as microbial pesticides. Much of the early effort was associated with the *Autographa* and *Brassica* NPVs. Most recently, they have turned their attention to the codling moth granulosis virus. It was recently registered by the West German government and named "Granusal" (Dickler & Huber, personal communications).

In California, farmers developed a non-profit cooperative called the "Association for Sensible Pest Control, Inc." (ASPC), in order to obtain the codling moth granulosis virus (CMGV). The farmers were willing to do this after it became obvious that industry was not going to develop CMGV. Sandoz, Inc., experimented with CMGV in the early 1980s and then abandoned the program. A fledgling venture capital company known as MicroGeneSys, became involved with CMGV in the mid-part of the decade. After three years, they shelved the CMGV project and concentrated their research on finding a vaccine against the AIDS virus. Both companies had released material for field testing under an EPA Experimental Use Permit (EUP) and field results with the experimental CMGV products was good. Organic farmers in particular, wanted continuous access to CMGV so they organized ASPC. Their participation provides funds to assist with CMGV R&D and registration costs. This effort will help hasten the day when CMGV will be registered and available as a commercial microbial insecticide. The current EUP was issued to the University of California, Berkeley Campus (UCB) under the direction of the author. UCB is the "potential registrant". More marriages between industry, government, growers and consumers (you and me) are needed to develop microbial pesticides and other alternatives to toxic chemical pesticides.

Market size is also affected by the competition created by the availability of cheaper and easy to use chemical pesticides. Chemical pesticide sales in turn, are influenced by federal and state government programs and policies. The majority of people giving farmers pest control advice are chemical pesticide-oriented. When an investment is at stake, they normally recommend the use of toxic chemical pesticides mainly because they were trained to do so. In these situations, there is little concern for the environmental problems and deleterious side effects caused by the use of toxic chemical pesticides. Congress can influence state and federal agencies to hire a representative number of biological and microbial control-oriented specialists (e.g. USDA/ARS, Cooperative Extension). There are very few pest control strategies available that utilize microbial and other biological control agents as the main weapons to suppress major pests. Congress should employ its powers to influence state and federal agencies to develop programs and policies that encourage the use of biological control methods and products. Congress should use its influence to encourage USDA and state agricultural experiment stations to allocate a significant amount of resource to the development of biological and microbial control methods and products.

The Natural Research Council of the US National Academy of Sciences recently made several recommendations regarding alternative agriculture including: "..include wider adoption of..biological pest control.."and "..lower-cost management strategies that use fewer off-farm and synthetic chemical inputs..." "Future farm programs should offer no new incentives to manage these and other fragile lands in a way that impairs environmental quality." "A set of guidelines for assessing the benefits of pesticides under regulatory review should be developed. This procedure must include a definition of beneficiaries as well as an assessment of the costs and benefits of other available pest control alternatives." " Cosmetic and grading standards should be revised to emphasize the safety of food and deemphasize appearance and other secondary criteria."

Large-Scale Production

While it is true that many insect pathogens are difficult or thus far impossible to mass produce. Their are many that lend themselves to established fermentation technology (bacteria, fungi) and in vivo production systems using semisynthetic media (baculoviruses). The basic technology is developed and continually being improved. There is always the possibility that insect tissue cultures systems may someday provide an economical way to produce insect pathogens for use as microbial pesticides. Of course, production improvements come faster when their is greater demand. In 1976, Sandoz, Inc. was the first in the USA to develop a factory to produce a baculovirus microbial insecticide (Elcar) on a large scale. The failure of Elcar (*Heliothis* NPV) as a product was due to marketing and competition and not to the production methods. In Brazil, the government agriculture research arm EMBRAPA, successfully produced the velvet bean caterpillar NPV for distribution on 1000s of acres of soybean each year starting in 1986 (Moscardi, personal communication). Also, in Brazil, there are private firms producing insect fungi-based- insecticides for control of insect pests (Homoptera) on sugarcane and pasture. The research effort establishing the use of the fungi was accomplished through a Food and Agriculture (FAO) sponsored country program during the 1970s.

Using Microbial Pesticides

Microbial pesticides differ from chemical pesticides in many ways too numerous to mention here. Probably most important, with the exception of the fungi, is that all have to be ingested. The fungal spores may infect via ingestion or contact. Once ingested by a susceptible host there is an incubation period lasting several hours before the host dies. Although the microbial pesticide does not kill rapidly, the afflicted host may become sick and stop feeding several hours before it dies. In contrast, chemical pesticides often kill the pest right away. On the other side of the coin, microbial pesticides have many pluses and when compared over the entire growing season or for several seasons they usually end up outperforming chemical pesticides both in cost and crop protection. This is so mainly because they do not produce any of the environmental perturbations caused by toxic chemical pesticides. Over a 5 year period the codling moth granulosis virus outperformed azinphosmethyl in a commercial pear orchard (Falcon & Berlowitz, unpublished). In another 5-year study Bt outshone chemical pesticides for the control of spruce budworm in the Canadian forest (Morris, personal communication).

Developing Their Full Potential

One reason for the success of toxic chemical pesticides is due to the ability of a well financed chemical company to produce large quantities of a standardized experimental product. The experimental product is rapidly distributed to field specialists through an organized network for testing under a variety of conditions. Data on efficacy, toxicity, formulation and utility are rapidly gathered and adjustments made to the product as needed to perfect it. Therefore, once registered, much experience and know-how about the product already exists. With the exception of the Bt complex, Elcar is the only microbial insecticide for use in agriculture to have gone through the process described above. The private industry expenses for this were mostly borne by International Mineral & Chemical Corp. in the 60s and early 70s and later by Sandoz, Inc.

With most candidate microbial pesticides, only small amounts are produced and this is done by each researcher in his/her laboratory for his/her personal use. Seldom is there standardization of procedures or products. Field testing is limited to a few small plots. Unless a private company becomes interested in acquiring the candidate microbial pesticide, the project will end after a few years and the candidate microbial pesticide will be put on the shelf. One way to overcome this problem may be for the federal government to establish a central microbial pesticide development center much as it does biological warfare research centers. Such a center would receive candidate microbial pesticides. These would be mass produced and formulated into standardized experimental products and made available for distribution to cooperating insect specialists in the world to be tested on the same crop/s in a standardized way. Registration work for promising candidates would be completed at the center. The registered product would then be available for production and marketing by private industry under license to the government. Licensing fees thus collected would be retained by the center to offset costs.

Overcoming Human Fears

The registration process must be designed to provide all of the data needed to assure everyone that a candidate microbial pesticide is indeed non-hazardous. Education programs should also be employed. The importance of useful microbial agents that humans come in contact with every day should be emphasized (i.e. cheeses, breads, beer, yogurt, sour dough, wine, etc.).

Some of the greatest fears humans have are related to environmental pollution. The concern of EPA is that a pesticide, when used in accordance with widespread and commonly recognized practice, will not cause (or significantly increase the risk of) unreasonable adverse effects to humans or the environment (section 3 (c)(5) and (7) of FIFRA). Toxic chemical pesticides are always registered with a tolerance level based on the hazard they represent. On the other hand, all microbial pesticides registered to date are "exempt from a tolerance". This means they have been shown to be "non-hazardous" and will not cause unreasonable adverse effects to humans and the environment. This factor alone should provide whatever justifications are needed to do all possible to facilitate the industrialization of microbial pesticides as alternatives to toxic chemical pesticides.

ACKNOWLEDGEMENTS

I gratefully acknowledge the assistance and support provided by my research associate, Arthur Berlowitz.

REFERENCES

1.   Reilly WK (1989) Administrator, US Environmental Protection Agency, Address: Improving upon nature: The promise and pitfalls of biotechnology. At: Industrial Biotechnology Association, Washington, DC, October 13, 1989

2.   Falcon LA (1985) In: Hoy MA, Herzog DC (eds) Biological Control in Agricultural IPM Systems. Academic Press, NY, pp 229-242

3.   Falcon LA (1976) In: Smith RF, Mittler TE, Smith CN (eds) Annual Review of Entomology. Palo Alto, CA, pp 305-324

© 1990 Elsevier Science Publishers B.V. (Biomedical Division)
Pesticides and alternatives, editor J.E. Casida

VIRAL INSECTICIDES: PROFITS, PROBLEMS, AND PROSPECTS

JÜRG HUBER

Biologische Bundesanstalt für Land- und Forstwirtschaft
Institut für biologische Schädlingsbekämpfung, D-6100 Darmstadt, Germany FR

One of the main principles in integrated pest management is the use of specific pesticides for a directed control of the few pest species that surpass the economic damage threshold. The intention is to leave the ecosystem in a given crop as undisturbed as possible, taking advantage of the natural enemies present in an intact fauna. For reasons given below, most chemical insecticides are wide spectrum pesticides and fit therefore very poorly into that scheme. It is obvious that in integrated control programs a single use of a broad spectrum pesticide can annihilate the effect of all the other selective control measures. The lack of selective insecticides is therefore a major problem in integrated control programs in agriculture and forestry. Fortunately enough, nature itself has produced highly specific insecticides: the insect viruses.

INSECT VIRUSES

Viruses pathogenic for insects do not represent a taxonomic unit. We find viruses capable of infecting insects in such different virus families as Iridoviridae, Parvoviridae, Poxviridae, Reoviridae and Baculoviridae (1). In most of these families there are also members which infect vertebrates or even plants; with one exception, the family of the baculoviruses. This lack of evidence for the occurrence of baculoviruses in non-arthropod hosts is sustained by the absence of baculovirus incidence from the publications of medical, veterinary and phytopathology science. Baculoviruses have been isolated from crustacea and mites, but mostly from insects. The absence from non-arthropod organisms is already a strong indirect evidence for the safety of baculoviruses for man and environment (2). Their specificity is outstanding: viruses from the family of Baculoviridae, which represent about 60% of the more than 1100 insect viruses isolated till today, usually infect a few closely related insect species only. For some of them just a single susceptible host is known (3).

Baculoviruses are characterized by double stranded circular DNA included in rod-shaped capsids which are formed mostly in the nucleus of the host cells (4). As a feature in common with some insect viruses from other virus families, the virions of most baculoviruses are contained within the matrix of proteinaceous particles, the so called occlusion bodies, which provide protection against adverse physical and chemical factors in the environment (5). This protective coat allows the virus to kill its host within very short time without jeopardizing its own existence, permitting survival also outside of the host cell. The good protection of the viruses within the occlusion body also is of great advantage for the use of these viruses as biological insecticides. Since they are so resistant, they can be applied like chemical pesticides.

USE IN PEST CONTROL

Baculoviruses have several properties which make them ideally suited for use in integrated plant protection programmes. Table 1 lists a few attributes of viral insecticides, positive as well as negative ones (6). Basically, baculoviruses can be used for plant protection in three different ways: a) the so called insecticidal approach, i.e. release of massive amounts of baculoviruses for immediate control of the target pest. b) the classical biological control strategy which is the introduction of viruses into a pest population for long term control and c) the management of natural occurring viruses by designing the crop management in such a way as to favour the outbreak of virus epizootics (7).

Table 1: Some attributes of viral insecticides with regard to their use in plant protection and to their commercialization.

positive	negative
• highly selective: environmentally and ecologically safe; harmless to beneficials — less problems with secondary, man made pests.	▪ highly selective: in case of other pests in the same crop sometimes additional control measures necessary; small sales potential — not attractive for commercialization.
• no residue problems.	▪ short persistence of foliar deposits.
• persists and multiplies in pest population, giving long term control.	▪ affects mostly larval stage of insect only.
• effective even at a very low dosage.	▪ relatively slow acting; no knock-down effect.
• not known to induce major resistance.	▪ considerable attention to timing and application necessary.
• production technology simple, suited for cottage type industry.	▪ production labor-intensive — not amenable to conventional microbial techniques.
• conventional application techniques can be used.	▪ preparations have to be registered.

World-wide, little more than a dozen baculoviruses are registered for use as biological insecticides in forestry and agriculture (for review see 8). Whereas in the United States of America and in Canada most of the registrations are held by government agencies, in Europe 5 virus preparations are being produced and sold by private companies: in Finland, Great Britain, Switzerland and Germany. This number seems small with regard to the considerable potential of baculoviruses. It has been estimated that "baculoviruses can be used against about 30% of the major pest species interfering with food and fibre production in the world" (9).

LIMITATIONS AND PROBLEMS

It cannot be denied that a wider use of insect viruses in pest control meets with some difficulties. So far, viral insecticides have hardly been promoted because of their environmental advantages, but mostly only when conventional chemical control has failed, due to problems with residue on food or resistance of the pest population.

One of the main reasons why viral pesticides have met little acceptance by the agricultural practice so far, lies in the dilemma that, whereas the main advantage of using selective insecticides are at an environmental and social level, there is usually no immediate economic benefit for the farmer as the direct consumer of the product. As table 1 shows, viral insecticides do not have only positive features for use in plant protection. As profitable and desirable selectivity is from an ecological view point, as problematic and hindering it is with regard to the economics of the commercialisation of viral pesticides. In most countries, insect viruses have to be officially registered for use as insecticides and are subjected to the same regulations as chemical pesticides. Therefore, the expenses for their commercialisation are in the same order of magnitude as for conventional insecticides. But, due to their selectivity, their market size and their sales potential is rather limited and the manufacturer is forced to charge a high prize for his product.

In addition to that, the application of selective pesticides requires a vast amount of know-how from the side of the farmer about the biology of the pest species and the antagonists in the crop and is therefore not as easy as the use of broad spectrum chemicals. Since the effect of the virus on the target pest usually is not as quick and thorough as that of most chemical insecticides, more attention has to be given to the timing and application of the sprays. All this makes the use of selective pesticides for the farmer more cumbersome and more costly (10). As figure 1 tries to illustrate, the farmer therefore has mostly to deal with the negative side of selective pesticides, whereas most of the benefit is on the side of the public. Nobody can blame the farmer that he is not particularly keen to pay for somebody else advantages. Even if he would be willing to do so, he could not survive in a world governed by commerce.

120

Figure 1: The ecological and the economical aspect of viral insecticides as an example for selective pesticides.

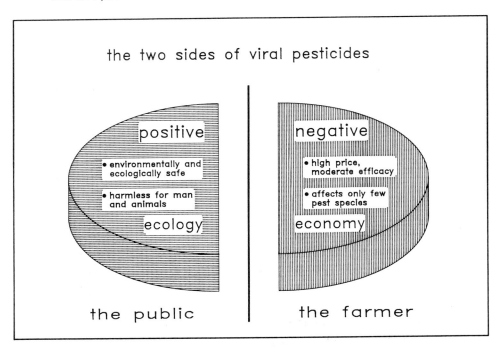

FUTURE PROSPECTS

A exit out of this dilemma of the two sides of selective pesticides can only be brought forward either by the consumer or by the government. If the consumer rejects agricultural products which are produced with the help of broad spectrum pesticides, the farmer is forced to change his pest management practice. But this means at the same time that the consumer has to accept higher prices for his products. This would be a change from within the market situation.

Only the government has the possibility to change the framework of the market from the outside through regulations, taxes and subsidies. It could, for instance, rise taxes on environmentally disruptive preparations or pay subsistence for less harmful products. The government could also ban the use of a given broad spectrum chemical, if other environmentally safer products are available for the same purpose. It is obvious that this too would lead to higher prices for the products of agriculture.

In short, either the farmer is forced to abandon the cheap broad spectrum pesticides, or the use of environmentally safe pesticides is made profitable to the farmer. Only then, selective insecticides, as for instance viral preparations, will be as widely esteemed and used in the future as they should be with regard to our environment.

Recently, advances in genetic engineering have pinned ones hope on this novel techniques to improve some of the pesticidal qualities of insect viruses (11). It has been suggested to create viruses which a) exhibit a broader host range, b) produce a toxin for faster kill, c) show increased virulence or d) have a better environmental stability than their naturally occurring "parent" viruses. Technically this way is feasible, but in view of the general apprehension of genetic engineering, release of such recombinant viruses into the environment probably will meet great public resistance. Since, as we have seen above, the main hindrance for a wider use of insect viruses is not lack of a efficacy, this would not solve the problem anyhow.

Whereas insect viruses are met with great reluctance in industrialized countries, they have a great potential for use in third world nations. Their production technique is simple; they can be produced in a cottage type industry, using local resources. Viral pesticides offer the possibility for developing countries to produce their own insecticides, becoming less dependant from chemical insecticides which they have to buy for foreign currency from industrialized nations. This has been recognized and the potential of insect viruses is already being exploited in countries like Brazil, Guatemala, Thailand, Columbia, Zimbabwe and so on.

To summarize, future promotion of viral insecticides can help third world nations to lessen their economical difficulties whereas it can support the industrialized world in overcoming its ecological and environmental problems.

REFERENCES

1. KRIEG, A., 1973: Arthropodenviren. Georg Thieme Verlag, Stuttgart, 328 pp.

2. BURGES, H.D., CROIZIER, G., and HUBER, J., 1980: A review of safety tests on baculoviruses. Entomophaga **25**, 329-340.

3. GRÖNER, A., 1986: Specificity and safety of baculoviruses. In: GRANADOS, R.R. and FEDERICI, B.A. (eds.): The Biology of Baculoviruses. Vol. I: Biological Properties and Molecular Biology. CRC Press, Inc., Boca Raton, Florida, p 177-202.

4. GRANADOS, R.R. and FEDERICI, B.A. (eds.), 1986: The Biology of Baculoviruses. Vol. I: Biological Properties and Molecular Biology. CRC Press, Inc., Boca Raton, Florida, 275 pp.

5. JAQUES, R.P., 1977: Stability of entomopathogenic viruses. Misc. Publ. Entomol. Soc. Am. **10**(3), 99-116.

6. HUBER, J., 1986: Use of baculoviruses in pest management programs. In: GRANADOS, R.R., and FEDERICI, B.A. (eds.): The Biology of Baculoviruses. Vol. II: Practical Application for Insect Control. CRC Press, Inc., Boca Raton, Florida, p 181-202.

7. HUBER, J., 1988: Einsatzmöglichkeiten von Baculoviren im Pflanzenschutz. Mitt. Biol. Bundesanst. Land- und Forstwirtsch. Berlin-Dahlem **246**, 167-177.

8. CUNNINGHAM, J.C., 1988: Baculoviruses: Their status compared to Bacillus thuringiensis as microbial insecticides. Outlook on Agric. **17**(1), 10-17.

9. FALCON, L.A., 1980: Economical and biological importance of baculoviruses as alternatives to chemical pesticides. In: Proc. Symp. "Safety Aspects of Baculoviruses as Biological Insecticides". 13-15 Nov. 1978, Jülich. Bundesministerium für Forschung und Technologie, Bonn, p 27-46.

10. HUBER, J., 1987: Hochselektive Pflanzenschutzmittel am Beispiel der Insektenviren. In: Bundesminister für Ernährung, Landwirtschaft und Forsten (ed.): Biologischer Pflanzenschutz. Schriftenr. Bundesmin. Ernährung Landwirtschaft Forsten, Reihe A: Angewandte Wissenschaft **344**, 73-80. (Landwirtschaftsverlag GmbH, Münster-Hiltrup)

11. POSSEE, R.D., CAMERON, I.R., ALLEN, C.J., and BISHOP, D.H.L., 1988: Experiences with the first field release of genetically engineered viruses. Schr.-Reihe Verein WaBoLu **78**, 165 - 186. (Gustav Fischer Verlag, Stuttgart)

© 1990 Elsevier Science Publishers B.V. (Biomedical Division)
Pesticides and alternatives, editor J.E. Casida

VIRUS INSECTICIDES: GENETIC ANALYSIS OF *PANOLIS FLAMMEA* NUCLEAR POLYHEDROSIS VIRUS

MATTHEW D. WEITZMAN, ROBERT D. POSSEE AND LINDA A. KING
School of Biological & Molecular Sciences, Oxford Polytechnic, Gypsy Lane, Oxford OX3 OBP and NERC Institute of Virology & Environmental Microbiology, Mansfield Road, Oxford OX1 3SR, U.K.

INTRODUCTION

Increasing and warranted concern about the immediate and long term effects on the environment of the use of chemical control agents has prompted attempts to develop alternatives to chemical insecticides. Insect viruses probably offer the greatest potential in the biological control of economically important pests[1]. Most of the examples of natural epizootics controlling insects in the field are from the family *Baculoviridae* and therefore these viruses are an ideal choice for bio-control agents. Baculoviruses have been used since the turn of the century as naturally occurring insecticides and over a dozen are now commercially available.

Isolated principally from diseased Lepidoptera, Hymenoptera and Diptera, the major advantage of baculoviruses is their high degree of specificity. In 1973 a joint WHO-FAO meeting on insect viruses[2] endorsed the development and use of baculoviruses as pest control agents. In addition to their specificity they are safe to handle, relatively cheap to produce, widely distributed in nature, stable in storage, easy to apply, non-polluting, show no problems of resistance and are harmless to plants, vertebrates and other beneficial insects[2].

BACULOVIRUS BIOLOGY

Based on structural considerations the baculoviruses have been divided into three subgroups, with the nuclear polyhedrosis viruses (NPVs) constituting subgroup A of the family *Baculoviridae*[3]. The conventional nomenclature system is based on the virus morphology and on the insect host from which the virus was originally isolated[4]. Over 800 different baculovirus isolates have been reported of which less than 20 have been studied in any detail[5]. The virus genome consists of a covalently closed circular molecule of double stranded (ds) DNA, with sizes ranging from 80-220 Kilobase-pairs (Kbp)[6]. The virion consists of a lipid membrane enveloping a rod-shaped nucleocapsid, with a dsDNA core. The NPVs may package one (single nucleocapsid, SNPV) or many (multiple nucleocapsid, MNPV) nucleocapsids within each virus particle[3]. The virus particles are further packaged into large protein occlusion bodies (OBs; 1-4μm diameter) termed polyhedra because of their polyhedral morphology[3,6].

Polyhedra play an important role in the natural life cycle of the virus, providing a stable entity for horizontal transmission between insects. The viral occlusions protect the embedded virus particles from environmental factors that would otherwise rapidly lead to inactivation e.g. ultra violet light. When an infected caterpillar dies, millions of polyhedra remain in the decomposing tissue and on plant leaves, where they can be ingested by other larvae when feeding. Infectious virions are released when polyhedra break down in the presence of the alkaline digestive fluids of the host midgut[6]. Virus attachment and cell invasion occurs initially in the gut and virions can be found fused with the membranes of microvilli on midgut epithelial calls[7]. Following fusion the nucleocapsid is expelled into the cytoplasm and migrates to the cell nucleus where replication begins. Infection is spread to other insect tissues by the extracellular virus (ECV), which is released into the haemolymph[8]. An infected insect larva can contain 1×10^9 polyhedra inclusion bodies (pibs) and eventually the larval body collapses, liberating the polyhedra[9].

The development of insect cell culture systems has enabled detailed analyses of the replication events at the molecular level. However, relatively few baculoviruses have been adapted to growth in cell culture[10] and the majority of intracellular studies on replication and gene expression have been performed with the *Autographa californica* (Ac) (alfalfa looper) MNPV, in a cell line derived from *Spodoptera frugiperda*. There is a complex and often transient appearance of many virus induced polypeptides which have been divided into four phases of gene expression[11]. The crystalline matrix of polyhedra consists of a single polypeptide (polyhedrin) of molecular weight 29000 daltons. Polyhedrin is one of the very late proteins and is synthesised in the final phase of gene expression at 15-72 hours post-infection (hpi). In this phase polyhedrin becomes the most abundant protein, comprising 20-50% of the total cell protein by 70 hpi. Expression of very late genes is controlled by an efficient upstream promoter, in which there appears to be a common 12 bp sequence that has been found in all very late gene promoters sequenced to date[12].

PANOLIS FLAMMEA NUCLEAR POLYHEDROSIS VIRUS (PfMNPV)

The Pine beauty moth *Panolis flammea* (Lepidoptera; Noctuidae) is a major pest of lodgepole pine, *Pinus contorta*, a species grown commercially on a large scale in the United Kingdom[13]. The *P. flammea* nuclear polyhedrosis virus (PfMNPV) was originally isolated from infected insects in a natural epizootic and has since been evaluated as a biological insecticide for controlling this economically important pest in Scotland[9]. The virus belongs to subgroup A of the baculoviruses and packages multiple nucleocapsids into virus particles. The virus genome is relatively large (145Kbp) and has been shown to have a high degree of homology to the *Mamestra brassicae* (Mb) MNPV[14]. No suitable semi-synthetic diet has yet been found for laboratory culturing of *P. flammea* larvae and large scale rearing on foliage is not feasible. Therefore larvae of the closely related cabbage moth *M. brassicae* (Lepidoptera; Noctuidae) are used as an alternative heterologous host species for producing the virus *in vivo* in production runs for field control[9,15].

The original virus isolate was shown to consist of a mixture of two strains PfMNPV(A) and PfMNPV(B) which vary in proportion according to the host larvae in which the virus is propagated. PfMNPV(A) predominates in *M. brassicae* and PfMNPV(B) is more successful in the original host *P. flammea*. This is obviously undesirable during large scale production for use as an insecticide as the virus strain which is most successful against the *P. flammea* pest, decreases when the virus is grown in *M. brassicae* larvae. It does, however, provide an opportunity to study at the molecular level factors affecting host range in insect baculoviruses.

It is essential that only purified and fully characterized virus preparations are considered for use in field applications. The two strains of PfMNPV have been separated into pure clones by using low dose mortality infections of *M. brassicae* and *P. flammea* larvae [J.Cory and B.Green, unpublished data]. Each baculovirus to be used in field control requires detailed investigation of biochemical and biophysical properties and reliable methods of identifying isolates recovered in the field. The construction of restriction endonuclease maps and characterization of virus DNA, forms the basis for more advanced molecular studies in baculoviruses. The genomes of the two PfMNPV strains have been analysed with a series of restriction enzymes and physical maps constructed. Comparison between the two maps has identified variable regions which may contain factors determining host specificity. Secondary digests and Southern hybridizations have been used to pinpoint and analyse these regions of variation. The degree of relatedness between the two viruses and other baculoviruses has been determined by reciprocal dot blot hybridization analysis.

MATERIALS AND METHODS

Viruses and insects. *Panolis flammea* MNPV was originally isolated from *P. flammea* larvae collected in Scotland in 1979[9]. The virus was produced in the laboratory in cultures of the cabbage moth *M. brassicae* maintained on a modification of Hoffman's Tobacco hornworm diet[16]. Polyhedra and virus particles were purified from infected larvae as described by Harrap *et al.*[17].

Virus DNA purification and restriction enzyme digestion. Virus DNA was extracted from purified virus particles by lysis in sarkosyl and centrifugation in caesium chloride gradients[18]. The DNA was digested with restriction endonucleases using conditions recommended by the suppliers (Bethesda Research Laboratories or Boehringer Corporation Ltd.). The fragments were analysed in 0.6-1.0% agarose gels using a Tris-borate buffer system[19]. Gels were dried down under vacuum at 80°C and exposed to X-ray film for autoradiography.

Radiolabelling of virus DNA. For size determinations DNA fragments were end-labelled using an *Escherichia coli* DNA polymerase I Klenow fragment fill-in reaction[19]. Lambda DNA digested with restriction enzymes and then end-labelled with [^{32}P]dNTPs provided molecular size standards. For hybridizations virus DNA was labelled to high specific activity (10^8 cpm/µg) using the nick translation method[20].

Dot blot hybridizations. Virus DNA was denatured and applied to nylon filters as described by Possee and Kelly[14]. Baculovirus DNA (40ng) was applied per dot and several replica spots were made for each virus sample. After exposure to X-ray film the radioactive spots were cut from the filter and counted in a liquid scintillation counter.

RESULTS AND DISCUSSION

Restriction endonuclease analysis of PfMNPV(A) and PfMNPV(B) DNA

The DNA purified from each pure virus strain was digested with *Asp*718, *Bam*HI, *Bgl*II, *Hin*dIII, *Sma*I and *Xho*I. The DNA fragments were end-labelled with ^{32}P *in vitro* and then analysed in agarose gels. The size of each DNA band was estimated by comparison with ^{32}P-labelled lambda DNA fragments. Simultaneous gel electrophoresis of restriction enzyme digests of virus genomes, highlighted variation between the two. Differences within the digestion profiles, identified variable restriction fragments for further detailed analysis. With the aid of secondary digests and Southern hybridizations, restriction enzyme analysis facilitated construction of a physical map of PfMNPV(B) and comparison with that for the PfMNPV(A) strain[14] (Fig. 1). The maps appear to be fairly similar but show definite regions of variation between the two strains.

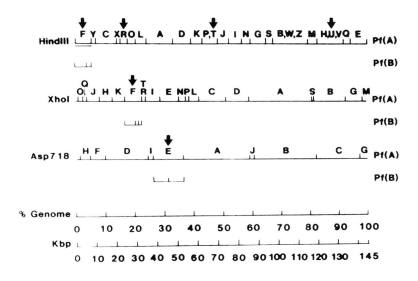

Fig. 1. Comparison of the linearized physical map of PfMNPV(A) DNA for HindIII, XhoI and Asp718 with PfMNPV(B) DNA. The arrows above the PfMNPV(A) map indicate restriction fragments absent from PfMNPV(B) digest profiles. The lower lines show hybridizations of PfMNPV(B) variable fragments to PfMNPV(A) DNA. The underlined HindIII fragment F contains the polyhedrin gene.

Homology between baculovirus DNAs

The degree of homology between PfMNPV(A), PfMNPV(B), MbMNPV and AcMNPV was assessed using dot blot hybridization methods[14]. To each filter several replica spots were applied for each unlabelled baculovirus DNA. Hybridizations with each nick-translated baculovirus DNA provided reciprocal comparisons and were carried out in the presence of 20% and 50% formamide. Salmon sperm DNA was also included as a control. After washing at conditions equivalent to that used for hybridization, the filters were exposed to X-ray films for autoradiography. To quantify the ^{32}P-labelled DNA hybridized to filter bound DNA, the radioactivity in each spot was measured in a liquid scintillation counter. The apparent percentage homology between viral DNAs was calculated as described in Fig.2. In 20% formamide at 37°C stable hybrids should be formed at 65% sequence homology, while 85% homology is required in 50% formamide[21]. The AcMNPV DNA shared very low sequence homology to the other baculovirus DNAs (homology ranged from about 2.5-4.8% in 20% formamide and 0.25-0.9% in 50% formamide). The PfMNPV viruses seem to share more DNA homology with MbMNPV (about 34.5-50% homology in 20% formamide and 21-26% in 50% formamide). In reciprocal hybridization comparisons in both 20% and 50% formamide concentrations, PfMNPV(A) and PfMNPV(B) were virtually 100% homologous.

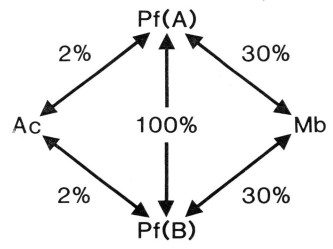

Fig. 2. Summary of reciprocal comparisons for dot hybridizations between AcMNPV, MbMNPV, PfMNPV(A) and PfMNPV(B) in both 20% and 50% formamide concentrations. Percentage homology was calculated as follows: (mean cpm hybridized to heterologous DNA / mean cpm hybridized to homologous DNA) x 100. The mean cpm hybridized to salmon sperm DNA was subtracted from each value.

CONCLUSIONS

Construction of restriction endonuclease maps enables identification of virus isolates after field releases for pesticide control. Isolates of the virus can be classified as either PfMNPV(A) or PfMNPV(B) based on the electrophoretic migration of the polyhedrin gene as determined by Southern hybridization. The polyhedrin genes of the two PfMNPV strains reside on different restriction fragments after digestion with *Hin*dIII, as detected by hybridization with the homologous polyhedrin gene sequence of AcMNPV (data not shown). Mapping pure clones of both PfMNPV(A) and PfMNPV(B), provides a baseline for measuring genetic variation in both viruses and recombination between the two strains.

Comparison of the restriction maps of the two strains has identified regions of variation within the PfMNPV viruses. These variable regions may contain host-determining factors that lead to the differences in biological activity of the two viruses.

The use of restriction enzymes for comparing virus DNA genomes is too stringent a criterion for assessing the degree of genetic relatedness because only a very small proportion of the genome is sampled and the enzymes have such a high specificity. Hybridization methods are therefore often employed for broader comparisons of viral genomes. Dot blot hybridization analysis demonstrated that PfMNPV(A) and (B) share very little DNA homology with AcMNPV and slightly more with MbMNPV. The very high level of homology (almost 100%) shared by PfMNPV(A) and PfMNPV(B) in the reciprocal comparisons in both 20% and 50% formamide suggests that the virus strains are very closely related.

Certain baculoviruses (e.g. AcMNPV) have been modified by genetic engineering in attempts to improve their efficacy as insecticides[22]. Future genetic manipulations include the possibility of improving the potential and speed of action of baculoviruses as biological control agents by the incorporation of insect toxin or hormone genes. PfMNPV is particularly attractive as a candidate for genetic manipulation as it is already used as a natural biological insecticide. The studies presented in this paper act as prerequisites to genetic engineering, providing detailed knowledge of the viruses' genetic organization.

ACKNOWLEDGEMENTS

We thank Barbara Southall for photography and Bernadette Green for supplying the PfMNPV(B) isolate. Matthew Weitzman was supported by a NERC-CASE studentship.

REFERENCES

1. Maromorosch K, Sherman KE (eds) (1985) Viral Insecticides for Biological Control. Academic Press, New York

2. World Health Organization (WHO) (1973) WHO Technical Report Series No.531, Geneva

3. Matthews REF (1987) Intervirology 17:52-54

4. Moore NF, King LA, Possee RD (1987) Insect Sci Applic 3:275-289

5. Martignoni ME, Iwai PJ (1981) In: Burges HD (ed) Microbial Control of Pest and Plant Diseases 1970-80. Academic Press, New York, pp 897-911

6. Kelly DC (1982) J Gen Virol 63: 1-13

7. Keddie BA, Aponte GW, Volkman LE (1989) Science 243:1728-1730

8. Faulkner P (1981) In: Davidson EW (ed) Pathogenesis of Invertebrate Microbiological Diseases. Allanheld, Osmun & Co Ltd, New Jersey, pp 3-33

9. Entwistle PF, Evans HF (1987) In: Leather SR, Stoakley JT, Evans HF (eds) Population Biology and Control of the Pine Beauty Moth. Forestry Commission Bulletin 67, pp 61-68

10. Cameron IR, Possee RD, Bishop DHL (1989) TIBTECH 7:66-70

11. Doerfler W, Bohm P (eds) (1986) The Molecular Biology of Baculoviruses, Current Topics in Microbiology & Immunology Vol 131, Springer-Verlag, Berlin

12. Fraser MJ (1989) *In vitro* Cell Dev Biol 25:225-235

13. Watt AD, Leather SR (1988) In: Berryman AA (ed) Dynamics of Forest Insect Populations. Plenum Publishing Corporation, pp 243-266

14. Possee RD, Kelly DC (1988) J Gen Virol 69:1285-1298

15. Kelly PM, Entwistle PF (1988) J Virol Meth 19:249-256

16. Hunter FR, Crook NE, Entwistle PF (1984) In: Grainger JM, Lynch JM (eds) Microbial Methods for Environmental Biotechnology. Academic Press, New York and London, pp 323-347

17. Harrap KA, Payne CC, Robertson JS (1977)Virology 79:14-31

18. Brown D, Bud HM, Kelly DC (1977) Virology 89:317-327

19. Maniatis T, Fritsch EF, Sambrook J (1982) Molecular Cloning: A Laboratory Manual. Cold Spring Harbor Laboratory, New York

20. Rigby PWJ, Dieckmann M, Rhodes C, Berg P (1977) J Mol Biol 113:237-251

21. Howley PM, Israel MA, Law M, Martin M (1979) J Biol Chem 254:4876-4883

22. Bishop DHL, Harris MPG, Hirst M, Merryweather AT, Possee RD (1989) In: BCPC Mono.43 Progress and Prospects in Insect Control, pp 145-155

© 1990 Elsevier Science Publishers B.V. (Biomedical Division)
Pesticides and alternatives, editor J.E. Casida

Use of a nuclear polyhedrosis virus (NPV) to control *Spodoptera littoralis* in Crete and Egypt

KEITH A JONES

Overseas Development Natural Resources Institute, Central Avenue, Chatham Maritime, Chatham, Kent ME4 4TB (UK)

INTRODUCTION

Spodoptera littoralis (Boisduval), the Egyptian cotton leafworm, is a polyphagous pest that attacks a variety of vegetable, fodder and fibre crops. Brown and Dewhurst[1] list 115 species of plants that are attacked, at least 87 of which are of economic importance. The insect is widely distributed throughout Africa and the Middle East but it is in the Mediterranean region that it is regarded as a recurrent major pest.

Control of this insect, as with most major pests, is normally by using chemical insecticides although there are exceptions. In Egypt, for example, control of the pest on cotton is achieved primarily by large teams of children searching the cotton at intervals of three days to collect and destroy egg-masses[2]. Even here though chemical insecticides are being used increasingly to supplement this mechanical control.

The ever increasing use, and often mis-use, of chemical insecticides has led to a number of well publicised problems. The broad spectrum nature of most chemical pesticides means that non-target organisms, including mammals, birds and beneficial insects, are often effected. The contamination of the environment and the presence of toxic residues on fruit, vegetable and fodder crops have all been highlighted in recent years[3,4]. Destruction of beneficial insects has sometimes led to increased pest problems, often from a previously unimportant pest[3,5,6]. Also there is the problem of pesticide resistance; *S. littoralis* is notorious for the rapid development of resistance and some resistance has been reported to most classes of insecticides[7,8]. This has meant that resistance management programmes are necessary which limit the use of the different classes of insecticides. Such a system is in operation in Egypt where, for example, pyrethroids can only be used against *S. littoralis* on cotton once a season[9].

All of these problems have led to a great interest in developing alternative, non-chemical pesticides (biopesticides). One of the

most promising groups of biopesticides are insect pathogenic
viruses.

INSECT VIRUSES FOR PEST CONTROL

The potential of insect viruses for pest control has been
reviewed by a number of authors (for example see refs 10-13, also
see Huber in this volume); most have pointed out that on the basis
of specificity and safety the Baculoviruses (which include the
NPVs) are the most suitable group of viruses for use in pest
control programmes. Baculoviruses are harmless to non-target
organisms, including beneficial insects and do not leave any toxic
residues. Another advantage is that the cost of development is
likely to be much lower than for chemical insecticides (the cost of
developing Elcar[R], a commercial preparation of *Heliothis* NPV was
estimated by Ignoffo[14] to be between two and five times less than
the cost of developing a chemical insecticide). However the
potential market for baculoviruses is much smaller than for most
chemical pesticides that reach the market[15] and therefore the
developmental cost advantage of baculoviruses is offset. Also, of
relevance to the work of ODNRI, the large scale production of
baculoviruses relies on an *in vivo* system in which live larvae are
infected with the virus and harvested after a period of incubation.
The technology involved in this is highly labour intensive and
suitable for developing countries.

There are also disadvantages of baculoviruses. One of the most
important is the slow speed of action. Infected 1st instar larvae
take at least 3 days to die and older larvae longer. During this
period there is not usually any significant reduction in feeding.
Also the virus needs to be ingested to infect the larvae. These
two characteristics mean that some damage does occur to an infested
crop before control is achieved. This effectively limits the use
of viruses to crops on which some damage is acceptable. The narrow
host range of baculoviruses has also been quoted as barrier to
commercialisation of viral pesticides[15,16], although this can be
overcome by using a mix of viruses in crops with a complex of pests
or by selection or alternatively, genetically engineering virus
strains which are effective against several pest species. A
further disadvantage which is often cited as a drawback to
commercialisation of insect viruses is the need to produce
baculoviruses in live insects. This process is unattractive to

many large companies because of high labour costs[11,17] but as mentioned previously where there is a ready supply of labour, as in developing countries, this is not considered a problem.

DEVELOPMENT OF *S. littoralis* NPV

ODNRI has been assessing the potential of using a NPV to control *S. littoralis*. The virus was purified and characterised from field collected larvae obtained from Egypt and was subjected to a limited safety testing regime under a contract funded by the UKs Overseas Development Administration. This confirmed that the virus was harmless to mammals[18,19].

Laboratory tests were then carried out in the UK to establish the potency of the virus to the host insect. The virus was shown to be extremely infective to *S. littoralis* with a LD_{50} for neonate larvae ranging from 1 to 5 polyhedral inclusion bodies (PIB)/insect depending on the bioassay method used[20,21]. Larger larvae are less susceptible with an LD_{50} of greater than 5000 PIB/insect for ten day old larvae[20]. However, because bigger larvae eat more, in a virus-sprayed field large larvae will ingest more contaminated foliage than small larvae and therefore the difference in LD_{50} is largely offset. For example it has been estimated that a 6th instar noctuid larva eats approximately 86% of all the food ingested during the larval stage whereas a 1st instar larva eats approximately 0.06%[22]; thus when feeding on contaminated foliage a sixth instar larva will consume about 1400 times the amount of virus compared with a 1st instar. Although this is something of a simplification, it has been demonstrated for *S. exigua* by Smits[23] that increased feeding compensates for the decrease in virus susceptibility in the first four larval instars. Field application rates do not, therefore, have to be greatley increased to account for the lower susceptibility of larger larvae.

The effect of several common formulation additives was also tested, these included a wetting agent (Teepol), commercially available UV protectants (Tinopals[R] and Shade[R]) and molasses. None was found to be insecticidal or to inactivate the virus[20]. Tinopal[R] and molasses were shown to be effective UV protectants under field conditions[20,21]. In the few experiments undertaken with Shade[R] little evidence of effective UV protection was found[20,] but this additive has been used extensively in the application of Gypsy moth NPV[24].

Field trials were then undertaken, initially on lucerne in Crete to determine whether application of the virus in the field would result in larvae mortality. Subsequent large scale and replicated trials were carried out on cotton in Egypt to compare the use of virus with the standard methods of control.

FIELD TRIALS

Crete

In Crete field trials were carried out in collaboration with the Institute of Subtropical and Olive Trees, Chania. The trials were located near the village of Episkopi on the northern coast of Crete about 10km west of Rethimnon in an area of lucerne fields that were interspersed with plots of vegetables, groundnuts, olives and pasture. The virus was applied as a highly purified aqueous suspension formulated with 12% Shade[R], 5% Sorbo[R] (used as a thickener to keep the virus in suspension), 1% National Resin sticker, 0.5% Teepol and 0.001% Tinopal RBS 200[R]. The formulated virus was applied at weekly intervals at a rate of 4.8×10^{11} PIB/ha in a volume of 2.5 l/ha using a Turbair X[R] ULV sprayer.

Due to the variation between fields in both crop quality and husbandry replicated trials were not possible, but the results obtained showed that the application of virus resulted in high levels of larval mortality. This supplemented the the natural control resulting from parasitism (Table 1).

TABLE 1

MORTALITY OF LARVAE COLLECTED FROM THE FIELD

Treatment	% Parasitism	% Virus
Untreated Control	4.3 (0 - 9)	3.6 (0 - 9)
Virus Sprayed	15.0 (5 - 27)	52.0 (37 - 71)

However, the beneficial effect of this was often masked by the ingress of large larvae migrating from surrounding untreated fields which had been harvested. These large larvae would totally destroy the crop before succumbing to viral infection. A protective barrier consisting of cypermethrin and a sodium fluorosilicate groundbait around the edge of virus treated fields prevented the invasion of these larvae. The application of virus to fields treated with a barrier resulted in fewer late instar larvae (Table 2) and significantly less damage compared with untreated controls.

Using a damage scoring system of 0=no damage to 6=all foliage
eaten, the mean score at the end of the season for the virus
sprayed fields was 2.8 compared with 5.3 for the untreated fields.
Untreated fields with an insecticide barrier were also included in
the trial and although they had a low damage score (2.3) they also
had much lower larval infestations as a result of a lower rate of
oviposition (Table 2).

TABLE 2

NUMBER OF EGG-MASSES AND LATE INSTAR LARVAE IN VIRUS TREATED
LUCERNE FIELDS IN CRETE

Treatment	Egg-masses[*]	Larvae (4th-6th)[+]	Larvae/egg-mass
Untreated	744	1836	2.46
Virus + barrier	589	693	1.18
Untreated + barrier	321	887	2.76

[*]Hatched egg-masses sampled using 1m² eggboards[26]
[+]Total in 12 x 0.25m² quadrats

If all fields were treated with virus the use of a barrier would
not be necessary as the population would be prevented from
increasing to give large numbers of late instar larvae. Control,
however, was not complete and was variable. This was attributed to
poor penetration of the spray into the crop. The least control was
on the better crops where the lucerne was lush and the crop canopy
dense and spray targets placed in these fields confirmed little of
the spray reach the lower canopy of the crop.

   The trial also demonstrated another advantage of using viruses
for pest control which could, and in some cases is, exploited.
This is the rapid spread of virus infection amongst the insect
population throughout the whole area. Over a six week period
virus-infected larvae were found in most of the fields in the trial
area (figure 1).   Where no virus-killed larvae were found the pest
population was low. This contrasted with a similar area of lucerne
at Drapanias (approximately 70km to the west of the virus trial
area) which was not sprayed with virus but had a similar pest
attack to that found at Episkopi. At Drapanias only two virus-
killed larvae were found during the same six week period.
Obviously the epizootic at Episkopi was initiated by the
application of virus (at two sites totaling 4 fields); these

136

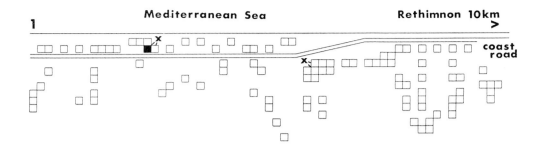

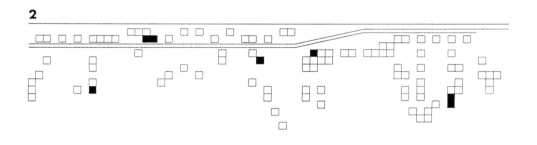

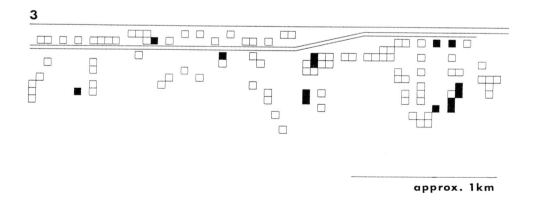

approx. 1km

Fig. 1. Spread of NPV infection amongst *S. littoralis* over a six
week period on lucerne in Crete.   □ = Lucerne fields
    ■ = Lucerne fields containing virus-killed larvae
    x = Fields sprayed with NPV

137

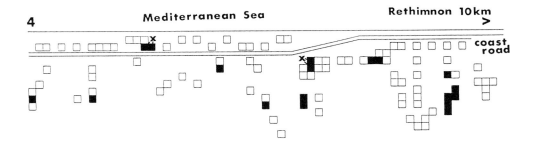

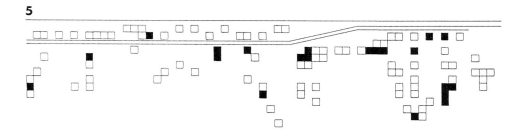

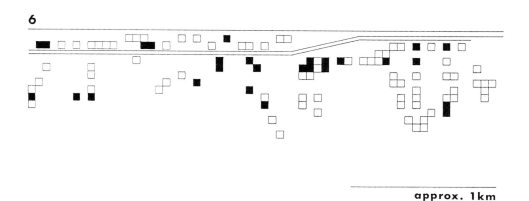

approx. 1km

Fig. 1 cont. Spread of NPV infection amongst *S. littoralis* over a
six week period on lucerne in Crete.   □ = Lucerne fields
   ■ = Lucerne fields containing virus-killed larvae
   x = Fields sprayed with NPV

acted as loci from which the virus spread. This spread was
probably a result of a combination of factors including man and
animals moving between fields, wandering infected larvae
transferring the virus to adjacent fields and action of wind and
rain. Birds probably carry the virus over longer distances by
ingesting dead or infected larvae; NPVs have been shown to pass
unharmed through the digestive tracts of several bird species[25].
This longer distance transfer sets up new loci of infection.

It was concluded that the use of NPV to control *S. littoralis* on
lucerne was only feasible if a significant amount of damage was
acceptable. More effective and consistent control might be
possible with improved application and/or the use of a feeding
attractant in the formulation. Several feeding attractants were
tested in the field (Table 3) and a suspension of grassmeal was
found to be the most effective. Laboratory tests showed that a
commercially available attractant, Coax, was also effective[20]. A
solid ground-bait based on bran and grassmeal was shown to be
effective in attracting late instar larvae[26] and epizootics were
initiated in the field by placing virus contaminated bait into
heavily infested fields. It is possible that the epizootic effect
could be exploited in a pest control strategy for *S. littoralis* on
lucerne by giving a general reduction in the pest population
throughout the area, thus reducing the need for other control
methods.

TABLE 3
FIELD TEST OF FEEDING ATTRACTANTS ON LUCERNE

Treatment	% Increase (±SE) in Feeding compared to untreated control*
Grassmeal	31.36 (±7.2)
Wheatgerm	26.05 (±0.65)
Molasses	-10.15 (±13.07)
Groundbait[26]	18.3 (±9.09)
Celacol M2500[R]	4.85 (±9.65)

*Single leaflet painted with solution/suspension under test.
Leaves scored 24 hr later as eaten or undamaged

Unfortunately area wide application of virus was not carried out
in Crete due to difficulties in organisation. Large-scale and
replicated trials were, however, carried out in Egypt.

Egypt

    In Egypt the trials were carried out in collaboration with the
Egyptian Academy of Sciences and the Ministry of Agriculture.
Areas of cotton in the Fayoum Governorate 80 km south of Cairo and,
in the Delta to the north of Cairo, were sprayed with virus. The
trials showed that the application of a purified aqueous suspension
of virus at a rate of 5 x 10^{12} PIB/ha was as effective in reducing
damage to cotton as either the collection of egg-masses or the use
of chemical insecticides[27]. The virus was formulated with 10%
molasses (which was readily available in Egypt and as well as being
an effective UV protectant possibly also acted as a sticker), 0.5%
Tecpol and 0.001% Tinopal RBS 200[R]. The mortality due to virus of
larvae collected from sprayed fields three days after application
was 88.3, 79.4 and 80% for 1st, 2nd and 3rd instar larvae
respectively[28].

    It is essential to target hatching larvae to minimise crop
damage. On cotton in Egypt newly emerged larvae are normally
located on the undersurface of the leaves toward the top of the
plant[29]. Accurate spray application was therefore the key to
effective control. The spray was applied at a rate of 140 l/ha
through a cotton tailboom fitted to a CP3[R] knapsack sprayer. Both
this system and an experimental spinning disc sprayer which charged
the spray electrostatically (the APE-80)[30] gave good cover on the
undersurface of the cotton leaves. In the upper region of the
plant the electrostatic sprayer and the knapsack sprayer with
tailboom (or a modified lance which mimicked the tailboom)
deposited 30 - 45%[31] and 30 - 40%[32,33] respectively of the total
amount of spray received by the leaves onto the undersurface. In
contrast the cover on the undersurface of the leaves from a
conventional spinning disc sprayer (Micron Mini Ulva[R]) was <1%[31].
The system used by the prototype electrostatic sprayer would offer
the great advantage of lowering spray volume, but unfortunately it
is not yet commercially available.

    The trials also demonstrated that the insect predator population
was maintained in virus treated fields, which was in sharp contrast
to fields sprayed with insecticide[34]. As a result of predation
from the large numbers of beneficial insects found in cotton fields
in Fayoum, even in the absence of any control measures more than
10,000 *S. littoralis* egg-masses per hectare are required before

there is any significant damage[35]. Application of virus
supplements rather than replaces this natural biological control.

Recently trials have been undertaken using a wettable powder
formulation, which consists of freeze-dried virus-infected insects
with a bulking agent (china clay) and a wetting agent (Etocas 30[R])
adsorbed to a synthetic silica (Neosyl[R]). No further additives
were necessary to improve persistence as previous field research
had shown that the insect debris present in the unpurified virus
was an effective UV screen and sticker[21]. Physical loss and UV
inactivation are the two main factors which determine the
persistence of this virus on cotton in Egypt[36]. These trials
confirmed that application of virus was as effective as the
collection of egg-masses. It was also demonstrated that the
formulation would persist on the cotton plant for at least two
weeks[21].

The formulation is being produced on a pilot scale at the Plant
Protection Research Institute, Cairo using techniques which ensure
an acceptably low level of bacterial contamination and a standard
product[34,37]. It is planned to spray virus on 50 - 100 ha of
cotton during the 1990 field season.

CONCLUSIONS

The trials in Crete and Egypt have demonstrated that the use of
an NPV can be an effective control agent for *S. littoralis*. While
this research has demonstrated some of the limitations of using
baculoviruses, such as the slow kill (particularly of large larvae)
and the need for accurate and effective application, it has been
shown that these disadvantages can be overcome. The trials have
also demonstrated the advantages of using insect viruses such as
host specificity, lack of damage to beneficial insect populations,
and the epizootic effects.

It has been shown that the virus can be produced and formulated
locally in a developing country, and a simple formulation has also
been developed using cheap ingredients. This formulation is
effective, relatively persistent and safe.

In conclusion this research has confirmed that baculoviruses
could, and should, play an important role in integrated pest
management.

ACKNOWLEDGEMENTS

I would like to acknowledge the help of staff at ODNRI, the Institute of Sub-Tropical and Olive Trees and the Plant Protection Research Institute who have either provided facilities or assisted in carrying out this work. I would like to thank Jerry Cooper and Mary Jones for making useful comments on the manuscript.

REFERENCES

1. Brown ES, Dewhurst CF (1975) Bull Ent Res 65:221-262

2. Hosny MM (1980) Outlook in Agriculture 10:204-205

3. Bull D (1982) A Growing Problem. Pesticides and the Third World Poor. Oxfam, Oxford

4. Youdeowei A, Service MW (1983) Pest and Vector Management in the Tropics. Longman, Harlow Essex

5. Kurstak E, Tijssen P (1982) In: Kurstak E (ed) Microbial and Viral Pesticides. Marcel Dekker, New York, pp 3-32

6. Ahmed AH, Elhag EA, Bashir NHH (1987) Trop Pest Manag 33:67-72

7. Clapham WBJnr (1980) Agric Environ 5:201-211

8. El-Guindy MA, Madi SM, Keddis ME, Issa YH, Abdel-Sattar MM (1982) Int Pest Control 124:6-11,16-17

9. Jackson GJ (1986) In ICI Plant Protection Division, Entomology and Plant Pathology Research and Development. Presentations to the 1986 British Crop Protection Conference - Pests and Diseases. British Crop Protection Council, Croydon, pp 135-141

10. Tinsley TW (1979) Ann Rev Ent 24:63-87

11. Entwistle PF, Evans HF (1985) In Kekut GA, Gilbert LI (eds) Comprehensive Insect Physiology, Biochemistry and Pharmocology vol. 12. Pergamon Press, Oxford, pp 347-412

12. Falcon LA (1985) In Hoy MA, Herzog DC (eds) Biological Control in Agricultural IPM Systems. Academic Press, London, pp 229-242

13. Payne CC (1986) In Franz JM (ed) Biological Plant and Health Protection. Biological Control of Plant Pests and Vectors of Human and Animal Diseases. Gustav Fisher Verlag, Stuttgart, pp 183-200

14. Ignoffo CM (1973) Exp Parasitol 33:380-406

15. Huber J (1986) In Granados R, Federici B (eds) The Biology of Baculoviruses vol. II. Practical Application for Insect Control. CRC Press, Boca Raton, pp 181-202

16. Hunter FR, Crook NE, Entwistle PF (1984) In Grainger JM, Lynch JM (eds) Microbial Methods for Environmental Biotechnology. Society for Applied Bacteriology, London, pp 323-347

17. McKinley DJ (1981) In Proceedings of the International Workshop on *Heliothis* Management Nov 1981. ICRISAT, Patancheru, India, pp 123-135

18. Carey D, Harrap KA (1980) In Kurstak E, Maramorosch K, Dubendorfer A (eds) Invertebrate Systems *in vitro*. Elsevier, Amsterdam, pp 441-450

19. McKinley DJ (1980) Ecol Bull (Stockholm) 31:75-80

20. McKinley DJ (1985) Nuclear Polyhedrosis virus of *Spodoptera littoralis* (Boisd.) as an infective agent in its host and related insects. PhD thesis, University of London

21. Jones KA (1988) Studies on the persistence of *Spodoptera littoralis* NPV on cotton in Egypt. PhD thesis, University of Reading

22. Goodyear R (1978) A. G. Bull 2. Dept Agric NSW, Australia

23. Smits PH (1986) In Samson RA, Vlak JM, Peters D (eds) Fundamental and Applied Aspects of Invertebrate Pathology. Foundation for the Fourth International Colloquium of Invertebrate Pathology, Wageningen, pp 616-619

24. Lewis F, Yendol WG (1981) In Doanne CC, McManus ML (eds) The Gypsy Moth: Research Toward Integrated Pest Management. USDA Technical Bulletin 1584, pp 503-512

25. Entwistle PF (1982) In Invertebrate Pathology and Microbial Control. Society of Invertebrate Pathology pp 344-351

26. Campion DG, Ellis PE, Hunter-Jones P, McKinley DJ, McVeigh, Murlis J, Paton EM, Brimacombe L, Bettany BW, Cavanagh GG, Jordon J (1980) Pheromones and Viruses in the Control of the Egyptian Cotton Leafworm *Spodoptera littoralis* (Boisd.) and Trials with Pheromones of the Olive Moth *Prays oleae* (Bern.) in Crete, Report for 1977. COPR unpublished report, ODNRI, Chatham, Kent.

27. Topper C, Moawad G, McKinley D, Hosny M, Jones K, Cooper J, El-Nagar S, El-Sheik M (1984) Trop Pest Manag 30:372-378

28. El-Sheik M (1984) The NPV of *Spodoptera littoralis* (Boisd.): An Evaluation of its Role for the Pest Management in Egypt. PhD Thesis, Cairo University

29. Khalifa A, Iss-hak RR, Foda ME (1982) Res Bull 1749. Fac Agric, Ain Shams University, Cairo

30. Arnold AJ, Pye BJ (1981) Proc. 1981 Brit. Crop Prot. Conference. - Pests and Diseases. BCPC, Croydon, pp 661-666

31. Cooper JF (1983) A Comparison Between the Distribution of Charged and Uncharged Spray Droplets on Young Cotton Plants. Unpublished Report, ODNRI, Chatham

32. Cooper JF, Topper C, McKinley DJ, Jones KA (1981) Spraying Techniques for the Application of *Spodoptera littoralis* Virus on Egyptian Cotton. Unpublished Report, ODNRI, Chatham

33. Cooper JF, Jones KA (1989) Spray Nozzle Comparison on Cotton in Egypt with Implications for Scaling Up Virus Application. Unpublished Report, ODNRI, Chatham

34. McKinley DJ, Moawad GM, Jones KA, Grzywacz D, Turner C (1989) In Green MB, de B. Lyon DJ (eds) Pest Management in Cotton. Ellis Horwood, Chichester, pp 93-100

35. Hosny MM, Topper CP, Moawad GM, El-Saadany GB (1986) Crop Prot 5:100-104

36. Jones KA, McKinley DJ (1987) Aspects Appl Biol 14:323-334

37. Jones KA (1988) Aspects Appl Biol 17:425-433

© 1990 Elsevier Science Publishers B.V. (Biomedical Division)
Pesticides and alternatives, editor J.E. Casida

STATUS AND POTENTIAL OF <u>BACILLUS</u> <u>THURINGIENSIS</u> FOR CONTROL OF HIGHER DIPTERA, CYCLORRHAPHA

R.E. GINGRICH

Entomology Unit, Joint FAO/IAEA Programme, Agency's Laboratories
A-2444 Seibersdorf (Austria)

INTRODUCTION

Many species of insects among the Cyclorrhapha such as the house fly, face fly, latrine fly, biting flies and myiasis producing types are serious pests involved with animal and human health whereas some, such as tsetse flies, are vectors of major diseases. Other important species in the group, the fruit flies, are among the most widespread and damaging agriculture pests, attacking more than 250 varieties of fruits and vegetables in all parts of the world. Generally, control of these flies today still depends primarily on synthetic chemical insecticides. Alternative methods involving attractant chemicals and devices have in limited instances been effective. The sterile insect technique, first used for eradicating the screwworm, has been especially successful for eradicating other species of Cyclorrhapha, but the technique has limitations that prevent universal application. For example, suppression of wild pest populations to levels permitting practical releases of sterile males still requires considerable quantities of insecticides. Other biological control methods have been examined but none are yet available for routine use. There are no pathogens registered for application.

PRESENT STATUS

Among the many potential pathogens for Diptera control the spore forming bacterium, <u>Bacillus</u> <u>thuringiensis</u> (Bt), is as a result of extensive experimental investigation, a highly viable candidate for development as a control agent. It is widespread throughout the world, is versatile in that it exists in many varieties producing multiple types of entomopathogenic agents and it has a well founded reputation for safety to man and other nontarget organisms. It occurs commonly as spores in soil but has never been reported to cause natural epizo-otics among the higher Diptera. It is not a highly infectious pathogen and only occasionally occurs naturally in sufficient concentrations to cause significant mortality. In laboratory bioassays LC_{50} values are commonly in millions of spores per insect. Nevertheless a laboratory mass rearing colony of the horn fly, <u>Haematobia</u> <u>irritans</u>, became unintentionally infected and eventually decimated by Bt (1). The bacterium cycled in the horn fly colony presumably via spores as evidenced by bioassays of isolates from dead insects which revealed insecticidal activity in the heat labile, insoluble portion of whole fermentation beers. Usually spores, the transmission agent, do not build up in insect cadavers and though they can remain viable in soil for at least 10 years, they are readily inactivated by heat and ultraviolet light and, therefore, of low residium in natural environments. Thus, for control purposes Bt is rarely used as an innoculate, but rather as an inundative agent.

B. thuringiensis produces various agents that are pathogenic for insects and thereby potentially useful for control. Besides infectious spores, there are also various types of entomopathogenic metabolites produced. Delta-endotoxin, the most well known and widely used of these metabolites, is contained in a protein parasporal crystal formed in vegetative cells at the same time the spore is produced. Under alkaline conditions the crystal dissolves and protoxins are released, which in turn are activated by proteolytic enzymes in the susceptible insect gut to produce an active endotoxin. Most of the commercially available Bt products are based on these endotoxins, which apparently through variations in chemical structure show a degree of specificity toward many insect species, mostly among the Lepidoptera. Isolates producing endotoxin active against the potato beetle and some nematocerous Diptera are now also known. The near neutral pH of the gut of many cyclorrhaphous insect species does not provide the environment for crystal dissolution and, therefore, probably accounts for the near lack of endotoxin activity.

There is evidence of pathogenicity of endotoxins for adult medflies but at low levels and only when ingested with spores (2). Activity from endotoxin, as well as from an unidentified insoluble agent, has been reported against larval horn flies by an isolate of the israelensis variety of Bt (3). However, similar activity by a subculture of the same isolate could not be repeated against medflies, but rather a highly active heat stable exotoxin was detected (4). This exotoxin precipitated with heavy metals in the tap water and appeared in the sediment of the fermentation beer. Possibly the unidentified insoluble agent reported active against horn fly larvae was precipitated exotoxin, but unfortunately the heat stability of the unidentified agent was not determined. Furthermore, there is confusion about the identity of the isolate because israelensis has never been reported to produce heat stable exotoxin. Another subculture of the isolate with the same numerical designation, obtained from the original culture collection, did not produce it. Thus, the identity of the variety of Bt involved in the report and the present status of δ-endotoxin activity for higher Diptera remains unclear.

On the other hand the activity of an exotoxin, referred to variously as thermostable exotoxin, fly factor and β-exotoxin has been repeatedly reported (5). Although well known for its effects on flies, β-exotoxin is a general toxin and not selective in its activity for either insects or vertebrates. The parenteral LD_{50} value of acute toxicity for mice is only 30 times less than that for wax moth larvae. As the early nomenclature implied, β-exotoxin is water soluble and stable to 120°C. It is produced and excreted into the medium during maximal bacterial growth before the start of sporulation. Usually prepared from high yielding isolates of H-serotype 1 (variety thuringiensis), it is produced in most serotypes and its presence or absence is not a taxonomic character. The molecular weight is near 700. During the past 20 years the structural formula of the compound has been defined, it and its analogs have been synthesized and the mode of activity explained. Studies in vitro showed that β-exotoxin inhibits bacterial DNA dependent RNA polymerase. When injected into mammals the exotoxin affects the terminal stages of RNA biosynthesis. As a structural analog of ATP and acting as a competitive inhibitor it is not properly a toxin and is now termed thuringiensin. Although not active when applied perorally to mammals, as it is readily deactived by intestinal phosphorylases, its use as an insecticide has been banned in many countries. However, the USSR and other East European nations have successfully used products based on thuringiensin against many pest species of higher Diptera without apparent complications. Recent attempts by a commercial producer to register an exotoxin product for control of cotton pests were stymied when the EPA categorized the product as a chemical. Such a designation involves millions of dollars to perform the studies required for registration rather than the few thousand dollars required for a Bt product based on endotoxin.

While the experimental evidence for mammalian pathogenicity of parenterally applied thuringiensin is clear, the safety of heat stable exotoxin as an insecticide is not. The early works were done on supernatants of fermentation beers, which besides thuringiensin, contained other soluble substances with physiological activity. Such substances could account for discrepancies in reported vertebrate toxicity of Bt products applied orally. For example in comparative studies purified thuringiensin and culture supernatants differed in effects on DNA synthesis in human cell cultures; pure exotoxin was not cytotoxic even at very high concentrations (6). The insecticidal activity of pure thuringiensin and crude supernatants can even differ depending on the isolation methods used to obtain the pure compound. Bioassays of an experimental thuringiensin product, fractionated by high pressure liquid chromatography (HPLC), revealed two widely separated eluants that were both active against adult medflies (7). Also, insecticidally active eluants of HPLC fractionated supernatants from other Bt isolates had rf values that were different from thuringiensin.

Further conflicting evidence arises from the spectrum of host activity. Bioassays of the autoclaved insoluble fermentation fractions of more than 300 Bt isolates revealed many that produced exotoxins with differences in spectrum of activity against horn fly larvae and immature biting lice (8). The exotoxins appeared in the insoluble fractions because they had precipitated with heavy metals in the water used to prepare the fermentation medium. Some isolates produce exotoxin that precipitate more readily than others grown under the same conditions. Both horn fly larvae and the biting lice are susceptible to thuringiensin but heat stable exotoxins produced by some of the test isolates killed only 1 or the other of them. Further nonconformity in activity spectrum occurred when these same heat stable agents were later bioassayed against medfly adults, another insect susceptible to thuringiensin. Also, comparison of isolates with high but different insecticidal activity showed that fermentation supernatants of some were acutely toxic to mice when injected intraperitoneally while others were not.

Thus, evidence that (1) thuringiensin may in some cases be only a part of the total insecticidal component in the fermentation supernatant while in other cases it may not be involved at all, (2) insecticidally active fractions separated by HPLC have different migration speeds and (3) crude fermentation supernatants from different isolates have different spectra of susceptible hosts and differences in toxicity to mice points strongly to heterogeneity among the soluble exotoxins produced by Bt. The possibility of finding safe compounds should encourage further investigations to develop exotoxins as insect control agents. Their soluble nature and high potency would allow economically advantageous low volume applications and they are not labile to heat and UV radiation as are spores and δ-endotoxins. Exotoxin could even be produced and harvested as a by-product from isolates that are fermented to produce spores and crystals.

Because of their chemical and physical characters exotoxin can be more versatilely applied that endotoxins. When fed to poultry and ruminants in their diet ration as an insoluble salt they passed unchanged through the digestive tract and were deposited in the feces where they prevented the development of copraphagous insects (9). In combination with an organic insecticide and applied to sheep as an aerosol, they were effective against 1st stage larvae of the sheep nose bot (10). Sprayed onto the wool of sheep they prevented strike establishment by larvae of the Australian sheep blow fly (11). By a means

unclear at present exotoxin is also apparently taken up by sucking insects as
evidenced by their activity against mites and bugs on plants.

POTENTIAL

   As for the future, we can expect that increasing efforts to develope Bt
endotoxin as an insect control agent will continue and be applied more to the
major pests among the Cyclorrhapha. Certainly genetic engineering will play an
important role. Plasmid borne, protein crystal-coding genes for several serotypes have been cloned. This has led to investigations of the base sequences of
the genes and their regulatory regions, determinations of the location of the
genes in different subspecies, analyses of DNA flanking genes, comparisons of
crystal protein genes in different strains and subspecies and investigations of
the mechanisms regulating gene expression. Information gained will lead to ways
of altering the spectrum of endotoxin activity and make it possible to engineer
strains of Bt to produce crystals that can be activated in insects where the pH
of the gut contents is near neutral. Developing methods to stabilize endotoxin
in the non-crystalline form would also increase their versatility of activity.
Genetic manipulation will lead to increased activity and greater stability of
the endotoxin under field conditions. Uncoupling endotoxin formation from the
sporulation process will allow its expression and excretion during the vegetative growth phase and, thereby, increase the amount produced. Genes coding for
endotoxin production, already cloned it other bacteria species and in plants,
will be exploited, not only to increase production, but also to induce
production in other natural food sources of target pest insects.

   Present studies are revealing the heterogeneity of exotoxins, which when
explored further could lead to the development of types that are safe for
vertebrates. Once achieved a new aspect of Bt could be opened for controlling
higher Diptera.

   Nutrients and physical conditions for increased production of the exotoxin
will be determined. Formulators will take advantage of their physical
characters to make them efficient and effective control agents in the field.
Genetic studies will allow manipulation to achieve target specificity.

   Feeding attractants, known for adults of many species of higher Diptera will
be formulated with Bt and used to increase contact with less dispersal of the
pathogen. Low volume application of such baits besides reducing environmental
stress will also reduce the quantities of pathogens needed and costs for
applying them. By increasing ingestion, feeding attractants can also increase
the effectiveness of only moderately active pathogens.

   Bacillus thuringiensis, has the potential to produce widely diverse types of

148

active agents simultaneously, which will be of great economic advantage.
Furthermore, when 2 or more active agents are combined in a single treatment
they offer the prospect of efficient, safe and effective control of specific
target pests with reduced likelyhood of inducing resistance in the pest.

ACKNOWLEDGEMENTS

I am grateful to B. Butt and D.A. Lindquist for reviewing and to Ms. E. Pereira
for assistance in preparing and for typing the manuscript.

REFERENCES

1. Gingrich RE (1984) In: Cheng TC (ed) Comparative Pathobiology, Vol 7. Plenum
   Publishing Co, New York, pp 47-57

2. Gingrich RE, El-Abbassi TS (1988) In: Proc Internatl Symp, Vienna, pp 77-84

3. Temeyer KB (1984) Appl Environ Microbiol, Vol 47, pp 952-955

4. Gingrich RE Unreported observation

5. Sebesta K, Farkas I, Horska K (1981) In: Burges HD (ed) Microbial Control
   of Insects and Mites. Academic Press, London, New York, pp 249-181

6. Carlberg G (1973) PhD Dissert, Univ Helsinki, 90 pp

7. Gingrich G Unreported observations

8. Dulmage et al (1981) In: Burges HD (ed) Microbial Control of Insects and
   Mites. Academic Press, London, New York, pp 193-222

9. Laird M (1971) In: Burges HD, Hussey NW (eds) Microbial Control of Insects
   and Mites. Academic Press, London, New York, pp 387-406

10. Sartbaev SK (1977) Biologicheskie Metody Bor, pp 47-48

11. Cooper DJ, Pinnock DE, Were ST (1985) Proc 4th Australasian Conf on Grassl
    Invest Ecol, Fuicolu College, Canterbury, pp 236-243

© 1990 Elsevier Science Publishers B.V. (Biomedical Division)
Pesticides and alternatives, editor J.E. Casida

CONSTRUCTION OF *BACILLUS THURINGIENSIS* STRAINS WITH IMPROVED INSECTICIDAL
PERFORMANCES BY GENETIC EXCHANGE, AND ENHANCEMENT OF THE BIOLOGICAL
ACTIVITY OF A CLONED TOXIN GENE BY *IN VITRO* MUTAGENESIS

JEAN-CHRISTOPHE PIOT (1), CINDY LOU JELLIS (2), THIERRY BRUYERE (1),
DENIS BASSAND (1), JAMES R. RUSCHE (3) AND DANIEL P. WITT (3)

(1) Sandoz Ltd, Agro Research, CH-4002 Basle, Switzerland,
(2) Repligen-Sandoz Research Corporation, 128 Spring Street, Lexington MA 02173 USA,
(3) Repligen Corporation, One Kendall Square, Cambridge, MA 02139 USA.

INTRODUCTION

Bacillus thuringiensis (*Bt*) is a spore-forming, Gram-positive bacterium, which is pathogenic to
many Lepidoptera, Diptera, and Coleoptera species. The biological activity is essentially due to a
crystallized protein, called protoxin, which is produced during sporulation. When ingested by a
susceptible insect, the protoxin is quickly dissolved in the midgut, and activated by proteases,
leading to a highly insecticidal principle, the delta-endotoxin (DET). The protoxin and the DET of the
strains which are active on Lepidoptera have a molecular weight of approx. 135 kdal and 65 kdal,
respectively. The genes coding for the protoxin are localized on large plasmids, although, in some
strains, they also can be observed on the bacterial chromosome (1, 6).

Bt, which has been used for about thirty years on a large scale for crop protection, has amply
demonstrated a remarkable ability to effectively control many lepidopterous species detrimental to
crops and forests. Due to its high insecticidal activity and reliability, *Bt* is essential everywhere pests
have acquired resistance to chemical insecticides, or in any situations where residues of pesticides
are a concern. Moreover, because of its selectivity, *Bt* has a minimal impact on the equilibrium of
some fragile ecosystems (4).

However, despite these unquestionable qualities, *Bt* suffers from some weaknesses, which
explain its relatively limited success so far:

- The level of insecticidal activity of *Bt* is not sufficient on some economically important pests, like
Heliothis and *Spodoptera* species.

- The range of activity of *Bt* is sometimes perceived as being too narrow, for instance, when a
complex of pests is present in a crop. In such cases, the microorganism has to be used in
combination with chemical pesticides.

- The users very often consider that the persistence of *Bt* in the field is too short. Treatments have
to be repeated at brief intervals. As a result, the profitability and practicality of the microorganism are
impaired.

In order to correct these weak points, it is still possible, as it was successfully done in the past, to search in the nature for new strains of *Bt*, exhibiting the desired properties. However, this approach remains quite uncertain and, if intensified, might become very costly. Therefore, more rational and more economical ways are needed.

One of these ways is certainly the genetic engineering of *Bt*. Several years ago, Sandoz established a research team aimed at the improvement of the insecticidal properties of *Bt*, using the most advanced techniques of the bacterial genetics.

Two main approaches have been selected: The first one exploits the opportunities offered by intraspecific and interspecific conjugation, whereas the second one applies the techniques of molecular biology to modify genes and to clone them into various microorganisms.

CONSTRUCTION OF STRAINS BY CONJUGATION

Material and Methods

High-frequency plasmid transfer by a conjugation-like mechanism has been shown to take place naturally between certain *Bt* strains (2). Since high-frequency transfer, or simply transfer ability, does not seem to be a general feature among the various *Bt* subspecies, we applied the method described by Lereclus et al. (3), which takes advantage of the broad-host-range conjugative plasmid pAMβ1 from *Streptococcus faecalis*. This plasmid, which can be transmitted to numerous Gram-positive and Gram-negative bacteria, confers resistance to a group of antibiotics, including erythromycin. Plasmid pAMβ1 has been shown (3) to promote the transfer of indigenous plasmids from *Bt* subsp. *kurstaki* (strain HD-73) and *subtoxicus* to a plasmid-cured derivative of subsp. *kurstaki* (strain HD-1 cryB).

Bioassay. Thirty (3 x 10) 2nd instar larvae of *Trichoplusia ni* (cabbage looper), *Spodoptera littoralis* (Egyptian cotton leafworm), *Phaedon cochleariae* (mustard beetle), and thirty (3 x 10) 1st instar larvae of *Heliothis virescens* (tobacco budworm) were fed with leaves, which were previously sprayed with an aqueous suspension of 10^8 spores/ml. The treated foliage was Chinese cabbage for the first three above mentioned species, and cotton for *Heliothis* larvae. Mortality was recorded 5 and 7 days later, respectively.

Results

Transfer of pAMβ1 from *S. faecalis* to *Bt* strains belonging to subsp. *kurstaki* (HD-1, HD-73, NRD-12), *aizawai* (HD-137), *israelensis* (HD-500) and *tenebrionis* (BI 258-82) was achieved by using the filter-mating technique (3). Each of these strains was used as donor in mating experiments with spontaneous antibiotic-resistant recipients derived from the same four subspecies.

Except for intervarietal crosses involving *Bt* subsp. *israelensis* as the donor, in which survival of the recipient strains was very low, transfer of pAMβ1 was obtained with frequencies ranging from 10^{-6} to 10^{-3} transcipients per recipient cell.

Analysis of the plasmid content, extracted from a number of transcipients (50-200) of each intervarietal mating, showed that cotransfer of various sets of small (less than 10 Mdal) indigenous plasmids took place in 5 to 60 % of the selected strains.

Various transcipients were obtained in mating experiments between strains of *Bt* subsp. *kurstaki* (HD-73) and *tenebrionis*, producing bipyramidal and flat quadratic crystals, respectively.

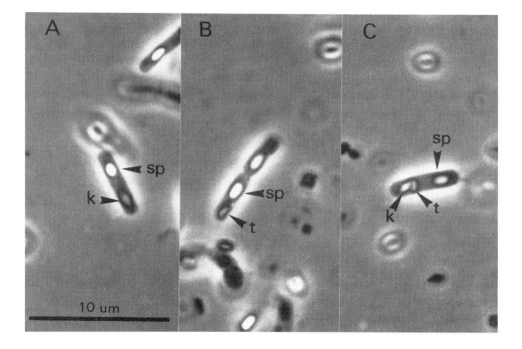

Fig. 1. Sporulating cells of parental and hybrid strains
  A: *Bt* subsp. *kurstaki* (HD-73)   sp: spore
  B: *Bt* subsp. *tenebrionis* (Bl 256-82)   k: *kurstaki*-type crystal
  C: Hybrid strain L21004   t: *tenebrionis*-type crystal

Microscopic examination of sporulated cultures of purified transcipients showed that some hybrid strains produced both types of parasporal bodies (Fig. 1). Plasmid content analysis confirmed that the 50 Mdal plasmid from HD-73, bearing the gene coding for DET, had been transferred (Fig. 2).

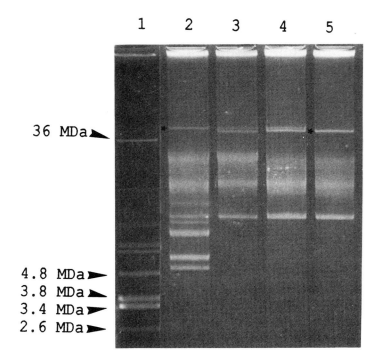

Fig. 2. Plasmid content of parental and hybrid strains
        Lane 1:   Molecular weight markers
        Lane 2:   Donor strain *Bt* subsp. *kurstaki* (HD-73)
        Lanes 3 & 4:   Hybrid strain L21004
        Lane 5:   Recipient strain *Bt* subsp. *tenebrionis* (BI 256-82)
        DET genes are located on plasmids indicated by a *.

    <u>Bioassay</u>. A bioassay of these hybrid strains was performed on the larvae of 5 insect species. Approximately 30 strains showed interesting insecticidal properties. The best one, L21004, is active on lepidopterous larvae, like the parental strain subsp. *kurstaki*, and on coleopterous larvae, like the parental strain subsp. *tenebrionis* (Fig. 3). Moreover, the combination of the genetic elements of the parental subspecies confers an additional activity on *Spodoptera littoralis*, a noctuid moth which is not controlled by the parental strains (Fig. 3).

MUTAGENESIS OF DELTA-ENDOTOXIN GENES

Material and Methods

    In designing our approach for mutagenesis, the following points were taken into consideration:
    1) mutagenize and evaluate mutations in one defined section of the gene at a time,

2) generate a limited number, 2 or 3, of changes within a given target area in at least 90 % of the clones and

3) use results from the region directed mutagenesis experiments to follow with a more site-directed approach.

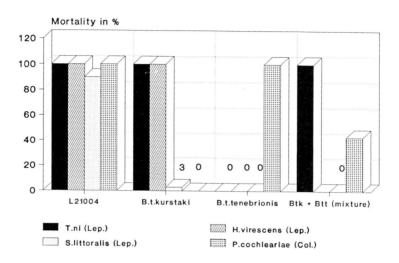

Fig. 3. Hybrid strain L21004: Larvicidal activity on 3 Lepidoptera and 1 Coleoptera species (Dose: 100 millions spores per ml spray)

Fig. 4 shows plasmid prAK, containing the amino-terminal part of a cryIA(b) gene isolated from *Bt* subsp. *kurstaki* (5.3 type gene). The cloned DNA can be divided into 5 segments from 342bp to 683bp in length using the restriction enzymes shown. These regions were classified as conserved or variable based on the degree of amino acid homology with a number of DET genes. We opted to target conserved segments of the gene for the first round of mutagenesis.

Bisulfite and formic acid were used to achieve a wide range of possible amino acid substitutions within specified regions of the DET gene. Bisulfite is a single strand mutagen which converts cytosine to uracil by deamination (7). This change results in a transition of cytosine to thymine, or guanine to adenine depending upon whether the sense or the antisense strand is mutagenized. Formic acid depurinates DNA by breaking N-glycosyl bonds (5). Polymerization across this template using the "error prone" polymerase reverse transcriptase most commonly results in transversions as purines are usually inserted opposite the site of damage.

154

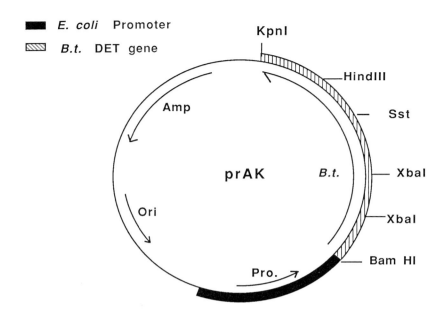

Fig. 4. Template used for Mutagenesis.- *E. coli* expression vector carrying the truncated crylA(b) gene of *Bt* subsp. *kurstaki*. Restriction enzymes shown were used to define targets for mutagenesis.

Bioassay. Twenty 2nd instar larvae of *Heliothis virescens* (tobacco budworm) were fed with artificial diet, to which a suspension of the candidate microorganism had previously been incorporated (8). The diet was dispensed into plastic trays of 20 cavities, each cavity receiving one larva. Six serial dilutions per microorganism were prepared, each dilution being 1:2 of the preceeding one, and each being used to treat one tray. Mortalities were recorded 7 days later, and they were used to estimate the LC50 by Logit analysis. Relative toxicity was then calculated, dividing the LC50 of the standard (BT-301) by the LC50 of the candidate microorganism, and multiplying this quotient by 100.

Results

By treating single stranded DNA (in heteroduplex molecules) with bisulfite for 30 minutes, we obtained between 2 and 3 base changes per clone in the specified region(s). Similarly, by altering the amount of time that single stranded DNA was exposed to formic acid, we were able to achieve a range of mutation densities as illustrated in Fig. 5. A number of improvements were necessary in order to achieve these high densities.

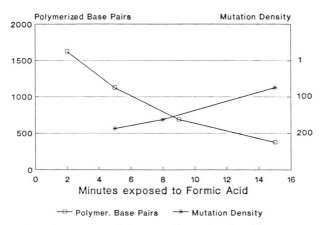

Fig. 5. Damage / misrepair mutagenesis by exposition to formic acid

E. coli strains transformed with mutation-containing prAK DNA were grown up in YT/Amp media to stationary phase. Random clones were selected for DNA sequence analysis. An average mutation frequency of 2 changes per target region in at least 90 % of the clones was a prerequisite for proceeding to in vivo bioassays.

Bioassay. From approx. 7000 E. coli strains tested on Heliothis larvae, eleven strains showed at least a five-fold increase in insecticidal activity compared to a truncated toxic protein consisting of the first 723 amino acids of the Bt subsp. kurstaki HD-1 protoxin. In a related set of experiments we discovered that this wild-type truncated toxin was as much as ten-fold less active than the full length DET gene product (also of the cryA(b) type) that we cloned from Bt subsp. wuhanensis. We were interested in screening some of our mutations in the background of this clone to see if the increased activity could be transferred.

Eleven full-length mutant Bt subsp. wuhanensis DET genes were cloned for expression in E. coli and the results from bioassays with these toxins are shown in Fig. 6. Insecticidal activity of the full-length mutants was increased up to five-fold as compared to the wild-type clone in strain BT301.

Interestingly, all the up-mutations were clustered in two preferential regions of the studied segments. The up-mutants differ from the native toxin by the substitution of one to three amino acids.

CONCLUSION

The present study has shown that conjugation technique can successfully be used to construct Bt strains characterized by ranges of activity which are substantially extended beyond the simple juxtaposition of the ranges of the parent strains. A good example is the strain L21004, which not

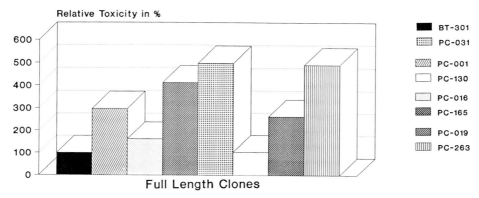

Fig. 6. Up-mutants: insecticidal activity of full length clones on 2nd instar larvae of *Heliothis virescens* (7 days after treatment)

only exhibits good insecticidal activity on lepidopterous and coleopterous species susceptible to the parent strains, but additionally controls species such as *Spodoptera littoralis*, which are not affected by the microorganisms used as donors and recipients in this conjugation.

The other facet of the present study, i.e. the mutagenesis of the DET gene, resulted in the construction of a number of mutants cloned in *E. coli*, which were up to five times more toxic to *Heliothis* larvae than the wild-type DET gene expressed in *E. coli*.

ACKNOWLEDGEMENTS

The authors are most grateful to Professor D. Karamata (Institut de Génétique et de Biologie microbiennes, University of Lausanne) for his invaluable scientific guidance, which made possible the realization of the first part of this work. We thank C. Dennis, N. Beerman, R. Kurzman, R. Gobeli and M. Koenig for their skillful technical assistance.

REFERENCES

1. Aronson AI, Beckman W, Dunn P (1986) Microbiol Rev 50:1-24
2. Gonzalez JM Jr, Brown BS, Carlton BC (1982) Proc Natl Acad Sci 79:6951-6955
3. Lereclus D, Menou G, Lecadet MM (1983) Mol Gen Genet 191:307-313
4. Luethy P, Wolfersberger G (1986) Swiss Biotech 4:18-20
5. Meyers RM *et al* (1985) Science 229:242-247
6. Miller KL, Ling AJ, Bulla LA Jr (1983) Science 219:715-721
7. Shortle D, Botstein D (1983) Methods enzymology 100:457-468
8. Dulmage TH, Boening OP, Rehnborg CS, Hansen GD (1971) J Invertebr Pathol 18:240-245

Molecular biology

© 1990 Elsevier Science Publishers B.V. (Biomedical Division)
Pesticides and alternatives, editor J.E. Casida

MOLECULAR BIOLOGY AND ENTOMOLOGY: AN EXCITING INTERPHASE

A.S. ROBINSON

IMBB, FORTH, P.O. B. 1527, 711 10, Heraklion, Crete, Greece

INTRODUCTION

Molecular biology can trace its origins back to the 1940s with discovery by Oswald Avery that DNA was the "transforming principle". Subsequently, following the elucidation of the structure of DNA it became possible to determine the sequence of nucleotides in DNA, restriction enzymes and ligases were discovered, autonomous circular DNA molecules were described and sequences of DNA were found which could move within the genome. The development of molecular biology, especially within the last 10 years has been of such speed and relevance that it has had an enormous impact on many scientific disciplines. The molecular biology in *Drosophila melanogaster* including the cloning and characterization of many important genes has paved the way for the expansion of molecular biology into entomology. The discovery of large amounts of non-coding DNA in insect genomes whilst initially of little relevance to the wider field of entomology is guaranteed to impinge on the way we assess many insect population processes.

The decisive breakthrough for entomology came with the crucial demonstration of efficient and now routine germ-line transformation in *Drosophila melanogaster*. This opened up for the entomologist the possibility of being able to manipulate the genomes of insects of economic importance with the aim of devising new methods of control or of improving existing methods. It would also enable the enormous "gene bank" of *D. melanogaster* to be exploited and thereby reducing dependence of long term classical genetic studies on pest insects.

This report aims at a synthesis of some aspects of molecular biology as they relate to the various fields of expertise in entomology.

SPECIATION

Phylogenetic analysis of insect populations is often hampered by the lack of suitable characters amenable to population analysis. Molecular methods using restriction enzyme mapping may offer a way out of this impasse. At the molecular level two classes of DNA can be exploited namely mitochondrial DNA and highly repetitive nuclear DNA.

Mitochondrial DNA

As mitochondrial DNA is of crucial importance for cellular function it would be expected to show high conservation. However, it has been clearly demonstrated that animal mitochondrial DNA shows rapid rates of evolution at levels 5-10 times higher than single copy nuclear DNA[6]. It could therefore be a very useful molecule for studying speciation in recently diverged populations. In animals the mitochondrial genomes are relatively small e.g. 16.2 kb in the mouse and 18.4 kb in *D. melanogaster*. The genomes in the mouse, cow and human have been completely sequenced. In *D. melanogaster* and probably in most insects, mitochondrial DNA shows maternal inheritance[33]. A physical map of DNA at the molecular level can be obtained by breaking it at defined poins using restriction enzymes. A restriction map identifies these points of breakage along the DNA molecule. Changes in base sequence in the molecule can lead to alternate positions of breakage and hence to a change in the restriction map.

Using mitochondrial DNA restriction maps, it has been possible to determine the phylogenetic relationships between three subspecies in the *Glossina morsitans* complex[38]. A small fragment of the mitochondrial DNA (ca 750 bp) was cloned and maternal inheritance of this fragment was shown. By comparing the restriction maps both within and flanking the cloned sequence it was possible to confirm preliminary conclusions based on isoenzyme analysis on the relationships between the three subspecies.

Highly Repeated DNA Sequences

The genomes of most eukaryotes contain large quantities of repetitive DNA which does not code for protein, in fact only a small percentage of the DNA functions in the classical way of DNA→RNA→protein. In Drosophila this is less than 20%. Repetitive DNA is evolutionary labile and related species of Drosophila differ enormously in the quantity and quality of this type of DNA. It has even been argued that in cereals the accumulated sequence differences may actually be a cause of speciation and not simply a consequence of it[11]. The function of this repetitive DNA is unclear at the present but if it does have important evolutionary consequences then it would be a useful parameter for the analysis of evolutionary population processes.

An analysis of highly repetitive DNA has been carried out in the mosquito *Aedes scutellaris* subgroup using nine cloned highly repeated sequences[22]. By comparing the abundance of these sequences in the different sub-species, phylogenetic relationships could be established and compared with enzyme and mating studies. While in general agreeing with the established sub-divisions, important differences were found. They concluded that even though rapid changes in abundance of repeated sequences could be demonstrated within the sub-group, correlation with the results of other methods used to assess species affinity led to several incongruities.

C-VALUE AND r AND K SELECTION

The C-value is the mass of DNA in the haploid cell. The relationship of this value to the morphological complexity of organisms and to the number of proteins synthesized presents molecular biology with irreconcilable differences as the bulk of the DNA in the nucleus in non-protein coding DNA of uncertain function. However, it does appear that there is a correlation between the amount of DNA in the cell and the type of reproductive strategy adopted by the organism. Species under intense r selection (short generation time, early reproduction and small size) have low C-values whereas organisms under more relaxed selection (K strategists) have longer generation times and slow development and have high C-values[7,8]. As the concepts of r and K strategies can be important in determining the pest status of an insect population, their partial correlation with a quantitative factor would provide a valuable tool.

MOLECULAR TAGGING

Many ecological and insect control studies involve the release and recapture of marked individuals. Marking is usually carried out by the administration of a recognizable external pigment. Conventional genetic markers cannot be used because they are frequently associated with reduced fitness under field conditions.

Recently a baculo-virus of *Autographa californica*, which was being used for the biological control of this pest, was marked by the insertion of a small sequence of non-host DNA. The sequence consisted of a non-coding synthetic oligonucleotide, 80 nucleotides long, with stop codons in all six reading frames and no ATG codons[3]. This enabled the released virus to be differentiated from the native virus and it also enabled the survival in nature of the released viral genome to be monitored. In principle this technique could be expanded to include insects. It would be particularly useful when ecological data is rrequired on the long term integration of released insects into an ecosystem. Detection techniques at the moment are not sufficiently routine to allow for mass screening of many individuals from field populations. However, considering that developments in molecular technology are extremely rapid, this restriction could soon be lifted.

DEVELOPMENTAL TIMES

While at first sight, the relationship between development time and molecular biology is not obvious one example will serve to highlight the important interface between them. Heat shock protein genes (hsp) are activated by an environmental stress and were first identified as responding to heat induced stress. They are known to exist in plants, animals and microbes. The proteins coded for by these genes prevent the expression of genes concerned with cellular function and in so doing may protect the organism against the stress.

It has been suggested that during laboratory colonization such genes may be lost[41]. If laboratory populations are used to determine the effect of temperature on reproductive capacity then erroneous conclusions may be drawn. This error will be compounded when such data is used to predict temperature thresholds for insect pests of stored products.

GENETIC TRANSFORMATION

Transposable Elements

Transposable elements were analysed in detail in prokaryotes in the late 1960's and they wre shown to be discrete sequences of DNA that could exist at different places on the bacterial genome or on plasmids. They vary n length from 0.76 kb to 38 kb and are characterized by having the same nucleotide sequences at each end (inverted terminal repeats). They code for an enzyme (or enzymes) transposase which is involved with the mobility of the element. They can also contain other functional genes e.g. for antibiotic resistance. The genetic evidence for transposable elements in eukaryotes was provided by McClintock[19] but her results remained in an intellecual vacuum until the molecular analysis of transposable elements in prokaryotes became available. Subsequent studies have revealed the presence of many transposable element families in *Drosophila* and yeast.

Transposable elements are included in the moderately repetitive component of nuclear DNA which constitutes 10% of the genome in Drosophila. It has been suggested that most if not all of the middle repetitive DNA families are extremely mobile[42]. The frequency with which members of different families transpose varies and appears to be under both genetic and environmental control. Insertion of an element in a gene leads to loss of function and mutation. Many spontaneous mutations in *D. melanogaster* have been shown to be caused by insertion of transposable elements. The most well studied transposable elements in *D. melanogaster* are the *copia* element[34].

P Elements and Hybrid Dysgenesis

In *D. melanogaster* the P transposable element induces the hybrid dysgenesis syndrome which is characterized in the F_1 from a particular cross by increased mutation, male recombination, chromosome breakage and gonodal dysgenesis; many F_1's are in fact sterile[17]. The syndrome is only seen when males carrying the elements are crossed with females lacking them, the reciprocal cross is normal. In the dysgenic state the P element becomes derepressed as the females have no P-element suppressor in the egg cytoplasm. The P element in *D. melanogaster* has been cloned, it is 2.9 kb long and contains 4 non-overlapping reading frames which would suggest that it codes for 4 proteins[28]. Other members of the P-element family have arisen by internal deletions[28].

Transformation using Transposable elements

The ability of the P element to integrate in DNA has been exploited to enable germ line transformation of *D. melanogaster* to be carried out. (In other words the integration of functional foreign DNA in the germ line). Individuals that gain new genetic information from the addition of foreign DNA are transgenic. For transformation two P elements are used, one defective and carrying the required gene, the other being an intact element. These are injected into pre-blastoderm eggs 0-90 min after laying. The intact element produces transposase for the integration of the defective P elements carrying the required gene[35,37].

This technique is now routine in *D. melanogaster* with transformation frequencies varying from 10-60%. The P element appears to integrate at random in the genome and the transferred genes show good tissue and stage specificity. Integration is generally stable. One element inserted into heterochromatin showed good expression, therefore in *D. melanogaster* all the information needed to regulate gene expression may be within the gene locus. Chorion genes from the silkworm, *Bombyx mori*, have even been integrated into the *D. melanogaster* genome and showed to be correctly regulated[24]. The P element from *D. melanogaster* has also been able to transform *D. simulans*[36], *D. hawaiiensis*[4] and recently 3 mosquitoe species[20,23,25]. However in these last three cases, the molecular analysis of the transformants showed clearly that the integration events were not P-mediated.

Prodigious efforts both in *Ceratitis capitata*[31,21] and *Lucilia cuprina* have failed to demonstrate P-element transformation. The recent demonstration by Rio (pers comm) of a host factor goes some way to explain the restriction of mobility in heterologous systems.

The *hobo* element in *D. melanogaster* has now been used to effect transformation (Gelbart pers. comm) and it is clearly worthwhile to extend this work into pest insects. Indeed preliminary attempts in both *An gambiae* (S. Miller pers com) and *C. capitata* (Louis pers comm) have already been started.

Transposable elements as control agents

When transposable elements transpose they increase their copy number in the genome and therefore are at an advantage over other DNA sequences; they have as such been considered as genetic parasites[10,30]. As indicatead above, P elements in certain crosses cause hybrid dysgenesis resulting in hybrid sterility due to derepression of P elements. It might be possible to selectively inactivate the gene for the repressor *in vitro* but maintain the mobility. Such an irrepressible element would increase in frequency and it could cause a lowering of population fitness.

The occurrence of F_1 sterility and other hybrid phenomena when insect populations from different origins are mated might indicate the presence of transposable elements. This observation could be exploited to try to identify and clone such elements in pest insects.

Transposable elements as a transporting mechanism

The ability of P elements to transpose can be used to manipulate gene frequencies by seeding a susceptible population with individuals containing P elements. In Drosophila, population models[39] and laboratory studies[16] have shown the potential of this technique. Two classes of gene could be considered, deleterious (for the insect) of beneficial (for us). Genes which have dominant effects on viability and fitness would be very relevant for insect control. An example would be the defective testes-specific tubulin gene (B2tD) which causes male sterility in *D. melanogaster*[15]. Recent developments in the cloning of sex-switching genes in *D. melanogaster* also open the possibilty for the manipulation of insect populations. These types of genes show in general good conservation and thus should be functional when switched between species. A corollory to this approach is to use beneficial genes which would lead to the replacement of a pest form by an innocuous strain.

INSECTICIDE RESISTANCE

Insecticide resistance has been intensively studied from genetic and biochemical standpoints and much is now known. It is clear that the phenomenon presents a multi-facetted response of the insect when subject to continuous selection pressure as a result of exposure to an insecticide. Many mechanisms have been genetically analysed and biochemically unravelled and have demonstrated that resistance is due to pre-adaptive genetic variability. In the majority of cases resistance has been shown to be determined by a single locus and two general mechanisms have been found, namely alteration at the site of action and increased detoxification[29]. An example of the former is modification of the target enzyme acetylcholinesterase causing resistance to organophosphates and carbamates. In these cases the mutation is likely to be a localized event resulting in a small change in the amino acid sequence of the protein. For the second case, increased detoxification occurs as a consequence of the increased rate of metabolism of the insecticide to non-toxic products. In other words more of an already present enzyme is produced. There is now substantial biochemical evidence[9,12] that this type of resistance is mediated via gene amplification. Indeed Mouches et al.[26] succeeded in cloning the gene responsible for organophosphorous resistance in Culex quinquefasciatus and showed that a resistant strain had 250 times more copies of an esterase gene than the susceptible strain.

The phenomenon of insecticide resistance is extremely accessible to molecular analysis as the genetics and biochemistry are well known and gene products coded for by resistance genes can be obtained in relatively large amounts.

Introduction of Insecticide Resistance Genes into Beneficial Insects

Using classical selection techniques considerable progress ahs been made in the selection of insecticide resistance in phytoseiid mites. The predator mite Metaseiulus occidentalis has been selected in the laboratory for permethrin and carbaryl resistance and releases of these resistant mites in the field were successful[13]. Expansion of this approach to other parasites and predators is hampered by the apparent absence of resistance and the difficulties incumbent in the laboratory selection for resistance. The classical approach is also limited to intra-strain selection methods. Gene transfer of insecticide resistance genes offers a way out of the dilemma. Transposable elements would be used and cloned resistance geens would be incorporated into defective P elements for stable transformation[1,29].

Resistance genes against most insecticides are now available within the arthropod kingdom and providing the relevant protein can be purified in sufficient amounts any resistance gene should be able to be cloned. Unfortunately D. melanogaster cannot provide a "gene bank" for genes of this type as very little insecticide work has been done in this species. However, the gene coding for the wild-type acetylcholinesterase in *D. melanogaster* has already been cloned during a chromosome walk[2] and more recently in *An stephensi* (Malcolm pers comm).

A second case for the transfer of insecticide resistance genes could be made for bees because of their importance as pollinators and susceptibility to insecticides. Classical selection for resistance would be a very laborious task as considerable effort would be needed to rear and analyse the progeny of each fertile queen[40]. Gene transfer by injection of fertilized eggs would be a very efficient way of achieving this goal.

It should also be mentioned that the cloning of insecticide resistance genes in pest insects could open the way for the monitoring at the DNA level the presence of insecticide resistance genes in natural populations[5].

New Insecticides

It is now considered that the next generation of insecticides will be based on neuropeptides[18,32,14]. These peptides perform key functions as chemical messengers which regulate all aspects of insect behaviour. At the moment only four neuropeptides have been discovered in insects but many more are awaiting analysis[32]. The fact that these peptides are gene products opens up new possibilities of insect control in that these chemicals are amenable to biotechnological manipulation and production.

THE ENVIRONMENTAL PROBLEM

If the development of some of these molecular techniques proceeds as expected then eventually insects containing recombinant DNA will have to be released into the environment where they will be subject to the same regulations as other biological material. The initial and understandable caution in the field of recombinant DNA technology has to some extent been replaced with a realization that where genetic engineering is confined to debilitating bacterial strains for the production of particular substances very little environmental risk is posed. This is even more so when physical containment can be easily guaranteed.

However, this period of tacit acceptance wil be jolted somewhat when organisms, plants, bacteria, viruses of insects, will be released into the environment. Recombinant plants, bacteria and viruses are in many cases at this threshold and although some have made it to the other side, it has not been an easy process.

The community response to the type of science proposed here must always be taken into account so that a situation does not arise in which much time and money has been expended on a successful project which then is faced with unsurmountable problems of acceptance for application.

ACKNOWLEDGEMENTS

I thank Prof. F.C. Kafatos for comments on the text. The secretarial help of Georgia Houlaki is gratefully acknowledged.

REFERENCES

1. Beckendorf, J.K. and Hoy, M.A. (1985) In: Biological Control in Agriculatural IPM Systems, Eds, R. Herzog and M.B. Hoy. Academic Press 1985.
2. Bender, W., Spierer, P. and Hogness, D.S. (1983) J. Mol. Biol. 168: 17-33.
3. Bishop, D.H.L. (1986) Nature 323: 496.
4. Brennan, M.D., Rowan, R.G. and Dickinson, W.J. (1984) Cell 38: 147-151.
5. Brown, T.M. and Brogdon, W.G. (1989) Ann. Rev. Entomol. 32: 145-162.
6. Brown, W.M., George, M. and Wilson, A.C. (1979) Proc. Natl. Acad. Sci. 76: 1967-1971.
7. Cavalier-Smith, T. (1978) J. Cell Sci. 34: 247-278.
8. Cavalier-Smith, T. (1982) Ann. Rev. Biophy. Bioeng. 11: 273-302.
9. Devonshire, A.L. and Sawicki, R.M. (1979) Nature 280: 140-141.
10. Doolittle, W.F. and Sapienza, C. (1980) Nature 284: 601-603.
11. Flavell, R.B. (1982) In: Genome Evolution. Eds. G.A. Dover and R.B. Flavell, Academic Press, London: p.p. 301-325.
12. Hyrien, O. and Buttin, G. (1986) Trends in Genetics. Nov. 1986 pp. 275-276.
13. Hoy, M.A. (1984) Proc. VI Int. Congr. Acarology. Elsevier, p.p. 27-36.
14. Kelly, T.J., Masler, E.P. and Menn, J.J. (1990) These proceedings.
15. Kemphues, K.J., Raff, R.A., Kaufman, T.C. and Raff, E.L. (1979) Proc Natl. Acad. Sci. 76: 3991-3995.
16. Kidwell, M.G., Novy, J.B. and Feeley, S.M. (1981) J. Hered. 72: 32-38.
17. Kidwell, M.G. (1983) In: The Genetics and Biology of Drosophila. M. Ashburner, H.L. Carson and J.N. Thompson Jr. (Eds.) Vol 3c. Academic Press, London pp. 125-154.
18. Kirschbaum, J.B. (1985) Ann. Rev. Entomol. 30: 51-70.
19. McClintock, B. (1957) Cold Spring Harbour Symp. Quant. Biol. 21: 197-215.
20. McInnis, P.O., Tam, S.Y.T., Grace, C.R., Helmann, L.J., Courtwright, J.B. and Kumaran, A.K.. (1988) IAEA Symposium "Modern Insect Control: Nuclear Techniques and Biotechnology, Vienna 1987, pp. 251-256.
21. McGrave, V., Carlson, J.D., Miller, B.R. and Beaty, B.J. (1988). Amer. J. Trop. Med. Hyg. 39: 502-510.
22. McLain, D.K., Rai, K.S. and Fraser, M.J. (1986) Ann. Entomol. Soc. Am. 79: 784-791.
23. Miller, L.H., Sakai, R.K., Romans, P., Gwadz, R.W., Kantoff, P. and Coon, N.G. (1987) Science 237: 779-781.
24. Mitsialis, A.A. and Kafatos, F.C. (1985) Nature 317: 453-456.
25. Morris, A.C., Eggleston, P. and Crampton, J.M. (1989) Med. Vet. Entom. 3: 1-7.
26. Mouches, C. and 7 authors (1986) Science 233: 771-780.
27. Mouches, C. (1987) Proc II Int. Symp. Fruit Flies, Greece 1986 (Ed) A.P. Economopoulos, Elsevier, p.p. 245-251.

28. O'Hare, K. and Rubin, G.M. (1983) Cell 34: 25-35.

29. Oppenoorth, F.J. (1985) In: Comprehensive Insect Physiology, Biochemistry and Pharmacology. (Eds) G.A. Kerkut and L.I. Gilbert. Vol. 12. Pergamon 1985.

30. Orgel, L.E. and Crick, F.H.C., (1980) Nature 284: 604-607.

31. Robinson, A.S. Savakis, C. and Louis C. (1988) IAEA Symposium "Modern Insect Control: Nuclear Techniques and Biotechnology", Vienna 1987. pp. 241-250.

32. O'Shea, M. (1986) In: Approaches to New Leads for Insecticides. (Eds.) C.H. van Keyserlingk, A. Jager and Ch. van Szcyepanski. Springer Berlin, pp. 131   151.

33. Reilly, J.G. and Thomas, C.A. (1980) Plasmid 3: 109-115.

34. Rubin, G.M. (1983) In: Mobile Genetic Elements. Ed. J. Shapiro. Academic Press. Chap. 8.

35. Rubin, G.M. and Spradling, A.C. (1982) Science 218: 348-353.

36. Scarvarda, A.C. and Hartl, D. (1984) Proc. Natl. Acad. Sci. 81: 715-717.

37. Spradling, A.C. and Rubin, G.M. (1982) Science 218: 341-347.

38. Trick, M. and Dover, G.A. (1984) Can. J. Genet. Cytol. 26: 692-697.

39. Uyenoyama, M.,. (1985) J. Theoret. Biol. 27: 176-201.

40. Whitten, M.J. (1978) In: "Genetics in Relation to Insect Managment", pp. 93-97. Rockefeller Foundation 1979.

41. Whitten, M.J. (1986) Ann. Ent. Soc. Amer. 79: 766-772.

42. Young, M.W. (1979) Proc. Natl. Acad. Sci. 76: 6274-6276.

Biological and integrated control

© 1990 Elsevier Science Publishers B.V. (Biomedical Division)
Pesticides and alternatives, editor J.E. Casida

THE USE OF *METARHIZIUM ANISOPLIAE* FOR CONTROL OF SOIL PESTS

D.E. PINNOCK

Department of Entomology, Waite Agricultural Research Institute, The University of Adelaide, P.M.B. 1, Glen Osmond, South Australia 5064, (Australia).

Soil insect pests often are difficult to control, because the control effect usually must be of long duration, the insect moving through the soil may detect and avoid the control agents, and the soil environment may cause binding or decomposition of an applied toxicant.

Until recently, effective control of soil insect pests was provided by various chlorinated hydrocarbon insecticides which were persistent in the soil and relatively inexpensive. However, increasing problems of pest resistance and increasing concerns over pesticide residues and effects on non-target organisms has resulted in a search for alternative control agents.

One recent development is the application of controlled-release formulations of insecticides such as chloropyrifos®, which under some circumstances provide long-term control and at the same time avoid some of the problems associated with chlorinated hydrocarbon insecticide residues.

Yet another approach to the control of soil insect pests is the use of the entomopathogenic fungus *Metarhizium anisopliae*. *M. anisopliae* is a hyphomycete fungus long recognised as a pathogen of insects, and the cause of "green muscadine" disease of many insect species. It was one of the first insect pathogens to be produced for insect control, with the experiments of Metchnikoff in the late nineteenth century being particularly significant.

Many species of soil insect pests have been found in the field naturally infected with *M. anisopliae*. The fungus can be readily isolated from this field material, and cultured on a wide variety of mycological media. The fungus occurs in many more or less distinct physiological strains, each with its own range of host specificity, virulence, temperature tolerances, enzyme and toxin production. From a library of strains, it is thus possible to select a particular strain, usually by bioassay and by some set of physiological characters, for development as a pest control agent.

The selected *M. anisopliae* strain can be mass produced and incorporated into a carrier or formulation appropriate to the field requirements. This type of development is proceeding in various countries, and in Australia is directed towards control of "cockchafers" or scarabeid larvae, (Coleoptera: Scarabeidae), which are pests of pastures and others of sugar cane; or of soldier fly larvae, (Diptera: Inopinae, Stratiomyidae) and other soil inhabiting insect pests.

The Australian Black Headed Pasture Cockchafer, *Aphodius tasmaniae*, is reported to destroy 2 million hectares of pasture annually. Its control with *M. anisopliae* has now

172

reached the stage of registration field trials. The fungus is applied as a bait, which is taken by the foraging *A. tasmaniae* larvae into their tunnels, where infection occurs and the fungus kills the insect. After the death of this insect, the fungus grows and sporulates on the cadaver. Protected in the soil environment, it provides carry-over of *M. anisopliae* to effect control the following year.

Examples of field mortality of *A. tasmaniae* larvae caused by application of bait contain 1.3 x 10^{15} conidiospores/ha are given for two field sites in figures 1 and 2 (Coles and Pinnock, 1984).

A different approach is taken in the development of *M. anisopliae* for control of insect larvae attacking sugar cane. In Australia the most important genera are *Antitrogus, Dermolepida* and *Lepidiota* (Coleoptera: Scarabaeidae), and *Inopus* (Diptera: Inopineae, Stratomyidae).

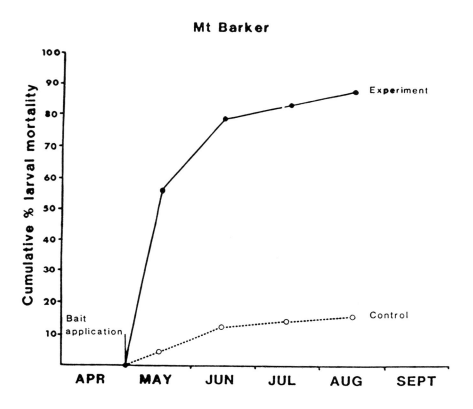

Fig. 1.   Control of *Aphodius tasmaniae* by *Metarhizium anisopliae* bait formulation, Mount Barker, South Australia.

Unlike *A. tasmaniae*, these sugar cane pests do not forage on the soil surface, but remain under the soil throughout the larval development. For effective control, the selected *M. anisopliae* strain must be applied directly into the soil, where it will remain until contact is made with a target insect. The carrier or formulation must therefore provide a protective and sustaining vehicle to maintain the viability and infectivity of the fungus for long periods of time. Various formulations have been found which do this, and field viability of more than two years has been achieved. Also, the selection of the *M. anisopliae* strain to be used includes criteria such as the quantity of conidiospores produced on the dead larvae, as well as the strain's virulence measured by bioassay. These criteria, together with tests of compatibility
of the selected strains with the fertilisers and other agricultural chemicals used in the sugar cane industry, has resulted in the development of strains with excellent potential as control agents for major cane pests in Australia (Samuels, Pinnock, Featherstone and Bull, 1988, in press,

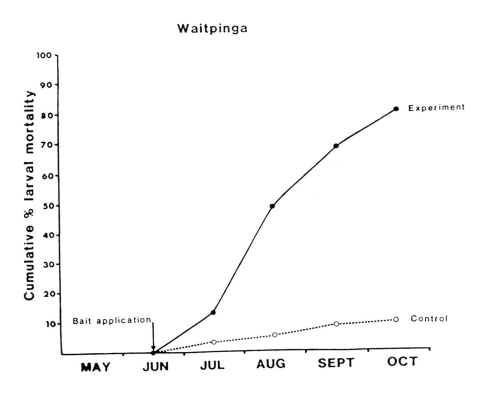

Fig. 2. Control of *Aphodius tasmaniae* by *Metarhizium anisopliae* bait formulation, Waitpinga, South Australia.

Samuels, Pinnock and Allsop, 1989) and early indications are that substantial increases in yield up to 100% may be achieved where *M. anisopliae* is applied to infested sugar cane.

The examples given above show that *M. anisopliae* can be developed as a control agent for soil pests which is effective under field conditions. However, to become an operational control measure, the cost of the *M. anisopliae* produced must be acceptable to the industry and farmers using it. Our experience suggests that the two greatest factors affecting production costs are the capitalisation of the production and formulation plant, and the material costs of the carrier in the product formulation. With improved fermentation technology, the actual material cost of producing the fungus itself is now relatively low. For example, our experience shows that the material and energy costs to produce a batch of 12.5 tonnes of primary *M. anisopliae* culture by fermentation on brewery waste liquor is approximately $A350 at 1987/88 prices. To formulate this batch of fungus into a simple cereal-based carrier would add a further $A1,800 in carrier material costs alone. This quantity is sufficient to treat over 250 ha of crop or pasture. Estimates vary on the cost of a production facility to produce *Metarhizium* commercially, but an average estimate would be approximately $A3 million, plus the cost of a packaging system suited to market requirements.

Against these costs must be considered the advantages of *M. anisopliae* as a control agent. The selected strains are relatively specific to the insect pests in the soil environment to which they are applied. The fungus can be regarded as safe to other organisms, including man, and has no deleterious residue or food-chain accumulation effects. The duration of control has been shown to be adequate under field conditions where the fungus has been tested, and the target pests seem not to avoid the *M. anisopliae* formulation.

In summary, *M. anisopliae* is considered to have considerable potential as a control agent for a variety of soil inhabiting insect pests, and its commercial production is now being considered in Australia.

REFERENCES
1.   Coles, R.B., Pinnock D.E. (1984). Current status of the Production and Use of *Metarhizium anisopliae* for Control of *Aphodius tasmaniae* in South Australia. Proc. IVth Aust. appl. ent. Res. Conf., 357-361, Government Printer, Adelaide, South Australia.

2.   Samuels, K.D.Z., Pinnock, D.E., Featherstone, N.E., Bull, R.M. (1989). Entomophaga (in press).

3.   Samuels, K.D.Z., Pinnock, D.E. and Allsop, P.G., (1989). J. Aust. ent. Soc. **28**: 69-74.

© 1990 Elsevier Science Publishers B.V. (Biomedical Division)
Pesticides and alternatives, editor J.E. Casida

TOXORHYNCHITES MOSQUITOES: FLYING INSECTICIDES WHICH DO NOT POLLUTE THE ENVIRONMENT

MASUHISA TSUKAMOTO and MASAHIRO HORIO
Department of Medical Zoology, School of Medicine, University of
Occupational & Environmental Health, Kitakyushu 807 (Japan)

BIOLOGICAL CONTROL OF MOSQUITOES USING MOSQUITOES

The development of a new chemical insecticide requires much time and a great financial investment without any assurance of whether the target pests will eventually develop resistance to this new chemical. Once resistance has developed, application of increased amounts of the chemical may cause economic problems as well as pollution of the environment.

Many mosquito species are considered to be pests of medical importance because not only are they a nuisance but they are also vectors of diseases through their blood sucking. Mosquitoes belonging to the genus *Toxorhynchites*, however, are a group of beneficial insects because 1) their larvae are predators of those of other mosquitoes, especially *Aedes* spp., which are vectors of filariasis, dengue, yellow fever, and so on; 2) adults of *Toxorhynchites* do not suck the blood of human beings or animals but suck only nector from flowers; and 3) adults can fly anywhere and seek out oviposition sites where larvae of *Aedes* breed. The interesting idea to use *Toxorhynchites* larvae as potential biological control agents to aedine mosquitoes has been discussed since 1911[1-4], and experiments have been carried out in laboratory[5] or fields[3,6,7]. Some species of *Toxorhynchites* have actually been introduced on several Pacific islands to control *Aedes* mosquitoes since 1929[8-10]. The results of these trials, however, have not been as successful as hoped[4,11].

INTRODUCTION OF A NEW APPROACH

We have analyzed the major causes why the biological control of *Aedes* by *Toxorhynchites* has not been successful, and have come to the conclusion that the old concept considering that biocontrol using *Toxorhynchites* being difficult should be abandoned and a new concept should be established viewing *Toxorhynchites* mosquitoes as "living and flying insecticides". The major reason for the failure or limitation in such biological control was the difficulty in colonization and subsequent mass breeding of suitable species or strains of *Toxorhynchites* because of their double-bladed characteristics of being carnivorous and cannibalistic.

Habitats for many species of the genera *Anopheles* and *Culex* are usually open and large aquatic environments, such as ponds, ground pools, ditches, or ricefields, where the application of chemical insecticides or other control methods should be easily applied. Breeding places for larvae of most aedine mosquitoes, in contrast, are limited to shaded, scattered, and small aquatic environments, such as tree holes, leaf axils, bamboo stumps, cut and/or split bamboos, rock holes, coconut shells, snail shells, rainwater tanks, drum-cans, tin cans, flower vases, ant-traps, and other artificial containers to which application of chemical insecticides, though not impossible, would be more difficult. Since adults of the predator themseves seek suitable oviposition sites, the cost of searching out and the spraying insecticides to these complicated breeding sites of aedine mosquitoes in the natural environment would be saved.

Now it is possible, as is described later, to colonize many species or strains of *Toxorhynchites* and to produce on a large scale for inundative releases to an area where a mosquito-borne disease is epidemic or endemic. Thus, the obviously beneficial use of *Toxorhynchites* as a natural biological control agent should be re-evaluated from environmental and economic viewpoints.

PREVIOUS DIFFICULT ASPECTS OF USING *TOXORHYNCHITES* FOR BIOCONTROL
Establishment of a laboratory colony from field-collected materials.

For laboratory colonization, it is desirable to start from at least 30 individuals to keep gene pool rich. It has, however, been difficult to collect enough larvae or pupae of *Toxorhynchites* species from the natural environment. Besides, the materials collected from natural environments often develop asynchronously[12] (some larvae requiring several months to become adults in the laboratory), and hence only a few males and females of a similar age might be available to produce progeny in establishing a laboratory colony. Most of our laboratory colonies have actually been started from only a few individuals.
Mass breeding after colony establishment.

Frequent releases of a large number of individuals to an area necessitate the efficient mass breeding of larvae in laboratory. Since larvae of *Toxorhynchites* are carnivorous, a constant supply of preys is essential. Without sufficient live food, cannibalism will result in the rapid decrease in number of predator larvae, and only the strongest individual will survive especially in a small place. Such a character, while effective for natural selection in evolution, is inconvenient for laboratory mass breeding. Certain species of *Toxorhynchites* have shown violent cannibalistic or "killing" traits, and in such cases mass breeding may not be possible. The larvae of some species, however, rarely display cannibalism although they are carnivorous.
Selection of the most suitable species or strain of *Toxorhynchites*.

Even if mass breeding of an established strain is successful, this does not necessarily mean that this colony is suitable to biologically control a target vector of disease. Since the colonization of *Toxorhynchites* mosquitoes has, in the past, been very difficult, any colony that could be established was used for biological control in any place needed. Overcoming these laboratory colonization problems for most species has now made it possible to choose an appropriate species or strain for a given place and time.

Introduction of *Toxorhynchites* colony to a new area.

Merely the "introduction" to and "field colonization" in a new environment are not enough to assure biological control of a vector. Even though the newcomer will successfully establish a field colony there, it will maintain just an equilibrium between the predator and its prey. Co-existence of the predator with the prey, therefore, will never result in eradication of the vector from the area. To achieve eradication of a disease, a large and successive numbers of suitable strain or species of *Toxorhynchites* must be released as "living and flying insecticides" until the absolute number of patients will decrease to a certain low level in such area.

KNOWHOW FOR MASS PRODUCTION OF *TOXORHYNCHITES*

New techniques are necessary to establish a local laboratory colony thought most appropriate to control the target vector of a certain disease. Establishment of a new colony of *Toxorhynchites* in the laboratory required finding answers to the following major questions:

How to collect as much materials as possible from fields?

Set up of many artificial oviposition traps at or near natural habitats is quite helpful for this purpose. Old automobile tires act as a good oviposition trap because of its black color and its long retention of rainwater.

How to enhance mating in a laboratory cage?

Natural mating. Mating is obviously the first step in production of off-spring. Some species or colonies easily copulate within a laboratory cage (20 x 30 x 20 cm or 70 x 70 x 80 cm) while others do not. A black cover with a top window (about 10-15 cm in diameter) is effective in enhancing flights of both sexes towards the window, and frequently induces their copulation[13]. Under a laboratory condition, however, males and females of some species of *Toxorhynchites* often do not copulate for a long time after their emergence.

Artificial mating. In such cases artificial mating is necessary to obtain fertilized eggs at least for the next generation. The procedure for this is:

1) A 4-5 day old female is lightly anaesthetized with ethyl ether and placed put on her back. 2) Gentle petting of the female terminalia with those of a decapitated male under light anaesthesia will result in connection of two sex organs (in the case of *Tx. minimus* the decapitation is not neccessary). 3) After several seconds of "hanging-up" of the linked partners, the female will drop down, indicating the end of copulation. From a brief few seconds in *Tx. minimus* to several minutes in *Tx. bengalensis* may be required (unpublished data).

How to induce or enhance oviposition?

Some species readily lay eggs in an artificial water container in a cage, while others do not. Some caged species lay eggs on water surface in any container, while cut bamboo and/or bamboo internodes with a small hole have proven more effective for oviposition in other instances. We must determine what factor(s) is the most effective inducer for or attractant of oviposition:

container color? size? shape? depth of water? micro-scale difference in humidity? micro-scale difference in temperature? light reflection? chemical attractants?, and so on. In general, dark, deep-walled containers are preferable to shallow ones for ovitraps. In special cases, females of *Toxorhynchites* frequently project their eggs towards the lens of a camera inserted into a cage to take pictures. Females of *Tx. klossi*, a pitcher plant dweller, prefer the red color for oviposition (unpublished data).

Confinement of a conceived female in a small beaker (for example, 100 ml), the inside of which is covered with moist soft tissue paper, has also sometimes been quite effective in getting a large number of eggs (unpublished data). Adult females usually begin oviposition within a few days after sexual maturation. Some special cases, however, require at least one month for oviposition after successful copulation and maturation of the ovary; the reason for this is not yet known.

How to prevent cannibalism among larvae of *Toxorhynchites*?

As stated, certain species have a strong cannibalistic tendency, while others have none or only a weak tendency. The latter can be easily "educated" for successful mass breeding. Matured larvae of some species attack any moving organism, not to eat but to kill. This "killing" behavior makes these particular species unsuitable for laboratory mass breeding although the character is quite useful for actual biological control of a vector in the field.

"Infant education": An adequate number of 1st instar larvae of the prey (such as *Ae. aegypti*) should be provided just prior to the hatch of 1st instar larvae of *Toxorhynchites*. Several hours after hatching, the predator larvae will then attack only the prey and later will recognize each other as being of the same species. After such "infant education" to the 1st instar larvae of *Toxorhynchites*, cannibalism can be prevented to some extent by providing a large number of 1st instar larvae of the prey. The effect of this "training" remains until the 4th instar stage even when their population density is high, hence the mass breeding of predators can be successfully accomplished. Starting from 100 larvae at the 1st instar stage, average rates of emergence to adults are around 96-98% in mass breeding.

When individually reared larvae (without "education") are placed in the same container, however, violent cannibalism will begin immediately, even if enough prey is supplied. Lack of prey at earlier stages results in rapid decrease of the predators. In some species we have not been able to "educate" at all, and in such cases mass breeding is impossible; instead, the troublesome and time-consuming individual breeding is required.

How to efficiently and constantly provide a large number of prey?

Larvae of almost all predator species recognize and attack only living or moving organisms as prey. In the laboratory, larvae of *Aedes aegypty* can be used for this purpose because of its easiness in maintenance. Larvae of *Tx. klossi* are exceptional: they prowl about and eat dead bodies of other insects or their debris in the bottom of the pitcher. They can, therefore, develop

without being given living prey, whereas they also eat living prey as usual.
How to synchronize growth of a colony during developmental stages?

In cases of individual breeding, the larval developmental period varied from rapid to very slow, making it inconvenient to maintain a colony, especially one with a small population. However, mass breeding allows the synchronous and rapid development of larvae, and this made it easy to produce a large number of pupae or adults of the same age. Under standard laboratory conditions (26°C, 14 hr illumination and 10 hr dark), the total developmental period of many species is 17.6–21.0 days: 1.8–2.4 days as the egg, 13–15 days for larval stages, 5–6 days for the pupal stage, 4–7 days for sexual maturation, and 1–3 days prior to oviposition[13]. In exceptional cases, oviposition of *Tx. metallicus* will occur about one month after mating, and in the case of *Tx. leicesteri* we must wait even longer (unpublished data).

NECESSITY FOR BASIC RESEARCH ON *TOXORHYNCHITES* BIOLOGY

The ecology of *Toxorhynchites* is still not completely known. Different species and sometimes even different strains within a single species have different ecological characters or behavior. Some species live on plains (either urban or rural, coastal or inland) and others in forests or mountainous areas. Their habitats may be tree holes, bumboo stumps or internodes, coconut shells, leaf axils, pitcher plants, or various artificial containers. If the vector to be controlled lives in an urban condition, a colony of *Toxorhynchites* must be selected which prefers or at least can tolerate an urban polluted environment. Selection of the predators for insecticide resistance may be useful under urban circumstances. If a target vector normally breeds in leaf axils of plants, a predator which also breeds in leaf axils should be used. To select the most suitable colony, therefore, the mass breeding of a variety of colonies of *Toxorhynchites* should be attempted.

To achieve successful biological control, more intensive and extensive studies on the basic biology of *Toxorhynchites* are necessary, covering such aspects as taxonomy, genetics, ecology, biochemistry, molecular biology, physiology, toxicology, and so on.

Taxonomy and distribution: Seventy-six taxa of the genus *Toxorhynchites* have been reported in the world to date[14-18]. Forty-two of these belong to the subgenus *Toxorhynchites* in Asia, New Guinea, and South Pacific; and 13 taxa in Africa; 4 taxa to the subgenus *Ankylorhynchus* in South America; and 17 taxa of the subgenus *Lynchiella* in North and South Americas.

The taxonomic situation among local populations of so-called "*Tx. splendens*" is complicated. A colony collected from Palawan Island did not produce F_1 progeny after crosses with that from another island, Mindanao, or that from Thailand, or *Tx. amboinensis* (Hawaii strain). However, the latter can produce offspring after crossing with either Mindanao colony or the Indian colony of *Tx. splendens* (unpublished data).

LABORATORY COLONIES OF *TOXORHYNCHITES*

Up to 1981, only 6 species or subspecies of *Toxorhynchites* have been established as laboratory colonies: *Tx. brevipalpis*[19], *Tx. amboinensis*[10], *Tx. rutilus septentionalis*[20], *Tx. splendens*[21], *Tx. r. rutilus*[22], and *Tx. inornatus*[23]. Soon colonization of 3 Japanese species (*Tx. towadensis*, *Tx. okinawensis*, and *Tx. manicatus yaeyamae*) was reported in 1985[13]. More recently 8 species have also been successfully colonized (unpublished data). The following species and strains are routinely maintained in our laboratory:

Tx. towadensis	3 strains	Yakushima Is., Japan, since 1983;
		Mt. Hikosan, Japan, since 1984;
		Mt. Tateyama, Japan, since 1987.
Tx. okinawensis#	1 strain	Okinawa-Hontou, Japan, since 1984.
Tx. amboinensis	1 strain	Hawaii [from Philippines], since 1982.
Tx. splendens	6 strains	Palawan, Philippines, since 1981;
		wl/wl (white larval mutant), Philippines, since 1981;
		Bangkok, Thailand, since 1983;
		Selangor, Malaysia, since 1986;
		Poona, India, since 1987;
		Rathunapuna, Sri Lanka, since 1987.
Tx. yamadai	1 strain	Amami-Ohshima, Japan, 1985.
Tx. aurifluus#	1 strain	Taiwan, China, since 1988.
Tx. minimus*#	1 strain	Rathunapuna, Sri Lanka, since 1987.
Tx. bengalensis*#	1 strain	Sylet, Bangladesh, since 1988.
Tx. metallicus*	1 strain	Selangor, Malaysia, since 1986.
Tx. klossi*	3 strains	Gunung Jerai, Malaysia, since 1986;
		Cameron Highland, Malaysia, since 1986;
		Genting Highland#, Malaysia, since 1986.
Tx. quasiferox	1 strain	Selangor, Malaysia, since 1986.

Species marked with * require individual rearing, and those with # require artificial mating under the laboratory conditions. Colonies once established but later terminated for various reasons are:

Tx. yaeyamae#	1 strain	Yaeyama Is., Japan, 1983–1986.
Tx. gravelyi*	1 strain	Doi Suthep, Thailand, 1983–1986.
Tx. splendens	4 strains	Chang Mai, Thailand, 1983–1987;
		Chanthaburi, Thailand, 1984–1986;
		Ilomavis, Philippines, 1981–1986;
		Palawan leaf axil, Philippines, 1981–1986.
Tx. amboinensis	1 strain	Luzon, Philippines, 1983–1984.

NECESSITY OF A PILOT FIELD APPLICATION TRIAL

The large number of *Toxorhynchites* adults to be released, the mosquitoes should be looked upon as a living and flying insecticide, but one that will not cause environmental contamination or pollution. Therefore, even several consecutive releases may be safely made until the absolute number of patients of a target disease is reduced to a minimal number in the area of concern.

Most of the questions mentioned above have largely been overcome on a laboratory scale. A small-scale pilot trial for field application should now be done in those tropical countries where vectors of various diseases like filariasis, dengue, or yellow fever are common. The cost for this natural biological control should be compared to that using chemical methods and evaluated together with the environmental benefits.

ACKNOWLEDGEMENTS

This investigation was supported in part by Grants-in-Aid for Overseas Scientific Surveys from the Ministry of Education, Science and Culture, Japan: Projects entitled "Phylogenic Studies on Mosquito Fauna of Southeast Asia" (Nos. 56041048, 58041058, and 61041070) and entitled "Zoogeographical Studies on the Medically Important Diptera in Southwest Asia" (Nos. 6204103 and 63041058).

REFERENCES
1. Colledge WR (1911) Proc Roy Soc Queensl 13:121-131
2. Buxton PA, Hopkins GHE (1927) Mem Lond Sch Hyg Trop Med No. 1. 121 pp
3. Muspratt J (1951) Bull Entomol Res 42:355-370
4. Steffan WA (1975) Mosq Syst 7:59-67
5. Chuah MLK, Yap HH (1984) Trop Biomed 1:145-150
6. Trpis M (1973) Bull WHO 49:359-365
7. Gerberg EJK, Visser WM (1978) Mosq News 38:197-200
8. Paine RW (1934) Bull Entomol Res 25:1-32
9. Peterson GD, Jr (1956) J Econ Entomol 49:786-789
10. Nakagawa PY (1963) Proc Hawaii Entomol Soc 18:291-293
11. Bay EC (1974) Ann Rev Entomol 19:441-453
12. Steffan WA, Evenhuis NL (1981) Ann Rev Entomol 26:159-181
13. Horio M, Tsukamoto M (1985) Jpn J Sanit Zool 36:87-93
14. Knight KL, Stone A (1977) A Catalog of the Mosquitoes of the World (Diptera: Culicidae). Thomas Say Found Publ 6. 611 pp
15. Steffan WA, Evenhuis NL (1985) J Med Entomol 22:421-446
16. Evenhuis NL, Steffan WA (1977) J Med Entomol 23:538-574
17. Tsukamoto M (1989) Jpn J Trop Med Hyg 215-228
18. Toma T, Miyagi I, Tanaka K (1989) J Med Entomol (in press)
19. Trpis M, Gerberg EJ (1973) Bull WHO 48:637-638
20. Trimble RM, Corbet PS (1975) Ann Entomol Soc Amer 68:217-219
21. Furumizo RT, Cheong WH, Rudnick A (1977) Mosq News 37:664-667
22. Focks DA, Hall DW, Seawright JA (1977) Mosq News 37:751-755
23. Barker-Hudson P [cited by Pal R, Ramalingam S (1981) WHO/VBC/81.799]

Pesticides and alternatives, editor J.E. Casida

A MODEL FOR TESTING THE FOOD CHAIN TOXICITY OF LOW-LEVEL
CONCENTRATIONS OF PESTICIDES IN HOST-PARASITOID-SYSTEMS

FRANK WOLF-ROSKOSCH and INGOLF SCHUPHAN*

Department of Ecological Chemistry, Federal Biological Research
Centre for Agriculture and Forestry, 1000 Berlin 33, FRG

INTRODUCTION

An essential requirement for the application of selective working
pesticides in an integrated pest management is to identify those of
the pesticides which possess beneficial insect preserving properties. Therefore an increasing number of tests has been developed recently to evaluate reproducibly the **contact toxicity** of spray films,
as derived from pesticide application, on beneficial insects (HASSAN
et al. 1988). Besides mortality effects the tests also elucidate
sublethal influences of the tested agents on the beneficial capacity.

Investigations with endoparasitic hymenoptera however showed that
pesticides act poisonous even when taken up by the beneficial insect
via the food chain (plant-host-endoparasite) in acute non-toxic doses (SCHÄRER 1983; HOFFMANN 1984; WOLF-ROSKOSCH und SCHUPHAN 1986).
Such effects are significant in the field if pest insects repopulate
a treated area and the beneficial insects - predators or parasitoids
- feed continuously on them.

Screening tests to investigate such **food chain toxicities** of pesticides for beneficials are lacking in the present testing practice.

FOOD CHAIN MODEL SYSTEM AND PESTICIDE APPLICATION

The aim to test the food chain toxicity in series reproducibly
necessitate the use of selected model food chains in the laboratory.
That implies that the complexity of natural influences must be reduced for standardization purpose.

184

Test insects

 Two endoparasitic hymenoptera, Apanteles glomeratus L. (Braconidae)
and Pteromalus puparum L. (Chalcididae), along with the host of
both, Pieris brassicae L. (Lepidoptera, Pieridae), were chosen as
test organisms. Both beneficials are known as important antagonists
(gregarious parasitoids) of this cabbage pest. As they parasitize
different developmental stages of the host (Apanteles: larval parasitoid, Pteromalus: pupal parasitoid) they are parts of two on principle different model food chains. As first trophic level Brassica
oleracea L. (savoy cabbage) was the nutrition plant of the host.

Test performance

 The application of the test agent to the food chain complex take
place in specifically constructed cages of stainless wire netting
(Fig.1). The Pieris-larvae (groups of 10) are fed during their last

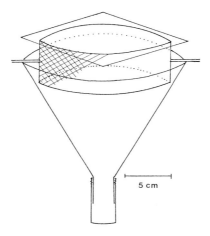

Fig. 1. Test cage with glass funnel and vial for faeces collection

larval stage (L5) for 5 days with cabbage leaves treated with the
chemical. The caterpillars of the Apanteles test are singly parasitized during their L1-stage and kept under breeding conditions till
they are reaching L5. In the case of the Pteromalus test feeding of
the test compound is performed to nonparasitized caterpillars during
the fifth instar. Parasitization follows just after pupation of the
Pieris-larvae.

 The test compounds are dissolved in suitable solvents (e.g. metha-

nol) and applicated in geometrically defined concentrations (mg in-
gredient/kg leaf mass) to standardized savoy leaf disks (diameter
60 mm, punched without middlerip, two disks put together as a sand-
wich, treated sides inwards).

The experimental conditions are: 20 $\pm$ 0.5ºC, 70 - 80 % R.H. and
16:8 photoperiod (10000 lux; Osram L 65 W/30S). One experiment consists of 5-7 cages in which the caterpillars are fed daily with
freshly prepared disk sandwiches. Leaf disks treated only with the
solvent are given to the control group. The faeces are collected and
weighed daily.

REARING METHODS

The cultivation of savoy plants is performed in an air-conditioned
greenhouse at 18 - 20ºC and 60 - 70 % RH up to the 10-leaf stage
(additional 6000 lux, Osram HQI-TS 400 W, are used during the short
day period).

Imagines of Pieris are kept in a cage (60x60x80 cm) under LD 16:8
photoperiod conditions, changing the temperature 25 - 30ºC by day to
20ºC by night (WOLF-ROSKOSCH 1989, FELTWELL 1982, JUNNIKKALA 1966,
DAVID 1957, DAVID and GARDINER 1952). Larvae rearing is performed
for maintenance in groups of 50 at potted cabbage plants (20ºC, 60-
70 % RH, LD 18:6 photoperiod, 4000 lux), yet for testing purpose in
clear plastic boxes of 20x20x6 cm (WOLF-ROSKOSCH 1989).

Imagines of Apanteles are kept under caterpillar rearing conditions in tubes of acrylic glass (length 20 cm, diameter 15 cm, covered with a nylon stocking; feed: 10 % honey solution). Rearing is
performed for maintenance by introducing about 100 L1-Pieris larvae
into the tubes for several minutes. Single parasitization of L1 larvae is necessary for the experiments (WOLF-ROSKOSCH 1989).

Adults of Pteromalus are kept like Apanteles. For maintenance as
well as for experiments at times one pupa of Pieris is brought together with 1 female and 2 males in a petridish for 5 days (WOLF-
ROSKOSCH 1989).

TEST STRATEGY

Range finding
  In course of testing chemicals or pesticides respectively in host-
parasite systems the sensitivity of the host against the chemical
is to take into consideration. Thus in the beginning of the beneficial organism test a range finding is essential to find those concentrations the host can survive as a nutrient basis as well as a
transferring link for the test compound. Therefore the "non-lethal
level" of Pieris (nonparasitized) is determined. That means the
highest concentration of the chemical (mg ingredient/kg feed substrate) is defined by which no mortality of Pieris is evident. The
resulting surviving range submits suitable marks for the determination of the upper niveau of concentration for the parasite test.
Moreover sublethal effects on Pieris are partly perceptible (stage
weights, faeces production). Thus "sublethal range" and "no-visible-
effect level" of the test substance can be estimated by regression
analysis. These values may give an idea till which lower concentration level parasite influencing effects of the test agent are to be
expected.

Sensitivity of the host Pieris (effective concentration - EC50)
  The size and dynamic of a pest population decisively depends on
the influence of antagonists, but also on the sensitivity of the
pest itself referring to the chronically consumed mortality causing
agents. From this point of view the knowledge of the sensitivity of
the host is connected also with the biocoenotic significance of the
results received from the pest-parasite complex studies. Therefore
the corresponding EC50 is determined as a parameter of the developmental success of the pest at different agent concentrations. In
this connection the methodically important "non-lethal level" is
less suitable as a standard value figure from a statistical point of
view.

Sensitivity of the beneficials (effective concentration - EC50)
  The impairment of the successful development of the beneficial
insects, developing inside the host larvae or pupae serves as a
parameter for the detection and quantification of a toxic impact of
the test chemical. Thus the capability of the beneficial insect to
reach the imaginal stage under chemical burden is measured. Using

the mortality data obtained under different experimental concentrations the effective concentration of the test chemical is determined, which reduces the developmental success of the beneficial endoparasite to 50% as to the control (EC50). The values are computed by probit analysis according to FINNEY (1971).

Ecotoxicological assessment

The ecotoxicological assessment of a pesticide applied in agro-ecosystems should implicate following aspects:
1. The acute and chronic toxicities against selected beneficial insects, including risk valuation in consideration of degradation and residue formation in the field.
2. Evaluation of the biocoenotic effect of the agent on the pest-beneficial complex, with special regard to the pest as the reproduction basis of the entomophagous organisms.

Moreover data recording considering different developmental stages of the pest-beneficial complex along with comparative evaluation of all available test results (different chemicals and organisms) may reveal toxical effects dependent on the structural features of the test agent (structure-effect dependence). This is of basic importance to the recognizing of selective properties of special chemical classes or agent structures respectively.

TEST RESULTS

The established model was proved with two physico-chemical and structural different model compounds - LINDANE and PARATHION. The most important results of the test program with Pieris, Apanteles and Pteromalus are given in Tab. 1 and Fig. 2 and 3.

Food chain toxicity of LINDANE and PARATHION

The testing of LINDANE and PARATHION resulted in a high food chain toxicity for both **beneficial insects** Apanteles and Pteromalus by the two pesticides (Tab. 1; Fig. 2 and 3). The EC50-values amount clear below 1.0 mg/kg (ingredient/kg). Besides the data show that LINDANE own a significant higher food chain toxicity compared with PARATHION.

Relating to the **pest** Pieris LINDANE and PARATHION exhibit a very different toxic effect in kind and extent. LINDANE demonstrates a

188

TABLE 1

RESULTS OF THE FOOD CHAIN TESTING OF LINDANE AND PARATHION

Compound		LINDANE	PARATHION
Pieris lethal range (mg/kg)		> 0.63 (0.84*)	> 0.41 (0.45*)
sublethal range (mg/kg)		0.04 – 0.63	–
no-visible-effect range (mg/kg)		< 0.04	≤ 0.41
mortality at 0.5 mg/kg (%)		0.0	30.0
EC_{50} (mg/kg) (95% confidence limits)		1.26 (1.06 – 1.50)	0.55 (0.52 – 0.60)
Apanteles mortality at 0.5 mg/kg (%)		56.0	24.4
EC_{50} (mg/kg) (95% confidence limits)		0.45 (0.39 – 0.54)	0.56 (0.55 – 0.57)
Pteromalus mortality at 0.5 mg/kg (%)		53.2	13.1
EC_{50} (mg/kg) (95% confidence limits)		0.48 (0.47 – 0.49)	0.68 (0.67 – 0.77)

mg/kg = mg active ingredient/kg cabbage leaves; * lowest concentration tested exhibiting host (pest) mortality

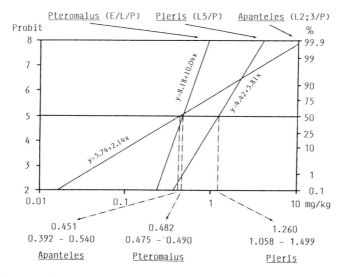

Fig. 2. EC50 of LINDANE: Estimation of the effective concentration (mg compound/kg cabbage leaves) which reduces the developmental success of Pieris, Apanteles and Pteromalus to 50% (including 95% confidence limits, probit analysis according to FINNEY (1971)). E = eggs; L = larvae; P = pupae

comparatively low toxicity (EC50 above 1.0 mg/kg), combined with a relatively late action namely in the pupal stage (Fig.4). Moreover

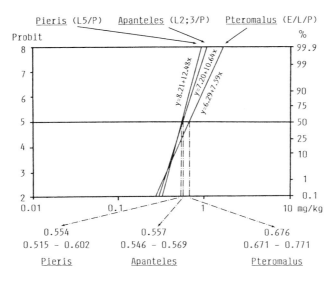

Fig. 3. EC50 of PARATHION: Estimation of the effective concentration (mg compound/kg cabbage leaves) which reduces the developmental success of Pieris, Apanteles and Pteromalus to 50% (including 95% confidence limits, probit analysis according to Finney (1971)). E = eggs; L = larvae; P = pupae

the pesticide exhibits a pronounced sublethal effect (reduction of faeces excretion), which is established even in the ppb-region

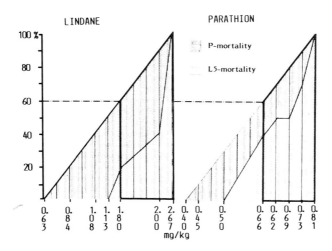

Fig. 4. Mortality of Pieris: Larvae (L5), pupae (P) and total mortality in tests with LINDANE and PARATHION (each conc.: n=10)

(Tab.1). In contrast PARATHION effects <u>Pieris</u> to a greater extent
(EC50 far below 1.0 mg/kg) and documents a distinct killing effect
mainly affecting the larval stage (Fig. 4).

<u>Sensitivity of beneficials and pest</u>
    The test results document the highly more sensitive reaction of
both beneficial insect species against **LINDANE**, taken up via food
chain, compared to <u>Pieris</u> (Tab. 1; Fig. 2). The EC50-values determined differ nearly for a threefold. The endoparasites <u>Apanteles</u> and
<u>Pteromalus</u> nearly show the same sensitivity. In the case of **PARATHI-
ON** a comparable high sensitivity of <u>Apanteles</u> and the pest <u>Pieris</u>
can be shown in contrast to a significant lower sensitivity of the
beneficial <u>Pteromalus</u> (Tab. 1; Fig. 3). All three EC50-values amount
below 1.0 mg/kg.

DISCUSSION OF TEST RESULTS

<u>Food chain toxicity of the test chemicals: Apanteles and Pteromalus</u>
    The high food chain toxicity of LINDANE and PARATHION on the endo-
parasitic beneficials <u>Apanteles</u> and <u>Pteromalus</u> - by very low contamination of the first nutrition level - is caused by different reasons:
1. Known insecticidal action; 2. Direct uptake into the host (no
integument barrier); 3. Summing up of the total compound burden in
the host-parasitoid system through chronic uptake; 4. Function of
the contaminated host haemolymph as feed and environment of the
weakly sclerotisized endoparasite (oral, epidermal and tracheal uptake of the compounds).

    The relatively higher food chain toxicity of LINDANE can be ex-
plained easily by the accumulation of the chemical in the food
chain "cabbage-host-endoparasite" (that means the increasingly high
enrichment within the different trophic levels). In contrast PARA-
THION is successively degraded (HOFFMANN 1984). Different behaviour
in enrichment and excretion of both pesticides in insect organism,
ultimately responsible for accumulation and degradation in food
chains, is attributed especially to the physico-chemical properties
as persistence, metabolism and water/lipid solubility (HOFFMANN und
SCHUPHAN, 1986).

Food chain toxicity of the test chemicals: Pieris

The definitely lower toxic effect of LINDANE (EC50: 1.26 mg/kg) on
the pest Pieris in comparison with PARATHION (EC50: 0.55 mg/kg) can
be related clearly to the high storage of LINDANE into the fatbody.
It is likely that the extensive storage of LINDANE prevents the coming up of toxical doses in the caterpillar during a wide range of
applied concentrations. During metamorphosis the stored compound is
released successively and causes late intoxication. That seems to be
verified by observing relatively low larval toxicity by testing LIN-
DANE whereas the initial pupal mortality rises till 50% and domi-
nates nearly the whole toxic range (Fig. 4). In contrast PARATHION
is more toxic to the larvae. The pupal mortality generally does not
exceed 30%.

Sensitivity of beneficials and pest: LINDANE

The distinctly higher LINDANE sensitivity of the beneficials compared to the pest can be explained by the greater accumulation of
the chemical in the food chain "Brassica - Pieris-host - endoparasite" in relation to the chain "Brassica - Pieris (nonparasitized)"
(HOFFMANN 1984). The reason for the enrichment in nonparasitized
Pieris can be explained by accumulation in the fatbody of the caterpillar. However such a (voluminous) fatbody is lacking in Pieris-
larvae which are parasitized by Apanteles-larvae (FÜHRER and KEJA,
1976). The evident enrichment of LINDANE in the parasitized Pieris-
larvae and further in Apanteles can be attributed to the endoparasitic larvae taking over the functional role of the lacking fatbody, especially during the fifth instar of the host. In additional
experiments it could be shown that the amount of ^{14}C-LINDANE taken
up by parasitized Pieris-larvae is of the same magnitude as in nonparasitized Pieris-larvae. Subsequently three quarters of LINDANE
quantity are located in the Apanteles-larvae when leaving the host!
This underlines the fatbody function of the endoparasite Apanteles
within the host. Corresponding to the relatively low biomass of the
endoparasites the much higher LINDANE concentration in the beneficial organism in comparison to the nonparasitized caterpillar is
evident.

The unexpected similar LINDANE sensitivity of Apanteles and Pteromalus, parasitizing different host stages, must be seen as a result
of the comparable high residual burden of both host-parasite comple-

xes ultimately understandable in consideration of the total transfer of the compound from Pieris larva to pupa (HOFFMANN 1984). Furthermore the range of increasing LINDANE toxicity relating to Pteromalus is very small in contrast to that of Apanteles.

Sensitivity of beneficials and pest: PARATHION

Similar toxicities of PARATHION for Pieris and Apanteles, showed
by nearly identical EC50-values, correspond to the lacking storage
behaviour of the compound in the tested pest and beneficial organisms (HOFFMANN 1984). Obviously toxical effects are caused mainly
in connexion with the passing processes (incorporation, metabolization and excretion) of the compound in pest or host larva respectively, and ultimately depends on the whole quantity of the chemical
chronically applied. This is different in the case of Pteromalus
showing a higher EC50-value (lower toxicity) of the chemical compared with Apanteles and Pieris (Fig. 3). As a result of metabolism
and excretion of PARATHION by Pieris larva (HOFFMANN 1984), Pteromalus is affected only by PARATHION (or metabolites) residues stored
in low concentration in host pupa. Different to Apanteles the pupal
parasite is not influenced by the daily administered chemical.

ECOTOXICOLOGICAL ASSESSMENT

The dissimilar hostphysiological properties of larval and pupal
stages of Pieris suggest contrary host-endoparasite systems, which
in the one case confront the beneficial organism from the beginning
with the total amount of the applicated chemical (Apanteles) and in
the other case much later, when the uptake of the chemical has fi-
nished and parts of the chemical were excreted and metabolized (Pteromalus). Using both systems might be of great interest (importance)
for the realistic assessment of the toxic risks of pesticides for
beneficial organisms. In addition selective properties dependent
on structural characteristics might be elucidated, helpful for further developments in integrated pest management.

The ecochemical and toxicological results pointed out demonstrate
undesirable enrichment of LINDANE combined with chronic toxical effects on the test beneficials. The ecotoxicological valuation of
the chronic toxicity results give a clear preference to PARATHION,

because of the fast metabolization and excretion as well as the absence of detectable chronic effects on the tested beneficial insects by concentrations little below the EC50. Therefore PARATHION rather than LINDANE might enable pests and beneficials to survive and restore a population below the economic threshold if the usage of a non-selective compound would be indispensable.

ACKNOWLEDGEMENT

The financial support of the Deutsche Forschungsgemeinschaft (DFG) is gratefully acknowledged.

REFERENCES

DAVID, W.A.L. (1957): Breeding Pieris brassicae L. and Apanteles glomeratus L. as experimental insects.- Z. Pflkrankh., Pflsch. 64, 572-577

DAVID, W.A.L. and B.O.C. GARDINER (1952): Laboratory breeding of Pieris brassicae L. and Apanteles glomeratus L.- Proc. R. Ent. Soc. Lond. 27, 54-56

FELTWELL, J. (1982): Large white butterfly. The biology, biochemistry and physiology of Pieris brassicae L.- Dr. W. Junk Publishers, The Hague, Boston, London

FINNEY, D.J. (1971): Probit analysis.- Cambridge: University Press, 3. ed., 333 pp.

FÜHRER, E. and T.D. KEJA (1976): Physiologische Wechselbeziehungen zwischen Pieris brassicae L. und dem Endoparasiten Apanteles glomeratus L. Der Einfluß der Parasitierung auf Wachstum und Körpergewicht des Wirtes.- Ent. exp. & app. 19, 287-300

HASSAN, S.A., F. BIGLER, H. BOGENSCHÜTZ, E. BOLLER, J. BRUN, P. CHIVERTON, P. EDWARDS, F. MANSOUR, E. NATON, P.A. OOMEN, W.P.J. OVERMEER, L. POLGAR, W. RIECKMANN, L. SAMSOE-PETERSEN, A. STÄUBLI, G. STERK, K. TAVARES, J.J. TUSET, G. VIGGIANI and A.G. VIVAS (1988): Results of the fourth joint pesticide testing programme carried out by the IOBC/WPRS-Working Group "Pesticides and Beneficial Organisms".- J. Appl. Ent. 105, 321-329

HOFFMANN, E. (1984): Untersuchungen zum ^{14}C-Pestizid-Transfer beim Schädlings-Nützlings-Paar Pieris brassicae L. und Apanteles glomeratus L.- Wiss. Hausarbeit, Fachbereich Biologie der Freien Universität Berlin, 105 pp.

HOFFMANN, E. und I.SCHUPHAN, (1986): Ökochemisches Verhalten und ökotoxikologische Wirkung von Lindan, Parathion, Monolinuron und Hexachlorbenzol nach chronischer Aufnahme im Schädlings-Nützlings-paar Großer Kohlweißling (Pieris brassicae L.) und Kohlweißlings-Brackwespe (Apanteles glomeratus L.).- J. Appl. Ent. 102, 154-164

JUNNIKKALA, E. (1966): Effect of braconid parasitization on the nitrogen metabolism of Pieris brassicae L.- Ann. Acad. Sci. Fenn., Ser. A, IV. Biologica 100, 1-83

SCHÄRER, E. (1983): Entwicklung und Erprobung eines terrestrischen Modell-Ökosystems bestehend aus einer Vegetationskammer und einem Agrarökosystem-Modellausschnitt für quantitative ökochemische Verhaltensstudien von Umweltchemikalien.- Mitt. Biol. Bundesanst. Land-Forstwirtsch. Berlin-Dahlem, H. 215, 171

WOLF-ROSKOSCH, F. (1989): Entwicklung eines Testmodells zur Prüfung der Nahrungsketten-Toxizität von Pflanzenschutzmitteln an Parasitoiden im Laboratorium.- Dissertation, Freie Universität Berlin

WOLF-ROSKOSCH, F. und I. SCHUPHAN (1986): Entwicklung von Testmodellen zur Erfassung nahrungskettenbedingter Pflanzenschutzmitteleinflüsse auf endoparasitische Nutzarthropoden während der Larvalentwicklung.- Mitt. Biol. Bundesanst. Land-Forstwirtsch. Berlin-Dahlem, H. 232, 307

© 1990 Elsevier Science Publishers B.V. (Biomedical Division)
Pesticides and alternatives, editor J.E. Casida

INTEGRATION OF CHEMICAL AND BIOLOGICAL METHODS FOR MOSQUITO AND FILTH FLY
CONTROL

RICHARD C. AXTELL

North Carolina State University, Raleigh, NC 27695-7613, USA

INTRODUCTION

The interrelationships of mosquitoes and filth flies with humans, livestock
and the environment present challenges to designing and executing control
programs for those arthropod pests and disease-vectors worldwide. Filth flies
refers to the house fly and other related muscoid flies breeding in animal
manure and other organic wastes. The densities of these pest populations are
significantly affected by human activities involving altering the environment,
producing livestock and poultry in high density confined systems, and the
handling and disposal of organic wastes.

Control of these pests is not a simple process. Different species with
unique biological traits are involved and there are regional and climate
differences. Control is further complicated by the shift of human populations
into semirural areas in proximity to animal production facilities of increasing
complexities. It is more and more apparent that control of mosquitoes and filth
flies requires a management approach utilizing an integration of chemical and
biological agents with cultural methods (1, 2). Among the factors fostering
this realization are: (1) shortage of new effective insecticides and/or
application methods, (2) development of resistance to insecticides, (3) problems
with insecticide residues in animal tissues and the environment, (4) changes in
animal production to high density, confined systems which create severe manure
disposal problems and associated high pest populations, (5) the encroachment of
people into agricultural areas, and (6) greater awareness of ecology and the
environment. In this context, greater use of biological control agents is
inevitable, but these agents must be meshed with chemical control which will
continue to be of importance.

Of particular significance is the realization that mosquitoes and filth flies
can not be eradicated and that it is necessary to maintain suppression measures
in an integrated pest management (IPM) program designed to keep these pest
populations at acceptable low levels. The concept of IPM in relation to
mosquito control and to livestock production has been discussed and diagrams
provided to illustrate the interrelationships (1-3, 6). Recent reviews of the

biological control of mosquitoes (11, 26) and filth flies (36) provide extensive lists of references. Further references on the impact of agriculture and associated waste management on mosquito populations are provided in refs. 33, 39, and 40. For an illustrated presentation on filth fly management and references see ref. 5.

Progress in the integration of chemical and biological methods for mosquito and filth fly control is illustrated by two examples from our research on integrated control at North Carolina State University. These examples are: (1) the potential use of the fungal pathogen, *Lagenidium giganteum* (Oomycetes, Lagenidiales) for mosquito control and (2) the use of parasites and predators for control of the house fly, *Musca domestica* (Diptera, Muscidae) in poultry production facilities.

MOSQUITO CONTROL

The aquatic fungus, *Lagenidium giganteum*, produces swimming zoospores (and oospores which in turn produce zoospores) which readily attach to mosquito larvae, invade the haemocel, and the proliferating mycelia rapidly kill the larvae. In the asexual cycle, sporangia develop and produce vesicles, each yielding 12-15 zoospores which infect other mosquito larvae and repeat the cycle. In the sexual cycle, oospores are produced and germinate asynchronously, even after years of dry storage, to produce zoospores to infect more larvae. Consequently, the fungus may persist in a suitable habitat for months or even years and cycles of epizootics result. The life cycle has been elucidated (10) and the complexities of oosporogenesis and germination investigated but many questions remain unresolved (22, 23, 25). The fungus is specific to mosquito larvae (and some closely related Chaoboridae) and has a high level of safety since it is nontoxic to mammals, birds and plant life (24, 41). An application for registration of *L. giganteum* for mosquito control has been made to the U. S. Environmental Protection Agency (EPA) by the State of California. The World Health Organization (WHO) has ranked *L. giganteum* as the most promising fungus for mosquito control and is supporting research on it.

Problems exist in the practical use of this biocontrol agent. The fact that the fungus may persist in a habitat for long periods is attractive (18, 19). In practice, however, it is likely to be erratic in the degree of persistence and supplemental chemical control would be required. Changing water quality and temperature can be significant factors affecting fungal survival. The fungus

does not tolerate very much organic pollution with, for example, lack of
survival in water with the COD (chemical oxygen demand) much above 150 mg/l or
salinity above ca. 0.5 ppt (20, 27, 30). The fungus may be adversely affected
by insecticides applied to the water specifically for mosquito control, or other
pesticides in the water as a result of contamination from nearby agricultural
activities.

The impact of selected pesticides on two isolates of the fungus have been
demonstrated (31). The zoospore production in both isolates was less tolerant
than mycelial growth to most of the pesticides tested. The most toxic
pesticides to one or both isolates were captan, gamma-BHC, DDT, toxaphene,
chlorpyrifos, and fenthion. Those pesticides produced at least 10% inhibition
of mycelial growth rate or completely inhibited zoospore production at
concentrations below 5 parts per million (ppm). The least toxic pesticides
(causing less than 10% mycelial inhibition and no inhibition of zoospore
production at concentration greater that 50 ppm) were diflubenzuron, permethrin,
temephos, and propoxur. Pesticides of intermediate toxicity were malathion,
carbaryl, methoprene, alachlor and atrazine. The two isolates differed
substantially in their tolerance of malathion, chlorpyrifos, toxaphene,
carbaryl, propoxur, permethrin, and methoprene. At the rates of application
commonly used for control of mosquito larvae, methoprene, fenthion, malathion,
and temephos would probably be compatible with both isolates of *L. giganteum*.
Field studies are needed to confirm compatibilities, however. These results
suggest that it should be feasible to use combinations of the biocontrol agent
and insecticides or insect growth regulators (IGRs) in an integrated mosquito
control program.

The use of the bacterial agents *Bacillus thuringiensis israelensis* (*Bti*) and
B. sphaericus for control of mosquito larvae is likely to increase with the
introduction of new isolates and genetically engineered forms. *Bti* is widely
used for mosquito control and *B. sphaericus* is on the verge of being marketed.
With proper timing of applications, those agents can be compatible with *L.
giganteum* in the habitat. We have found that, if the mosquito larvae survives
for sufficient time, the fungus can proliferate in the larvae infected with
bacteria and the cadavers will become a source of fungal innoculum. Thus,
bacterial and fungal agents can be compatible. To use these agents, along with
selected chemicals as needed, in an integrated mosquito control program will
require sophisticated mosquito population monitoring and timing of applications.

Improvements in the production and formulation of *L. giganteum* will enhance its potential use in an integrated control program. Production of the asexual stages of the fungus in simple, inexpensive media is possible and we use a water extract of sunflower seeds (SFE) for both liquid and solid (agar) culture (17, 21). Other natural products could be used. The storageability and effective life of the fungus is enhanced by encapsulating the fungal presporangia in calcium alginate. With these alginate beads we have obtained prolonged release of zoospores and infection of mosquito larvae for up to 15 days after applying to the habitat even after the beads have been stored for 2 or 3 months (9, 37). In contrast, fungus from the cultures when directly applied to the habitat will produce zoospores for only up to 24 hours. Thus, formulation of this biocontrol agent presents potential for enhancing its persistence and making it more practical to use it in combination with chemical agents in a control program.

This example of research in progress with *L. giganteum* illustrates the potential for integration of one or more biological agents with chemical agents for mosquito control. It illustrates that combinations of methods should be feasible and beneficial. Since the characteristics of the aquatic habitat will vary greatly, the integrated approach will fit some situations and not be feasible in others. Where the integrated approach can be used, this should lengthen the duration of acceptable control resulting from initial treatments, reduce overall costs of control, and reduce the rate of resistance development to chemicals by the mosquitoes.

An integration of biological and chemical methods will require a high level of monitoring of the water quality of the habitat and the mosquito population together with the ability to predict trends. This will be necessary to properly decide what, if any, biological agent and/or chemical should be introduced and the timing of those applications. Computer simulation models of mosquito-pathogen population dynamics are being developed to facilitate such an integration of control methods.

HOUSE FLY CONTROL

Hymenopterous (Pteromalidae) parasites, mites (Macrochelidae, Uropodidae and Parasitidae) and beetles (Histeridae) are major natural enemies of house flies developing in animal manure, especially in poultry houses (4, 5, 7). These biocontrol agents attack other muscoid flies as well as the house fly. Together they significantly suppress house fly populations and, therefore, it is vital to integrate them with chemicals in an integrated fly control program. The most research has been in poultry production systems, mainly caged-layer houses where house flies are a major problem.

The most common parasites are species of the genera *Muscidifurax* and *Spalangia* (38). All of the species have essentially the same life cycle and similar rates of development. The female oviposits through the puparium and deposits an egg on the surface of the fly pupae where the parasite develops through three instars, pupates and cuts a hole in the puparium to emerge as an adult after 2-4 weeks. There is usually only one parasite produced from a fly pupae. However, the parent parasite destroys additional fly pupae by probing with the ovipositor and feeding on exudate. These parasites are able to search in relatively dry manure and locate the fly pupae at various depths, depending on the parasite species. The ovipositing female, by mechanisms that are not understood, is able to detect a previously parasitized fly pupae and there is very little superparasitism.

The predaceous mites in poultry manure are most commonly *Macrocheles muscaedomesticae* (Macrochelidae), *Fuscuropoda vegetans* (Uropodidae) and, to a lesser extent, *Poecilochirus monospinosis* (Parasitidae) which has been investigated very little compared to the other species (4, 7, 12, 15, 42). These mites prey on the eggs and/or larvae (first instar) of the house fly and are found in the upper portions and on the surface of the poultry manure where those stages of the fly are most common. The adult female macrochelid is phoretic on the adult fly and is thereby distributed to new microhabitats. The uropodids are phoretic as specialized deutonymphs and the parasitids as normal deutonymphs, with both more often attached to beetles than flies. These mites may reach extremely high populations in manure of moderate moisture so that it accumulates in piles. In semi-liquid manure, the mite population can not survive while fly larvae readily develop. The histerid beetle, *Carcinops pumilio*, develops high populations in poultry manure in the absence of excessive moisture, and preys on eggs and larvae (first instar) of the house fly (12, 15). The beetle tends to be distributed slightly deeper in the manure than the mites so there is complimentary rather than competitive predation.

The impact of insecticides used for fly control on the beneficial parasites and predators depends on the selectivity of the chemical and the mode of application. The pteromalid parasites are likely to be susceptible to fly control chemicals used as mists or sprays, although data are limited. Due to the inadequate information on the resting habits of these parasites, the effects of residual surface treatments in poultry houses are unknown. Under confined laboratory test conditions, most residual treatments for fly control are toxic to the parasites. Toxicant-baits formulated specifically for house fly control appear not to be attractive to the parasites, but data are lacking.

In the case of manure-inhabiting predaceous mites and beetles, direct application of insecticides to the manure for control of fly larvae is usually devastating. Larvicides that are effective against house fly larvae are about equally effective against the predator *M. muscaedomesticae* and, although experiments have not been reported, probably also against *C. pumilio* (4, 5, 7). There is one notable exception, cyromazine, which is highly toxic to fly larvae but essentially non-toxic to the macrochelid mites and histerid beetles (8). Thus, it is possible to have selective chemicals although little effort has been directed to identifying such compounds.

Adverse non-target effects on the manure-inhabiting predaceous mites and beetles may be achieved by selective application methods directed against the adult house flies and by avoiding any larviciding. Use of toxicant-baits does not harm the predator population, provided the baits are placed in restricted areas and not allowed to get into the manure. Formulations containing methomyl and muscalure are commonly available, effective, and should not affect the predator population if properly used. Unfortunately, the baits are often scattered in the poultry house with resultant contamination of the manure. Use of coarse sprays for residual applications to only the upper parts of the poultry house can be accomplished with little or no drift onto the manure. Since the house flies tend to rest in the upper parts of the structure at night, this restricted application can be effective. Use of insecticide-disinfectant mixtures for whole house treatment is common but should not be done because the chemicals in a mixture often lose their potency and if effective would have undesirable non-target effects (14). An alternative to spraying is brush-on or "painted" spot treatments of limited amounts of upper surface areas with sugar-toxicant mixtures, such as alfacron. As mentioned previously, data are lacking on the impact of these measures on the parasite population under field conditions.

Further research may reveal other biocontrol agents of value in suppressing house fly populations. Under some conditions the fungus *Entomophthora muscae* is promising (35). Some steinernematid and heterorhabditid nematodes are effective against the house fly in laboratory tests, but are ineffective in the field because the nematodes survive only a short time in poultry manure (13, 34).

The presence of these biological control agents against the house fly must be encouraged and enhanced by habitat manipulation (manure management) and the selective use of chemicals in order to have an integrated fly control program (4). Routine monitoring of the house fly population (e.g., by spot cards or baited jug traps), abundance of predators and parasites, and manure condition is essential to the operation of such a program (28). More data are critically needed on the non-target effects of fly control chemicals and application methods to support this integrated control approach. Computer simulation models of predator, parasite, and house fly population dynamics are being developed (16, 29, 32) as components of a fly management model.

SUMMARY

These examples of incorporation of biological and chemical measures in the control of mosquitoes and filth flies suggest the future path for research and development of control strategies. Integration of these methods will be increasingly necessary to obtain practical, economic, and environmentally acceptable pest control, and to combat the problem of insecticide resistance. More emphasis in pesticide research and development should be placed on evaluating the non-target effects of new chemicals, formulations, and application methods, in order to develop the most effective uses in mosquito and fly IPM programs and thereby extent the useful life of those chemicals in the field. Further development of computer simulation models and their incorporation into expert systems for decision-making is needed to facilitate the planning and execution of integrated biological and chemical control methods.

ACKNOWLEDGEMENTS

Research at NCSU was supported by the North Carolina Agricultural Research Service. Research on fungal agents for mosquito control was supported by NIH Grant AI 20886 and the UNDP/World Bank/WHO Special Programme for Research and Training in Tropical Diseases; filth fly control research was supported by USDA-Cooperative States Research Service Grants 86-CSRS-2-2889 and 89-341-3-4240.

REFERENCES CITED

1. Axtell RC (1979) Mosq News 39:709-718

2. Axtell RC (1981) In: Knapp FW (ed) Systems Approach to Animal Health and Production: A Symposium. Univ Kentucky, Lexington, pp 31-40

3. Axtell RC (1983) Mosq News 43:122-125

4. Axtell RC (1986) Poult Sci 65:657-667

5. Axtell RC (1986) Fly Control in Confined Livestock and Poultry Production. Tech Monogr, Ciba-Geigy Corp, Greensboro, North Carolina, 59 p

6. Axtell RC (1986) Entomol Soc Am Misc Publ 61:1-9

7. Axtell RC, Arends JJ (1990) Annu Rev Entomol 35:101-126

8. Axtell RC, Edwards TD (1983) Poult Sci 62:2371-2377

9. Axtell RC, Guzman DR (1987) J Am Mosq Contr Assoc 3:450-459

10. Brey PT (1985) J Invertebr Pathol 45:276-281

11. Chapman HC, ed (1985) Biological Control of Mosquitoes. Bulletin 6, Am Mosq Contr Assoc, Lake Charles, Louisiana, 218 p

12. Geden CJ, Axtell RC (1988) Environ Entomol 17:735-744

13. Geden CJ, Axtell RC, Brooks WM (1986) J Med Entomol 23:326-332

14. Geden CJ, Edwards TD, Arends JJ, Axtell RC (1987) Poult Sci 66:659-665

15. Geden CJ, Stinner RE, Axtell RC (1988) Environ Entomol 17:320-329

16. Geden CJ, Stinner RE, Kramer DA, Axtell RC (1989) Environ Entomol 19:in press

17. Guzman DR, Axtell RC (1986) J Am Mosq Contr Assoc 2:196-200

18. Guzman DR, Axtell RC (1987) J Am Mosq Contr Assoc 3:211-218

19. Guzman DR, Axtell RC (1987) J Am Mosq Contr Assoc 3:442-449

20. Jaronski ST, Axtell RC (1982) J Med Entomol 19:255-262

21. Jaronski ST, Axtell RC (1984) Mosq News 44:377-381

22. Kerwin JL, Washino RK (1986) Can J Microbiol 32:294-300

23. Kerwin JL, Washino RK (1987) J Am Mosq Contr Assoc 3:59-64

24. Kerwin JL, Dritz DA, Washino RK (1988) J Econ Entomol 81:158-171

25. Kerwin JL, Simmonds CA, Washino RK (1986) J Invertebr Pathol 47:258-270

26. Lacy LA, Undeen AH (1986) Annu Rev Entomol 31:265-296

27. Lord JC, Roberts DA (1985) J Invertebr Pathol 45:331-338

28. Lysyk TJ, Axtell RC (1986) J Econ Entomol 79:144-151

29. Lysyk TJ, Axtell RC (1987) Can Entomol 119:427-437

30. Merriam TL, Axtell RC (1982) J Med Entomol 19:388-393

31. Merriam TL, Axtell RC (1983) Environ Entomol 12:515-521

32. Mann JA, Axtell RC, Stinner RE (1990) Med Vet Entomol 4:in press

33. Mulla MS, Mian LS, Gratz NG (1987) J Agric Entomol 4:97-131

34. Mullens BA, Meyer JA, Georgis R (1987) J Econ Entomol 15:56-60

35. Mullens BA, Rodriquez JL, Meyer JA (1987) Hilgardia 55:1-41

36. Patterson RS, Rutz DA, eds (1986) Entomol Soc Am Misc Publ 61:1-174

37. Patel KJ, Rueda LM, Axtell RC (1990) J. Am Mosq Contr Assoc 5:in press

38. Rueda RM, Axtell RC (1985) Tech Bull 278, North Carolina Agric Res Serv. Raleigh, 88 p

39. Rutz DA, Axtell RC (1978) Tech Bull 256, North Carolina Agric Expt Sta, Raleigh, 32 p

40. Rutz DA, Edwards TD, Axtell RC (1980) Mosq News 340:403-409

41. Siegel JP, Shadduck JA (1987) J Econ Entomol 80:994-997

42. Wise GU, Hennessey MK, Axtell RC (1988) Ann Entomol Soc Am 81:209-224

© 1990 Elsevier Science Publishers B.V. (Biomedical Division)
Pesticides and alternatives, editor J.E. Casida

COMPARATIVE STUDY OF A MASS TRAPPING METHOD AND VARIOUS BAIT
SPRAYS FOR THE CONTROL OF THE OLIVE FRUIT FLY – FIRST YEAR
RESULTS

T. BROUMAS, G. HANIOTAKIS, C. YAMVRIAS, and G. STAVRAKIS
Benaki Phytopathol. Instit., Kifissia, 14561 Athens, Greece

INTRODUCTION

Control of the olive fruit fly, <u>Dacus</u> <u>oleae</u> (Gmelin) in Greece
is based today on the use of organophosphorus insecticide either
in bait or cover sprays. During the last few years the most common method used is the application from the air of very low volume bait sprays (10 litters of bait per Hectare) due to its low
application cost. The constant use of such wide spectrum insecticides over extended areas, has caused serious side effects and
stimulated extensive research toward the development of alternative control methods. The development of an effective and specific trap which could be used for the control of this pest has
been given special consideration. Scientists in Greece and other
Mediterranean countries have devoted a considerable amount of
their effort to this goal (Allen, 1976; Broumas et al., 1983,
1986, 1987; Cirio et al., 1979; Delrio, 1982; Economopoulos,
1979, 1986; Hameiri, 1971; Haniotakis 1986; Haniotakis et al.
1982, 1986; Zervas, 1986). In these efforts a variety of traps
based on one or more of the available olive fly attractants (sex,
food, and visual), have been used. Comparative studies have
shown that the combination of food attractants and pheromones in
the same trap is the best for control purposes in regard both to
efficacy and environmental safety (Haniotakis, 1987, and unpublished data). A method of mass trapping based on such a trap has
been developed and is being gradually introduced into actual practice. In a continuing effort to improve the efficacy of this
method various formulations of food attractants and pheromones
are being tested. In the present tests the efficacy of traps
utilizing food attractants and pheromones in liquid form was tested and compared with the efficacy of sprays with three different baits.

MATERIALS AND METHODS

The tests were conducted during 1988 in two locations i.e. at

Mazi and Tanagra both of the Viotia district. The olive trees in both locations were of medium size of a large fruit variety (megaritiki) grown for oil production. Fruit load during 1988 was medium to full. In each location the following treatments were tested:

1. Mazi:

a) Mass trapping – Traps were plywood boards 15 X 20 X 0.4 cm dipped for 30 min. in a water solution containing deltamethrin (decis 0.25%) 0.1% a.i., sugar 10% as phagostimulant, and glycerine 10% as hygroscopic substance. Half of the traps were baited with a food attractant (dacona, Phytophyl, Athens, Greece), 10% water solution in 500 cc plastic bottles with two 3 mm holes in the lid. The other half were baited with the same food attractant dispenser plus a dispenser (Vioryl S.A. Athens Greece) containing 50 mg of a mixture of two pheromones, i.e. one male sex attractant and a female aggregation pheromone with additional arrestant and aphrodisiac properties. Traps were installed on June 23 at a density of one per tree, alternately in regard to the type of bait. All traps and the containers of food attractants were replaced on August 23. The new containers had a 2.5 cm opening for higher evaporation rates.

b) Bait sprays with bait containing insecticide, and food attractant (dacona)

c) Bait sprays with bait containing insecticide, food attractant (entomella, Phytophyl, Athens, Greece), and pheromones (polycore, Biological Control Systems LTD, U.K.).

d) Bait sprays with bait containing insecticide and pheromones (polycore).

In all bait sprays the insecticide fenthion (lebaycid E.C. 50%) was used at a concentration of 0.3% a. i. Both types of food attractants were used at a concentration of 2%, and polycore 40 mg per tree.

Sprays, 400 cc of bait per tree, were applied from the ground with a hand operated sprayer.

The completely randomized design was applied with three replicates per treatment. Each replicate consisted of a block of approx 350 olive trees. All olive trees of the area (approx. 4.000) were used in the test except about 400 trees which were at a distance of about 1 km from the main orchard.

The evaluation of the methods compared in these tests was based on adult pest population density records during the experimental period, on fruit infestation levels, and on the number of spray applications which were required in order to keep fruit infestation below economic threshold levels.

Adult population density was measured through a network of four McPhail Traps per experimental block checked every 5 days. McPhail traps were baited with a 2% ammonium sulfate solution which was renewed at every check.

In the mass trapping blocks, 8 sticky traps (plywood rectangles as above coated with adhesive), 4 of each attractant type, were also placed per block, in addition to the McPhail traps, for an estimation of the number of adult flies killed by the insecticide treated traps.

Fruit infestation levels were measured 4 times during the experimental period i.e. on August 1, September 25, October 20, and November 12. At each sampling date fruit samples, 40 – 50 per tree, were collected at random from 10 trees, properly marked for this purpose, per experimental block.

2. Tanagra:

a) Mass trapping as described above but only one orchard with approx. 700 trees was used as one block. In this orchard the mass trapping method has been applied continuously during the last five years in order to compare its effectiveness with that of aerial bait sprays but mainly in order to study its long term effects on the agroecosystem. The traps were placed on July 4. The orchard where the mass trapping method was applied is isolated from all sides except South in which direction the closest olive orchard was at a distance of about 500 m.

b) Bait sprays applied from the air with bait containing insecticide and food attractant as above. The air sprays were applied in an area of about 50.000 olive trees by the special service for olive protection of the Ministry of Agriculture.

Pest population densities were measured here through a network of 10 McPhail traps in the mass trapping orchard and 40 such traps in the air sprayed orchard. Traps in both orchards were checked every 5 days. Fruit infestation levels were measured 3 times in the mass trapping orchard, i.e. on September 15, October 20, and November 9, and two times in the sprayed orchard, i.e. on October 20, and November 9. Samples of 50 – 100 fruit per tree were collected from 10 – 15 marked trees per treatment at each sampling date.

208

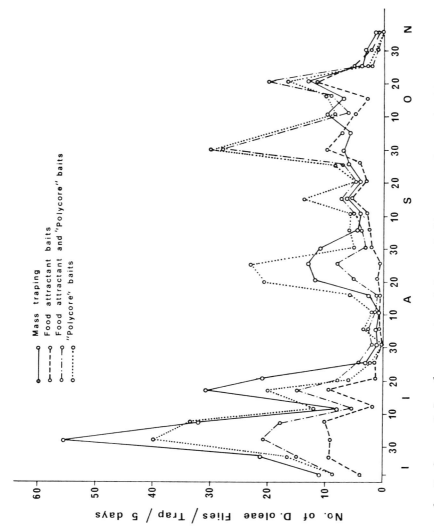

Fig. 1. Numbers of *D. oleae* captured in McPhail traps placed inside orchards protected by mass trapping and various bait sprays. Means of 12 traps. Mazi, 1988.

209

Three bait sprays were applied in the sprayed orchard on July 7, September 13, and October 21. No sprays were applied in the mass trapping orchard. The amount of bait used per spray was 10 liters per hectare which contained 90 g a.i. of fenthion (lebaycid 50% E C), and 600 g of food attractant (dacona).

RESULTS AND DISCUSSION
Mazi

Fig. 1 shows population fluctuations of D. oleae in the various treatments throughout the experimental period based on McPhail trap catches. Population fluctuations were great even between blocks of the same treatment. This resulted in the need to apply different numbers of sprays in different blocks. Spray applications were decided on the basis of pest population levels in combination with other parameters such as fruit infestation levels, the insect stage inside the fruit, and adult female physiological stage. Thus the average number of sprays applied per treatment was as follows: Mass trapping 0.3 (only one block was sprayed on July 30); food bait sprays 2; food and sex bait sprays 3; and sex bait sprays 2.7.

Table 1. shows fruit infestation levels in the various treatments.

Although no significant differences were observed between treatments the trends indicate that baits containing polycore not only did not improve the effectiveness of the sprays, which was the aim of its addition, but had negative results. It should be pointed out, however, that in the case of food and polycore bait the first application on July 5, which is considered critical for subsequent population suppression, had limited effect because dacona, the food attractant used, was reacting with the polycore to form a precipitate which was interfering with the performance of sprayers. In subsequent sprays the food attractant entomella was used, which dos not react with the polycore It should be emphasized also that the 400 tree olive orchard which was at a distance of about 1 km from the experimental orchard and in which only one bait spray with food attractant and insecticide was applied at the beginning of October, the fruit infestation level was 59.7 ± 16.1. This infestation level was obtained from a fruit sample collected from 10 trees with 100 – 150 fruit collected at random per tree.

TABLE 1. Percent fruit infestation by D. oleae in orchards protected by: Mass trapping (MT), sprays with food attractant baits (FBS), sprays with food attractant and pheromone baits (F+PHBS), and sprays with pheromone baits (PHBS). Means of 3 replicates. Mazi, 1988.

Sampling Date	MT[1]	FBS[2]	F+PHBS[3]	PHBS[4]
Aug. 1	0.50[5]	0.40	1.30	1.00
Sept.25	2.00	0,70	2.30	1,80
Oct. 20	9.30	6.20	12.30	18.80
Nov. 12	5.40	7.80	12.90	14.40

1. Application of an average of 0.3 supplementary baite sprays
2. " " 2.0 " " "
3. " " 3.0 " " "
4. " " 2.7 " " "
5. No significant differences were found between treatments for each sampling date, Duncan's Multiple Range Test, P = 95

Table 2. shows the numbers of D. oleae flies captured per trap per 5 days in the two types of sticky traps used for mass trapping i.e. traps baited with food attractant and traps baited with food attractant and pheromones, as well as in McPhail traps during various time intervals characterized by differences in environmental conditions, mainly ambient temperatures and R.H. levels, which are known to effect trap efficacy.

During the period of high temperatures and low R.H. (July – September) McPhail traps caught more flies of both sexes than sticky traps. Haniotakis, Fitsakis and Papadimitrakis (unpublished data) have found similar results which were due to low evaporation rates of food attractant dispensers used in sticky traps (plastic bags containing ammonium bicarbonate salt) and that the efficacy of these traps can be enhanced by using a different formulation of food attractant with higher evaporation rates. During the same period, food attractant containers had two small holes which propably did not allow optimal evaporation rates and pheromone dispensers have limited effectiveness due to reduced

TABLE 2. Number of Dacus oleae flies captured per trap per 5 days in McPhail traps, sticky traps baited with food attractant, and sticky traps baited with food attractant and pheromones all of which were located in mass trapping blocks. Means of 4 replicates. Mazi, 1988.

Number of flies captured by

Period	Block Number	McPhail Traps			Food Attractant			Food Attract. & Pher.		
		Males	Females	Total	Males	Females	Total	Males	Females	Total
June 28 – Sep. 16	1	1.3	0.9	2.2	0.4	0.1	0.5	1.1	0.2	1.3
	2	2.9	2.0	4.9	0.5	0.2	0.7	1.0	0.3	1.3
	3	20.4	12.7	33.1	1.1	0.8	1.9	1.6	0.8	2.4
	Total	24.6	15.6	40.2	2.0	1.1	3.1	3.7	1.3	5.0
Sept.17 – Nov. 9	1	3.9	3.3	7.2	1.8	1.9	3.7	12.7	2.3	15.0
	2	2.8	2.2	5.0	2.0	1.2	3.2	5.9	1.6	7.5
	3	5.3	3.6	8.9	8.9	6.6	15.5	17.6	7.5	25.1
	Total	12.0	9.1	21.1	12.7	9.6	22.4	36.2	11.4	47.6

sex activity of the insect. During the period of lower temperatures and higher R.H. (September – November) sticky traps with
food attractant caught about the same numbers of flies as McPhail
traps while sticky traps with food attractants and pheromones
caught more flies. The improvement of the performance of the
food plus pheromone trap during this period must be attributed to
the presence of pheromones and to maximum sex activity of the
insect (Haniotakis and Vassiliou – Waite 1987).

2. Tanagra

Fig. 2. shows D. oleae population fluctuations in the trap-
pingand spraying areas throughout the experimental period. Cha-
raclteristic is the substantial drop of fly population which followed every spray in the sprayed orchard and the installation of
traps in the mass trapping orchard. From mid July to mid August,
fly populations were low, which is usually the case in the area
during hot and dry summers. From the end of August to the mid of
September, populations increased mainly in the mass trapping
orchard but did not exceed economic threshold levels. A last
population increase was observed during the month of October,
which was more pronounced this time in the sprayed orchard.

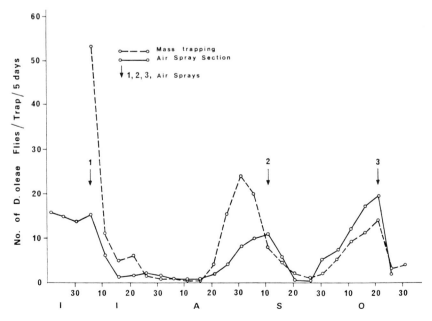

Fig. 2. Numbers of D. oleae captured in McPhail traps placed inside orchards
protected by mass trapping and air bait sprays. Means of 10 and 40
traps respectively. Tanagra, 1988.

Table 3. shows fruit infestation levels both in the mass trapping and sprayed orchards.

TABLE 3. Percent fruit infested by D. oleae in orchards protected by mass trapping and aerial bait sprays. Tanagra 1988.

Sampling Date	Mass trapping	Aerial Bait Sprays[1]
Sept. 9	0.40 + 0.81	—
Oct. 20	6.10 + 3.44	4.60 + 3.68
Nov. 9	13.30 + 7.92	10.80 + 9.35

1. Sprays applied on July 7, Sept. 13, and Oct. 21.

Maximum fruit infestation levels (13.3 in the mass trapping and 10.8 in the sprayed orchards) was observed in the sample collected on November 11. Fruit infestation in samples collected on the same day from the orchard at a distance of about 500 m south of the mass trapping area was found to be 60.1 + 12.6. This high infestation could be attributed to a possible inadequate spraying due to the proximity of this to the village of Tanagra, which pilots try to avoid.

CONCLUSIONS

Taking under consideration the results of these experiments as well as similar ones carried out during the last seven years, the following conclusions can be drawn: Control of the olive fly can be achieved with a mass trapping method combining various semiochemicals and mainly food attractants and pheromones. Crop protection levels are reduced with increasing pest population densities and over certain levels supplementary measures such as bait sprays must be applied. Such supplementary measures are usually required in small areas (hot spots) where environmental conditions favor the development of high insect populations. Continuous application of the mass trapping method in an orchard over a number of years tends to gradually decrease pest population densities to levels which allow a reduction of trap density

without reducing the effectiveness of the method. Gradual increase of beneficial fauna in the mass trapping orchards has also
been observed (Michelakis, unpublished data).

ACKNOWLEDGEMENTS

The authors would like to thank the agronomists, P. Mavroudis
for substantial technical assistance, and V. Ziogas and A. Ioan-
nou for their assistance in administrative matters.

REFERENCES

1. Allen WW (1976) Insecticide treated yellow boards for con-
    trol of Dacus oleae (Gmel.) In: UNDP/SF/FAO Project GR:60-
    525 Report on chemical control investigation 52 pp 1976

2. Broumas T, Liaropoulos C, Katsoyannos P, Yamvrias C, Hanio-
    takis G, Strong F (1983) Control of the olive fruit fly in a
    pest management trial in olive culture. Proc. International
    Symposium of the CEC/IOBC on fruit flies of economic impor-
    tance, Athens 16-19 Nov 1982 (Cavalloro R, ed), AA Balkema,
    Rotterdam, pp 585-592

3. Broumas T, Haniotakis G, Liaropoulos C, Yamvrias C (1986)
    Experiments on the control of the olive fruit fly by mass
    trapping. Proc. International Joint Meeting on integrated
    pest control in olive groves, Pisa, Italy 3-6 Apr 1984
    (Cavalloro R, Grovetti A, eds) pp 411-419

4. Broumas T, Haniotakis G (1987) Further studies on the con-
    trol of the olive fruit fly by mass trapping. Proc. II In-
    tern Sympos on fruit flies, Crete Sept 1986 pp 561-565

5. Cirio V, Vitta G, Gentili PA, Cecchini G (1979) Confront fra
    cinque tipi di trappale cromotrapiche per la cattura degli
    adulti di Dacus oleae Gmel. Publicazione 587 della Divisione
    RAD/APPL Lab Valor Colt Indust NEN CSH, Caraccia, Roma,
    Italia pp 230-242

6. Delrio G (1982) Esperienze di lotta integrata in olivicol-
    tura in Sardegna. Proc. l'etat d'avancement des travaaux et
    echange d'informations sur les problemes poses par la lutte

integrees en oleiculture, Antibes 4-6 Nov 1981, INRA, France pp 73-85

7.   Economopoulos A (1979) Application of color traps for Dacus oleae control. Proc. International Symposium of IOBC/WPRS on Integrated Control in Agriculture and Forestry, Vienna 8-12 Oct 1979 pp 552-559

8.   Economopoulos A, Raptis A, Stavropoulos A (1986) Control of Dacus oleae by yellow sticky traps combined with ammonium acetate slow-release dispensers. Entomol Exp Appl 41:11-16

9.   Hameiri Y (1971) Color traps for the trapping of the olive fruit fly. Report to the Israeli Ministry of Agriculture, 7 pp

10. Haniotakis GE (1986) Control of the olive fruit fly, Dacus oleae by mass trapping: present status - prospects. OEPP/EPPD Bulletin 16 pp 395-492

11. Haniotakis GE, Kozyrakis E, Bonatsos C (1986) Control of the olive fruit fly, Dacus oleae Gmel. (Dipt. Tephritidae) by mass trapping: pilot scale feasibility study. J Appl Entomol 101:343-352

12. Haniotakis GE, Mazomenos BE, Hardakis IM (1982) Monitoring and control of the olive fruit fly with pheromone traps. Proc. Reunion du Group d'experts de CEC sur l'etat d'avance-ment des travaux et echange d'informations sur les problemes poses par la lutte integree en oleiculture, Antibes 4-6 Nov 1981 INRA France pp 46-60

13. Haniotakis GE, Vassiliou-Waite A (1987) Effect of combining food and sex attractants on the capture of Dacus oleae flies. Entomologia Hellenica 5:27-33

14. Zervas G (1984) Effect of continuous mass trapping on Dacus oleae population suppression. Proc. CEC/IOBC Ad-hoc Meeting on Fruit Flies of Economic Importance, Hamburg 23 Aug 1984 pp 75-80

© 1990 Elsevier Science Publishers B.V. (Biomedical Division)
Pesticides and alternatives, editor J.E. Casida

CONTRIBUTION TOWARD THE DEVELOPMENT OF AN INTEGRATED CONTROL

METHOD FOR THE CORN STALK BORER, Sesamia nonagrioides (Lef.)

JOHN. A. TSITSIPIS

Institute of Biology, "Democritos" National Center for Scientific
Research, P.O. Box 60228, GR-15310 Aghia Paraskevi, Greece*

INTRODUCTION

  The corn stalk borer, Sesamia nonagrioides (Lef.) (Lepidoptera,

Noctuidae) is an important pest of maize in the circummediterranean

countries. The larvae can cause extensive damage to the stalks as

well as to the ears of maize, depending on the year and the planta-

tion time. The insect overwinters as diapausing last larval instar

and the first adults appear, in Greece, from the beginning of March

to the beginning of May for mild and cold areas respectively. The

insect can complete three, and a partial fourth, generations per

year [1]. The population density is very low in the first two gene-

rations. The third generation, however, gives a high and abrupt peak

in the second half of August and the first half of September. The

adult population pattern is different in other south european count-

ries. In France, a high adult density shows in May-June [2], while

in Sardinia high populations appear in June-July and the first part

of August [3]. Mild winters presumably allow high insect survival

and hence high initial insect population. In Greece, the later the

sowing date the higher is the risk for heavy attack. The late corn,

sown after the harvest of wheat, is very susceptible to attack when

the insect has reached high population levels. In certain years,

the crop can be completely destroyed as was the case in Larissa,

Central Greece, in 1982 [4]. Even in early crops, damage can become

significant.
----
* Present address: University of Thessaly, GR-38110 Volos, Greece

The usual ways of controlling the insect has been the use of insecticides. The efficiency of chemical treatments is, however, very often questionable, since timely applications are very important.
The female deposits the egg masses in the interphase between the
leaf collar and the stalk. The young larvae spend 2-5 days in the
area of the egg deposition (Tsitsipis and Thanopoulos, unpublished
data) and than they enter the stalk. It is only, therefore, during
this short period the larvae can be reached by insecticides. Even
for optimal chemical control, adequate knowledge of the biology of
the insect is necessary. The thermal constant for the insect has
been previously calculated to be about 590 day-degrees, for development on an artificail medium, while for maize the respective value
was found to be 617 [5]. Sex pheromone blends have been published
for S. nonagrioides [6,7,8] and they have been proposed for monitoring as well as for possible control by mass-trapping [8]. Infestation of maize by the insect in 1984 in Greece, in certain cases,
was very high reaching 97 % of the plants and 50 % of ears infested,
with a high degree of infestation [9]. High stalk infestation seemed to affect very adversely yields [9]. A program of OP insecticidal applications, in a late crop, timing them according to data of
light trap captures, showed that reasonable protection can be provided by three applications (23 % ear infestation compared to 62.5 %
in the control) [9]. An egg parasitoid, Platytelenomus busseolae
(Gahan) (Hymenoptera, Scelionidae) was found to parasitize S. nonagrioides eggs to levels as high as 28-43 % in the area of Istiaea,
Evoia, in Central Greece [10]. Additionally, a larval parasitoid,
Lydella thompsoni (Herting) (Diptera, Tachinidae), has been reported
in Greece [11], though its role has not been investigated.

The present paper deals with a comparison of adult monitoring by
light and/or pheromone traps, the estimation of yield losses due to

insect attack, the control of the insect by synthetic pyrethroids. Finally, the available information will be discussed in relation to the development of an IPM program for the corn stalk borer.

MATERIAL AND METHODS

Population monitoring of the corn stalk borer was studied in two kinds of traps. The first was a light trap, Pennsylvania type, with a 15 Watt BL tube and the second a plastic pheromone trap (in three replicates), modified "International Pheromones" type (Phytophyl Co. Ltd., 16 Averoff Str., Athens, Greece). In both kinds, a small portion of a plaquette of a slow release formulation of dichlorvos (DDVP), exchanged every month, served as killing agent. The light trap was serviced three times a week and the pheromone traps twice a week. The pheromone traps were charged with 100 µg of a pheromone blend [8], composed of Z-11-hexadecenyl acetate, Z-11-hexadecenal, Z-11-hexadecenol and dodecyl acetate found at a 10:1:1:2 ratio, impregnated on a polypropylene dispenser (antibiotic bottle cap) exchanged once a month.

To study the effect of insect infestation on the crop, artificial infestation, with two ready to hatch egg masses (with about 100 eggs each), was made on plants at 10 different stages of development initiated on June 4th, when the plants had 4-5 leaves, and repeated at weekly intervals. Each plant growth stage represented a different treatment and it received one infestation. There were 27 plants in each treatment and the experiment was set up in a completely randomized block design in the Experimental Field of the Aliartos Agriculture Experimental Station of the Ministry of Agriculture. At harvest time, all plants were evaluated for stalk and ear infestation, expressed as percent of the total infested by the larvae. The seed weight of each ear was also considered.

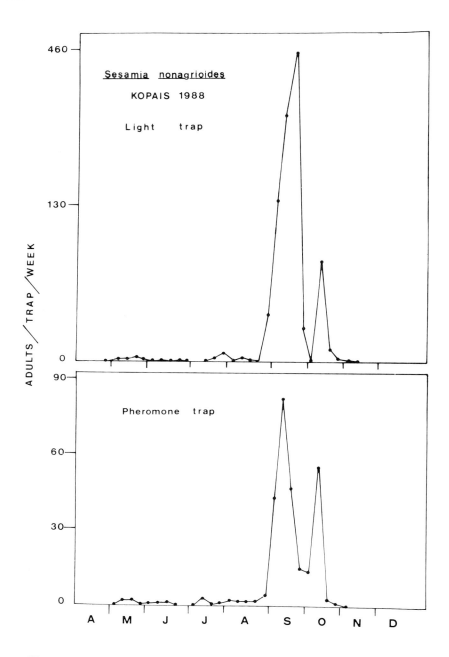

Fig. 1. Adults of *Sesamia nonagrioides* caught in light and pheromone traps in Central Greece (Kopais) in 1988.

An experiment was done to test a spray program with a synthetic pyrethrine (deltamethrine, 2.5 % a.i. in a 70 ml/100 l water solution) against the corn stalk borer in the Experimental Field of the Aliartos Experimental Station of the Ministry of Agriculture. The program included a combination of two to four insecticidal applications at three week intervals. The first spray was done 10 days after the initiation of the abrupt population increase in the first part of August. It was scheduled to follow two days after irrigagation to avoid insecticide washing. The experiment was set up in a completely randomized block design in four blocks. Each treatment included four rows of 25 corn plants in each. The lines were 80 cm apart and the plants were 20 cm fron each other. Only the two median ones were considered for evaluation the other serving as buffer lines. The application was made with a mechanical sprayer and care was given to bathe the plant, especially the stalk, with the spraying solution. The following treatments were applied: two early, two intermediate, two late, three early, three late and four sprays. At harvest, ten plants from each block were examined and the percent stalk and ear infestation as well as the ear seed weight were recorded.

RESULTS

Adults trapped in the area of Kopais, Central Greece, in light and pheromone traps during 1988 are shown in Fig. 1. The trapping period in the former was from the end of April to the beginning of November, while in the pheromone traps it started one week later and ended one week earlier. The pattern of captures was practically similar, the same population density trend followed by the two. However, the maximum values were much higher in the light trap than in the pheromone trap in the first peak that occurred in the second

week of September (cf. 460 to 85, though the latter catch only males). In the second peak, however, the relationship was different
and in favor of the pheromone trap (cf. 90 to 56). Monitoring the
corn stalk borer, for many years, in practically all corn producing
areas in Greece, it has been found [1, 9, 13, 14] that the seasonal
appearance and the population density follow a more or less similar
pattern. During the first two generations (April to July),the population remains at very low levels and then it abruptly rises to very
high values from mid-August to end September with a usually second
peak appearing in October. Very seldom are there, however, occasions of high population levels in the beginning of the trapping season as was the case in Western Peloponnese (Varda) in 1988 (Fig. 2).

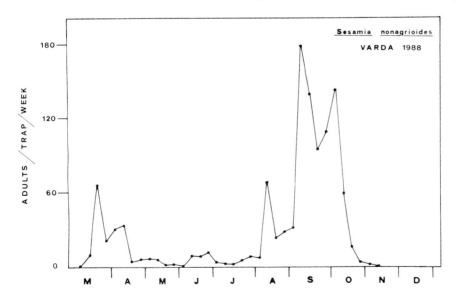

Fig. 2. Males of Sesamia nonagrioides caught in pheromone
traps in W. Peloponnese (Varda) during 1988.

The effect of the insect infestation on the degree of damage to
the stalks, ears and yield in corn is shown in Table I. The results
show that the very young plants suffer high stalk infestation and a
small part of them bear ears. The ear infestation was nil or very

TABLE I.

Relationship between corn growth stage and S. nonagrioides field infestation. A completely randomized block design in 27 blocks. Treatments concerned artificially infested plants by ready to hatch eggs at weekly intervals. First infestation was made on June 4, 1987.

Plant growth stage	% infestation		Plants with ear	Dry seed weight per ear (gr)
	Stalks	Ears		
1. 4-5 leaves	42.6	0	8	82.6
2. 7-9 leaves	25.9	0	17	68.6
3. 7-9 leaves	37.2	4.5	12	66.8
4. 9-10 leaves	55.0	0	2	50.0
5. 1.7 m high	17.5	3.6	14	79.3
6. 2.0 m high	33.5	13.0	11	82.5
7. 2.5 m high	17.5	40.0	19	87.5
8. Flowering	28.8	32.8	16	65.4
9. Milk stage	18.2	16.0	19	80.8
10. End of milk	22.5	36.0	16	95.8
11. Control	4.5	0	19	95.0

low until the 1.70 m high growth stage. Their yield was, however, adversely affected by early infestation indicating an intervention in the plant physiology. The infestation of ears was very high when it occurred one week before flowering and during flowering. During the latter stage, the yield is considerably lowered. Infestation at milk stage and later does not influence yields.

The results of the protection of corn by the spray program are shown in Table II. Two late applications resulted in high ear infestation and low yield. Then, it followed the treatment with two early sprays. Two intermediate ones provided good protection and so did three or four sprays. The data show that two to three applicacations can secure good degree of crop protection. The two sprays should be done, however, early to protect from heavy insect population loads.

DISCUSSION

Comparison of the two kinds of traps showed that they both give

224

TABLE II.

A spray program on late sown corn, variety "ARIS", with deltamethrine against S. nonagrioides. The program included 2-4 applications
beginning August 20 and repeated every 21 days until October 22.
Experiment was done in a completely randomized block design in 4
blocks.

| Treatments | | % infestation | | Dry seed weight per |
		Stalks	Ears	ear (g)
1+2*	(2)	23.7	16.4	176.6
2+3	(2)	8.2	10.9	183.2
3+4	(2)	29.4	56.3	122.9
1+2+3	(3)	6.1	14.1	188.5
2+3+4	(3)	7.0	16.8	176.8
1+2+3+4	(4)	1.8	15.3	185.4
Control	(0)	79.4	68.7	103.2

* Numbers denote spray sequence chronologically: 1= spray done on
   20-8-87, 2= on 10-9-87, 3= on 6-10-87 and 4= on 22-10-87. Numbers in parentheses show the number of applications.

similar population trends of S. nonagrioides. The pheromone trap is
easier to use than the light trap (no electricity required, practically species specific) and it can be used for population monitoring
in an IPM program. The host-plant relationships showed that the
plant growth stage shortly before and at flowering are more sensitive for yield reduction due to insect infestation than before or after those stages. With the normal crop, sown in mid-April, this
stage is reached in July, long before the sharp population increase
of the insect. In formulating a control strategy, when there are no
high populations during this period, and this is usually the case,
no measures are necessary to be taken. If, however, a late crop is
under consideration, flowering falls during the period of population
outbreak and control measures are indispensable. Control tactics
should be also considered when the population, in the beginning of
the flight period, is high. The late crop being vulnerable to heavy
infestation can be protected by a program of two to three insecticidal applications by synthetic pyrethroids. The first application is

timed about 10 days from the initiation of the population increase, as can be monitored by pheromone trapping. The degree of crop protection by synthetic pyrethroids was found to be better than by organophosphates [9].

Integral parts of an IPM program are: population monitoring, temperature-development relationship, insect ecophysiology regarding diapause, host-plant relationships for the development of an insect appearance and risk forecasting model, existence of an insecticidal application program based on population data, role of possible biological control agents and eventually the use of biotechnical methodologies for control. For forecasting, the following information gives material to build the model. Adult population monitoring is possible by pheromone trapping. The thermal constant for development has been found to range between 769 and 836 day-degrees for development in plants (with a developmental threshold temperature of 10.2 °C) [16], under our conditions, a value considerably lower than the one given earlier for France [5]. Part of the larval population, hatching in late June, enters diapause and practically all larvae hatching in the end of August diapause. The form of diapause is an oligopause [2] and it terminates early in the winter (late December to end January) [16]. After the attainment of this physiological stage, day-degrees can start accumulating for larval and pupal development. The first adult occurrence can be predicted and verified by trapping. Depending on the severity of the winter, the first emergences can occur, in mild climate areas, in the end of February and in colder ones in early May. In mild winters, early appearance of adults comes before corn is present and the fate of the short living adults is doomed. Only a small portion of the population can oviposit in alternate, non preferable, hosts such as reeds, Typha sp., when available. Following the winter temperatures, it is pos-

sible, on many occasions, to predict adult emergence and time sowing
accordingly to avoid presence of maize. In very cold winters (temperatures below 6-8 °C), a large part of the population is killed and
the early crop does not encounter any pest problems.

The control strategy can include cultural methods, such as burning
of the crop remnants and plowing after the harvest to kill off large part of the overwintering generation. Two inportant biological
control agents could prove to be of importance. The egg parasitoid
P. busseolae was found in the area of Istiaea and in smaller numbers
in other areas in Greece. It was the first record of the parasitoid
in Europe and it seems it can provide a good density dependant factor for population regulation of S. nonagrioides. High parasitism rates have been recorded (Fig. 3) [10]. It appears it can be

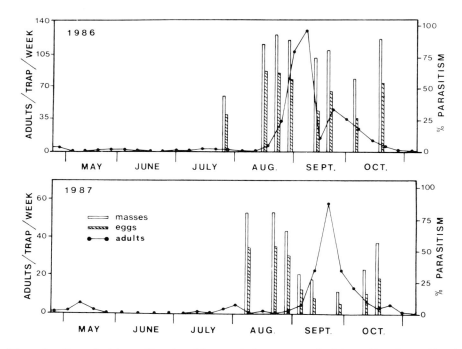

Fig. 3   Population fluctuation of S. nonagrioides (left ordinate,
●————●) and percent parasitism (right ordinate) of its egg masses
(▭) and its eggs (▨) by P. busseolae, in the area of Istiaea
during 1986, 1987 [10].

used in a control program [17, 18; Alexandri and Tsitsipis, unpublished data]. A larval parasite of S. nonagrioides and O. nubilalis, L. thompsoni, has been found in many areas in Greece. A survey recorded the lepidopterous species of the family Noctuidae, Archanara geminipuncta Haworth, Archanara dissoluta Treitschke, Archanara spargani Esper and Nonagria typhae Thunberg, obligatory intermediate hosts of the parasite, attacking hydrobiotope plants such as, Phragmites communis, Typha sp., Sparganium sp. [12], found in many maize agroecosystems [Tsitsipis and Galichet, unpublished data]. In reach biotopes, e.g. the Evros Delta, the populations of the insects were more abundant indicating a high parasite activity (36 % O. nubilalis parasitism) while in poor ones parasitism was low (0.8 % in Larissa, Central Greece). It is possible to increase parasitism by managing the alternative host plants (usually weeds) properly. Finally, the pheromones can be used for control purposes either by applying the mass trapping [8], or the mating disruption technique. The latter probably has better chances for success as has been shown in other lepidoptera. The use of pheromones could become compatible with the use of parasitoids. The eggs that would be deposited by mated females could be parasitized by P. busseolae. The insecticides could be used at the end of the period, after mid-August, if the other two techniques, initiated very early when the pest populations are very low, cannot keep the population at low levels. New insecticides such as chitin synthesis inhibitors, often compatible with parasites, could be tested for efficient borer control.

ACKNOWLEDGEMENTS

    Partial support by the No. 1110 EEC Contract is ackowledged. I thank M. Alexandri, A. Fantinou, R. Thanopoulos, F. Stathopoulos, B.

228

Papadopoulos and B. Demopoulos for assistance.

REFERENCES

1.	Tsitsipis JA, Gliatis A, Mazomenos BE (1984) Med Fac Landbouww Rijksuniv Gent 49:667-674

2.	Galichet PF (1982) Agronomie 2:561-566

3.	Prota R, Cavalloro R (1973) Studi Sassar Ann Fac Univ Sassari 21:407-426

4.	Gliatis A (1983) Rep Hell Min Agr 13pp (mimeo)

5.	Hilal A (1981) Bull OEPP 2:107-112

6.	Sreng I, Maune B, Frérot B (1985) C R Acad Sci III 301:439-442

7.	Rotundo G, Tonini C, Capizzi A, Maini S (1985) Boll Lab Ent Agr Fillipo Silvestri 42:191-206

8.	Mazomenos BE, Vardas D (1988) In: Cavalloro R, Sunderland KD (eds) Integrated Crop Protection in Cereals. Balkema AA, Rotterdam, Brookfield, pp 179-186

9.	Tsitsipis JA (1988) In: Cavalloro R, Sunderland KD (eds) Integrated Crop Protection in Cereals. Balkema AA, Rotterdam, Brookfield, pp 171-177

10.	Alexandri MP, Tsitsipis JA (1990) Entomophaga 35: (in press)

11.	Stavrakis GN (1973) 4th Balkanic Plant Protection Conference, Athens, 24-27 September.

12.	Galichet PF, Riany M, Agounke D (1985) Entomophaga 30:315-328

13.	Tsitsipis JA, Gliatis A, Saltzis B, Stathopoulos F, Mouloudis S, Stefanakis M, Papastefanou S, Christoulas C, Papageorgiou G, Katranis N, Economou D (1990) Proc 1st Panhell Entomol Meet Hell Entomol Soc (In press)

14.	Tsitsipis JA, Alexandri M (1989) Acta Phytopathologica and Entomologica (In press)

15.	Eizaguirre M, Riba M, Rosell A, Guerrero A (1989) In: Current Status of Insect Monitoring and Attractants, Working Group "Use of Pheromones and Other Semiochemicals in Integrated Control". OILB/SROP Bull XII/2 p 40

16.	Thanopoulos R, Tsitsipis JA (1989) Proc 3rd Panhell Entomol Meet Hell Entomol Soc (In press)

17.	Bin F, Johnson NF (1982) In: Les Trichogrammes. Les Colloques de l' INRA No 9:275-287

18.	Bin F, Maini S (1984) In: XVII Internal Congr Entomol, Hambourg, Abstr vol p. 777

© 1990 Elsevier Science Publishers B.V. (Biomedical Division)
Pesticides and alternatives, editor J.E. Casida

A NEW APPROACH TO WHITEFLY CONTROL IN CRETE - GREECE

S. E. MICHELAKIS
Institute of Subtropical Plants and Olive Tree Chania-Crete-Greece

INTRODUCTION

   The greenhouse whitefly Trialeurodes vaporariorum Wests (fam, Aleyrodidae) is
an important pest in many vegetable crops and on ornamentals. Although widespread
in the glasshouses of Europe, it was unknown until recently in Crete where almost
one third of the greenhouses of Greece exist. The whitefly problem appeared for
the first time in Crete in 1978 and has now expanded to all areas of the island
where plastic houses are present (3). For the control of this insect several chemicals (e.g.organophosphorous compounds and synthetic pyrethroids) are used in
many applications which are sometimes repeated every week especially after the
increase of the temperature in spring. To reduce insecticide use, efforts were
made recently to enclose the parasite Encarsia formosa Gaham against this pests.
The aim of this experimental work was to study the possibility of controlling
T. vaporariorum with the combination of biological and biotechnical methods and
with the least use of chemical insecticides in the unheated plastic greenhouses
of Crete.

MATERIALS AND METHODS

   The experiments were carried out in plastic commercial unheated greenhouses of
about 700 m² each and in a glasshouse of about 200 m² heated only during the cold
nights of the winter. The greenhouses were planted with tomatoes during the cultivating periods 1987-88 and 1988-89 and each cultivating period started in Septem-
ber-October and lasted up to May-June of the following year. In the first experiment Vydate (oxamyl 10%) was applied at a dose of 1 gr per plant during the beginning of the cultivation (in November) and later in spring four releases of
E. formosa were made with 2000 individuals in each release at intervals of about
fifteen days. In the second experiment the effectiveness of yellow traps was tested with two installations during autumn and spring. The traps were picnic plates
of 20 cm diameter. These commercial plastic greenhouses were compared to similar
nearby plastic greenhouses with the same vegetable under the same conditions which
received the usual treatments from the grower. The results from the treatments
were estimated by measuring the changes in the whitefly population by counting
directly the adult white flies of the three top leaves from 10% of the plants.
During spring 1989 in the semiheated glasshouse and in a randomized complete
block design with four blocks (replicates) the following treatments were tested,
all applied on February 10. a. yellow sticky traps installed with a distance of

230

about 2 m between them and at the level of the top of the plants b. the systemic carbamate pesticide Vydate G (oxamyl 10%) in granules at a dose of 1 gr per plant with this application repeated twice more. c. E. formosa releases at two times and d. the control. The parasitization rate was followed by weekly samplings from the lower parts of the tomato plants where the parasitized (black scales) and the unparasitized stages of whitefly were counted.

RESULTS AND DISCUSSION

During the cultivating period 1987-88 the effects of Vydate, E. formosa and yellow sticky traps were tested in different plastic unheated greenhouses. After application of Vydate the white fly population dropped from 17.7% infestation to around 2-3% of the infested top leaces (Fig. 1.).

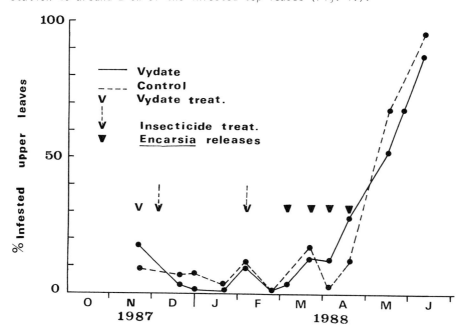

Fig. 1. **Evolution of whitefly population in two plastic houses in Kamisiana.**

This infestation remained low until the beginning of March when the Encarsia parasite releases started. The parasitism was 27.9% in the middle of May and reached 48,4% at the beginning of June. The white fly population remained relatively low up to the beginning of April then it increased very rapidly after the middle of April and remained high up to the end of the cultivating period. In the other greenhouse, without Vydate application, the whitefly population followed a similar curve but after having received two chemical treatments.

Yellow sticky traps in the other experiment established early in the cultivating period 1987-88, i. e. November 3, resulted in a drop of the white fly population (Fig. 2). The effect of the traps(in combination with the cool temperatu-

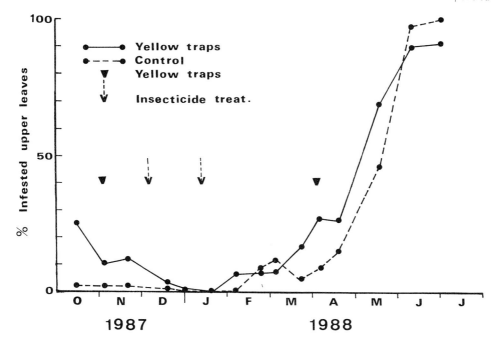

Fig. 2. Evolution of whitefly population in two plastic houses in Kamisiana.

res of the winter which kept the white fly population low) lasted up to the beginning of April. After that period although a new set of yellow traps was installed on of April 4, the white fly population increased very rapidly because of favorable weather and almost reached 100% infested top leaves.

Comparing the effects of different treatments i.e. yellow traps, Vydate and Encarsia, on the control of the white fly shows (Table I) that the effect of the yellow traps was the most rapid and their action was able to keep the white fly population low up to the end of March. The white fly population was higher in the plots treated with Vydate than with the traps, but this difference was not significant; it was necessary however to repeat the Vydate treatments in almost monthly intervals. In the plots with Encarsia the white fly population was even higher than on the previous treatments and this was propably due to the delay of parasite releases. The white fly population continously increased in the plots treated with Encarsia and only a small decrease was shown after two applications of Savona solution (Safer Agrochem LTD, Ontario, Canada).

The first black scales observed in the plots treated with E. formosa were found
on February 28 that is 18 days after the first release of the parasite. At the

TABLE I
Effects of Traps, Vydate and Encarsia on the Mean Number of Whitefly Adults per
Plant.

Date	Traps	Vydate	Encarsia	Control
February 23	2.0a	4.8a	20.1b	22.6b
February 26	4.5a	7.0a	24.5ab	34.8b
March 1	7.0a	13.6a	10.2a	47.6b
March 5	9.5a	20.7a	9.0a	53.8b
April 3	59.4a	69.1a	56.0a	238.0b

Means in the same line followed by the same letter are not significantly
different (Duncan 0.05).

beginning the parasitism was different among the different blocks but it increased later and reached the level of about 70% parasitisation around the end of
April (Fig. 3).

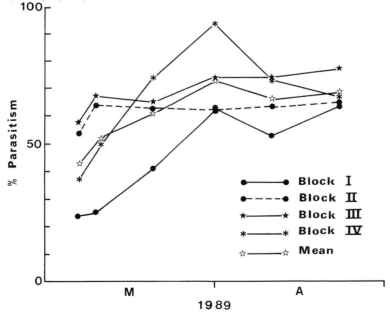

Fig. 3 Evolution of whitefly parasitism caused by E.formosa

The preference of adults of the greenhouse whitefly for yellow colour was shown by Lloyd (1921) and since then experiments were conducted in several places to develop monitoring and control methods by using yellow sticky traps (1, 3, 5). The yellow traps are compatabile with E. formosa and give good protection from T. vaporariorum (7). The efficiency of the yellow sticky traps seems to be higher in the Mediterranean region having favorable temperatures and also plenty of sunshine which in our area, even in winter rarely drops below 3-4 hours per day. The same type of yellow traps used in combination with quinomethionate in Sicily gave the best control in comparison to other commonly used insecticides (6). Successful application of Vydate on the other hand, was demonstrated by Dunne and Donovan (1977) when they found that two treatments in Ireland reduced excessive whitefly numbers to a sufficiently low level for subsequent biological control to be established from April introduction of parasites. They considered that integration of Vydate with Encarsia could insure the success of biological control. The results obtained from the experiments described above show that the number of chemical treatments against T. vaporariorum can be reduced during all of the cultivating period until around April. The chemical treatments can be replaced during this period by the yellow sticky traps. This is more true for the climatic conditions of Crete with its mild weather and abundant sunshine which increases the mobility of the insects and therefore the effectiveness of the traps. Vydate used in granules in soil applications is also useful to supprese white fly populations during the same period. There is however a great increase of the T. vaporariorum population during the last two months of the cultivating period and even the combined action with E. formosa at that time is not able to keep the pest insect population at a low level.

REFERENCES
1. Grill D. 1979. La couleur contre certains insectes de serre. Phytoma 305:36
2. Lloyd L. 1921. Notes on colour tropism et Asterochiton (Aleyrodes) vaporariorum Westwood. Bull. Ent. Res. 12 355-359.
3. Michelakis S. 1982. The whitefly problem in Crete, Greece, the first experiments with Encarsia formosa in the plastic houses of the Island Bull. IOBC/WPRS 1983/VI/3 :15-24.
4. Nusifora A. and Michelakis S. 1988. Progress in the development of integrated control of vegetable crops in the Mediterranean area Proc. CEC/IOBC/EPPO Inter. Joint Confer. On Integrated Crop Protection Ed. Cavalloro R. and M. J. Way pp. 138-146.
5. Nusifora A. and Vacante V. 1980. Premiers resultats d'un projet de protection integree des cultures en serre au moyen de pieges chromotropique jaunes. Colloque sur la Protection Integree des Cultures. Valence 18-19 Juin.

234

6. Vacante V. 1982. Effetto comparato di trappole chromotropiche e chinometionato, araffronto con insetticidi di sintesi, nella lotta contro Trialeurodes vaporariorum (Westw) From "Atti giornate fitopathologiche 1982" Vol. 3 Edit. University Library of Bologna p.p. 295-300.
7. Von de Veire M. and Vacante V. 1984. Greenhouse whitefly and leaf miner control by the combined use of the colour attraction system with the parasite wasp. Encarsia formosa (Gaham). Med. Fac. Laud Rijks Gent. 49 (1): 107-114.

EFFECTIVENESS OF BUPROFEZIN, FLUFENOXURON, ETHOFENPROX AND MIXTURES
OF QUINOMETHIONATE WITH PYRETHROIDS ON GREENHOUSE WHITEFLY *TRIALEU-
RODES VAPORARIORUM* (HOMOPTERA:ALEYRODIDAE)

N. E. RODITAKIS
Plant Protection Institute, 711 10 Heraklion Crete Greece

INTRODUCTION

The greenhouse whitefly *Trialeurodes vaporariorum* West has consisted the main insect problem to most greenhouse crops since 1979.
Firstly it faced succesfully with conventional insecticides as methomyl and meninfos but soon these replaced by pyrethroids. Now ten
years later the growers ask for more and more effective compounds
presumably due to resistance developed by the overuse of such insecticides. In order to overcome these problems we have recently adapted an integrated control programme for greenhouse pests in tomatoes under local greenhouse conditions using a mass trapping method
in combination with parasite *Encarsia formosa* and some pestisides
as quinomethionate, mancozeb and oxamyl Roditakis and Vakalounakis
1985. This integrated control programme failed to other greenhouse
crops as cucumber, melons and egg plants as we ought to face a
complex of pests as mites, thrips and leafminers.

We need new compounds as yet in consideration of their safety
to enviroment, human health beneficial pests and effectiveness to
harmfull pests. Under this view we tried to evaluate some new compounds and mixtures in order to be used in an integrated control
programme in greenhouses.

Some new chitin synthesis inhibitors have very selective effect
on Homoptera especielly on sucking insects. Kinoprene controlled
succesfully 2nd and 3rd nymphal stage of greenhouse whitefly but
it was safe to aphelinid parasite *Encarsia formosa* Roditakis N. E.
1984b. Buprofezin a novel chitin synthesis inhibitor is considered
to be a selective control agen by inhibiting incorporation of
N-acetyl-D-(1-H) glucose-amino into chitin Izawa et al 1985. Buprofezin also inhibits the prostagladin formation which may cause
suppression of oviposition Uchida et all 1987. It has a very selective activity on sucking insects as whiteflies Yasui et all 1985,
Ishaaya et all 1988, plant hoppers Nagata 1986 and scale insects
Yarom et all 1988.

Flufenoxuron is an acylurea chitin synthesis inhibitor with a

broader range of action on mites and lepidopteran insects but safe
to beneficial pests. Perugia et all 1987, Anderson et all 1987.

Ethophenprox is also a new insecticide consisted of C, H, O safe
to birds, fishes, mamalians and some beneficial species.

Quinomethionate is a fungicide with side effects on insects and
mites. Having a high ovicidal action on whitefly eggs and a great
effectiveness on crawlers is suitable for an integrated control
programme in greenhouses in combination with pyrethroids Roditakis
N.E. 1984a, Yasui et all 1985. As such the range of effectiveness
of pyrethroids is broadened to all life stages of whiteflies and
the risk of a sudden burst of mites is eliminated.

MATERIALS AND METHODS

In a special greenhouse of ca.150m^2 consisted of 32 blocks of
2.5m^2 each separated by nylon curtains all around, 256 tomatoe
seedlings were tranplanted. Six to seven days later the tomatoe
plants were artificially infested by 100-120 adults of greenhouse
whitefly per plant. The adults were transfered in greenhouse by
small glass cylinder CAN containing 50-60 newly emerged adults. The
whiteflies were reared on beans and cucumbers in an experimental
greenhouse, originated from Tybaki area one of the main greenhouse
areas of Crete (7.000.000m^2). These whiteflies have treated with a
variety of insecticides amongst pyrethroids deltamethrine and cy-
permethrine were the most frequent used. There was reared for four
to five succesive generations without any insecticide application.

The experimental design was a four completed randomized blocks.
In each block eigh treatments were arranged and eight tomatoe plants
were transplanted in two rows in each plot. A weekly spray schedu-
le was initiated 15 days after transplanting in order to cover a 60
day period Table 1. Deltamethrine was used as a reference insecticide because it was firstly used against whiteflies but was put
aside the latest years. Therefore eight applications were totally
applied on each treatment.

A census of whitefly adults was taken by direct counting of
whitefly adults on 40 top apical leaflets. There was sampled four
plants per plot (that means 10 leaflets per plant) just prior to
spraying. At this case 160 top apical leaflets were counted per
treatment at weekly intervals.

TABLE I

Pesticides used against greenhouse whitefly *Trialeurodes vaporario-rum* West

	Common name	Trade name	a.i %	Company	ppm	
1.	Buprofezin	Applaud WP	25	Nichino	a.	100
					b.	200
2.	Flufenoxuron	Cascade EC	5	Shell	a.	200
					b.	400
3.	Cyfluthrin +	Baythroid +	5	Bayer		50
	Quinomethionate	Morestan	25	Bayer		82.5
4.	F.C.R. 4545 +	Buldoc K.E.C.	3.5	Bayer		35
	Quinomethionate		25			250
5.	Ethofenprox	Trebon E.C.	30	Mitsui		120
6.	Deltamethrin	Desis E.C.	2.5	Hoechst		17.5

Immature stages (eggs & nymphs) were recorded at 15 day intervals removing four 1.0cm diam. leaf discs from top leaflets per sampled plant (16 leaf discs/plot) by a corky borer and counting them under a stereoscope. A total 64 leaf disks per treatment were examined bi-weekly. The mortality of immature stages was recorded 22 days after release of whitefly and dead insects were counted under a stereosko-pe. A total 1.600 individuals was examined per treatment from 16 leaf random sampled.

As tolerable pest density was taken 5 adults of whitefly per top leaflet that means 450-500 adults per plant on average (Roditakis N. unpublished).

There was used a Knapsack sprayer TECHNOMA and the solution of insecticides gradually increased from 2 to 10 Kgs per treatment 35 days after transplanting.

RESULTS

Both doses of buprofezin (100 ppm and 200 ppm) caused a gradually decrease of adults and stage density with no significant statistical difference Fig. 1a, 2a, Table 2. In the first generation the adult mean density was lower (12.3-17.0) than the initial established (120-140) (number of adult/leaflet in parenthesis) as the stage density (90 in the initial generation and 10 in the second) Table 2.

TABLE 2

Mean number of adults of GWF per leaflet at weekly intervals

a.a Treatments	ppm	pre-treatm.	1/9	16/9	22/9	1/10	8/10	15/10	23/10	30/10
					Generation					
1. Buprof. a.	100	140	33.6 a	15.8 a	12.6 d	17.0 b	25.7 cde	1.35 b	2.26 b	3.8 c
b.	200	120	27.8 b	13.0 a	7.9 d	12.3 b	13.0 de	1.00 b	2.19 b	2.7 c
2. Flufenox. a.	200	132	25.7 b	12.5 a	48.2 c	112.5 a	45.5 bc	2.42 a	7.63 b	24.3 bc
b.	400	124	26.4 b	13.3 a	92.3 a	112.5 a	64.0 b	3.07 a	9.64 b	31.8 bc
3. Cyfl.+ Quin.	50+82.5	95	8.8 d	3.8 b	14.9 d	15.0 b	7.2 e	2.63 b	3.95 b	7.55 bc
4. FCR 4545+Quin.	35+250	120	2.0 e	0.81 b	4.12 d	3.7 b	2.5 e	0.9 b	0.74 b	1.14 c
5. Ethofen.	120	142	21.8 bc	11.6 a	93.2 a	125.0 a	38.0 bcd	6.98 a	32.0 a	76.9 a
6. Deltam.	17.5	131	17.9 c	10.2 a	64.7 b	112.0 a	100.0 a	3.6 a	24.3 a	39.7 b

Means followed by the same letters are not significantly different by

Duncan's multiple range test (P=0.05)

Date of applications 31/8, 8/9, 15/9, 21/9, 30/9, 7/10, 14/10, 20/10

Buprof. = Buprofezin

Flufenox. = Flufenoxuron

Cyfl. = Cyfluthrine

Quin. = Quinomethionate

Ethofen.= Ethofenprox

Deltam. = Deltamethrine

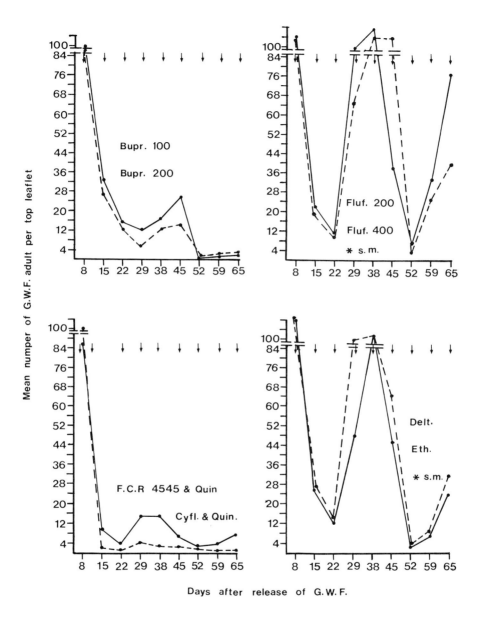

Days after release of G.W.F.

Fig. 1. Mean numper of greenhouse whitefly adults per top tomato leaflet at weekly intervals. Bupr. = buprofezin, Fluf. = flufeno-xuron, Cyfl. = cyfluthrin, Quin. = quinomethionate, Delt. = delta-methrine, Eth. = ethofenprox.
s.m. = sooty mould growth   = application

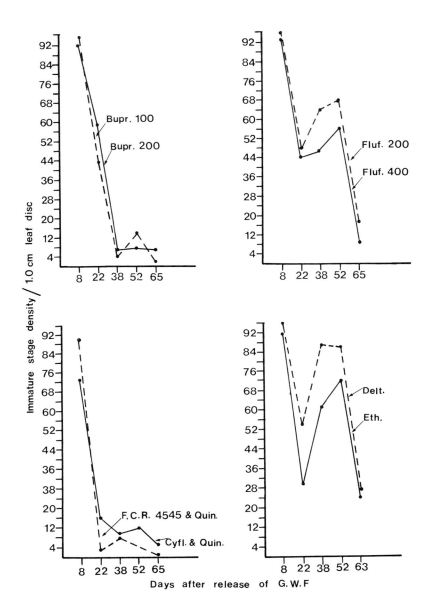

Fig. 2. Mean number of immatures stages (eggs, nymphs) per 1.0 cm
leaf disc at 15 days intervals Bupr. = buprofezin, Fluf. = flufenoxuron, Quin. = quinomethionate, Cyfl. = cyfluthrin, Delt. =
deltamethrine, Eth. = ethofenprox.

241

The subsequent second generation was almost eliminated (mean 2.7-3.8 adults/leaf) Table 2. The stage density was redused 88.5% and 93.6% at 100 ppm and 200 ppm concentrations respectively while the initial adult density reduced 90% and 88% at 100 ppm and 200 ppm respectively Table 3, 4.

TABLE 3
Reduction (%) of stage density (eggs + nymphal stages) of greenhouse whitefly per leaf disc 1.0 cm diam. in the first generation after five applications at weekly intervals.

a.a.	Treatments	% reduction
1.	F.C.R. 4545 + Quinomethionate	94
2.	Buprofezin 200 ppm	93.6
3.	Buprofezin 100 ppm	88.5
4.	Cyfluthrin + Quinomethionate	84
5.	Ethofenprox	65
6.	Flufenoxuron 200 ppm	49
7.	Flufenoxuron 400 ppm	41
8.	Deltamethrine 17.5 ppm	40

TABLE 4
Reduction (%) of whitefly adults per leaflet after eight applications at weekly intervals.

a.a.	Treatments	% reduction
1.	F.C.R. + Quinomethionate	97
2.	Buprofezin 100 ppm	90
3.	Buprofezin 200 ppm	88
4.	Cyfluthrin + Quinomethionate	85
5.	Ethofenprox	44
6.	Flufenoxuron 200 ppm	16
7.	Flufenoxuron 400 ppm	10
8.	Deltamethrine 17.5 ppm	8.9

The total days remained below the threshold (5 adult/leaf) were the latest 22 days Table 5.

TABLE 5
Number of days that GWF remained below the threshold (5 adults/
leaflet) throughout the experiment.

a.a.	Treatments	Days
1.	F.C.R. 4545 + Quinomethionate	60
2.	Cyfluthrin + Quinomethionate	28
3.	Buprofezin 100 ppm	22
4.	Buprofezin 200 ppm	22
5.	Flufenoxuron 200 ppm	7
6.	Flufenoxuron 400 ppm	7
7.	Deltamethrine 17.5 ppm	7
8.	Ethofenprox 120 ppm	0

The number of latest nymphal stages were the lowest all the others
treatments after 30, 45 and 60 days after artificial infestation
Table 6.

TABLE 6
Number of the latest nymphal stages of GWF per leafdisc 1cm diam.
in 30, 45 and 60 days after the articicial infestation.

a.a.	Treatments/Days	30		45		60	
1.	Buprofezin 100 ppm	0.0	a	0.0	a	1.4	a
2.	Buprofezin 200 ppm	0.0	a	0.0	a	2.1	a
3.	F.C.R. 4545 + Quinom.	4.8	b	1.7	a	1.7	a
4.	Cyfluthrine + Quinom.	5.0	b	6.8	b	5.5	b
5.	Flufenoxuron 400 ppm	9.5	b	4.4	b	9.1	b
6.	Flufenoxuron 200 ppm	36.6	c	3.1	b	17.1	bc
7.	Deltamethrine 17.5 ppm	52.5	c	5.06	b	24.1	c
8.	Ethopenprox 120 ppm	83	d	17.6	c	27.5	c

Means followed by the same letters are not siginificcantly
different by Duncan's multiple range test (P=0.05)

   The mixture F.C.R. 4545 + Quinomethionate (formulated) reduced
more rapidly the mean adult density as stage density than the other
and remained below threshold all the period of test fig. 1b, Table
5. A small recovery was noticed in the first generation but in the

second one not at all fig. 1b. The reduction (%) of mean stage density per 1.0 cm diam. leaf disc was the highest (94%) as the buprofezin 200 ppm (93.6%) while the mean adult density drastically reduced (97%) at the end of the experiment Table 3, 4.

The mean number of latest nymphal stages per leaf disc was very low (1.7) with no statistical significant difference with the mixture cyfluthrin + quinomethionate all the period and both buprofezin concentrations 45 and 60 days after initial infestation Table 6.

The other mixture cyfluthrin + quinomethionate prepared just before applications reduced the mean adult density a little more higher than the F.C.R. 4545 + quinomethionate one Fig. 1b. The first generation was well discriminated but the adult density (15) and stage density (12) was low with no statistical significant differences with F.C.R. 4545 + quinomethionate mixture Fig. 1b, 2b, Table 2. The second generation is slightly recovered and the reduction (%) of the stage density was high 84% in the first generation while the initial established adults redused also 85% Fig. 1b, Table 3, 4. The total days remained below the threshold was 28 Table 5.

The effectiveness both the flufenoxuron, concentrations, the new insecticide ethofenprox and reference one deltamenthrine was unstisfactory. The adult population was extremely high during the first generation and we applied two supplementary application with pirimiphos - ethyl and deltamethrin to avoid possible displacements to neighbour plots. There after mean adult density remained at about the same level of the initial established Fig. 1c, 1d and there are not significant differences amongst them Table 2. At the end of the experiment (30/10) both flufenoxuron concentrations gave better results than ethofenprox and deltamethrine while deltamethrine also was more effective than ethofenprox Table 2. However all these adult densities were upper the threshold and the total days remained below threshold were seven to both flufenoxuron concentrations and deltamenthrine and zero to ethofenprox Table 5. The mean stage density was moderatly reduced (40-65%) as initial adult density (8.9-44%) Table 3, 4. The mean number of latest stages was also high enough so resulted sooty mould growth on lower leaves in flufenoxuron and ethofenprox plots in 55 days and deltamenthrine one in 60 days after initial infestation Fig. 1c, 1d, 2c, 2d. Table 6.

Ovicidal action of buprofezin was varied 4.3-9.1%, flufenoxuron 1.7-3.3%, ethofenprox 2.5%, deltamethrine 1.5% while the mixtures of quinomethionate 21.5-23.2%. The larvicidal action (L_1-L_3) of the pesticides tested was very high (100%) both the buprofezin treatments, the mixtures of quinomethionate with cyfluthrin (90%) and F.C.R. 4545 (94), moderate both the flufenoxuron treatments (50-60), deltamethrine (40) and low to ethofenprox (21) Table 7.

TABLE 7
Mortality (%) of eggs and nymphal stages observed on tomatoe leaves in the greenhouse after four applications at weekly intervals.

a.a	Treatments	Eggs	Nymphal stages $I_1 + I_2 + I_3$
1.	Buprofezin 100 ppm	4.3	100
2.	Buprofezin 200 ppm	9.1	100
3.	Flufenoxuron 200 ppm	1.7	56
4.	Flufenoxuron 400 ppm	3.3	60
5.	Cyfluthrin + Quinomethionate	23.2	90
6.	F.C.R. 4545 + Quinomethionate	21.5	94
7.	Ethofenprox 120 ppm	2.5	21
8.	Deltamethrine 17.5 ppm	1.5	40

Side effects was noticed a. on green garden looper *Plusia chalcites* with flufenoxuron, the mixtures cyfluthrin + quinome-thionate, F.C.R. 4545 + quinomethionate and deltamethrine. b. on lefminer *Liriomyza bryoniae* both the mixtures of quinomethionate, deltamethrine and ethofenprox while buprofezin was unaffective both upper insects.

A few parasitism (5-25%) was observed on buprofezin and flufe-noxuron mixtures while the pradator *Macrolophus calliginosus* He-miptera was established to buprofezin and flufenoxuron plots.

DISCUSSION
The mixture F.C.R. 4545 + quinomethionate was clearly the most effective insecticide against adults and nymphs of greenhouse whi-tefly. Therefore the quinomethionate broadened the effectiveness

of the F.C.R. 4545 to all life stages and having also fungicide
and miticide traits was prooved a useful polydynamic pesticide in
a integrated control programme.

The ovicidal action (21.5%) observed under greenhouse was possibly dued to quinomethionate. Quinomethionate is an excelent ovicide
(95-100%) and larvicide mainly on crawlers (100%) and second nymphal
stage (51%) Nakazawa et all 1978, Roditakis N. 1985, Yasui et all
1985.

The other mixture cyflythrin + quinomethionate was also the same
effective as the F.C.R. 4545 + quinomethionate. It must be noticed
that a weekly spray programme both these mixture is extemely lethal
to parasites and predators of whitefly. We must investigate the
appropriate interval between applications in order to permitt the
colonization of beneficial pests. On the other hand they were very
effective on leam-miners and green garden looper.

Amongst juvenil analogs buprofezin was the most effective. According to mortality data buprofezin was the same effective on the
first three nymphal stages as pyrethroids. Its gradual action was
dued to absense of adulticidal action and the population reduction
resulted through its high effectiveness on crawlers and subsquent
two nymphal stages, Buprofezin has a low ovicidal and adulticidal
action but affect the hatchability of egg laid by the adults (14.1%)
Yasui et all 1985, 1987. The hatchability of eggs laid also on
sprayed tomatoes leaves was very low while the survival of larvae
hatched was negligible Yasui et all 1987. These results demonstrate
that buprofezin at 100 ppm at weekly intervals is very effective
and suppress high whitefly infestation on greenhouse tomatoes in
40 days.

The hymenopterus parasite *Encarsia formosa* was observed on all
plots of buprofezin parasitized the latest nymphal stage. At the
end of the experiment the parasitism was greatly reduced possibly
due to absence of suitable hosts. Juvenile hormone analogs are
usually safe for this parasite. Some chitin synthesis inhibitors
safe for adults and pupae of *Encarsia* was lethal to new hatching
larvae inside the surving hosts. This resulted a lower parasitism
on treated plots with juvenil hormone analogs than the untreated
ones Domen and Wiegers 1984. How the buprofezin acts exaxtly to
Encarsia must be investigated. The predator *Macrolophus calliginosus* was also observed in all plots. There after it must be concluded that buprofezin is suitable for an integrated control programme.

246

We must take under condideration the it was unaffective on leafminer *Liriomyza bryoniae* and green garden looper *Plusia chalcites* Esper.

The deltamethrine a pyrethroid used against whitefly the latest 10 years prooved unaffective in 17.5 ppm, concentration, 50% higher of the recommended dose. It was presumably due to resistance developped through the repeated applications.

REFERENCES

1. Collmann GL, All J.N. (1981). Biological impact of contact insecticides and insect growth regulators on isolated stages og the greenhouse whitefly (Homoptera:Aleyrodidae). Journal of Econ. Entom. 75:863-867.

2. Domen P.A., Wiegers G.L. 1984. Selective effects of a chitin synthesis inhibiting insecticides (CME 134-01) on the parasite *Encarsia formosa* and its whitefly host *Trialeurodes vaporariorum*. Med. Fac. Londbouwn. Rijksuniv Gent 49/3a:745-750.

3. Elhaq E.A., David J.H. (1983). Reistance of greenhouse whitefly (Homoptera:Aleyrodidae) to insecticides in selected Ohio greenhouses. Journal of Econ. Entom. 76:945-948.

4. Ishaaya I., Z. Mendelson and V. Melamed Madjan (1988). Effect of buprofezin on embryogenesis and progeny formation of sweet potato whitefly (Homoptera:Aleyrodidae). Ent. Soc. of America 81: 781-784.

5. Izawa Y., Uchida, T. Sugimoto & T. Asai (1985). Inhibition of chitin biosynthesis by buprofezin analogs in relation to their activity controlling *Nilaparvata lugens* Stal Pestic. Bioch. Physiol. 24: 343-347.

6. Michelakis St. (1983). The whitefly problem in Crete Greece. The first experiment with *Encarsia formosa* on the plastic houses of the island OILB SROP 3:15-24.

7. Naba K., Nakazawa K. (1982). Long term effects of byprofezin spray in controlling the greenhouse whitefly *Trialeurodes vaporariorum* Westwood in vinylhouse **tomatoes**. App. Ent. Zool. 18(2): 284-286.

8. Nagata T. (1986). Timing of buprofezin application for control of the brown planthopper *Nilaparvata lugens* Stal (Homoptera:Delphacidae). Appl. Entomol. Zool. 21: 357-362.

9. Roditakis N.E. (1984a). Evaluation of the effectiveness some pesticides on whitefly population and isolated stages of greenhouse whitefly *Trialeurodes vaporariorum* West 3rd Conference for vegetables and flowers under greenhouses Abstracts 51.

10. Roditakis N.E. (1984b). Evaluation of fluvalinate, methomyl and Kinoprene on the greenhouse whitefly *Trialeurodes vaporariorum* West (Homoptera:Aleyrodidae). Entomolog. Hellenica 2:25-30.

11. Roditakis N.E., Vakalounakis D.J. (1985). The integrated control of greenhouse whitefly *Trialeurodes vaporariorum* West, on greenhouse in Crete. Proceedings of a meeting of the EC Experts Group Heraklion 24-26 1985:137-144.

12. Uchida M., Y. Izawa & T. Sugimoto (1987). Inhibition of prosta-
    gladin biosynthesis and oviposition by an insect growth regula-
    tor, buprofezin, in *Nilaparvata lugens* Stal. Pestic. Biochem.
    Physiol. 27: 71-75.

13. Yarom I., Daniel Blumberg and I. Ishaaya (1988). Effects of
    buprofezin on California Red Scall (Homoptera:Diaspididae) and
    Mediterranea black scale (Homoptera:Coccidae) 81:1581-1585.

14. Yasui M., Manoru F., Maekawa S. (1985). Effects of buprofezin
    on different decelopmental stages of the greenhouse whitefly
    Trialeurodes vaporariorum West (Hompotera:Aleyrodidae) Appl.
    Ent. Zool. 20(3): 340-347.

15. Yasui M., Fukada M., Maekawa S. 1984. Effects of buprofezin on
    reproduction of the greenhouse whitefly *Trialeurodes vaporario-
    rum* (Westwood) (Homoptera:Aleyrodidae) App. Ent. Zool. 22:
    266-271.

Hormones and neuropeptides

© 1990 Elsevier Science Publishers B.V. (Biomedical Division)
Pesticides and alternatives, editor J.E. Casida

ECDYSTEROID AGONISTS AS NOVEL INSECT GROWTH REGULATORS

KEITH D. WING AND HAROLD E. ALLER
Research Labs, Rohm and Haas Co., 727 Norristown Rd., Spring House,
Pennsylvania, 19477 (U.S.A.)

INTRODUCTION

The agrochemical business is becoming increasingly mature. Trends for the
near future include rapidly increasing R&D costs, industrial consolidation as
manifested by mergers and streamlining of organizations, and increasing
difficulty in penetration of the major agricultural markets by new chemicals
(1). The search for new agrochemical agents is slowed by more rigorous
regulatory requirements and increasing public scrutiny. Nevertheless, novel
chemicals at competitive costs will still be needed to provide continued
economic control, lowered environmental disruption and to combat resistant
target organisms.

A new class of insect growth regulators (IGR's), distinct from the juvenile
hormone mimics and benzoylphenylurea IGR's, has been discovered recently (2)
which seem to fulfill many for these criteria. These compounds, represented
by RH-5849 (1,2-dibenzoy, 1-tert-butyl hydrazine), have the unique
characteristic of mimicking the invertebrate molting hormone 20-
hydroxyecdysone (20-OHE) in both Drosophila melanogaster Kc (3) and Plodia
interpunctella imaginal disc cells in vitro, and in Manduca sexta larvae in
vivo (4). Recent data indicate that RH-5849 may be a useful prototype
insecticide for the control of certain agriculturally important Lepidoptera
and Coleoptera, that it is effective foliarly and systemically against both
insecticide-susceptible and resistant pests, and that it is relatively safe to
mammals and nontarget organisms. These compounds are also of interest to
endocrinologists, since they are the first nonsteroidal ecdysone agonists.

MATERIALS AND METHODS
Ecdysone agonist assays in vitro

Ecdysone assays using intact fruitfly Drosophila Kc cells have been
described previously (3). Ecdysone receptor (ER) assays using the potent
ecdysteroid ^{3}H-ponasterone A and cytosolic or nuclear extracts from Kc cells
or Indian meal moth Plodia interpunctella IAL-PID2 imaginal disc cells were
performed according to published procedures (3,5).

Ecdysone agonist assays in vivo

Ecdysone agonist assays using either intact tobacco hornworm Manduca sexta or ligated abdomens therefrom were described previously (4).

Whole insect bioassays

Whole insect bioassays were performed according to standard procedures as described in the Results section.

RESULTS

Previously published work using well-established ecdysone bioassays with intact Kc cells has shown that RH-5849 is less potent than the molting hormone 20-OHE by a factor of over 100-fold (3). These assays include monitoring hormone agonist-induced process elaboration (morphological differentiation), inhibition of proliferation, and induction of acetylcholinesterase. When tested as a competitor on the Kc cell cytosolic ER, RH-5849 is 30-fold less potent than the hormone. However, Scatchard plots and both kinetic on-rate k_a and off-rate k_d experiments yield data indicating that RH-5849 binds to some common domain in the ER with the ecdysteroid ^{3}H-ponasterone A. In addition, sublines of Kc cells selected for resistance to either 20-OHE or RH-5849 display cross-resistance to both compounds and a decreased specific activity of ER. These data provide evidence for the biochemical and cellular action of RH-5849 at the ecdysone receptor (3).

Recently, data parallel to that described above have been obtained with ER preparations from nuclear extracts of Plodia cells. Fig. 1a show the effect of 1 μM RH-5849 on the Scatchard plot of specific ^{3}H-ponasterone A binding to these extracts. As had previously been observed with Kc cell ER preparations, binding isotherms in the presence of RH-5849 show an increased equilibrium dissociation constant K_d, while the maximum binding concentration B_{max} remains the same. Kinetic experiments likewise show a decreased on-rate k_a of ^{3}H-ponasterone A binding to the Plodia receptor in the presence of RH-5849, while the off-rate k_d remains the same (Wing, unpublished data). Fig. 1b shows competitive binding isotherms for unlabelled ponasterone A, 20-OHE, RH-5849 and alpha ecdysone to the Plodia ER. After transformation of the EC_{50} via the Cheng-Prusoff equation (using the experimentally determined K_d for ^{3}H-ponasterone A), the estimated K_d's for the above compounds are 0.0032, 0.21, 0.49 and 4.6 μM, respectively. These data demonstrate the presence of ER activity from a lepidopteran source, which binds RH-5849 and ecdysteroids in a manner similar to that described for the dipteran Kc cells.

We find, however, that although 20-OHE is consistently more potent in the above-mentioned in vitro assays, RH-5849 is a much more effective ecdysone agonist in either intact lepidopteran larvae or isolated abdomens therefrom.

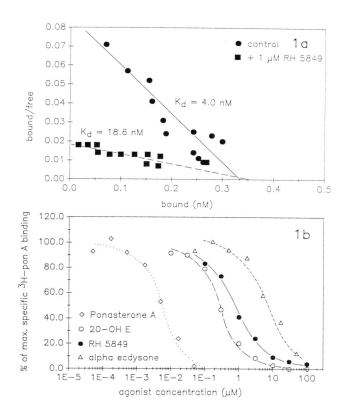

Fig. 1. The effect of RH-5849 on binding isotherms of ^{3}H-ponasterone A (141 Ci/mmole) to <u>Plodia</u> IAL-PID2 cell nuclear extracts (23°C). a) Scatchard plot of binding in the presence and absence of 1 μM RH-5849. b) Competition of unlabelled ligands with 2.7 nM ^{3}H-ponasterone A.

The tobacco hornworm <u>Manduca</u> has proven to be a valuable model in these studies because of its large size, because its epidermis responds sensitively and reproducibly to hormonal stimuli, and because a substantial body of knowledge exists on its endocrinology. In bioassays utilizing intact early last larval instar hornworm larvae, treatment with high dosages of 20-OHE causes a characteristic head capsule apolysis (slippage of the original cuticle forward upon morphogenesis of developing head tissues lying underneath). This is a morphological response normally occurring at peak titers of 20-OHE. We observe that RH-5849 is far more potent than 20-OHE in such assays; if the compounds are injected, RH-5849 at a 53-fold lower dose causes an equivalent molting response; if administered orally, as would be the usual route of uptake in a field situation, RH-5849 is >670-fold more potent (4). Thus far, we have observed authentic molting responses to RH-5849 at any

larval lepidopteran instar and at any time within an instar; RH-5849 also
appears to be able to break pupal diapause in Manduca (C.M. Williams, personal
communication). RH-5849 is not behaving as a trophic hormone for the
production of endogenous ecdysone, because a) treatment of intact larvae
actually leads to a decline in immunoreactive ecdysone titer and b) we observe
that RH-5849 potently induces molting even in ligated abdomens, which lack a
biosynthetic source of the ecdysteroids (4). The ecdysonergic effects of
RH-5849 and/or its analogs have been manifested in a wide diversity of
lepidopteran species in a variety of lab and field situations; in addition
RH-5849 initiates ecdysone-like responses in intact Plodia cells and cabbage
looper Trichoplusia ni IAL-TND1 imaginal disc cells (H. Oberlander, personal
communication) and in cells from the forest tent caterpillar Malacosoma
disstria (A. Retnakaran, personal communication). Thus, a substantial body of
evidence is accumulating which argues that RH-5849 is behaving as a bona fide
ecdysone in Lepidoptera.

Clearly, one important contributing factor to RH-5849's higher efficacy on
intact Lepidoptera or their tissues is its superior absorption and metabolic
stability, relative to ecdysones. The synchronization of physiological events
involved in the insect molting process is highly precise, and is critically
dependent upon an adequate concentration of receptors in the appropriate
tissues, a rapid rise and then an equally precipitous fall in the hormone
titer. Many of the target tissues such as the gut and fat body contain highly
active enzymes involved in metabolism and clearance of the ecdysones,
especially soon after a molt (6).

It appears that RH-5849 is refractory to many of these enzymatic mechanisms
and in fact after ingestion the compound is absorbed efficiently and rapidly
into the hemolymph and epidermis. Pharmacokinetic experiments show that peak
hemolymph concentrations of 16 μM authentic RH-5849 occur 6 hrs after oral
administration of 10 μg/gr body weight of ^{14}C-RH-5849 (4). Even higher levels
of compound are observed in the epidermis between 6 to 12 hours., with lower
amounts in the gut contents, gut tissues and fat body (though the highest
levels of compound are excreted intact in the feces; Wing, unpublished
data). Other metabolites identified thus far by thin-layer chromatography,
reversed-phase high performance liquid chromatography, and gas chromatography-
mass spectrometry are ring-hydroxyllated RH-5849 and hippuric acid (Wing and
Westmoreland, unpublished data). Available information from the literature
indicate that orally administered 20-OHE would be rapidly metabolized and
excreted; this is apparently corroborated by our observation that even a 700-
fold mass excess of 20-OHE relative to molt-inducing levels of RH-5849 have no
effect on last instar Manduca larvae.

RH-5849 thus seems to behave as a rapidly absorbed, relatively persistent ecdysone agonist which binds to ER's throughout the body cavity of Lepidoptera with moderate affinity. After binding, those ER's in the epidermis initiate a molt which leads to premature cuticle synthesis, especially around the head region where occlusion of the functional mouthparts can cause a feeding inhibition within 24 hrs. The apparent relation between the ability of 28 RH-5849 analogs to bind to Drosophila Kc cell ER and their ability to elicit premature head capsule apolysis in Manduca larvae is shown in Fig. 2 (4). These data, in combination with those described above, argue that this ecdysonergic effect is the primary toxic action of these compounds in Lepidoptera. Although RH-5849 has been shown to have toxicity towards certain Coleoptera and Diptera as well, it is currently unknown at the physiological level whether ecdysonergic effects are involved.

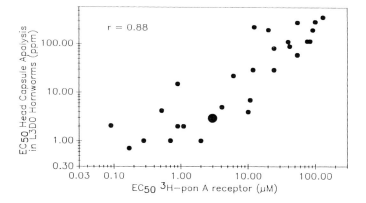

Fig. 2. Relation between apparent binding affinity of 28 RH-5849 analogs to the Kc cell ER and the ability of those analogs to induce premature molting in newly ecdysed third instar Manduca sexta. The large point indicates RH-5849. (Copyright 1988 by the AAAS).

It is important to note that the benzoylphenylureas Dimilin and CGA-112913 fail to bind to ecdysone receptors, do not cause differentiation of ecdysone-sensitive Kc cells, and do not initiate molting in either intact Manduca larvae or their isolated abdomens. Thus although these compounds may disrupt ecdysone-initiated cuticle deposition, they do not mimic the hormone itself and thus apparently differ from RH-5849 in their actions.

Laboratory and field studies show that RH-5849 is efficacious against agricultural pests. The field efficacy of RH-5849 on the lyonetid leafminer Leucoptera scitella (apples, Italy) is shown in Table 1. This pest responds poorly to Dimilin treatment and may be resistant. However it is controlled by the more recent benzoylphenylurea teflubenzuron and by economic levels of RH-5849 (2).

TABLE I

CONTROL OF <u>LEUCOPTERA</u> <u>SCITELLA</u> ON APPLES

Compound	Foliar Dose (kg/l)	First Generation (29 day observ.)		Second Generation (15 day observ.)	
		No. mines/ 100 leaves	% control	No. mines/ 100 leaves	% control
RH-5849	0.6	9.8	93	11.7	86
	1.2	0.7	100	3.8	95
Diflubenzuron	1.25	107.0	28	39.9	53
Teflubenzuron	0.6	7.3	95	4.9	94
Untreated	-	149.0	-	84.0	-

RH-5849 is also plant systemic, a feature which further distinguishes it from benzoylphenylureas. This is illustrated in Table 2., where effective control of both susceptible southern armyworm and Mexican bean beetle and pyrethroid-resistant Colorado potato beetle is achieved by low levels of soil-applied RH-5849 (2).

TABLE II

SYSTEMIC ACTIVITY OF RH-5849 SOIL DRENCH APPLICATION

Pest (instar)	Crop	Plant Uptake Interval (days)	LC_{50} (mg/l) after exposure for specified days	
			3	6
Spodoptera eridania	lima bean	7	0.5	0.5
(L3)		14	0.6	0.5
Epilachna varivestis	lima bean	7	2.7	1.2
(L3)		14	2.0	1.5
Leptinotarsa	tomato	7	0.5	0.3
decemlineata (L2)		14	>2.0	0.4

In addition, the acute mammalian toxicity of RH-5849 is minimal; the rat oral LD_{50} is 435 mg/kg, the rat dermal LD_{50} is >5000 mg/kg; and it is negative in the Ames mutagenicity test. It is also essentially nontoxic to fish and birds; and although Crustacea are also known to use ecdysones for their molting processess, it appears to be safe to <u>Daphnia</u> (acute 48 hr. LC_{50} 7 mg/l, life cycle LC_{50} 0.5 - 1.0 mg/l) (2) as well as to newly hatched crayfish <u>Procambarus clarkii</u> (LC_{50} > 60 mg/l, Wing and Slawecki, unpublished data). Thus RH-5849 has the characteristics one would wish for in an environmentally compatible insecticide.

In conclusion, RH-5849 and its certain of its analogs hold considerable promise as novel IGR's acting at a new invertebrate-specific target site, the ecdysone receptor. These compounds appear to have sufficient insecticidal efficacy and toxicological safety characteristics to be considered viable candidates for commercial development. Further, they show that unique biochemical lesions may be revealed by the application of physiological/biochemical techniques within the insecticide discovery environment; one may speculate that judicious use of molecular cloning technology will also be instrumental in small molecule pesticide discovery.

ACKNOWLEDGMENTS

The authors wish to acknowledge contributions in synthetic chemistry by Dr. A. Hsu, the technical assistance of Messrs. W. James and R. Slawecki, and the Rohm and Haas Insecticide Group and Profs. Peter Cherbas and Carroll Williams for helpful discussions.

REFERENCES

1. Finney JR (1988) In: Brighton Crop Protection Conference - Pests and Diseases. The British Crop Protection Council, Surrey, pp. 3-14.

2. Aller HE, Ramsay JR (1988) In: Brighton Crop Protection Conference - Pests and Diseases. The British Crop Protection Council, Surrey, pp. 511-517.

3. Wing KD (1988) Science 241: 467-469

4. Wing KD, Slawecki RA, Carlson GR (1988) Science 241: 470-472.

5. Sage BA, O'Connor JD (1985) Meth. Enzymol. 111: 458-468.

6. Koolman J, Karlson P (1985) In: Kerkut GA,, Gilber LI (eds) Comprehensive Insect Physiology Biochemistry and Pharmacology, Vol. 7. Pergamon, Oxford, pp. 343-361.

© 1990 Elsevier Science Publishers B.V. (Biomedical Division)
Pesticides and alternatives, editor J.E. Casida

A MOLECULAR BIOLOGICAL APPROACH TO THE DIPTERAN JUVENILE HORMONE SYSTEM: IMPLICATIONS FOR PEST CONTROL

STEPHEN C. TROWELL, MARION J. HEALY, PETER D. EAST, MIRA M. DUMANCIC, PETER M. CAMPBELL, MARK A. MYERS AND JOHN G. OAKESHOTT

CSIRO Division of Entomology, G.P.O. Box 1700, Canberra, A.C.T. 2601, Australia.

INTRODUCTION

The juvenile hormone (JH) signalling system is particularly attractive to target in the search for alternatives to conventional insecticides. The system is unique to insects and it regulates events which are crucial to the insect, namely development and reproduction. Also, it is already the target of a class of insecticidal agents, the juvenoids (1), which are extremely effective in certain circumstances. Research on the JH signalling system may improve the range of available juvenoid agents and also may provide candidate genes that, when combined with a suitable delivery system, will constitute novel insecticidal agents. The JH system therefore presents research challenges of both a fundamental and a practical commercial nature.

Juvenile hormones are a closely-related family of at least five sesquiterpenoid molecules produced by the insect corpus allatum (CA). While JH III has been found in all insect orders described to date (2), other forms, such as the bisepoxide molecule found in the higher Diptera (3), are more restricted in their distribution. The significance of the variable JH forms between and within orders is unclear, although there are suggestions that some other components of the system are also order specific.

In the larval or nymphal stages, JH acts to maintain the juvenile state through the various moults. The specification of the final moult is brought about by a drop in JH titre, which is due to the combination of reduced synthesis and increased degradation of JH (4). In the adult insect, JH is important for the development and function of the male and female accessory glands and for the synthesis of yolk proteins and their uptake by the developing oocytes (5). In addition, differentiation of the various morphs in polymorphic insects (e.g. termites) is under JH control (6).

Our research interests are focussed on three processes within the JH signalling pathway in Diptera (see Fig. 1). These comprise the signals controlling the synthesis and release of JH from the CA, the receptor mechanisms that give rise to tissue-specific responses to JH and the control of JH titre through enzymatic degradation. The titres and role of JH in the higher Diptera have been technically difficult problems to address even in the recent past. New results demonstrating the synthesis of two forms of JH in dipteran CA (3) and the first reported isolation of a putative intracellular JH receptor from a *Drosophila* cell line (7) indicate that these problems may be largely overcome. The accessibility of *Drosophila* to molecular genetic manipulation therefore makes this and related Diptera informative and tractable model species for these studies.

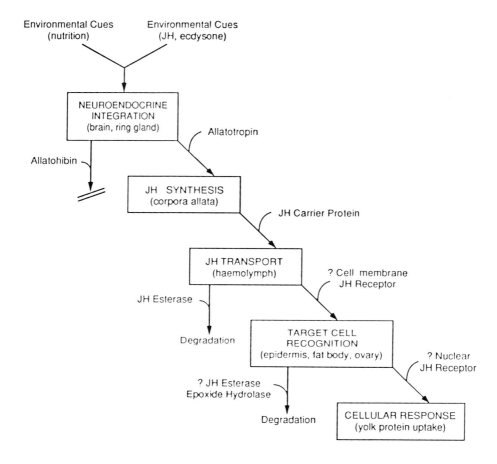

Fig.1. The cascade of events from induction of JH biosynthesis to its metabolism and cellular effects, demonstrating the points at which the effect of JH may be regulated.

In the first section of this paper we review the current state of knowledge about molecules constituting the JH signalling system. We also outline the strategies being adopted to identify, characterize and isolate the component molecules in dipteran species. The second section describes present and prospective approaches to manipulating components of the JH system to generate novel agents and strategies for controlling pest insects.

MOLECULAR AND CELLULAR BIOLOGY OF THE JUVENILE HORMONE SYSTEM

Control of Juvenile Hormone Biosynthesis

The regulation of JH titre at the level of synthesis and release by the CA involves a complex, multicomponent pathway. In no case are precise mechanisms understood, and indeed the variability among taxa suggests that the relative importance of specific factors may also differ. However, recent research indicates that the nervous system is the source of neuropeptide hormones which act on the CA to modulate JH biosynthesis at different stages of development.

The chemical identity of most of the signals which modulate CA activity is not known. It is clear that both positive and negative regulation is involved although to date it has not been possible to distinguish between neurosecretion and direct neural transmission, since most experiments have involved physical disruption of axonal pathways to the CA. Most attempts to isolate and characterize the stimulatory (allatotropin) and inhibitory (allatostatin/allatohibin) factors have utilised homogenates of brain or brain-retrocerebral complexes and therefore do not distinguish between humoral and paracrine secretions.

Allatostatins/Allatohibins. Two types of negative regulatory activity have been described (8). Allatohibins reduce the rate of JH biosynthesis whereas allatostatins act to maintain low levels of synthesis in unstimulated glands. Factors which act via the haemolymph and by neural pathways have been described in several species, and four peptides that have allatostatic activity have been isolated from the cockroach, *Diploptera punctata*. The peptides are 8 to 13 amino acids in length and show sequence similarity at their carboxyl termini (9).

Allatotropins. Allatotropic activity has been identified in the immature stages of the wax moth, *Galleria mellonella* (10) and the tobacco hornworm, *Manduca sexta* (11). In the latter case the active component was specific for the synthesis of the JH III homologue and was localized to specific neural tissues. The factor appeared to be a protein on the basis of heat lability and protease sensitivity, with an apparent size of 40 kDa estimated by gel filtration chromatography.

Allatotropic factors have also been partially characterized in adults of *Locusta migratoria* and *M. sexta*. Factors from *L. migratoria* are of neural origin (12, 13 and 14) and at least one is proposed to be a peptide. A 13 residue peptide purified from the heads of pharate adult *M. sexta* (15) was shown to have strong allatotropic activity *in vitro* in both native and synthetic forms. Significantly, this allatotropin had no effect on JH biosynthesis by CA isolated from larval and pupal stages of *M. sexta* nor from the adult stages of three other insect orders. It did, however, stimulate synthesis of JH by the CA of another adult female moth, *Heliothis virescens*, suggesting that the activity may be specific to adults in the Lepidoptera.

Limited evidence for allatotropic activity in oocyte maturation in adult females was provided by surgical experiments on *D. melanogaster* (16,17) and *Aedes aegypti* (18). Surgical destruction of neurosecretory cells of the brain and extirpation of the corpora cardiaca indicate that this neuroendocrine axis regulates oocyte maturation in many species of higher Diptera (19, 20 and 21).

In many dipterans, terminal oocyte development requires a protein meal (22). Flies fed only a sugar-water diet fail to develop mature oocytes and application of a JH analogue can overcome

262

this effect, at least in *Phormia regina* (23). This apparent hormonal gating of oocyte development provides an excellent experimental system that we are exploiting in the Australian sheep blowfly, *Lucilia cuprina*, to investigate the molecular mechanism of action of JH in regulating oocyte maturation.

Our research strategy in this and the two projects outlined below consists of: (a) isolation of the protein/peptide of interest by conventional biochemical methods, (b) determination of amino acid sequence from purified polypeptide, (c) synthesis of oligonucleotides based on peptide sequence and (d) use of these oligonucleotides for either direct screening of appropriate cDNA libraries or as primers for amplification of specific sequences from genomic or cDNAs by the polymerase chain reaction, for subsequent use as hybridization probes. Purified proteins and peptides will also be used to generate antibodies. We anticipate that the specific antibody and nucleic acid probes thus obtained will be valuable reagents for detailed physiological and cell biological studies of these components of the JH signalling pathway in Diptera.

Juvenile Hormone Receptors

Insect JHs have small, simple structures which can encode little information yet they have a multiplicity of physiological effects. Like steroid hormones, they therefore require complex molecular adapters to mediate their effects. Because of the lipid nature of JHs and the fact that they control or modulate gene expression, it is generally assumed that JH receptors will prove to be soluble DNA-binding proteins similar to the family of steroid hormone receptors. The assumption is strengthened by similarities in structure between the JHs and retinoic acid, which is known to interact with a receptor related to those of the steroid hormone family (24).

Two classes of proteins that bind JH have been described. One class shows low affinity for the hormone and is typified by haemolymph JH binding proteins, which also occur as intracellular proteins since they are synthesized in the fat body and sequestered by the ovaries (25, 26 and 27). The other class comprises soluble, high affinity, exclusively cellular juvenile hormone binding proteins (cJHBPs) which have been reported to occur in a number of insect tissues. Possible receptor status has been claimed for a number of them which have dissociation constants for complexes with natural or synthetic ligands ranging down to 10^{-9} M (28, 29, 30, 31, 32, 33, 34, 35, 36 and 37). Similar cJHBPs have been detected in a cultured *Drosophila* cell line (7, 38 and 39). Putative receptor molecules with nuclear sources have also been identified (32, 40).

Molecular biological techniques promise a route to isolation of the receptors for JH and the corresponding genes in the face of significant technical hurdles. Four stages may be defined in this process: identification and characterization of binding sites intrinsic to target tissues using ligand-binding assays; tagging and identification of the binding proteins in crude tissue extracts, using photoaffinity analogues of JHs; purification of selected binding proteins, microsequencing of portions of the proteins and use of the partial amino acid sequence data to identify and isolate the cognate genes and to generate antibodies against the binding proteins. When these steps are complete, it should be possible to probe both the relationship of the cJHBP in question to other lipid and steroid hormone receptors and to determine experimentally whether it functions as a genuine JH receptor. Radiolabelled analogues of the JHs, which are now commercially available, have been a prerequisite for the first stage of the program whilst the synthesis of a variety of radioactive photoaffinity analogues of the JHs and juvenoids (41, 42 and 43) has made the second and third stages of the program feasible. To date, the entire process has not been completed for any cJHBP from any insect tissue. The greatest advances appear to have been made with the cJHBP from the *D. melanogaster* Kc cell line and *M. sexta* larval epidermis. In both cases it is anticipated that a partial sequence for the JHBP will be obtained in the near future. We are now applying a similar program to cJHBPs of tissues from higher dipterans. Our aim is to exploit the advantages for biochemical work of *Lucilia cuprina*, namely large size and ease of culture, whilst utilising the homology with *D. melanogaster* to enable the molecular genetic aspects of the project to be pursued in that species.

Juvenile Hormone Esterase

It has been proposed that, at least in some orders (e.g. Lepidoptera), JH degradation plays a key role in regulating the titre of JH (4). Although several metabolic pathways may be implicated (44), only two have been studied in any detail, namely hydrolysis of the epoxide moiety and hydrolysis of the ester group. Ester hydrolysis plays a major role in Lepidoptera (45) while both pathways are utilised by Diptera (46, 47). In this paper we describe only ester hydrolysis. The epoxide hydrolytic pathway has been reviewed in (4).

Ester hydrolysis has been most studied in the Lepidoptera, where it is a soluble protein probably synthesized in the fat body (48). It is secreted into the larval haemolymph, where it occurs in high levels, with almost insignificant activity in other tissues. In contrast, JH esterase activity in dipterans has been identified both in microsomal and soluble protein extracts. The activity in dipteran larval haemolymph is very low (49), although activity has been found in the larval fat body (50) and body wall (51).

JH esterase is expressed at defined stages of the life cycle. Haemolymph activity increases just prior to the larval-pupal moult in both Diptera and Lepidoptera (45, 51) in order to reduce JH titres and allow pupal development to proceed. In Lepidoptera two activity peaks, induced by different factors, occur in the final larval instar and are associated with this transition. The first activity peak is induced by a 'head factor', other than JH, while the second peak is induced by JH itself (2, 52 and 53). This suggests that JH esterase synthesis in larvae may be under both neuroendocrine and endocrine control. Studies of JH esterase in homogenates of fat body of Lepidoptera (48) and whole bodies of *Drosophila* (54) reveal that enzyme activity levels gradually increase until about the middle of pupal life. Levels then gradually fall until JH esterase is at very low levels in newly eclosed adults, where the enzyme acts to modulate the gonadotrophic functions of JH.

While the data outlined above provide indirect evidence that the enzyme modulates JH titre, more direct evidence is revealed in studies where topical application of larvae with inhibitors of JH esterase leads to delayed pupation and malformed organisms (55). It is therefore clear that JH esterase modulates JH titre and it is also likely that the disruption of either preadult or adult JH esterase activity may enable development of novel control agents and strategies. The means by which molecular analysis of the JH esterase gene could lead to novel insecticides are outlined in a later section. Here we discuss the progress of the molecular analysis of JH esterase.

The cloning of the gene that encodes a JH esterase of *H. virescens* has been reported recently.(56). A cDNA library was screened with an oligonucleotide probe derived from the amino acid sequence of the N-terminus of the purified protein. The gene gives rise to a mRNA of 3.0kb with the protein having a signal peptide, as predicted for a secreted protein. The size of the mature protein, 61 kDa, is in close agreement with the M_r predicted from electrophoresis. Variability within the *H. virescens* JH esterase gene is suggested by the presence of three polyadenylation sites and changes at three bases in the region encoding the N-terminal 35 residues amongst three sequenced cDNA clones. Substantial variation is also seen at the protein level both within *H. virescens* and between two closely related *Heliothis* species, suggesting that JH esterase has some degree of species specificity.

We have initiated a project to characterise the JH esterase gene in higher Diptera in which its regulation and possibly function will differ from Lepidoptera. Our experimental approach to cloning the JH esterase gene is similar to that outlined for the allatotropins, and the initial step involves the purification of the JH esterase protein. Our work to date has focussed on identifying the *Drosophila* JH esterase and two approaches have been adopted. First, several lines of evidence suggest that two esterases of fast electrophoretic mobility may correspond to JH esterase (P.M.C. and M.M.D., unpublished). The developmental pattern of their expression is very similar to a putative JH esterase described for *D. virilis* (54) and also parallels that for the JH III titre in *D. melanogaster* (57). In addition, the enzymes are insensitive to the effects of diisopropyl phosphorofluoridate, a property characteristic of JH esterases in other organisms (4) and both esterases are sensitive to the inhibitor 3-octylthio-1,1,1,-trifluoropropan-2-one, proposed to inhibit specifically JH esterases in lepidopterans (58). The ability of these proteins to hydrolyse JH has not been demonstrated directly, however. The second approach has used a radiometric partition assay to measure directly hydrolysis of JH. The hydrolytic activity is predominantly located in the pupal cytosolic fraction, but in adults is found in the microsomal fraction. Native PAGE analysis of the hydrolytic activity reveals that it does not correspond to the esterase identified as the *D. virilis* JHE homologue. Current studies are directed towards characterizing the putative JHEs identified by electrophoretic and radiometric assays to determine their relationship.

POSSIBLE APPLICATIONS IN INSECT CONTROL
Molecular Analysis of Physiology

The JH signalling pathway presents an obvious target for control strategies based on genetic engineering technology but this will only be possible when the mode of action of each factor in the pathway is understood. As described above, the isolation of the relevant peptides and genes will provide us with a battery of immunological and nucleic acid reagents with which to probe the sites of production and action of these molecules and to begin a concerted attack on the biochemical and pharmacological aspects of the JH signalling pathway in dipteran insects. Such studies will be necessary not only for the design of novel insecticidal compounds but may also form an important part of the case for registration of these products by government regulatory agencies.

The regulation of JH synthesis can be addressed at several levels. First, the isolation of an allatotropic peptide will elucidate the mechanism by which the allatotropic signal is transmitted across the CA plasma membrane. Several studies have implicated cAMP as a second messenger for both allatotropins and allatostatins.(59, 60), suggesting the involvement of a G-protein linked receptor system. Second, biochemical studies of JH biosynthesis and comparison with cholesterol and isoprenoid synthetic pathways in vertebrates have suggested that HMG-CoA reductase might be the rate-limiting step and therefore the point of regulation of JH synthesis. Accordingly, it was proposed that reversible phosphorylation of HMG-CoA reductase might provide a mechanism for the regulation of JH synthesis (61). Third, the mechanism of JH release from the CA is unknown. However, it has been demonstrated (62) that in L. migratoria high concentrations of potassium ions stimulate JH release and that the effect was dependent on calcium ions; although it was not possible to distinguish between calcium mediated vesicle release and calcium as a second messenger in a signal transduction pathway. The isolation of the neuroendocrine signalling molecules and their receptors will provide the opportunity to investigate these processes directly at the cellular level.

As with regulation of JH synthesis by neuroendocrine factors, little is known of the receptor-mediated mechanism of action of JH, although the existence of both cytoplasmic and nuclear receptors has been claimed (32, 40 and 63). To date, two different membrane-protein-mediated cellular responses to JH have been described, involving Ca^{2+} and protein kinase C in the male accessory glands of D. melanogaster (64) and a membrane Na^+, K^+-ATPase in ovarian follicle cells of Rhodnius prolixus (65). Clearly isolation and purification of the JH receptors will be necessary for a complete understanding of these phenomena.

JH esterase in Lepidoptera is postulated to lower circulating JH levels in the haemolymph. In Diptera haemolymph JH levels are very low and it is unclear if the esterases have the same functions in this tissue. Although JH esterase has been detected in the peripheral tissues of D. hydei (51), the role of JH esterase in target tissues has not been addressed in any insect. The role, if any, of JH esterase in degrading receptor bound JH in target tissues can be addressed directly using reagents generated by molecular biological studies.

In vitro Expression Systems

Cloning and sequencing of the genes that encode allatotropins, allatostatins, allatohibins, juvenile hormone receptors and the degradative enzymes would make them available for insertion into in vitro expression systems. The nuclear polyhedrosis viruses (NPVs) from Autographa californica or Heliothis should be suitable for this purpose since it is possible to generate large quantities of foreign proteins from engineered NPVs in compatible cell culture systems (66, 67).

Two sets of advantages would flow from the application of this technology. First, generation of the unmodified proteins would have utility in determining the structure of important regions of the proteins such as ligand- or receptor-binding surfaces. The information would be valuable in the biorational design of novel insecticides. Existing molecular genetic technology would allow the creation of modified or chimaeric proteins which could be expressed in order to test models of ligand-receptor interactions. This approach could be applied to an allatotropin stimulating a cell-surface receptor or to a JH binding soluble intracellular receptor or to the resultant complex interacting with nuclear binding sites.

The second advantage to flow from *in vitro* expression of one of these genes would be its value as a laboratory tool in the screening of modified or novel insecticides. This can be illustrated for the case of the juvenile hormone receptor. An assay based on the effect exerted by a ligand on the interaction of the ligand-receptor complex with DNA or nuclear proteins might allow efficient preliminary screening of JH agonist and antagonist activities. A true JH antagonist would be a particularly valuable innovation because juvenoid insecticides by their nature are only useful where the larval stage of the pest is not the principal cause of damage. In other cases currently available juvenoids may actually be detrimental because they prolong the damaging larval stage. The ideal target of such research would therefore be an anti-JH agent since no commercial agents of this type are yet available.

Genetic Engineering Applications

Several properties of the JH system recommend its use in novel approaches to insect pest control involving genetic engineering. First, JH is essentially restricted to arthropods, and some individual components of the JH signalling system are specific down to the genus level at least. Organisms engineered with selected components of the system should therefore satisfy the target specificity criteria required for their registration as insecticidal agents. Second, several critical components of the system are unmodified peptide or protein products of single genes and as such are readily amenable to recombinant DNA and genetic engineering technologies. Third, these single gene components are implicated in diverse aspects of JH metabolism, encompassing its synthesis, action and degradation. A wide range of approaches should therefore be possible to disrupt JH metabolism using genetic engineering technologies.

Importantly also, this flexibility in terms of components of the JH system which could be targeted for disruption is paralleled by the increasing flexibility of the genetic engineering technology by which such disruption could be achieved. The amount of the relevant gene product could be increased by judicious use of synthetic promoters (68); or it could be decreased, by the use of appropriately designed antagonistic antisense or ribozyme genes (69); or its function could be altered qualitatively, for example by site-directed *in vitro* mutagenesis of its catalytic domains (70). Moreover, potentially at least, there are several alternative routes by which these strategically adapted gene products could be delivered to an insect. These options include the engineering of the pest insect itself, of viruses infecting the pest, or of the beneficial species to be protected from the pest.

What then are the prospects for the practical application of these various theoretical possibilities for disrupting the JH system by genetic engineering? In terms of cloned genes available for genetic engineering, a gene encoding a JH esterase has recently been cloned from *Heliothis* (56) and we are currently working to clone its dipteran parallels. The allatotropin peptide from

Manduca (15) and 4 allatostatic peptides from *Diploptera punctata* have been purified and sequenced (9) and synthetic genes encoding these relatively small molecules could be constructed readily. A putative receptor protein has recently been purified from *Drosophila* Kc cells (7) and we and others are now purifying them from other sources; the characterization of these proteins will permit the cloning of the corresponding genes. Several of the JH receptors, the allatotropin and the JH esterase may be life-stage- and species-specific in their activity. Nevertheless, at least some suitable genes affecting JH production, action or degradation are now available for engineering, or soon will be.

Of the various genetic engineering technologies for exploiting these cloned resources, the engineering of the pests themselves or the beneficial species requiring protection would seem less promising than the engineering of the viruses infecting the pests. The technology to engineer insects is currently limited to a few species of *Drosophila* (71). Even if the technology could be generalised to other insects, and presuming genes could be inserted to disrupt processes like JH metabolism, the problem would still remain that the deleterious engineered genotypes would not persist or spread in the pest populations. This same problem has beset attempts to develop autocidal genetic control systems using classical genetics. The problem can be overcome using various elements promoting meiotic drive (see for example 72 with *L. cuprina*) but the virus-based strategy below would generally be simpler.

The technology to engineer beneficial species requiring protection is available for several farm animals and dicotyledonous plants, and a degree of insect resistance has been engineered into some crop plants with the gene encoding a *Bacillus thuringiensis* toxin and some genes encoding protease inhibitors (73). One essential criterion for insecticidal genes expressed in this way is that their products either be direct gut poisons like the *B. thuringiensis* toxins or the protease inhibitors, or that they be small enough to reach their target sites across the gut membranes. Large proteins like JH receptors or JH esterase do not meet this criterion. Allatotropin may be small enough to cross the gut membrane, but we are unaware of bioassay results to test this possibility.

The most promising engineering technology with which to disrupt JH metabolism probably involves the NPVs. Such viruses infect the larvae of many pest Lepidoptera and several wild-type NPVs have already been used as biological insecticides (74). Their efficacy as insecticides has generally been limited by their slow rate of kill and low pathogenicity against middle- or late-instar larvae, but these problems could be overcome by engineering the viruses with larvicidal genes. The technology to engineer NPVs is well established (75) and genes disrupting JH metabolism could be expected to have larvicidal effects if engineered into the NPVs. For example, overproduction of JH esterase in larvae infected with an NPV containing a JH esterase gene should reduce JH titres and induce precocious or aberrant moults. Larvicidal effects might also result from infection with NPVs engineered with several other components of the JH system, but without greater understanding of their modes of action, their precise effects are difficult to predict.

268

REFERENCES

1.   Staal, G.B. (1986). Ann. Rev. Entomol. 31: 391-429.

2.   de Kort, C.A.D. and Granger, N.A. (1981). Ann. Rev. Entomol. 26: 1-28.

3.   Richard, D.S., Applebaum, S.W., Sliter, T.J., Baker, F.C., Schooley, D.A., Reuter, C.C., Henrich, V.C. and Gilbert, L.I. (1989). Proc. Natl. Acad. Sci. USA. 86: 1421-1425.

4.   Hammock, B.D. (1985). In: Kerkut, G.A. and Gilbert, L I. (eds) Comprehensive Insect Physiology, Biochemistry and Pharmacology. Pergamon Press, Oxford. Vol. 7 pp. 431-472.

5.   Koeppe, J.K., Fuchs, M., Chen, T.T., Hunt, L.M., Kovalick, G.E. and Briers, T. (1985). In: Kerkut, G.A. and Gilbert, L.I. (eds) Comprehensive Insect Physiology, Biochemistry and Pharmacology. Permagon Press, Oxford. Vol. 8. pp 165-203.

6.   Staal, G.B. (1982). Ent. Exp. Appl. 31:15-23.

7.   Wang, X., Chang, E.S. and O'Connor, J.D. (1989). Insect Biochem. 19: 327-335.

8.   Tobe, S.S. and Stay, B. (1985). Advances Insect Physiol. 18: 305-432.

9.   Woodhead, A.P., Stay, B., Seidel, M.A. and Tobe, S.S. (1989). Proc. Natl. Acad. Sci. U.S.A. 86: 5997-6001.

10.   Granger, N.A. and Borg, T.K. (1976). Gen. Comp. Endocrinol. 29: 349-359.

11.   Granger, N.A., Mitchell, L.J., Janzen, W.P. and Bollenbacher, W.E. (1984). Mol. Cell. Endocrinol. 37: 349-358.

12.   Ulrich, G.M., Schlagintweit, B., Eder, J. and Rembold, H. (1985). Gen. Comp. Endocrinol. 59: 120-129.

13.   Rembold, H., Schlagintweit, B. and Ulrich, G.M. (1986). J. Insect Physiol. 32: 91-94.

14.   Gadot, M., Rafaeli, A. and Applebaum, S.W. (1987). Archives Insect Biochem. Physiol. 4: 213-223.

15.   Kataoka, H., Toschi, A., Li, J.P., Carney, R.L., Schooley, D.A. and Kramer, S.J. (1989). Science. 243: 1481-1483.

16.   Bouletreau-Merle, J. (1974). J. Insect Physiol. 20: 2035-2041.

17.   Postlethwait, J.H. and Shirk, P.D. (1981). Amer. Zool. 21: 687-700.

18.   Hagedorn, H.H., Turner, S., Hagedorn, E.A., Pontecorvo, D., Greenbaum, P., Pfeiffer, D., Wheelock, G. and Flanagan, T.R. (1977). J. Insect Physiol. 23: 203-206.

19.   Thomsen, E. (1951). J. Exp. Biol. 29: 137-172.

20.   Lea, A.O. (1975). J. Insect Physiol. 21: 1747-1750.

21.   Bouletreau-Merle, J. (1976). J. Insect Physiol. 22: 933-940.

22.   Barton Brown, L., van Gerwen, A.C.M. and Roberts, J.A. (1986). Int .J. Invert. Reproduction and Development. 10: 179-186.

23.   Fraenkel, G. and Hollowell, M. (1979). J. Insect Physiol. 25: 305-310.

24.   Evans, R.M. (1988) Science 240: 889-895.

25.   Engelmann, F. (1981) In: Pratt, G.E. and Brooks, G.T. (eds) Juvenile Hormone Biochemistry. Elsevier, North Holland Biomedical Press. pp 233-240.

26.   Van Mellaert, H., Theunis, S. and De Loof, A. (1985). Insect Biochem. 15: 655-661.

27.   Rayne, R.C. and Koeppe, J.K. (1988). Insect Biochem. 18: 667-673.

28.   Schmialek, P., Borowski, M., Geyer, A., Miosga, V., Nündel, M., Rosenberg, E. and Zapf, B. (1973). Z. Naturforsch. 28c: 453-456.

29.   Klages, G., Emmerich, H. and Peter, M.G. (1980). Nature 286: 282-285.

30.   Engelmann, F. (1981). Mol. Cell. Endocrinol. 24: 103-112.

31. Engelmann, F. (1984). In: Engels, W. (ed) Advances in Invertebrate Reproduction. Elsevier, Amsterdam. pp 177-184.

32. Engelmann, F., Mala, J. and Tobe, S.S. (1987). Insect Biochem. 17: 1045-1052.

33. Roberts, P.E. and Wyatt, G.R. (1983). Mol. Cell. Endocrinol. 31: 53-69.

34. Wisniewski, T.R. and Kochman, M. (1984). FEBS Lett. 171: 127-130.

35. Roberts, P.E. and Jefferies, L.S. (1986). Arch. Insect Biochem. Physiol. (Supplement) 1: 7-23.

36. Riddiford, L.M., Osir, E.O., Fittinghoff, C.M. and Green, J.M. (1987). Insect Biochem. 17: 1039-1044.

37. Wisniewski, T.R., Wawrzenczyk, G., Prestwich, G.D. and Kochman, M. (1988). Insect Biochem. 18: 29-36.

38. Chang, E.S., Coudron, T.A., Bruce, M.J., Sage, B.A., O'Connor, J.D. and Law, J.H. (1980). Proc. Natl. Acad. Sci. USA. 77: 4657-4661.

39. Chang, E.S., Bruce, M.J. and Prestwich, G.D. (1985). Insect Biochem. 15: 197-204.

40. Osir, E.O. and Riddiford, L.M. (1988). J. Biol. Chem. 263: 13812-13818.

41. Prestwich, G.D., Singh, A.K., Carvalho, J.F., Koeppe, J.K. and Kovalick, G.E. (1984). Tetrahedron 40: 529-537.

42. Prestwich, G.D. and Wawrzenczyk, C. (1985). Proc. Natl. Acad. Sci. USA. 82: 5290-5294.

43. Prestwich, G.D., Koeppe, J.K., Kovalick, G.E., Brown, J.J., Chang, E.S., and Singh, A.K. (1985). Meth. Enzymol. 111: 509-530.

44. Hammock, B.D., Mumby, S.M. and Lee, P.W. (1977). Pestic. Biochem. Physiol. 7: 261-272.

45. Jones, D., Jones, G., Wing, K.D., Rudnicka, M. and Hammock, B.D. (1982). J. Comp. Physiol. 148: 1-10.

46. Ajami, A.M. and Riddiford, L.M. (1988). J. Insect. Physiol. 19: 635-645.

47. Yu, S.J. and Terriere, L.C. (1978). Pestic. Biochem. Physiol. 9: 237-246.

48. Wing, K.D., Sparks, T.C., Lovell, V.M., Levinson, S.O. and Hammock, B.D. (1981). Insect Biochem. 11: 473-485.

49. Wilson, T.G. and Gilbert, L.I. (1978). Comp. Biochem. Physiol. 60A: 85-89.

50. Korochkin, L.I., Ludwig, M.Z., Poliakova, E.V. and Philinova, M.R. (1987). Sov. Sci. Rev. F. Physiol. Gen. Biol. 1: 411-466.

51. Klages, G. and Emmerich, H. (1979). J. Comp. Physiol. 132: 319-325.

52. Sparks, T.C. and Hammock, B.D. (1979). J. Insect. Physiol. 25: 551-560.

53. Jones, G. and Hammock, B.D. (1983). J. Insect Physiol. 29: 471-475.

54. Rauschenbach, I. Yu, Lukashina, N.S., Budker, V.G. and Korochkin, L.I. (1987). Biochem. Genet. 25: 687-704.

55. Sparks, T.C. and Hammock, B.D. (1980). Pestic. Biochem. Physiol. 14: 290-302.

56. Hanzlik, T.N., Abdel-Aal, Y.A.I., Harshman, L.G. and Hammock, B.D. (1989). J. Biol. Chem. 264: 12419-12425.

57. Sliter, T.J., Sedlak, B.J., Baker, F.C. and Schooley, D.A. (1987). Insect Biochem. 17: 161-165.

58. Hammock, B.D. Abdel-Aal, Y.A.I., Mullin, C.A., Hanzlik, T.N. and Roe, R.M. (1984). Pestic. Biochem. Physiol. 22: 209-223.

59. Aucoin, R.R., Rankin, S.M., Stay, B. and Tobe, S.S. (1987). Insect Biochem. 17: 965-969.

60. Feyereisen, R. and Farnsworth, D.E. (1987). Insect Biochem. 17: 939-942.

61. Feyereisen, R. (1985). In: Kerkut, G.A. and Gilbert, L.I. (eds) Comprehensive Insect Physiology, Biochemistry and Pharmacology. Pergamon Press, Oxford. Vol. 8. pp 391-429.

62. Dale, J.F.and Tobe, S.S. (1988). Physiological Entomology. 13: 21-27.

63. Goodman, W.G. and Chang, E.S. (1985). In: Kerkut, G.A. and Gilbert, L.I. (eds) Comprehensive Insect Physiology, Biochemistry and Pharmacology. Pergamon Press, Oxford. Vol. 7. pp 491-510.

64. Yamamoto, K., Chadarevian, A. and Pellegrini, M. (1988). Science. 239: 916-919.

65. Ilenchuk, T.T. and Davey, K.G. (1987). Insect Biochem. 17: 1085-1088.

66. Smith, G.E., Fraser, M.J. and Summers, M.D. (1983). J. Virol. 46: 584-593.

67. Maatsura, Y., Possee, R.D., Overton, H.A. and Bishop, D.H.L. (1987). J. Gen. Virol. 68: 1233-1250.

68. Guarino, L.A. and Summers, M.D. (1986). J. Virol. 61: 2091-2099

69. Haseloff, J and Gerlach,W.L. (1988). Nature 334: 585-591.

70. Lindberg, R.L.P. and Negishi, M. (1989). Nature 339: 632-634.

71. Engels,W.R. (1989). In: Berg, D.E. and Howe, M.A. (eds) Mobile DNA. Am. Soc. Microbiol. Washington D.C. pp 437-478

72. Foster, G.G., Vogt,W.G., Woodburn, T.L. and Smith, P.H. (1988). Theor. Appl. Genet. 76: 870-879

73. Meeusen, R.L. and Warren, G. (1988). Ann. Rev. Entomol. 34: 373-381.

74. Cunningham, J.C. (1988). Outlook on Agriculture 17: 10-17.

75. Luckow, V.A. and Summers, M.D. (1988). Biotechnology 6: 47-55.

© 1990 Elsevier Science Publishers B.V. (Biomedical Division)
Pesticides and alternatives, editor J.E. Casida

271

THE EFFECT OF METHOPRENE ON RNA AND CHITINOLYTIC ENZYMES SYNTHESIS AND ON ECDYSTEROID TITER IN SOME INSECTS

ELI SHAAYA

Division of Stored Products, The Volcani Center, Bet-Dagan 50250, Israel.

KLAUS-D. SPINDLER

Institute of Zoology, University of Düsseldorf, D-4000 Düsseldorf 1, West Germany.

INTRODUCTION

Insect growth regulators (IGRs) are highly selective insecticides which interfere with normal insect growth and development. The juvenile hormone analogues (JHAs) are the most extensive group of IGRs which by mimicking the natural juvenile hormone, have a wide range of novel biological effects on insects. In particular, they cause arrest and/or disruption of metamorphosis, which results in the formation of supernumerary larvae or nonviable larval-pupal or pupal-adult intermediates [1,2]. The discovery of JHAs and their biological, chemical, and economic prospects, have been reviewed extensively [3,4,5]. This paper deals with the effect of methoprene, a potent juvenile hormone analogue, on RNA and chitinolytic enzymes synthesis and on ecdysteroid titer in some insects.

Fig. 1. Chemical structure of juvenile hormone I and methoprene.

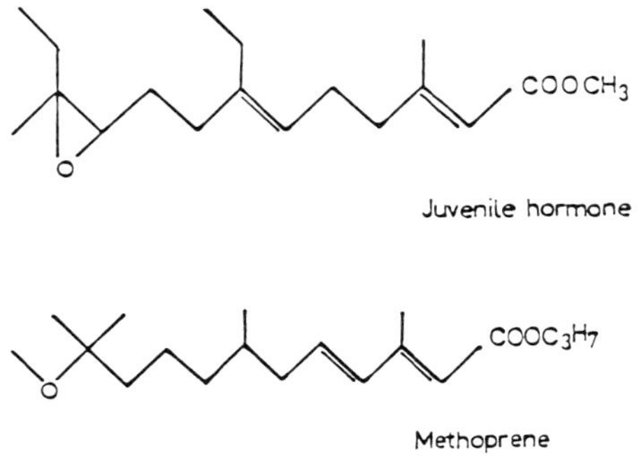

Juvenile hormone

Methoprene

RESULTS AND DISCUSSION

Effect of Methoprene on Egg Production

The JHA, methoprene (Fig. 1) interferes with the normal development of Ephestia cautella eggs so that young larvae die shortly before or after they hatch from the eggs. Ephestia cautella embryos which exhibit high sensitivity to this compound are embryos prior to blastokinesis, aged 0-30 hours. When given to young eggs age 0-4 hours for a period of 24 hours, methoprene caused mortality in 60% of the newly emerged larvae and only 15% of the treated eggs developed into normal adults. Older eggs (after blastokinesis) which received the same treatment, were found to be less susceptible to this JHA (Fig. 2).

Embryos exposed to methoprene throughout their entire embryonic development starting from the preblastokinesis stage displayed results similar to those described above (data not shown). Parallel results were obtained with the older embryos (short and long term exposure to methoprene were found similarly less susceptible to the compound). This is consistent with the finding that the JH or JHA block embryonic development in other lepidopteran insects and Diptera [6,7,8].

Methoprene was found to have no effect on the production of ecdysteriods during embryonic development in Ephestia cautella. Measuring the ecdysteroid titer during this period in control and treated eggs showed that in both cases the ecdysteroid titers increased on day 2, reaching a maximum on day 3, about one day prior the hatching of the eggs (Fig. 3). The higher concentration of ecdysteroids measured in the treated eggs may be due to the difficulty in measuring the precise age of the eggs. It should be noted that in locusts ecdysone in the early stages of embryogenesis is produced either through hydrolysis of maternal conjugates or through hydroxylation of ecdysone precursors. Only later in the post-blastokinetic embryo can ecdysone be produced by the differentiated prothoracic gland [9].

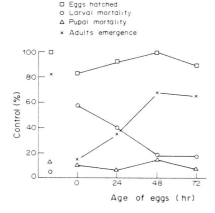

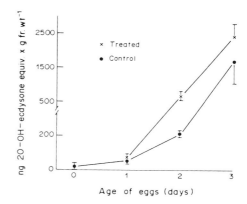

Fig. 2. Change in sensitivity
to methoprene during embryonic
development of Ephestia. Eggs
were exposed to the JHA
impregnated on Whatman No.1
filter paper (1g/m²) for a
period of 24 hr at various
ages. The mortality of eggs,
larvae and pupa were recorded
[10].

Fig. 3. Ecdysteroid
concentration in control and
methoprene treated eggs of
Ephestia. Eggs were exposed to
the JHA (1g/m²) until they
were used for the test. The
vertical lines denote SE [10]

EFFECT OF METHOPRENE ON LARVAL AND PUPAL DEVELOPMENT

Methoprene was also found to inhibit metamorphosis and caused
the production of giant larvae when it was applied to larvae
prior to the wandering stage. However, it did not prevent
pupation when it was given to larvae shortly before pupation, but
did prevent adult emergence of the treated larvae. The same
results were obtained when it was applied to young pupae. Studies
to determine the sensitivity of Ephestia cautella larvae during
the last larval instar (duration 8 days) showed that the compound
inhibits metamorphosis and causes production of giant larvae when
it is given to larvae within the first 4 days following the last
larval molt. Older larvae were found unresponsive to methoprene

274

and seemed to pupate normally, however, total mortality resulted
in the subsequent pupal stage (Table 1). From dissecting the dead
pupae it was concluded that the block in development occurred in
the pharate adult stage. The change in sensitivity to methoprene
in the last larval instar occurred after the appearance (shortly
before wandering) of a small ecdysteroid peak (Fig. 4A) and
correlated to the production of giant hetero-disperse nuclear RNA
in the epidermal cells (Table 1). In larvae treated with
methoprene the small ecdysteroid peak, as well as the main peak,

	Larvae introduced to methoprene, days following the final larval moult						
	1	2	3	4	5	6	7
Pupation %	0	0	0	15	80	100	100
Adult emergence (%)	–	–	–	0	0	0	0
HnRNA formation in control larvae	–	–	–	–	±	+	+

TABLE I
Change in sensitivity of Ephestia to methoprene during the last
larval instar [10].

could not be detected (Fig. 4B). Instead, a number of small
ecdysteroid peaks were measured. The appearance of these
ecdysteroid peaks might well be due to the extra molt found to
occur during the production of giant larvae. Depression in
ecdysteriod production as a result of juvenile hormone or JHA
treatment has also been found in other endopterygote insects such
as Galleria [11]. This effect might be related to methoprene
inhibiting the production of PTTH, a hormone which stimulates the
prothoracic glands to produce ecdysone [12,13]. Another
possibility exists in which JHA directly suppresses the
production of ecdysone in the prothoracic glands [14]. It should
also be mentioned that Nighout [15], Berreur et. al. [16], and
Shaaya [17], proposed that the small peak of ecdysteroids in the
last larval instar (Fig. 4A) is responsible for the genetic
switchover which occurs during development of larva to pupa. This

peak is also responsible for the permanent shut off of
larval-specific genes such as those which code for larval
cuticular proteins and for the larval pigment insecticyanin
[18,19].

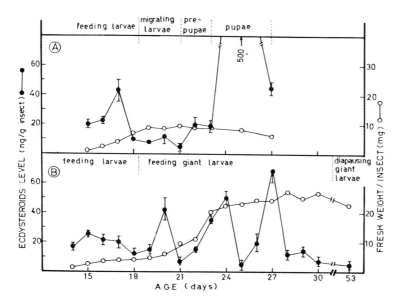

Fig. 4. Ecdysteroid titers during the fourth larval instar of
Ephestia in control (A) and methoprene treated larvae age 13 days
(B). Each larva received topically 10 μg JHA in 1μl
acetone. Controls received 1μl acetone alone. Vertical lines
denote SD [20].

The sensitivity of the pupae to methoprene was also found to be
age dependent. Methoprene was lethal when given to young pupae,
0-1 day old but less effective when given to older pupae
(Fig. 5). Measuring the ecdysteroid titer during pupal-adult
development in control and treated pupae showed that the
ecdysteroid titer of animals treated 2 days prior to pupation
was found to be considerably lower than in control animals
(Fig. 6). This was not the case when the JHA was given to pupae
age 0-10 hours. In this developmental stage JHA was found to have
no pronounced effect on the ecdysteroid titer with the exception

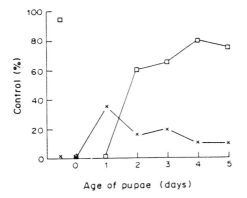

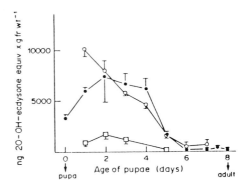

Fig. 5. Change in sensitivity to methoprene during pupal-adult development of <u>Ephestia</u>. Each pupa received 6µg JHA in 1µl acetone at the various ages. ▫———▫ Normanl adults; x———x non viable adults [10].

Fig. 6. Ecdysteroid concentration in control and methoprene treated larvae of <u>Ephestia</u> before and after pupation. The animals received 6µg JHA in 1µl acetone. (●———●) Control; (▫———▫) larvae treated 2-3 days prior to pupation; (o———o) pupae treated 0-5hr after pupation. The vertical lines denote SE [10].

that higher amounts of ecdysteriods were measured in day 1 treated pupae compared to control pupae (Fig. 6). Our data show that animals treated with JHA shortly before or after pupation seem to undergo normal metamorphosis although they die shortly before adult emergence. It is interesting to note that though in Lepidoptera the prothoracic gland is the source of ecdysteroids in the larvae shortly before pupation and also in young pupae [11], we could detect a profound decrease in ecdysteroid titer only when the JHA was given shortly before pupation. It seems that the lethal effect of methoprene cannot only be due to the lack of ecdysteroid production during pupal development.

EFFECT OF METHOPRENE ON RNA SYNTHSIS

Changes in RNA synthesis in the epidermal cells of last instar larvae of <u>Ephestia cautella</u>, <u>Manduca</u> <u>sexta</u>, and <u>Calliphora</u> <u>vicina</u> were followed. Just prior to the wandering stage, total RNA synthesis was depressed for about 30 hours (Fig. 7) and [21,22].

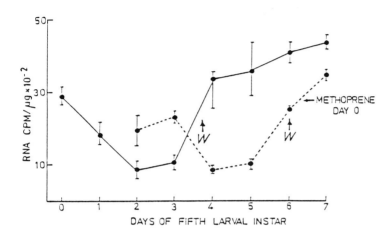

Fig. 7. Comparison of [³H] uridine incorporation into epidermal RNA of control last 5th-instar <u>Manduca</u> larva to larva treated with 10µg methoprene at day 0 of last instar. (●----●) Treated larvae; (●———●) Control; W; Wandering stage; Vertical lines denote SD.

The shut down of RNA synthesis including that of rRNA (Fig. 8, three and four days after the last larval molt) appears to be one of the first metamorphic responses to ecdysteroids in the absence of juvenile hormone and permits the loss of ribosomes.
In <u>Calliphora</u>, this change caused a reduction in 60% of the bulk RNA in the epidermal cells [21]. Following this depression period, pupally committed epidermal cells synthesize a new type

278

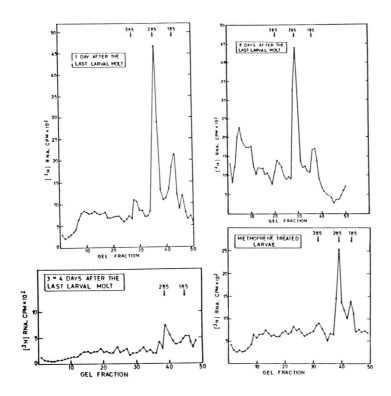

Fig. 8. Electrophoretic separation of _Ephestia_ epidermal RNA
synthesized in vitro in the last larval instar during 1hr [³H]
uridine pulse in control and methoprene treated larvae. Larvae were
transferred to a culture medium containing 25 ppm methoprene
immediately after the final larval molt and killed six days later.

of RNA termed hetero-disperse nuclear RNA (HnRNA) (Fig. 8, six
days after the last larval molt) and [21,22]. Although this RNA
species contains mRNA precursors and other turning over nuclear
RNA, all of its functions are not well understood [23]. The
coincidence of HnRNA synthesis with the cessation of larval-
specific mRNA synthesis shortly prior to the appearance of
pupal-specific mRNAs [18], suggests that it could play a role in
the permanent shutting off of larval-specific genes and/or
unmasking of the previously unexpressed pupal genes. The
appearance of this RNA species when RNA synthesis first resumes

is one of the first manifestations of pupal commitment.
Methoprene was found to prevent these changes in RNA synthesis
when it was given to young larvae. In <u>Manduca</u> <u>sexta</u> wandering was
delayed for 2 days and the depression of RNA synthesis was found
to occur 2 days later if larvae in the early last instar were
treated with the JHA (Fig. 7). Methoprene was also found to
prevent the shift in RNA synthesis and the production of giant
HnRNA (Fig. 8, methoprene treated larvae). This was expected as
methoprene was found to depress the small ecdysteroid peak (Fig.
4B). This peak was shown to induce the synthesis of this HnRNA
[24].

THE INFLUENCE OF METHOPRENE ON THE ACTIVITIES OF CHITINOLYTIC
ENZYMES

If the JHA was present in the culture media from the beginning
of the last larval instar of <u>Ephestia</u> <u>cautella</u>, the animals were
unable to pupate and they showed low levels of ecdysteroid titers.

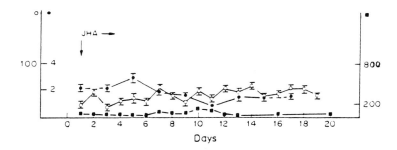

Fig. 9. Titer of ecdysteroids (■;ng 20-OH-ecdysone equiv.x g wet
wt^{-1}), chitinase activity (●;cmpxmg protein^{-1}) and N-acetylglucosaminidase activity (o;mU x mg protein^{-1}) of <u>Ephestia</u> continuously
treated with methoprene. Vertical lines denotes SD [25].

In additon, the activity of the chitinolytic enzymes, chitinase
and N-acetylglucosaminidase was also very low (Fig. 9). It
should be noted that in control animals the rise in chitinase
activity in the last larval instar begins 2 days before pupation

and the activity curve shows a peak followed by a steep decrease
at pupation. During the pupal stage there is fluctuation of the
enzyme activity (figure not shown) similar to the JHA treated
larvae (Fig. 10).

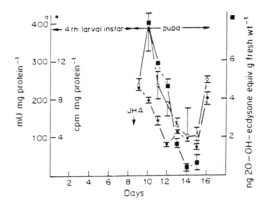

Fig. 10. Titer of ecdysone (■), chitinase activity (●) and
N-acetylglucosaminidase activity (o) of Ephestia, treated once at
the first day of pupal life with 6μg methoprene. Vertical lines
denote SD [25].

In contrast to the chitinase activity curve, the main peak of the
activity of N-acetylglucosaminidase was reached at the second day
of the pupal stage (figure not shown). When methoprene was given
once topically on the first day of the pupal stage (Fig. 10) no
differences in either ecdysteroid titer or specific enzyme
activities could be seen in comparison to control animals. The
treatment of Ephestia cautella with methoprene showed quite
different effects depending on the time of application.
Methoprene must be applied before the small ecdysteroid peak in
order to prevent the rise in the activity of chitinolytic
enzymes. At the same time it also prevents the appearance of the
small ecdysteroid peak. The small ecdysteroid peak is known to be
responsible for the physiological changes which are necessary for
pupal development as discussed before. This might also be true
for the increase in activity of chitin degrading enzymes. The
question arises whether methoprene acts directly on the levels of
chitinolytic enzymes activities or only indirectly via changes in

the titer of ecdysteroids. The latter seems to be more probable since there is a pronounced time-lag between application of methoprene and its effect. In addition, different schedules of JHA treatment always led to a similar change in the titers of ecdysteroids and chitin degrading enzymes [25]. Such a direct effect of ecdysteroids on the level of chitinolytic enzymes has been also described in other insect [26, 27].

Acknowledgments

We wish to thank Mrs. S. Plotkin and Mrs. D. Goldman for assistance in preparing the manuscript. We are also very grateful to the Alexander-von- Humboloh-Stiftung for financial support.

REFERENCES
1. Hollingworth RM (1976) In: Wilkinson CF (ed) Insecticide Biochemistry and Physiology. Plenum Press, New York, pp 431-506

2. Sehnal F (1976) In: Gilbert LI (ed) The Juvenile Hormones. Plenum Press, New York, pp 301-321

3. Slama K (1974) In: Slama K, Romanuk M, Sorm F (eds) Insect Hormones and Bioanalogues. Springer Verlag, Vienna, pp 90-281

4. Staal GB (1975) Annu Rev Entomol 20:417

5. Retnakarn A, Granett J and Ennis T (1985) In: Kerkut GA and Gilbert LI (eds) Comprehensive Insect Physiology, Biochemistry and Pharmacology. Pergamon Press, New York Vol. 12, pp 529-601.

6. Retnakaran A (1970) Can Ent 102:1592-1596

7. Riddiford LM (1970) Devl Biol 22:249-263

8. Smith R and Arking R (1975) J Insect Physiol 21:723-732

9. Hoffmann JA, Lagueux M, Hetru C, Charlet M, and Goltzene F (1980) In: Hoffman JA (ed) Progress in Ecdysone Research. Elsevier/North-Holland, Amsterdam, pp 431-465

10. Shaaya E, Spindler-Barth M, and Spindler KD (1986) Insect Biochem. 16: 181-185

11. Sehnal F, Maroy P, and Mala J (1981) J. Insect Physiol 27:535-544

12. Chippendale GM (1977) A Rev Ent 22:121-138

13. Takeda (1978) Gen Comp Endocr 34:123-131

14. Ciemior KE, Sehnal F, and Schneiderman HA (1979) Z angew Ent 88: 414-425

15. Nijhout HE (1976) J Insect Physiol 22:453-463

16. Berreur P, Porcheron P, Berreur-Bonnefont J, and Simpson P (1979) J exp Zool 210:347-352

17. Shaaya E (1979) Hoppe-Seylers Z Physiol Chem 360:445-449

18. Riddiford LM (1982) Devl Biol 92:330-342

19. Riddiford LM, Backmann A, Hice RH, and Rebero J (1986) Devl Biol 118:82-94

20. Lazarovici P, Shapira D, Pisarev V, and Shaaya E (1984) Archs Insect Biochem. Physiol. 1:409-415

21. Shaaya E (1976) Insect Biochem 6:553-559

22. Shaaya E and Riddiford LM (1988) J Insect Physiol 34:655-659

23. Sekeris CE (1985) J theor Biol 114:601-604

24. Shaaya E and Levenbook L (1982) Insect Biochem 12:663-667

25. Spindler-Barth M, Shaaya E and spindler KD (1986) Insect Biochem 16: 187-190

26. Spindler KD (1983) In: Scheller K (ed) The larval serum proteins of insects. Theime Verlag, Stuttgart pp. 135-150

27. Chen AC (1987) Archs Insect Biochem. Physiol. 6:267-277

© 1990 Elsevier Science Publishers B.V. (Biomedical Division)
Pesticides and alternatives, editor J.E. Casida

INSECT NEUROPEPTIDES: NEW STRATEGIES FOR INSECT CONTROL

THOMAS J. KELLY, EDWARD P. MASLER AND JULIUS J. MENN
Insect Reproduction Laboratory, Plant Sciences Institute, USDA, ARS,
Beltsville, Maryland 20705 (U.S.A.)

I. HISTORY AND OVERVIEW

Biologists have long recognized the importance of chemical messengers for transferring information and regulating development or homeostasis within organisms. In fact, it was seventy years ago when Kopec [1,2] first demonstrated endocrine activity in an invertebrate, the gypsy moth, Lymantria dispar. His discovery of a "pupation factor", secreted by the brain, was the first indication anywhere in the animal kingdom that nervous tissue could produce hormones [3]. This initial observation of neurohormonal regulation was subsequently verified for numerous physiological processes in vertebrates and invertebrates. In insects these neurohormone-regulated processes include growth, development, molting, reproduction, diapause, behavior, color change, metabolism, ion and water balance, and muscle contraction [4-17] (Fig. 1). Known neurohormone-regulated processes in insects now number over 30 and continue to be identified at a rapid pace [15].

Although the rate of identification of these processes expanded rapidly during the 1950's and 1960's, it was not until 1975 that the first insect neuropeptide, proctolin (Arg-Tyr-Leu-Pro-Thr-OH), was structurally characterized 1975 [18]. Since that time over 40 additional insect neurohormones have been sequenced, most within the past five years [10,11, 13,16,17,19,20] (Table 1).

As the class Insecta is the largest class in the animal kingdom, insect neuropeptides may be expected to possess a high degree of structural and functional diversity. This diversity has already been demonstrated for three insect neuropeptide families: adipokinetic/hyperglycemic, myokinins, and prothoracicotropic hormones [15]. The proliferation of structually identi-fied insect neurohormones promises to escalate as a result of advances in bioassay and separation technology and the attendant implications for insect control.

284

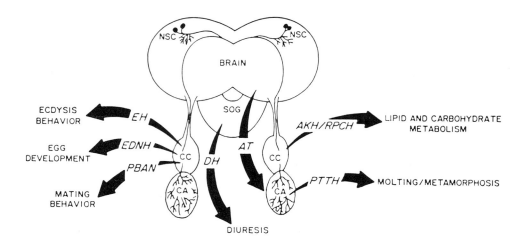

Fig. 1. Sites of presumed synthesis and/or release for structurally identified insect neuropeptides. For further information see [6,17]. In the case of
PTTH, the synthetic neurosecretory cells and identified axons from Manduca
sexta [79] have also been included as an example. Synthetic neurosecretory
cells have also been identified in the lateral [80] and medial [81] regions
for M. sexta EH, with the gut proctodeal nerve acting as the neurohemal release
site for the medial cells during larval and pupal ecdyses. Myotropins and
PDHs have not been included. See Table 1 for full names of abbreviated
neuropeptides. NSC, neurosecretory cell; SOG, suboesophageal ganglion; CC,
corpus cardiacum; CA, corpus allatum.

The primary method for demonstrating a neurohormone-regulated process has
been by inactivation of the process by ablation of sites of neurohormone
synthesis or release (i.e. neurohemal), or through in vitro incubation of
target tissues. Reactivation of function is established by injection or in
vitro addition of extracts prepared from neurohormonal tissues. In many cases,
the simplest and most sensitive of these bioassay systems have been used for
purification of the neurohormone. In recent years, these techniques have been
supplemented and often simplified by the use of selected vertebrate and
non-insect invertebrate antibodies that are cross-reactive with insect
neurohormones. Through the use of antibody-based techniques, such as immuno-
cytochemistry, radioimmunoassay and affinity chromatography, cross-reactivity
with neurosecretory cells in insect tissue has been demonstrated [13,21],
and insect neurohormones have been purified. Other antibody-based approaches
have also been utilized [22].

II. ISOLATION, CHARACTERIZATION, AND IDENTIFICATION OF INSECT NEUROPEPTIDES

Since the initial isolation of proctolin from Periplaneta americana [23], which required more than 100,000 cockroaches (125 kg) to yield 180 µg of pure peptide, open column chromatographic and manual sequencing techniques have been supplanted by high performance liquid chromatography [24], FAB-MS, MS/MS, and gas-phase sequencing techniques [11,16,17,19]. These methods are more sophisticated and operationally simpler than those used for proctolin. Less than 1/1000 of the amount of material required for manual sequencing is now sufficient for gas-phase sequencing. The effort involved in collecting and preparing starting material has also been refined somewhat by techniques developed to isolate localized regions of the brain/neurohemal complex without tedious dissection of neuropeptide-producing tissues [19]. This initial effort eliminates much of the massive amount of non-specific material present in whole body or even head extracts, where, for example, twenty million B. mori heads were required to purify 4K-PTTH-II [25]. The techniques currently available for purification of insect neuropeptides have been recently reviewed [19]. Although these techniques require much less starting material and effort than that required 15 years ago, the effort is still considerable, and further refinements in sensitivity and simplicity can be expected.

Recently, a powerful technique, nucleic acid hybridization, was employed with insect neurohormones to identify peptide neurohormone primary structures from species for which the amino acid sequence was not previously determined [26-28]. This technique promises to revolutionize insect neuropeptide characterization and simultaneously provide us with knowledge of the regulation of synthesis and processing of insect neurohormones (see section IV).

III. IMPORTANCE OF NEUROPEPTIDE PRIMARY STRUCTURE AND PROHORMONE SEQUENCES

Determination of the primary structure of a neuropeptide is paramount to the development of methods of insect control based on neuropeptide chemistry and metabolism. From the primary structure, existing methods can be utilized to isolate receptors [29] and degradative enzymes [30,31], useful in develop- ment of agonistic/antagonistic analogs which may block in vivo activity. No receptors have yet been isolated for insect neuropeptides. However, it is envisioned that receptors could be utilized for rapid screening of super- agonists and antagonists of insect neuropeptides and for the design of insect peptidomimetics, as is being done with vertebrate and especially human peptide neurohormones. Short of the availability of insect neuropeptide receptors, in vivo and in vitro assays have been utilized as screens for structure/activity studies. Such activities in insects have been carried out primarily with the AKH/RPCH and myotropin families since these peptides were the first insect

TABLE 1. REPRESENTATIVES FROM CLASSES OF CHEMICALLY-IDENTIFIED, BIOLOGICALLY ACTIVE INSECT NEUROPEPTIDES

General Class[1]	Result of Disruption	Examples[2]	Source	Structure[3]	Number Identified	Ref.
Myotropins[4]	—[5]	Leucokinin I (Lem-K-I)	Leucophaea maderae	DPAFNSWG-NH₂	8	[82]
	—[5]	Leucopyrokinin (Lem-PK-I)	"	pQTSFTPRL-NH₂	1	[83]
	—[5]	Leucosulfakinin (Lem-SK-I)	"	EQFEDY(SO₃)GHMRF-NH₂	4	[84]
	—[5]	Leucomyosuppressin (Lem-MS)	"	pQDVDHVFLRF-NH₂	1	[85]
AKH/RPCH Family	depressed sugar and lipid metabolism	Adipokinetic Hormone I (Lom-AKH-I)	Locusta migratoria	pQLNFTPNWGT-NH₂	13	[86]
Ecdysiotropins	failure to initiate the molting and/or egg development process	4K-PTTH-II (Bom-PTTH-II)	Bombyx mori	A chain: GIVDECCLRPCSVDVLLSYC-OH B chain: pQQPQAVHTYCGRHLARTLA-DLCWEAGVD-OH	3 4	[87][88]
Eclosion Hormones[6]	failure to initiate the ecdysial process	(Mas-EH)	Manduca sexta	NPAIATGYDPMEICIENCAQ-CKKMLGAWFEGPLCAESCIKF-KGKLIPECEDFASIAPPLNKL-OH	2	[89][90]

TABLE 1. REPRESENTATIVES FROM CLASSES OF CHEMICALLY-IDENTIFIED, BIOLOGICALLY ACTIVE INSECT NEUROPEPTIDES (CONTINUED)

General Class[1]	Result of Disruption	Examples[2]	Source	Structure[3]	Number Identified	Ref.
Diuretic Hormones	water retention, toxemia	(Lom-DH)	Locusta migratoria	CLITNPRG-NH$_2$ CLITNPRG-NH$_2$	1	[91]
	"	(Mas-DH)	Manduca sexta	RMPSLSIDLPMSVLRQKLSLE-KERKVHALRAAANRNFLNDI-NH$_2$	1	[92]
Pigment-Dispersing Hormones	—[7]	(Rom-PDH)	Romalea microptera	NSQIINSLLGLPKLLNDA-NH$_2$	2	[93]
Allatotropin[8]	failed development in all stages	(Mas-AT)	Manduca sexta	GFKNVEMMTARGF-NH$_2$	1	[94]
Pheromone Biosynthesis Activating Neuropeptide	failure to mate	(Hez-PBAN)	Heliothis zea	LSDDMPATPADQEMYRQDPE-QIDSRTKYFSPRL-NH$_2$	1	[95]

1 See [11,17] for a list of all chemically identified neuropeptides in each class. See also [96] for Bombyx mori ecdysiotropin, Bombyxin IV; [97] for Locusta migratoria neuroparsin B; [98] for two Aedes aegypti and [99] for one Schistocerca gregaria myotropin-related neuropeptides.

2 See [100] for definition of nomenclature.

3 Underlined letters indicate conserved amino acids for that group.

4 This class also includes proctolin (RYLPT-OH) [18].

5 The effect of disruption is not known, if any, and would be difficult to determine since these neuropeptides are generally distributed and have not been selectively blocked. Except for Lem-MS, which is inhibitory, these neuropeptides stimulate hindgut contraction. The C-terminal sequence of Lem-SK and Lem-MS is related to FRMFamide [101]. A FLRFamide/LMS-related peptide was recently isolated from Schistocerca gregaria [99] and has cardioinhibitory activity. Diuretic/antidiuretic activity was also recently demonstrated [102].

6 The entire sequence of Bombyx mori eclosion hormone has recently been determined [56].

7 The effect of disruption has not been determined. The function of these neuropeptides in insects is unknown.

8 The primary structures of Diploptera punctata allatostatins were recently determined [103,104].

neuropeptides isolated and their sequences are short, making rapid and relatively cheap synthesis of numerous analogs possible. These studies were recently reviewed [15] and show that, at least for the AKH/RPCH family, amino acid positions 1, 4, and 8 are critical for binding, and are the only conserved amino acids (Table 1) for this family (also see [32] for studies on proctolin; [33] for the AKHs; [34] for the sulfakinins).

Studies on neuropeptide degradative enzymes are also relatively sparse for insects and have been restricted to proctolin and AKH (reviewed by [15,16]). Available reports indicate a short half-life (ca. 1 min) for proctolin, with degradative pathways involving primarily aminopeptidase and aminodipeptidase-type metalloproteases, suggesting that similar rapid processing would occur with other insect peptides possessing unblocked N- and C-termini. In the AKH/RPCH family, with pyroglutamate (pGlu)-blocked N-termini and amidated C-termini, examination of Periplanetin CC-2 showed that the major degradation was due to endopeptidases when solubilized extracts of fat body or Malpighian tubules were used. The half-life was ca. 1 hour [35,36]. Persistence of Periplanetin CC-2 was much longer in the hemolymph. With Schistocerca gregaria AKH-I (the same as Lom-AKH-I, Table 1), the major cleavage was at the internal Asn-Phe bond [37]. No insect neuropeptide-degrading enzymes have been isolated to date, but assays utilizing radiolabelled neuropeptides should make this possible.

Studies on synthesis and processing of insect neuropeptides are also sparse with the only major study limited to AKH [38,39]. The localization of AKH synthesis and processing to the glandular lobe of the Locusta migratoria CC, where it may be the major, or possibly only, processed neuropeptide, presented a unique opportunity to investigate neuropeptide biosynthesis. In the brain and other major ganglia, where many other insect neuropeptides are synthesized, the neurosecretory cells (NSCs) are mixed, thus making processing studies diffi-cult. This localization of AKH has allowed the direct study of prohormone processing through the use of in vitro radiolabelling techniques. Two 8.4-kD prohormones (P1 and P2) are synthesized in the CC and converted, apparently directly, into AKH-I and -II with the liberation of two other 6.5-kD AKH-precursor-related peptides, APRP-I and -II. Isolation of the specific processing enzymes and analysis of their specific cleavage sites should be possible with this system through the use of amino acid specific radiolabelled prohormones combined with homogenates of the glandular lobe of the CC. Although, with the exception of the above studies, there is no information on processing of insect neuropeptides, substantial insight can be gained from studies of vertebrate and non-insect invertebrate systems [40-47]. In particular, the relevant points are: 1) similar preprohormones may be processed

differently by different tissues, 2) preprohormones contain N-terminal
sequences of 12-30 primarily hydrophobic amino acids (signal sequence) for
transport across membranes of the endoplasmic reticulum, 3) many preprohormones
are polyproteins containing duplicate sequences of identical peptides and/or
more than one sequence of different peptides, 4) major processing enzymes are
trypsin-like endopeptidases that specifically recognize basic amino acids (Arg,
Lys), and 5) many post-translational modifications occur, such as glycosylation, phosphorylation, methylation, acetylation, sulfation and amidation.
Amidation of peptides is probably the most thoroughly studied neuropeptide
processing step [48], and is clearly required for activity of many vertebrate
peptide neurohormones. This may be the case, as well, for many insect
neurohormones, that are also amidated (Table 1).

IV. ALTERNATIVES TO PURIFICATION

   Although the isolation and sequencing of neuropeptides have been simplified
over the years, the techniques of molecular biology promise to further simplify
the determination of insect neuropeptide primary structures and prohormone
sequences. The primary method for determining pro- and preprohormone sequences
in vertebrates has been through sequencing of genes or complementary cDNAs
[49]. To utilize this methodology, the amino acid sequence of at least one
member of a family of peptide neurohormones must first be determined. Nucleic
acid probes can then be developed to screen cDNA and/or gene libraries prepared
from the original, related or evolutionarily distant species. With the
availability of more and more neuropeptide amino acid sequences and nucleic
acid probes from vertebrates and non-insect invertebrates, numerous libraries
from different non-insect species have been probed and homologous sequences
isolated. This approach has been used recently to isolate the Drosophila
melanogaster gene that encodes multiple neuropeptides related to FMRFamide [26,
28] and the gene for drosulfakinin (related to vertebrate cholecystokinin and
Lem-SK-I, Table 1), also from D. melanogaster [27]. The methods involved have
been described [49], although numerous variations have recently been reported
for increasing sensitivity and specificity. These new methods include
amplification of specific genomic DNA, cDNA and/or mRNA sequences by
sequence-specific primers, e.g. the polymerase chain reaction (PCR) [50] and
its modifications, mixed oligonucleotide primed amplification of cDNA(MOPAC)
[51], GAWTS (genomic amplification with transcript sequencing) [52], and RAWTS
(RNA amplification with transcript sequencing) [53]. Neurohormone-specific cDNA
has also been produced by in situ primed amplification of specific mRNA [54].
We have utilized some of these techniques in our laboratory to screen gypsy
moth brain and egg cDNA libraries using oligonucleotide probes for allatotropin

(AT) and pheromone biosynthesis activating neuropeptide (PBAN) (Davis et al., unpublished results). Probe sequences were based on the published amino acid sequences for Mas-AT and Hez-PBAN (Table 1). We have also produced by MOPAC, oligonucleotides of ca. 60 and 84 bases from our gypsy moth brain cDNA library based on the primary structures of 4K-PTTH-II A and B chains (Table I) (Davis et al., unpublished results).

Recently, gene sequences were published for Bom-4K-PTTH-II [55], Bom-EH [56], Mas-EH [57] and Mas-AKH [58]. Determination of these sequences was based on the previous isolation and sequencing of the respective peptide neurohormones, followed by nucleic acid probe synthesis and screening of cDNA and/or gene libraries. These published nucleotide sequences can now be used to develop nucleic acid probes for the isolation of homologous genes from other species. An additional advantage of having these published nucleotide sequences is that probe synthesis can be based directly on these sequences, eliminating consideration of genetic code redundancy, a necessary consideration when preparing probes based on the amino acid sequence.

Preprohormone sequences determined from sequenced neuropeptide genes or cDNAs can be used to predict sites of post-translational processing, such as cleavage [46], glycosylation (glycosylation of asparagine residues requires the sequence Asn-XXX-(Ser,Thr), [40], and amidation (often requires the sequence peptide-Gly-basic residues(s), [48]. Cloning technology has also been the primary method for determining receptor sequences [59] and even for demonstrating proper neuropeptide processing by specific enzymes [60]. There is little doubt that gene technology will be useful in future studies on insect neuropeptides.

V. POTENTIAL EXPLOITATION OF NEUROPEPTIDES FOR INSECT CONTROL

There is a growing need for environmentally-safe and more selective methods of insect pest control. Insect resistance to present chemical control agents continues to rise, the cost of developing these agents continues to increase, and public pressure continues to mandate reductions in chemical pesticide use [61-64]. Although pest insects are mainly controlled by chemical pesticides, the use of selective, biodegradable control agents, compatible with IPM practices is increasing [64]. Agents that interfere with insect neuropeptide synthesis or action would fit into IPM practices, because 1) neuropeptides can be highly selective in their action, 2) they are active at extremely low concentrations (10^{-9} to 10^{-15}M), 3) they can be easily engineered by gene technology, and 4) they can presumably be delivered directly to the insect through vector systems. The tactics for exploitation of neuropeptides that are envisioned include 1) developing inhibitors of processing enzymes, such as the

human drug, captopril, that inhibits the conversion of the inactive decapep-
tide, angiotensin I into the active octapeptide, angiotensin II [65], 2)
developing peptidomimetics, such as the non-peptide inhibitor of cholecystokinin reported by Evans et al. [66], 3) developing inhibitors of degrading
enzymes, such as thiorphan, an inhibitor of the enkephalin degrading enzyme,
enkephalinase A [67], and 4) delivering natural neuropeptides or their
agonists/antagonists via vector systems directly to the insect. All of these
tactics have been considered previously [9,12,15,16,61,64,68], and further
details can be found therein. A few areas deserve further consideration,
however.

For the intensely studied field of human neuropharmacology, drugs that affect
neuropeptide synthesis or action, such as captopril, and the cholecystokinin
peptide-mimic reported by Evans et al. [66], are rare [69]. In fact, captopril
took 20 years to design and develop [68]. Thus the cost to produce these
inhibitors may be high and similar efforts for developing pest control agents
for agriculture may not be cost effective, unless cheaper screening methods can
be developed. Furthermore, the peptide-like structures of these inhibitors
limit penetration and absorption, making it unlikely that native peptides can
be used as control agents. Similarly, non-peptide mimics, agonists or
antagonists, may also possess some of the non-utilitarian properties of their
natural peptide prototypes. Further details on the potential of enzyme
inhibitors or peptidomimetics to insect control can be found in recent reviews
[9,12,15,16,69].

Another problem associated with peptides is that the majority of active mimics contain non-natural amino acids or derivatives which cannot be made by
recombinant DNA techniques [69]. Thus, their utilization in vector delivery
systems would not be possible. There is still the possibility that continuous
administration of natural neuropeptides could be deleterious, but, as yet, no
studies have examined the effects of continuous administration of insect
neuropeptides by vector systems, since the genes have only recently been
isolated. There are, however, other possible alternatives for blocking
neurohormone synthesis and/or action.

Two alternatives which have been suggested for use in vector systems to
inhibit neurohormone action are production of antipeptides or peptide
antibodies [9]. Secretion of either of these factors by vector systems at the
appropriate time in vivo would presumably block neuropeptide action by binding
to the natural neurohormone. The feasibility of the antipeptide approach was
demonstrated by Bost et al. [70] for ACTH and gamma-endorphin. Unlike the
antibody system, it would not require insertion of multiple genes into the
vector. Following the report by Blalock and Smith [71] that codons on the

sense strand, which code for hydrophilic amino acids, are complemented on the antisense strand by codons for hydrophobic amino acids, and vice-versa, Bost et al. [70] synthesized antipeptides that bind selectively to the natural hormones. Recently, naturally occurring antihormones were demonstrated for human FSH [72]. In this case, the degree of glycosylation may be important, which might present a problem for synthesis in vector systems (see below).

A third alternative, a potential method for blocking neuropeptide synthesis, is the use of antisense RNA in vector systems. Antisense RNAs have been shown to block in vivo translation [73] and, therefore, might be expected to block neuropeptide synthesis in vector-infected cells, if appropriate sequences were incorporated into the vectors and expressed in a cellular region that allowed binding to sense RNA. According to Strickland et al. [73], at least for specific inhibition of mRNA translation in maturing mouse oocytes, the greatest inhibition is obtained with sequences complementary to the 3' non-coding region of the mRNA.

All of these alternatives for developing methods to inhibit neuropeptide synthesis and/or action, and other methods involving gene technology described previously, have the added advantage that site-directed mutagenesis can be used to study the effects of deletions, additions, and modifications in amino acid or nucleotide structure.

The use of vector systems for expressing insect neuropeptides, agonists or antagonists would seem to hold much promise for insect control. Vector systems, specifically the baculoviruses, have a number of traits that recommend them for inclusion in insect control strategies: 1) Specificity — There are approximately 500 known varieties of baculoviruses with most types having limited host ranges specific to lepidopterans, the major group of economic pests of crops and trees [74,75]; 2) Developed Technology — Two types of baculoviruses, Autographa californica nuclear polyhedrosis virus (AcMNPV) and Bombyx mori nuclear polyhedrosis virus (BmNPV), have already been engineered to express foreign proteins and peptides [76,77], many of which were biologically active and were expressed as fusion or nonfusion products at levels up to 500 mg/liter in cell culture and 1 mg/larva in vivo; 3) Acceptability — Four NPVs have already been registered for use by the EPA [64]. Current knowledge of the development and potential use of baculovirus expression vectors has been recently reviewed [76,77]. In spite of this promise, however, many problems remain in the use of baculovirus expression vectors for insect control. There are issues of environmental safety and persistence/non-persistence. Some of these issues may be resolved in the scheduled release (summer, 1989) of the first genetically-engineered baculovirus in Geneva, New York [74,75]. Problems exist in obtaining uniformly high levels of expression in vivo, since the mechanisms regulating expression of foreign genes in baculoviruses have not been determined. It is now believed that expression is dependent on the particular gene expressed [76,77]. Further efforts are necessary to develop vectors which penetrate the gut and express the foreign gene more rapidly, since the currently utilized polyhedrin site is one of the last sites expressed in NPV replication [74-77]. A fuller understanding of the glycosylation process is warranted [76,77] in NPV replication. While many of the processing steps in the synthesis of proteins and peptides, such as signal peptide cleavage, amidation, internal cleavage and even RNA splicing, occur normally in baculovirus-infected insect cell lines or whole insects, glycosylation is restricted to N-glycosylation with the addition of high-mannose type oligosaccharides, lacking sialic acid, galactose and fucose residues common to vertebrate glycoproteins. However, when foreign genes coding for glycosylated products, such as interleukin 3, were expressed by baculovirus systems, their products still showed full biological activity [77]. Efforts are necessary to elucidate the mechanisms of baculovirus-induced insect mortality and molt inhibition, since the recent discovery of a baculovirus-produced ecdysteroid UDP-glucosyl transferase implicated in blocking molting by the fall armyworm, Spodoptera frugipeida [78] indicates that non-engineered baculoviruses naturally produce factors which affect the insect endocrine system. These natural factors might be complemented or augmented by other factors engineered into baculoviruses, such as neurohormone genes.

The potential for developing new methods of pest control through the disruption of neuropeptide regulating systems holds great promise for meeting the requirements of specificity, non-persistence, health and environmental safety. Only further research will determine the possible utility of neuropeptide technology in selective insect control.

ACKNOWLEDGEMENTS

We thank Bruce Black, Mark Holman and Alexej Borkovec for helpful comments on manuscript preparation, Carol Robinson for initial typing and literature search and Carol Masler for artwork.

REFERENCES

1. Kopec S (1917) Bull Int Acad Cracovie B:57
2. Kopec S (1922) Biol Bull Woods Hole 42:323
3. Scharrer B (1987) Ann Rev Entomol 32:1
4. Truman JW, Taghert PH (1983) In: Krieger DT, Brownstein MJ, Martin JB (eds) Brain Peptides. John Wiley & Sons, New York, pp 165-181
5. Borkovec AB, Kelly TJ (eds) (1984) Insect Neurochemistry and Neurophysiology. Plenum Press, New York

294

6. Cook BJ, Holman GM (1985) In: Kerkut GA, Gilbert LI (eds) Comprehensive Insect Physiology, Biochemistry and Pharmacology, Vol. 11. Pergamon Press, New York, pp 531-593

7. Mordue W, Morgan PJ (1985) In: Kerkut GA, Gilbert LI (eds) Comprehensive Insect Physiology, Biochemistry and Pharmacology, Vol. 7. Pergamon Press, New York, pp 153-183

8. Borkovec AB, Gelman DB (eds) (1986) Insect Neurochemistry and Neurophysiology-1986. Humana Press, Clifton, New Jersey

9. Keeley LL, Hayes TK (1987) Insect Biochem 17:639

10. Thorpe A, Duve H (1987) NATO Ser. A, Life Sciences 141:133

11. Holman GM, Wright MS, Nachman RJ (1988) ISI Atlas of Science: Plants and Animals 1:129

12. Keeley LL, (1988) In: Hedin PA, Menn JJ, Hollingworth RM (eds) Biotechnology for Crop Protection. American Chemical Society, Washington, D. C., pp 147-159

13. Thorpe A, Duve H (1988) In: Ganten D, Pfaff D (eds) Stimulus-Secretion Coupling in Neuroendocrine Systems, Current Topics in Neuroendocrinology, Vol. 9. Springer-Verlag, New York, pp 185-230

14. Borkovec AB, Masler EP (eds) (1989) Insect Neurochemistry and Neurophysiology-1989. Humana Press, Clifton, New Jersey, In press

15. Keeley LL, Hayes TK, Bradfield JY (1989) In: Borkovec AB, Masler EP (eds) Insect Neurochemistry and Neurophysiology-1989. Humana Press, Clifton, New Jersey, In press

16. Menn JJ, Borkovec AB (1989) J Agr Food Chem 37:271

17. Holman GM, Nachman RJ, Wright MS (1990) Ann Rev Entomol 35: In press

18. Starratt AN, Brown BE (1975) Life Sci 17:1253

19. Schooley DA, Kataoka H, Kramer SJ, Toschi A (1989) In: Borkovec AB, Masler EP, (eds) Insect Neurochemistry and Neurophysiology -1989. Humana Press, Clifton, New Jersey, In press

20. Platt N, Reynolds SE (1988) In: Lunt GG, Olsen RW (eds) Comparative Invertebrate Neurochemistry. Cornell University Press, Ithaca, pp 175-226

21. DeLoof A (1987) Entomol Exp Appl 45:105

22. Holder FC, Lwoff L, Wicker C, Goltzene F, Meister MF, Zachary D, Reichhart JM (1988) Intl J Invert Reprod Develop 14:105

23. Brown BE, Starratt AN (1975) J Insect Physiol 21:1879

24. Esch FS, Ling NC, Bohlon P (1983) Methods Enzymol 103:72

25. Ishizaki H, Mizoguchi A, Hatta M, Suzuki A, Nagasawa H, Kataoka H, Isogai A, Tamura S, Fujino M, Kitada C (1987) In: Law JH (ed) Molecular Entomology. Alan R. Liss, New York, pp 119-128

26. Nambu JR, Murphy-Erdosh C, Andrews PC, Feistner GJ, Scheller RH (1988) Neuron 1:55

27. Nichols R, Schneuwly SA, Dixon JE (1988) J Biol Chem 263:12167

28. Schneider LE, Taghert PH (1988) Proc Natl Acad Sci USA 85:1993

29. Venter JC, Harrison LC (eds) (1984) Molecular and Chemical Characterization of Membrane Receptors. Alan R. Liss, New York

30. McKelvy JF (1983) In: Krieger DT, Brownstein MJ, Martin JB (eds) Brain Peptides. John Wiley & Sons, New York, pp 117-133

31. McKelvy JF, Blumberg S (1986) Ann Rev Neurosci 9:415

32. O'Shea M, Adams M (1986) Adv. Insect Physiol 19:1

33. Orchard I (1987) J Insect Physiol 33:451

34. Nachman RJ, Holman GM, Haddon WF, Hayes TK (1989) Peptide Research 2:171

35. Skinner WS, Quistad GB, Adams ME, Schooley DA (1987) Insect Biochem 17:433

36. Schooley DA, Quistad GB, Skinner WS, Adams ME (1987) In: Greenhalgh R, Roberts TR (eds) Pesticide Science and Biotechnology. Blackwell Scientific Publications, Oxford, pp 97-100

37. Isaac RE (1988) Biochem J 255:843

38. Hekimi S, O'Shea M (1987) J Neurosci 7:2773

39. Hekimi S, O'Shea M (1989) J Neurosci 9:996

40. Herbert E, Uhler M (1982) Cell 30:1

41. Loh YP, Gainer H (1983) In: Krieger DT, Brownstein MJ, Martin JB (eds) Brain Peptides. John Wiley & Sons, New York, pp 79-116

42. Steiner DF, Docherty K, Chan SH, Segundo BS, Carroll R (1983) In: Koch D, Richter D (eds) Biochemical and Clinical Aspects of Neuropeptides: Synthesis, Processing, and Gene Structure. Academic Press, New York, pp 3-13

43. Douglass J, Civelli O, Herbert E (1984) Ann Rev Biochem 53:665

44. Loh YP, Brownstein MJ, Gainer H (1984) Ann Rev Neurosci 7:189

45. Andrews PG, Brayton K, Dixon JE (1987) Experientia 43:784

46. Fisher JM, Scheller RH (1988) J Biol Chem 263:16515

47. Joosse J, Geraerts WPM (1989) In: Borkovec AB, Masler EP (eds) Insect Neurochemistry and Neurophysiogy-1989. Humana Press, Clifton, New Jersey, In press

48. Eipper BA, Mains RE (1988) Ann Rev Physiol 50:333

49. Douglass J, Herbert E (1989) In: Conn, PM (ed) Neuroendocrine Peptide Methodology. Academic Press, New York, pp 57-65

50. Saiki RK, Gelfand DH, Stoffel S, Scharf SJ, Higuchi R, Horn GT, Mullis KB, Erlich HA (1988) Science 239:487

51. Lee CC, Wu X, Gibbs RA, Cook RG, Muzny DM, Caskey CT (1988) Science 239:1288

52. Stoflet ES, Koeberl DD, Sarkar G, Sommer SS (1988) Science 239:491

53. Sarkar G, Sommer SS (1989) Science 224:331

54. Tecott LH, Barchas JD, Eberwine JH (1988) Science 240:1661

55. Iwani M, Kawabani A, Ishizaki H, Takahashi SY, Adachi T, Suzuki Y, Nagasawa H, Suzuki A (1989) Develop Growth & Differ 31:31

56. Suzuki A, Nagasawa H, Kono T, Sato B, Kamito T, Tanaka H, Sakagami Y, Mizoguchi A, Ishizaki H, Fugo H (1989) In: Borkovec AB, Masler EP (eds) Insect Neurochemistry and Neurophysiology-1989. Humana Press, Clifton, New Jersey, In press

57. Horodyski FM, Riddiford LM, Truman JW (1989) Proc Natl Acad Sci USA: In press

58. Bradfield JY, Keeley LL, (1989) J. Biol Chem 264:12791

59. Kaufman DL, Tobin AJ (1984) In: Venter JC, Harrison LC (eds) Molecular and Chemical Characterization of Membrane Receptors. Alan R. Liss, New York, pp 241-259

296

60.   Thomas G, Thorne BA, Hruby DE (1988) Ann Rev Physiol 50:323

61.   Menn JJ, Hendrick CA (1985) In: Hilton JL (ed) Agricultural Chemicals
      of the Future. Beltsville Symposium in Agricultural Research, Vol.8.
      Rowman & Allanheld, Totowa, New Jersey, pp 247-265

62.   Menn JJ, Hollingworth RM (1985) In: Kerkut GA, Gilbert LI (eds)
      Comprehensive Insect Physiology, Biochemistry and Pharmacology, Vol.
      12. Pergamon Press, New York, pp 1-8

63.   Geissbuhler H, d'Hondt C, Kunz E, Nyfeler R and Pfister K (1987) In:
      Greenhalgh R, Roberts TR (eds) Pesticide Science and Biotechnology.
      Blackwell Scientific Publications, Oxford, pp 3-14

64.   Menn JJ, Christy AL (1989) In: Schnoor JL (ed) US/USSR Symposium on
      Fate of Pesticides and Chemicals in the Environment. Wiley-
      Interscience, New York, In press

65.   Ondetti MA, Rubin B, Cushman DW (1977) Science 196:441

66.   Evans BE, Bock MG, Rittle KE, DiPardo RM, Whitter WL, Veber DF,
      Anderson PS and Freidinger RM (1986) Proc Natl Acad Sci USA 83:4918

67.   Roques BP, Fournie-Zaluski MC, Soroca E, Lecomte JM, Malfroy B, Llorens
      C, Schwartz J-C (1980) Nature 288:286

68.   Menn JJ (1985) J Pesticide Sci 10 (special issue):372

69.   Kempe TG (1989) In: Borkovec AB, Masler EP (eds) Insect Neurochemistry
      and Neurophysiology-1989. Humana Press, Clifton, New Jersey, In press

70.   Bost KL, Smith EM, Blalock JE (1985) Proc Natl Acad Sci USA 82:1372

71.   Blalock JE, Smith EM (1984) Biochem Biophys Res Commun 121:203

72.   Dahl KD, Bicsak TA, Hsueh JW (1988) Science 239:72

73.   Strickland S, Huarte J, Belin D, Vassalli A, Rickles RJ, Vassalli J-D
      (1988) Science 241:680

74.   Lewis R (1989) Genet Engin News 9:1

75.   Wood HA, Hughes PR, van Beek N, Hamblin M (1989) In: Borkovec AB, Masler
      EP (eds) Insect Neurochemistry and Neurophysiology-1989. Humana Press
      Clifton, New Jersey, In press

76.   Luckow VA, Summers MD (1988) Bio/Technology 6:47

77.   Maeda S (1989) Ann Rev Entomol 34:351

78.   O'Reilly DR, Miller LK (1989) Science 245:1110

79.   O'Brien MA, Katahira EJ, Flanagan TR, Arnold LW, Haughton G,
      Bollenbacher WE (1988) J Neurosci 8:3247

80.   Copenhaver PF, Truman JW (1986) J Neurosci 6:1738

81.   Truman JW, Copenhaver PF (1989) J Exp Biol: In press

82.   Holman GM, Cook BJ, Nachman RJ (1986) Comp Biochem Physiol 84C:205

83.   Holman GM, Cook BJ, Nachman RJ (1986) Comp Biochem Physiol 85C:219

84.   Nachman RJ, Holman GM, Haddon WF, Ling N (1986) Science 234:71

85.   Holman GM, Cook BJ, Nachman RJ (1986) Comp Biochem Physiol 85C:329

86.   Stone JV, Mordue W, Batley KE, Morris HR (1976) Nature 263:207

87.   Nagasawa H, Kataoka H, Isogai A, Tamura S, Suzuki A, Ishizaki H,
      Mizoguchi A, Fugiwara Y, Suzuki A (1984) Science 226:1344

88.   Nagasawa H, Kataoka H, Isogai A, Tamura S, Suzuki A, Mizoguchi A,
      Fugiwara Y, Suzuki A, Takahashi SY, Ishizaki H (1986) Proc Natl Acad Sci
      USA 83:5840

89. Marti T, Takio K, Walsh KA, Terzi G, Truman JW (1987) FEBS Lett 219:415

90. Kataoka H, Troetschler RG, Kramer SJ, Cesarin BJ, Schooley DA (1987) Biochem Biophys Res Comm 146:746

91. Proux JP, Miller CA, Li JP, Carney RL, Girardie A, Delaage M, Schooley DA (1987) Biochem Biophys Res Commun 149:180

92. Kataoka H, Troetschler RG, Li JP, Kramer SJ, Carney RL, Schooley DA (1989) Proc Natl Acad Sci USA 86:2976

93. Rao KR, Mohrherr CJ, Riehm JP, Zahnow CA, Norton S, Johnson L, Tarr GE (1987) J Biol Chem 262:2672

94. Kataoka H, Toschi A, Li JP, Carney RL, Schooley DA, Kramer SJ (1989) Science 243:1481

95. Raina AK, Jaffe H, Kempe TG, Keim P, Blacher RW, Fales HM, Riley CT, Klun JA, Ridgway RL, Hayes DK (1989) Science 244:796

96. Maruyama K, Hietter H, Nagasawa H, Isogai A, Tamura S, Suzuki A, Ishizaki H (1988) Agric Biol Chem 52:3035

97. Girardie J, Huet J-C, Pernollet J-C , Girardie A (1989) In: Borkovec AB, Masler EP (eds) Insect Neurochemistry and Neurophysiology-1989. Humana Press, Clifton, New Jersey, In press

98. Matsumoto S, Brown MR, Crim JW, Vigna SR, Lea AO (1989) Insect Biochem 19:277

99. Robb S, Packman LC, Evans PD (1989) Biochem Biophys Res Comm 160:850

100. Raina AK, Gade G (1988) Insect Biochem 18:785

101. Greenberg MJ, Payza K, Nachman RJ, Holman GM, Price DA (1988) Peptides 9 (Suppl.):125

102. Hayes TK, Ford MM, Keeley LL (1989) In: Borkovec AB, Masler EP (eds) Insect Neurochemistry and Neurophysiology-1989. Humana Press, Clifton, New Jersey, In press

103. Woodhead AP, Stay B, Seidel SL, Khan MA, Tobe SS (1989) Proc Natl Acad Sci USA 86:5997

104. Pratt GE, Farnsworth DE, Siegel NR, Fok KF, Feyereisen R (1989) Biochem Biophys Res Commun 163:1243

Natural products

© 1990 Elsevier Science Publishers B.V. (Biomedical Division)
Pesticides and alternatives, editor J.E. Casida

ANT SECRETIONS AS A SOURCE OF NATURAL PRODUCT MODELS FOR
POSSIBLE PEST CONTROL AGENTS

ROBERT F. TOIA

Pesticide Chemistry and Toxicology Laboratory, Department of Entomological
Sciences, University of California,Berkeley, CA 94720, (USA)

INTRODUCTION

Exocrine gland secretions from arthropods, and in particular those from
members of the Formicoidea, have received substantial attention from both
chemists and biologists and continue to do so. These secretions are now
recognized as a rich source of remarkably varied natural products ranging from
the structurally most simple of the carboxylic acids to complex hydrocarbons,
terpenoids, alkaloids and proteins. Ants are highly social insects and much of
the stimululus to chemical investigations in this field has been provided by
considerations of their complex behavioral patterns and the chemical factors
eliciting them. Moreover, since the components of these secretions, be they
classified as venoms, attractants or repellents, elicit biological responses of
varying specificities, they may be viewed as potential agents for insect and
other pest control.

General observations in the area of insect chemistry are by no means new. For
example, an acidic material, later characterized as formic acid, was noted as a
product from dry distillation of Formica rufa as early as the 17th century (1).
Notwithstanding this, perhaps the most rapid advances have occurred in this
field in the last three decades, primarily as a result of the progress and
refinement in analytical methodology, particularly with GC and GC-MS methods. A
recent analytical development which may also prove useful in future studies is
supercritical fluid chromatography.

It is noteworthy that much of the work has been carried out using glandular
material, viz: material extracted directly from glands dissected from the
species of interest. Under these circumstances, there is no doubt as to the
origin of the compound(s) being investigated. In some instances, the chemical
isolations have been accompanied by behavioural studies. A measurable biological response is often a useful aid in fractionation procedures while also
allowing a more precise definition of the biological function(s) of the com-
pound(s) and the gland from which they derive. Excellent general reviews of
the chemistry of insect secretions have been published by Attygalle and Morgan
(2) and of their biosynthesis, by Blum (3).

In relation to potential model pesticidal materials from ant secretions this
discussion will concentrate primarily on volatiles from members of the Dolicho-

derinae, Formicinae, Ponerinae and Myrmicine sub-families. A number of classes of compounds are worthy of comment.

IRIDOIDS

From an historical perspective iridoids, a cyclopentanoid-based group of monoterpenes which are now known to occur widely in both flora and fauna, should be considered first. An early and definitive review of insect iridoids is that by Cavill and Clark (4). The first compound of this class to be isolated from an ant secretion was iridomyrmecin (1), reported in 1950 by Pavan and his co-workers (5) as a result of their investigations into the anal gland of *Iridomyrmex humilis*, a member of the Dolichoderinae. They assigned structure to this monoterpene lactone, and noted that it had antimicrobial activity. A second paper from this group on iridomyrmecin appeared in 1952 (6). This attracted further attention since the compound was now reported to be insecticidal and, in particular, to be active against some DDT-resistant species. Moreover, it had lower mammalian toxicity than DDT; 1.5 g/kg compared with 0.2 g/kg, mouse oral LD_{50}, respectively. Substantial interest in the study of insect secretions ensued in general and within a relatively short period, in contemporary studies in Australia and Italy (7,8), a range of further iridoids was identified from various members of the Dolichoderinae and Formicinae. These included iridodial (2) dolichodial (3), isoiridomyrmecin (4) and isodihydronepetalactone (5) (9-12). In relation to their biological function, these compounds are considered to comprise part of the defense secretions from the various species from which they are isolated, possibly acting as fixatives for some to the more volatile components also present (see below) (4). It is interesting to note the close structural relationship of these compounds to nepetalactone (6), an iridoid

reputed to be the active constituent of the catmint plant, *Nepeta cataria* (13).

OTHER ALIPHATIC COMPOUNDS

Ants of the Dolichoderinae and Formicinae have also been a source of a variety of other low molecular weight aliphatic carbonyl compounds including heptan-2-one (7), 4-methylhexan-2-one (8), 6-methylhept-5-en-2-one (9), 2-methylheptan-4-one (10), tri-, penta- and heptadecan-2-one (11, 12, and 13, respectively), 4-methylheptan-3-one (14), 2,6-dimethyl-5-heptenal (15), 2,6-dimethyl-5-hepten-1-ol (16), E- and Z-citral (17), citronellal (18) and farnesal (19). These compounds are also considered to be part of the ants defence secretion complex, possibly functioning as alarm pheromones. Several are quite effective knockdown agents; for example, 6-methylhept-5-en-2-one has a reported EC$_{50}$ of 1.33 µL/L (female housefly, 2.5 hr)(4). In more recent work similar compounds, in particular 4-methyl-3-heptanone (14), 4,6-dimethyl-3-nonanone (20) and 4,6-dimethyl-3-octanone (21), were found in *Dasymutilla occidentalis* and other

mutillid wasps and suggested to function as allomones against the ants that are the major potential predators of these wasps (14).

In addition to cuticle waxes and related compounds, ants produce a number of interesting hydrocarbons including a variety of small cyclic molecules. For example, in our recent study on the volatiles from the whole-body extract of *Iridomyrmex discors*, 1-methylcyclopentene (22), 1-methyl-2-ethylcyclopentane (23) and 2-methylcyclopent-1-ene-carboxaldehyde (24) were observed (15). A further compound, also new insofar as its identification in insects was concerned, was geranylacetone (25) (15). Other compounds noted but which have been previously reported from other species of *Iridomyrmex* were 2-acetyl-3-methyl-cyclopentene (26), 1,3,3-trimethyl-2,7-dioxabicyclo[2.2.1]heptane (27) (plus an isomer), methylheptenone (9), 2-(3-methylcyclopentyl)propional (28), iridodial

(2) (various isomers) and isodihydronepetalactone (5) (15).   At this time, neither the biological function nor the spectra of activities of these new compounds has been established.   Related low molecular weight cyclopentanoids have been reported in other members of the Dolichoderinae, in particular, in *Azteca* species (16).   All of these compounds pose interesting biogenetic questions and it is noteworthy that 25 bears the same relationship to farnesal (19) as does the widely occurring 6-methylhept-5-en-2-one (9) to citral (17). In a recent biosynthesis study using *Iridomyrmex purpureus* as the test organism, methylheptenone (9) was shown to be a degraded terpenoid (17).

22	23	24	25

26	27	28

CHROMONES AND RELATED AROMATICS

Chromones occur naturally in insects, plants, fungi, lichens and marine organisms, and have a wide spectrum of biological activities associated with them.   For example, 3-methylchromone (29) and its derivatives have muscle relaxant (18) and spasmolytic (19) properties and a vasodilator effect on coronary blood vessels (20).   Furthermore, 3-methylchromone causes hypothermia in mice (21), hypotension in rats (20), and potentiates the hypnotic effect of some drugs (21).   Of particular relevance to this discussion is the observation that a derivative of 2-methylchromone, lepraric acid (30), has antimicrobial action against *Escherichia coli*, *Candida albicans*, *Staphylococcus pyogenes*, *streptococcus pyogenes*, *and Salmonella typhimurium*   (22) and 2-ethylchromone (31) exhibits slight insecticidal activity against body lice (23).

A series of related aromatics are also worthy of comment.   The isocoumarin, mellein (32) occurs widely in insects and fungi and has an impressive array of

29 R = Me	30	31 R = Et	32

biological effects associated with it (24), including growth inhibition of corn seedlings (25). In termites it is considered to be a component of their defense secretion (26). Within the Ponerinae sub-family, mellein has been noted to occur in *Rhytidoponera chalybea* and *R. victoriae* (27), while the related 2-hydroxy-6-methylacetophenone (33) has been found in *R. aciculata* (28), 2,5-dimethylchromone (34) in *R. metallica* (29), and 2,4-dihydroxyacetophenone (35)

in *R. chalybea* (27). While these aromatics may be considered useful as chemo-taxonomic markers, as noted earlier for similar aromatics isolated from various *Hypoclinia* species (Dolichoderinae) (30), their biological function(s) in the Ponerinae have not been ascertained. Speculation suggests that they might function as antimicrobial agents in relation to control of bacteria in the nest and the brood since various acetophenone derivatives are active as antioxidants (31), antimicrobial (32), antimalarial (33) and antiseptic (34) agents. Although aromatics of these types have been the subject of various biosynthetic investigations in microorganisms, their biosynthesis in insects and, in par-ticular in ants, has only recently been addressed. Feeding studies to *R. aciculata* and *R. chalybea* using appropriately labeled ^{14}C-acetic acid followed by isolation and degradation procedures to locate the positions of label have shown the acetophenone derivatives and mellein, respectively, to be, as antici-pated, polyketide derived (35 and 27, respectively).

PYRAZINES

The pyrazines (36) are another class of compound which occur widely in insects

(including the Hymenoptera, Coleoptera, Lepidoptera and Diptera), plants, marine organisms, fungi and in raw and cooked foodstuffs. They are used commercially as flavoring and odor components. In ants, bees and wasps they frequently occur in the mandibula glands, and in some ant species also the venom resevoir. In common with the types of compounds discussed above, they elicit a range of biological responses. In ants they function as trail, alarm or sex pheremones or are components of the defense secretions (36). The pyrazines from the Ponerinae are noteworthy; in particular the volatile extractives from the head

of *Rhytidoponera metallica* contains twelve pyrazines, ten of which have been
identified (37-46). To date, these represent the most structurally complex set

of such compounds isolated from an insect source (37). Although this work was
not carried out at a glandular level, it is likely that these compounds origin-
ate in the mandibula glands and that they form part of an alarm or trail
pheromone.

The biosynthesis of pyrazines has been studied in fungi (36) but their origins
insofar as the pathways by which they arise in insects remain unknown. The
topic area of insect pyrazines has recently been reviewed by Brophy (38).

Trimethylpyrazine (47) has been shown to be active against *Staphylococcus
aureus* and *Escherichia coli* (20) and other alkyl derivatives are reputed to have

fungicidal activity (19). However, to date, there appears to be no literature
describing the insecticidal activity or otherwise of compounds of this class.
Given that pyrazines are biologically active at extremely low levels, they may
warrant further attention in this context.

PYRROLINE, PYRROLIDINE and PIPERIDINE ALKALOIDS

The 2,5-dialkylpyrroline (48), 2,5-dialkylpyrrolidine (49) and 2,6-dialkyl-
piperidine alkaloids (50) are the three classes of compounds occuring in ants

which have attracted most interest in recent years from the point of view of
their potential pesticidal activity. These bases are found, along with other
nitrogenous components, in the poison glands of species of the *Solenopsis* (fire

ants) and *Monomorium* genera (both of the Myrmicine sub-family). These ants are well known for the painful stings that they can inflict on humans, but in addition to the allergenic factors, the venoms also have antibacterial, anti- fungal and insecticidal properties. These ants have been the subjects of extensive chemical investigations, and a number of excellent reviews are available (39, 40, 41). Specific mention should be made of the large number of naturally occurring disubstituted piperidines since preliminary evaluation

51 R = C_9H_{19}
52 R = $C_{11}H_{23}$

showed the C_9 and C_{11} homologs (both isomers) (51 and 52, respectively) to compare favourably, overall, with the commercial fungicides 10-undecenoic acid and griseofulvin (41). The 2,6-dialkylpiperidines also show contact insecti- cidal activity against species of *Reticulitermes* termite, and similar results are noted for the 2,5-dialkylpyrrolines and pyrrolidines. For example, *cis*- and *trans*-6-undecyl-2-methylpiperidine (52) both have reported LD_{50} values against termite workers of 0.6 µg/mg, a level of toxicity that is in the same general range as that of nicotine (0.5 µg) (41). In a recent publication (42) on the venom alkaloids from several species of European *Monomorium* two pyrrolines (53

53 $R_1 = (CH_2)_7CHCH_2$ $R_2 = (CH_2)_4CHCH_2$
54 $R_1 = C_9H_{19}$ $R_2 = (CH_2)_4CHCH_2$

55 $R_1 = (CH_2)_7CHCH_2$ $R_2 = (CH_2)_4CHCH_2$
56 $R_1 = C_9H_{19}$ $R_2 = (CH_2)_4CHCH_2$
57 $R_1 = C_9H_{19}$ $R_2 = C_8H_{13}$

and 54) and three pyrrolidines (55-57) were observed. The pyrrolines showed little toxicity to *Monomorium* ants, but were active against a wide range of other insects, including *Reticulitermes*, *Locusta migratoria*, *Pieris napi* and *Musca domestica*. The insecticidal activity of these compounds has formed the basis for at least one patent, as agents for termite control (42, 43).

CONCLUSIONS

At the present time, a considerable body of information is available on the chemistry of ant secretions, particularly in relation to chemotaxanomic con- siderations. For some species the associated biological phenomena have been explored, but this is not generally the case. Moreover, very limited toxico- logical evaluation of the exocrine secretions has been reported and only little screening appears to have been documented in the literature. The intitial interest in insect secretions as possible pest control agents, as exemplified by the iridoids, may well have been doused at the time by the development of the organophosphate and carbamate pesticides. However, with the ever-increasing need to develop more selective and environmentally acceptable control agents, the plethora of naturally occurring ant-derived compounds warrants close scrutiny as a source for possible models.

ACKNOWLEDGMENT

The preparation of this manuscript was supported, in part, by United States National Institutes of Health grant number ES00049.

REFERENCES

1. Fisher S reported by Ray J (1671) Phil. Trans. Roy. Soc. London 1670: 2063; cited in Cavill GWK, Robertson PL (1965) Science 149:1337

2. Attygalle AB, Morgan ED (1984) Chem. Soc. Reviews 13:245

3. Blum MS (1987) Ann. Rev. Entomol. 32:381

4. Cavill GWK, Clark DV (1971) In: Jacobson M, Crosby DG (eds) Naturally Occurring Insecticides. Marcel Dekker, New York

5. Pavan M (1950) Proceed. Eighth Intern. Congr. Entomol. 863

6. Pavan M (1952) Trans. Ninth Intern. Congr. Entomol. 321

7. Cavill GWK, Ford DL, Locksley HD (1956) Aust. J. Chem. 9:288

8. Trave R, Pavan M (1956) Chimica Ind. Milano 38:1015

9. Cavill GWK, Hinterberger H (1960) Aust. J. Chem. 13:514

10. Meinwald J, Chadha MS, Hurst JJ, Eisner T (1962) Tetrahedron Lett.:29

11. Cavill GWK, Clark DV (1967) J. Insect Physiol. 13:131

12. Cavill GWK, Hinterberger H (1961) Aust. J. Chem. 14:143.

13. Bates RB, Eisenbraun EJ, McElvain SM (1958) J. Amer. Chem. Soc.80:3420

14. Fales HM, Jaouni TM, Schmidt JO, Blum MS (1980) J. Chem. Ecol. 6:895

15. Cox M, Brophy JJ, Toia RF (1989) J. Nat. Prod. 52:75

16. Wheeler JW, Evans SL, Blum MS, Torgerson RL (1975) Science 187:254

17. Kim JH, Toia RF (1989) J. Nat. Prod. 52:63

18. Bradel-Gay Y, Guiroy P, Bourillet F (1962) Therapie 17:1211

19. Prino G, Procopio P (1960) Boll. Chim. Farm. 99:79

20. Crepax P, Volta A (1957) Studi Urbinati Fac. Farm. 31:82; cited in Chem. Abs. 57:1489i

21. Prino G (1958) Farmaco (Pavia) Ed. Sci. 13:619; cited in Chem. Abs. 53:20552h

22. Soviar, K (1971) Acta Fac. Pharm. Univ. Comeniana 20:27; cited in Chem. Abs. 76:123969z

23. Eddy GW, Carson NB (1946) J. Econ. Entomol. 39:763

24. Hill RA (1986) In: Herz W, Grisebach H, Kirby GW, Tamm Ch (eds) Fortschr. Chem. Org. Naturst. Springer-Verlag, New York 49:1, and references therein

25. Devys M, Bousquet JF, Skajennikoff M, Barbier M (1974) Phytopathol. 81:92

26 Blum MS, Jones TH, Howard DF, Overal WL (1982) Comp. Biochem. Physiol. Sect. B 71B:731

27. Sun CM (1988) PhD Thesis, Univ. New South Wales, Australia

28. Brophy JJ, Cavill GWK, Duke RK (1983) Insect Biochem. 13:503

29. Brophy JJ, Sun CM, Tecle B, Toia RF (1988) J. Nat. Prod. 51:99

30. Blum MS, Jones TH, Snelling RR, Overal WL, Fales HM, Highet RJ (1982) Biochem. Systematics Ecol. 10:91

31. Bors W, Michel C, Saran M (1984) Biochim. Biophys. Acta 796:312

32. Leifertova I, Hejtmankova N, Hlava H, Kudrnacova J, Santavy F (1975) Acta Univ. Palacki. Olomuc. Fac. Med. 74:83; cited in Chem. Abs. 85:14611s

33. Thompson PE, Moore AM, Reinertson TW, Bayles A (1953) Antibiotics and Chemotherapy 3:399

34. Fujikawa F, Sawaguchi G, Takimura M (1952) J. Pharm soc. Japan 72:1033

35. Tecle B, Brophy JJ, Toia RF (1986) Insect Biochem. 16:333

36. Brophy JJ, Cavill GWK (1980) Heterocycles 14:477

37. Tecle B, Sun CM, Brophy JJ, Toia RF (1987) J. Chem. Ecol. 13:1811

38. Brophy JJ: In Atta-Ur-Rahman (ed) Studies in Natural Product Chemistry   (in press)

39. Jones TH, Blum MS, Fales HM (1982) Tetrahedron 38:1949

40. Blum MS (1985) In: Hedin PA (ed) Bioregulators from Pest Control. ACS Symposium Series 276:393. ACS Washington DC

41. Blum MS (1988) In: Cutler HG (ed) Biologically Active Natural Products-Potential use in Agriculture. ACS Symposium Series 380:438. ACS Washing ton DC

42. Bacos D, Basselier JJ, Celerier JP, Lange C, Marx E, Lhommet G, Escoubas P, Lemaire M, Clement JL (1988) Tetrahedron 29:3061

43. Clement JL, Lemaire M, Lange C, Lhommet G, Celerier JP, Basselier JJ, Cassier P (1984) French Patent Application No. 84/6980; Fr. Demande FR 2563696 (CI. AOIN49/00)

© 1990 Elsevier Science Publishers B.V. (Biomedical Division)
Pesticides and alternatives, editor J.E. Casida

SYNTHESIS AND COMPARISON OF UNNATURAL trans-B/C ROTENOIDS WITH THE NATURAL cis-STEREOISOMERS

M.J. BEGLEY, L. CROMBIE, HAMID bin HADI AND J.L. JOSEPHS

Dept. of Chemistry, The University, Nottingham, NG7 2RD, U.K

'Derris' is an insecticide of long-standing, and interest in it has lately undergone something of a revival probably because it is a botanical insecticide and therefore more acceptable in some quarters. A major commercial source is plants of the genera Derris and Lonchocarpus, and the main insecticidal principle is rotenone (1) which is found along with other related substances constituting the rotenoid group. They are based on the core structure (2). The cis-B/C fusion of rotenone was deduced in our laboratory many years ago,[1] and this, and the remaining configurative details for the molecule, were later confirmed by our X-ray structure for 8'-bromorotenone.[2] Surprisingly, the cis- fusion is thermodynamically stable relative to the trans- and this appears to be due in part to relief of the 1-H to 12-C=O interaction in the cis-isomer, though torsional factors may also be involved.

All known natural rotenoids belong to the stable cis- series and indeed the trans-fusion has been completely unknown among enolisable rotenoids for more than 50 years, though it is represented in trapped unenolisable form e.g. by an isorotenolone (3)[3] and a C-12a methylation product (4).[4] Because of the considerable geometrical differences between the cis - and trans- structures, comparison of their biological activities is of interest. cis-Rotenoids have bent ridge-tile like structures whereas the trans- structures are flatter and more extended.

THE SYNTHESIS OF ENOLISABLE trans-B/C-ROTENOIDS.

A group of rotenoid syntheses converge on a 6a,12a-dehydrorotenoid [e.g. 6a,12a-dehydroisorotenone (5)] as the precursor to the final rotenoid. A standard procedure is then reduction with sodium borohydride which effects not only 1,4- reduction but furthur 1,2-reduction leading to a 12-hydroxy rotenoid:[5] this must then be carefully reoxidised. In order to improve and shorten this procedure we tried reducing agents other than sodium borohydride and found that diisobutylaluminium hydride (DIBAL) in toluene/THF (-78° to 20°C) successfully gave 1,4-reduction without the ensuing 1,2-. The product was not however the well-known (±)- cis-isorotenone (6) m. p. 162-163°C, despite having a similar m.p. (160-163°C) since there was a marked depression in mixed m.p. Its NMR spectrum differed from that of cis-isorotene, though depending on the acidity of the deuteriochloform solvent it gradually changed

(1)

(2)

(3) R = OH
(4) R = Me

to that of the latter and clearly belonged to the unstable (±)-trans-series (7). The compound is more stable in d6-acetone or d6-benzene.

Other trans-rotenoids were then prepared by a similar method.[6] 6a,12a-Dehydrorotenone itself (8) retains a chiral R-centre at 5' so the DIBAL procedure gives a pair of trans- diastereoisomers separable by chromatography and crystallisation into the 6aS,12aR,5'R- (9) and 6aR,12aS,5'R- (10)forms. The former is readily recognisable as the trans- form of natural rotenone since epimerisation at12a with acid gives the familiar cis-rotenone (6aS,12aS,5'R) (1), identical with the natural material.   [Note that base treatment racemises 6a and 12a via beta elimination].   The chromen (±)-trans-deguelin (11) was similarly made using DIBAL: it was moderately stable to chromatography on silica (hexane/ethyl acetate) and spectral data were collected in acetone as it was readily epimerised to (±)-cis-deguelin in deuteriochloform.

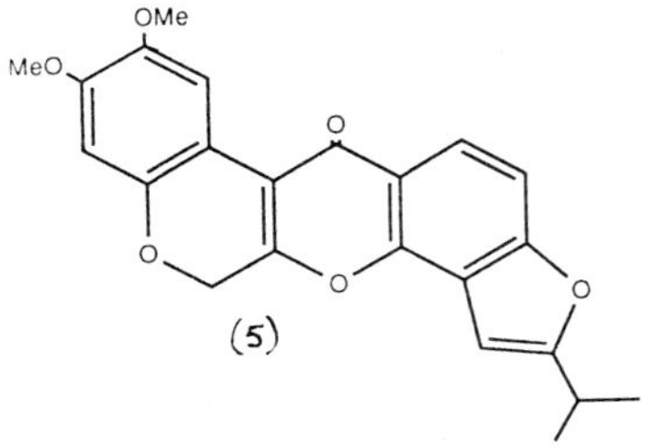

(5)

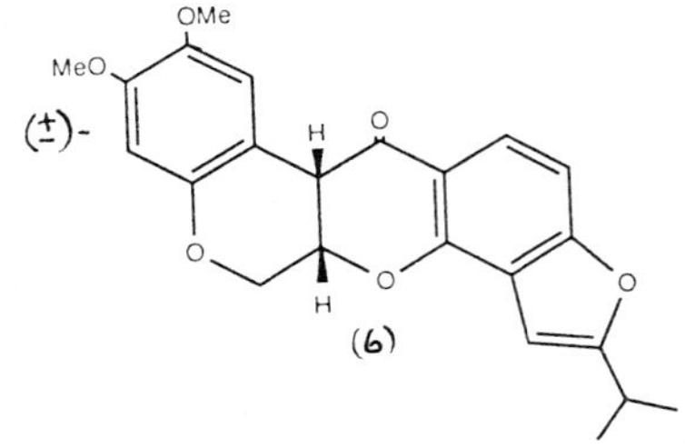

(±)- (6)

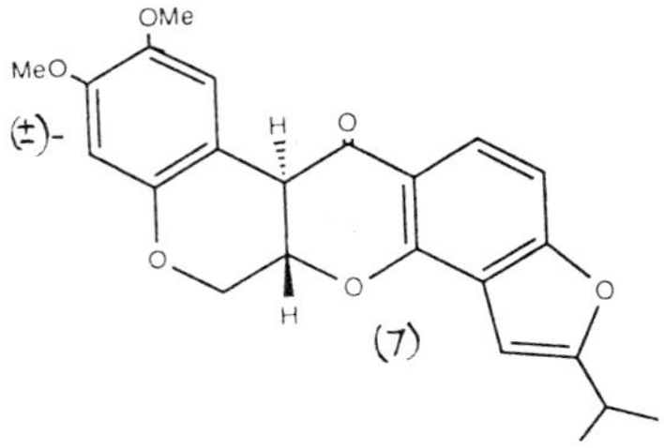

(±)- (7)

(8)

(9)

(10)

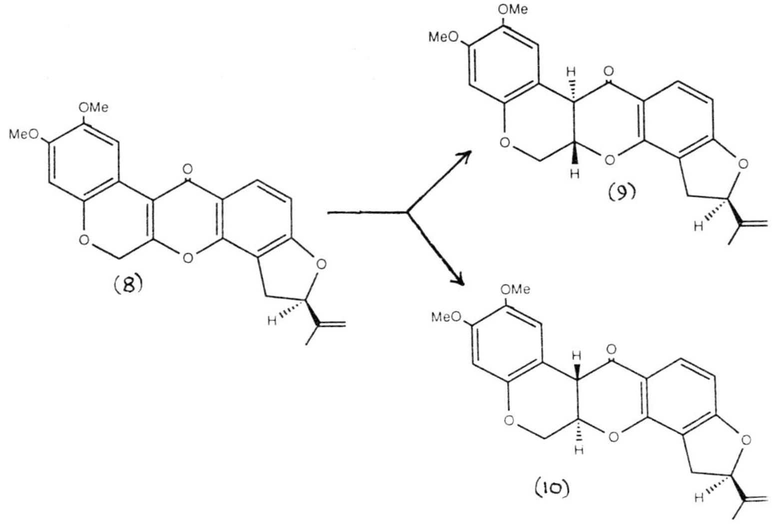

From the corresponding 6a.12a-dehydro compound, the (±)-core compound of the rotenoid series (13) was made by DIBAL reduction. It was found to be more unstable than the other _trans_-rotenoids made, being unstable even in d6-acetone; NMR data could however be obtained in d6-benzene. The greater stability of the methoxylated ring-A compounds may be attributable to the electron donating groups destabilising the stilbene structures formed on enolisation. As an example of an 11-hydroxy _trans_- rotenoid, 6a,12a-dehydrotoxicarol was converted into (12). This too was an unstable compound, being converted into the _cis_-isomer in a few minutes in d6-acetone. The increased instability relative to deguelin is presumably due to internal acid catalysis by the hydroxyl chelated to the 12- C=O, promoting enolisation.

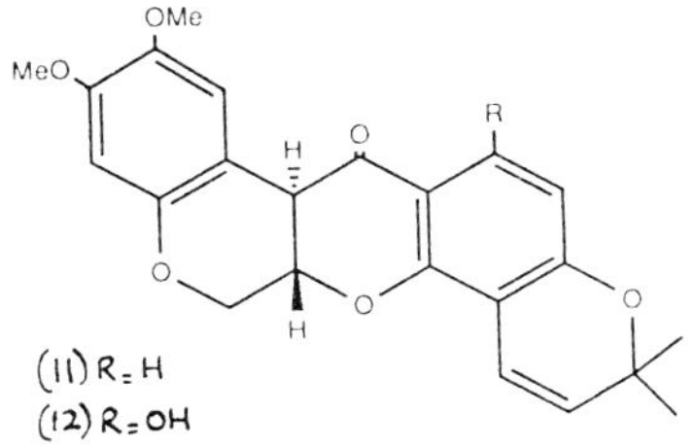

(11) R = H
(12) R = OH

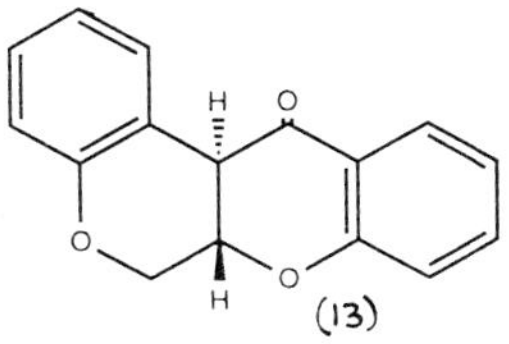

(13)

X-RAY DATA FOR cis- AND trans-ISOROTENONE

(±)-_cis_-Isorotene (6) crystallised in triclinic form with four molecules per unit cell and two crystallographically independent molecules of very similar molecular geometry and conformation. The bent _cis_- shape is shown in Fig.(1a) and (1b) . (±)-_trans_-Isorotenone (7) also crystallised in triclinic form with two symmetry related molecules per unit cell and its

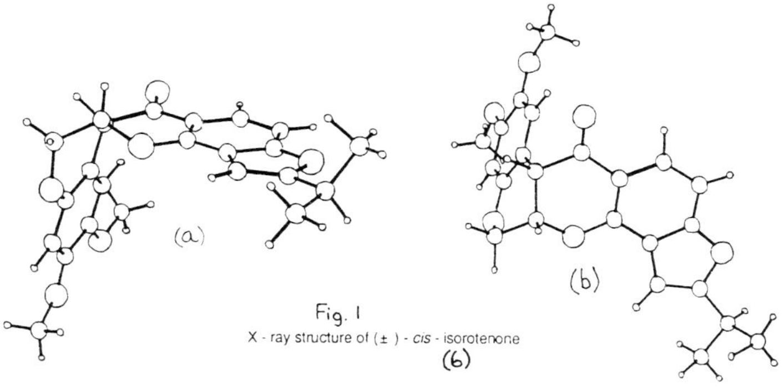

Fig. 1
X - ray structure of (±) - _cis_ - isorotenone
(6)

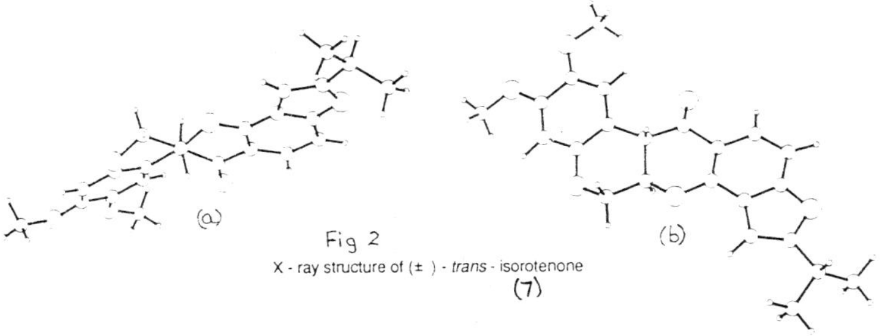

Fig 2
X - ray structure of (±) - _trans_ - isorotenone
(7)

flatter and more extended shape is shown in Fig, (2a) and (2b). The major change in molecular shape consequent upon the change in stereochemistry at the B/C-ring junction is conveniently expressed by the dihedral angle between the two aromatic rings which is 158° for the trans-molecule and 99° and 101° for each of the crystallographically distinct cis-molecules. In the trans-compound there is a close non-bonded contact between the C-1 hydrogen and the C-12 carbonyl oxygen of 2.40A. The cis-stereochemistry allows this contact distance to be increased to 2.48A and 2.56A in the two types of molecule. The strain of the contact is indicated by expansion of the C-1a,C12a,C-12 bond angle to 118.4° (cis-forms : 111.4° and 111.8°) and the C-12a,C-12,carbonyl-O bond angle to 124.9° (cis-forms : 119.4° and120°) in the trans-form.

SPECTROSCOPIC CRITERIA FOR DIFFERENTIATING cis- AND trans-ROTENOIDS.
1. The C-1 hydrogen resonates near 6.7 for the cis- and 7.6 for the trans-.
2. For the cis- J6a,12a is about 4Hz, for the trans-about12Hz.
3. For the cis- J6Hb,6a is about 4Hz, for the trans-about10Hz.
4. For the cis-J6Ha,6Hb is about 10Hz, for the trans-about 12Hz.

THE 12-alpha-HYDROXY-COMPOUNDS OF THE ISOROTENONE SERIES WITH cis- AND trans-B/C-FUSIONS.
These (±) compounds, being unenolisable, have stable B/C fusions. The cis- representative (14) was readily prepared by sodium borohydride reduction of (±)-cis-isorotenone (6): the reagent approaches from the less hindered side giving an alpha-hydroxyl. On the other hand approach of the reagent to (±)-trans-isorotenone is less hindered and can occur from either face. Two products, the 12-alpha (15) and -beta (16) were formed and separated and significant NMR data for the three compounds is shown.

12-α- cis- B/C   (14)   12-α-trans B/C (15)   12-β-trans B/C (16)

ASSAY FOR INHIBITION OF MITOCHONDRIAL RESPIRATION.
The insecticidal effects of rotenoids is usually ascribed to their inhibitory effects on the mitochondrial respiratory chain. It therefore seemed of interest to compare the activities of cis- and trans- rotenoids, and this work was carried out in the Biochemistry Laboratories of Wellcome Research, Berkhamsted[7] using blowfly flight-muscle mitochondrial particles, assaying the conversion of NADH to NAD. Results are expressed in the Figure as IC50 values. It is apparent from the data for cis-(6aS,12aS,5'R)- and trans-(6aS,12aR,5'R)-rotenone (1) and (9) that despite the strong change in molecular geometry the loss in activity by changing to the unnatural trans-fusion is not substantial. This is borne out again in the case of the (±)-isorotenones (6) and (7). The (±)-12-alpha-hydroxy compounds (14) and (15) both have

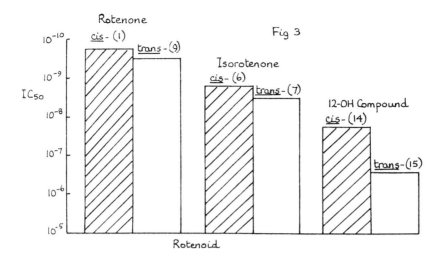

Fig 3

substantially diminished activity, though the relationship between cis- and trans-B/C isomers is similar. Further studies on structure-activity relationships are in progress.

We thank Dr. J.B. Weston (Wellcome) for his interest in this work.

REFERENCES

1 G. Buchi, L. Crombie, P.J. Godin, J.S. Kaltenbronn, K.S. Siddalingaiah and D.A. Whiting, J. Chem. Soc., 1961,2843.
2 M.J. Begley, L. Crombie and D.A. Whiting, J. Chem. Soc., Chem. Commun., 1975, 850.
3 L. Crombie and P.J. Godin, J. Chem. Soc., 1961, 2861.
4 G.R. Brown and D. Wright, Experientia, 1976, 32/3, 277.
5 M. Miyano and M. Matsui, Bull. Agric. Chem. Soc., Japan, 1958, 22, 128: Chem. Ber.,1958, 91, 2044.
6 M.J. Begley, L. Crombie, A. Hamid bin Hadi and J.L. Josephs, J. Chem Soc. Perkin Trans I, 1989,204.
7 We thank Dr. C.J. Brealey for these results.

© 1990 Elsevier Science Publishers B.V. (Biomedical Division)
Pesticides and alternatives, editor J.E. Casida

HERITABLE TRICHOME EXUDATE DIFFERENCES OF RESISTANT AND SUSCEPTIBLE GERANIUMS

Donald S. Walters, Richard Craig, and Ralph O. Mumma

Departments of Entomology and Horticulture, Pennsylvania State University, University Park, PA.

INTRODUCTION

Glandular trichomes have been associated with insect and mite resistance in a substantial number of plant species[2]. Perhaps the most studied glandular trichomes are those of potatoes and tomatoes, where the exudate has been demonstrated to be important in insect defense through a variety of mechanisms including physical entrapment, toxicity and repellency[1,5,12].

The garden geranium, *Pelargonium xhortorum*, possesses tall glandular trichomes. Winner used bioassays to assess resistance of 2000 progeny from crosses of resistant and susceptible lines to the twospotted spider mite[13]. He observed heritable differences in mite resistance among inbred geranium lines and proposed a genetic model for the inheritance of resistance. Subsequent studies have shown that resistant plants have larger numbers of tall glandular trichomes than susceptible lines and produce greater amounts of trichome exudate[11]. The exudate from the tall glandular trichomes of resistant geraniums has been identified as chiefly C_{22} and C_{24} unsaturated anacardic acids (6-[(Z)-10'-pentadecenyl]salicylic acid ($C_{22}H_{34}O_3$) and 6-[(Z)-12'-heptadecenyl]-salicylic acid ($C_{24}H_{38}O_3$)[4,10].

Anacardic acids have been reported from other plants of the *Anacardiaceae*, *Ginkgoaceae* and *Myristacaceae* families[3,6,8,14]. The high concentration of anacardic acids in geraniums with the *cis* ω-5 double bond is somewhat unusual, but *Knema elegans* is also known to produce ω-5 anacardic acids in small amounts[6].

Bioassays to assess the mortality and behavior of the foxglove aphid (*Acyrthosiphon solani*) on geraniums indicated that mite resistant and susceptible plant lines were also resistant and susceptible to the aphids[9]. The critical importance of the exudate in defense was demonstrated when the exudate was removed from leaves of resistant geranium plants with a basic aqueous wash as the leaves then became aphid susceptible[9].

While the exudate observed on trichomes from resistant plants is a viscous liquid, the exudate of susceptible geraniums has a crystalline clumped appearance and is solid to the touch. Utilizing capillary chromatography and a newly available and superior liquid phase (90% biscyanopropyl-10% phenyl cyanopropyl), we have reanalyzed the tall trichome exudate from susceptible and resistant geranium lines. In addition, the inheritance of the exudate composition was evaluated by analyzing parental and F_1 generations of two well characterized inbred lines, one resistant and one susceptible.

MATERIALS AND METHODS
Chemical Analysis of Trichome Exudate

Anacardic acids were rinsed from the geranium leaf surfaces with a 0.008M carbonate/0.077M bicarbonate buffer (pH 9.0). Leaves at the third and fourth nodes from the apical meristem were removed and extracted for 20 min in the buffer with shaking on a mechanical wrist shaker. The extract was acidified (pH $\leq$ 2.0 using concentrated HCl) and partitioned with 5 ml of methylene chloride with shaking in a 20 ml vial. The organic solvent was removed, evaporated to dryness and the residue redissolved in 0.5 ml ethyl ether. Following selective methylation of the carboxyl using a 5 min diazomethane treatment at room temperature[10], the monomethylated extract was analyzed using an RTX-2330 capillary column (10 m, 0.25 mm I.D., 0.25 μ film thickness) employing splitless off-column injection with H_2 carrier in a back pressure regulated mode (23.5 PSI) and a four minute initial temperature hold at 160°C followed by a 5° per minute program to 230°C. A Varian 3700 gas chromatograph was used in conjunction with an HP 3390A integrating recorder. Peak identifications were verified by GC/MS[10].

Exudate was collected and analyzed from 8 vegetatively propagated plants of resistant line 71-17-7 (17-7), 6 of resistant line 71-18-6 (18-6) and 8 of susceptible line 71-10-1 (10-1)[4,7,11,13]. In addition to the above analyses, plants from other inbred lines determined to be mite susceptible by earlier workers[4,7,13] were analyzed using the aforementioned buffer extract and GLC analysis. Also, an individual trichome extract was made of the crystalline exudate on the trichome tips of inbred line 10-1. A pasteur pipette drawn to an extremely fine diameter was filled with methylene chloride, and used to extract trichomes on an individual basis. The technique is the same as that described previously[10] except that only the columnar shaped pillars of material on the trichome head were extracted and not the trichomes themselves.

Determination of the Heritability of Exudate Composition

Inbred diploid lines 17-7 and 10-1, which have been the most intensively studied were used to evaluate the inheritance of the trichome exudate composition. Both lines were self-pollinated and the resulting plants were evaluated for exudate compositions. An additional self-pollinated generation of 17-7 was also analyzed. F_1 hybrids were produced from reciprocal cross-pollinations of individual selections of each line. Three separate F_1 hybrid combinations were evaluated in this study. Since the research was conducted over several years, seeds from the same self- or cross-pollination usually were sown more than once. For example, the F_1 hybrid 10-1 x 17-7 was grown twice in 1987 and in 1988. Plants were analyzed at the seedling stage, but reanalysis of about 15% of the plants at maturity confirmed that exudate composition was stable. A summary of the geranium families analyzed is as follows:

Genetic Background	Family Number Code (Number of Plants)
1st generation self of 17-7	87-5(4), 88-51(13)
2nd generation self of 17-7	88-2(8)
1st generation self of 10-1	87-13(4), 87-14(4)
	88-10(10), 88-50(10)
F_1 generation of 17-7 x 10-1	87-6(6), 88-5(8)
F_1 generation of 10-1 x 17-7	87-16(11), 88-11(10)
	88-52(10), 87-17(6)

Plant Propagation and Growth Conditions

Plants were pollinated using standard practices. Seeds were manually scarified and sown 3/8" deep in once leached Metro Mix® 215 in 50 slot plug trays, irrigated and placed under artificial illumination in growth chambers for one week before they were moved to the greenhouse. Seedlings were maintained in the plug trays

320

throughout the experiment and fertilized and irrigated as needed. Chemical analysis of the plants began at 6-8 weeks of age.

RESULTS AND DISCUSSION
Comparison of Exudate Composition Among Resistant and Susceptible Lines
Light microscope examination of tall glandular trichomes of resistant and susceptible geraniums revealed important differences in their appearance. Exudate on the glandular trichomes of resistant plants completely covered the head of the trichome in a seemingly uniform layer (Fig. 1A), was usually light yellow to orange in color and sticky to the touch. On the other hand, exudate on trichomes of susceptible plants appeared as a clear to light yellow semisolid, was physically located on the top of the head of the glandular trichome, was not sticky to the touch and appeared rigid in form (Fig. 1B).

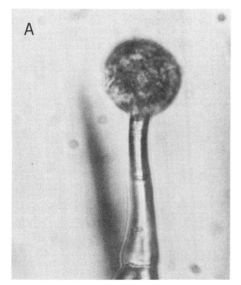
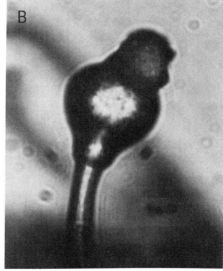

Fig. 1. Photomicrograph of typical tall glandular trichome from resistant (A) and susceptible (B) geraniums (*Pelargonium xhortorum*)

The separation of the unmethylated anacardic acids utilizing a 1.5% SP2250/1.95% SP2401 packed column is presented in Fig. 2A. Packed column GLC had been used previously to analyze the exudate from various plant lines[11]. Fig. 2, panels B and C, shows the gas chromatograms of the monomethylated exudate from resistant and susceptible geranium plants utilizing a polar-phase RTX 2330 capillary column (Restek, Inc., Bellefonte, PA). Both lines possess saturated and unsaturated anacardic acids. Saturated side chain anacardic acids had been previously detected in the glandular trichome exudate of resistant plants in mass spectrometric analysis[10]. Other capillary columns possessing different stationary phases (5 and 35% phenyl; carbowax) were evaluated, but could not equal the separation obtained with the RTX 2330 column.

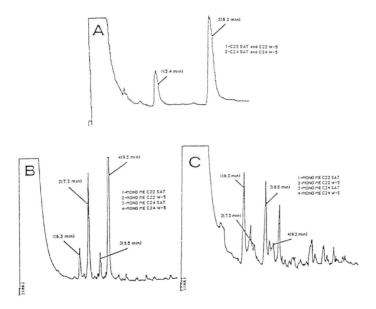

Fig. 2. GLC analysis of: (A) anacardic acids from resistant geraniums (17-7) utilizing a packed column; (B) monomethylated anacardic acids from resistant geraniums (17-7) utilizing an RTX-2330 capillary column; and (C) monomethylated anacardic acids from susceptible geranium (10-1) utilizing an RTX-2330 capillary column.

322

The analysis of 17-7 showed the expected predominance of ω-5 unsaturated anacardic acids, but also showed a lower but very important contribution, 13.4%, from the saturated analogs (Fig. 3; Table I). Inbred line 18-6, which is also resistant, has a similar exudate composition with about 90% of the exudate composed of C_{22} and C_{24} ω-5 anacardic acids. In contrast, 77.4-80.0% of the C_{22} and C_{24} compounds present in the exudate of line 10-1 are made up of the saturated analogs. Analysis of a number of other plants of this same line (10-1) during the course of other experiments not presented here indicates these values are typical and conserved under a variety of environmental conditions. As demonstrated in earlier studies, line 10-1 produces a very low amount of exudate[11]. The other compounds present in the 10-1 exudate are also believed to be anacardic acids (Fig. 2C). Plants from other lines evaluated as mite susceptible (71-15-4, 71-13-3 and 71-13-1) showed the same type of exudate composition as that exhibited by line 10-1, the saturated compounds comprising a majority of the exudate in all cases (Table I). Finally, the results of the methylene chloride, capillary tube extraction of the solid exudate clumps on line 10-1 showed the same type of composition as the rest of the analyses of susceptible plants. The saturated compounds are the predominant materials present in the exudate of plants designated as mite and aphid susceptible.

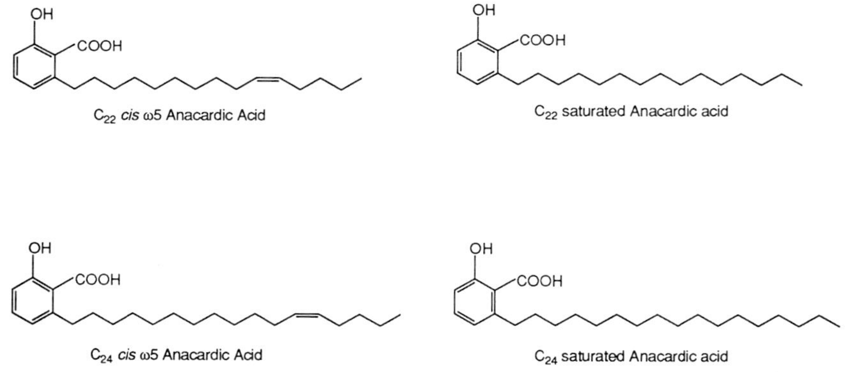

C_{22} cis ω5 Anacardic Acid

C_{22} saturated Anacardic acid

C_{24} cis ω5 Anacardic Acid

C_{24} saturated Anacardic acid

Fig. 3. Structures of predominant compounds of resistant geranium trichome exudate.

TABLE I.
RELATIVE PERCENTAGE COMPOSITION OF SATURATED (C_{22} AND C_{24}) AND
UNSATURATED (ω-5) ANACARDIC ACIDS IN TRICHOME EXUDATES FROM
SUSCEPTIBLE AND RESISTANT GERANIUM LINES AS ANALYZED BY
CAPILLARY GAS CHROMATOGRAPHY.

No. of		C_{22} Compounds		C_{24} Compounds	
Plant Line	Plants	Sat	ω-5 Unsat	Sat	ω-5 Unsat
71-17-7 (Resistant)	8				
% (S.E.)		13.4(1.4)	86.6(1.4)	8.6(1.1)	91.4(1.1)
range		7-17	83-93	4-11	89-96
71-18-6 (Resistant)	6				
% (S.E.)		9.4(1.4)	90.6(1.4)	10.7(1.9)	89.3(1.9)
range		6-13	87-94	4-15	85-96
71-10-1 (Susceptible)	12				
% (S.E.)		77.4(4.4)	22.6(4.4)	80.0(4.8)	20.0(4.8)
range		58-97	3-42	58-100	0-42
71-13-3 (Susceptible)	2				
% (S.E.)		78.5(1.5)	21.5(1.5)	78.0(2.0)	22.0(2.0)
range		77-80	20-23	76-80	20-24
71-15-4 (Susceptible)	2				
% (S.E.)		88.0(4.0)	12.0(4.0)	76.5(1.5)	23.5(1.5)
range		84-92	8-16	75-78	22-25
71-10-1 (Individual Trichome Exudate)		76	24	80	20

Inheritance of Exudate Composition

Analysis of the self-pollinated progeny of lines 17-7 and 10-1 demonstrate the
heritability of exudate composition (Fig. 4). Like their parent, first and second
generation self-pollinated progeny (S_1 and S_2 families 87-5, 88-2, 88-51) of 17-7

produce exudate with a low proportion of saturated C_{22} anacardic acid relative to the total C_{22} compounds present (both ω-5 unsaturated and saturated). Likewise, offspring of 10-1 (families 87-13, 87-14, 88-10, 88-50) produce mostly saturated C_{22} compounds in the trichome exudate like 10-1. There is no overlap in the two groups so that the proportion of saturated C_{22}/total C_{22} can be used to discriminate between the 17-7 and 10-1 phenotypes. Although they are not presented, analysis of the C_{24} anacardic acids in these families parallels the results of the C_{22} analysis quite closely. F_1 hybrids of 17-7 and 10-1 exhibit a proportion of saturated C_{22} anacardic acid very similar to that of their resistant 17-7 parent (Fig. 5). Again there is no overlap of the susceptible and F_1 phenotype with respect to the proportion of saturated C_{22} anacardic acid. Thus, a plot of this nature is capable of separating the 10-1 phenotype from those of both the 17-7 and the F_1 hybrids of these two lines.

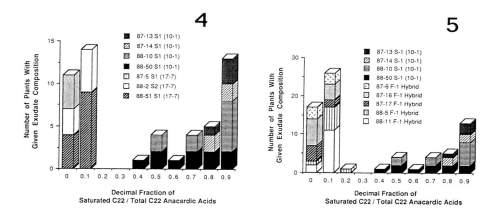

Fig. 4. Distribution of self-pollinated progeny of 17-7 and 10-1 with respect to the proportion of saturated C_{22} to total C_{22} anacardic acids present in the trichome exudate.

Fig. 5. Distribution of F_1 hybrid families and families from self-pollination of 10-1 with respect to the proportion of saturated C_{22} to total C_{22} anacardic acids present in the trichome exudate.

While 17-7 type plants and F_1's are similar with respect to the proportion of saturated C_{22} anacardic acid in their exudate, there are distinct differences in the exudate composition in terms of the proportion of ω-5 C_{22} anacardic acid to the total ω-5 anacardic acids present (C_{22} and C_{24}). As reported by Gerhold[4], in line 17-7 about 35% of the ω-5 unsaturated compounds are C_{22} with the remainder C_{24}. Our analysis supports Gerhold's assertion: the eight resistant 17-7's analyzed here produced exudate with a mean 34.5% ω-5 C_{22}/total ω-5 anacardic acids (C_{22} and C_{24}). All the 17-7 offspring fall in the range from 25 to 37% with a fairly even distribution over the range (Fig. 6). In contrast to the 17-7 phenotype, the F_1 hybrids of 10-1 and 17-7 produce exudate that contains higher amounts (37-64%) of the ω-5 C_{22} compound relative to its ω-5 C_{24} companion (families 87-6, 87-16, 87-17, 88-5, 88-11, 88-52). With the exception of one plant the proportion of ω-5 C_{22} is greater than 40% in all six combinations of the F_1 analyzed. In general, the ω-5 C_{22} compound is present in amounts greater than or equal to the ω-5 C_{24} compound. Of great importance is the fact that again there is no overlap between the 17-7 phenotype and the F_1 phenotype with respect to the proportion of ω-5 C_{22}/total ω-5 anacardic acids.

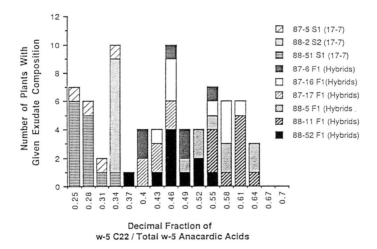

Fig. 6. Distribution of F_1 hybrid families and families from self-pollination of 17-7 with respect to the proportion of ω-5 C_{22} to total ω-5 anacardic acids (C_{22} and C_{24}) present in the trichome exudate.

The reason for not including the saturated C_{24}/total C_{24} proportion in Figs. 4 and 5 can now be justified. It appears that the F_1's produce a reduced amount of ω-5 C_{24} which gives rise to the increase in the proportion of ω-5 C_{22}/total ω-5 anacardic acids we have just seen. This decrease also results in an increase in the proportion of saturated C_{24}/total C_{24} compounds and tends to obscure differences between predominantly saturated exudate (10-1 type) and predominantly unsaturated exudate (17-7 type). Therefore, the proportion of saturated C_{22} is a better discriminator between phenotypes than the proportion of saturated C_{24}.

The difference in exudate composition between lines was previously undetected because of lack of chromatographic resolution and is of major importance to the physical properties of the exudate and the functioning of the resistance mechanism. The impact of the double bond on the physical properties of these anacardic acids is similar to that observed in the desaturation of stearic acid to oleic acid. At room temperature, stearic acid is a crystalline solid while oleic acid is a viscous liquid. It is not surprising that the anacardic acids of geraniums, similar in many physical and chemical respects to fatty acids, should behave in a similar manner.

The plants are able to exert control over the composition of the exudate. It may be that the 10% contribution of saturated material in the resistant type exudate is not an accidental bypassing of the ω-5 biosynthetic pathway, but an important evolutionary adaptation to provide proper viscosity of the exudate. Earlier work has demonstrated the efficacy of the geranium trichome exudate as a sticky trap[11]. Obviously, a solid exudate will be ineffective in providing any sort of physical entrapment type of resistance. A solid exudate will also be less effectively applied to a potential pest in a resistance mechanism based on toxic properties. It is apparent that the change from exudate consisting primarily of unsaturated ω-5 anacardic acids to exudate with a large percentage of saturated compounds has tremendous impact on the effectiveness of the resistance mechanism. The unusual ω-5 double bond position present in these anacardic acids appears to be in part a device utilized by the geraniums to adjust the physical state of the trichome exudate to meet the plants' requirements as a defensive agent.

ACKNOWLEDGEMENTS

This work was supported in part by Northeastern Regional Project NE-115 and the United States Department of Agriculture Grant No. 87-CRCR-1-2423. Appreciation is expressed to Jody Harman and Cindy Goudy for assistance.

REFERENCES

1. Dimock MB, Kennedy GG (1983) Ent Exp Appl 33:263-268
2. Duffey SS (1986) In: Juniper BE, Southwood TR (eds) Insects and the Plant Surface. Edward Arnold Ltd, Baltimore, MD, pp 151-173
3. Gellerman JL, Schlenk H (1988) Anal Chem 40:739-743
4. Gerhold DL, Craig R, Mumma RO (1984) J Chem Ecol 10: 713-722.
5. Gregory P, Ave DA, Bouthyette PY, Tingey WM (1986) In: Juniper BE, Southwood TR (eds) Insects and the Plant Surface. Edward Arnold Ltd, Baltimore, MD, pp 173-183
6. Spencer GF, Tjarks LW, Kleiman R (1980) J Nat Products 43:724-730
7. Stark RS (1975) Morphological and Biochemical Factors Relating to Spider Mite Resistance in the Geranium. (Ph.D. Thesis) University Park, Pennsylvania, Pennsylvania State University
8. Tyman JHP, Tychopoulos V, Chan P (1984) J Chromatog 303:151-163
9. Walters DS (1988) Biochemical and Morphological Characteristics Involved in the Pest Resistance Mechanism of Geraniums. (Ph.D. Thesis), University Park, Pennsylvania, Pennsylvania State University
10. Walters DS, Minard R, Craig R, Mumma RO (1988) J Chem Ecol 14:743-751
11. Walters DS, Grossman HH, Craig R, Mumma RO (1989) J Chem Ecol 15:357-372
12. Weston PA, Johnson DA, Burton HT, Snyder JC (1989) J Am Soc Hort 114:492-498
13. Winner BL (1975) Inheritance of resistance to the two-spotted spider mite, *Tetranychus urticae* (Koch) in the geranium *Pelargonium Xhortorum* (Bailey). (M.S. Thesis), University Park, Pennsylvania, Pennsylvania State University
18. Yalpani M, Tyman JHP (1983) Phytochem 22:2263-2266

EFFECTS OF SOME FEEDING INHIBITORS ON TWO HOMOPTERAN INSECT PESTS <u>NILAPARVATA LUGENS</u> AND <u>ACYRTHOSIPHON PISUM</u>

R.M.WILKINS, E.OKELLO-EKOCHU, K.JEEVARATNAM AND D.WECHAKIT

Department of Agricultural and Environmental Science, University of Newcastle upon Tyne, Newcastle upon Tyne, NE1 7RU, U.K.

INTRODUCTION

Many natural and synthetic compounds inhibit feeding (antifeedants) or show repellent activity on plant feeding arthropods[1,2]. The presence of such compounds in or on the host has been demonstrated to reduce food intake[3], disturb the normal feeding rhythm[4] and to result in the slowing of development and decreasing of reproductive rate [5,6] of insect pests. Such compounds have also been shown to reduce the transmission of some pest viruses by vectors[7].

The action on the target insect may range from true antifeeding or repelling through to hormone or other metabolic disturbances. For the purpose of this paper, the word antifeedant is used to cover a range of unknown activities involved with feeding inhibition or suppression.

Most studies on antifeedants have predominantly been performed against Lepidopteran and Coleopteran insect larvae. Following the discovery of rice brown planthopper (<u>Nilaparvata lugens</u>) resurgence after insecticide application and the development of biotypes which can feed on resistant varieties, Heinrichs,[8] recommended the identification of compounds with ovicidal action or which act as antifeedants or repellents and their application within an integrated pest management (IPM) approach.

This study was conducted to determine the antifeedant activity of some naturally occurring and synthetic compounds against the rice brown planthopper (BPH), <u>Nilaparvata lugens</u> Stal (Homoptera: Delphacidae), and the pea aphid, <u>Acyrthosiphon pisum</u> Harris (Homoptera: Aphididae).

MATERIALS AND METHODS

Compounds tested

The compounds tested were neem oil, citronella oil, eucalyptus oil, marcosa oil, turpentine, azadirachtin, n-dodecanoic acid, n-decanoic acid, 2-(2-methylaminoethyl)-pyridine, 3-(methylaminomethyl)-pyridine, cadaverine, 1,8-diaminooctane, spermine, polyethyleneimine, carbendazim, benomyl, cypermethrin, permethrin, carbofuran, chlormequat, fentinhydroxide and polygodial. Each test consisted of a range of dilutions and a control. All controls were treated with diluent (water containing Triton X-100 at 0.3% for the oils or at 0.05% with acetone (10%) for other compounds) only. Reagent or technical grade materials (except the plant oils) were used.

Experimental insects

Brachypterous adult female BPH of uniform size and age were obtained from a stock colony of insects reared on the BPH-susceptible rice variety 'Taichung Native 1'(TN1) in plastic cages (30x45x30cm) kept in a greenhouse at $25-30^0$C and 70%RH. Before each test, insects were confined in 2.5cm diameter by 1.5cm long test tubes (five insects per test tube) and starved for three hours. A water soaked paper was provided to prevent the insects from dessicating.

Apterous adult A.pisum from a laboratory culture maintained on broad bean plants (Vicia faba L var Imperial White Windsor) at greenhouse conditions of 20-25ºC, 60-70%RH and 24 hour supplementary flourescent light were used in the aphid tests. Aphids were removed from the plants using a small moistened brush and starved for 2-3 hours in plastic petri dishes before each test.

Experimental plants

The BPH-susceptible rice variety TN1 used in the BPH experiments were reared in isolation in a greenhouse at the Univeristy experimental station. Potted plants of the same size and age (2 months) were taken for the various tests.

Two week old bean plants, V.faba, also reared at the University experimental station were used in the aphid experiments. They were grown in 9cm diameter pots, four plants per pot.

Assay for Antifeedant Activity Against BPH

Efficacy Feeding activity of BPH was determined by honeydew production using either
theparafilm sachet[9] or by the filter paper method[10]. However, the sachet method was
slightly modified by differential weighing of the sachet with and without honeydew on a
0.001mg sensitive balance, instead of measuring the volume of honeydew using
micropipettes.

Tests solutions were prepared in diluent as % concentration (w:v or v:v). Test
solutions were applied to rice plant stems ($10cm^2$) using a small paint brush. Repeated
applications, where needed, were made to achieve the desired loading/surface deposit
($\mu g/cm^2$). Solutions were allowed to evaporate to dryness before reapplying. All
treatments in pots were arranged in a randomised block design. Each treatment was
replicated at least three times, with five insects per replicate. All experiments were
conducted under controlled environmental conditions of 27–90%RH, over 24 hours.

To assess the effect of a compound as an antifeedant, the amount of honeydew excreted
(mg or mm^2 of the area stained on filter paper) in the control and treated were
compared and the effect on feeding activity defined as:

$$\% \text{ Inhibition} = \frac{\text{amount of honeydew excreted in control} - \text{amount of honeydew excreted in treated}}{\text{amount of honeydew excreted in control}} \times 100$$

Persistence The method, design and conditions adopted were the same as in the efficacy
tests above. Plants were assessed for antifeedant activity at intervals of 0,1,3,5 and 7
days after treatment (DAT) (up to 14 days in some experiments). Some compounds were
combined with an equal weight of a latex containing polyethyleneglycol (PEG) and
polyvinyl acetate (PVAc) in equal proportions by weight, and diluted with distilled water
to the desired concentration.

Systemic activity The soil-free roots of individual rice plants were immersed in a
beaker containing 50ml of a test solution. Each treated plant was replicated four
times. The control was treated with distilled water only. The conditions of the
experiment and the method of assessment were the same as in the rice stem treatment
tests.

332

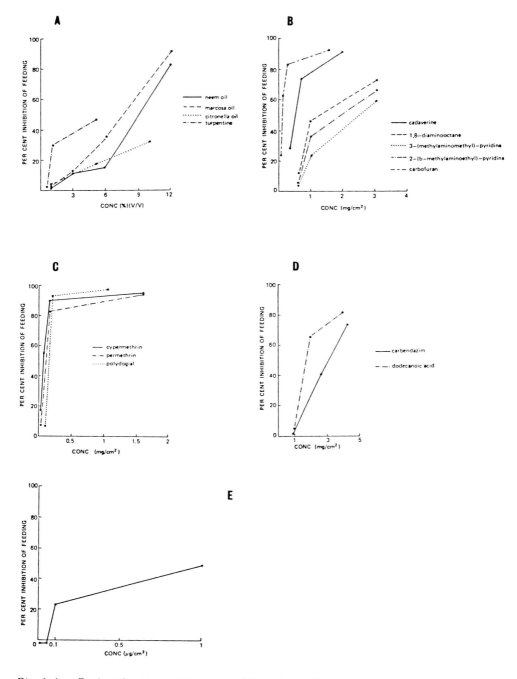

Fig 1 A – E. Antifeeding activity of (A) oils, (B) amines and a carbamate insecticide, (C) pyrethroids and polygodial, (D) a fungicide and a carboxylic acid, (E) azadirachtin, against BPH

Aphid Feeding Deterrence Tests

Complete leaves of similar size (ca. 15cm^2) and age cut from two week old bean plants were used. One of a pair of leaflets from the same leaf was treated with the test solution. Solutions were evenly coated onto both the abaxial and adaxial surfaces of the leaflets using a 1ml capacity pipette. The other leaflet was treated with diluent only. Leaves were left to dry.

A hole was made through a plastic petri dish base. This petri dish base was then placed within another un-perforated base leaving some space at the bottom for distilled water. Each leaf, bearing two leaflets, was then placed with it's petiole protruding into the distilled water through the hole made in the upper petri dish base. Ten aphids were then centrally placed in each petri dish base containing the leaves. The lids were gently pressed down so that the aphids were enclosed in an aphid-proof chamber with an equal choice of treated and untreated leaflets.

Treatments were arranged in a randomised design. Each petri dish containing the leaf and aphids represented one replicate. Each treatment was replicated four times. All experiments were conducted in a controlled temperature room at 25°C, 70%RH and 16 hour light for 24 hours. The position of the insects on the leaflets was taken to indicate their preference. Aphids at this time not on the leaf or not feeding were excluded from assessment, hence allowing the proportion of feeding to non-feeding adult aphids to be based on only those insects that remained on the leaf surface. All data were subjected to an arc-sin transformation, analysis of variance (ANOVA) and the Student-Newman-Keuls (SNK) multiple range test.

RESULTS

Antifeedant activity of plant essential oils

In the BPH studies, the percent feeding inhibition increased with increasing concentration of the test compound (Fig 1), with 12% neem and marcosa oils causing up to more than 80% feeding inhibition. The efficacy ranking of the oils based on the minimum dosage applied to the rice plant stem to produce a significant reduction in honeydew excretion compared to the control, at the 5% level of significance according to the Duncans multiple range test, was: turpentine $>$ marcosa $>$ neem $>$ citronella (Table 1). However, high concentrations of turpentine and citronella oils show phytotoxic activity to rice.

334

Table 1

Minimum concentration applied to rice plant stem to produce a significant reduction in
honeydew production, by BPH, from control at the 5% level – DMRT*

compound	concentration	compound	concentration
neem	6% v:v	carbendazim	2580 µg/cm^2
marcosa	6% v:v	permethrin	80 µg/cm^2
citronella	10% v:v	cypermethrin	16 µg/cm^2
turpentine	1% w:v	carbofuran	15 µg/cm^2
cadaverine	360 µg/cm^2	dodecanoic acid	2000 µg/cm^2
1,8-diaminooctane	1140 µg/cm^2	polygodial	210 µg/cm^2
3-(methylaminomethyl)-pyridine	1160 µg/cm^2	azadirachtin	1 µg/cm^2
2-(2-methylaminoethyl)pyridine	1180 µg/cm^2		

*Duncans Multiple Range Test

Azadirachtin, a constituent of neem oil from seed of Azadirachta indica A.Juss,
was active at concentrations of 0.1µg/cm^2 and above. Concentrations below this
did not show activity significantly different from control (Fig 1E).

In the aphid feeding deterrence tests, the inhibitory activity of the oils
was: citronella>turpentine>neem>eucalyptus, with citronella oil being about
twice as active as either neem or turpentine at a concentration of 2.5% (Table
2). Eucalyptus oil had no apparent effect on the aphids.

Antifeedant activity of amines

Against the BPH, all the four amines tested caused over 50% feeding
inhibition, reaching 90% with cadaverine, at concentrations of 2-3000µg/cm^2
(Fig 1B). At this concentration however, some phytotoxicity on rice was
evident. Cadaverine was the most effective of the four amines tested requiring a
much lower minimum dosage to produce a significant reduction in honeydew
production from control (Table 1). Spermine and polyethyleneimine had no
antifeedant activity against BPH (data not included).

Against the pea aphid, 2-(2-methylaminoethyl)-pyridine was over 60% more
active than 3-(methylaminomethyl)-pyridine at a concentration of 1.8µg/cm^2
(Table 2).

Table 2

Feeding deterrence of the pea aphid, A.pisum, on broad bean leaves.

Compound	Concentration	Mean no.(+SE) on treated leaflets[ab]		Percentage deterred[c]
control	–	44.8	(+0.2)	–
2-(2-methylaminoethyl)-pyridine	1.8 μg/cm^2	4.6	(+4.6) ***	89.7
3-(methylaminomethyl)-pyridine	1.6 μg/cm^2	35.4	(+3.9) *	21.0
dodecanoic acid	2.6 μg/cm^2	26.7	(+3.6) ***	40.4
	1.3 μg/cm^2	24.0	(+8.1) **	46.4
	0.6 μg/cm^2	32.6	(+4.1) **	27.7
n-decanoic acid	4.4 μg/cm^2	30.4	(+2.2) ***	32.1
	2.2 μg/cm^2	32.4	(+4.2) **	27.7
neem oil	10% v:v	15.8	(+5.6) ***	64.7
	5% v:v	20.4	(+2.0) ***	54.5
	2.5% v:v	25.8	(+4.3) ***	42.4
	1.2% v:v	29.3	(+4.5) ***	34.6
citronella oil	2.5% v:v	0	***	100.0
	1.2% v:v	4.6	(+4.6) ***	89.7
	0.6% v:v	34.2	(+2.0) **	23.7
turpentine	10% v:v	0	***	100.0
	5% v:v	13.5	(+7.9) **	69.9
	2.5% v:v	26.1	(+8.9) *	41.7
eucalyptus oil	no significant differences			

a   arc-sin transformed data
b   differences significant from untreated : * P = 0.05; ** P = 0.01; *** P = 0.001.

Only data where treated differed from untreated are indicated.
c   (number feeding on control – number feeding on treated leaflets) X 100
            number feeding on control

Antifeedant activity of pesticides

All the insecticides tested against the BPH caused over 80% feeding inhibition at concentrations of 200μg/cm^2 and above (Fig 1B & C). Carbofuran and cypermethrin exhibited the most activity of the pesticides (Table 1). Carbandazim was only effective at high concentrations (Fig 1D & Table 1). Benomyl, fentin hydroxide, and chlormequat had no antifeedant activity against BPH (data not shown).

Activity of other compounds

Dodecanoic acid treatment of rice plants resulted in the inhibition of feeding of BPH at high concentrations (Fig 1D), when some phytotoxicity occurred. Against the pea aphid, both dodecanoic acid and n-decanoic acid were active, n-decanoic acid being half as active as dodecanoic acid (Table 2).

Polygodial treatment resulted in a very significant reduction in BPH feeding comparable to that of the insecticides (Fig 1C & Table 1) although concentrations of more than $500\mu g/cm^2$ were phytotoxic.

Persistence of antifeedants

The activities of marcosa and neem oils were similar and for both agents persisted for up to 7DAT (Table 3). Among the amines, 2-(2-methylaminoethyl)-pyridine and 3-(methylaminomethyl)-pyridine were effective for 5 DAT (Table 3). The activity of cadaverine was more persistent than that of its less volatile analogue, 1,8-diaminooctane, even at half concentration (Table 3).

A combination of either cypermethrin or cadaverine with latex[11] improved the persistence of activity of either compound against BPH (Table 3). Feeding on rice plants treated with a combination of cadaverine and latex was less at 7 DAT than on freshly treated plants. The amount of feeding at 7 DAT on plants treated with cadaverine plus latex was nearly equal to that on plants treated with cadaverine alone immediately after treatment. Insects on rice plants treated with a combination of neem oil and latex fed nearly two times less at 14 DAT than at 1 DAT. Feeding at 14 DAT was nearly equal to that at 1 DAT on plants treated with neem oil alone[11].

TABLE 3

Days after treatment (DAT) when reduction of honeydew excretion, by BPH, ceased to be significantly different* from control

Compound	Concentration	DAT	Compound	Concentration	DAT
neem	12% v:v	7	3-(methylaminomethyl)-pyridine	$3500\mu g/cm^2$	5
marcosa	12% v:v	7			
cadaverine	$700\mu g/cm^2$	1	2-(2-methylaminoethyl)-pyridine	$3500\mu g/cm^2$	5
cadaverine + latex	$700\mu g/cm$	7			
			1,8-diaminooctane	$1100\mu g/cm^2$	3
cypermethrin	$80\mu g/cm^2$	5	cypermethrin + latex	$80\mu g/cm^2$	7

* P = 0.05

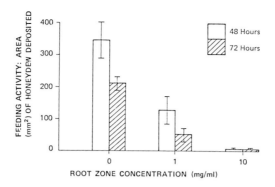

Fig 2 Systemic activity of cadaverine against BPH

Systemic activity of an antifeedant

This experiment, conducted to determine the systemic activity of cadaverine, showed that 48 hours after treatment (HAT), a concentration of 10mg/ml caused a significant reduction in feeding by BPH compared to either 1mg/ml or control. There was also a significant difference between 1mg/ml and control (Fig 2).

DISCUSSION

The responses of the rice brown planthopper (BPH) and the pea aphid to some feeding deterrents were investigated. The experiments were conducted primarily to screen for antifeedant activity of various types of compounds on a comparative basis.

In the study on the BPH, parafilm sachets[9] and filter paper[10] were used to collect and measure honeydew excretion in a no-choice design. In the aphid feeding deterrence experiments, the results were expressed as percent feeding deterrence as the tests were performed in a choice design, which is probably more sensitive than a no-choice design[12].

The results obtained with the plant essential oils, especially neem, are in general agreement with those obtained by other researchers. Food intake by newly emerged BPH, whitebacked planthopper (WBPH), Sogatella furcifera, and the rice green leafhopper (GLH), Nephotettix virescens, has been shown to decrease with increasing neem oil concentration, thus indicating antifeedant activity [13]. Growth and development of hopper nymphs was also greatly retarded on plants sprayed with neem oil. Neem oil caused a greater reduction in the amount of honeydew excreted by BPH than in the present experiment[14]. This is probably due to BPH biotype difference[15] or source of neem[16]. Gill and Lewis (1972) reported that azadirachtin at 0.5 ppm and above caused 100 per cent feeding inhibition of Schistocerca gregaria on young bean plants[17]. Eucalyptus oil had no apparent effect on the aphids, possibly due to rapid dissipation over 24 hours.

Cadaverine was a better antifeedant than the other amines, at least against the BPH. Although all the four amines tested have a strong odour, cadaverine possesses a higher volatility and hence may act both as repellent and antifeedant. The results on cadaverine, however, contrast with those of Sogawa (1971) who reported that cadaverine-2HCl (1000 ppm) dissolved in 5% sucrose, had no antifeedant activity against BPH[18]. It is assumed that the physical properties of cadaverine-2HCl are different from those of the cadaverine free base used in this study. Sucrose may also act with cadaverine-2HCl to stimulate feeding in BPH because the average number of honeydew droplets using a combination of cadaverine 2HCl and 5% sucrose was greater than in the control (5% sucrose). In further experiments we found that cadaverine was more effective than a combination of cadaverine and dodecanoic acid. It is possible that the combination of these two compounds may result in the formation of a salt which neutralises the activity of both compounds.

Although cypermethrin and permethrin are potent insecticides, it has been suggested that their sublethal effects (mainly antifeedant and repellent activity) are valuable aspects of crop protection [19]. Pyrethroids have been shown to exhibit antifeedant and/or repellent activity against the diamondbacked moth, Plutella xylostella [5,20], the two-spotted spider mite Tetranychus urticae [21] and Pieris brassicae larvae [22]. Jackson and Wilkins (1985) showed that topical dosages of fenvalerate around the LD_5 value stimulated reproduction in Myzus persicae, while sub-lethal deposits below the LD_5 value depressed the fecundity of the aphids[23]. In contrast, the antifeeding effect of carbofuran against WBPH (EC50: $0.15\mu g/cm^2$) was about 300 times less than the carbofuran concentration used for BPH here [24].

Yoshihara et.al. (1980) showed that oxalic acid, a dicarboxylic acid, inhibited the sucking activity of BPH on rice plants[4]. It was observed that carboxylic acids were deterrent to the settling and larviposition of M.persicae[25].

Polygodial has been shown to reduce virus transmission by M.persicae in potato, beet and cauliflower[7]. Its potential use as a field crop protection agent has been demonstrated by Pickett et.al. (1986) who showed that 50g/ha of polygodial gave effective control against the barley yellow dwarf virus and consequently increased barley yield from 3.83 to 5.22 tonnes/hectare[26].

One of the requirements for the practical use of antifeedants in crop protection is their persistence[1]. The reason for the low persistence of the amines, except cadaverine, is not clear, although rapid degradation remains a possibility. It is not known whether the plant oils and cadaverine would persist for longer than 7 days since long term experiments were not conducted. Ladd et.al. (1978) demonstrated that neem oil applied to soybean seedlings against the Japanese bettle remained active for up to two weeks[27].

An improvement in the effectiveness of deterrent compounds could be achieved by incorporation into polymers. The latex used here contained two polymers; polyethylene glycol and polyvinyl acetate. The potential use of such formulations in controlling plant virus vectors has been demonstrated in the field[28] by Wilkins et.al. (1984). They showed that the disease control activity of carbofuran could be enhanced by formulation with pine kraft lignin in soil applied granules.

REFERENCES

1   Jermy T, (1971) Acta Phytopathologica Academia Scientiarum Hungaricae 6 (1-4):253-260.

2   Chapman RF, (1974) Bulletin of Entomological Research 64:339-369.

3   Montgomery ME, Arn H (1974) Journal of Insect Physiology 20:413-421.

4   Yoshihara T, Sogawa K, Pathak MD, Juliano BO, Sakawa S. (1980) Entomologica Experimentalis et Applicata 27:149-155.

5   Kumar K, Chapman RB (1984) Pesticide Science 15:344-352.

6   Griffiths DC, Greenway AR, Lloyds L (1978) Bulletin of Entomological Research 68:613-619.

7   Gibson RW, Rice AD, Pickett JA, Smith MC, Sawicki RM, (1982) Annals of Applied Biology 10:55-59.

8   Heinrichs EA (1977) The brown planthopper threat to rice production in
     Asia. Paper presented at the 3rd Asia-Pacific science, brown planthopper
     symposium, Bali, Indonesia, July 22-23.

9   Pathak MD, Saxena RC, Heinrichs EA, (1982) Journal of Economic Entomology
     75:194-195.

10   Paguia P, Pathak MD, Heinrichs EA (1980) Journal of Economic Entomology 73:
     35-40.

11   Wilkins RM, Wechakit D, Okello-Ekochu E (1989) Proceed Intern Symp Control
     Rel Bioact Mater 16:267-268, Controlled Release Society Inc.

12   Schoonhoven LM (1982) Entomologica Experimentalis et Applicata 31:57-69.

13   IRRI Annual Report (1983) p.192.

14   Saxena RC, Liquido NJ, Justo HA (1980) Neem oil, a potential antifeedant for
     the control of the rice brown planthopper Nilaparvata lugens. Proceedings
     of the 1st neem conference, Battach-Egern, pp 171-188.

15   Sogawa K (1981) Applied Entomological Zoology 16 (2):129-137.

16   Jacobson M (1986) Natural resistance of plants to pests: Roles of
     allelochemicals, ACS Washington DC, pp 220-232.

17   Gill JS, Lewis CT (1971) Nature (London) 232:402-403.

18   Sogawa K (1971) Applied Entomological Zoology 6 (4):215-218.

19   Ruscoe, CNE (1977) Pesticide Science 8:236-242.

20   Ho SH (1984) Proceedings of the British Crop Protection Conference, Pests
     and   Diseases, 2:553-558.

21   Penman DR, Chapman RB (1983) Entomologica Experimentalis et Applicata
     33:71-78.

22   Tan K (1984) Pesticide Science 12:619-626.

23   Jackson A, Wilkins RM (1985) Pesticide Science 16:364-368.

24   Liu G, Wilkins RM (1987) International Rice Research Newsletter 12
      (6):24-25.

25   Sherwood MH, Greenway AR, Griffiths DC (1981) Bulletin of Entomological
      Research 71:133-136.

26   Pickett JA, Dawson GW, Griffiths DC, Hassanali A, Merritt LA, Mudd A, Smith
      MC, Wadhams LJ, Woodcock CM, Zhang Zhong-ning (1986) In: Pesticide Science
      and Biotechnology (Greenhalgh R and Roberts T R (Eds)). Proceedings of the
      Sixth International Congress of Pesticide Chemistry, pp 125-128.

27   Ladd JL, Jacobson M, Buriff CR (1978) Journal of Economic Entomology
      71:810-813.

28   Wilkins RM, Batterby S, Heinrichs EA, Aquino GB, Valencia S (1984) Journal
      of Economic Entomology 77:495-499.

Insecticides and acaricides

© 1990 Elsevier Science Publishers B.V. (Biomedical Division)
Pesticides and alternatives, editor J.E. Casida

PYRETHROID INSECTICIDES AND HUMAN WELFARE

MICHAEL ELLIOTT

AFRC Institute of Arable Crops Research, Rothamsted Experimental Station,
Harpenden, Hertfordshire, AL5 2JQ, U.K.

INTRODUCTION

   The human race (about 4 billion people in 1975, predicted to be 6 billion
by the end of this century) shares the earth's resources with many other
organisms, including about 1 million insect species. Of the latter, some 1%
may be regarded as pests, because in various ways, they remove 1/4 to 1/3 of
the food we produce, attack crops, transmit debilitating diseases to man and
cattle, and destroy vast areas of forests. Any measures by which the adverse
consequences of insect action can be diminished must be a valuable contribution
to human welfare.

   Much research has attempted to discover means of controlling insects without
direct application of insecticides; however, so great is the problem that no
alternative measures without serious social or economic consequences have been
found that are universally adequate or even generally applicable.

   Therefore insecticides, now inevitably used frequently and broadly, should
possess the most favourable combination of properties attainable, including
high activity to the pest species (to permit low rates of application and so
not contaminate the environment) complemented by low potency to benevolent or
predator non-target insect species or other organisms such as man or mammals.

BOTANICAL INSECTICIDES

   Botanical insecticides (nicotine, rotenone and pyrethrum, Figure 1) were some
of the first effective materials used to control insects, but all had some
disadvantages. Nicotine was frequently more toxic to mammals than to the
insect pest (as indicated by the relative magnitude of the median lethal doses)
and special precautions when applying it were essential. In practice rotenone
(derris), despite more favourable properties, controlled only a relatively
small spectrum of insect pests adequately and was not readily available.
Pyrethrum was very safe under all normal conditions and controlled a wide range
of insects, with rapid action against flying pests. However, it was much too
unstable in air and light and too expensive to combat pests of agricultural
crops and insects that transmitted diseases such as malaria and sleeping
sickness.

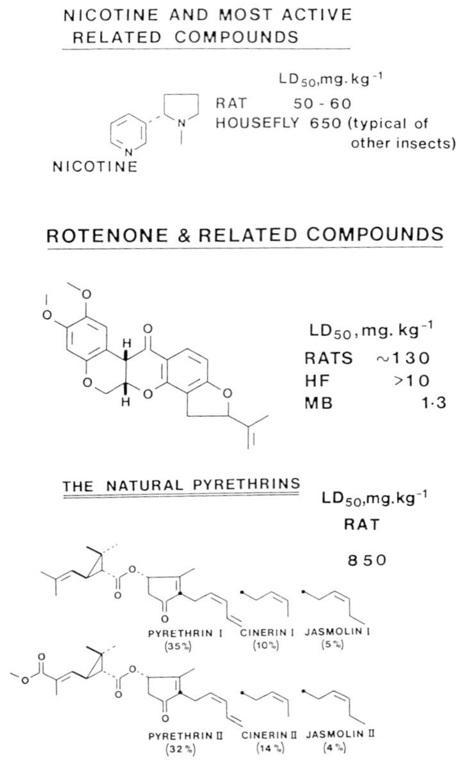

DDT

Müller's discovery (Switzerland, 1939) (1) of the insecticidal properties of DDT remains probably the most significant event in the history of insect-control, which, for the first time, was possible with residual films of a readily available contact insecticide - direct spraying was no longer necessary. The numerous successful applications of DDT such as the spectacular management of the incipient typhus epidemic in Naples in 1944 led to its widespread use throughout the world to a peak consumption of 100,000 tons per year in the late 50's.

OTHER SYNTHETIC INSECTICIDES

The properties of DDT - easy to manufacture on a large scale, effective against many insect pests, and relatively harmless to mammals, stimulated research to find comparable products.

NICOTINE AND MOST ACTIVE RELATED COMPOUNDS

LD_{50}, mg.kg^{-1}

RAT   50 - 60

HOUSEFLY 650 (typical of other insects)

NICOTINE

ROTENONE & RELATED COMPOUNDS

LD_{50}, mg.kg^{-1}

RATS ~130

HF   >10

MB   1·3

THE NATURAL PYRETHRINS

LD_{50}, mg.kg^{-1}

RAT

850

PYRETHRIN I   CINERIN I   JASMOLIN I
(35%)   (10%)   (5%)

PYRETHRIN II   CINERIN II   JASMOLIN II
(32%)   (14%)   (4%)

Fig. 1.

None with the unique combination of qualities possessed by DDT were discovered but other chlorinated insecticides (lindane, aldrin, dieldrin, endosulfan and toxaphene, for example) were introduced as their potential benefits were recognized. Organophosphates (e.g. parathion, fenitrothion, azinphosmethyl, dimethoate) and carbamates (carbaryl, aldicarb) with various advantages (for example, systemic activity) were developed. As the world economy expanded, the need for more food and other agricultural crops, often grown as monocultures on a large scale, led to greater dependence upon synthetic insecticides. By 1974, the annual value of these products was ca. 900m. Apprehension about the persistence of organochlorine compounds (160m) led to greater reliance on the less stable organophosphates (500m) and carbamates (220m); in contrast the pyrethrum, nicotine and rotenone consumed was valued at only about 18m annually.

RESISTANT INSECTS

With continued, unregulated application of insecticides, insects began to develop high levels of resistance in many areas on numerous crops where large quantities of organochlorines, organophosphates and carbamates were used. About 35% of total production was applied to cotton, 20% to the soil, 15% to orchards and vines and 15% to various tropical and sub-tropical crops. In some cotton areas, lepidopterous pests (the bollworm, Heliothis zea, and the tobacco budworm, Heliothis virescens) became so resistant that control was lost or was only possible with such high levels of organophosphates (e.g. parathion) repeatedly applied that the health of the operators was endangered. The situation was desperate in some cotton growing regions of Mexico and Texas by 1977; cotton farms were abandoned and the entire economic and sociological structure of several regional communities was affected.

PHOTOSTABLE PYRETHROIDS

In response to this crisis, emergency registration of two photostable pyrethroids, fenvalerate and permethrin, was granted. Both these new insecticides had been developed in 1973 - fenvalerate by the Sumitomo Chemical Company in Japan and permethrin at Rothamsted Experimental Station in the United Kingdom. There a fundamental study of the relationship between insecticidal activity and chemical structure had been initiated by Charles Potter in 1948 (2).

The new compounds controlled the resistant cotton pests very successfully at field rates below those required by the longer established products and operators were less at risk from the smaller mammalian toxicities of the synthetic pyrethroids (see Table 1, below). The favourable combination of properties demonstrated in these circumstances, and comparable experiences elsewhere, encouraged and stimulated the rapid commercial development of the more photostable synthetic pyrethroids, including compounds such as deltamethrin, at its introduction the most powerful insecticide known (2).

TABLE 1 COMPARISON OF SOME INSECTICIDES

	Effective field rate g/hectare	LD_{50} (rats) mg/kg	Acceptable daily intake (man) mg/kg
Permethrin	100-150*	430-4000*	0.05*
Fenvalerate	25-250	450*	0.02*
Deltamethrin	10-25	140-5000*	0.01*
Parathion	>500	3.6-13*	0.005*
Endosulfan	>500	76-240	0.008*
DDT	>750	120*	0.02 *
Carbaryl	250-2000*	850*	0.01 *

* Source: The Pesticide Manual, ed. C. R. Worthing, 1987

ORIGIN OF SYNTHETIC PYRETHROIDS

The natural pyrethrins, extracted from the flowers of <u>Tanacetum</u> <u>cinerariae-</u>
<u>folium</u>, grown in Kenya and recently in Tasmania, are in some respects, ideal
insecticides. They act rapidly against many insect pest species, but are
harmless to mammals under all normal conditions. They are unstable in air and
light and therefore do not persist in the environment, but are consequently not
suitable for controlling pests of agricultural crops.

Many aspects of the structures of the natural pyrethrins (Figure 1) had been
established in the period 1910-1916 by the Swiss chemists Staudinger and
Ruzicka, who published their work in 1924. One of their stated objectives was
to find simple and effective synthetic insecticides. Although they could not
make the structure they assigned to the alcoholic component (Figure 2), with
remarkable insight they conceived that an ester of the natural acid with an
allyl substituted cyclopentanolone might be effective. That the cuminyl and
piperonyl but not the unsubstituted, benzyl chrysanthemates were active was a
very significant indicator for future developments.

La Forge, Schechter and co-workers in the U.S.D.A. developed the Swiss work by
revising the structure of the alcoholic components and, in a most important
advance, synthesized cyclopentenolones, in particular, one with the simpler
allyl side chain. This gave the important synthetic

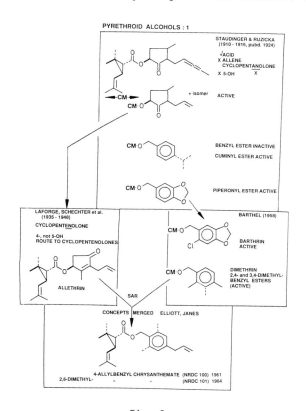

Fig. 2.

pyrethroid allethrin, still widely used today especially in mosquito coils and
mats. Some years later, Barthel from the same laboratory, examined further
benzyl esters and found enhanced activity in 6-chloropiperonyl chrysanthemates
and especially in 2,4- and 3,4-dimethyl benzyl esters.

BIORESMETHRIN

At Rothamsted, consideration of these results and conclusions from earlier synthetic work led to our discovery that 4-allylbenzyl chrysanthemate had enhanced activity and, later that the related 2,6-dimethyl ester was effective against a broader spectrum of pests.

Also at Rothamsted Charles Potter organised a comparison of the natural pyrethrins with allethrin isomers (kindly donated by La Forge) against a number of insect species. A wide range of relative potencies (Figure 3 shows typical results) was detected. Except against houseflies, compounds with the natural 2-pentadienyl side chain appeared more effective than those with the simpler allyl group. In the absence at the time of synthetic routes giving ready access to compounds with a Z-pentadiene we examined compounds with phenyl groups, hoping that for biological activity these might simulate the function of the diene.

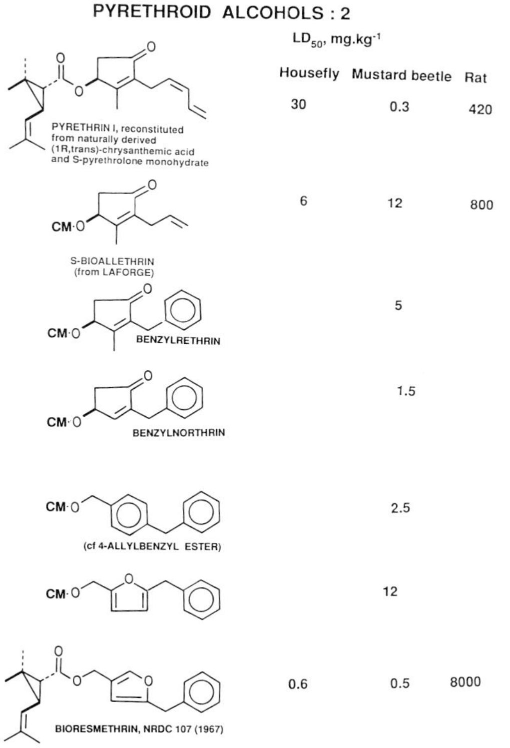

Benzylrethrin was indeed somewhat more active than the corresponding allyl compound. The even greater potency of benzylnorthrin indicated that modification of the alcohol nucleus might also be an advantage. Then synthesis and testing of many related compounds including 4-benzyl benzyl chrysanthemate led, <u>via</u> the benzylfurfuryl ester, to the much more active 5-benzyl-3-furylmethyl chrysanthemate,

PYRETHROID ALCOHOLS : 2

LD_{50}, mg.kg^{-1}

	Housefly	Mustard beetle	Rat
PYRETHRIN I, reconstituted from naturally derived (1R,trans)-chrysanthemic acid and S-pyrethrolone monohydrate	30	0.3	420
S-BIOALLETHRIN (from LAFORGE)	6	12	800
BENZYLRETHRIN		5	
BENZYLNORTHRIN		1.5	
(cf 4-ALLYLBENZYL ESTER)		2.5	
		12	
BIORESMETHRIN, NRDC 107 (1967)	0.6	0.5	8000

Fig. 3.

bioresmethrin, the first synthetic pyrethroid with activity comparable to that of pyrethrin I to a range of insect species and the valuable property, not anticipated at the time of development, of considerably diminished mammalian toxicity (see third column in Figure 3).

350

PHOTODECOMPOSITION OF RESMETHRIN

CASIDA et al.

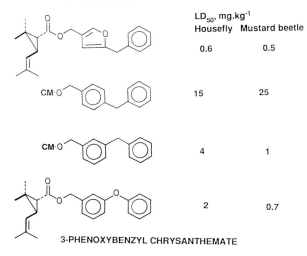

Fig. 4.

Bioresmethrin and the related (±)-cis, trans chrysanthemate, resmethrin were synthesized commercially but were not sufficiently stable in air and light signifi- cantly to extend the range of application for pyrethroids. The photo- labile centres were estab- lished to be the trans methyl group in the

iso-butenyl side chain and the furan nucleus (3) (Figure 4) by Professor John E. Casida in the University of California at Berkeley.

PHOTOSTABLE PYRETHROIDS:PERMETHRIN

Somewhat later (Figure 5) a survey of compounds synthesized en route to bioresmethrin suggested that 3-benzyl benzyl; as well as the 4-benzyl benzyl chrysanthemate made earlier, should be examined. The 3-isomer was more active, so the related 3-phenoxy compound was prepared to assess the function, for activity, of the methylene grup between the aromatic rings. The 3-phenoxy compound was potent, so by this sequence we reached the significant 3-phenoxy-

PYRETHROID ALCOHOLS : 3 (1969)

	LD$_{50}$, mg.kg^{-1} Housefly	Mustard beetle
	0.6	0.5
CM·O	15	25
CM·O	4	1
	2	0.7

3-PHENOXYBENZYL CHRYSANTHEMATE

Fig. 5.

benzyl esters at about the same time as, but quite independently of, the Sumitomo group.

The furan alcohol was found to be more effec- tive for examining the influence on insecticidal activity of changes in the acid components of esters (Figure 6) than allethrolone, which had been used in many earlier studies. With it the potency of cis (e.g. cismethrin) as well as of trans-chrysanthemates was confirmed. The enhanced activity of the ethanochrysanthemate reported for RU 11,679 stimulated us to examine alternative side chains including Z-butadienyl and, en route to ethynyl, monochlorovinyl. The activity of the latter led to the more active dichlorovinyl compound shown, derived from an analogue of chrysanthemic acid in which the side chain methyl groups had been replaced by isosteric chlorine atoms.

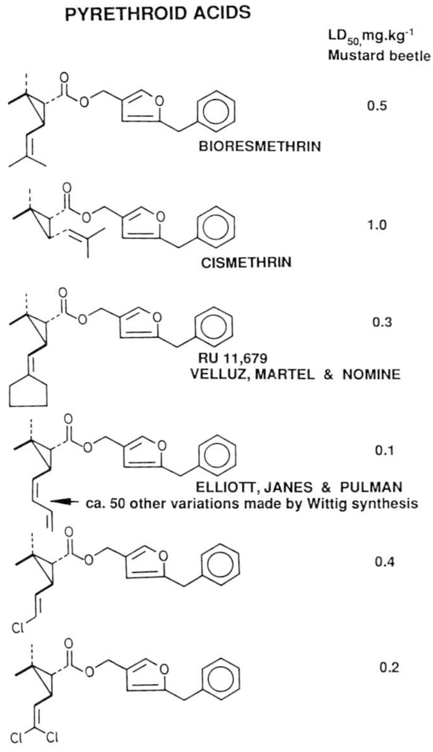

When Casida's work on the photo-lability of resmethrin was reviewed in relation to these results, it appeared that in an ester of the above analogue of chrysanthemic acid with 3-phenoxybenzyl alcohol, the sensitive centres in bioresmethrin would have been replaced by groups each potentially more stable in air and light. This combination (Figure 7, permethrin, R=H) which provided under experimental conditions more than twenty times longer persistence than bioresmethrin was also more active than would have been predicted from established relationshps. Several lines of investigation were pursued to exploit this finding of a more photostable ester which yet retained valuable qualities of the natural pyrethrins.

PYRETHROID ACIDS

LD_{50} mg.kg^{-1}
Mustard beetle

BIORESMETHRIN — 0.5

CISMETHRIN — 1.0

RU 11,679
VELLUZ, MARTEL & NOMINE — 0.3

ELLIOTT, JANES & PULMAN — 0.1
ca. 50 other variations made by Wittig synthesis

0.4

0.2

Fig. 6.

DELTAMETHRIN

One approach was based on an investigation of the influence of α-substituents on the activity of benzyl and related chrysanthemates. Chen and Barthel (Figure 7) detected no important improvement derived from α-substitution of piperonyl chrysanthemate; methyl or ethynyl did not increase the activity of 5-benzyl-3-furylmethyl chrysanthemates. However, the Sumitomo chemists made the important discovery that ethynyl or cyano, respectively, did not diminish or actually increased the activity of benzyl benzyl or 3-phenoxybenzyl chrysan-themates and related esters. We found that making a comparable substitution in permethrin (to give cypermethrin, Figure 7) more than doubled insecticidal activity, which was already significantly greater than that of most known compounds.

ORIGIN OF α-CYANOBENZYL ESTERS

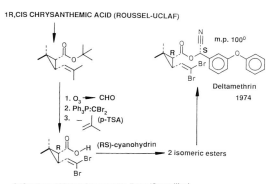

	Chen & Barthel,1956
R = Alkyl	
Alkenyl	
Cyclohexyl	
Aryl	

R = Me   Elliott & Janes, 1965
R = ·≡   BASF, 1968

BASF, 1968

R = ·≡ or ·≡N
X = CH₂ or O   Sumitomo, 1973

Other cyclopropanecarboxylates

LD$_{50}$, mg.kg^{-1}
Mustard beetle

R = H   0.25   PERMETHRIN

R = CN   0.09   CYPERMETHRIN

Fig. 7.

A new chiral centre having been introduced at the α-position in cypermethrin and related compounds, it became both interesting and important to determine the relative potency of the two optical isomers. After failing to resolve the parent alcohol itself, we decided to esterify the racemic alcohol with a resolved pyrethroid acid, hoping then to be able to separate the isomeric esters produced. Based on experience that pyrethroid esters of cis-cyclopropane acids sometimes crystallized more readily than trans forms and the relatively high melting points of bromo-compounds, we chose to make the IR, cis-dibromo vinyl acid and derived esters (Figure 8). Starting from [IR,cis]-chrysanthemic acid generously given to us by Dr. Martel of Roussel-Uclaf, we prepared the resolved dibromo acid by the route shown. After some time and manipulation, one of the isomers crystallized and had a m.p., after recrystallization, of 100°. This isomer, subsequently called

OPTICAL RESOLUTION OF CYANOHYDRIN ESTERS
SYNTHESIS OF DELTAMETHRIN (NRDC 161)

1R,CIS CHRYSANTHEMIC ACID (ROUSSEL-UCLAF)

m.p. 100°

Deltamethrin
1974

1. O₃ ➝ CHO
2. Ph₃P:CBr₂
3. ─ (p-TSA)

(RS)-cyanohydrin ───➤ 2 isomeric esters

S (Confirmed X-Ray) Cyanohydrin Ester (Crystalline)
R Cyanohydrin Ester (Liquid) from aldehyde + HCN with D-Oxynitrilase

	Relative Potency*	Life in Soil** (months)
DELTAMETHRIN	400	1
DDT	1	48

* Mean for 10   **Depending
insect species   on conditions

Fig. 8.

deltamethrin (Decis commercially) was, when discovered, the most potent known insecticidal compound, natural or synthetic. Thanks to their established proficiency in synthesis of chiral compounds and various pyrethroids, the chemists of Roussel-Uclaf rapidly developed the manufacture of deltamethrin under license from The National Research Development Corporation (now British Technology Group). Deltamethrin quickly assumed a unique place in the armoury of available insecticides; Figure 9 shows the active isomers in related commercial compounds subsequently developed in various research centres.

ACTIVE ISOMERS IN SOME PHOTOSTABLE PYRETHROIDS

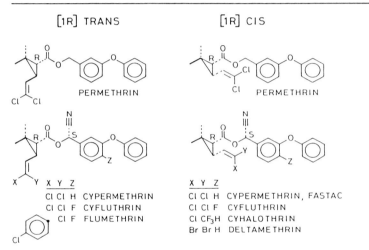

Fig. 9.

FENVALERATE

The other important range of photostable synthetic pyrethroids includes fenvalerate discovered by chemists at the Sumitomo Chemical Company; it, with permethrin, was first given emergency registration for use on cotton. In screening a range of esters of the furan alcohol, or related 3-phenoxybenzyl alcohol, the Sumitomo chemists detected activity in derivatives of α-ethyl phenyl acetic acid (Figure 10). Optimization of this lead gave fenvalerate, the α-cyano-3-phenoxybenzyl ester of α-isopropyl-4-chlorophenyl acetic acid, now available in the resolved S, S-form, asana.

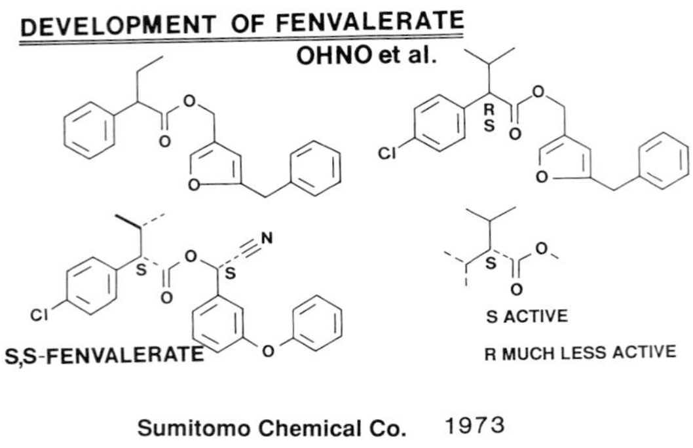

354

DEVELOPMENT OF FENVALERATE
OHNO et al.

S,S-FENVALERATE

S ACTIVE
R MUCH LESS ACTIVE

Sumitomo Chemical Co.   1973

Fig. 10.

SELECTIVE POTENCY OF PYRETHROIDS

A desirable property of insecticides is great potency towards insects combined with small toxicity to mammals, a characteristic possessed by natural
and synthetic pyrethroids. This is associated with their ability to penetrate
rapidly and interact with their site of action in insects; deltamethrin, for
example, affects the sodium channels in nerve membranes at concentrations down
to 10^{-12}M. In contrast, following external or oral administration to mammals, pyrethroids are largely converted by hydrolytic or oxidative attack to
polar metabolites which are eliminated in the faeces or urine unchanged, or as
conjugates, before sensitive sites are reached (Figure 11).

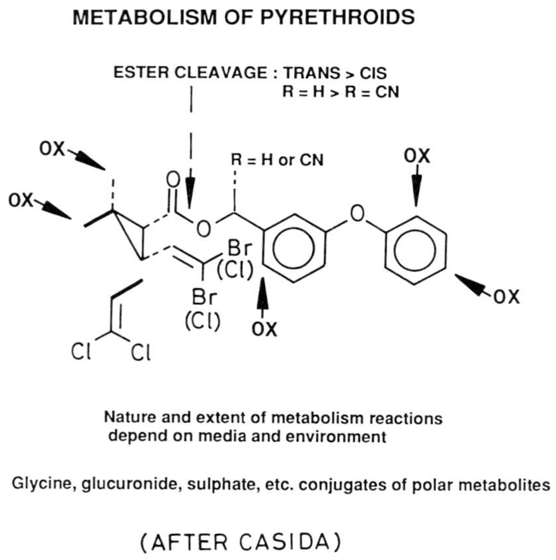

METABOLISM OF PYRETHROIDS

ESTER CLEAVAGE : TRANS > CIS
R = H > R = CN

R = H or CN

Nature and extent of metabolism reactions
depend on media and environment

Glycine, glucuronide, sulphate, etc. conjugates of polar metabolites

(AFTER CASIDA)

Fig. 11.

355

Comparable mechanisms ensure that synthetic pyrethroids do not survive unchanged in the environment, where polar metabolites are produced by appropriate biotic systems; this behaviour differs from that of DDT and other chlorinated insecticides, from which, persistent, apolar metabolites are produced.

PRESENT STATUS OF PYRETHROID INSECTICIDES

Synthetic pyrethroids developed from permethrin (Figure 9) or fenvalerate (Figure 10) are estimated to have been used to treat more than 70 m. ha of agricultural crops in 1987. In financial terms (Figure 12) their contribution to human welfare by controlling insects infesting crops and cattle and transmitting diseases rose during little more than a decade at least 40 fold to above $1300 million per year, with more than $800 million directly derived from the research project initiated by Charles Potter at Rothamsted in 1948 and the chemical studies by Stanley H. Harper at University College, Southampton from 1942.

Applications of pyrethroids (1987)

	%
Cotton	46
Fruit and vegetables	22
Other crops	17
Animal	9
Non-agricultural	6

Value: $ 1345m.

BTG-licensed compounds : $ 820m.

Source: County NatWest Wood Mac

Fig. 12.

REFERENCES

1. For a recent account, see K. Mellanby in Progress and Prospects in Insect Control, BCPC Monograph No. 43, ed. NIR. McFarlane, 1989, p 1

2. For many leading references, see The Pyrethroid Insecticides, Edited by John P. Leahey, Taylor and Francis, London and Philadelphia, 1985; Elliott, M., Janes, N.F., and Potter, C. (1978) Annual Review of Entomology, 23, 443; Elliott, M., and Janes, N.F. (1979) Chemical Society Reviews, 7, 473

3. Ueda, K., Gaughan, L.C., and Casida, J.E. (1974) J. Agr. Food Chem., 22, 212

Pesticides and alternatives, editor J.E. Casida

357

LONG-ACTING PYRETHRIN FORMULATIONS

G. G. ALLAN[1] AND T. A. MILLER[2]
University of Washington, AR-10, Seattle, Washington, U.S.A.

The durability of the insecticidal action of natural and synthetic pyrethrins is rapidly diminished by the action of sunlight and oxygen. These degradation pathways can be closed off by a liquid alkyl aryl silicone-based formulation containing an antioxidant and an ultraviolet light stabilizer. The enhanced period of insecticidal effectiveness of this new type of formulation has been demonstrated by the use of dog fleas and ticks.

INTRODUCTION

Every pesticide applied in real life situations is subject to various degradative influences from the moment of application (1). These usually comprise oxidation, leaching, volatilization, hydrolysis, microbial breakdown, and ultraviolet irradiation by sunlight. The contribution that each of these may make to the destruction of the pesticide is fundamentally determined by the features of the chemical structure of the pesticide. When these destructive factors are recognized, controlled release delivery systems can be developed (2) which function by reducing the extent of degradation for a given time period while simultaneously permitting an adequate amount of pesticide to reach the target organism. The design of a particular controlled released system will, of course, be determined by the chemical characteristics of the pesticide to be delivered. In this paper, the development of such a system for natural and synthetic pyrethrins (3) is reported within the context of the control of ectoparasites on dogs.

1. To whom enquiries should be addressed.
2. Present address; Zoecon Corp., Dallas, Texas.

DISCUSSION

   Biologically active agents for the control of ticks and fleas on pet dogs
are the basis of an important industry. Initially, organophosphates, and
subsequently carbamates, were used for this purpose (4). More recently,
there has been a growing unease over the use of these highly toxic
substances on pets in home situations. This concern is leading to their
substitution by the safer pyrethrins which are not terato-, carcino- or
muta-genic.

   Unfortunately, a major disadvantage of these substances is their poor
stability in the environment, which is often only a few hours. As early as
the 1930's there has been interest in extending the period of effectiveness
of natural pyrethrins. The first efforts included the addition of
antioxidants and ultraviolet absorbers but these were not notably
successful (5). More recently, Miskus and Andrews (6) studied the
decomposition rates of two natural pyrethrins, pyrethrin I and cinerin I,
during exposure to sunlight in the presence of UV screening agents. Test
formulations were prepared and these included a variety of organic
solvents. The best stability was obtained with mineral oil containing an
antioxidant. However, the destruction of both of the natural pyrethrins
was very substantial after exposure to sunlight for only 4 hours. A
similar low degree of stability was observed for the synthetic pyrethrin,
allethrin, under the same test conditions. This durability of
effectiveness is clearly inadequate for a formulation intended to control
fleas and ticks on a dog.

   To develop such a formulation it is necessary to enhance the stability of
pyrethrins. This requires that the molecules be kept apart so that
reaction between pyrethrins is diminished. In principle, this can be
accomplished by dissolution of the pyrethrins in a suitable polymer to
afford a solid solution (7). Because of the cosmetic restrictions implied
by a system suitable for application to the hair of a dog, one class of
initial candidates evaluated was the polydimethylsiloxanes. However, the
solubility of the pyrethrins in all of the dimethylsiloxanes tested (from
very low to very high molecular weight) was very poor.

   In an attempt to overcome this solubility deficiency the dialkylsiloxanes
were substituted by a low molecular weight alkyl aryl siloxane. This
polymer transpired to be a good solvent for the pyrethrins and also for the
other additives needed to offset the degradative effects of oxygen and
ultraviolet radiation. As a result the period of effectiveness of the

pyrethrin was increased from about 4 hours to 21 days. Furthermore, the
alkyl aryl siloxane, due to its characteristic low viscosity, combined the
desired cosmetic effect with ease of application. In addition, the
hydrophobicity of the polymer enabled the coating on the dog's hair to
withstand removal by rain and other sources of water.

EXPERIMENTAL

Materials

The insecticides used were commercial products generously gifted by the
MGK Co. Minneapolis, MN. They comprised the 20% w/w natural pyrethrum
extract in kerosene (Pyrocide 175), as well as the synthetic deltamethrin,
phenothrin, d-trans-allethrin, permethrin, tetramethrin, cypermethrin,
resmethrin, and dimethrin. The synergists used with the foregoing were
piperonyl butoxide and n-octylbicycloheptenedicarboximide (MGK 264) and
these were also donated by the MGK Co.

The antioxidant employed was commercial grade butylated hydroxytoluene
(BHT) which was likewise provided by the MGK Co.

The ultraviolet protectants added to the formulations were also donated
commercial products, 2-ethylhexyl-p-dimethylaminobenzoate (Escalol 507, Van
Dyk & Co., Inc., Belleville, N.J.) and 2-ethylhexyl-2-cyano-3,3-diphenyl
acrylate (Uvinul 539, BASF Corp., Parsippany, N.J.).

The repellents used were likewise commercial products, di-n-propyl
isocinchomeronate (MGK R326) and 2,3,4,5-bis-(2-butylene)-tetrahydro-2-
furaldehyde (MGK R11) again gifted by the MGK Co.

The alkyl aryl siloxane matrices were all products of the Dow Corning
Corp., Midland, MI, and carried the number designations DC-550, DC-704 and
DC-710.

Methods

In a typical preparation, the insecticide (pyrethrum, 100 mg), synergists
(piperonyl butoxide, 370 mg; MGK 264, 610 mg), repellents (MGK R11, 200 mg;
MGK R326, 200 mg), UV protectants (Escalol 507, 250 mg; Uvinul 539, 250 mg)
and the siloxane (Dow Corning DC-704, 510 mg) are admixed sequentially with
a stirred solution of BHT (200 mg) in isopropanol (96.51 g). The mixture
also contains petroleum distillates (400 mg) from the pyrethrum concentrate
(Pyrocide 175) as well as a fragrance (400 mg).

In the animal test procedure, 10 dogs, randomly divided into 2 groups of
5, were exposed to infestation by fleas and ticks by placing on their coats
newly emerged, unfed dog fleas (Ctencephalides) and ticks (Rhipicephalus).

One group of dogs was then treated with the above formulation (6.2 mL/kg of body weight) while the other was left untreated to serve as a control group. Each of the treated dogs was lightly misted over its complete body surface, with a gloved hand being drawn across the coat of the animal in a direction opposite to the lay of the hair. Thereafter, the hair coats of both groups were examined at various time intervals, without removing or harming the insects, to determine the number of fleas and ticks surviving. Both groups of dogs were repeatedly reinfestated with new fleas and ticks and following each infestation the dogs were examined to measure the establishment and survival of these new parasites.

RESULTS

The data in Table I shows the extended efficacy secured by the alkyl aryl siloxane formulation.

Table I

THE DURATION OF EFFECTIVENESS OF PYRETHRUM IN AN ALKYL ARYL SILOXANE MATRIX FOR THE SUPPRESSION OF REPEATED TICK AND FLEA INFESTATIONS.

		Average Number of Fleas and Ticks Surviving			
Time (Days)	Infest/ Treat	Ticks		Fleas	
		Treated	Control	Treated	Control
-1	Infest				
0		17.2	14.2	30.8	21.6
	Treat				
3 h		9.0	14.2	0	19.8
5 h		3.0	13.2	0	19.6
1		2.0	12.0	0	16.8
2		0.2	11.2	0	15.2
5		0.8	11.0	0	12.6
	Reinfest				
6		2.2	20.4	0	36.0
8		1.2	19.8	0	35.0
	Reinfest				
9		2.8	21.0	0	33.4
12		1.6	20.8	0	34.4
	Reinfest				
13		4.4	22.4	0.2	42.2
16		3.2	16.6	0.2	32.6
	Reinfest				
17		6.8	28.8	2.0	49.0
21		4.2	24.4	0	43.8
	Reinfest				
22		8.4	29.4	4.6	48.2

In another test, conducted for comparative purposes, a standard commercially available flea spray containing insecticide, synergist and repellent at higher levels but without the antioxidants, the UV light protectants or the alkyl aryl siloxane was used to treat a group of dogs infested with fleas and ticks of the same species previously used.

The data in Table II show that although the commercial formulation produced an immediate kill of the parasites, the killing action was very short-lived and the dogs rapidly became reinfested with fleas and ticks.

Table II.

THE DURATION OF EFFECTIVENESS OF A COMMERCIAL PYRETHRUM SPRAY PRODUCT FOR THE SUPPRESSION OF REPEATED TICK AND FLEA INFESTATIONS

		Average Number of Fleas and Ticks Surviving			
Time (days)	Infest/ Treat	Ticks		Fleas	
		Treated	Control	Treated	Control
-1	Infest	27	37	114	95
0	Treat				
1		0	38	6	125
2		0	42	7	108
5	Reinfest				
6		5	64	39	114
8	Reinfest				
9		91	63	150	150

The alkyl aryl siloxane employed in the foregoing experiments (Dow Corning DC-704) was the discrete chemical compound, tetramethyltetra-phenyltrisiloxane, MW 484, which has a viscosity of 39 centistokes at 25 C.

To determine if there were significant differences between the performance of various alkyl aryl siloxanes in pyrethrin formulations a comparison of three commercially available silicone products was undertaken. These were Dow Corning DC-550, DC-704 and DC-710. Dow Corning DC-550 is a dimethyldiphenylsiloxane of MW 750 which has a viscosity of 125 centistokes at 25 C. Dow Corning DC-710 is a methylphenylsiloxane of MW 2600 with 56% methyl groups, 44% phenyl groups, and a viscosity of 500 centistokes at 25 C.

Formulations, differing only in the siloxane used, were prepared as specified above. Each formulation was applied to a test group of four dogs at an average dose rate of 6.2 mL/kg of body weight as before. Another group of four dogs served as a control. The performance of these three formulations is summarized in Tables III and IV. These data do not show great differences in efficacy though the highest molecular weight and most viscous siloxane does seem to be slightly superior to its lower molecular weight congeners.

Similar formulations based on alkyl aryl siloxanes were prepared with the various synthetic pyrethroids previously listed (5).

Table III

COMPARISON OF THE CAPABILITIES OF THREE SILOXANES TO EXTEND THE DURATION OF EFFECTIVENESS OF PYRETHRUM FOR THE CONTROL OF FLEAS ON DOGS

Time after treatment	Group Flea Counts (F) and Treatment Efficacies (E_f)*						
	Control	DC-550 Spray		DC-704 Spray		DC-710 Spray	
	F	F	E_f	F	E_f	F	E_f
Pre-treatment	59	81	--	70	--	55	--
3 h	55	0	100	0	100	0	100
5 h	52	0	100	0	100	0	100
1 day	47	0	100	0	100	0	100
2	50	0	100	0	100	0	100
5	38	0	100	0	100	0	100
Reinfest							
6	63	0	100	0	100	0	100
8	63	0	100	0	100	0	100
Reinfest							
9	75	0	100	4	94.7	3	96
12	66	0	100	3	95.5	1	98.5
Reinfest							
13	94	29	69.2	17	81.9	16	83
16	90	14	84.4	19	78.9	5	94.4
Reinfest							
17	118	30	74.6	43	63.6	22	81.4
21	114	16	86	39	65.8	13	88.6

*The efficacy in the treated groups for the first 5 days post-treatment was measured by comparing flea burdens before and after treatment. After reinfestation on the 5th day, efficacies were measured by comparison of the flea burdens of treated and control dogs.

TABLE IV

COMPARISON OF THE CAPABILITIES OF THREE SILOXANES TO EXTEND THE DURATION OF
EFFECTIVENESS OF PYRETHRUM FOR THE CONTROL OF TICKS ON DOGS

	Group Tick Counts (F) and Treatment Efficacies (E_t)*						
Time after treatment	Control	DC-550 Spray		DC-704 Spray		DC-710 Spray	
	F	F	E_t	F	E_t	F	E_t
Pre-treatment	80	70	- -	103	- -	65	- -
3 h	77	12	82.9	17	83.5	16	75.4
5 h	75	8	88.6	6	94.2	6	91
1 d	79	0	100	2	98.1	1	98.5
2	81	0	100	1	99	1	98.5
5	34	0	100	0	99	0	100
Reinfest							
6	108	1	99.1	3	97.2	4	96.3
8	95	0	100	0	100	0	100
Reinfest							
9	115	3	97.4	9	92.2	3	97.4
12	92	0	100	5	94.6	1	98.9
Reinfest							
13	121	12	90.1	18	85.1	12	90.1
16	122	2	98.4	18	85.2	6	95.1
Reinfest							
17	123	22	82.1	37	69.9	10	91.9
21	107	19	82.2	32	70.1	9	91.6

*The efficacy in the treated groups for the first 5 days post-treatment was
measured by comparing tick burdens before and after treatment. After
reinfestation on the 5th day, efficacies were measured by comparison of the
tick burdens of treated and control dogs.

CONCLUSION

A new environmentally acceptable dimension in pesticide science and
technology has been established by this demonstration that the effective
life of pyrethrins can be significantly extended by dissolution in a
biodegradable alkyl aryl siloxane containing a dissolved antioxidant as
well as protectants against ultraviolet radiation.

REFERENCES

1. Allan GG, Chopra CS, Friedhoff JF, Gara RI, Maggi MW, Neogi AN,
    Roberts SC, Wilkins RM, (1973) Chemtech 4:171

2. Heller J, Harris F, Lohmann D, Merkyl H, Robinson J (1988) Eds.,
    Proc. 15th International Symposium on Controlled Release of Bioactive
    Materials, Basel, Switzerland 1988. The Controlled Release Society
    Inc. Lincolnshire, Illinois

3. Casida JE (1973) Pyrethrum, The Natural Insecticide.
    Academic Press, New York

4. Greenberg J (1980) In: Abstracts of the 7th International Symposium on
    Controlled Release of Bioactive Materials, Ft. Lauderdale, Florida.
    The Controlled Release Society Inc. Lincolnshire, Illinois

5. Allan GG, Miller TA (1987) U.S. Patent 4,668,666
    and references therein cited

6. Miskus RP, Andrews TL (1972) J Ag Food Chem 20(2):313

7. Allan GG, Neogi AN (1972) Int Pest Control 14:21

© 1990 Elsevier Science Publishers B.V. (Biomedical Division)
Pesticides and alternatives, editor J.E. Casida

BENZOYLPHENYL UREAS AND OTHER SELECTIVE INSECT CONTROL AGENTS - MECHANISM AND
APPLICATION

I. ISHAAYA
Department of Entomology, Agricultural Research Organization, The Volcani
Center, Bet Dagan 50250, Israel

I. INTRODUCTION

   Benzoylphenyl ureas act on insects of various orders by inhibiting chitin
formation (40,45,87,100), thereby causing abnormal endocuticular deposition and
abortive molting (72). Studies of the mode of action of diflubenzuron
[1-(4-chlorophenyl)-3- (2,6-diflubenzoyl)urea] (DFB) revealed that the compound
alters cuticle composition - especially that of chitin (45,87) - thereby
affecting the elasticity and firmness of the endocuticle (34,36). The reduced
level of chitin in the cuticle seems to result from inhibition of biochemical
processes leading to chitin formation (40,87,106). It is not clear whether
inhibition of chitin synthetase is the primary pathway for the reduced level of
chitin, since in some studies benzoylphenyl ureas do not inhibit chitin
synthetase activity in cell-free systems (20,23,66). An interesting suggestion
related to the biochemical mode of action of benzoylphenyl ureas was put forward
by Mitsui et al. (70,71), who showed that DFB inhibited the transport of
UDP-N-acetylglucosamine across the midgut epithelium in the cabbage armyworm.
These authors proposed that the catalytic site of chitin synthetase is located
on the outer surface of the membrane, and as such the substrate must cross the
plasma membrane in order to interact with the enzyme. Mauchamp and Perrineau
(65) indicated that protein and chitin microfibrils are not associated after
treatment with benzoylphenyl ureas. Consistent reports indicate the possibility
that benzoylphenyl ureas might affect the hormonal balance in insects, thereby
resulting in physiological disturbances such as the inhibition of DNA synthesis
(25,69,99), alteration in carbohydrases and phenoloxidase activity (43,45), and
suppression of microsomal oxidase activity (115,116). Excellent reviews have
been published recently reporting available data relating to biochemical and
biological modes of action of benzoylphenyl ureas (21,22,37,90).

   DFB, the most thoroughly investigated compound of this type, affects the
larval stage (35). It acts mainly by ingestion, but in some species it
suppresses fecundity (5,91) and exhibits ovicidal and contact toxicity
(9,10,42,110). The search for potent acylureas has led to the development of new
compounds such as chlorfluazuron (IKI-7899, CGA 112,913, PP 145) (39),
teflubenzuron (CME-134) (15), and hexafluron (XRD-473) (92) (Fig. 1), which are
considerably more potent than DFB on various agricultural pests (11,12,49-51).

Benzoylphenyl ureas affect the larval stages which are actively synthesizing chitin. Hence, the adults of non target species, e.g. parasites and predators, are seldom affected. Parasites of the housefly Musca domestica and the gypsy moth Lymantria dispar are not affected by DFB (1,97,98). In some cases parasite larvae inside treated hosts are sensitive to DFB but the adults are not affected (16,33). Predatory mites and adult predators are not appreciably affected when fed on treated larvae (2,16,56). However, of serious concern regarding benzoylphenyl ureas in the environment is their effect on crustacean species. Cladocerans are very sensitive, copepods are susceptible to some extent, while ostracods are unaffected at the levels of DFB used for controlling pests (4,73,102). Further assays are needed to evaluate potency of the new compounds on non-target organisms and to neutralize their effect on crustacean species.

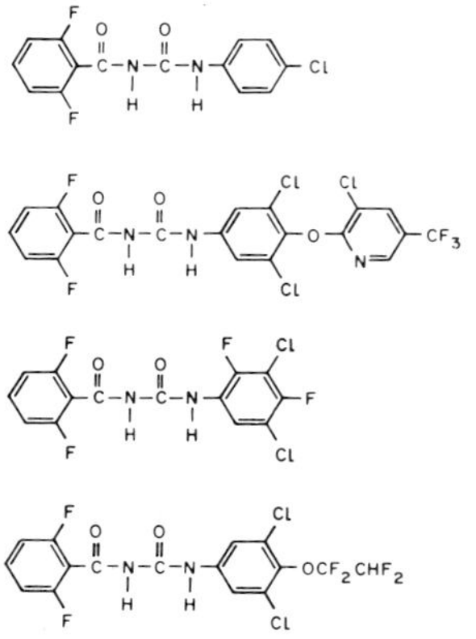

Fig. 1. Structure of four benzoylphenyl urea compounds. From top,
diflubenzuron, chlorfluazuron,
teflubenzuron, hexafluron.

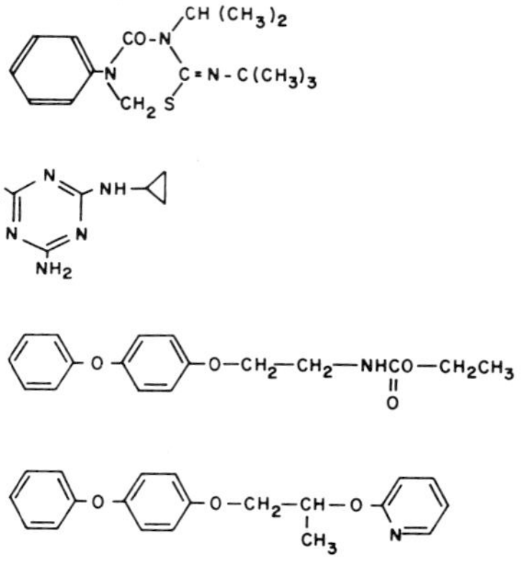

Fig. 2. IGRs other than
benzoylphenyl ureas. From top,
buprofezin, cyromazine, fenoxycarb,
pyriproxyfen.

Parallel to the development of benzoylphenyl ureas, a novel chitin synthesis inhibitor, buprofezin (Applaud, 2-tert-butylimino-3-isopropyl-5-phenylperhydro--1,3,5-thiadiazine-4-one; Fig. 2) has developed (6,57). It acts specifically on homopteran pests such as the greenhouse whitefly Trialeurodes vaporariorum, the sweetpotato whitefly Bemisia tabaci (44,48,112,113), the brown planthopper Nilaparvata lugens (7,55,74), and the citrus scales Aonidiella aurantii and Saissetia oleae (44,111). Whiteflies are important pests of cotton and vegetables. In some cases they transmit viruses and are considered limiting factors for growing agricultural crops. The brown planthopper is an important pest of rice in the Far East. Most of these pests have developed resistance to conventional insecticides and buprofezin is an important addition enabling continuing production of various agricultural commodities. Buprofezin is harmless to aphelinid parasites such as Encarsia formosa and Cales noaki

(29,62,108), and to predacious mites (3), and as such it is considered a
selective insecticide.

Other insect growth regulators (IGRs) of agricultural importance are the
triazine compound cyromazine and the juvenoid analogs fenoxycarb and
pyriproxyfen (Fig. 2). Cyromazine, extremely effective against dipteran species,
acts at the apolytic stage, affecting thereby the ecdysis process, but has no
effect on chitin synthesis (27,93). Fenoxycarb and pyriproxyfen act as juvenile
hormones, affecting specifically scale insects and egg fertility (8,63,81-83).

This report concentrates on biochemical and biological aspects, not covered by
previous reviews, relating to detoxification, synergism, mode of resistance and
potency of benzoylphenyl ureas along with available biological and biochemical
information of buprofezin and other recent IGRs of agricultural importance.

II. BENZOYLPHENYL UREAS

Biochemical Processes Affecting Stability and Potency

The search for potent acylureas led to the development of chlorfluazuron
(IKI-7899), teflubenzuron (CME-134), and hexafluron (XRD-473), which are
considerably more potent than DFB against various agricultural pests
(11,15,39,49-51,92). The high toxicity of some acylureas results from their high
retention in the insect as a result of rapid transport from the gut into the
larval tissues and/or of lower detoxification (32,38,75,76). In assays carried
out with Tribolium castaneum (51), hexafluron, teflubenzuron and chlorfluazuron
were 4- to 23-fold more toxic than DFB and exhibited similar toxicity on both
malathion-susceptible (bb) and -resistant (CTC-12) strains. On the other hand,
DFB was considerably less toxic to the resistant strain (Table I), which seems
to be due to DFB's susceptibility to the relatively high oxidative and
hydrolytic activities present in this strain (109). Accordingly, the potency of
the new acylureas relative to DFB increased considerably in the CTC-12 strain,
reaching ratios of 14- to 23-fold at LC-95 (Table I). These results agree with
those given in other reports (17,78,88) on a possible cross resistance between
organophosphorus compounds and DFB. On the other hand, chlorfluazuron,
teflubenzuron and hexafluron which are relatively stable to detoxifying enzymes,
show in the Tribolium assay, similar potency on malathion-susceptible and
-resistant strain (Table I). The relative toxicity of the test compounds on both
Tribolium strains was hexafluron > teflubenzuron ⩾ chlorfluazuron > DFB.

Assays using radiolabeled DFB and chlorfluazuron applied to fourth-instar
Tribolium larvae (30), revealed a rapid elimination of DFB (T1/2 ∼7 h) as
compared with chlorfluazuron (T1/2 > 100 h) (Fig. 3). This was followed by a
respective increase in labeled residues of DFB, as compared with chlorfluazuron,

TABLE I.

LC-50 and LC-95 VALUES OF FOUR CHITIN SYNTHESIS INHIBITORS OBTAINED WITH
MALATHION-SUSCEPTIBLE (bb) AND -RESISTANT (CTC-12) STRAINS OF TRIBOLIUM
CASTANEUM. [after Ishaaya et al., (51)].

Compounds	bb	CTC-12
	LC-50, in ppm (and potency relative to DFB)	
Hexafluron	0.068a* (7.1)	0.070a (10.2)
Teflubenzuron	0.092b (5.2)	0.104b (6.9)
Chlorfluazuron	0.106b (4.5)	0.108b (6.7)
Diflubenzuron	0.480c	0.720c
	LC-95, in ppm (and potency relative to DFB)	
Hexafluron	0.108a (9.8)	0.116a (22.6)
Teflubenzuron	0.148b (7.2)	0.188b (14.0)
Chlorfluazuron	0.150b (6.8)	0.176b (14.9)
Diflubenzuron	1.060c	2.63c

Data are means of 15-20 replicates of 15 first-instar larvae kept on a diet
containing various concentrations of the test compound. Cumulative larval and
pupal mortality was determined
*Within the same group and column, data followed by same letters do not differ
significantly at P=0.05.

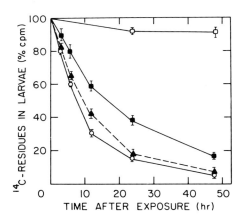

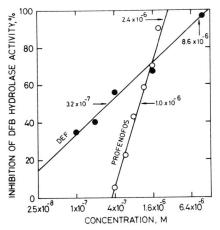

Fig. 3. Retention of ^{14}C residues in
larvae treated with chlorfluazuron
compared with diflubenzuron with and
without the esterase inhibitors DEF
and PSCP. Chlorfluazuron (□); DFB (o);
DFB + DEF 100 ppm (■), DFB + PSCP 100
ppm (▲) [after Gazit et al. (30)].

Fig. 4. The inhibitory effect of profenofos and DEF in vitro on the
hydrolysis of diflubenzuron by larval
gut hydrolase(s). Arrow designates
I-50 and I-95 values, i.e., concentrations resulting in 50 and 95%
enzyme inhibition, respectively
[after Ishaaya and Degheele (46)].

in the feces (30). Similar differences between the retention of DFB and
chlorfluazuron were observed in the Egyptian cotton leafworm, Spodoptera

littoralis (38,75,76). Addition of esterase inhibitors such as phenyl saligenin cyclic phosphonate (PSCP) and S,S,S-tributylphosphorothioate (DEF) to the diet, increased the retention time for half-lives of DFB in Tribolium larvae from 7 h to 9.5 and 18 h, respectively (Fig. 3). Furthermore, addition of 100 ppm DEF to the diet, increased the toxicity of DFB either in T. castaneum or S. littoralis (30,47), which was probably due to inhibition of DFB hydrolase activity (46). Profenofos and DEF synergized the toxicity of DFB in Platynota stultana (31) and S. littoralis (46), but not of the more stable chlorfluazuron (30). On the other hand, in M. domestica and in the boll weevil Anthonomus grandis, oxidation seems to be the major route for DFB detoxification (18,19,88,89), since oxidase inhibitors in these insects synergized the toxicity of DFB to a greater extent than esterase inhibitors. Apparently the predominant pathway for benzoylphenyl urea detoxification in insects, whether hydrolytic or oxidative, depends largely on the species involved. Synergists based on the inhibition of benzoylphenyl urea detoxification may increase toxicity or overcome resistance due to decreased metabolism.

Detoxifying Enzymes and their Importance in Resistance Development

   A primary consideration in the use of any novel insect control agent is development of resistance, in particular in species that are resistant to commonly used insecticides. Resistant strains of M. domestica to conventional insecticides are variously cross-resistant to DFB (17,78,88). On the other hand, the more stable acylureas, hexafluron, chlorfluazuron and teflubenzuron, are equally toxic to strains of T. castaneum that are either resistant or susceptible to malathion (50,51). A field strain of S. littoralis, which was over 100-fold more resistant to pyrethroids and organophosphorus showed a mild cross resistance ($\sim$5-fold) to teflubenzuron (Table II). Perng and Sun (85) reported that the resistant diamondback moth Plutella xylostella showed negligible (two- to threefold) cross resistance to teflubenzuron. The high potency of these IGRs on insect pests which have developed resistance to conventional insecticides, along with their low toxicity to man and natural enemies, render these compounds important components in IPM programs.

   Increased metabolic activity in insects is an important sign of resistance. The degradative pathways of DFB in a laboratory model ecosystem by algae, snails, caterpillars and mosquito larvae are almost entirely through cleavage between the carbonyl and amide groups of the urea bridge to form hydrolytic products (68). The major metabolites found in soil are 4-CPU and 2,6-difluorobenzoic acid (77). In addition, DFB can be hydroxylated in the aniline or the benzoic ring to form polar materials which can be conjugated and rapidly eliminated from the body (18,19,53,54). Part of the DFB residue found in the excreta of insects is unextractable in nonpolar solvent (18,19,101) and consists of conjugated polar materials which are products of DFB metabolism. Hydrolytic cleavage seems to be a major route for DFB detoxification in S. littoralis. Hence, an optimized assay for determining DFB hydrolase activity has been developed (46). This assay can be used for monitoring resistance in S. littoralis due to DFB or other acylureas application.

TABLE II

TOXICITY OF CHLORPYRIPHOS, CYPERMETHRIN AND TEFLUBENZURON FOR LABORATORY (S) AND FIELD (R) STRAINS OF Spodoptera littoralis [after Ishaaya and Klein (47)].*

Compound	Strain	Slope ± SE	LC-50	R/S ratio
Chlorpyriphos	S	5.60±0.47	1.5×10^{-4}	120
	R	2.90±0.34	1.8×10^{-2}	
Cypremethrin	S	1.78±0.22	6.1×10^{-5}	102
	R	0.35±0.05	6.2×10^{-3}	
Teflubenzuron	S	0.96±0.37	3.0×10^{-5}	5
	R	0.55±0.12	1.6×10^{-4}	

*Adapted with permission from Journal of Economic Entomology.

The DFB hydrolase assay in S. littoralis (46) is optimized in a 0.4 ml reaction mixture consisting of 0.1 ml enzyme solution (equivalent to 50 mg gut weight and approximating 0.5 gut of sixth-instar and 0.9 mg protein), 0.2 ml 0.1 M glycine-NaOH buffer at pH 9.0, 0.1 ml H_2O or 0.1 ml aqueous inhibitor solution, and ^{14}C uniformly labeled DFB at the aniline ring (0.5 nmol, equivalent to 10,000 cpm) in 4 ul ethanol. The test tubes are incubated at $37^{o}C$ for 2 h and then freeze-dried with a Virtis lyophilizer. DFB and its hydrolized metabolites of each assay are extracted three times with 0.5 ml acetonitrile and three times with 0.5 ml methanol. The combined extracts are concentrated under vacuum to a volume of 100 ul. Reference compounds consisting of 20 ug of DFB, 4-CA, and 4-CPU are added to each test assay. The concentrated extract is applied to a TLC aluminum sheet of silica gel 60 F254 (Merck No. 5554) and chromatographed with ethyl acetate: dichloromethane (70:30). Autoradiography with X-ray films (Agfa-Gevaert, type Osray M3) is used for detecting ^{14}C-labeled compounds, and UV light (254 nm) for detecting the reference compounds. Using this optimized assay, a high level of metabolites was obtained after 2 hours reaction (Table III), resulting in 8.6, 1.4 and 9.0% of 4-CA, 4-CPU and polar materials, respectively. Total inhibition of DFB hydrolase activity was obtained after addition of 10^{-5} M of either DEF or profenofos (Fig. 4).

Further studies are needed to optimize enzyme assays important in detoxifying the more recent benzoylphenyl ureas and to establish their importance in monitoring resistance after benzoylphenyl urea application.

TABLE III.

EFFECT OF REACTION TIME ON DIFLUBENZURON HYDROLASE ACTIVITY AS EXPRESSED BY THE PERCENTAGE OF METABOLITES PRODUCED [after Ishaaya and Degheele (46)].

Reaction time (h)	DFB and metabolites (% of total recovery)				
	DFB	4-CA	4-CPU	Polar materials	Others
0	100.0	0	0	0	0
0.5	92.9	4.2	0.4	1.7	0.8
1.0	85.5	7.6	0.7	4.4	1.8
2.0	77.7	8.6	1.4	9.0	3.3
4.0	67.0	11.6	1.5	14.4	5.5

III OTHER IGRs OF AGRICULTURAL IMPORTANCE: BIOLOGICAL AND BIOCHEMICAL ASPECTS

Parallel to the development of benzoylphenyl ureas, several other IGRs of agricultural importance have been developed, such as buprofezin, cyromazine and the juvenoid analogs fenoxycarb and pyriproxyfen (Fig. 2).

Buprofezin, a novel IGR acts by inhibiting chitin formation (55,104) specifically on homopteran pests. It affects developmental stages and in some cases oviposition and egg fertility (48,111-113). The effect on egg production seems to result from inhibition of biochemical processes leading to prostaglandin formation (105). A recent study of the biochemical mode of action of buprofezin (59) revealed that apolysis and the subsequent cell proliferation of the epidermis are unaffected, while the digestion of the old endocuticle and the deposition of the new cuticle are severely inhibited. This was accompanied by elevation of the molting hormone, 20-hydroxy ecdysone. Hence, disturbances in hormonal balance is suggested to be the primary cause for the observed inhibition of ecdysis (59). Studies carried out in our laboratory indicated that buprofezin suppresses embryogenesis and progeny formation of B. tabaci, a very important pest of cotton (Table IV). The estimated concentration for 50% inhibition of egg hatch was 0.0015% a.i. in the spray solution, and that for 50% cumulative larval mortality (LC-50) was 0.0006% a.i. All pupae produced normal adults (48). Hence, the compound exerts its effect only on egg hatch and on the larval stage. It has no ovicidal activity, but suppresses embryogenesis through adults. The length of exposure of the whitefly females to buprofezin corresponds well with the suppression of egg fertility. Adult females, exposed for up to 5 h to cotton seedlings treated with 62.5 ppm laid eggs with a

372

fertility similar to that of the control, but those exposed for a period of >24
h laid infertile eggs (48). A good correlation between the length of adult
exposure to buprofezin and egg fertility was observed also with T. vaporariorum
(113). Part of buprofezin's efficiency resulted from its vapor phase. Assays
carried out with B. tabaci (24) indicated that 96 and 57% of 1st-instar larvae
died after they were placed at a distance of 2 and 4 cm, respectively, from
leaves treated with 0.045% a.i. buprofezin. On the other hand, the translaminer
effect of this concentration induced ~25% mortality. Hence, vapor phase and
contact toxicity are major factors for controlling B. tabaci. The high potency
of buprofezin on whiteflies and citrus scales (111) along with its low toxicity
to natural enemies, render this compound an important component in IPM programs
in cotton fields and citrus groves.

TABLE IV.
EFFECT OF BUPROFEZIN ON OVIPOSITION, EGG HATCH AND PUPATION OF BEMISIA TABACI
UNDER GREENHOUSE CONDITIONS [after Ishaaya et al. (44)].

Concentration in spray solution, % a.i.	X + SEM		
	Oviposition, eggs/♀	Egg hatch, %	Pupation, %
Control	5.9+0.6a	66+4a	65+5a
0.0004	7.6+0.5a	49+2b	42+6b
0.0016	6.7+0.8a	30+4c	8+4c
0.0064	5.8+0.9a	14+2d	0d
0.025	5.8+0.9a	–	0d

Cotton seedlings were sprayed to runoff with various concentrations of
buprofezin. Effect on oviposition, egg hatch and pupation was then determined.
a-dWithin columns, figures followed by the same letter do not differ
significantly at P=0.05.

Cyromazine, a novel triazine IGR, acts specifically on dipteran species
(28,41,79,80,93,107,114). It inhibits apolysis and ultimately ecdysis. However,
the procuticle continues to be secreted, resulting in a gross thickening of the
cuticle (27). The cuticle of treated larvae exhibits disoriented microfibrils
and is subjected to abnormal sclerotization and melanization. It is suggested
that the primary mode of action of cyromazine is via the hormonal system (27).
Cyromazine is very effective for controlling dipteran pests such as the
serpentine leafminer Liriomyza trifolli (79,80,93,114), the sheep blowfly
Lucilia cuprina (27,28), the mosquito Culex quinquefasciatus (14) and M.
domestica (13,86).
Fenoxycarb, a juvenile hormone analog (JHA) (Fig. 2), inhibits last stages of
embryogenesis and, larval and pupal development (26,63). In general, application
of a JHA suppresses corpora allata activity (60,61,103) or interferes with

ecdysone biosynthesis (64,94-96). Fenoxycarb is effective against citrus scales
such as <u>Ceroplastes</u> <u>floridensis</u>, <u>Chrysomphalus</u> <u>aonidum</u>, <u>A.</u> <u>aurantii</u> and <u>S.</u> <u>oleae</u>
(81,82), and the pine scale pest <u>Matsucoccus</u> <u>josephi</u> (67). In <u>Heliothis</u>
<u>virescens</u>, it affects egg viability and early stages of larval development (63).
The compound has no effect on hymenopteran parasites of citrus scale pests (81),
but affects the developmental stages of <u>Chilocorus</u> <u>bipustulatus</u> when the
coccinelid feeds on treated scales (82).

A more recent JHA, pyriproxyfen (Fig. 2), was found to be more effective than
fenoxycarb on the housefly and the common mosquito (52) and to have promising
results on cockroaches, whiteflies and citrus scale pests (8,58,84).

The diversity of selective IGRs available today for controlling agricultural
pests in cotton, citrus and vegetables enables their use in IPM programs
incorporating biological control.

ACKNOWLEDGMENT

My appreciation is expressed to Sara Yablonski and Zmira Mendelson for expert
technical assistance and Malka Nehorai for typing the manuscript. I thank Nihon
Nohyaku Company, Tokyo, the Israel Cotton Board, and Makhteshim Chemical
Company, Be'er Sheva, for their support. This article is contribution no.
2758-E, 1989 series, from the Agricultural Research Organization, Bet Dagan,
Israel.

REFERENCES
1. Ables JR, West RP, Shepard M (1975) J Econ Entomol 68:622-624
2. Anderson DW, Elliott RH (1982) Can Ent 114:733-737
3. Anonymous (1985) Applaud 25WP on <u>Trialeurodes</u> <u>vaporariorum</u>,Technical Information, Nihon Nohyaku, May 1985
4. Apperson CS, Schaefer CH, Colwell AE, Werner GH, Anderson NL, Dupras EF, Jr, Longanecker DR (1978) J Econ Entomol 71:521-527
5. Armabourg Y, Pralavario R, Dolbeau C (1977) Rev Zool Agric Pathol Veg 76:118-126
6. Asai T, Fukada M, Maekawa S, Ikeda K, Kanno H (1983) Appl Entomol Zool 18:55-552
7. Asai T, Kijihara O, Fukada M, Maekawa S (1985) Appl Entomol Zool 20:111-117
8. Ascher KRS, Eliyahu M (1988) Phytoparasitica 16:15-21
9. Ascher KRS, Nemny, NE (1974) Phytoparasitica 2:131-133
10. Ascher KRS, Nemny, NE (1976) Pestic Sci 7:447-452
11. Ascher KRS, Nemny, NE (1984) Phytoparasitica 12:13-27
12. Ascher KRS, Yathom S, Nemny NE, Tal S (1989) Z PflKrankh PflSchutz 96:60-70

374

13. Awad TI, Mulla MS (1984) J Med Entomol 21:419-426

14. Awad TI, Mulla MS (1984) J Med Entomol 21:427-431

15. Becher HM, Becker P, Prokic-Immel R, Wirtz W (1983) 10th Int Congr Pl Protection, Brighton, pp 408-415

16. Broadbent AB, Pree DJ (1984) Environ Entomol 13:133-136

17. Cerf DC, Georghiou GP (1974) J Agric Food Chem 22:1145-1146

18. Chang SC (1978) J Econ Entomol 71:31-39

19. Chang SC, Stokes JB (1979) J Econ Entomol 72:15-19

20. Cohen E (1985) Experientia 41:470-472

21. Cohen E (1987) In: Wright JE, Retnakaran A, (eds) Chitin and Benzoylphenyl Ureas. Dr W Junk Publishers, Dordrecht, pp 43-73

22. Cohen E (1987) Ann Rev Entomol 32:71-93

23. Cohen E, Casida JE (1980) Pestic Biochem Physiol 13:129-136

24. De Cock A, Ishaaya I, Degheele D, Veierov D (1989) J Econ Entomol, submitted

25. DeLoach JR, Meola SM, Mayer RT, Thompson JM (1981) Pestic Biochem Physiol 15:172-180

26. Dorn S, Frischknecht ML, Martinez V, Zurfluh R, Fischer U (1981) Z PflKrankh PflSchutz 88:269-75

27. Friedel T, Hales DF, Birch D (1988) Pestic Biochem Physiol 31:99-107

28. Friedel T, McDonell PA (1985) J Econ Entomol 78:868-873

29. Garrido A, Beitia I, Gruenholz S (1984) Brit Crop Protection Conf - Pests and Diseases, Brighton, pp 305-310

30. Gazit Y, Ishaaya I, Perry AS (1989) Pestic Biochem Physiol 34:103-110

31. Granett J, Hejazi MJ (1983) J Econ Entomol 76:403-406

32. Granett J, Robertson J, Retnakaran A (1980) Ent. Exp Appl 28:295-300

33. Granett J, Weseloh RM (1975) J Econ Entomol 68:577-580

34. Grosscurt AC (1978) J. Insect Physiol 24:827-831

35. Grosscurt AC (1978) Pestic Sci 9:373-386

36. Grosscurt AC, Anderson SO (1980) Proc K ned Akad Wet 83C:143-150

37. Grosscurt AC, Jongsma B (1987) In: Wright JE, Retnakaran A (eds) Chitin and Benzoylphenyl Ureas. Dr W Junk Publishers, Dordrecht, pp 75-99

38. Guyer W, Neumann R (1988) Pestic Biochem Physiol 30:166-177

39. Haga T, Tobi T, Koyanagi T, Nishiyama R (1982) Abstracts, 5th Int. Congr. Pesticide Chemistry (IUPAC), Kyoto, P IID-7

40. Hajjar NP and Casida JE (1979) Pestic Biochem Physiol 11:33-45

41. Hall RD, Foehse MC (1980) J Econ Entomol 73:564-569

42. Holst H (1975) Z Pflkankh PflSchutz 82:1-7

43. Ishaaya I, Ascher KRS (1977) Phytoparasitica 5:149-158

44. Ishaaya I, Blumberg D, Yarom I (1989) Med Fac Landbouww Rijksuniv Gent 54:in press

45. Ishaaya I, Casida JE (1974) Pestic Biochem Physiol 4:484-490

46. Ishaaya I, Degheele D (1988) Pectic Biochem Physiol 32:180-187

47. Ishaaya I, Klein M (1990) J Econ Entomol 83: in press

48. Ishaaya I, Mendelson Z, Melamed-Madjar V (1988) J Econ Entomol 81:781-784

49. Ishaaya I, Nemny NE, Ascher KRS (1984) Phytoparasitica 12:193-197

50. Ishaaya I, Yablonski S (1987) In: Wright JE, Retnakaran A (eds) Chitin and Benzoylphenyl Ureas. Dr W Junk Publishers, Dordrecht, pp 131-140

51. Ishaaya I, Yablonski S, Ascher KRS (1987) In: Donahaye E, Navarro S (eds) Proceedings of the Fourth International Working Conference on Stored-Product Protection. Caspit, Jerusalem pp 613-622

52. Itaya N (1987) SP World, Sumitomo Pyrethroid, No. 8, pp 2-4

53. Ivie GW (1978) J Agric Food Chem 26:81-89

54. Ivie GW, Wright JE (1978) J Agric Food Chem 26:90-94

55. Izawa Y, Uchida M, Sugimoto T, Asai T (1985) Pestic Biochem Physiol 24:343-347

56. Jones D, Snyder M, Granett J (1983) Ent Exp Appl 33:290-296

57. Kanno H, Ikeda K, Asai T, Maekawa S (1981) British Crop Protection Conference - Pests and Diseases, Brighton, pp 56-69

58. Kawada H (1988) SP World, Sumitomo Pyrethroid, No. 11, pp 2-4

59. Kobayashi M, Uchida M, Kuriyama K (1989) Pestic Biochem Physiol 34:9-16

60. Kramer SJ, Stall GB (1981) In: Pratt GE, Brooks GT (eds) Juvenile Hormone Biochemistry. Elsevier, Biomedical Press, pp 425-437,

61. Lohri-Kaelin M, Masner P (1981) In: Pratt GE, Brooks GT (eds) Juvenile Hormone Biochemistry. Elsevier, Biomedical Press, pp 403-413

62. Martin NA, Workman P (1986) Proc. 39th N.Z. Weed and Pest Control Conf, pp 234-236

63. Masner P, Angst M, Dorn S (1987) Pestic Sci 18:89-94

64. Masner P, Hangartner W, Suchy M (1975) J Insect Physiol 21:1755-1762

65. Mauchamp B, Perrineau O (1987) In: Wright JE, Retnakaran A (eds) Chitin and Benzoylphenyl Ureas. Dr W Junk Publishers, Dordrecht, pp 101-109

66. Mayer RT, Chen AC, DeLoach JR (1981) Experientia 37:337-338

67. Mendel Z, Rosenberg U (1988) J Econ Entomol 81:1143-1147

68. Metcalf RL, Lu P-Y, Bowlus S (1975) J Agric Food Chem 23:359-364

69. Mitlin N, Wiygul G, Haynes JW (1977) Pestic Biochem Physiol 7:559-563

70. Mitsui T, Hitturu T, Nobusawa C, Yamaguchi I (1985) J Pestic Sci 10:55-60

71. Mitsui T, Nobusawa C, Fukami J-I (1984) J Pestic Sci 8:19-26

72. Mulder R, Gijswijt MT (1973) Pestic Sci 4:737-745

73. Mulla MS, Majori G, Darwazeh HA (1975) Mosquito News 35:211-216

74. Nagata T (1986) Appl Entomol Zool 21:357-362

75. Neumann R, Guyer W (1983) 10th Int Congr Plant Prot, Brighton, pp 445-451

76. Neumann R, Guyer W (1987) Pestic Sci 20:147-156

77. Nimmo WB, de Wilde PC, Verloop A (1984) Pestic Sci 15:574-585

78. Oppenoorth FJ, Van Der Pas LJT (1977) Ent Exp Appl 21:217-228

79. Parrella MP (1983) J Econ Entomol 76:1460-1464

80. Parrella MP, Robb KL, Christie GD, Bethke JA (1982) Cal Agric 36:17-19

81. Peleg BA (1982) Phytoparasitica 10:27-31

82. Peleg BA (1983) Entomophaga 28:367-372

83. Peleg BA (1988) J Econ Entomol 81:88-92

84. Peleg BA (1988) Hassadeh 68:1321-1324 (in Hebrew)

85. Perng FS, Sun CW (1987) J Econ Entomol 80:29-31

86. Pochon J-M, Casida JE (1983) Ent Exp Appl 34:251-256

87. Post LC, de Jong BJ, Vincent WR (1974) Pestic Biochem Physiol 4:473-483

88. Primprikar GD, Georghiou GP (1979) Pestic Biochem Physiol 12:10-22

89. Primprikar GD, Georghiou GP (1982) J Agric Food Chem 30:615-618

90. Retnakaran A, Wright JE (1987) In: Wright JE, Retnakaran A (eds) Chitin and Benzoylphenyl Ureas. Dr W Junk Publishers, Dordrecht,pp 205-282

91. Sarasua MJ, Santiago-Alvarez C (1983) Ent Exp Appl 33:223-225

92. Sbragia RJ, Bisabri-Ershadi B, Rigterink RH (1983) 10th Int Congr Plant Protection, Brighton, pp 417-424

93. Schlapfer T, Cotti T (1986) British Crop Protection Conf - Pests and Diseases Brighton, pp 123-128

94. Sehnal F, Maroy P, Mala J (1981) J Insect Physiol 27:535-544

95. Shaaya E, Riddiford LM (1988) J Insect Physiol 34:655-659

96. Shaaya E, Spindler-Barth M, Spindler K-D (1986) Insect Biochem 16: 181-185

97. Shepard M. and Kissam JB (1981) J Georgia Entomol Soc 16:222-227

98. Skatulla VU (1975) Auzeiger fur Schadlingshunde Pflanzenschutz Umweltschutz 48:145-147

99. Soltani N, Besson MT, Delachambre J (1984) Pestic Biochem Physiol 21:256-264

100. Sowa BA and Marks EP (1975) Insect Biochem 5:855-859

101. Still GG, Leopold RA (1978) Pestic Biochem Physiol 9:304-312

102. Tester PA, Costlow JD, Jr (1981) Mar Ecol Prog Ser 5:297-302

103. Tobe SS, Stay B (1979) Nature (London) 281:481-482

104. Uchida M, Asai T, Sugimoto T (1985) Agric Biol Chem 49:1233-1234

105. Uchida M, Izawa Y, Sugimoto T (1987) Pestic Biochem Physiol 27:71-75

106. Van Eck WH (1979) Insect Biochem 9:295-300

107. Williams RE, Berry JG (1980) Poultry Sci 59:2207-2212

108. Wilson D, Anema BP (1988) British Crop Prot Conf - Pests and Diseaes, Brighton, pp 175-180

109. Wool D, Noiman S, Manheim D, Cohen E (1982) Biochem Genet 20:621-636

110. Wright JE, Harris RL (1976) J Econ Entomol 69:728-730

111. Yarom I, Blumberg D, Ishaaya I (1988) J Econ Entomol 81:1581-1585

112. Yasui M, Fukada M, Maekawa S (1985) Appl Entomol Zool 20:340-347

113. Yasui M, Fukada M, Maekawa S (1987) Appl Entomol Zool 22:266-271

114. Yathom S, Ascher KRS, Tal S, Nemny NE (1986) Israel J Entomol 20:85-93

115. Yu SJ, Terriere LC (1975) Life Sci 17:619-625

116. Yu SJ, Terriere LC (1977) Pestic Biochem Physiol 7:48-55

© 1990 Elsevier Science Publishers B.V. (Biomedical Division)
Pesticides and alternatives, editor J.E. Casida

CHITIN SYNTHESIS INHIBITORS: EFFECT ON CUTICLE STRUCTURE AND COMPONENTS

DANNY DEGHEELE

Laboratory of Agrozoology, Faculty of Agricultural Sciences, Coupure Links, 653, B-9000 Gent (Belgium)

INTRODUCTION

An overview of effects caused by and the mode of action of benzoylphenyl ureas and buprofezin (Applaud, 2-*tert*-butylimino-3-isopropyl-5-phenylperhydro-1,3,5-thiadiazine-4-one) on insects is given in the contribution of I Ishaaya in this issue. These compounds are called chitin synthesis inhibitors (7,11,13,21,22,25,26,27). Their activity will be followed in the cuticle of some insects; special attention will be given to the fine structure as well as chitin and protein contents.

EFFECT ON THE FINE STRUCTURE OF THE CUTICLE

All the benzoylphenyl ureas inhibit the deposition of post-ecdysial lamellae in the procuticle during the phase of inter-moult of the larval instars. Buprofezin, on the contrary, probably exerts its effect only at the moment of apolysis when the new procuticle is to be formed.

Diflubenzuron [1-(4-chlorophenyl)-3-(2,6-difluorobenzoyl) urea] also seems to interfere with the formation of the protein epicuticle, which is missing in some areas in sixth-instar *Mamestra brassicae* larval cuticle (Figs. 1 and 2). This is rather abnormal, because the protein epicuticle does not contain chitinous microfibrils (24) and was already secreted, together with pre-ecdysial procuticle, before application of diflubenzuron. This compound does not only exert an effect on the deposition of protein epicuticle after application, but also on the existing pre-ecdysial procuticle. The wax filaments are not affected and the thickness of the cuticle is similar to that of the untreated *M. brassicae* larva.

The effect of diflubenzuron can occur very quickly and resulted in complete inhibition of the post-ecdysial procuticle in the third instar *Plutella xylostella* larva. In figure 3, only 5 lamellae instead of 13 in the control are observed in the procuticle after injection of diflubenzuron to the newly ecdysed third-instar. This number of lamellae corresponds exactly with the number at ecdysis, which means that the activity of the epidermis has been blocked almost immediately by diflubenzuron, and neither chitin nor protein has been deposited. The epidermis cell contains many fusing multivesicular bodies, indicating that all metabolic activity has stopped.

Diflubenzuron does not only inhibit the formation of the post-ecdysial lamellae of the procuticle in a sixth instar *Spodoptera littoralis* larva, but also interferes with the protein epicuticle and the pre-ecdysial lamellae already deposited at the moment of ecdysis and diflubenzuron application (Fig. 4). This

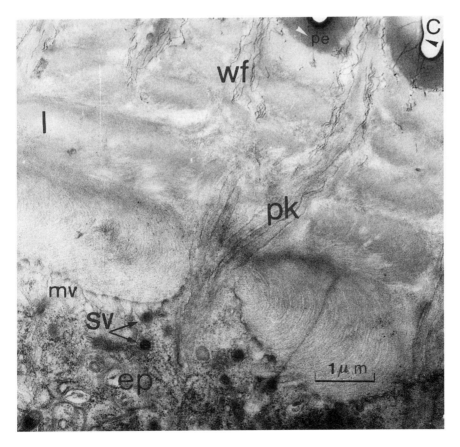

Fig. 1.   Fine structure of the integument of sixth instar *Mamestra brassicae* larva 96 h: cuticulin (c) and protein epicuticle (pe); lamellae (l) of the procuticle; wax filaments (wf); pore canals (pk); microvilli (mv) and secretion vesicles (sv) of the epidermis (ep)

effect is similar to that in *M. brassicae* (Fig. 2). The post-
ecdysial cuticle of diflubenzuron-treated fourth instar *Manduca
sexta* larvae also has a granular structure and is devoid of
lamellae (14); in addition, the epidermal cells extruded cytoplasm apically. However, in our laboratory these has never been
observed.

The effect is dose dependent in *S. littoralis* : lower concentrations of diflubenzuron do not influence the protein epicuticle
and pre-ecdysial lamellae which become loosely structured (15).
A good correlation between toxicity and the degree of chitin

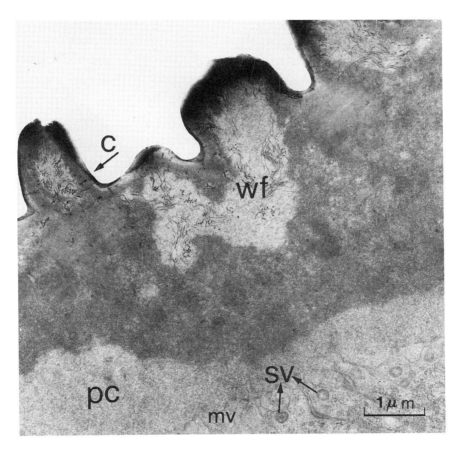

Fig. 2. Fine structure of the integument of sixth instar
Mamestra brassicae larva 96 h, injected diflubenzuron just after
ecdysis: cuticulin (c); wax filaments (wf) in the non-lamellate
procuticle (pc); microvilli (mv) and secretion vesicles (sv)

inhibition has also been indicated in *Oncopeltus fasciatus* (13).

It has been shown that the muscle attachment to the cuticle (cuticulin layer) is influenced by diflubenzuron in *S. littoralis*: no digestion either of the tonofibrillae or the old cuticle (20). This explains why larvae have difficulties or fail to shed off the old cuticle at the moment of ecdysis.

The effect of diflubenzuron in the integument of a *Leptinotarsa decemlineata* larva can be observed in the procuticle and the epidermis (Fig. 5). The procuticle is very thin in comparison

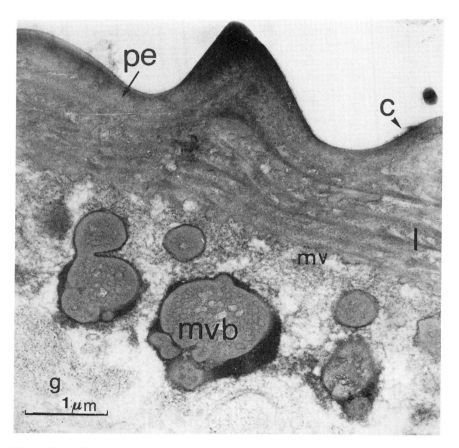

Fig. 3. Fine structure of the integument of third instar *Plutella xylostella* larva 78 h, injected diflubenzuron just after ecdysis: cuticulin (c) and protein epicuticle (pe) unchanged; only 5 lamellae (l) in the procuticle; disturbed microvilli (mv); fusing multivesicular bodies (mvb) and glycogen (g) in the epidermis

with that of the control and has no lamellar structure. Sometimes some helicoidal arrangement could be observed; this could
indicate an uncomplete and disturbed formation of chitin microfibrils. The procuticle can also have an amorphous structure, this
is probably caused by a higher diflubenzuron concentration (16).

Also diflubenzuron treatment of the earlier *Anthonomus grandis*
pupal stage interfered with deposition of the lamellate cuticle
by eliminating or reducing the lamellar structure (23). Elimination of already deposited procuticle lamellae has also been

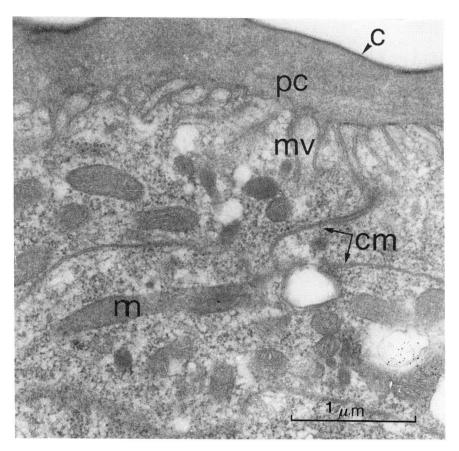

Fig. 4. Fine structure of the integument of sixth instar *Spodoptera littoralis* larva 144 h, injected diflubenzuron just after
ecdysis: cuticulin (c); procuticle (pc) without lamellae; microvilli (mv); cell membrane (cm) and mitochondria (m)

382

observed in diflubenzuron treated larvae of *M. brassicae, S. littoralis* and *L. decemlineata.*

Application of diflubenzuron (50 mg a.i./kg of diet) to first instar *Musca domestica* larvae resulted in a delayed effect of ecdysis to the second instar: in untreated larvae ecdysis occurs at approximately 36 h (18,19); whereas in figure 6 no ecdysis after 48 h was observed in treated larvae. Diflubenzuron does not only

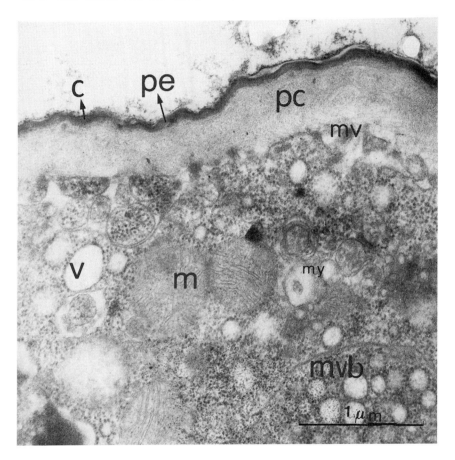

Fig. 5.   Fine structure of the pre-ecdysial integument of a pharate second instar *Leptinotarsa decemlineata* larva fed on potato leaves, treated with diflubenzuron (50 mg a.i./l = LC$_{50}$-value) during 72 h: cuticulin (c); protein epicuticle (pe); procuticle (pc) with apparently no lamellar appearance nevertheless some helicoidal arrangements of microfibrils can be observed.   The microvilli (mv) miss their regular outlines and membrane plaques; cytoplasm with large mitochondria (m) and vacuoles (v), myeline figures (my) and multivesicular bodies (mvb), indicating the near death of the cell

prevent the formation of a normal lamellate appearance in the
procuticle of *Lucilia cuprina* larvae, but also interferes with
the deposition of epicuticle (4,5). The effect of diflubenzuron
on the epicuticle was also be observed in *M. domestica*, *M. brassicae* and *S. littoralis*. Diflubenzuron seems to have an effect
on the digestion of the old procuticle of *M. domestica*: no looser
structure of the endocuticle or formation of an ecdysial membrane

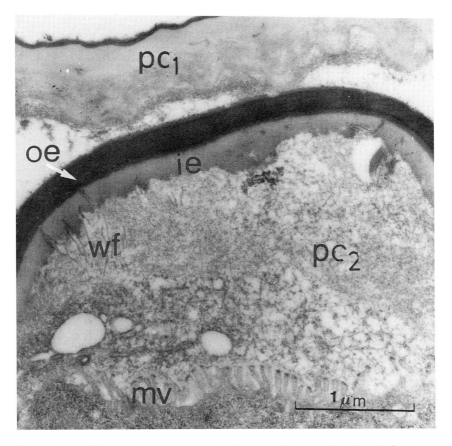

Fig. 6.   Fine structure of the cuticle of first-instar   *Musca
domestica* larva 48 h, fed on a diet mixed with diflubenzuron (50
mg a.i./kg).   The first instar procuticle (pc₁) is only partly
digested, which prohibits ecdysis (untreated larvae are ecdysed
at approximately 36 h).   Outer (oe) and inner epicuticle (ie) are
regularly formed.   The second instar procuticle (pc₂) is seen as
an amorphous layer, containing wax filaments (wf) as in untreated
larvae.   The microvilli (mv) have a normal regular shape and size
with dense plaques at the tips

384

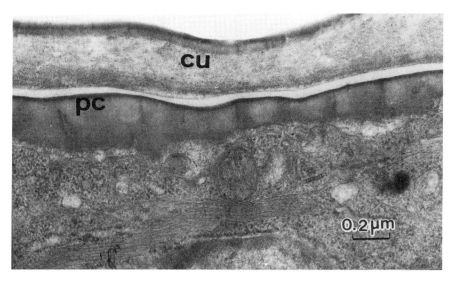

Fig. 7. Fine structure of third instar *Trialeurodes vaporariorum*
larva 72 h, fed on tomato leaves treated with buprofezin (5 mg
a.i./l): old cuticle (cu); procuticle (pc) of the pharate pupa
without lamellae

has been observed during moult events (Fig. 6). The deposition
of the new epicuticle (outer and inner) is not influenced, even
wax filaments, extending from the procuticle to the inner side of
cuticulin, can still be observed. On the other hand, no pre-
ecdysial lamellae of the procuticle are formed, only an amorphous
mass is seen as procuticle after withdrawing of the microvilli.

Buprofezin does not exert an appreciable effect on the cuticle during the phase of intermoult of third instar *Trialeurodes
vaporariorum* larvae at a concentration of 5 mg a.i. /l after 72 h
feeding on treated tomato leaves (Fig. 7). On the contrary, at
the time of apolysis to the pharate pupa buprofezin clearly
interferes with cuticle formation: the procuticle is non lamellate and is irregular in thickness at higher concentration (80 mg
a.i./l). The microvilli are irregular and vacuoles are present
in the cytoplasm. The failure of new cuticle deposition in
fifth instar *Nilaparvata lugens* nymphs occurred just before the
death caused by buprofezin, no histological effect was observed
during intermoult (28).

EFFECT ON CHITIN AND PROTEIN CONTENTS OF CUTICLES

The chitin contents of cuticles commonly falls within the range
25 to 50 per cent of the cuticular dry weight (12). The relative

proportions of chitin and protein in cuticles change during cuticulogenesis. In *Locusta migratoria migratoriodes* the cuticle deposited immediately after apolysis contains 90 to 95 per cent protein but as cuticle synthesis and deposition proceed this drops to about 70 per cent and the chitin content rises to about 30 per cent (6).

Figure 8a illustrates the effect of diflubenzuron (100 mg a.i./kg of diet) on the cuticular dry weight of fourth instar *M.*

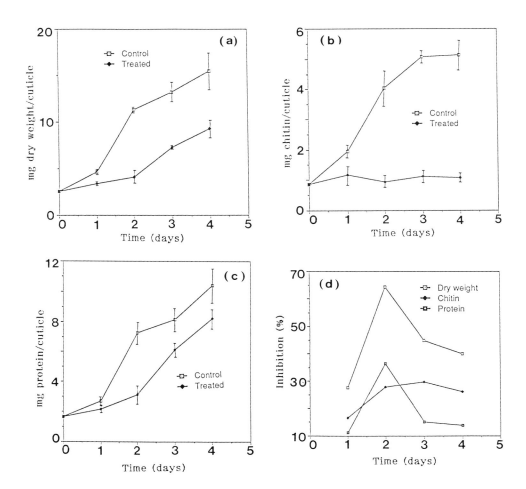

Fig.8. Cuticular dry weight, chitin and protein content, and inhibition per cent of fourth instar *Manduca sexta* larva, fed on either untreated or diflubenzuron-treated diet (100 mg a.i./kg) (vertical bar = SD) (3)

sexta larvae: 15.5 mg in the control and 9.3 mg in the treated larva on day four (last day of the fourth-instar). Chitin build-up was inhibited from day 1 on in the treated larva (Fig.8b). The chitin percentage in the untreated larva was 57 on day 1 and decreased to 36 on day 4; however in the treated larva the amount decreased from 42 per cent on day 1 to 12 on day 4. So the chitin level *in situ* was considerably lower in the treated larvae. The amount of protein removed by hydrolysis in untreated larvae was greater than that of diflubenzuron-treated larvae (Fig.8c). This also indicates an effect of diflubenzuron on protein synthesis. The protein inhibition closely followed the contour of dry weight inhibition and the chitin inhibition re-mained constant from day 2 on (Fig 8d).

A reduction in cuticle dry weight and protein synthesis and a severe inhibition of chitin synthesis has been observed after treatment in:

a) *S. littoralis* with diflubenzuron, triflumuron [1-(4-trifluoro-methoxyphenyl)-3-(2-chlorobenzoyl)urea], teflubenzuron [1-(3,5-dichloro-2,4-difluoro-phenyl)-3-(2,6-difluorobenzoyl)urea] or chlorfluazuron [1-(3,5-dichloro-4-(3-chloro-5-trifluoromethyl-2-pyridyloxy)phenyl)-3-(2,6-difluorobenzoyl)urea] (1,9)

b) *L. decemlineata* with diflubenzuron, chlorfluazuron, tefluben-zuron, triflumuron or hexaflumuron [1-(3,5-dichloro-4-(1,1,2,2-tetrafluoroethoxy)-phenyl)-3-(2,6-difluoro-benzoyl)urea] (16,17)

c) *Spodoptera exigua* with diflubenzuron (30)

d) *Heliothis virescens* with chlorfluazuron (8)

The amount of chitin deposited and the amount of protein stabilized within the cuticle of *L. migratoria* was also greatly reduced by diflubenzuron (29). A direct effect by diflubenzuron on cuticle protein synthesis was also found in *L. cuprina* (5). Although diflubenzuron arrested chitin synthesis in the elytra of *L. decemlineata*, cuticle protein synthesis and deposition conti-nued also (10).

A variation in degree of the effect of benzoylphenyl ureas on the cuticle dry weight, chitin and protein synthesis can be caused partly by the cuticle preparation techniques; however, the possibility that it may merely reflect differences in insect susceptibility beside dosage effects should also be considered.

Benzoylphenyl ureas apparently affect the production of all cuticlular proteins. However, electrophoretic analysis demonstrated non or only minor qualitative changes of soluble protein patterns in treated and untreated larvae; moreover a lower protein concentration is usually observed in the treated ones. This has been observed after application of (a) benzoylphenyl urea(s) to *S. littoralis* (2,9), *L. decemlineata* (16,17), *M. sexta* (3), *H. virescens* (8) and *S. exigua* (30). On the contrary, electrophoretic analysis showed, next to similar protein patterns, a similar density in both diflubenzuron-treated and untreated *L. cuprina* larvae (5).

Considering the effects of the benzoylphenyl ureas on the fine structure of the cuticle and the determination of chitin and protein, it can be concluded that the primary mode of action of benzoylphenyl ureas apparently is linked to direct and rapid inhibition of chitin synthesis in the integument. Reduction in chitin content led to a decrease in protein stabilized within the cuticle.

REFERENCES

1. Auda M, El Saidy MF, Degheele D (1988) Med Fac Landbouw Rijksuniv Gent 53: 175-183

2. Auda M, El Saidy MF, Degheele D (1988) Med Fac Landbouw Rijksuniv Gent 53: 185-193

3. Auda M, El Saidy MF, Janssens S, Degheele D (1989) Med Fac Landbouw Rijksuniv Gent 54: 1009-1018

4. Binnington KC (1985) Tissue Cell 17: 131-140

5. Binnington KC, Retnakaran A, Stone S, Skelly P (1987) Pestic Biochem Physiol 27: 201-210

6. Cassier P, Porcheron P, Papillon M, Lensky Y (1980) Ann Sci Nat Zool Biol Anim 14: 51-65

7. Cohen E (1987) In: Wright JE, Retnakaran A (eds) Chitin and Benzoylphenyl Ureas. Dr W Junk Publishers, Dordrecht, pp 43-73

8. El-Refai SA, Degheele D (1988) Med Fac Landbouw Rijkuniv Gent 53: 211-217

9. Emam AK (1989) Ph D thesis Fac Landbouw Rijksuniv Gent 160 pp

10. Grosscurt AC (1978) Pestic Sci 9: 373-386

11. Grosscurt AC, Jongsma B (1987) In: Wright JE, Retnakaran A (eds) Chitin and Benzoylphenyl Ureas. Dr W Junk Publishers, Dordrecht, pp 75-99

12. Hackman RH (1987) In: Wright JE, Retnakaran A (eds) Chitin and Benzoylphenyl Ureas. Dr W Junk Publishers, Dordrecht, pp 75-99

13. Hajjar NP, Casida JE (1979) Pestic Biochem Physiol 11: 33-45

14. Hassan AEM, Charnley AK (1987) J Insect Physiol 33: 669-676

15. Hegazy G (1984) Ph D thesis Fac Landbouw Rijksuniv Gent 105 pp, 181 fig

16. Hegazy G, De Cock A, Auda M, Degheele D (1989) Med Fac Landbouw Rijksuniv Gent 54: 89-101

17. Hegazy G, De Cock A, Degheele D, Salem H (1989) Med Fac Landbouw Rijksuniv Gent 54: 103-114

18. Hegazy G, Degheele D (1988) Med Fac Landbouw Rijksuniv Gent 53: 225-235

19. Hegazy G, Degheele D (1990) J Insect Physiol, submitted

20. Hegazy G, Degheele D (1990) Med Fac Landbouw Rijksuniv Gent 55, submitted

21. Hunter E, Vincent JFV (1974) Experientia 30: 1432-1433

22. Ishaaya I, Casida JE (1974) Pestic Biochem Physiol 4: 484-490

23. Leopold RA, Marks EP, Eaton JK, Knoper J (1985) Pestic Biochem Physiol 24: 267-283

24. Locke M (1969) J Morph 127: 7-40

25. Post LC, de Jong BJ, Vincent WR (1974) Pestic Biochem Physiol 4: 473-483

26. Retnakaran A, Wright JE (1987) In: Wright JE, Retnakaran A (eds) Chitin and Benzoylphenyl Ureas. Dr W Junk Publishers, Dordecht, pp 205-282

27. Sowa BA, Marks EP (1975) Insect Biochem 5: 855-859

28. Uchida M, Asai T, Sugimoto T (1985) Agric Biol Chem 49: 1233-1234

29. Vincent JVC, Clarke L (1985) Entomol Gener 11: 15-24

30. Van Laecke K (1988) M Sc thesis Fac Landbouw Rijksuniv Gent 152 pp

© 1990 Elsevier Science Publishers B.V. (Biomedical Division)
Pesticides and alternatives, editor J.E. Casida

SEARCH FOR NEW INSECTICIDES: A RATIONAL APPROACH THROUGH INSECT MOLECULAR NEUROBIOLOGY

YVES PICHON

Département de Biophysique, Laboratoire de Neurobiologie Cellulaire et Moléculaire du CNRS. F-91198 GIF SUR YVETTE CEDEX (France)

INTRODUCTION

During the past twenty years, our approaches to pest control have changed considerably. Amongst the various factors responsible for this evolution are a better knowledge of the biology of the pests and of their equilibrium with predators and parasites, the development of molecular genetics and genetic engineering and a better definition of the mode of action of existing pesticide molecules.

The development of new insecticide molecules has been closely associated to a better definition of the various target sites, most of them in the central nervous system, and with the active search for biologically active natural compounds acting specifically on these target sites. Insect neurobiology provides specific tools for these studies.

An emerging new branch of neurobiology, namely molecular neurobiology, which combines molecular biological techniques, biochemistry and sophisticated electrophysiological techniques enables precise studies of the dynamic properties of the protein molecules which constitute the targets of most insecticide molecules. Molecular neurobiology has already significantly improved our knowledge of the fundamental properties of the ionic channels and receptors in the nervous system of both vertebrate and invertebrate species. In our opinion, this approach is susceptible to enable considerable progresses to be made in the rational design of insecticide molecules in the near future.

TARGET SITES OF MAJOR INSECTICIDE MOLECULES

The present commercially available as well as putative insecticide molecules, have a limited number of target sites (1). Most of these sites are located in the nervous system. The axonal sodium channels appear to be the main target site of Organochloride insecticides such as DDT and derivatives and pyrethroid insecticides (allethrin, bioallethrin, resmethrin, bioresmethrin, permethrin, fenvalerate, cypermethrin, deltamethrin etc.). The effect of the molecule is to delay the turning-off of the voltage-dependent sodium conductance, resulting in the production of negative after potentials and repetitive activity and/or to increase the resting sodium conductance of the membrane, resulting in membrane depolarization and action potential block (2-4). The Acetylcholine receptor and associated ionic channel is the site of action of nicotine and cartap, whereas

390

the inhibitory GABAergic transmission is the main target of lindane, cyclodienes and cage convulsants and probably the secondary target of pyrethroids and avermectins. The aminergic system (mainly octopaminergic) is the target of formamidines and imidazolines whereas organophosphates and carbamates act on acetylcholinesterases. A more thorough knowledge of the fundamental properties of these target sites and of a few others (glutamate receptors and the voltage-dependent calcium and potassium channels) will undoubtly facilitate the understanding of their interaction with known or putative insecticide molecules and help in answering questions related to selectivity and resistance mechanisms.

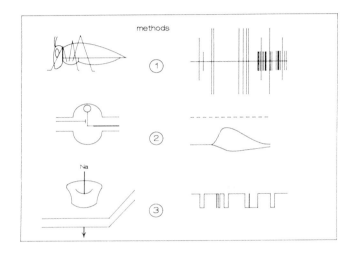

Fig.1 Schematic representation of the results obtained by various electro-physiological methods. (1) 'in situ' recording from intact insects or from isolated nerve truncs of fast biphasic action potentials corresponding to several neurones with different patterns of activity (3 in this example). (2) Intracellular recording from large neurones or axons such as those illustrated in the left panel reveals resting potentials (difference between the dotted line and the continuous line at the beginning of the trace) and synaptic potentials corresponding to the stimulation of a presynaptic neurones (the excitatory synaptic potential which corresponds to a depolarization is shown as an upward deflection whereas the inhibitory synaptic potential which corresponds to a hyperpolarization is shown as a downward deflection). (3) The activity of the single sodium channel which is illustrated as a funnel-like structure crossing the lipid bilayer in the left panel can be recorded with the 'patch-clamp' technique and consists into a succession of step changes of the currrent from the zero (closed) level to a constant (open) level. The (inwardly directed) sodium current is represented as a downward deflection.

MOLECULAR NEUROBIOLOGY: A COMBINATION OF TECHNIQUES.

To determine the dynamic properties of the molecules which are essential in the various functions of the nervous system, molecular neurobiology combines several sophisticated techniques which are now available in a few laboratories in the United States, Japan and also in Europe: Molecular biology (cloning and sequencing of the proteins), electrophysiology (electrical activity associated with nerve function, action potentials, synaptic potentials, ionic currents and conductances, ionic current noise, single channel activity), biochemistry (binding assays and flux measurements) and computer analysis and modelling. The results which can be obtained are sufficiently precise to enable the detection of small differences between various species or changes in the same species following mutations or genetic manipulations.

ELECTROPHYSIOLOGY: ON LINE MONITORING OF NERVE ACTIVITY

A wide range of electrophysiological techniques are available to study in real time (millisecond range) the dynamic properties of the insect nervous system (Fig.1). Nerve impulses which correspond to the almost simultaneous opening and closing of a large number of voltage-dependent sodium channels can be recorded from nerve trunks or ganglia in situ or in vitro using extracellular electrodes (1) Resting membrane potential as well as action potentials or synaptic potentials can be monitored using intracellular microelectrodes impaled into large cell bodies or giant axons (2) or from isolated giant axons. Ionic currents corresponding to the opening and closing of a large number of channels can be recorded from the same cells using the 'voltage-clamp' technique. Detailed informations concerning the activity of a single ion channel can be obtained with the so-called 'patch-clamp' technique: the single channel currents are very small (one to a few picoamperes) and appear usually as square all or none events (3).

MOLECULAR NEUROBIOLOGY OF THE SODIUM CHANNELS

To illustrate how Molecular Neurobiology has already significantly improved our knowledge of the fundamental properties of the ionic channels and receptors in the nervous system of insects , we have chosen one of the major target sites of the present insecticides: the sodium channel, its proposed structure and its activity in a deltamethrin treated neurone.

The sodium channel protein

The sodium channel protein has been isolated from the eel electroplax, mammalian brain and muscles and drosophila brain (5). It is large polypeptide of about 260 kDa containing around 2000 aminoacids. It contains four homologous internal repeats of about 300 aminoacids (I to IV, fig.2). Each repeat contains 6 hydrophobic regions which are believed to be the membrane spanning regions S1 to S6, one of which (S4) is positively charged (it posseses 4 to 8 basic

aminoacids, arginine or lysine located at every third position) and is supposed
to be the voltage sensor.

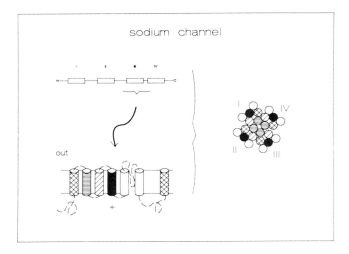

Fig.2: Proposed structure of the sodium channel. Upper left panel: the sodium
channel α-subunit is made of a string of 4 internally homologous repeats
indicated by the boxes labelled I-IV linked by cytoplasmic bridges. Lower left
panel: Each repeat (here repeat III) is made of 6 membrane spanning segments
shown here as a linear sequence of cylinders (S1 to S6) where the black cylinder
marked with a + sign is S4, the proposed voltage sensor. The cross-hatched
cylinder on the right corresponds to repeat IV. The interrupted line correspond
to the hydrophilic links between the membrane spanning segments. Right panel:
Proposed structure of the sodium channel (viewed the top, perpendicular to the
membrane). The pore would be located in the middle, surrounded by the 4 units
of homology. The transmembrane segments are shown as circles and are filled as
in the lower left panel.(modified from 6 and 7).

Deltamethrin induced single sodium channel activity

   As mentioned in the introduction, the depolarizing effect of pyrethroid
molecules correpond to an increase of the resting sodium conductance. Fig. 3
shows the activity of a single sodium channel induced by 1 μM deltamethrin
applied onto a cultured insect neurone. The properties of these channels are
different from those of normal voltage sensitive sodium channels (voltage-
dependency, selectivity, time course and conductance).

CONCLUSION

   The above examples illustrate some of the potentialities of molecular
neurobiology in the field of insecticide research. Other insect channels and
receptors are being characterized and studied and can now be compared with
their vertebrate counterparts (see 8). Most of them are highly conserved in

evolution but significant differences are also found which could be used to design new and selective insecticides.

This rational approach should not however be considered as a substitute for the more traditional techniques, but rather as an alternative and as an additional step in the search for novel insecticides, and in long term planning of insecticide research. Since it requires the knowledge of the possibitilies as well as of the limitations of a wide variety of techniques, it is reasonable to assume that its use will be, at leat momentarily, restricted to a few Institutions (mainly academic). The future probably resides, here again, in a collaboration between University and Industry.

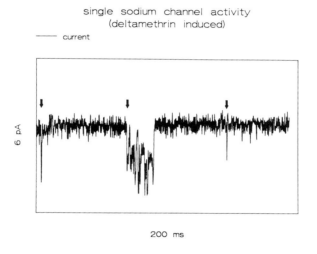

Fig. 3. Single sodium channel activity induced by 1 µM deltamethrin in a cockroach neurone. Arrows indicate the openings. Note the complex nature of the second event.

REFERENCES

1.   Casida JE (1989) Pesticide mode of action: implications of a finite number of biochemical targets. This volume.

2.   Pichon Y, Guillet JC, Heilig U, Pelhate M (1985) Pesticide Sci 16:657-640

3.   Pichon Y, Pelhate M (1985) in: StJohn JB, Berlin E, Jackson PE (eds) Frontiers in Membrane Research in Agriculture. Beltsville Symposium 9. Rowman and Allanheld, Totowa, pp 421-438.

4.   Pichon Y, Pelhate M, Heilig U. (1987) in: Hollingworth RM, Green MB (eds) Sites of Action of Neurotoxic Pesticides. ACS, Washington, pp 219-225.

5.   Salkoff L, Butler A, Wei A, Scavarda N, Baker K, Pauron D, Smith C (1987) TINS 10:522-527.

6. Noda M, Ikeda T, Kayano T, Suzuki H, Takeshima H, Kurasaki M, Takahashi H, Numa S (1986) Nature 230:188-192

7. Aldrich RW (1989) Nature 339:578-579

8. Lunt GG (1988) Neurotox '88: Molecular Basis of Drug and Pesticide Action. Excerpta Medica, Amsterdam

© 1990 Elsevier Science Publishers B.V. (Biomedical Division)
Pesticides and alternatives, editor J.E. Casida

EXPLOITATION OF MITE BIOCHEMICAL TARGETS BY ACARICIDES

CHARLES O. KNOWLES

Department of Entomology, University of Missouri, Columbia, Missouri 65211 (USA)

INTRODUCTION

Plants are exposed to numerous stresses that affect adversely their growth, development, and maturation, and therefore their yield and utility as agricultural commodities. Some of these stresses arise from the interaction of plants with herbivorous mites. In this regard, several groups of mites are problematic, and the spider mites are among the most devestating (1). Spider mites are remarkably adaptable and have colonized successfully areas in many climatic regions. They have a wide host range; one species, for example, attacks over 150 crops worldwide. Their destructive power is related to a high reproductive potential and to the fact that they are "genetically plastic" with new races or strains continually being formed. In 1968, spider mites were referred to as the causative agents of a worldwide plague (2). The available evidence suggests that spider mites are even more of a problem today than in 1968. Moreover, spider mite populations thrive under warm, dry conditions; thus with the trend toward global warming, mite problems can be expected to worsen. Other mites also share with the spider mites some of these features with the result that pest mite populations generally are extremely difficult to manage.

Acaricides currently are essential components of mite management programs and will likely remain so for the foreseeable future. Most acaricides in use, like insecticides, are products of industrial empirical screening programs. In addition to discovering the acaricidal activity of certain members of the major classes of insecticides, these programs have yielded some specific acaricides. However, empirical screening is not as productive today as in the past, and a current trend is the attempt to synthesize new pesticides based on known biochemical and physiological differences between target and nontarget species. This approach to pesticide discovery is somewhat feasible with insecticides because the data base on insect biochemistry and physiology is substantial and is growing rapidly. In contrast, this approach is not possible with acaricides because the data base on mite biochemistry and physiology is woefully lacking. Also, the limited information that is available suggests that biochemical and physiological differences exist between insects and mites making it unlikely that rationally designed insecticides will have acaricidal action.

In contrast to the commercial insecticides that come from relatively few chemical classes, acaricides are found in many different groups (3). Their structural diversity will be illustrated with examples of some of these acaricides.

396

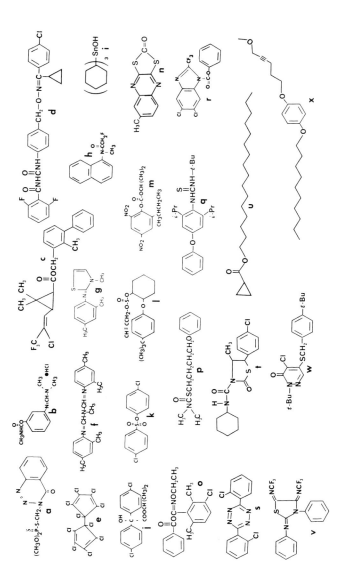

Fig. 1. Chemical structures for some acaricides.

The biochemical targets of acaricides will be mentioned with emphasis on those
few cases where this information has been obtained from mites. If little or no
data from mites are available, effects on insects and even other organisms will
be mentioned. In the context of potential sources of biochemical targets available for exploitation by acaricides, the mite nervous system has received the
most attention. Therefore, the current status of our knowledge of mite neurochemistry will be assessed.

ACARICIDES AND THEIR BIOCHEMICAL TARGETS

Acaricides are chemicals used to control pest arthropods in the subclass
Acari which is comprised of ticks and mites, the latter including both animal
and plant feeding species. It should be pointed out that some differences
exist in the response of the animal parasitic ticks and mites and the herbiv-
orus mites to acaricidal chemicals and that this paper is concerned mainly
with the latter organisms. The acaricides can be divided into the insectoacaricides and the specific acaricides. The distinguishing characteristic
between the two types is that at practical rates insectoacaricides are active
against both insect and acarine species, while the activity of specific acaricides is confined to acarines and usually to herbivorous mites.

Among the many organophosphates and carbamates are those that are active
against plant feeding mites. Azinphosmethyl (Fig. 1a) and formetanate hydro-
chloride (Fig. 1b) are examples of an organophosphate and carbamate, respectively, that have marked acaricidal activity. It seems that organophosphates and
carbamates owe their toxic action in mites mainly to inhibition of cholinester-
ase (ChE). This conclusion is based on the fact that ChE activity of several
mite species was inhibited in vitro by many of these compounds (4-21) and that
ChE activity was inhibited in vivo following exposures of twospotted spider mites
(TSSM), Tetranychus urticae Koch, to malathion (5) and formetanate (7).

Some pyrethroids have acaricidal action, but herbivorous mites generally are
not as susceptible to these compounds as are insects and animal parasitic mites
and ticks. In fact a problem encountered in the use of pyrethroid insecticides has been the induction of mite outbreaks (22,23). The early photostable
compounds, such as permethrin, cypermethrin, and fenvalerate, possess little
activity against herbivorous mites at rates used to control insects. Later
compounds like fenpropathrin, flucythrinate, and fluvalinate, are active, buc
chiefly against immature forms. However, bifenthrin (Fig. 1c), a relatively
new pyrethroid, has outstanding acaricidal and insecticidal activities (24).
Pyrethroids are neurotoxic in insects since they interfere with the voltage-
sensitive sodium channels associated with nerve membranes (25); however, no
studies of pyrethroid action in mites have been reported.

Diflubenzuron, the first substituted benzoylphenylurea introduced, is mainly insecticidal with acaricidal activity only against eriophyid mites (26). Optimization programs, however, have yielded compounds with much improved activity against mites. Examples are flufenoxuron and flucycloxuron (Fig. 1d) which are active against most important herbivorous mites and some insects. Flucycloxuron exerts its toxic action in insects by inhibiting the synthesis of chitin in immature stages (26). Its activity in mites also is confined to immatures, suggesting a mechanism of action similar to that in insects (27).

Several organochlorine compounds are toxic to mites. Endrin, although chiefly a broad spectrum insecticide, has been used widely to control the recalcitrant cyclamen mite, Stenotarsonemus pallidus (Banks) (28). Dienochlor (Fig. 1e) is a specific acaricide. Although the actions of these compounds in mites have not been examined, endrin has been found to antagonize the binding of dihydropicrotoxinin to nerve components of American cockroach, Periplaneta americana (L.), brain (29) and to inhibit weakly the calcium-magnesium ATPase activity of bertha armyworm, Mamestra configurata Walker, adult brain (30), whereas dienochlor has been observed to inhibit both sodium-potassium and magnesium ATPase activities of bluegill fish brain (31).

Amidine acaricides, of which chlordimeform was the forerunner, include the formamidines amitraz (Fig. 1f) and sulfamidine and the cyclic amidine cymiazole (Fig. 1g). Amitraz, like chlordimeform, is lethal to all life stages of most acarines but has a much narrower spectrum of lethal activity against insects (32,33). However, sublethal effects on feeding, dispersal, and reproduction can be observed in both acarine and some insect species (32,34). In insects, parent formamidines or certain of their metabolites or both have been shown to interact with octopamine and other biogenic amine receptors (35,36), and it seems likely that perturbation of octopaminergic transmissions in mites is involved in some of the actions of formamidines in these organisms, though definitive evidence is not yet available (34). Cymiazole, a compound whose mechanism of action apparently has not been studied, has shown acaricidal activity against two parasitic mites, Acarapis woodi (Rennie) and Varroa jacobsoni Oudermans, of honey bees, Apis mellifera L. (37,38).

Fluenethyl and Nissol® (Fig. 1h) are two organofluorines that have acaricidal activity. Fluenethyl had a rather short commercial life, and the use of Nissol has been confined mainly to Japan. Both compounds have been shown to cause accumulation of citrate in TSSM and house flies, Musca domestica L., and it was concluded that inhibition of aconitase by their monofluoroacetic acid metabolite was mainly responsible for the toxic action (39,40).

Several organotins including cyhexatin (Fig. 1i), fenbutatin oxide, and azocyclotin are specific acaricides. Cyhexatin inhibited TSSM magnesium ATPase at low concentrations but was stimulatory at high concentrations (41).

The carbinoles are specific acaricides and include dicofol, chlorobenzilate, chloropropylate (Fig. 1j), and bromopropylate. Chlorobenzilate interfered with the binding of the muscarinic acetylcholine (ACh) receptor antagonist quinuclidinyl benzilate (QNB) to membranes from house fly brains (42) and inhibited sodium-potassium and magnesium ATPases of bluegill fish brain (31).

Several organosulfurs have acaricidal activity. They include the sulfonate ovex or chlorfenson (Fig. 1k); the sulfone tetradifon; the sulfides tetrasul and chlorbenside; and the sulfites aramite and propargite (Fig. 1l). Ovex, chlorbenside, and aramite have been shown to inhibit ATPases from TSSM or bluegill fish brain or both (31,41).

Dinitrophenol derivatives such as dinocap, binapacryl, dinobuton (Fig. 1m), and dinitrocyclohexylphenol also have acaricidal activity. Little is known of their specific action in mites, but dinitrophenols are uncouplers of oxidative phosphorylation in other organisms (43).

There is a substantial number of other synthetic organic acaricides. They include oxythioquinox (Fig. 1n), a quinoxaline (44); benzomate (Fig. 1o), a benzohydroximate (45); fenothiocarb (Fig. 1p), a thiocarbamate (46); diafenthiuron (Fig. 1q), a thiourea (47); fenazaflor (Fig. 1r), a benzimidazole (48); clofentazine (Fig. 1s), a tetrazine (49); hexythiazox (Fig. 1t), a oxothiazolidinecarboxamide (50); cycloprate (Fig. 1u), a cyclopropanecarboxylate (51); flubenzimine (Fig. 1v), a diaryl thiazolidine (52); NC-129 (Fig. 1w), a pyridazinone (53); JH-388 (Fig. 1x), an alkyl, aryl ether (54); and others. Although a few of these compounds also possess some insecticidal activity, most are specific acaricides. Some are toxic to all life stages; others are active mainly against immature stages. Except for oxythioquinox, which was shown to bind irreversibly to TSSM homogenates (55) and to inhibit Madagascar cockroach, Gromphadorhina portentoso, phosphodiesterase (56), and fenazaflor, which was shown to uncouple TSSM oxidative phosphorylation (57), little information is available on their mode of action.

Several products isolated from microorganisms have acaricidal activity. Tetranactin, a macrotetrolide antibiotic isolated from the culture broth of the actinomycete Streptomyces aureus, was the first pesticidal antibiotic commercialized, having been marketed in Japan in 1973 (58). Tetranactin is toxic to adults of several pest mites; however, it is inactive against mite eggs and insects. Its action, which was elucidated on preparations of a tolerant cockroach species, is thought to be due to uncoupling of oxidative phosphorylation by virtue of its ability to complex with potassium ions (58).

The nikkomycins, secondary metabolites from a strain of Streptomyces tendae, possess acaricidal, insecticidal, and fungicidal activities (59,60). The acaricidal activity of certain members of this group, e.g., nikkomycins X, Z, and B, is expressed chiefly against eggs and immature stages of spider mites. The nikkomycins are structurally similar to uridine diphospho-N-acetyl-D-glucosamine and have been shown to be competitive inhibitors of chitin synthesis in the Tribolium confusum Jacquelin duVal and Phycomyces blakesleeanus assays (59). Inhibition of chitin synthesis is consistent with the lesions produced in nikkomycin-treated twospotted spider mites (61,62); however, effects on oogenesis also suggest an influence on protein synthesis (62).

The avermectins are macrocyclic lactones isolated from the fermentation broth of Streptomyces avermitilis; some, e.g., abamectin, possess good activity against mites and some insects (63). Their mode of action in mites apparently has not been examined, but they have been shown to open directly putative chloride channels in American cockroach muscle and central nervous system (29).

The Bacillus thuringiensis β-exotoxin or thuringiensin is an acaricide and insecticide. It acts as a growth regulator and also as an inhibitor of protein synthesis in insects and mites (64).

It is obvious that our knowledge of the mode of action of acaricides in mites is very limited. The major reason for this paucity of information is related to the small size of these organisms. Since dissection of discrete tissues is impractical, biochemical studies often must use whole homogenates of many mites and some biochemical systems have proven to be very difficult to assay under these conditions. Moreover, symptoms of acaricide poisoning in mites are not easily discerned making it difficult to establish causal relationships between in vitro biochemical effects and some manifestations of toxicity. Therefore, organisms other than mites, e.g., insects, have often been used in the study of acaricides. Studies of this type can yield valuable information in some cases. However, to conclude from such studies that a biochemical effect observed in a nonacarine will be of toxicological consequence in a mite could be problematic. Before definitive conclusions can be drawn regarding the mode of acaricidal action of a particular compound, the biochemical lesion should be demonstrated in mites and the effect(s) should be correlated with toxicity, the above difficulties encountered when working with these organisms notwithstanding.

MITE NEUROCHEMISTRY

The mite nervous system has been the subject of some research. The existence in mites of a cholinergic system seems certain, because the presence in some of these organisms of several of the essential components has been demonstrated. Further, the high toxicity to mites of compounds such as organophosphates and carbamates that are known to exert their action in other organisms by perturbation of cholinergic transmission lends support to this contention. The enzyme

ChE, which is responsible for degradation of ACh, was the initial component of this system to be examined in mites. In 1955, Casida (20) showed that whole homogenates of the grain mite, Acarus siro L., hydrolyzed several esters of choline and that ACh deacetylation was inhibited to some extent by the carbamate eserine and the organophosphate tetraethylpyrophosphate. This appears to be the initial demonstration of ChE activity in a mite species. However, most of the research on mite ChE's has been done on spider mites. Substrate specificity studies with the TSSM, carmine spider mite, T. cinnabarinus (Boisduval), Kanzawa spider mite, T. kanzawai Kishida, and the citrus red mite, Panonychus citri (McGregor), have revealed that the hydrolysis rate of choline and thiocholine esters decreased in the order propionyl>acetyl>butyryl (8,11,18,19,65, 66), except for that in an organophosphate resistant strain of carmine spider mite which decreased in the order acetyl>propionyl>butyryl (18). Acetyl-β -methylcholine (MeCh) was hydrolyzed more slowly than the choline esters by TSSM (11,19). ChE substrate specificity has been examined in only two mite species other than spider mites. The wet grain mite, Sancassania berlesei (Michael) degraded choline esters in the order acetyl>butyryl>propionyl (19,67), whereas the order was acetyl>propionyl>butyryl for the bulb mite, Rhizoglyphus echinopus (Fumouze and Robin) (68). Both mites also hydrolyzed MeCh. Moreover, these two mite species were tolerant to several organophosphates (19,69). Apparently the esteratic site of ChE's in mites with target site resistance to organophosphates is smaller than that in susceptible mites (18,19). This view is supported by the fact that dimethyl-substituted organophosphates are usually much better than diethyl-substituted compounds as inhibitors of ChE from organophosphate tolerant mites (18,19,68). Thus it seems that in mites the typical ChE substrate specificity pattern is that observed in organophosphate susceptible strains with propionylcholine being the preferred acylcholine ester in in vitro assays. However, the significance of this observation relative to the endogenous acylcholine substrate currently is inexplicable.

Early studies indicated that hydrolysis of ACh by mite ChE was not inhibited by excess substrate (11,70,71). However, a more recent study using partially purified ChE demonstrated excess substrate inhibition and suggested that interpretation of some of the results of earlier studies was confounded by the contribution of more than one ACh-hydrolyzing enzyme (15). A fascinating observation on mite ChE's was that of Blank and Osborne (19) who reported that TSSM and wet grain mite homogenates each contained separate enzymes that hydrolyzed ACh and MeCh. They also indicated that the ChE that hydrolyzed MeCh (acetyl-β -methylcholinesterase) was more susceptible than was the ChE that hydrolyzed ACh (acetylcholinesterase) to inhibition by organophosphates. These unusual observations were made on the basis of additivity of ACh and MeCh activities

in mixed substrate experiments using the Hestrin technique and on the fact that
MeCh hydrolyzing activity from the two mite species was more sensitive to inhibition in vitro by two organophosphates than was that of ACh (19). Electrophoretic studies did not substantiate this interpretation, although several ChE
isozymes were found in preparations from both mite species (67). Thus, the evidence upon which the observation of the two types of mite ChE's rests is tenu-
ous, and more research along these lines clearly is necessary before this interpretation can be generally accepted. Finally it should be mentioned that some
mite ChE's do not appear to be especially sensitive to eserine. For example, a
final eserine concentration of 1.0 mM yielded only 20% inhibition of ACh hydrolysis by bulb mite homogenates (68). However, some spider mite ChE's are inhibited by this carbamate (8,11,12,15). It is noteworthy that classical insect
acetylcholinesterases hydrolyze cholinesters in the order acetyl>propionyl>buty-
ryl, show excess substrate inhibition, and are sensitive to eserine (72).
Therefore, some differences between mite and insect ChE's apparently exist.

ACh, the endogenous substrate for ChE in insects, has been found in extracts
of TSSM at a concentration of 25 µg/g whole mites (73), and Mehrotra (74) suggested that if cholinesters other than ACh were present in TSSM, they must be
present in very low concentrations. Both ACh and MeCh were reported in extracts
of wet grain mite homogenates (75). Subsequent research using similar techniques confirmed the presence in this species of ACh but not MeCh (67).

Choline acetyltransferase (CAT) is the enzyme responsible for synthesis of
ACh. TSSM homogenates synthesized ACh from radioactive choline in presence of
an acetyl donor (74), and acetylated six analogs with dimethyl or diethyl N-sub-
stituents (76). Bulb mite homogenates fortified with choline and radioactive
acetyl coenzyme A (AcCoA) also synthesized ACh, indicating the presence of CAT
in this mite species (68).

ACh receptors are essential components of a cholinergic system, and only one
study in this area with mites has been conducted. Huang and Knowles (77)
studied the binding of tritiated QNB to the 5,000 g pellet from bulb mite homogenates. Specific binding, as defined by atropine, had high affinity and was
rapid, saturable, and reversible. QNB specific binding was strongly inhibited
by muscarinic antagonists and agonists but not by nicotinic ligands. Therefore,
the presence in bulb mite of putative muscarinic ACh receptors seems likely.

With regard to mite aminergic systems, Knowles et al. (78) subjected bulb mite
extracts to high performance liquid chromatography coupled to an electrochemical
detector and demonstrated the presence of octopamine (OCT) at 2.3 ng/g and dop-
amine (DA) at 4.3 ng/g wet weight. Epinephrine, norepinephrine, tyramine, N
-methyldopamine, N-acetyldopamine, and 5-hydroxytryptamine (5-HT), if present,
were below the limits of detectability (∿0.1 ng/g).

Monoamine oxidase (MAO) and N-acetyltransferase (NAT) are two enzymes that inactivate biogenic amines. Beeman et al. (79) found that homogenates of the
cheese mite, Tyrophagus putrescentie (Schrank), degraded tryptamine (TRY); formation of the aldehyde metabolite indicated the presence of MAO activity. Scott
and Knowles (80) observed that bulb mite homogenates degraded 2-phenylethylamine
(PEA)>TRY>5-HT>OCT. Because activity toward PEA was inhibited almost completely
by 0.1 mM pargyline and tranylcypromine, two known MAO inhibitors, they indicated that Type B MAO was present in bulb mites. This conclusion was corroborated by Kadir and Knowles (81) who found that PEA metabolism by bulb mite
homogenates was preferentially inhibited by deprenyl, a selective inhibitor of
Type B MAO, but not by clorgyline, a selective Type A MAO inhibitor.

When fortified with AcCoA, cheese mite (79) and bulb mite (81) homogenates
degraded TRY and PEA, respectively, to their corresponding N-acetyl metabolites,
indicating the presence of NAT activity in these two acarine species. Bulb mite
homogenates also possessed NAT activity toward TRY, DA, OCT, and 5-HT, but PEA
clearly was the preferred in vitro substrate. Thus, cheese mites and bulb mites
possess at least two enzymes capable of inactivating biogenic amines. This is
especially interesting since attempts to demonstrate the presence of MAO in insects often have not been successful, and it is currently thought that NAT and
not MAO is the major biogenic amine inactivating enzyme in insects (82).

There have apparently been no published studies of putative aminergic receptors in mites. The presence of a GABAergic system in mites can only be inferred
from the fact that certain organochlorine and avermectins, which are toxic to
insects and which interfere with insect GABAergic transmission, also are toxic
to some mites. Little else has been published on mite neurochemistry.

SUMMARY AND CONCLUSIONS

New acaricidal chemicals as well as other control measures are needed for successful management of pest mite populations. As far as chemicals are concerned,
most of the major groups of insecticides contain compounds that also are active
against mites; however, there are compounds from a number of other groups that
are active against mites but not against insects (specific acaricides). Therefore, it appears that mites are vulnerable to more diverse types of chemicals
than are most insects. This variance in susceptibility to chemicals between
mites and insects is indicative of biochemical and physiological differences
between them and suggests that more intensive research on acaricide mode of
action and on mite biochemistry and physiology might generate information that
could be used in the design of novel, specific acaricides. An enhanced data
base such as this also could contain information on mites that would be helpful
in the search for alternatives to chemical acaricides. In any event, it is

404

clear that both the search for new targets for acaricide chemicals and for alternatives to chemicals will require a substantive data base, particularly in the areas of physiology and biochemistry. Management of pest mite populations in the 21st Century will be a most difficult and challenging endeavor.

ACKNOWLEDGEMENT

This paper is a contribution from the Missouri Agricultural Experiment Station, Columbia, MO. Journal Series No. 10914.

REFERENCES

1. Jeppson LR, Keifer HH, Baker EW (1975) Mites Injurious to Economic Plants, Univ of Calif Press, Los Angeles

2. Anonymous (1968) Chemagro Courier, No. 2, 24-25, 31

3. Knowles CO (1975) In: Street JC (ed) Pesticide Selectivity. Marcel Dekker, New York, pp 155-176

4. Voss G, Matsumura F. (1964) Nature 202:319-320

5. Matsumura F, Voss G (1964) J Econ Entomol 57:911-917

6. Herne DHC, Brown AWA (1969) J Econ Entomol 62:205-209

7. Knowles CO, Ahmad S (1971) Pestic Biochem Physiol 1:445-452

8. Aziz SA, Knowles CO (1974) J Kans Entomol Soc 47:239-243

9. McEnroe WD (1963) In: Naegele JA (ed) Advances in Acarology. Comstock Pub Assoc, Ithaca, New York, Vol 1, pp 214-224

10. Voss G, Dauterman WC, Matsumura F (1964) J Econ Entomol 57:808-811

11. Voss G, Matsumura F (1965) Can J Biochem 43:63-72

12. Smissaert HR (1964) Science 143:129-131

13. Smissaert HR (1965) Nature 205:158-160

14. Ballantyne GH, Harrison RA (1967) Entomol Exptl Appl 10:231-239

15. Smissaert HR, Voerman S. Oosterbrugge L, Renooy N (1970) J Agric Food Chem 18:66-75

16. Schoneich D (1970) Zeit Angew Zool 57:97-119

17. Zahavi M, Tahori AS (1970) Biochem Pharmacol 19:219-225

18. Zahavi M, Tahori AS, Klimer F (1971) Molec Pharmacol 7:611-619

19. Blank RH, Osborne GO (1979) N Z J Agric Res 22:491-496

20. Casida JA (1955) Biochem J 60:487-496

21. Hastings FL, Dauterman WC (1976) J Econ Entomol 69:69-72

22. Penman DR, Chapman RB (1988) Exptl Appl Acarol 4:265-276

23. Gerson U, Cohen E (1989) Exptl Appl Acarol 6:29-46

24. Plummer EL (1984) In: Magee PS, Kohn GK, Menn JJ (eds) Pesticide Synthesis Through Rational Approaches. ACS Symposium Series 255, Washington DC, pp 297-320

25. Soderlund DM, Bloomquist JR (1989) Ann Rev Entomol 34:77-96

26. Grosscurt AC, ter Haar M, Jongsma B, Stoker A (1988) Pestic Sci 22:51-59

27. Scheltes P, Hofman TW, Grosscurt AC (1988) Proc Brighton Crop Protection Conf 1:559-566

28. Helle W (1984) In: Griffiths DA, Bowman CE (eds) Acarology VI. Ellis Horword, England, Vol 1, pp 122-131

29. Matsumura F, Tanaka K, Ozoe Y (1987) In: Hollingworth RM, Green MB (eds) Sites of Action for Neurotoxic Pesticides. ACS Symposium Series 356, Washington DC, pp 44-70

30. Luo M, Bodnaryk RP (1988) Pestic Biochem Physiol 30:155-165

31. Cutkomp LK, Desaiah D, Koch RB (1972) Life Sci 11:1123-1133

32. Knowles CO (1982) In: Coats JR (ed) Insecticide Mode of Action. Academic Press, New York, pp 243-277

33. Knowles CO (1983) In: Miyamoto J, Kearney PC (eds) Pesticide Chemistry: Human Welfare and the Environment. Pergamon Press, Oxford, Vol 1, pp 265-270

34. Knowles CO (1987) In: Hollingworth RM, Green MB (eds) Sites of Action for Neurotoxic Pesticides. ACS Symposium Series 356, Washington DC, pp 174-190

35. Hollingworth RM, Johnstone EM (1983) In: Miyamoto J, Kearney PC (eds) Pesticide Chemistry: Human Welfare and the Environment. Pergamon Press, Oxford, Vol 1, pp 187-192

36. Downer RGH, Gole JWD, Orr GL (1985) Pestic Sci 16:472-478

37. Eischen FA, Vergara C, Dietz A, Cardoso-Tamez D (1988) Apidologie 19:367-376

38. Eischen FA, Cardoso-Tamez D, Dietz A, Ware GO (1989) Apidologie 20: 41-51

39. Johannsen FR, Knowles CO (1972) J Econ Entomol 65:1754-1756

40. Johannsen FR, Knowles CO (1974) Gen Pharmacol 5:101-110

41. Desaiah D, Cutkomp LK, Koch RB (1974) Life Sci 13:1693-1703

42. Shaker N, Eldefrawi A (1981) Pestic Biochem Physiol 15:14-20

43. Corbett JR (1974) The Biochemical Mode of Action of Pesticides, Academic Press, Inc., New York

44. Sasse KA (1960) Hofchen-Briefe 13:197

45. Ando M (1978) Japan Pestic Inf No. 34, 14-21

46. Ogawa H, Miyaki T, Tamaru M, Fujimori K (1981) Appl Entomol Zool 16:335-344

47. Streibert HP, Drabek J, Rindlisbacher A (1988) Proc Brighton Crop Protection Conf 1:25-32

48. Anonymous (1969) Fisons Corp. Technical data sheet for Lovozal miticide

49. Brooker PJ, Parsons JH, Reid J, West PJ (1987) Pestic Sci 18:179-190

50. Anonymous (1984) Japan Pestic Inf No. 44, 21-24

51. Staal GB, Ludvik GF, Nassar SG, Henrick CA, Willy WE (1975) J Econ Entomol 68:91-95

52. Bluett DJ, Wainwright A (1981) Proc 1981 British Crop Protection Conf 75-81

53. Hirata K, Kudo M, Miyake T, Kawamura Y, Ogura, T (1988) Proc Brighton Crop Protection Conf 41-48

54. Puppin O, Caprioli V, Longoni A, Massardo P, Reggiori F (1983) Proc. 1983 Brit Crop Protection Conf 437-444

55. Aziz SA, Knowles CO (1973) J Econ Entomol 66:1041-1045

56. Rojakovick AS, March RB (1976) Pestic Biochem Physiol 6:10-19

57. Corbett JR, Wright BJ (1970) Pestic Sci 1:120-123

58. Ando K (1979) Japan Pestic Inf No. 36, 36-40

59. Cruger W, Frommer W, Goelker C, Kaiser J-W, Moeschler H-F, Salcher O, Schedel M, Wehlmann H (1985) Pflanzenschutz-Nachrichten 38:305-348

60. Zoebelein G, Kniehase U (1985) Pflanzenchutz-Nachrichten 38:203-304

61. Mothes U, Seitz K-A (1982) Pestic Sci 13:426-441

62. Mothes-Wagner U (1984) Pestic Sci 15:455-461

63. Campbell WC, Burg RW, Fisher MH, Dybas RA (1984) In: Magee PS, Kohn GK, Menn JJ (eds) Pesticide Synthesis Through Rational Approaches. ACS Symposium Series 255, Washington DC, pp 5-20

64. Anonymous (1988) Abbott Labs Technical data sheet for DiBeta miticide, insecticide

65. Voss G (1959) Naturwiss 46:652

66. Motoyama N, Saito T (1968) Botyu-Kagaku 33:77-80

67. Blank RH (1976) Ph.D. Thesis. University of Canterbury, New Zealand

68. Errampalli DD, Knowles CO (1989) Unpublished results

69. Knowles CO, Errampalli DD, El-Sayed GN (1988) J Econ Entomol 81:1586-1591

70. Voss G (1960) Naturwiss 47:400-401

71. Dauterman WC, Mehrotra KN (1963) J Insect Physiol 9:257-263

72. Chadwick LE (1963) In: Eichler O, Farah A (eds) Handbuch der Experimentellen Pharmacologie. Springer-Verlag, Berlin, Vol XV, pp 741-798

73. Mehrotra KN (1961) J Insect Physiol 6:180-184

74. Mehrotra KN (1963) In: Naegele JA (ed) Advances in Acarology. Comstock Pub Assoc, Ithaca, New York, Vol 1, pp 209-213

75. Moore DG (1973) M.S. Thesis. University of Canterbury, New Zealand

76. Mehrotra KN, Dauterman WC (1963) J Insect Physiol 9:293-298

77. Huang Z, Knowles CO (1989) Unpublished results

78. Knowles CO, McKee MJ, Hamed MS, Experientia, In press

79. Beeman RW, Matsumura F, Kikukawa T (1979) Comp Biochem Physiol 64C:149-151

80. Scott JA, Knowles CO (1985) Exptl Appl Acarol 1:227-233

81. Kadir HA, Knowles CO, Comp Biochem Physiol, In press

82. Evans PD (1980) In: Berridge MJ, Treherne JE, Wigglesworth VB (eds) Advances in Insect Physiology 15:317-473

Resistance mechanism

© 1990 Elsevier Science Publishers B.V. (Biomedical Division)
Pesticides and alternatives, editor J.E. Casida

RESISTANCE POTENTIAL TO BIOPESTICIDES AND CONSIDERATION OF COUNTERMEASURES

GEORGE P. GEORGHIOU

Department of Entomology, University of California, Riverside 92521 (U.S.A.)

INTRODUCTION

Increasing incidence of pest resistance to conventional insecticides, and widespread public concern over the effects of chemicals on man and the environment, have generated an enormous interest in biopesticides as alternative pest control agents. Biotechnology companies are committing substantial resources to the discovery and genetic improvement of microbial toxins, and young ambitious scientists are staking their careers on research ranging from mode of action to effective use strategies for these products. The total cost of insecticides used worldwide in 1985 was estimated to be $4.26 billion[1]. Biopesticides sales, which now represent less than 1% of that total, have been estimated to reach 50% by the year 2000[2].

Three types of biopesticides are of considerable current interest (Fig. 1): Toxin proteins produced by bacteria, e.g. *Bacillus thuringiensis* (*B.t.*); macrocyclic lactones (avermectins, Ivermectins) produced by the actinomycete *Streptomyces avermetilis*[3]; and baculoviruses, e.g. nuclear polyhedrosis and granulosis viruses[4]. For a detailed list the reader is referred to Carlton[5]. The present paper is concerned with the prospects and risks for development of resistance to biopesticides by target organisms, and possible measures for extending the effective life of these products. Because of time constraints, I shall limit myself to the class of biopesticides that have attracted the greatest attention, namely the toxin proteins produced by *B.t.*

The molecular biology, biochemistry and toxicology of the individual toxins are being researched intensively in several laboratories (for recent reviews see[6,7]). Various aspects of the subject have also been discussed in several symposia volumes[4, 8-10].

Bacillus thuringiensis, as typified by the subspecies *kurstaki*, produces toxins in a parasporal body during sporulation. The parasporal body consists of a single bipyramidal crystal, with or without a smaller cuboidal inclusion. The bipyramidal crystal is composed of one or more proteins with a molecular size of 135 kDa, while the cuboidal inclusion typically consists of a single protein of 65 kDa. Upon ingestion by an insect, the 135 kDa protein, actually a protoxin, is solubilized from the bipyramidal crystal and then cleaved by midgut proteases to produce an active 65 kDa toxin. The cuboidal inclusion

410

protein, also 65 kDa in size, is active upon solubilization, and is toxic without further processing.

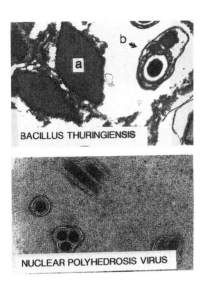

BACILLUS THURINGIENSIS

NUCLEAR POLYHEDROSIS VIRUS

AVERMECTIN B$_{1A}$

Fig. 1. Top: Electron micrograph of *Bacillus thuringiensis* subsp. *aizawa* bipyramidal crystal (a) and sporulated cell (b); middle: nuclear polyhedrosis virus nucleocapsids; bottom: chemical structure of Amermectin. (Top and middle photographs, courtesy of B. A. Federici).

It is known that the *B.t. kurstaki* strain HD-1, which is the one most commonly used in commercial preparations, contains at least three different toxin proteins[2]. In addition, the cuboidal inclusion contains one or two toxin proteins. Thus the parasporal body of *B.t. kurstaki* HD-1 contains at least four toxin proteins. Preparations from HD-1 are toxic to Lepidoptera.

411

Another subspecies, *B.t. israelensis* (*B.t.i.*) displays a spherical parasporal body containing at least four different proteins with sizes of, respectively 27.3, 65, 128, and 135 kDa[7,11]. Preparations from this subspecies are toxic to a small number of Diptera, especially mosquitoes and blackfly larvae. A third subspecies, *B.t. tenebrionis*, produces proteins that are toxic to a number of Coleoptera.

Concern over the probability for development of resistance to *B.t.* is understandable for a number of reasons. First, insects show considerable interspecific and intrapopulation variation in their susceptibility to *B.t.* toxins. Since a number of insect species are unaffected by certain subspecies and serotypes of *B.t.*, it would not be surprising if there also exist species with "marginal" sensitivity, which could easily be selected to a status of true, economic resistance[12]. Second, *B.t.* endotoxin preparations are currently being applied in the same fashion as synthetic pesticides. Thus, many of the biological, ecological and operational factors that influence the rate of development of resistance to synthetic insecticides[13,14] can be expected to also influence the development of resistance to biopesticides.

INFLUENCE OF MECHANISMS OF INSECTICIDE RESISTANCE

Insects have repeatedly demonstrated the ability to develop resistance to conventional insecticides. As reported in our latest compilation of information on the magnitude of resistance[15], at least 504 species of insects and mites are now resistant to one or more insecticides (Fig. 2).

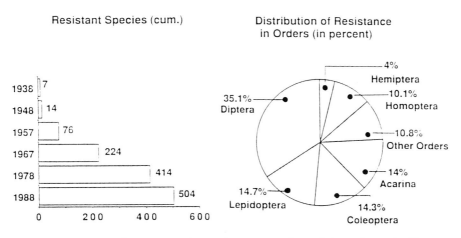

Fig. 2. Numbers of insecticide-resistant species of insects and mites arranged by decade (left), and their distribution in taxonomic Orders (right).

The majority of these species display multiple resistance, involving two or more classes of insecticide i.e. DDT, cyclodiene, organophosphate (OP), and carbamate, and at least 48 species now display resistance to pyrethroids, the last class of synthetic insecticides that has been introduced (Fig. 3).

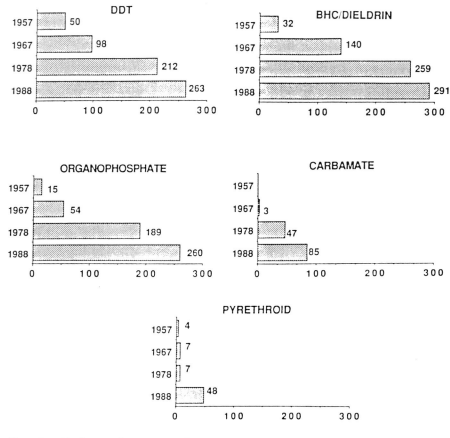

Fig. 3. Numbers of species of insects and mites with resistance to DDT, BHC/dieldrin, organophosphates, carbamates and pyrethroids, arranged by decade.

Since many of the economically important species are now multiply resistant and, therefore, possess genes for high levels of oxidase, esterase, and glutathione-S-transferase, it may be asked whether this background of metabolic systems enhances the probability of selection of resistance to $B.t.$

Fortunately, early work has demonstrated the absence of cross resistance to $B.t.$ in insecticide-resistant strains of insects. In a study by Sun et al.[16]

involving two strains of *Anopheles albimanus* and five strains of *Culex quinquefasciatus*, none showed cross resistance to *B.t.* despite the presence of high levels of resistance to OPs, carbamates, and pyrethroids due to multifunction oxidases, esterases, insensitive acetylcholinesterase (AChE) and kdr (Table I). These results have been extended by Carlberg & Lindstrom[17] who found that a *Drosophila melanogaster* strain resistant to DDT, BHC and nicotine was as susceptible to thuringiensin (β-exotoxin) as an insecticide-susceptible strain.

TABLE I

SUSCEPTIBILITY TO BTI IN MOSQUITOES RESISTANT TO CONVENTIONAL INSECTICIDES*

| | Insecticide | | BTI | |
Strain	Resistance Mechanism	Resistance Ratio (at LC_{50})	LC_{50} (ppm)	Resistance Ratio
	Culex quinquefasciatus			
Susceptible			0.15	
Propoxur-R	MFO	25	0.13	0.87
Temephos-R	Est.	320	0.07	0.47
t-permethrin-R	kdr	>4000	0.16	0.89
c-permethrin-R	kdr	450	0.12	0.80
	Anopheles albimanus			
Susceptible			0.86	
Parathion-R	AChE-R	84	1.0	1.2

*4th instars; 48-hr toxicity. (Source: Sun et al. 1980)

SELECTION FOR RESISTANCE TO *B.t.* IN THE LABORATORY

Selection of populations that have been colonized for extended periods of time are often unproductive, since such populations are at times subjected to unintentional bottle necks which restrict their genetic variability. However, if newly colonized, representative populations are employed, and selection consistently involves large numbers of individuals, such laboratory selections may reveal the types of resistance mechanisms that are likely to be obtained after more prolonged selection in the field.

Selection experiments with *B.t.* have been reported for at least 10 different species of insects (Table II). The lack of resistance development in several of these might be attributed to the use of highly inbred strains, or inadequate selection.

TABLE II
LABORATORY SELECTIONS OF VARIOUS SPECIES FOR RESISTANCE TO BACILLUS
THURINGIENSIS.*

Species	Toxin	Gen. (F)	R Level	Author	Year
Musca domestica	exotox.	27	none	Feigin	1963
" "	"	50	14x	Harvey	1965
" "	"	25	6x	Wilson	1968
Drosophila melanogaster	"	30	2.9x	van Herrewege	1969
" "	"	30	10x	Carlberg	1987
Aedes aegypti	endotox.	14	<2x	Goldman	1987
Culex quinquefasciatus	"	120	16.5x	Georghiou	1981-4
Anagasta kuehniella	"	7	none	Yamvrias	1962
Plutella xylostella	"	10	none	Deviendt	1976
Spodoptera littoralis	"	10	none	Sneh	1983
Ephestia cautella	"	21	7x	McGaughey	1988
Plodia interpunctella	"	3	3-29x	McGaughey	1985
" "	"	40	15-100x	McGaughey	1988
Heliothis virescens	"	14	20.5x	Stone	1989
	(130 kDa)				

*Adapted from Ref. 12.

Where some resistance was actually achieved, the levels
appeared to be low, thus contributing to optimism that resistance in field
populations, if selected, might not attain the levels observed with
conventional insecticides. However, more recently, a limited number of
studies have produced results showing that under certain conditions,
substantial resistance is likely to arise. By revealing the unique situations
under which selection could lead to resistance, these studies provide valuable
clues for designing resistance avoidance tactics and strategies.

Mosquitoes

We conducted four series of selections with *B.t.i.* on recently-colonized
populations of *C. quinquefasciatus* from southern California[18-21]. Series I, III
and IV were selected at about the 90% mortality level, whereas series II was
selected by gradually increasing pressure in an effort to prevent the possible
loss of any semi-recessive genes for resistance.

The four series of selections (I-IV) were maintained for 120, 36, 12 and 11
generations and attained maximal levels of resistance of 16.5x, 4.4x, 4.1x and

5.9x, respectively, at the LC_{95}. Resistance evolved far more slowly than had been experienced in earlier selections with conventional insecticides against this species in our laboratory. Series I and II initially produced increased susceptibility to *B.t.i.*, but beyond F_{10} a slowly evolving resistance became evident. In series I, which was maintained under selection pressure the longest, maximal resistance of 16.5x was obtained in the F_{46}, beyond which it maintained an oscillating plateau. Interestingly, when a subcolony, started from F_{92} of Series I, was subjected to further selection by a single toxin protein of *B.t.i.* (65 kDa), a substantial degree of resistance evolved relatively rapidly (20 generations). Resistance to the purified parasporal body (including all toxin proteins), however, remained relatively low (S.-M. Dai and S. S. Gill, personal communication). These results are consistent with work reported recently on *Heliothis virescens* referred to below.

The selections in series I-IV had no influence on susceptibility to OP insecticides. In fact, a low level of OP resistance, which existed in the respective parental population, was gradually lost in both the selected and control strains[22] in agreement with the known instability of esterase-mediated OP resistance in *C. quinquefasciatus*[23]. However, low levels of resistance to the carbamate propoxur and the pyrethroid permethrin, and a moderate level of resistance to DDT persisted in the *B.t.i.*-selected strain throughout the period of selection[22].

Tobacco budworm

Advances in molecular biology and genetic engineering during the past few years have stimulated considerable interest in genetic transformation of various organisms, especially plants, using toxin-encoding genes of *B.t.* Notable achievements have involved the transfer of toxin-encoding genes of *B.t.* subsp. *berliner* to tobacco plants, in which expression of the gene was sufficiently high to protect them from insect damage[24]. Likewise, the epiphytic bacterium *Pseudomonas fluorescens* has been transformed with the 130 kDa gene of *B.t.* subsp. *kurstaki*, var. HD-1.

Recently, Stone et al.[25] selected tobacco budworm, *H. virescens*, with lyophilized powder from the genetically engineered *P. fluorescens* strain by incorporating *P. fluorescens* powder into the diet of neonate larvae. A 24x level of resistance was obtained by generation F_7 and fluctuated between 13x and 20x thereafter. Interestingly, the selected strain showed only 3.6x resistance toward purified HD-1 endotoxin containing all four toxin proteins, and similarly low (3.8x) resistance to Dipel, a commercial product with the multiple toxins of HD-1. These results are in agreement with the observations on *C. quinquefasciatus* reported above.

Indianmeal moth

The most rapid and pronounced resistance to *B.t.* has been obtained through
laboratory selection of a strain of the Indianmeal moth, *Plodia interpunctella*
collected from grain silos in which *B.t.* was providing ineffective control[26,27].
Selection was based on seeding moth eggs in a larval medium in which a
concentration of *B.t.* (initially 62.5 mg/kg) was incorporated. A significant
level of resistance developed rapidly, mortality in the selected population
declining from 81% to 56% and 37% in the F_2 and F_3 generations, respectively.
Mortality fluctuated between 11% and 19% during generations F_5 to F_{15}. It was
calculated that these changes represented a 97x increase in LD_{50} within five
generations. When the selecting dose was increased to 500 mg/kg in a
subculture of F_{10}, resistance increased further to 310x. These results were
confirmed by additional selections on collections from Illinois, Iowa and
Nebraska[28]. Resistance was reported to be stable if selection was discontinued
after the resistance level had reached a plateau, but was unstable if
selection was interrupted earlier. On the basis of these results the authors
concluded that the Indianmeal moth could develop resistance to *B.t.* in storage
bins of treated grain "within a single season"[28].

Subsequent investigations on the spectrum of cross-resistance of *P.
interpunctella* to other *B.t.* isolates, revealed that cross resistance was
common toward isolates of subsp. *kurstaki* and *thuringiensis*, but rare or
absent toward subsp. *kenyae*, *galleriae*, *entomocidus*, *aizawai*, and *tolworthi*[29].

RESISTANCE TO *B.t.* IN FIELD POPULATIONS

Although *B.t.* subsp. *kurstaki* has been used in pest control in various
countries for some 20 years, especially against lepidopterous pests of
vegetable crops, no serious control failures have been reported to-date. A
possible explanation for this might be that *B.t.* treatments are not applied
consistently, many of the treated crops also receiving a number of
applications of conventional insecticides for control of pest species which
are not sensitive to *B.t.* Such discontinuity in use reduces the severity of
selection pressure and may be credited, in part, for the continuing
satisfactory performance of *B.t.*

Nevertheless, recent reports suggest a reduction of effectiveness of *B.t.*
against certain populations of the Indianmeal moth and the diamondback moth.
Treatment of certain farm grain bins and elevator silos by *B.t.* reduced
infestation of Indianmeal moth in wheat by only 50-60%[26,30]. It is not entirely
clear whether these difficulties are due to "marginal sensitivity" of certain
populations to *B.t.* (see above), or to the isolation of the grain storage
environment, which ensures more thorough selection of the populations. As

already described, further selection of a number of these populations in the
laboratory has provided clear evidence of resistance[27,28].

In Thailand, where the diamondback moth has become resistant to most
synthetic insecticides[31], B.t. is reported to have retained its effectiveness
despite increasing use[32]. However, concerns have been expressed regarding the
possible consequences of its overuse[33]. In the Philippines, Kirsch and
Schmutterer[34] reported "low efficacy" of a B.t. formulation (Thuricide HP)
against an isolated field population of P. xylostella and suggested that heavy
use of B.t. over several years may be responsible for the observed reduction
in effectiveness.

COUNTERMEASURES

It is apparent that despite early successes, the likelihood of resistance
to B.t. cannot be discounted. The development of resistance in the Indianmeal
moth, and the reported reduced effectiveness against populations of the
diamondback moth, indicate that some species are able to evolve resistance
against certain strains of B.t. It is also obvious, however, that the
existence of a variety of subspecies, strains, and toxins of B.t. offers
unique possibilities for countering the risks for resistance.

Principles for countering resistance to conventional insecticides have been
conveniently classified under three categories (management by moderation,
saturation, and multiple attack)[35,36], depending on whether (1) selection
pressure can be kept low and supplemented by non-chemical control measures
(moderation strategy); (2) the chemical can be applied at higher doses or with
synergists to render resistance functionally recessive (saturation strategy);
(3) different insecticides can be used in appropriate combinations or
rotations, taking advantage of low frequency of genes for resistance or of low
fitness in resistant individuals (multiple attack strategy). The rotation and
combination concepts appear especially appropriate in the case of B.t.

Based on the data available it is very likely that the use of two or more
toxins, encoded by different genes and acting at different receptor sites,
would allow fewer opportunities for survival in target populations, hence for
resistance, than the use of single toxins. This hypothesis is corroborated by
the high resistance obtained in C. quinquefasciatus and H. virescens through
laboratory selection with single toxins, and the preservation of relatively
high susceptibility in these strains to purified endotoxin. It is also
consistent with numerous field observations concerning the rapidity of
development of resistance to single-site acting pesticides (e.g. benzimidazole
fungicides) as opposed to multi-site acting products [e.g. those based on
copper, mercury, sulfur, etc. (review 37), and Cryolite insecticide].

418

Similarly, mathematical analysis and simulations indicate that simultaneous selection by two (or more) insecticides is more likely to delay the evolution of resistance than the tandem selection by these chemicals ([38], C. E. Taylor, personal communication, 1989).

These considerations are especially timely in view of the current interest to produce transgenic crop plants containing toxin-encoding genes of *B.t.*[39]. The risk for development of pest resistance, which may be expected to be high if such transgenic crop plants are grown on a large scale[40], would be even higher if single, instead of multiple, toxin genes are employed.

ACKNOWLEDGEMENTS

This investigation received financial support from the UNDP/WORLD BANK/WHO Special Program for Research and Training in Tropical Diseases, and from the University of California Mosquito Research Program.

REFERENCES

1.   Anonymous (1985) Farm Chemicals 148:26-34

2.   Wilcox DR, Shivakumar AG, Melin BE, Miller MF, Benson TA, Schopp CW, Casuto D, Gundling GJ, Bolling TJ, Spear BB, Fox JL (1986) In: Inouye M, Sarma E (eds) Protein Engineering: Applications in Science, Medicine and Industry. Academic press, London pp 395-413

3.   Burg RW, Miller BM, Baker EE, Birnbaum J, Currie SA, Hartman R, Kong Y-L, Monaghan RL, Olson G, Putter I, Tunac JB, Wallick H, Stapley EO, Oiwa R, Omura S (1979) Antimicrob Agents Chemother 15:361-367

4.   Granados RR, Federici BA, eds (1986) The Biology of Baculoviruses, Vol. I, CRC Press, Boca Raton, Florida

5.   Carlton BC (1988) In: Hedin PA, Menn JJ, Hollingworth RM (eds) Biotechnology for Crop Protection. American Chemical Society, Washington DC pp 260-279

6.   Höfte H, Whiteley HR (1989) Mibrobiol Reviews 53:242-255

7.   Federici BA, Lüthy P, Ibarra JE (1989) In: deBarjac H, Sutherland D (eds) Bacterial Control of Mosquitoes and Blackflies: Biochemistry, Genetics and Applications of *Bacillus thuringiensis* and *Bacillus sphaericus*. Rutgers University Press, New Brunswick, New Jersey

8.   Halvorson HO, Pramer D, Rogul M, eds (1985) Engineering Organisms in the Environment: Scientific Issues. American Society of Microbiology, Washington DC

9.   Hardy RWF ed (1987) Genetically Engineered Plants: Regulatory Considerations. Center for Science Information, San Francisco

10.   Headdin PA, Menn JJ, Hollingworth RM, eds (1988) Biotechnology for Crop Protection. American Chemical Society, Washington DC

11. Ibarra JE, Federici BA (1986) J Bacteriology 165:527-533

12. Georghiou GP (1988) In: Roberts DW, Granados RR (eds)
     Biotechology, Biological Pesticides and Novel Plant-Pest Resistance
     for Insect Pest Management. Boyce Thompson Institute for Plant
     Research, Ithaca, NY pp 137-145

13. Georghiou GP, Taylor CE (1977) J Econ Entomol 70:319-323

14. Georghiou GP, Taylor CE (1977) J Econ Entomol 70:653-658

15. Georghiou GP (1989) In: Moberg WK, LeBaron HM (eds) Fundamental
     and Practical Approaches to Combating Resistance. American Chemical
     Society, Washington DC (in press)

16. Sun C-N, Georghiou GP, Weiss K (1980) Mosquito News 40:614-618

17. Carlberg G, Lindstrom R (1987) J Invertebr Pathol 49:194-197

18. Georghiou GP (1981) In: Annual Report, Mosquito Control Research,
     University of California, pp 126-132

19. Georghiou GP (1983) In: Annual report, Mosquito Control Research,
     University of California, pp 86-90

20. Georghiou GP (1984) In: Annual Report, Mosquito Control Research,
     University of California, pp 96-99

21. Georghiou GP, Vazquez-Garcia M (1982) In: Annual Report, Mosquito
     Control Research, University of California, pp 80-81

22. Vazquez-Garcia M (1983) Ph.D. dissertation, University of
     California, Riverside

23. Georghiou GP, Lagunes A, Baker JD (1983) In: Miyamoto J, Kearney
     PC (eds) Fifth International Congress of Pesticide Chemistry,
     Kyoto, Pergamon Press, New York pp 183-189

24. Vaeck M, Reynaerts A, Höfte H, Janssens S, De Beuckeleer M, Dean C,
     Zabeau M, Van Montagu M, Leemans J (1987) Nature 327:33-37

25. Stone TB, Sims SR, Marrone PG (1989) J Invertebr Pathol 53:228-234

26. McGaughey WH (1985) J Econ Entomol 78:1089-1094

27. McGaughey WH (1985) Science 229:193-195

28. Mcgaughey WH, Beeman RW (1988) J Econ Entomol 81:28-33

29. McGaughey WH, Johnson DE (1987) J Econ Entomol 80:1122-1126

30. McGaughey WH, Dicke EB (1980) J Econ Entomol 73:228-229

31. Rushtapakornchai W, Vattanatangum A (1986) In: Proceedings of the
     1st International Workshop on Diamondback Moth Management. Taiwan
     pp 307-312

420

32.   Vattanatangum A (1988) In: Report of Meeting of Joint Research
       Project on Insect Toxicological Studies on Resistance to
       Insecticides and Integrated Control of the Diamondback Moth.
       Bangkok pp 8-13

33.   Miyata T, Sinchaisri N (1988) In: Report on Meeting of Joint
       Research Project on Insect Toxicological Studies on Resistance to
       Insecticides and Integrated Control of the Diamondback Moth.
       Bangkok pp 14-23

34.   Kirsch K, Schmutterer H (1988) J Appl Entomol 105:249-255

35.   Georghiou GP (1983) In: Georghiou GP, Saito T (eds) Pest
       Resistance to Pesticides. Plenum Press, New Yrok pp 769-792

36.   Glass EH ed (1986) Pesticide Resistance: Strategies and Tactics
       for Management. National Academy Press, Washington DC

37.   Ogawa JM, Manji BT, Heaton CR, Petrie J, Sonoda RM (1983) In:
       Georghiou GP, Saito T (eds) Resistance to Pesticides. Plenum Press,
       New York pp 117-162

38.   Mani GS (1985) Genetics 109:761-783

39.   Gasser CS, Fraley, RT (1989) Science 244:1293-1299

40.   Gould F (1988) BioScience 38:26-33

© 1990 Elsevier Science Publishers B.V. (Biomedical Division)
Pesticides and alternatives, editor J.E. Casida

BIOCHEMICAL AND DNA PROBING TECHNIQUES FOR MONITORING INSECTICIDE RESISTANCE
GENES

ALAN L DEVONSHIRE

AFRC Institute of Arable Crops Research, Rothamsted Experimental Station,
Harpenden, Herts, AL5 2JQ, United Kingdom

INTRODUCTION

The need for insecticide resistance monitoring programmes, and their
limitations, have been discussed by Roush and Miller (1). These programmes
have generally involved comparisons of LD_{50}'s or LD_{90}'s between field
populations and laboratory strains, and whilst useful for identifying a high
frequency of resistant individuals in the population such bioassays are very
inefficient for detecting incipient resistance. The use of a discriminating
dose of insecticide based on the LD_{99} of susceptible insects is better, but
even then as many as 1500 insects must be examined to be sure of detecting
resistance at a frequency of 1% in the population, and this is critically
dependent on the accuracy of the LD_{99} estimate. The number of insects would
fall dramatically (5-fold) if the dose were perfectly diagnostic (i.e. **all**
susceptible insects died and **all** resistant ones survived) but this is rare in
practice, and is unpredictable when new species are to be studied.

Whilst bioassays are essential for detecting resistance and measuring cross
resistance spectra, they can now be complemented by biochemical, immunological
and DNA probing techniques to identify resistance genes and their protein
products in individual insects (2,3). Such biochemical monitoring can give
more detailed information about the population being studied, but it is still
subject to the statistical considerations on sampling outlined above.

It is only when resistance has been confirmed by bioassay, and its
biochemical nature established that biochemical assays on individual insects
can be reliably employed to monitor resistance gene frequency. However, it is
important to remember that, unlike bioassays, which assess the insects'
response to the toxicant and thereby all the contributing biochemical and
physiological factors, biochemical assays can only give information about the
particular mechanisms chosen for study. This is restricted by our
understanding of the proteins responsible and by the methods available for
analysing them in the large numbers of insects necessary, which at present
relies predominantly on colour reactions for enzymes.

What then is the information required to justify the use of biochemical
assays for monitoring resistance genes? At its simplest, a thoroughly
established correlation between resistance and a particular biochemical marker
can support the use of that marker in resistance studies. However, since most

such assays involve the use of a model substrate *in lieu* of the insecticide, it
is preferable to confirm by detailed biochemical analysis that resistance is
caused by the enzyme being assayed (4,5). This is especially important for
polymorphic enzymes such as esterases and glutathione transferases, and it
should be done on each insect species to be studied if the credibility of this
approach is to be established and maintained.

In contrast, enzyme assays that measure directly the interaction between an
insecticide and its target protein can unequivocally identify a resistance
mechanism without needing further justification. However, at present this
applies only to acetylcholinesterase inhibition assays, and as discussed below
these are at the forefront of biochemical resistance monitoring. Even here, it
is not straightforward to equate the enzyme insensitivity factor directly with
the resistance factor in a bioassay since pharmacokinetic interactions with
common metabolic mechanisms can enhance or diminish the intrinsic resistance
due to the insensitivity of the target protein (6).

As with resistance monitoring based on bioassay, *in vitro* techniques must
also be capable of analysing many insects if a low frequency of resistance is
to be detected, and this has been facilitated by the development of 96-well
microplate technology. Whilst originally aimed primarily at immunoassay
techniques, the equipment is also well suited for the biochemical microanalysis
of many insects. A major recent development has been the kinetic microplate
reader, such as the Molecular Devices UVmax, and associated computer software
that enables the reactions in all 96 wells of the microplate to be monitored
simultaneously, and reaction rates computed rapidly from sequential readings
taken at intervals as short as five seconds (7). Complementing such
developments in 'high technology' is the availability of a simple manual device
for use with microplates that homogenizes 96 insects quickly and effectively,
and so allows rapid sample handling by use of multiple tip pipettors (8).

ENZYMES SUITABLE FOR RESISTANCE MONITORING
Degrading enzymes

Three major enzyme groups, the hydrolases, glutathione transferases and
mixed function oxidases, contribute to the degradation of insecticides, and
resistance can arise from changes in any of them (6). Unfortunately, none is
readily assayed in large numbers of individual insects by using insecticides as
substrates; to achieve the sensitivity needed would require the use of
radiometric and/or chromatographic assays to measure product formation (e.g.
aldrin epoxidation is measured using glc). Model substrates are therefore used
extensively since they give products that are readily assayed, usually
spectrophotometrically. It is quite straightforward to crush an insect and use
a model substrate to measure enzyme activity but as discussed above,

interpretation requires biochemical validation and correlation with bioassays. As examples of potential pitfalls, it has been shown that in houseflies the glutathione transferase responsible for conjugation of glutathione with the model substrate, CDNB (1-chloro-2,4-dinitrobenzene), is different from that effecting the dealkylation of diazinon (9); similarly, changes in the ubiquitous and variable naphthyl esterases need not reflect differences in insecticide hydrolysis or resistance (10).

Without doubt the enzyme group most widely assayed in resistance monitoring programmes are the esterases, and the substrates used most often are naphthyl esters. Resistance can be associated with substantial changes (increases or decreases) in activity of these enzymes sometimes involving quantitative changes in the titre of an enzyme due to gene amplification as in aphids (11,12) and mosquitoes (13), and sometimes involving mutation to give a modified enzyme that hydrolyses insecticides more effectively whilst also changing its catalytic activity to the model substrate, e.g. the mutant esterases of houseflies (6), blowflies (14) and mites (15). The esterase levels of insects taken from treated crops should be interpreted carefully since they can be influenced by *in vivo* inhibition of the enzyme(s). As an example, resistant whitefly with intrinsically high esterase activity that have survived exposure to an organophosphate residue on the crop have inhibited esterase levels characteristic of untreated susceptible insects (16). This inhibition can persist for several days even after the insects have been transferred to clean plants. It is clearly important to understand such effects if esterase measurements are to be used with confidence.

Target enzymes

In addition to those enzymes involved in the degradation of insecticides, resistance often involves changes in the target proteins themselves, rendering them less sensitive to disruption by the insecticide (6); this is best understood for acetylcholinesterase. Although there is considerable electro-physiological evidence for comparable changes in the sodium channels of insects showing nerve insensitivity to pyrethroids and DDT (often referred to as *kdr* or knockdown resistance), the biochemical basis remains to be established in each insect species (6). It is quite possible that nerve insensitivity could arise from a variety of biochemical causes, in which case it should be considered as a generic term comparable to 'metabolism'. Only when this mechanism is better understood biochemically can we hope to develop reliable and generally applicable methods for diagnosing it *in vitro*.

METHODS FOR CHARACTERIZING ENZYMES

The attributes of the methods already in use, or likely to become available in the foreseeable future, are summarized in Table I. A major consideration is

TABLE I

ATTRIBUTES OF *IN VITRO* METHODS FOR MONITORING INSECTICIDE RESISTANCE

Method	Simplicity/cheapness to: develop	validate	use	Robustness for field[b] use	Throughput	Sensitivity	Quality of information: Precision	Distinguishing: Enzyme forms	hetero- zygotes
Enzyme assays									
'Spot tests'									
filter paper	+++	+	+++	+++	+++	++	+	-	-
microplates[c]	+++	+	+++	+++	+++	+++	+++	-	-
Spectrophotometry	++	+	++	+	+	+++	+++	-	-
Electrophoresis[d]	+	+	++	-	+	+++	++	+++	++
Immunoassay[e]	-	+	+	+	+++	+++	+++	-	-
AChE kinetics[f]	+	+++	+	-	++	+++	+++	+++	+++
DNA probing[e]									
Dot blots	-	-	+	-	++	+	+	-	-
Southern blots	-	-	-	-	-	+	+	+++	+++

[a] worst, - + ++ +++, best; scores are based on a combination of experience and educated guesses, and are averaged over various circumstances (insect, enzyme, qualitative, large or small quantitative differences, precision required etc.).

[b] includes rudimentary laboratory facilities.

[c] attributes for microplates will vary greatly according to whether colour is assessed visually or by which type of microplate reader.

[d] scanning of electrophoresis gels is not practicable on the large scale required for such studies.

[e] data are available only for insects with amplified esterase genes; scores therefore represent the author's perception of these techniques' wider potential.

[f] using kinetic microplate reader; end point assays are simpler and more robust but the quality of information they give is not so good.

that they must be robust, especially if intended for 'field' use; this can be a limitation since the most incisive information comes from the more demanding biochemical techniques such as electrophoresis, accurate enzyme activity measurements or rapid enzyme kinetic analysis. 'Spot tests', including simple assays done in microtitre plates, give limited insight of the potentially diverse resistance mechanisms to be found in the field. Thus, the use of the simpler assays tends to engender simplistic interpretation. Ideally, biochemical assays should give quantitative data that can be analysed statistically to identify the multiple components in the population that can arise from both multiple alleles and multiple loci, together with their heterozygotes. The identification of heterozygotes as well as homozygotes for a resistance mechanism is particularly important since the former predominate in the critical early stages of resistance build up (17).

'Spot' tests

These have been used extensively to detect esterases and are considered to include not only the use of substrate-impregnated filter papers (18) but also assays done in tile wells (19) or microplates (20) that are assessed visually. They are aimed primarily at field use where they can give clearcut results if it is possible to define a 'discriminating activity' for identifying insects differing dramatically in enzyme content. However, if insects with the intermediate enzyme activities commonly found in the field are to be recognized with any degree of certainty, these simple assays must be assessed quantitatively. This is possible by using a densitometer to scan filter paper spots (21,22) or a microplate reader, but these adaptations dramatically reduce throughput, especially when using a portable battery-operated reader designed for manual use, and they can increase data handling requirements. It seems pointless to adopt the very simple and intrinsically less accurate filter paper spot test if it then becomes necessary to scan the filters in order to achieve useful results; the use of microplate assays is preferable, especially now that a rapid and efficient homogenizer is available for use in microplates (8), and multiple tip pipettors allow very rapid sample handling.

Another shortcoming of simple spot tests can be their sensitivity to temperature and this can be a major consideration when performing the assays in tropical regions. The end-point value for esterase assays can double on increasing the temperature from 20° to 30° in whitefly (Byrne and Devonshire, unpublished) or from 24° to 30° in mosquitoes (23). Although a correction can be made, e.g. by varying the incubation time according to the ambient temperature (23), this requires careful prior calibration for each esterase form and insect species to be studied.

Spectrophotometry

This has long been used to assess enzyme activities in individual insects

under temperature-controlled conditions (24). Assays can be based either on an
end point reading or by continuous recording of product formation. The former
allows higher throughput but linearity must be established beforehand. All
three relevant enzyme groups can be assayed in this way, e.g. mixed function
oxidases by the dealkylation of p-nitroanisole (25), glutathione transferases
(26) using CDNB or DCNB (3,4-dichloronitrobenzene), and esterases by the
hydrolysis of naphthyl esters (5,24). The continuous assay of naphthol
formation based on its UV (234 nm) absorption (5) is more flexible than the
established end point assay which relies on its reaction with a diazonium
salt. Mixed function oxidases can also be assayed fluorometrically by the
dealkylation of alkoxyresorufins (27). Although spectrophotometric assays
should remain a standard with which other methods are compared, they are
rapidly being replaced by the higher throughput, though less-precise, assays in
microplates. This has been stimulated by the recent availability of kinetic
microplate readers operating at wavelengths down to 340 nm.

Electrophoresis

Electrophoresis has also been used extensively for resistance monitoring,
primarily for studying esterases (19,28-31). It is a meeting point between
resistance monitoring and a well established technique for genetic analysis of
multiple forms of enzymes, usually of unknown evolutionary significance. The
technique serves two major roles; it can identify qualitative variants of an
enzyme that might be toxicologically significant but be indistinguishable in an
assay of total esterase activity. Secondly, it can detect small quantitative
changes in one particular isoenzyme that would otherwise be imperceptible
against the greater activity and variability of other isoenzymes if assayed in
a crude homogenate. For example in the peach-potato aphid, moderate levels of
resistance are caused by an increase of approximately four-fold in the amount
of one insecticide-detoxifying esterase (FE4) which cannot be unequivocally
distinguished in assays of total esterase activity but is clear when the
enzymes are visualized on electrophoresis gels (32). Allozymes of the
esterases associated with resistance in aphids (33) and mosquitoes (31) are
also revealed by electrophoresis. Similarly in houseflies, the presence or
absence (null allele) of an esterase ($E_{0.39}$) associated with resistance to
pyrethroids and some organophosphorus insecticides is only discernible after
electrophoresis (29). In blowflies, resistance to diazinon correlates with the
null allele of esterase E_3 which again requires electrophoretic analysis (14).

Disadvantages of electrophoresis include the time, equipment and expertise
required for reliable analysis, coupled with the semiquantitative nature of the
results which must be assessed subjectively; it is not practicable to produce
and handle quantitative data, on the large scale required, by using gel
scanning equipment. Although electrophoresis readily identifies 'allozyme

heterozygotes' it does not reliably distinguish 'null allele heterozygotes'
(29), nor individuals with similar degrees of gene amplification.

Immunoassay

This offers an attractive prospect for monitoring proteins involved in
resistance, but requires much more effort to develop; it is necessary not only
to identify the biochemical basis of resistance, but to purify sufficient of
the protein for preparing antibodies. In many cases this effort would not be
justified for enzymes that are readily measured by conventional colorimetric
assays. However immunoassays can serve the same purpose as electrophoresis by
allowing the relevant enzyme to be assayed without the background contribution
of other isoenzymes, so giving better resolution; they also have the advantage
of generating quantitative data. So far, this approach has been adopted only
for the amplified esterases of aphids (34) and mosquitoes (35), perhaps
reflecting the large amounts of these proteins available from the very
resistant insects.

The E4/FE4 immunoassay in aphids is similar to ELISA, but does not require
the second antibody/enzyme conjugate since the immobilized enzyme from the
aphid is readily detected by its own esterase activity (34). The assay has ten
times the throughput of electrophoresis and has been used for intensive studies
of resistance buildup and loss in aphid populations (reviewed in ref. 33).

An alternative approach based on dot-blot immunoassays on nitrocellulose
membranes was recently reported for estimating the esterase content of Culex
mosquitoes (35). This procedure appears to offer no advantage over microplate
immunoassay techniques; it suffers from large blot-to-blot variations, is not
so readily quantified, requires extensive serial dilutions of each homogenate
to achieve the range of sensitivity necessary, and in this case appears to give
no more information than conventional esterase determination. However, the
method might be more generally applicable to monitoring resistance caused by
proteins that are not readily detectable by their own intrinsic enzyme activity.

Although these examples in aphids and mosquitoes have established that
immunoassays can contribute to resistance monitoring, it remains to be seen
what impact they will have in detecting other less amenable resistance
mechanisms. A feature of immunoassays is their specificity, and this could be
a disadvantage since each mechanism is likely to require individual development
work. Thus there is no cross-reaction between the aphid E4 antiserum and
mosquito esterases (Devonshire and Moores, unpublished), and the antisera
against the two esterase types, A and B, of Culex do not cross-react (35).

Acetylcholinesterase inhibition kinetics

Acetylcholinesterase insensitivity measurements have long been a feature of
insecticide resistance research, but it is only in the last few years that such
assays have been applied to individual insects on a large scale in order to

measure resistance gene frequency in populations. Such studies, based on 'end-point' assays, distinguished sensitive and propoxur-insensitive forms of the enzyme in plant hoppers (36). Higher resolution was achieved by the first order kinetic analysis of inhibition progress curves for individual housefly acetylcholinesterase; this not only distinguishes multiple allelic forms of the enzyme, even when showing only low levels of insensitivity, but also identifies heterozygous insects from the curvature of the first order plot generated by the on-line microcomputer (37). However, set against this precision was the very low throughput of only 10-15 insects per hour. A method for detecting the extremely high insensitivity factors to propoxur in mosquitoes, again based on comparing 'end-point' assays of the enzyme in the presence and absence of this inhibitor (38), did not distinguish heterozygotes reliably and would be unlikely to detect other slightly insensitive forms of the enzyme.

Kinetic microplate readers can now enable assays that discriminate as well as the earlier kinetic method whilst giving the high throughput (100-200 insects per hour) required for population studies (7). Again, the acetylcholinesterase in each insect homogenate is assayed colorimetrically in the absence and presence of inhibitor and the on-line microcomputer fits linear regressions to the reaction curves; this *average* activity in the presence of inhibitor is then expressed as a percentage of the uninhibited rate, and distribution histograms generated for each population sampled. By determining the inhibition by more than one insecticide for each insect and expressing the data as bivariate plots instead of histograms, it is possible to distinguish all six genotypic combinations of a sensitive and two insensitive forms of the enzyme (7). Indeed, these methods have played a major role in establishing that the gene for this key enzyme in the nervous system can exist in multiple allelic forms within a species, not only in houseflies (37), but also in whiteflies and aphids (16,39). For arrhenotokous species such as whiteflies, analysis of the haploid males gives clearest results since they contain only one enzyme form. Whilst the method will clearly identify known heterozygotes, data for field-collected insects must be interpreted carefully since there may be other forms of the enzyme present. It seems likely that as these techniques are used more extensively, multiplicity of acetylcholinesterase forms will become apparent in many more species.

A variation on this technique has been proposed as a generic assay for detecting all types of resistance to organophosphates and carbamates (3). It involves exposure of insects *in vivo* to a dose of insecticide that will inhibit the acetylcholinesterase in susceptible insects after a predetermined time. Any insects showing residual acetylcholinesterase activity when homogenized are considered to have one or more resistance mechanisms that should then be identified by specific *in vitro* assays. The enzyme assay is thus used in place of the death of the insect as the 'response' in the bioassay. The value of this approach is difficult to assess from the limited reference to unpublished results in a review article (3).

DNA probes

The potential of DNA diagnostics for identifying resistance genes is obvious, but this technology should not be considered as a panacea. The mechanisms to be analysed in this way will require thorough characterization not only at the biochemical level but also by molecular biological methods, and in many cases it will be more straightforward to continue using biochemical monitoring techniques to complement bioassays. However, DNA probes will become an automatic spin off from the increasing fundamental research effort worldwide to understand the molecular genetics of resistance. This approach will no doubt benefit from the dramatic developments in medical diagnostics (40), although the economics of applying such techniques to many thousands of insects instead of people will not be so easily justified.

As with immunoassays, DNA probing of resistance genes has so far been developed only for insects producing very large amounts of esterase protein as a consequence of gene amplification. There is no advantage whatsoever in adopting this approach purely as an alternative to esterase assays. However, it has proved very useful for studying the esterase genes of *M. persicae* where very resistant aphid clones can spontaneously lose resistance as a consequence of producing some offspring in which the E4 genes remain amplified but are no longer transcribed (41). In esterase assays, such revertant aphids are indistinguishable from normal susceptible insects, but they do differ in that their amplified esterase genes can occasionally be 'switched on' again in some offspring (42). Insecticide selection can then act on the consequent variability leading to rapid recovery of resistance in these revertant clones, which does not occur in truly susceptible clones. Distinguishing the two types in field populations is therefore important, and this can now be achieved by complementing esterase immunoassays with DNA probing of dot blots, both done on each individual aphid (43).

The broader potential of DNA diagnostics for resistance genes is yet to be realized, but this work using the E4 DNA probe can give some indication of the applicability of the approach. Approximately 0.5 μg DNA is extracted from each aphid (i.e. 1 μg/mg insect); this is sufficient to detect, but not quantify accurately, the highly amplified genes in crude homogenates of individual insects by using dot blots. If the extracted DNA is to be digested with restriction enzymes and analysed by electrophoresis and Southern blotting, a more stringent cleanup procedure is necessary so that approximately 5 mg insect material is required (44). If single copy genes are to be studied, the specific sequences would probably need amplifying *in vitro* by the polymerase chain reaction (PCR) and this would add further complication and cost to the assays (40). Detecting qualitative changes in genes due to point mutations would then be feasible, but this would constitute the ultimate in specificity and be of very restricted value. DNA hybridization can be detected colorimetrically, e.g. by using biotinylated probes, but ^{32}P labelling gives better sensitivity (40) and this is a further constraint on the broad applicability of DNA diagnostics.

CONCLUSIONS

There is a place for all of these *in vitro* techniques for studying insecticide resistance, but they can only complement bioassays and not replace them. They will only detect particular resistance genes, a major limitation when used to monitor insect populations from the field, and one that is likely to become more important as increasingly specific methods such as immunoassays and DNA diagnostics are developed. Their greatest impact is likely to be on studying the buildup of known resistance genes in insect populations under various carefully defined conditions, as a means of developing and evaluating resistance management strategies.

ACKNOWLEDGEMENTS

I thank F J Byrne, L M Field and G D Moores for their useful comments on the manuscript.

REFERENCES

1. Roush RT, Miller GL (1986) J econ Ent 79:293-298
2. Brown TM, Brogdon WG (1987) Ann rev Entomol 32:145-162
3. Brogdon WG (1989) Parasitology Today 5:56-60
4. Devonshire AL (1977) Biochem J 167:675-683
5. Devonshire AL, Moores GD (1982) Pestic Biochem Physiol 18:235-246
6. Oppenoorth FJ (1985) In: Kerkut GS, Gilbert LI (eds) Comprehensive Insect Physiology, Biochemistry and Pharmacology, Vol. 12. Pergamon, Oxford, pp 731-773
7. Moores GD, Devonshire AL, Denholm I (1988) Bull ent Res 78:537-544
8. ffrench-Constant RH, Devonshire AL (1987) Biochem Genet 25:493-499
9. Clark AG, Shamaan NA, Sinclair MD, Dauterman WC (1986) Pestic Biochem Physiol 25:169-175
10. Hemingway J, Jayawardena KGI, Herath PRJ (1986) Bull WHO 64:753-758
11. Devonshire AL, Sawicki RM (1979) Nature 280:140-141
12. Field LM, Devonshire AL, Forde BG (1988) Biochem J 251:309-312
13. Mouchès C, Pasteur N, Bergé JB, Hyrien O, Raymond M, Robert de Saint Vincent B, de Silvestri M, Georghiou GP (1986) Science 233:778-780
14. Hughes PB, Raftos DA (1985) Bull ent Res 75:535-544

15. Anber HAI, Oppenoorth FJ (1989) Pestic Biochem Physiol 33:283-297

16. Byrne FJ, Devonshire AL, Rowland MW, Sawicki RM (1990) Proc 7th Int Congr Pestic Chem (IUPAC), in press

17. Roush RT, McKenzie JA (1987) Ann Rev Entomol 32:361-380

18. Pasteur N, Georghiou GP (1981) Mosq News 41:181-183

19. Sawicki RM, Devonshire AL, Rice AD, Moores GD, Petzing SM, Cameron A (1978) Pestic Sci 9:189-201

20. Brogdon WG, Beach RF, Stewart JM, Castanaza L (1988) Bull WHO 66:339-346

21. Rees AT, Field WN, Hitchen JM (1985) J Am Mosq Assoc 1:23-27

22. Pasteur N, Georghiou GP (1989) J econ Ent 82:347-353

23. Beach RF, Brogdon WG, Castanaza LA, Cordón-Rosales C, Calderón M (1989) Bull WHO 67:203-208

24. van Asperen K (1962) J Ins Physiol 8:401-416

25. Plapp Jr FW, Tate LG, Hodgson E (1976) Pestic Biochem Physiol 6:175-182

26. Oppenoorth FJ, van der Pas LJT, Houx NWH (1979) Pestic Biochem Physiol 11: 176-188

27. Vincent DR, Moldenke AF, Farnsworth DE, Terriere LC (1985) Pestic Biochem Physiol 23:171-181

28. Ozaki K, Kassai T (1970) Ent exp appl 13:162-172

29. Sawicki RM, Devonshire AL, Farnham AW, O'Dell K, Moores GD, Denholm I (1984) Bull ent Res 74:197-206

30. Chung TC, Sun CN (1983) J econ Ent 76:1-5

31. Pasteur N, Sinègre G, Gabinaud A (1981) Biochem Genet 19: 499-508

32. Devonshire AL (1975) Proc 8th Br Insectic Fungic Conf 1:67-73

33. Devonshire AL (1989) Pestic Sci 26:375-382

34. Devonshire AL, Moores GD, ffrench-Constant RH (1986) Bull ent Res 76:97-107

35. Beyssat-Arnaouty V, Mouchès C, Georghiou GP, Pasteur N (1989) J Am Mosq Cont Assoc 5:196-200

36. Hama H, Hosoda A (1983) Appl Ent Zoo 18:475-485

37. Devonshire AL, Moores GD (1984) Pestic Biochem Physiol 21:341-348

38. Hemingway J, Smith C, Jayawardena KGI, Herath PRJ (1986) Bull ent Res 76:559-565

39. Moores GD, Denholm I, Byrne FJ, Kennedy AL, Devonshire AL (1988) Proc Br Crop Prot Conf 1:451-456

40. Landegren U, Kaiser R, Caskey CT, Hood L (1988) Science 242:229-237

41. Field LM, Devonshire AL, ffrench-Constant RH, Forde BG (1989) FEBS Lett 243:323-327

42. ffrench-Constant RH, Devonshire AL, White RP (1988) Pestic Biochem Physiol 30:1-10

43. Field LM, Devonshire AL, ffrench-Constant RH, Forde BG (1989) Pestic Biochem Physiol 34:174-178

44. Field LM, Moores GD, Smith SDJ, Devonshire AL (1990) Proc 7th Int Congr Pestic Chem (IUPAC), in press

© 1990 Elsevier Science Publishers B.V. (Biomedical Division)
Pesticides and alternatives, editor J.E. Casida

INSENSITIVE ACETYLCHOLINESTERASE IN INSECTICIDE RESISTANT MOSQUITOES

B. C. BONNING
NERC Institute of Virology and Environmental Microbiology, Mansfield Road,
Oxford OX1 3SR, UK

As disease vectors of considerable public health importance, mosquitoes are the target of comprehensive control programmes worldwide. Culicine mosquito species include vectors of filariasis and numerous arboviruses such as yellow fever and dengue. Resurgence of malaria, transmitted by anopheline mosquitoes, is a major problem in many parts of the world: in 1981 there were an estimated 90 million cases, with associated loss of human life and capacity. Such problems are exacerbated by vector resistance to insecticides, which has increased in extent and intensity, considerably diminishing the effectiveness of vector control as an anti-malarial measure (1).

Of 113 mosquito species with insecticide resistance, multiple resistance, involving resistance to organochlorines, organophosphates, carbamates and pyrethroids, is known in at least 8 (2).Although more than 20 important vectors of malaria, have developed resistance to one or more insecticides, such chemicals still play a major role in the control of malaria transmission.

As for other insect pests, chemical control of mosquitoes has been directed primarily at disruption of nerve impulse transmission. In 1980, more than 96% of insecticidal production was composed of organophosphorus compounds, carbamates, chlorinated hydrocarbons and pyrethroids, all of which have deleterious effects on the nervous systems (3). DDT was initially used to great effect for mosquito control. However, widespread resistance to DDT and other chlorinated hydrocarbons along with environmental concern, lead to cessation of use of these compounds in many countries, and replacement with the more costly organophosphorus and carbamate insecticides. The target of these insecticides is acetylcholinesterase (AChE) which removes excess of the neurotransmitter acetylcholine (ACh) from the insect central nervous system synapses to prevent repetitive nerve firing. AChE catalyses hydrolysis of the ester bond in ACh.

Anticholinesterase agents inhibit AChE competitively by covalent binding. Organophosphorus compounds and carbamates interact with AChE in the same way as ACh, phosphorylating or carbamylating the same serine hydroxyl that ACh acylates. The critical difference is in the regeneration times of the active enzyme (4). Accumulation of ACh in the synaptic junction leads to desensitization and blocking of nerve impulse transmission. On exposure to organophosphorus or carbamate compounds, insects show hyperactivity, convulsions and paralysis.

Extensive use of these insecticides promoted the selection of altered AChE in numerous arthropods, notably ticks, mites, houseflies and leafhoppers (5), the broad cross-resistance conferred by this mechanism presenting a particular hazard to control efforts. In some species altered AChE is associated with a change in the catalytic activity. Decreased efficiency of AChE in its altered form provides increased opportunity for detoxification enzymes to operate on anticholinesterase agents. Metabolic detoxification of organophosphorus compounds may arise from direct enzymatic hydrolysis, or the action of glutathione S-transferase and/or mixed function oxidases. Carbamate insecticides are more susceptible to degradation by mixed function oxidases than by other mechanisms.

Seven mosquito species are reported to have the insensitive AChE mechanism of resistance (Table 1). Such resistance problems are epitomized in agricultural areas where organophosphorus insecticides (particularly methyl parathion and fenthion), and carbamates (carbaryl and propoxur), are applied to crops. These agrochemicals exert selection pressure on mosquitoes breeding in the fields or irrigaton systems. El Salvador and Western Nicaragua in Central America, the Adana region of Turkey, and the San Joaquin Valley in California are typical of such hazard areas.

TABLE 1

REPORTS OF INSENSITIVE AChE IN MOSQUITO SPECIES

Species	Location
Anopheles albimanus	El Salvador (6, 7)
An. atroparvus	Spain (8)
An. sacharovi	Turkey (9)
An. nigerrimus	Sri Lanka (10)
Culex pipiens	France (11, 12)
	Italy (13)
Cx. tritaeniorhynchus	Japan (14)
	Sri Lanka (15)
Cx. quinquefasciatus	Tanzania (15)

In anopheline mosquitoes, the major selecting agents for the altered AChE gene have been the carbamate insecticides, used as adulticides;   In the culicines, selecting agents have predominantly been organophosphorus compounds applied as larvicides. Fenthion, fenitrothion, temephos, malathion, chlorpyrifos, chlorfenvinphos, bromophos and diazinon are particularly widely used as larvicides against mosquitoes. The altered AChE mechanism is expressed in both adults and larvae of the mosquito species in which the mechanism is known. In all mosquitoes studied, greater resistance is conferred by altered AChE to carbamates than to organophosphorus insecticides, with a variable degree of insensitivity.

DETECTION OF RESISTANCE

WHO susceptibility tests are most commonly used for detection of resistance. However, concentrations defined by WHO for detection of resistant mosquitoes do not detect low levels of resistance and large numbers of insects are needed to establish the discriminating dose (16). Only one insecticide can be tested per insect, and false positives may arise due to behavioural factors, such as resting on the wire gauze of the WHO test kit avoiding contact with insecticide during testing (17).

Biochemical, immunological and molecular approaches are increasingly being applied to detection of specific resistance mechanisms (18). Such techniques when applied to large numbers of individuals within a population, provide an indication of resistance frequency. Multiple assays can be carried out on individuals to test for different resistance mechanisms but are used in conjunction with standard WHO resistance assays as specific tests for all mechanisms are not yet available.

Biochemical techniques for detection of altered AChE were initially based on reduced activity of the enzyme with the substrate acetylthiocholine iodide (ASCHI) in resistant insects such as the green rice leafhopper *Nephotettix cincticeps* (19). There are two drawbacks to this approach: Ambiguities arise due to variation in physiological parameters and background (17), and reduced substrate reactivity of the altered AChE is not a universal trait; in *Musca domestica*, a variant form of altered AChE with enhanced substrate activity has been identified (20).

A rapid and accurate technique devised for analysis of altered AChE in *M. domestica* (21) has been adapted for use on mosquitoes (22). Rates of reaction in the presence and absence of insecticide for homogenate aliquots of individual mosquitoes are measured continuously over a 5 minute period using a kinetic microtitre plate reader. In conjunction with use of a multiple homogenizer for simultaneous homogenization of up to 96 individual insects in wells of a microtitre plate (23) this technique permits rapid genotyping of a very large number of insects. It has been used for analysis of altered AChE frequency in *Anopheles nigerrimus* from Sri Lanka and *Culex pipiens* from Italy (24), and is applicable to blood fed mosquitoes with abdomens excised to avoid interference in the assay from blood cholinesterases and pigment.

The development of a reliable technique for genotyping with respect to the altered AChE mechanism of resistance, facilitates early detection of this type of resistance at low frequencies in mosquito populations, and will have widespread application in vector control programmes.

REFERENCES

1. World Health Organization (1986) Resistance of Vectors and Reservoirs of Disease to Pesticides. Technical Report Series 737; WHO Geneva

2. Brown AWA (1986) J Am Mosq Cont Assoc 2: 123-140

3. Lund AE (1985). In: Kerkut GA, Gilbert LI (eds). Comprehensive Insect Physiology, Biochemistry and Pharmacology 12: 9-51 Pergamon, Oxford

4. Eldefrawi AT (1985) In: Kerkut GA, Gilbert LI (eds). Comprehensive Insect Physiology, Biochemistry and Pharmacology 12: 115-130 Pergamon, Oxford

5. Oppenoorth FJ (1985) In: Kerkut GA, Gilbert LI (eds). Comprehensive Insect Physiology, Biochemistry and Pharmacology 12: 731-773 Pergamon, Oxford

6. Ayad H. Georghiou GP (1975) J Ec Ent 68: 295-297.

7. Hemingway J, Georghiou GP (1983) Pest. Biochem. Physiol. 19: 167-171.

8. Hemingway J, Davidson G (1983) Parassitologia 25: 1.

9. Hemingway J, Malcolm CA, Kissoom KE, Boddington RG, Curtis CF, Hill N (1985) Pest Biochem Physiol 24: 68-76.

10. Hemingway J, Jayawardena KGI, Herath PRJ (1986) Bull WHO 64: 753-758.

11. Wood RJ, Pasteur N, Sinegre G (1984) Bull Ent Res 74: 677-688.

12. Raymond M, Pasteur N, Fournier D, Cuany A, Bergé JB, Magnin M (1985) CRAS 14: 509-512.

13. Villani F, Hemingway J (1987) Pest Biochem Physiol 27: 218-228.

14. Takahashi M, Yasutomi K (1987) J Med Ent 24: 595-603.

15. Hemingway J, Smith C, Jayawardena KGI, Herath PRJ (1986) Bull Ent Res 76:559-566.

16. Curtis CF, Pasteur N (1981) Bull Ent Res 71: 153-161.

17. Brown TM, Brogdon WG (1987) Ann Rev Ent 32: 145-162.

18. Devonshire AL (1987) In: Ford MG, Holloman DW, Khanbay BPS, Sawicki RM (eds). Combating resistance to xenobiotics : Biological and chemical approaches. Ellis Horwood, Chichester-UK pp 239-255.

19. Miyata T, Saito T, Hama H, Iwata T, Ozaki K (1980) App Entomol Zool 15: 351-352.

20. Devonshire AL, Moores GD (1984) Pest Biochem Physiol 21: 336-340.

21. Moores GD. Devonshire AL, Denholm I (1988) Bull Ent Res 78: 537-544.

22. ffrench-Constant RH, Bonning BC (1989) Med Vet Ent 3: 9-16.

23. ffrench-Constant RH, Devonshire AL (1987) Biochem Genet 25 493-499.

24. Bonning BC (1989) Acetylcholinesterase and Insecticide Resistance in Mosquitoes. PhD thesis, University of London 197 pp.

ROLE OF GENE AMPLIFICATION IN INSECTICIDE RESISTANCE

NICOLE PASTEUR, MICHEL RAYMOND, YVES PAUPLIN, ERIC NANCE, DENISE HEYSE

Institut des Sciences de l'Evolution, Laboratoire de Génétique Université de Montpellier II, 34085 MONTPELLIER 2, France

CLAUDE MOUCHES
Département des Sciences Biologiques, Université de Pau Campus Universitaire, 66000 PAU, France

INTRODUCTION

In insects, one of the mechanisms of resistance to organophosphorous (OP) insecticides is increased detoxification mediated by enzymes which, in addition to their action on OPs, hydrolyze naphthyl esters. In mosquitoes of the genus *Culex* and in the aphid *Myzus persicae*, high activity of these enzymes (= esterases) is the result of amplification of the respective structural genes[1-3].

Gene amplification appears today as a fundamental and widely occurring mechanism to produce large quantities of proteins needed either at a critical developmental time or to counteract the effect of environmental stresses. Thus, it is the mechanism of resistance to drugs in cultured and tumor mammalian cells[4], in *Leishmania*[5] and in *Plasmodium*[6], to metallic ions in yeast and plants[7], to herbicide in alfalfa[8], to extreme cold in fishes[9], and there is little doubt that many other cases will be discovered in the future, especially with respects to resistance to pesticides and drugs.

Here, we will summarize the results obtained on *Culex* mosquitoes through collaborative programs involving our laboratories in Montpellier and Pau, INRA in Antibes (Dr. J. B. Bergé), and UCR in California (Prof. G. P. Georghiou). We will then attempt to examine the important characteristics of gene amplification with respects to the evolution and management of insecticide resistance.

ESTERASES IN CULEX MOSQUITOES

Two groups of esterases, A and B, have been identified in electrophoretic studies of single insect homogenates on the basis of their preferential hydrolysis of alpha- or beta-naphthyl acetate, respectively. Esterases A and B differ widely in their molecular structure[10] and immunological characteristics[11] (Table 1), indicating that they are encoded by distinct genes or families of genes.

TABLE 1
CHARACTERISTICS OF OVERPRODUCED ESTERASES IN *CULEX* MOSQUITOES[10,11].

	Esterases A	Esterases B
Substrate preference	-naphthyl acetate	ß-naphthyl acetate
Molecular structure	dimer	monomer
Size of native form	120 kDa	67 kDa
Size of denatured form	60 kDa	67 kDa
Cross reaction with		
esterase A1 antibody	yes	no
esterase B1 antibody	no	yes

Several electrophoretic forms exist in each group; some have low activity, others very high activity. Esterase B electromorphs of low activity are encoded by multiple codominant alleles of a single gene[12,13]. High activity of electromorphs B1, B2 and B4 in *Culex pipiens*, and B3 in *C. tarsalis* is due to an overproduction of the respective esterases[11,14], and this overproduction is the result of amplification of each structural gene[1,2,14]. A likely hypothesis is that all esterase B electromorphs are, or derive from, allelic forms of the same gene, and present data from the nucleotide sequences of esterase B1[15] and B2[16] genes seem to confirm the high similarity between these enzymes.

High activity of esterases B1, B2, B3 and B4 is inherited as single Mendelian characters[17,18,19]. In *C. pipiens*, 2-3% of insects with both esterase B1 and esterase B2 amplifications on a same chromosome can be recovered in the offspring of appropriate crosses, indicating that recombination can occur between amplified systems[18].

The amino acid sequence of esterase B1[15] presents strong homologies in its N terminal region with *Drosophila* and *Torpedo* acetylcholinesterases, human butyrylcholinesterase, *Drosophila* esterase 6, *Heliothis* juvenile hormone esterase, rabbit liver esterase, and rat thyroglobulin. The C terminal region of esterase B1, however, is very different from that of these enzymes (Fig. 1). The relationship beetween these enzymes indicates an independent evolution of several families (Fig. 2).

Fig. 1. Comparison of the amino acid sequences of *Culex* esterase B1 (B1EST) with *Heliotis* juvenile hormone esterase[30] (JUVH), *Drosophila* esterase 6[31] (DROESVI), *Torpedo* acetylcholinesterase[32] (TORACHE), human butyrycholinesterase[33] (HUSCHE), *Drosophila* acetylcholinesterase[34] (DROACHE), rat thyroglobulin[35] (THYROGL) beginning at amino acid 397, and rabbit liver esterase[36] (LIVEST). Amino acid sequences were aligned using Corbet[37] method; amino acids in black boxes are identical to those of esterase B1; those in dotted boxes correspond to conservative substitutions when compared to esterase B1.

```
JUVH                                            WQETNSRSVVAHLDSGIIRGV.PRSA
B1EST                                            MSLESLTVQTKYGPVRGK.RNVS
DROESVI                                          SDTDDPLLVQLPQGKLRGR.DNGS
TORACHE   MNLLTVSSLGVLLHL...........VVLC.....QADDHSELLVNTKSGKVMG..TRVP
HUSCHES   HSKVTIICIRFLFWF...........LLLCM.LIGKSHTEDDIITATKNGKVRG..MNLT
DROACHE   MAISCRQSVRLPMSLPLPLTIPLPLVLVLSLHLSGVCGVIDRLVVQTSSGPVRG..RSVI
THYROGL     ISTPSVHI.........................DSFGQL...QGGSQV..VKVG
LIVEST                                           HPSAPPVVDTVKGKVLGKFVSLE

JUVH      D.GIKFASFLGVPYAKQPVGELRFKELEP.LEPWDNILNATNEGPICFQ........TDVL
B1EST     LLGQEYVSFQGIPYARAPEGELRFKAPVP.PQKWTETLDCTQQWEPCYH............
DROESVI   .....YYSYESIPYAEPPTGDLRFEAPEPYKQKWSDYFDATKTPVACLQ.......WDQ.
TORACHE   VLSSHISAFLGIPFAEPPVGNMRFRRPEP.KKPWSGVWNASTYPNNCQQY..VDEQFPGF
HUSCHES   VFGGTVTAFLGIPYAQPPLGRLRFKKPQS.LTKWSDIWNATKYANSCCQN..IDQSFPGF
DROACHE   VQGREVHVYTGIPYAKPPVEDLRFKRPVP.AEPWHGVLDATGLSATCVQE..RYEYFPGF
THYROGL   TAWKQVYQLFGVPYAAPLAENRFQAPEV.LN.WTGSWDATKLRSSCWQ.........PG.
LIVEST    GFAQPVAVFLGVPFAKPPLGSLRFAPPQP.AESWSHVKNTTSYPPMCSSDAVSGHMLSEL

JUVH      YGRLMAASNREMSEACIYANIHVPWQSL...........................PRVRGT
B1EST     FDR..RLQKIVGCEDSLKINVFAK.................................EINPS
DROESVI   FTP..GANKLVGEEDCLTVSVYKP................................KNSKR
TORACHE   SGSEMWNPNREMSEDCLYLNIWVPSP.............................RPKST
HUSCHES   HGSEMTNPNTDLSEDCLYLNVWIPAP.............................KPKNA
DROACHE   SGEEIWNPNTNVSEDCLYINVWAPAKARLRHGRGANGGEHPNGKQADTDHLIHNGNPQNT
THYROGL   ....TRTPTPQISEDCLYLNVFVPEN..............................LVSNA
LIVEST    FTNRKENIPLKFSEDCLYLNIYTPAD..............................LTQRG

JUVH      TPLRPILVFIHGGGFAFGSGHEDLHGPEYLV.TKNVIVITFNYRLNVFGFLS..MN....
B1EST     TPL.PVMLYIYGGGFTEGTSGTELYGPDFLV.QKDIVLVSFNYRIGALGFLCCQSE....
DROESVI   NSF.PVVAHIHGGGAFMFGAAWQNGHE.NVMR.EGKFILVKISYRLGPLGFVS..TG....
TORACHE   T....VMVWIYGGGFYSGSSTLDVYNGKYLAYTEEVVLVGHSAGGASVHLQML..HGS....
HUSCHES   T....VLIWIYGGGFQTGTSSLHVYDGKFLARVERVIVVSMNYRVGALGFLALPGN....
DROACHE   TNGLPILIWIYGGGFMTGSATLDIYNADIMAAVGNVIVASFQYRVGAFGFLHLAPEMPSE
THYROGL   S....VLVFFHNTVEMEGSGGQLNIDGSILAAVGNLIVVTANYRLGVFGFLSSGSD....
LIVEST    R..LTVMVWIHGGGLMVGGAS..TYDGLALSAHENVVVVTIQYRLGIGGF.GFNID....

JUVH      .TTKIPGNAGLRDQVTLLRWVQRNAKNFGGDPSDITIAGQSAGASAAHLLTL..SKATEG
B1EST     .QDGVPGNAGLKDQNLAIRWVLENIAAFGGDPKRVTLAGHSAGAASVQYHLI..SDASKD
DROESVI   .DRDLPGNYGLRDQRLALKWIKQNIASFGGEPQNVLLVGHSAGGASVHLQML..RQDFGQ
TORACHE   ..QEAPGNVGLLDQRMALQWVHDNIQFFGGDPKTVTIFGESAGGASVGMHILL..SPGSRD
HUSCHES   ..PEAPGNMGLFDQQLALQWVQKNIAAFGGNPKSVTLFGESAGAASVSLHILL..SPGSHS
DROACHE   FAEEAPGNVGLWDQALAIRWLKDNAHAFGGNPEWMTFLGESAGSSSVNAQLM..SPVTRG
THYROGL   ...EVAGNWGLLDQVAALTWVQTHIGAFGGDPQRVTLAADRGGADVASIHLLITRPTRLQ
LIVEST    ........ELFLVAVN.RWVQDNIANFGGDPGSVTIFGESAGGQSVSILL...SPLTKN

JUVH      LFKRAILMSGTGMSYF.FTTSPLFAAYISKQLLQILGNQ...RDGSEEIHRQLIDLPAEK
B1EST     LFQRAIVMSGSTYSSW.SLTR.Q.RNWVEKLAKAIGWDG...QGGESGALRFLRAAKPED
DROESVI   LARAAFSFSGNALDPW.VIQKGA.RGRAFELGRNVGCES...AEDSTSLKKCLKSKPASE
TORACHE   LFRRAILQSGSPNCPWASVSVAEGRRRAVELGRNLNCN...LNSDEELIHCLREKKPQE
HUSCHES   LFTRAILQSGSFNAPWAVTSLYEARNRTLNLAKLTGCS....RENETQIIKCLANKDPQE
DROACHE   LVKRGMMQSGTMNAPWSHMTSEKAVEIGKALINDCNCNASMLKTNPAHVMSCMRSVDAKT
THYROGL   LFRKALLMGGSALSPAAIISPDRAQQQAAALAKEVGCP....NSSVQEVVSCFRQKPANI
LIVEST    LFHRAISESGVAL..LSSSLFRKNTKSLAEKIAIEAGCK....TTTSADMVHCLRQKTEBE
```

442

Fig. 1. (continued)

```
JUVH     L.NEANAVLIEQIG....LTTFLPIVESPLPGVTTIIDDDPEILIAEGRGKNVPLLIGFT
B1EST    IVAHQEKLLTDQDMQDDIFTPFGPTVE.PYLTEQCIIPKAPFEMARTA......WGDKID
DROESVI  LVTAVRKFLIFSYVP...FAPFSPVLE.PSDAPDAIITQDPRDVIKSGKFGQVPWAVSYV
TORACHE  LIDVEWNV......L..PFDSIFRFSFVP.VIDGEFFPTSLESMLNSGNFKKTQILLGVN
HUSCHES  ILLNEAFV......V..PYGTPLSVNFGP.TVDGDFLTDMPDILLELGQFKKTQILVGVN
DROACHE  ISVQQWN.........SYSGILSFPSAP.TIDGAFLPADPMTLMKTADLKDYDILMGNV
THYROGL  LNEAQTKL......L..AVSGPFHY.WGP.VVDGQYLRELPSRRLKRPLPVKVDLLIGGS
LIVEST   LMEVTLKMKFMALDL..VGDPKENTAFLTCVIDGVLLPKAPAEIYEEKKYNMLPYMVGIN

JUVH     SSECETFRNRLL...NFDLVKKIQDMPTIIIPPKLLFMTPPELLM...ELAKTIE.RKYY
B1EST    IMIGGTSEEGLLLLQKIKLHPELLSHPHLFLGNVPPNLKISMEKRI..EFAAKLK.QRYY
DROESVI  TEDGGYNAALLLKERKSGIVIDDLNERWLELAPYLLFYRDTKTKKDMDDDYSRKIK.QBYI
TORACHE  KDEGSFFLLYGAPG.FSKDSESKISREDFMSGVKLSVPHANDLGL...D.AVTLQYTDWM
HUSCHES  KDEGTAFLVYGAPG.FSKDNNSIITRKEFQEGLKIFFPGVSEFGK...E.SILFHYTDWV
DROACHE  RDEGTYFLLYDLIDYFDKDDATALPRDKYLEIMNNIFGKATQAER...E.AIIFQYTSW.
THYROGL  QDDGLINRAKAVKQ.FEESQGRTNSKTAFYQALQNSLGGEDSDAR...ILAAAIWYYSLE
LIVEST   QQEFGWIIVMQMLG.YPLSEGKLDQKTA.TELLWKSYP.IVNVSK...ELPPVAT.EKYL

JUVH     NGTI.SIDN...FVKSCSDGFYEYPALKLAQKRAETGGAPLYLYRFAYEGQNSIIKKVMG
B1EST    PDSIPSMENNLGYVHMMSDRVFWHGLHRTI.LARA.ARSRARTFVYRICLDSEFYNHYRI
DROESVI  GNQRFDIESYSELQRLFTDILFKNSTQESLDLHRKYGKSPAYAYVYDNPAEKGI.AQVLA
TORACHE  DDNNGI.KNRDGLDDIVGDHNVICPLMHFVNKYTKFGNG...TYLYFFNHRAS..NLVWP
HUSCHES  DDQRPE.NYREALGDVVGDYNFICPALEFTKKFSEWGNN...AFFYYFEHRSS..KLPWP
DROACHE  EGNPGY.QNQQQIGRAVGDHFFTCPTNEYAQALAERGAS...VHYYYFTHRTS..TSLWG
THYROGL  HSTDDYASFSRALENATRDYFIICPIVNMASLWARRTRG...NFFMY..HVPE..SYGHG
LIVEST   GGTDDPVKKKDLFLDMLADLLFGVPFVNVARHHRDAGAP...TYMYEYRYRTSFSSDMRP

JUVH     LNHE....GVGHIEDLTYVFKVNSMSEALHASPSENDVKMKNLMTGYFLNFIKCSQFTCE
B1EST    MMIDPKLRGTAHADELSYLF..SNFTQQVPGKETFEYRGLQTLV.DVFSAFVINGDPNCG
DROESVI  MRTDYDF.GTVHGDDYFLIF..ENFVRDVEMRPDEQIIS.RNFI.NMLADFASSDN...G
TORACHE  EWM.....GVIHGYEIEFVF.GLPLVKELN..YTAEEEALSRRIMHYWATFAKTGMPNEP
HUSCHES  EWM.....GVMHGYEIEFVF.GLPLERRDN..YTKAEEILSRSIVKRWANFAKIFMPNET
DROACHE  EWM.....GVLHGDEIEYFF.GQPLNNSLQ..YRPVERELGKRMLSAVIEFAKTGMPAQ.
THYROGL  S.L.....ELLA..DVQYAF.GLPFYSAYQGYFSTEEQSLSLKVMQYFSNFAKIFMPNYP
LIVEST   KTV.....IGDHGDEIFSVL.GAPFLKEG....ATEEEKLSKMVMKYWANFARNGMPNGE

JUVH     DNNSLE.VWPANNGMQYEDIVSPT.........IIRSK....EFA........SRQQDII
B1EST    MTAKGG.VVFEPNAQTKPTFKCLN.........IANDGVAFVDYP.......DADRLD.
DROESVI  SLKYGE.CDFKDSVGSE.KFQLLA..................IYI.....DAARIGS
TORACHE  HSQESKWPLFTTKEQKFIDLNTEPM..KVHQRLRVQMCVFWNQFLPKLLNATETIDEAER
HUSCHES  QNNSTSWPVFKSTEQKYLTLNTEST..RIMTKLRAQQCRFWTSFFPKVLEMTGNIDEAEW
DROACHE  ..DGEEWPNFSKEDPVYYIFSTDDKIEKLARGPLAARCSFWNDYLPKVRSWAGTCD.GDS
THYROGL  H.......EFSQKAAEFATP.....................WPDFVP......GAGGESYK
LIVEST   ..GLPQWPAYDYKEG.YLQIGATT...QAAQKLKDKEVAFWTEL................

JUVH     EFFDSFTSRSPL
B1EST    MWDAMYVNDELF
DROESVI  MW..MFRKLHE
TORACHE  QNKTEFHRWSSYMMHWKNQFDHY.SRHESCAEL
HUSCHES  EWKAGFHRWNNYMMDWKNQFNDYTSKKESCVGL
DROACHE  GSASISPRLQ..LLGIAALIYICAALRTKRVF
THYROGL  ELSAQLPNRQG.............LKKADCSF
LIVEST   .WAKEAAR................PRETEHIEL
```

Fig. 2. Hierarchical classification of various proteins related to *Culex* esterase B1 given by Corbet method. Names of proteins as in Fig 1.

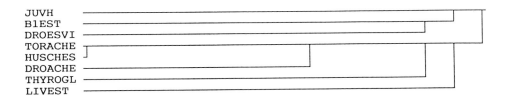

MOLECULAR ANALYSIS OF ESTERASES B AMPLIFICATIONS.

Although amplification of esterase B1 gene was suggested in 1980[20] to explain the correlated stepwise increase in esterase activity and OP resistance, it was demonstrated experimentally only in 1986[1].

Structure of esterase B1 amplification.

In all *Culex* strains studied thus far, there is co-amplification of the genomic sequences flanking the structural genes. In mosquitoes of the Tem-R strain with an amplified esterase B1 and of strain SeLax with an amplified esterase B2, each amplification unit covers more than 30 kb. In Tem-R mosquitoes, the amplification units are not all identical. Present data[15], using a 700 bp cDNA probe of the structural gene and a few restriction enzymes, suggest that they are formed of a constant 25 kb core (containing a single copy of the structural gene) which is flanked by fragments of variable length. Worth of noting are two sequences of repetitive DNA flanking the esterase B1 gene, CE1 on its 3' side, and CE2 on its 5' side. CE1 is also present in the 3' variable region of the amplification units[15], and present research is attempting to determine whether CE1 contains an origin of replication.

The structure of esterases B2 and B3 amplified systems is presently under investigation, but it is already clear that they are different from each other, and different from the esterase B1 system[2]. In contrast, there is a remarkable constancy among the amplified structures which encompass a particular esterase B gene. This is particularly striking in *Culex* in which esterase B2 gene is amplified: no variation in the size of the fragments generated by single[14] and double[16] digestions with various endonucleases was detected between mosquitoes captured in various USA states, Thailand, Pakistan, Ivory Coast, Egypt and France.

Since the sequences flanking non-amplified esterase B genes are highly variable (all strains thus far examined are different[16]), it seems that amplification of esterase B2 gene has been a unique event. This hypothesis is supported by population studies in France and California where esterase B2 appeared many years after a local, more efficient resistance mechanism was selected. This esterase was at first observed near Marseille airport[21] and the city of Los Angeles[22], respectively, suggesting a recent introduction from other parts of the world where it is common (Africa and Asia).

Chromosomal organization of esterase amplifications.

In situ hybridization of Tem-R metaphase chromosomes with esterase B1 cDNA probe has revealed that all the copies of the gene are grouped on a single chromosome, tentatively identified as chromosome II[23]. No double minute chromosome was found, an observation which agrees with the inheritance of high activity of esterase B1 (see above). Although other amplification systems have not yet been analyzed by this technique, their inheritance suggests that they are also on a single chromosome.

Tissue distribution and expression of esterase B amplifications

Amplification of esterase B1 has been observed in meiotic chromosomes prepared from testes, and in mitotic chromosomes prepared from embryos. Independent experiments have shown that it is also present in spermatozoa[24], as well as in larvae (from first to fourth instar), pupae, and adults[16]. Thus, it is very likely that all cells, in all tissues and at each developmental stage contain the amplified gene.

However, esterase B proteins are not present in all tissues[25]. In Tem-R insects, a large quantity of esterase B1 protein exists in tissues of the digestive tract and the malpighian tubules, in the hypodermis, and in neurons of the brain. Esterase B proteins are also present in digestive tissues and hypodermis, but not in neurons of resistant insects with esterase B2 or in susceptible insects; in susceptible mosquitoes esterase B quantity is much lower than in resistant insects.

Esterase B mRNA seems to be restricted to the tissues in which the protein is detected[25].

The tissue distribution differences in the localization and synthesis of the various amplified esterases B suggest that gene regulation may be modified during the amplification process.

ORIGIN OF ESTERASE B AMPLIFIED SYSTEMS

It is clear that the high amplification level (250-500 folds) of esterase B1 now observed in Tem-R mosquitoes was not a single step event. Evolution of resistance due to esterase detoxification in this strain has significantly increased over time[20]. Similar observations have been made in strains with esterases B2 and B4. Thus the amplification process seems to involved first the acquisition of a few copies of the gene, followed by the subsequent increase in this number of copies. The two phenomena may, or may not occur through a same process, and their frequency of occurrence may, or may not be identical.

The results described above show that, in the mosquitoes studied, there is no extrachromosomal elements containing the structural gene, and that if such structures have existed they were transient. Whether the initial amplification event was a simple duplication of the gene concerned, or the acquisition of a larger number of copies remain unknown. It can be noted that a *de novo* amplification of some 10 structural genes coding butyrylcholinesterase has been recently observed in a man exposed to parathion[27], and that this amplification occurred not only in somatic cells but also in gametes since it was transmitted to the son of this person.

Once initial amplification has been achieved, recombination events, as was demonstrated between chromosomes bearing different amplification systems, could increase the number of gene copies.

Further research on these problems must be undertaken, since it will permit to determine the rate of apparition of a new amplification, and the nature and frequency of subsequent increases in the number of gene copies that can be generated from this first amplification.

EVOLUTION OF AMPLIFIED SYSTEMS IN NATURAL POPULATIONS

To predict the evolution of amplification in natural populations, many questions in addition to those concerning the origin of amplification and its consequences on gene expression remain to be answered. Among them:

Is there a strict relationship between the amplification level and the quantity of esterase produced, as well as between the quantity of esterase produced and the resistance observed? In mammalian cells, the degree of amplification is not always correlated with

446

resistance. Similarly, in *Myzus persicae*, esterase E4 gene can be amplified but not expressed so that insects appear susceptible[28].

How stable are amplifications? Research on mammalian cell cultures have shown that there is a large variability of stability, reversion occurring in some cell lines and not in others. A recent study of *Myzus persicae*[28] has shown that reversion might be apparent, i. e. the amplification remains but the genes are not expressed, and that expression can be restored upon a single exposure to insecticide. In *Culex* mosquitoes of the Tem-R strain relaxation of selection has given a loss of resistance and amplification after 10-15 generations. Such a result was obtained in two independant experiments but not in a third one[29].

What are the fitnesses of the different amplification levels in relation to each others, in relation to susceptible genotypes, and in presence and absence of insecticides? Several studies indicate that Tem-R mosquitoes with high amplification of esterase B1 gene reach the adult stage much slower than mosquitoes of the susceptible reference strain, but presently no data permit to determine whether this is due to the amplification of esterase B1 gene or to some other differences in the genetic background of the insects tested.

REFERENCES

1. Mouchès C, Pasteur N, Bergé JB, Hyrien O, Raymond M, Robert de Saint Vincent B, de Silvestri M, Georghiou GP (1986) Science 233:778-780
2. Raymond M, Beyssat-Arnaouty V, Sivasubramanian N, Georghiou GP, Pasteur N (1989) Biochem Genet 27 (in press)
3. Field LM, Devonshire AL, Forde BG (1988) Biochem J 251:309-312
4. Stark GR, Wahl GM (1984) Ann Rev Biochem 53:447-491
5. Garvey EP, Santi DV (1986) Science 233:535-540.
6. Foote S.J., Thompson JK, Cowman AF, Kemp DJ (1989) Cell 57:921-930
7. Fogel S, Welch JW (1982) Proc Natl Acad Sci USA 70:5342-5346
8. Donn G, Tischer E, Smith JA, Goodman HM (1984) J Mol Appl Genet 2:621-635
9. Scott GK, Hew CL, Davies PL (1985) Proc Natl Acad Sci USA 82:2613-2617
10. Fournier D, Bride JM, Mouchès C, Raymond M, Magnin M, Bergé JB, Pasteur N, Georghiou GP (1987) Pest Biochem Physiol 27:211-217
11. Mouchès C, Magnin M, Bergé JB, de Silvestri M, Beyssat V, Pasteur N, Georghiou GP (1987) Proc Natl Acad Sci USA 84:2113-2116
12. Stordeur de E (1976) Biochem Genet 14:481-493
13. Pasteur N (1977) Thèse de Doctorat d'Etat, Université de Montpellier II, 162p
14. Beyssat-Arnaouty V (1989) Thèse de Doctorat, Université de Montpellier II, 226p

15. Mouchès C, Pauplin Y, Agarwal M, Lemieux L, Herzog M, Abadon M, Beyssat-Arnaouty V, Hyrien O, Robert de Saint Vincent B, Georghiou G.P., Pasteur N (submitted)
16. Raymond M (unpublished)
17. Georghiou GP, Pasteur N, Hawley MK (1980) J Econ Entomol 73:301-305
18. Wirth MC, Marquine M, Georghiou GP, Pasteur N (1989) J Med Entomol (in press)
19. Prabahker N, Georghiou GP, Pasteur N (1987) J Amer Mosq Control Assoc 3:473-475
20. Pasteur N, Georghiou GP, Ranasinghe LE (1980) Proc 48th Ann Conf Calif Mosq Vector Control Assoc, Anaheim, pp 69-73.
21. Magnin M (1986) Thèse de Doctorat, Université de Paris VI, 200p.
22. Raymond M, Pasteur N, Georghiou GP, Mellon RB, Wirth MC, Hawley M (1987) J Med Entomol 24:24-27.
23. Nancé E, Heyse D, Britton-Davidian J, Pasteur N (1990) Genome (in press).
24. Raymond M, Pasteur N (1989) Nucleic Acid Res 17:7116
25. Nancé E. (1990) Thèse de doctorat, Université de Montpellier II, in preparation
26. Mariani BD, Schimke RT (1984) J Biol Chem 259:1901-1910.
27. Prody CA, Dreyfus P, Zamir R, Zakut H, Soreq H (1989) Proc Natl Acad Sci USA 86:690-694.
28. Field AM, Devonshire AL, ffrench-Constant RH, Forde BG (1989) FEBS lett 243:323-327.
29. Ferrari J, Georghiou GP, personnal communication.
30. Hanzlik TN, Abdel-Aal YAI, Harshman LG, Hammock BD (1989) J Biol Chem 264:12419-12425.
31. Oakeshott JG, Collet C, Phillis RW, Nielsen KM, Russell RJ, Chambers GK, Ross V, Richmond RC (1987) Proc Natl Acad Sci USA 84:3359-3363.
32. Schumacher M, Camp S, Maulet Y, Newton M, MacPhee-Quigley K, Taylor SS, Friedmann T, Taylor P (1986) Nature 319:407-409.
33. Lockridge O, Bartels CF, Vaughan TA, Wong CK, Norton SE, Johnson LL (1987) J Biol Chem 262:549-557.
34. Hall L.M.C. Spierer P (1986) EMBO J 5:2949-2954.
35. Mercken L, Simon MJ, Swillens S, Massaer M, Vassart G (1988) Nature 316:647-651.
36. Korza G, Ozols J (1988) J. Biol Chem 263:3486-3495
37. Corpet F (1988) Nucleic Acid Res. 16:10881-10890.

PLANT PATHOGENS

© 1990 Elsevier Science Publishers B.V. (Biomedical Division)
Pesticides and alternatives, editor J.E. Casida

PROBLEMS AND PROSPECTS OF FUNGAL PLANT DISEASE CONTROL

S.G.GEORGOPOULOS
Lapapharm Inc., 73 Menandrou Str., Athens 104 37, Greece

Control of fungal diseases of crop plants is sought by five main routes :regulatory, cultural, biological, chemical, and host resistance. With the exception of some quarantine regulations for prevention of entry or eradication of pathogens, all other methods aim not at complete control, but at production of acceptable crops in a profitable way.

Cultural measures, such as sanitation, crop rotation, and avoidance of practices creating conditions favorable for disease development, may always help to reduce losses. In modern agriculture, however, such measures cannot always be taken, they seldom guarantee profitable crop production, and cannot be examined to any considerable extend in this short contribution.

BIOLOGICAL CONTROL

For the most part, biological control of plant pathogenic fungi has yet to be exploited. The successful, commercial-scale applications of single biological control agents against fungal diseases are very few and, certainly, not proportional to the amount of research that has been done in the last 30 years. The important examples are :

a. The inoculation of freshly cut pine stumps with the weak parasite *Peniophora gigantea* to prevent their invasion by the important pathogen *Heterobasidion annosum* and the spread of this destructive disease to nearby trees [13].

b. The inoculation of cankers on chestnut trees with hypovirulent strains of *Endothia parasitica,* so that, by anastomosis, hypovirulence is transmitted to the virulent strains present in the tissue and the cankers can heal. At present, 18,000 hectares of French chestnut forest are receiving this treatment [4].

c. The application of a preparation, containing spores of *Trichoderma harzianum* to pruning wounds of fruit trees as they are made, to protect against infection by *Stereum purpureum* [7].

Since the success stories with biocontrol agents are so few, little experience has been gained, in order to predict what types of complications may arise in the future. Workers in the field of biological control of fungal diseases have realised that considering the ecosystem as a whole rather than seeking a single factor against a given pathogen is more likely to give results. Some benefit has been derived from this approach, particularly in the case of soil-borne plant pathogens [1], but the complexity of the interactions involved makes it unlikely that there will be fast progress in this direction. Selectively enhancing antagonists in the soil microflora is often encouraging *in vitro*, but the results are not equally satisfying in the field.

The possibility of integrated control of fungal diseases is still under investigation. Experimentally, it has been possible to reduce the amount of fungicide required by integration with an antagonist considerably less sensitive than the pathogen to the particular chemical. Fungicide resistant strains of the biocontrol agent can be utilised in such efforts [12]. Research is also underway on the possibility of genetically engineering biocontrol agents and it is encouraging that several companies have projects to achieve this goal. Some optimism on the prospects of biological control of plant pathogenic fungi seems justified, but it appears that for the next 20 years at least the control of fungal diseases will continue to rely mainly on resistance breeding and fungicides.

USE OF RESISTANT VARIETIES

Resistance would appear the best long term solution to minimise crop loss from disease. However, satisfactory resistant varieties to rather few fungal diseases, mostly of annual crops, are available. Resistance breeding in perennial crops is time consuming and expensive and has met with only limited success. Further, most identified resistance genes are specific and do not affect susceptibility to even closely related pathogens. This is certainly a disadvantage of disease resistance compared to chemical control where a single compound may be effective against several, even unrelated pathogens.

To utilise host resistance, some knowledge on the genetics of the host-parasite interaction is needed, but for the majority of pairs of hosts and pathogens such knowledge is presently not available. The simplest genetical control of resistance is by single genes of large phenotypic effect. Such major genes are race-specific and can be overcome by pathogen races with matching pathogenicity. Particularly in the case of biotrophic pathogens which live in intimate contact with the host, major-gene resistance becomes ineffective after some time, so that resistance breeding must be a continuous process.

To overcome the difficulties created by the variability of the pathogens, resistance which is not controlled by major genes has been utilised in some cases. In this polygenic resistance, individual genes cannot be identified because in the segregating generations from a cross there is a continuous variation for levels of susceptibility. Once achieved, polygenic resistance usually remains effective for a long time, but the successful efforts of this type are not many and pathogen variability remains the main problem for disease control with resistant varieties.

The limitations of conventional plant breeding arise from the fact that only related species can be crossed and when a cross is made, the resulting randomisation of two complete genomes makes extensive back crossing necessary. These limitations can be overcome by the methods of molecular genetics which allow for introduction of a single gene or a set of genes, irrespective of its origin, into the chromosome of a higher plant [15]. The most developed vector for such transfers is the Ti-plasmid of *Agrobacterium tumefaciens* which, however, cannot be used with all plants, e.g. the cereals. Fast progress in this direction cannot be anticipated because, in order for a gene to be cloned, information about its biochemical product is required and for genes conferring disease resistance such information is generally not available [5]. It is also doubtful that non-host resistance may be utilised to solve disease control problems [8]. Possibilities for plant genetic engineering to help obtain disease resistant plants have been outlined by Willmitzer [15]. It is not anticipated that the new methods will soon replace conventional breeding, but they may at least increase its efficiency.

Finally, it must be mentioned that, in addition to utilising resistant plants, plant pathologists of the future may be able to immunize susceptible plants against disease. Though not well understood at present, an immune system is found in plants, which can systemically be immunized by restricted infection or exposure to chemicals which act as elicitors of resistance in susceptible plants [11]. The nature of the "immunity signal" which is graft transmissible and sensitizes the plant to react when challenged by the pathogen is not yet known. The effectiveness of immunization appears comparable to that of modern fungicides, but the economics do not make immunization a competitive method for plant disease control [11].

CHEMICAL CONTROL

The use of chemicals against fungal diseases in commercial practice began essentially 100 years ago with the discovery of bordeaux mixture. Very substantial progress has been made, so that we now have good fungicides for the control of most of the important fungal diseases, with the main exception of the vascular wilts and the root rots of woody perennials. Chemical disease control has won a central place in modern agriculture and today commercial production of a number of crops would be very difficult or even impossible without fungicides. In common with other crop protection chemicals, fungicides face the problems of possible adverse effects on man and his environment and of loss of effectiveness due to the development of resistance by target fungi.

Currently used fungicides are generally less toxic than most insecticides, when acute toxicity is considered, but most of the non-systemics which act as

multisite biochemical inhibitors have been identified as oncogenic or potentially oncogenic compounds. Probably, recognition of such activity would not
have been possible if the acute toxicity of the particular compounds was higher,
but it is low enough, so that large quantities can be fed to animals without
killing them. It is very alarming that, according to a recent report of the
Board on Agriculture of the U.S. National Research Council [3], 90% by weight
of the fungicides used in the U.S. are considered potential carcinogens. There
is fear that registration of some of the protective fungicides may be cancelled
for this reason and this would create tremendous disease control difficulties
in certain crops and certain areas because of the lack of economically viable
alternatives.

The importance of many multisite, suspect oncogenic fungicides is increased
by the fact that, even after many years of use, fungi show practically no
resistance to them [6]. In contrast, a number of pathogens have developed
resistance to new, single-site fungicides which are considered non-oncogenic
or more weakly oncogenic than the early protectants. Although no fungicide
has so far been lost because of resistance, pathogen variability with respect
to fungicide sensitivity tends to reduce the useful life of some highly effective compounds in the same way as variability with respect to virulence
creates the need for replacement of disease resistant varieties of crop plants.
Several serious fungicide resistance problems have arisen, particularly in
Europe [2] and Japan [10], where the use of fungicides is greater. However,
even with the single-site systemics, the resistance risk is not the same for
all fungicides. As in the case of host resistance to disease, effectiveness
is more easily lost if mutation of only one gene is required [6]. Unless a
significant loss of fitness is involved, the risk of sudden and complete
disease control failure is high with the major-gene control of fungicide
sensitivity.

In contrast, when mutations of many genes are required for a considerable
loss of sensitivity, as is the case with some fungicides, a lower resistance
risk is involved. Polygenic control of resistance which appears to be less
uncommon with fungicides than with insecticides, may give a gradual decrease
in effectiveness of the fungicide, but sudden and complete failures are unlikely,
so that the risk is considered to be low to moderate [6]. Existing evidence
indicates that whether major genes or polygenic systems control fungicide
sensitivity depends on the chemical rather than on the target fungus, although,
exceptionally, both types of genetic control may be found in the same fungus-
fungicide combination [9].

Despite the problems of toxicology and resistance, it is not expected that
fungicides will lose an importance for the control of plant pathogenic fungi

in the next 10-20 years. Advances in plant breeding, innovation in biological control, and progress in genetic engineering offer some promise for non-
chemical control of fungal diseases of plants in the future. However, the
existing problems with these alternative technologies will delay the adoption
of nonchemical methods and fungicides will continue to occupy a central part
in disease control. There is a critical need for toxicologically acceptable
new fungicides. At present, the viability of many of the site specific systemics is linked to their use in combination with the older multisite protectants
which may have to be withdrawn for toxicological reasons. Considering that
only a small fraction of the potential target sites has been exploited for
selective fungitoxic action within the fungal cell, there must be good possibilities for discovering new site-specific fungicides. Computer assisted
modelling may improve the rate of discovery to reduce costs and diversify
modes of action, so that fungal resistance from overuse of a few types of fungicides may be diminished.

One promising approach in the chemical control of fungal diseases is the use
of non-fungitoxic chemicals which, although not lethal or inhibitory to the
pathogen *in vitro*, may prevent infection or reduce disease severity. Already
compounds acting as antipenetrants or as inducers of host defence [14] have
proven successful in commercial practice. There is good reason to expect that
such compounds may prove less hazardous and less likely to lose effectiveness
because of pathogen variability than most of the fungitoxic chemicals currently
used in disease control.

REFERENCES

1. Baker F, Scher FM (1987) In: Chet I (ed) Innovative Approaches to Plant
    Disease Control. John Willey & Sons, New York, pp 1-17
2. Brent KJ (1988) In: Delp CJ (ed) Fungicide Resistance in North America.
    Amer Phytopathol Soc Press, St.Paul, Minn pp 9-11
3. Committee on Scientific and Regulatory Issues Underlying Pesticide Use
    Patterns and Agricultural Innovation (1987) Regulating Pesticides in
    Food. National Academy Press, Washington DC
4. Dubos B (1987) In: Chet I (ed) Innovative Approaches to Plant Disease
    Control. John Willey & Sons, New York, pp 107-135
5. Ellis JG, Lawrence GJ, Peacock WJ, Pryor AJ (1988) Ann Rev Phytopathol
    26:245-263
6. Georgopoulos SG, Skylakakis G (1986) Crop Protection 5:299-305
7. Grosclaude C (1983) Colloq l'INRA 18:115-118
8. Johnson R (1987) In: Day PR, Jelis GJ (eds) Genetics and Plant Patho-
    genesis. Blackwell Sci Publ, Oxford pp 311-322
9. Kalamarakis AE, Demopoulos VP, Ziogas BN, Georgopoulos SG (1989)
    Netherlands J Plant Pathol (in press)

456

10. Kato T (1988) In: Delp CJ (ed) Fungicide Resistance in North America. Amer Phytopathol Soc Press, St.Paul, Minn, pp 16-18

11. Kuc J (1987) In: Chet I (ed) Innovative Approaches to Plant Disease Control. John Willey & Sons, New York, pp 255-274

12. Papavizas GC, Lewis JA, Abd-El Moity TH (1982) Phytopathology 72:126-132

13. Parker EJ (1977) Europ J Forest Pathol 7:251-253

14. Sisler HD, Ragsdale N (1987) In: Lyr H (ed) Modern Selective Fungicides-Properties, Applications, Mechanisms of Action. VEB Gustav Fischer Verlag, Jena and Longman Group UK Ltd, London pp 337-353

15. Willmitzer L (1987) In: Chet I (ed) Innovative Approaches to Plant Disease Control. John Willey & Sons, New York, pp 353-364

© 1990 Elsevier Science Publishers B.V. (Biomedical Division)
Pesticides and alternatives, editor J.E. Casida

SOIL SOLARIZATION: A NON-CHEMICAL METHOD FOR THE CONTROL OF SOIL-BORNE PATHOGENS, WEEDS AND PESTS

JAACOV KATAN

Department of Plant Pathology and Microbiology, The Hebrew University of Jerusalem, Faculty of Agriculture, Rehovot 76100 (Israel)

INTRODUCTION

Control of soil-borne plant pathogens, pests and weeds is a prerequisite for achieving high and sustained yields. There are many approaches for attaining this goal, e.g. production of resistant cultivars, grafting on resistant stocks, use of biological and cultural methods of control, and application of conventional pesticides. However, soil disinfestation is among the most efficient methods of control. Soil disinfestation involves the eradication in soil of soil-borne propagules of the detrimental biotic agents, before planting. Therefore, drastic steps must be taken, with a high penetration capacity in the soil, in order to reduce the populations of pathogens and other pests at each soil site and to the desired depths. The two major approaches to soil disinfestation that have been followed since the end of the last century are the chemical (soil fumigation) and the physical (heating the soil to $70-100^0$C). Soil solarization (solar heating) is third and a relatively new non-chemical approach to soil disinfestation (1,2).

Chemical or physical disinfestation of the soil has advantages but also disadvantages. Among the formers are: (a) it is highly effective in controlling many pathogens, weeds and pests, and in certain circumstances it is the only effective means of control available; (b) some disinfestation methods give simultaneous control of several pathogenic fungi, nematodes and weeds; (c) it

458

reduces or even eliminates inoculum of pathogens; and (d) it results frequently in increased growth response, i.e., an increase in the yield beyond that attributable to disease control. The disadvantages or difficulties are: (a) it is usually drastic and non-selective, possibly resulting in the creation of a "microbial vacuum", in which case reinfestation may result in a severe outbreak of disease; (b) it is relatively expensive, because it necessitates sophisticated equipment, and for this reason is used mainly with high-value crops; (c) chemical disinfestation can be hazardous to the farmer and operator and detrimental to the environment, and requires strict safety precautions; and (d) beneficial microorganisms, e.g. mycorrhizae, may be adversely affected, and therefore any new alternative has to be assessed in the light of the above limitations.

SOIL SOLARIZATION (SOLAR HEATING), A NON-CHEMICAL MEANS OF CONTROL

The basic idea of soil solarization is to cover the soil with transparent polyethylene sheets during the hot season, thereby raising the soil temperatures and killing the pests. The polyethylene sheets, capture the solar energy. Therefore, the concept of soil solarization combines the heating principle as a killing agent for pest control with that of soil heating by polyethylene mulching. This concept is based on the observations of extension workers and growers in the Jordan Valley in Israel, that intensive heating occurs in mulched soils. It was developed into a control method by a team which included A. Greenberger, A. Grinstein and H. Alon (1). Additional information on this method can be found in more detailed reviews (3,4).

Soil solarization will be effective only in regions with an appropriate climate. Effective reduction of a pathogen population to a given depth and consequently control of the respective disease can be achieved under the following conditions: (a) soil mulching should be carried out during the period of high temperatures and intense solar irradiation; (b) the soil should be kept moist in order to increase thermal sensitivity of resting structures and to improve heat conduction; (c) a thin (25-30 um) polyethylene tarp is recommended, since it is both cheap and effective; (d) since the upper layers are heated more quickly and intensively than the lower ones, the mulching period should be extended sufficiently (usually 30 days or longer) to achieve pest control at all desired depths. The longer the mulching period, the deeper its effectiveness and the higher the pathogen killing rate (1,5). Typical maximal temperatures in solarized plots in which effective disease and weed control wase obtained, are within the range of 45-50 and 38-45^{0}C at depths of 10 and 20 cm, respectively, although higher temperatures have also been recorded.

Soil solarization differs in various aspects from soil disinfestation by artificial soil heating. The former can be carried out directly in the open field since there is no need to transport the heat from its source to the soil, while the latter is executed mainly in glasshouses. Since solar heating is done at relatively low temperatures, compared with artificial heating, its effect on living and nonliving soil components is likely to be less drastic.

Many studies have shown that solarization effectively reduces pathogen populations and disease incidence in various regions. In many cases these effects lasted for the whole season or even longer. The list of pathogens and diseases controlled by soil solarization is long, with the following serving as examples: Verticillium disease (of tomato, potato, eggplant, cotton, peanuts, pistachio, olive), Rhizoctonia disease (potato, onion, iris), Sclerotium rolfsii blight (peanuts), Pyrenochaeta lycopersici (tomato), P. terrestris (onion), Fusarium diseases (cotton, melon, tomato, onion, strawberry), the free – living nematode Pratylenchus thornei (potato), the parasitic weed Orobanche (carrot, eggplant, broadbean), pod rot (peanuts), and Ditylenchus dipsaci (garlic) (1-5). Disease control is usually accompanied by an increase in yield and quality. Yield increase is a function of the effectiveness of disease control as well as of the level of soil infestation and the damage caused to the crop by the disease. As expected, some pathogens are not controlled by solarization, e.g. <u>Macrophomina phaseolina</u>; the method is ineffective in controlling melon and pepper collapse in Israel, and variable in effectiveness against <u>Meloidogyne</u> spp. (3,4).

Weed control, a phenomenon discovered in solarized soils in the early experiments (1), is an additional benefit to disease control. An increasing number of studies of weed control by solarization have been carried out recently. In addition, solarization markedly reduces populations of the soil mite <u>Rhizoglyphus</u> <u>robini</u> (6).

BIOLOGICAL, CHEMICAL AND PHYSICAL CHANGES OCCURRING IN SOLARIZED SOIL

<u>Biological control</u>

Solarization controls numerous pathogens very effectively, in spite of the fact that temperatures in the solarized soil are not very high. Solarization stimulates biological control in the soil, during and after the solarization process, and several such mechanisms of control have been investigated (3,4,7-11). A few selected examples will be described. One important mechanism is the weakening effect (9,12). The basic assumption is that when a propagule of a pathogen is exposed to sublethal doses of a killing agent, it may be weakened and become more vulnerable to the soil organisms which, at a later stage, will attack and kill it. Hence, in spite of the fact that at zero time the pathogen population is only slightly affected by the sublethal dose, and seems viable, the population of the damaged and weakened propagules subsequently declines more rapidly than that of the intact, nontreated propagules. The weakening or stress concept is an old one and has been discussed thoroughly in the classical works of Garrett, as shown with <u>Armillaria</u> <u>mellea</u> (13). When this fungus is exposed to sublethal doses of CS_2, it becomes more easily colonized by <u>Trichoderma</u>. Sublethal heating weakens propagules of the pathogenic fungi <u>Sclerotium</u> <u>rolfsii</u>, <u>Fusarium</u> <u>oxysporum</u> f. sp. <u>niveum</u> and <u>A</u>. <u>mellea</u> (9,12,14). As a result, the populations of these pathogens are thus also disease incidence are reduced. The implications of this phenomenon are far beyond soil solarization. Thus, in the right situation, reducing the dosage of a disinfestant may enable us to reduce costs, and pollution of the environment, and avoid the creation of a biological vacuum in the soil.

Another phenomenon related to a beneficial microbial shift in the solarized soil is "induced suppressiveness". In many cases the solarized soil becomes resistant to reinfestation or reinvasion by a pathogen introduced into the previously solarized soil, which indicates that the solarized soil has become suppressive (4,7,10). This is supported by the observation that soil solarization frequently has a long-term effect in pathogen control which lasts for two or three seasons after solarization (5,15-17). Induced suppressiveness in solarized soils was associated with stimulation of lytic microorganisms, suppression of production of resting structures, and partial nullification of fungistasis (7).

Increased growth response (IGR)

It has been shown both with steamed and with fumigated soils that plant growth may be improved by such treatments even in the absence of known pathogens (11). Improvement of plant growth occurred in solarized soils even if they were not infested (18). One theory to explain this increased growth is that minerals are released, thereby improving the nutritional status of the soil. Chemical soil analyses confirmed this. In extracts of solarized soils, increased amounts of NO_3^-, NH_4^+, Ca_2^{++}, K^+ and soluble organic matter were recorded. These extracts also stimulated the growth of tomato seedlings (18). Stimulation of beneficial microorganisms in soil may also contribute to IGR. Populations of fluorescent pseudomonads (FP) increase greatly in the rhizosphere and tissues of plants growing in solarized soil (19). FP are beneficial microorganisms which in certain cases improve plant growth and control pathogens.

The phenomenon of plant growth stimulation in non-infested soils which are subjected to disinfestation treatments, raises the fundamental question of what is a healthy plant? Is it one grown in a non-infested soil, namely, a soil that is free from known soil-borne pathogens, or one grown in a disinfested soil? Plant health is a much broader concept than that of disease control, and producing a healthy plant is different from controlling a disease.

Simulation models of soil heating

Solar heating of the soil depends on climatic factors (e.g. solar radiation, temperature, air humidity and wind velocity), soil characteristics, and the polyethylene's properties (e.g. transmissivity to short- and long-wave atmospheric infrared radiation). Knowing these parameters may enable , with the aid of the appropriate equations, prediction of the temperature regime at a given depth. Mahrer (20) developed a one-dimensional numerical model for predicting the temperatures of polyethylene-mulched and -nonmulched soils. The predicted temperatures were very similar to the observed ones, the magnitude of error being $0.6-1.2^0$C. This model enables us to choose the appropriate climatic regions and the time of year most suitable for soil solarization, provided that data on pathogen heat-sensitivity and population density, at various depths, are available and adequately interpreted.

COMBINING SOIL SOLARIZATION WITH OTHER CONTROL METHODS

Combining pesticides, biocontrol agents and/or cultural practices with solarization should improve disease control. Whenever a pathogen is weakened by one treatment, a synergistic effect can be expected from dual treatments. Combining solarization with biocontrol agents might be especially effective in preventing reinfestation and in extending the effectiveness of disease control. Moreover, such combinations may permit reduced dosages of fumigation materials, or shorter duration of solarization. A combination of the antagonistic fungus Trichoderma harzianum and solarization delayed Rhizoctonia solani inoculum build-up and improved disease control (21). Especially interesting was the finding (22) that application of T. harzianum prevented reinfestation of methyl bromide-fumigated soil by S. rolfsii and

R. solani. Moreover, the combined treatments increased the crop yield. A rapid increase in the T. harzianum population in the fumigated soil apparently prevented soil colonization by the pathogen.

SOLARIZATION IN COOLER REGIONS

Various attempts have been made to adapt solarization in climatically marginal regions or periods of the year. Combining solarization with other methods of control is a promising approach for this purpose. Another approach, developed independently in Italy, Japan, and other countries, is to mulch the soil with polyethylene or vinyl inside closed glasshouses or plastic houses, in order to intensify soil heating (23,24). The improved heating and improved pathogen control in closed greenhouses was verified by both measurements and experimental approaches (25).

CONCLUDING REMARKS AND FUTURE STUDIES

A summary of the first decade (1976-86) of soil solarization (26) showed a marked proliferation of the method. During this period, research on soil solarization was extended to at least 24 countries, yielding at least 173 publications. Since then, the method has expanded. This indicates that soil solarization is effective, has great potential, and that there is a need for alternatives to the common methods of control. The use of soil solarization for disease control has its own advantages. It is a safe, non-chemical method that does not involve toxic residues, relatively inexpensive, simple and easy to use and to teach less-well-trained farmers to use. It can be applied over large areas by machine or in small plots by an individual worker. It is suitable for the developed countries, but has special advantages for the developing countries. However, this method has limitations as well: it can be used only in regions where the climate is suitable and the soil is free of crops for the month-long treatment. Also, for certain crops the method is too expensive with the present mode of application.

464

Various lines of research might be followed in an attempt to improve solarization and adapt it to a wider range of conditions. The method should be tested against additional important soilborne pests, and for other potential uses. Also, long-term field experiments should be carried out to seek any possible negative side effects, explore the possibility of using it for more than one season, and find ways to improve application and reduce its cost. Soil solarization should not be regarded as a universal method, but rather as an additional means of control which, if used correctly and in the right instances, can reduce pest damage safely, effectively and economically, and thereby contribute to increased food production. The full potential of soil solarization can be realized only if we continue with thorough studies in each region. The ultimate goal of any new method of control is to develop it for commercial use by the farmer. This requires interdisciplinary efforts, with the Extension Service playing a major role. Solarization is an additional option for use and inclusion in integrated pest management programs.

REFERENCES

1. Katan J, Greenberger A, Alon H, Grinstein A (1976) Phytopathology 66: 683-688

2. Katan J (1984) Br Crop Prot Conf 1189-1196

3. Katan J (1981) Ann Rev Phytopathol 19:211-236

4. Katan J (1987) In: Chet I (Ed) Innovative Approaches to Plant Disease Control, John Wiley & Sons, NY, pp 77-105

5. Pullman GS, DeVay JE, Garber RH, Weinhold AR (1981) Phytopathology 71:954-959

6. Gerson U, Yathom S, Katan J (1981) Phytoparasitica 9:153-155

7. Greenberger A, Yogev A, Katan J (1987) Phytopathology 77: 1663 - 1667

8. Katan JE, DeVay JE, Greenberger A (1989) In: Tjamos EC, Beckman CH (eds) Vascular Wilt Diseases in Plants. Springer-Verlag, Berlin, pp 493-499

9. Freeman S, Katan J (1988) Phytopathology 78: 1656 - 1661

10. Hardy GE, Sivasithamparam (1985) In: Parker CA, Rovira AD, Moore KJ, Wong PTW, Kollmorgen JK (eds) Biology and

Management of Soilborne Plant Pathogens. APS, St Paul, MN, pp 279-281

11. Cook RJ, Baker KF (1983) The Nature and Practice of Biological Control of Plant Pathogens. APS, St. Paul, MN

12. Lifshitz R, Tabachnik M, Katan J, Chet I (1983) Can J Microbiol 29:1607-1610

13. Garrett SD (1956) Biology of Root Infecting Fungi. Cambridge University Press, Cambridge

14. Munnecke DE, Wilbur W, Darley EF (1976) Phytopathology 66:1363-1368

15. Katan J, Fishler G, Grinstein A (1983) Phytopathology 73: 1215 - 1219

16. Abdel - Rahim MF, Satour MM, Mickail KY, El-Eraqi SA, Grinstein A, Chen Y, Katan J (1988) Pl Dis 72: 143 - 146

17. Davis J, Sorensen LH (1986) Phytopathology 76: 1021 - 1026

18. Chen Y, Katan J (1980) Soil Sci 130:271-277

19. Gamliel A, Hadar E, Katan J (1981) Proc 7th Congr Mediter Phytopath Union pp 72-73.

20. Mahrer, Y (1979) J Appl Meteor 18:1263 - 1267

21. Elad Y, Katan J, Chet I (1980) Phytopathology 70:418-422

22. Elad Y, Hadar Y, Chet I, Henis Y (1982) Crop Prot 1:199-211

23. Garibaldi A, Tamietti G (1984) Acta Hort 152: 237 -243

24. Kodama T, Fukai T, Matsumoto Y (1980) Bull Nara Pref Agric Exp Sta 11:41-52

25. Mahrer Y, Avissar R, Naot O, Katan J (1987) Agric For Meteor 41: 325-334.

26. Katan J, Grinstein A, Greenberger A, Yarden O, DeVay JE (1987) Phytoparasitica 15:229-255

© 1990 Elsevier Science Publishers B.V. (Biomedical Division)
Pesticides and alternatives, editor J.E. Casida

ADVANCES IN BIOLOGICAL CONTROL OF FUNGAL LEAF PATHOGENS
THROUGH FERMENTED ORGANIC SUBSTRATES AND MICROORGANISMS

HEINRICH C. WELTZIEN

Institut für Pflanzenkrankheiten, University of Bonn, Nussallee 9, 5300 Bonn,
Fed. Rep. Germany

Since Millardet (1) first developed Bordeaux mixtures as a fungicide in 1885
to control the grape downy mildew, Plasmopara viticola, chemical plant protection was developed based on pesticide application. The ideas of Pasteur (2)
and de Bary (3) were put in practise, that microbes can cause diseases, and
killing these organisms should result in health. Through the last 100 years
this principle was perpetuated, though more and more refined. It is only recent, that accumulating problems associated with the world wide use of pesticides cause scientists, practitioners, politicians and the general public to
demand the development of alternatives. It is generally hoped that new principles can be applied, avoiding some, if not all the negative effects known to
be caused by pesticides, while preserving or even improving the well known
benefits.

Our own research on biological control of plant diseases was started in 1985
and led us during the past years to gradually develop a novel approach. The
following postulates are considered as proven facts:

  1. Microbes and the metabolites can induce resistance in plants against
    pathogens.

The work of Kuc (4) and Schönbeck (5) with their respective research teams
offer rich evidence for induced resistance through microorganisms against
various host-pathogen-systems.

  2. Composted organic materials as soil amendments can suppress soil borne
    plant diseases in various environments.

There is enough evidence for these effects in the work of Hoitink (6) and
Lumsden et al. (7).

  3. In nature microbes on surfaces do not occur as single species colonies but
    in mixed conglomerates, forming bio-films with complex but rather stable
    interactions.

The work by Costerton et al. (8) has shown this for many microbial systems,
though data on plants were not yet presented. However, modern research on the
plant phyllosphere is in line with their findings (Fokkema)(9).

468

These reports and our empirical findings lead us to establish the following
hypotheses for an alternative system to maintain plant health:

1. Substrates, highly enriched with saprophytic soil microbes are likely to
   contain elicitors to induce resistance.
2. Composted organic material is a suitable source for microbial mixtures with
   the desired effects.
3. Plant surfaces treated with such microbe mixtures may also be protected
   against pathogens through bio-film like colonization.

We have tested these hypotheses during the past 4 years with various host
pathogen systems. The main results can be summarized as follows:

1. Soil amendment with composted manures does not only suppress soil borne
pathogens, but has significant depressive effects on two powdery mildews, if
inoculated under standardized conditions and compared against plants, cultivated
in field soil. The models used were Erysiphe graminis on wheat and barley (Budde
und Weltzien)(10) and Sphaerotheca fuliginea on cucumber (Samerski 1989, unpubl.)(table 1).

TABLE 1

THE EFFECT OF SOIL AMENDMENTS WITH COMPOSTED HORSE MANURE ON POWDERY MILDEW
OF WHEAT (ERYSIPHE GRAMINIS TRITICI) AND CUCUMBERS (SPHAEROTHECA FULIGINEA)
No. pustules on primary leaves after artificial inoculation,
check planted in field soil = 100.

| Pathogen-Host-System | Soil:Compost Ratio | | | | | | | | Literature |
	1:0	5:1	2:1	1:1	1:2	1:3	1:5	0:1	
E. graminis – winter barley	100	71	74	55	45		22	15	Budde und Weltzien (10)
E. graminis – wheat	100			54				35	Budde und Weltzien (11)
S. fuliginea – cucumber	100			76	69	59			Samerski 1989, unpubl.

2. Watery fermentation extracts from composts have highly significant suppressive effects on different host-pathogen-systems. So far the following
systems have been tried successfully (table 2).

TABLE 2

EFFICIENCY OF DISEASE SUPPRESSION AFTER PROPHYLACTIC APPLICATION
OF WATERY EXTRACTS FROM COMPOSTED ORGANIC MATERIAL

Pathogen-Host-System	Efficiency of disease suppression (%)	Literature
Phytophthora infestans - tomato leaves	90	Ketterer (12)
Plasmopara viticola - grape leaves	95	Weltzien et al. (13)
Pseudoperonospora cubense - cucumber leaves	66	Weltzien und Minassian, 1988, unpubl.
Pythium ultimum - alfalfa seedlings	59	Baumgart 1987, unpubl.
Uncinula necator - grape leaves	93	Ketterer und Weltzien (14)
Erysiphe graminis - barley leaves	75	Budde und Weltzien (10)
Erysiphe graminis - wheat leaves	59	Budde und Weltzien (10)
Erysiphe betae - sugar beet leaves	58	Samerski 1986, unpubl.
Sphaerotheca fuliginea - cucumber leaves	58	Samerski und Weltzien (15)
Botrytis cinerea - phaseolus bean leaves	70	Stindt und Weltzien (16)
Botrytis fabae - Vicia faba leaves	92	Medhin (17)
Venturia inaequalis - apple leaves	67	Tränkner und Kirchner- Bierschenk (18)
Phoma lingam - rape leaves	81	Paul 1989, unpubl.

3. Composts of different raw materials proved to be effective, though they may differ in their efficiency in comparative tests (table 3).

TABLE 3

THE EFFECTS OF EXTRACTS FROM COMPOSTS OF DIFFERENT RAW MATERIALS
ON PLANT DISEASE SUPPRESSION

Composted raw materials	% Efficiency of Disease Suppression		
	E. graminis [a] Barley	P. infestans [b] Tomato	B. cinerea [c] Phaseolus beans
Worm compost (commercial)	56		54
Green plants (mixed) + horse manure, 50:50	52		79
Green plants (mixed) + straw, 50:50	27		59
Household waste	38		
Cattle manure (sample 1) (commercial)	38		100
Cattle manure (sample 2) (commercial)	85		
Grape marc (commercial)	47		90
Horse manure	75	62	95
Hog manure		76	
Goat manure		70	

Literature: [a] Budde und Weltzien (10)
[b] Weltzien et al. (13)
[c] Stindt 1989, unpubl.

4. Until now, all extracts were based on watery suspensions. Compost-water-relations were varied between 1:3 and 1:10. Volumes prepared, varied between 1 and 5000 l. The mixtures were stirred thoroughly only once and then left for the remaining period at ambient temperatures. The extraction time ends by filtering of the broth through cheese cloth. The liquid is then applied with regular pesticide spray equipment. The volume used per plant or area is based on traditional plant protection recommendations. Table 4 summarizes some of the practices followed so far.

TABLE 4

EFFECTS OF VARIOUS EXTRACTION TIMES ON SUPPRESSION
OF PLANT DISEASE OR CONIDIA GERMINATION

Extraction time (Horse manure)	% Efficiency of Disease Suppression		
	E. graminis [a] Barley	P. infestans [b] Tomato	B. cinerea [c] Phaseolus beans
1 day		0	72
2 days		32	78
3 "	54		
4 "			80
6 "	41		
7 "		82	
8 "			86
14 "		89	
16 "			100
28 "		54	
32 "			100
3 months	56		
4 "	30		

Literature: [a]Budde 1989, unpubl.
[b]Ketterer 1989, unpubl.
[c]Stindt 1989, unpubl.

5. Most of our applications were only successfull, if used before inoculation
with the respective pathogen. However, there are indications for some curative
effects in the case of Botrytis leaf blight on phaseolus beans. For full efficiency of the extracts, some time must elapse between application and inoculation, called the "induction time". It is not necessarily characterized by the
development of induced resistance of the host but may as well be necessary for
the establishment of some microorganisms on the host surface, to establish bio-
film-like conglomerates, interacting directly with the pathogen's inoculum. Some
of the tested induction times are presented in table 5. It must be emphasized,
that the induction time becomes irrelevant under field conditions, where the
pathogen deposit can be considered a continuous process.

472

TABLE 5

EFFECTS OF THE TIME ELAPSED BETWEEN TREATMENT OF PLANTS WITH EXTRACTS
AND INOCULATION WITH THE PATHOGEN (= INDUCTION TIME) ON DISEASE SUPPRESSION
Efficiency: Untreated check =100

Induction time	% Efficiency of Disease Suppression		
	E. graminis [a)] Barley	P infestans [b)] Tomato	P. viticola [c)] Grape
1 hour			96
3 hours		62	98
4 "			92
1 day	39	88	
2 days	80	89	
3 "	60	80	

Literature: [a)+c)]Weltzien et al. (13)
[b)]Ketterer 1989, unpubl.

6. Induced resistance of the host and direct inhibitory effects on the pathogen have both been observed. So far powdery mildew diseases present the clearest
case for induced resistance, as no effects on the pathogens early development
were observed. Downy mildews and Botrytis are examples for direct inhibitions
but any additional effects on host reactions need further studies. Some of the
data obtained are presented in table 6.

7. In most cases, the efficiency of the extracts depended on the presence of
living microorganisms in the broth. If sterilized by heat or filtration, the
effect was largely lost. Some microorganisms isolated from the broth and cultivated under sterile conditions could induce similar effects, if suspended in
water and applied as the complex extract. Some of the best results achieved so
far were found, if the extracts were enriched with mixtures of selected microorganisms. Data presented in table 7 give evidence of these findings.

TABLE 6

INDUCTION OF HOST DEFENSE REACTIONS OR DIRECT INHIBITORY EFFECTS
CAUSED BY APPLICATION OF COMPOST EXTRACTS

Pathogen–Host–System	Effect caused	Efficiency (%)	Literature
Sphaerotheca fuliginea – cucumber leaves	general defense reactions	46	Samerski und Weltzien (15)
"	papilla formation	56	"
"	cell wall lignification	53	"
"	penetration	30	"
"	haustoria development	33	"
"	secondary hyphae development	50	"
"	conidiophore formation	25	"
"	sporulation	43	"
Erysiphe graminis – barley leaves	sporulation	56	Budde 1989, unpubl.
Erysiphe graminis – wheat leaves	sporulation	31	"
Phytophthora infestans	zoosporangia germination	64	Ketterer, 1989, unpubl.
Plasmopara viticola – grape leaves	zoosporangia germination	77	"
Pseudoperonospora cubense – cucumber leaves	zoosporangia germination	100	Winterscheidt 1989, unpubl.
Botrytis cinerea – phaseolus bean leaves	conidia germination	100	Stindt 1989, unpubl.

TABLE 7

EFFICIENCY OF NONE STERILE AND STERILE EXTRACTS FROM COMPOSTED ORGANIC MATERIAL
AGAINST DIFFERENT BIOLOGICAL SYSTEMS

Pathogen–Host–System	Extract used	Efficiency %	Literature
P. infestans – tomato leaves	horse manure, none sterile	82	Ketterer, 1989, unpubl.
"	horse manure, heat sterilized	0	"
"	horse manure, sterile filtration	10	"
P. viticola – grape leaves	cattle manure, none sterile	85	"
"	cattle manure, sterile filtration	42	"
P. cubense – cucumber leaves	horse manure, none sterile	90	Winterscheidt, 1989, unpubl.
"	horse manure, sterile filtration	5	"
E. graminis – barley leaves	horse manure, none sterile	85	Budde, 1989, unpubl.
"	horse manure, sterile filtration	44	"
S. fuliginea – cucumber leaves	horse manure, none sterile	56	Samerski, 1989, unpubl.
"	Horse manure sterile filtration	39	"

8. Successful disease control under field conditions was evident in several
cases. The result against Phytophthora infestans on potatoes in 1987 stand out,
as they were achieved during a very heavy epidemic. Control and yield data
compare favorably with those from fungicide treated plots. God results were also
found against Plasmopara viticola and Pseudopeziza tracheiphila on grapes and
against Botrytis cinerea on strawberries (table 8).

TABLE 8

FIELD EXPERIMENTS FOR PLANT DISEASE SUPPRESSION THROUGH APPLICATION
OF EXTRACTS FROM COMPOSTED ORGANIC MATERIALS, SELECTED MICROORGANISMS
AND MIXTURES OF BOTH

Host plant Disease	Material used	Efficiency %	Yield increase (control=100%)	Literature
Potato late blight	horse manure	5	98	Ketterer und Weltzien (12)
Potato late blight	horse manure + microorganisms	75	178	"
Potato late blight	microorganisms	71	161	"
Grape vine downy mildew	horse manure	75	374	Ketterer 1989, unpubl.
Grape vine downy mildew	horse manure + microorganisms	90	478	"
Winter barley powdery mildew	cattle manure	47	104	Budde 1989, unpubl.
Spring barley powdery mildew	grape marc	53	106	"
Spring barley powdery mildew	horse manure	40	106	"
Cucumber powdery mildew	horse manure	36	108	Samerski 1989, unpubl.
Strawberry grey mold	horse manure	50	126	Stindt und Weltzien (19)
Strawberry grey mold	cattle manure	70	121	Stindt und Weltzien (20)

CONCLUSIONS

One may conclude, that biological control of leaf and fruit diseases of plants is possible. None toxic microorganisms can be used. They act through induced resistance or as inhibitors of pathogen development. Composted organic materials are good sources of inhibitory, mixed microbe suspensions and for isolation of effective microorganisms. As the basic principle differs clearly from the traditional application of toxic chemicals, many of the problems related to chemical plant protection can be avoided. The system affects many different host pathogen combinations. It can be assumed, that others are also sensitive if tested with appropriate techniques. We have encouraging unpublished data from apple scab (<u>Venturia inaequalis</u>), <u>Phoma lingam</u> (Paul 1989, unpubl.) and various seed borne diseases such as <u>Pythium</u> spp. and even <u>Tilletia</u>. It is hoped, that some of the existing problems in todays plant protection can be resolved with this technology.

REFERENCES

1. Millardet P (1885) J d' Agr Pratique 2:707-710.

2. Pasteur L, Jourbert SF (1877) CR Soc Biol 85:101.

3. de Bary A (1863) Ann Sci Nat 4 Sér 20:1-148.

4. Dean RA, Kúc J (1986) Phytopath 76:186-189.

5. Schönbeck F, Dehne HW, Beicht W (1980) Z Pflanzenkrankh Pflanzenschutz 87:654-666.

6. Hoitink HAJ, Fahy PC (1986) Ann Rev Phytopath 24:93-114.

7. Lumsden RD, Lewis JA, Millner PD (1983) Phytopath 73:1543-1548.

8. Costerton WJ, Cheng KJ, Geesey GG, Ladd TJ, Nickel JC, Dasgupta M, Marrie TJ (1987) Ann Rev Microbiol 41:435-464.

9. Fokkema NJ, van den Heuvel (1986) Mircobiology of the phyllosphere. Cambridge Univ Press, Cambridge 392 pp.

10. Budde K, Weltzien HC (1988) Med Fac Landbouww Rijksuniv Gent 53:363-371.

11. Budde K, Weltzien HC (1988) Mitt BBA (Berlin-Dahlem) 245:366.

12. Ketterer N, Weltzien HC (1988) Mitt BBA (Berlin-Dahlem) 245:346.

13. Weltzien HC, Ketterer N, Samerski C, Budde K, Medhin G (1987) Nachrbl Dtsch Pflanzenschutzdienst 39:17-19.

14. Ketterer N, Weltzien HC (1987) Med Fac Landbouww Rijksuniv Gent 52:965-970.

15. Samerski C, Weltzien HC (1988) Med Fac Landbouww Rijksuniv Gent 53:373-377.

16. Stindt A, Weltzien HC (1988) Med Fac Landbouww Rijksuniv Gent 53:379-388.

17. Medhin G (1988) Wirtsresistenz und Erregeraggressivität am Wirt-Pathogen System Vicia faba L. - Botrytis fabae Sard.; Beitrag zur methodischen Verbesserung der Resistenzzüchtung. Landw Fakultät, Rhein Friedr Wilh Universität Bonn 79 pp.

18. Tränkner A, Kirchner-Bierschenk R (1988) Med Fac Landbouww Rijksuniv Gent 53:359-362

19. Stindt A, Weltzien HC (1988) Gesunde Pflanzen 40:451-454.

20. Stindt A, Weltzien HC. (1988) Mitt BBA (Berlin-Dahlem) 245:368.

© 1990 Elsevier Science Publishers B.V. (Biomedical Division)
Pesticides and alternatives, editor J.E. Casida

SUPPRESSION OF FUSARIUM WILT OF ADZUKIBEAN BY RHIZOSHERE MICRO-ORGANISMS

SHINSAKU HASEGAWA, NORIO KONDO* and FUJIO KODAMA*

Hokkaido Institute of Public Health, North 19, West 12 Northword, Sapporo #060, JAPAN and *The Hokkaido Central Agricultural Experiment Station, Naganuma, #069-13, JAPAN

AIM

Fusarium wilt of the adzukibean caused by *Fusarium oxysporum* f. sp. *adzukicola* is a serious and widespred disease in Hokkaido, northern part of Japan. This pathogen is a root-infecting fungus that spreads relatively slowly along the vessel by hyphal growth and causes necrotic, yellowing and wilt of the leaf and the stem of adzukibean[1-3]. In our work on Fusarium wilt of adzukibean, we have isolated microorganisms antagonistic to *F. oxysporum* f. sp. *adzukicola* FA-3 from the adzukibean rhizosphere, and report here: the isolation and identification of antagonists and their producing antifungal agents; and the efficacy of iso-ates or their antifungal agents as seed treatment to Fusarium wilt by *F. oxysporum*. f. sp. *adzukicola*[1,4-6].

ISOLATION AND IDENTIFICATION OF ANTAGONISTIC MICROORGANISMS AND THEIR PRODUCING ANTIFUNGAL AGENTS(Table 1)

We isolated antagonists to *Fusarium oxysporum* FA-3 from the rizoshere of adzukibean and other materials by the improved triple layer method[4]. One ml of diluted($10^3 - 10^5$ w/v) rizoshere soil of adzukibean were spread in plates with 1.5% agar and added the spore suspension of *F. oxysporum* FA-3 on the plates. These plates were incubated at 28 C for 2 to 4 days, and then the colonies with clear zone were picked up. These isolates were identified as *Pseudomonas aeruginosa*, *P. fluorescens*, *P. cepacia* *Streptomyces flaveus* and *Streptomyces* spp.[1,2,4-8]. These produced hemipyocianine, chlororaphin, phenazine-1-carboxylic acid[1,6], pyrrolnitrin[1,4], pyoluteorin[5,6], Antibiotic Y-1 (monazomycin like, 7) and water soluble unknowns.

Table 1 Isolated antaonists and their producing antifungal agents

Antagonist	Antifungal agents Source( )*1	Hemi-pyocianine	Chlororaphin	Phenazine-1-carboxylic acid	Pyrrolnitrin	Pyoluteorin
Pseudomonas						
aeruginosa S-1	Adzukibean(Rl)	(+)*2	+	+	–	–
S-7	Adzukibean(Rl)	+	+	+	–	–
SH-6	Soil	–	+	+	–	–
fluorescens S-2	Adzukibean(Rl)	–	+	(+)	–	–
Y-15	Melone(Rl)	–	–	–	–	+
NS-7371	lily(Rl)	–	–	+	+	–
cepacia B-17	Adzukibean(Rh)	–	–	–	+	–
1218	Beet(Rh)	–	–	–	+	–
Streptomyces						
sp. No. 2	Adzukibean(Rl)	Water soluble				
sp. B-6	Adzukibean(Rl)	Water soluble				
flaveus Y-1	River water	Antibiotic Y-1 (monazomycin like)				

*1 Sample source : (Rl), Rhizoplane; (Rh), Rhizosphere
*2 Antifungal agent: producing, +; trace, (+); no producing, -

Hemipyo-
cianine

Chlororaphin

Phenazine-1-
carboxylic
acid

Pyrrolnitrin

Pyoluteorin

Antibiotic Y-1
(Monazomycin
like)

in vitro ANTIFUNGAL ACTIVITIES OF MICROBIAL CULTURES AND ANTI-
FUNGAL AGENTS AGAINST *FUSARIUM OXYSPORUM* f. sp. *adzukicola* FA-3

Bioassay by reversed layer method(Fig. 1)(4) showed that 3
strains of Pseudomonads and *St. flaveus* Y-1(8) were highly inhibitory to *F. oxysporum* FA-3(Table 2). On agar spot inoculation
plates(Fig. 1)(4), *P. aeruginosa* S-7, *St. flaveus* Y-1 and
Streptomyces sp. No.2 showed highly inhibition and continuance
of antifungal activities. The minimum inhibitory concentration
(MIC) of pyrrolnitrin against *F. oxysporum* FA-3 was 3.13 ug/ml;
Antibiotic Y-1, 6.25 ug/ml; hemipyocianine, 50 ug/ml; chlororaphin and phenazine-1-carboxylic acid, 100 ug/ml; and water
soluble unknowns, 25-50 ug/ml(Table 2).

ANTIFUNGAL SPECTRUM OF MICROBIAL CULTURES AND ANTIFUNGAL AGENTS
(Table 3, 4)

The microbial cultures of isolates and their antifungal agents
strongly inhibited growth of *F. oxysporum* and also many other
plant pathogenic fungi: *F. solani*, *F. moniliforme*, *F. roseum*,
Biporaris sorokiniana, *Alternaria alternata*, *Cladosporium cucu-
merinum*, *Pyricularia oryzae*, *Pythium graminicolum*, *Verticillium
dahliae*, *Cylindrocarpon* sp., *Rhizoctonia solani*.

Antibiotic Y-1 was an effective inhibitor of all tested pathogens in culture. But pyrrolnitrin was much less effective

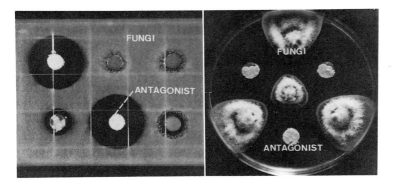

a. Reversed layer method   b. Agar spot inoculation method

Fig. 1 Antifungal activities of antagonists against <u>Fusarium oxysporum</u> FA-3

against *Fusarium* species than any other genera, and was totally
ineffectives against *F. oxysporum* f.sp. *cepae*. Also, phenazines,
such as hemipyocianine were did not inhibit strongly the growth
of *Fusarium* species. But the strains which produced phenazines
were active against *Fusarium* species and continued these strength
on the agar spot inoculation method. The specificity of the
strains for susceptibility against antifungal agents were recognized.

Table 2 The Inhibition effect of isolated antagonists and their antifungal agents against <u>Fusasrium oxysporum</u> FA-3

Antagonist	I. Antagonist agar disc		II. Antifungal agent	
	Reversed layer meth-od*1, 2days (inhibition zone, mm)	Agar spot inoculation method*2 (inhibition zone, mm)	Isolated antifungal agent	Minimum inhibitory concentration (μg/ml, 7days)
Pseudomonas aeruginosa S-7 (Brucella agar, 30 C, 4days)	30.0	9.5 +++(4days) ↓ 9.5 +++(7days)	Hemipyocyanine Chlororaphin Phenazine-1-carboxylic acid	100 200 200
Pseudomonas cepacia B-17 (Brucella agar, 30 C, 4days)	33.8	7.0 ++ (4days) ↓ 3.5 + (7days)	pyrrolnitrin	3.13
Pseudomonas fluorescens NS-7371 (Brucella agar, 30 C, 4days)	31.5	7.2 ++ (4days) ↓ 4.8 + (7days)	Pyrrolnitrin Phenazine-1-carboxylic acid	3.13 200
Streptomyces sp. No. 2 (YM agar*3, 30 C, 7days)	24.0	11.2 +++(4days) ↓ 9.5 +++(7days)	Crude--- water soluble	25
Streptomyces sp. B-6 (PDA*4, 30 C, 4days)	25.0	4.7 ++ (4days) ↓ 0.0 - (7days)	Crude--- water soluble	50
Streptomyces flaveus Y-1 (GS agar*5, 30 C, 7days)	31.2	10.7 +++(4days) ↓ 10.1 +++(7days)	Antibiotic Y-1 (Monazomycin like)	3.13

*1 Reversed layer method: <u>Fusarium oxysprum</u> FA-3 spores were used for
  bottom layer and 4 or 7 days culture agar discs of antagonists were
  used.
*2 Agar spot inoculation method: 7 days culture agar discs of <u>Fusarium
  oxysporum</u> FA-3 and 4 or 7 days culture agar discs of antagonists were
  used. Inhibition zone between the pathogen and the antagonist: +++≥
  9.0mm, 9.0>++≥5.0, 5.0>+≥2.0, 2.0>(+)>0.0, -=0.0
*3 YM agar: Yeast-malt agar
*4 PDA: Potato dextrose agar
*5 GS agar: Glycerol-soybean meal agar

The 3 Growth inhibition of the plant pathogens by the microbial cultures of antagonists*1

Phytopathogenic fungi*2	Antagonists											
Culture days	Pseudomonas aeruginosa S-7		Pseudomonas cepacia B-17		Pseudomonas fluorescens NS-7371		Streptomyces sp. No. 2		Streptomyces sp. B-6		Streptomyces flaveus Y-1	
	4	7	4	7	4	7	4	7	4	7	4	7
Fusarium oxysporum FA-3(adzukibean)*3	+++	+++	+++*5	+	++	++	+++	+++	++	++	+++	+++
Fusarium oxysporum FGH(adzukibean)	++	++	++	+	++	++	+++	+++	+	-	+++	+++
Fusarium oxysporum F-1(adzukibean)	++	++	++	-	++	++	+++	+++	-	-	+++	+++
Fusarium oxysporum f.sp.*4 spinacea H-18	++	++	++	++	++	++	+++	+++	+	-	+++	+++
Fusarium oxysporum f.sp.spinacea H-29	-	++	++	+	++	++	+++	+++	-	-	+++	+++
Fusarium oxysporum H-32(green pepper)	++	++	++	+	++	++	+++	+++	-	-	+++	+++
Fusarium oxysporum f.sp.fragariae H-34	+++	++	+	+	++	++	+++	+++	-	-	+++	+++
Fusarium oxysporum f.sp.melonis H-34	++	++	-	-	++	++	++	++	++	++	+++	+++
Fusarium oxysporum f.sp.lycopersici KF-244	++	++	++	-	-	+	+	++	-	-	+++	+++
Fusarium oxysporum f.sp.cepae KF-228	++	++	++	-	-	+	+	++	-	-	+++	+++
Fusarium oxysporum KF 854(lily)	+++	+++	++	-	++	+	+	++	++	+	+++	+++
Fusarium solani H-41(rice)	+++	+++	++	-	+++	++	+++	+++	-	-	+++	+++
Fusarium moniliforme H-24(rice)	++	++	++	-	+++	++	+++	+++	++	++	+++	+++
Fusarium moniliforme H-36(rice)	+++	+++	-	-	+++	+	+++	+++	-	-	+++	+++
Fusarium roseum H-35(wheat)	++	-	+++	++	-	-	+++	+++	-	-	+++	+++
Biporaris sorokiniana H-21(rice)	+++	+++	+++	+++	++	++	+++	+++	++	++	+++	+++
Alternaria alternata H-25(rice)	+++	+++	+++	+++	++	++	+++	+++	+++	+++	+++	+++
Cladosporium cucumerinum H-23(melon)	+++	+++	+++	+++	++	+	+++	+++	+++	+++	+++	+++
Pyricularia oryzae H-22(rice)	+++	+++	+++	+++	++	++	+++	+++	ND*6+	NT	+++	+++
Pythium graminicolum H-30(rice)	+++	++	+++	+++	++	++	+++	+++	+++	++	NT*7	
Verticillum dahliae H-28(strawberry)	+++	+++	+++	+++	++	++	+++	+++	NT		+++	+++
Cylindrocarpon sp. KF 846(lily)	+++	+++	+++	+++	+++	+++	+++	+++	++	++	+++	+++
Rhizoctonia solani H-31(potato)	-	-	+++	+++	++	++	+++	+++	++	++	+++	+++
Rhizoctonia solani KF 852(lily)	++	++	++	++	-	-	+++	+++	++	++	+++	+++

*1 Agar spot inocuration method: 7 days culture agar discs of phytopathogenic fungi and 4 days culture agar discs of antagonists, 7 days of actinomycetes were used.
*2 Microbial culture(culture agar disc): Potato dextrose agar(Difco) for phytopathogenic fungi, Brucella agar(Difco) for bacteria, Yeadt extract-malt extract agar(ISP medium No. 2) for actinomycetes, SG(Soybean-glycerol) agar for Streptomyces flaveus Y-1.
*3 Plant Source
*4 f. sp.: forma specialis
*5 Inhibition zone between the pathogen and the antagonist: +++≧9.0mm, 9.0>++≧5.0, 5.0>+≧2.0, 2.0>(+)>0.0, -=0.0
*6 ND: not detected.
*7 NT: not tested.

Table 4 Growth inhibition of the plant pathogens by the microbial cultures of antifungal agents

Phytopathgenic fungi	Antifungal agents — MIC (μg/ml)*1				
	Pyrrolnitrin	Pyoluteonin	Hemipyocianine	Phenazine-1-carboxylic acid	Antibiotic Y-1
Fusarium oxysporum FA-3(adzukibean)*2	3.13	25	50	100	6.25
Fusarium oxysporum FGH(adzukibean)	3.13	25	100	100	25
Fusarium oxysporum F-1(adzukibean)	3.13	25	100	50	12.5
Fusarium oxysporum f.sp.*3spinacea H-18	3.13	25	100	100	6.25
Fusarium oxysporum f.sp.spinacea H-29	3.13	25	100	100	6.25
Fusarium oxysporum H-32(green pepper)	3.13	12.5	200	50	12.5
Fusarium oxysporum f.sp.fragariae H-34	6.25	12.5	200	50	12.5
Fusarium oxysporum f.sp.melonis H-34	6.25	12.5	200	100	6.25
Fusarium oxysporum f.sp.lycopersici KF-244	6.25	25	200	100	25
Fusarium oxysporum f.sp.cepae KF-228	200	>200	>200	100	25
Fusarium oxysporum KF 854(lily)	12.5	25	>200	>200	12.5
Fusarium solani H-41(rice)	25	50	>200	>200	25
Fusarium moniliforme H-24(rice)	25	25	200	100	25
Fusarium moniliforme H-36(rice)	3.13	25	50	50	50
Fusarium roseum H-35(wheat)	3.13	12.5	>200	100	12.5
Biporaris sorokiniana H-21(rice)	0.78	6.5	100	100	0.39
Alternaria alternata H-25(rice)	0.78	3.13	>200	25	0.39
Cladosporium cucumerinum H-23(melon)	0.78	3.13	100	25	0.39
Pyricularia oryzae H-22(rice)	0.78	25	100	50	1.57
Pythium graminicolum H-30(rice)	3.13	12.5	>200	50	NT*4
Verticillium dahliae H-28(strawberry)	0.78	12.5	>200	25	3.13
Cylindrocarpon sp. KF 846(lily)	0.78	12.5	>200	25	1.57
Rhizoctonia solani H-31(potato)	0.39	400	>200	100	0.39
Rhizoctonia solani KF 852(lily)	1.56	400	>200	100	0.39

*1 MIC: Minimum inhibitory concentration(μg/ml), 7 or 14 days(27 C) culture on Potato dextrose agar(Difco)
*2 Plant Source
*3 f. sp.: forma specialis
*4 NT: not tested.

483

EFFICACY OF SEED BACTERIZATION WITH MICROBIAL CULTURES TO CONTROL OF FUSARIUM WILT OF ADZUKIBEAN

In greenhouse, treatment of the adzukibean seed with washed
bacterial cells of *P. cepacia* B-17 in *F. oxysporum* FA-3-infested
soil(Fig. 2) decreased the disease incidence from 76.3 to 8.8%

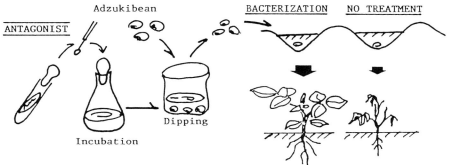

Fig. 2 Biological control of Fusarium wilt

| F.oxy. FA-3 | – | – | + | + |
| P.cep. B-17 | – | + | + | – |

Fig. 3 Effect of seed bacterization with <u>Pseudomonas</u> <u>cepacia</u> B-17 on
the control of Fusarium wilt of adzukibean caused by <u>Fusarium</u>
<u>oxysporum</u> FA-3*1

*1 Adzukibean: Hayate-syouzu,
   Treatment: Pathogenic fungi, <u>Fusarium</u> <u>oxysporum</u> FA-3(10^5spores/g soil);
   Antagonist, <u>Pseudomonas</u> <u>cepacia</u> B-17(10^8cells/ml solution).

(Fig. 3); *St. flaveus* Y-1, 9.0%; *P. aeruginosa* S-7, 11.6%; *Streptomyces* sp. No.2, 15.2%; and *P. fluorescens* NS-7371, 20.5% (Table 5).

In crop filed, treatment with *St. flaveus* Y-1 cultures decreased the disease incidence from 88 to 38%; *Streptomyces* sp. No.2, 41%; and *P. cepacia* B-17, 46%(Table 5). Methyl cellulose was used for injection of microbial cells at the time of seeding in field.

GROWTH OF MICROORGANISMS AND PRODUCTION OF ANTIFUNGAL AGENTS IN SOIL ON THE CONTROL OF FUSARIUM WILT OF ADZUKIBEAN(Fig. 4, Table 6)

In the case of low disease incidence, such as *P. cepacia* B-17 and *St. flaveus* Y-1, the increase of the number of antagonistic microorganisms and the decrease of the number of pathogen, *F. oxysporum* FA-3, in the rizoshere soil of adzukibean were recognized. The tightly relationship between the increase of antifungal agents and the decrease of disease incidence was not recognized. Washed microbial cells were as efficacious as whole cultures or culture filtrates, even though no or a few amount of antifungal agents were present when the seeds were treated. None of the treatments was phytotoxic to adzukibean.

Table 5   Effects of seed bacterization with antagonists on the control of adzukibean wilt caused by <u>Fusarium oxysporum</u> in green house and crop field*1

| | Disease incidence(%) | | |
| | Green house (36days) | Crop field (45days) | |
Antagonist*2	–	–	Me-cellulose
Pseudomonas aeruginosa S-7	11.6	63	60
Pseudomonas cepacia B-17	8.8	58	46
Pseudomonas fluorescens NS-7371	20.5	–*3	–
Flavobacterium sp. AB7	30.2	–	–
Acinetobacter calcoaceticus B28	77.0	85	–
Streptomyces sp. No. 2	15.2	92	41
Streptomyces sp. B6	65.0	82	–
Streptomyces flaveus Y-1	9.0	50	38
Without antagonist	76.3	88	88

*1 Adzuibean: Hayate-shozu in green house; Takara-shozu in crop field,
   Pathogenic fungi: <u>Fusarium oxysporum</u> FA-3, 10^5spores/g soil in green house; <u>Fusarium oxysporum</u> 10^3cells/g soil in crop field
*2 Antagonist: 10^8cells/ml solution
*3 Not tested.

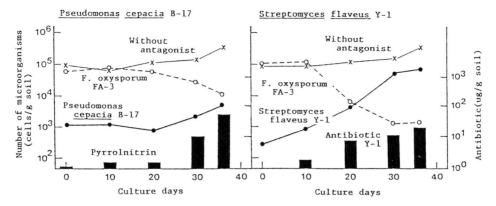

Fig. 4 Time course comparison of growth of microorganisms and production
        of antifungal agents on the control of Fusarium wilt of adzukibean
        in green house

Table 6 Growth of microorganisms and production of antifungal agents in
         rizoshere soil of adzukibean in green house

Antagonist	Number of cells/g soil		Production of antifungal agent (μg/g soil)	Disease incidence (%)
	Antagonist[*1] (days)0 10 20 30 36	F. oxysporum[*2] 0 10 20 30 36	0 10 20 30 36	
Pseudomonas aeruginosa S-7				11.6
Pseudomonas cepacia B-17				8.8
Pseudomonas fluorescens NS-7371				20.5
Acinetobacter calcoaceticus B-28				77.0
Streptomyces sp. No. 2				15.2
Streptomyces sp. B-6				65.0
Streptomyces flaveus Y-1				9.0
Without antagonist				76.3

[*1] 10^8cells/ml solutions of antagonists were used for seed bacterization.
[*2] 10^5cells/g soil of Fusarium oxysporum FA-3 were used.

486

The protective effect exhibited by treatment of adzukibean seed
with cultures of the antagonistic microorganisms may be due to
release of the antifungal agents by the gradual growth of the
microbial cells. Even though the concentration may be low, the
lysing cells may effect prolonged release and availability of the
antifungal agents during the critical period of seeding growth.

CONCLUSION

These results suggested that the isolates such as *P. cepacia*
B-17, *St. flaveus* Y-1 and *Streptomyces* sp. No.2 may be useful
as antagonists to *F. oxysporum* f. sp. *adzukicola* and may facilitate establishment of cultivation of healthy adzukibean. The
antagonisms exhibited by the microorganisms are possibly the
result of production of antifungal agents, which are themselves
effective in protecting agaist Fusarium wilt of adzukibean.

REFERENCES

1. Hasegawa S, Kodama F, Kaneshima H, Akai J (1987) J. Pharma-
    cobio-Dyn. 10s:57

2. Kodama F, Hasegawa S (1985) Kongetu no Nouyaku 30:22-27

3. Kondo N, Kodama F (1989) Shokubutu Boeki 43:28-33

4. Hasegawa S, Kamneshima H, Kodama F, Akai J (1986) Report of
    the Hokkaido Institute of Public Health 36:16-23

5. Hasegawa S, Kondo N, Kodama F (1989) Proceedings of 7th
    Symposium on the Development and Application of Naturally
    Occurring Drug Materials 7:67-70

6. Hasegawa S, Kondo N, Kodama F (1990) J. Pharmacobio-Dyn, in
    press.

7. Hasegawa S, Kamneshima H (1987) Report of the Hokkaido Insti-
    tute of Public Health 37:6-17

8. Hasegawa S, Kodama F, Nakajima M, Akai J, Murooka H (1987)
    Bull. Agr. & Vet. Med., Nihon Univ. 44:80-86

© 1990 Elsevier Science Publishers B.V. (Biomedical Division)
Pesticides and alternatives, editor J.E. Casida

INHIBITION OF SCLEROTIUM FORMATION IN PLANT PATHOGENIC FUNGI BY CERTAIN SULFHYDRYL COMPOUNDS AND THE PROSPECTS OF EXPLOITING THEM FOR THEIR CONTROL

CHRISTOS CHRISTIAS
Department of Biology, National Research Center "DEMOCRITOS", GR-153 10 Aghia Paraskevi Attikis, Greece.

INTRODUCTION

Certain Phytopathogenic soil fungi form sclerotia as resting structures. The sclerotia are small, usually spherical reproductive bodies produced asexually from mycelial hyphae. They play a very vital role in the biology of these fungi because they are the structures by means of which they survive for long periods of unfavorable conditions in nature (7,12,16).

The process of sclerotium formation involves three distinct developmental stages, namely, the Sclerotial Initials (SI) stage, the Development (D) and the Maturation (M) stage (8). It has been possible to inhibit the formation of sclerotia by the use of certain sulfhydryl compounds such as mercaptoethanol, thioglycolic acid, propyl mercaptan, 1- and 2-butyl mercaptan, benzyl mercaptan (4,5). These potent inhibitors of sclerotium formation are valuable tools for the study of the mechanism of sclerotium formation. At the same time they can be exploited in especially designed schemes for the control of these pathogens. This paper presents data on the effectiveness of these compounds in inhibiting the formation of sclerotia in some phytopathogenic fungi and discusses the prospect of controlling such pathogens through the use of specific inhibitors of sclerotium formation.

MATERIALS AND METHODS

Organisms

Two strains of Sclerotium rolfsii were used, one belonging to type R, sensu Henis and Chet (9), and another to type A. Type R was a cotton isolate while type A was isolated from Myoporum sp. Five additional plant pathogenic fungi were tested, namely, Sclerotium cepivorum, Sclerotinia minor, Sclerotinia sclerotiorum, Rhizoctonia _solani_ and _Botrytis cinerea_. Stock cultures of all fungi were kept on agar slants and renewed at 2-month intervals.

Growth Media

All isolates were grown in Potato Dextrose Agar (PDA). Occasionally the Joham's medium was also used (10). This medium contained (g/l.): glucose 40, K_2HPO_4 0.7, NH_4NO_3 1, KCl 0.15, $MgSO_4.7H_2O$ 0.2, $FeSO_4$ 0.002, $MnCl_2$ 0.002, $ZnSO_4$ 0.002, thiamine chloride 0.0001, Bacto agar (Difco) 20. The pH was adjusted to 7.0 and the medium autoclaved for 15 min at 121°C. The test compounds were incorporated into the growth medium to the desired concentration.

Chemicals

The following compounds, purchased from SIGMA Chemical Co., St. Louis, Missouri, USA, were tested for inhibitory activity on sclerotium formation: Mercaptoethanol, thioglycolic acid, propyl mercaptan, 1-butyl mercaptan, 2-butyl mercaptan, benzyl mercaptan and mercaptoethylamine. All other chemicals used were analytical reagent grade.

Growth conditions

The fungi were grown at 25°C in standard 9-cm Petri dishes containing 20 ml of nutrient agar medium. Mercaptoethanol, thioglycolic acid and mercaptoethylamine were incorporated into the agar medium at concentrations ranging from 0.3mM to 24mM. The compounds were added into the growth medium after autoclaving and when the temperature had dropped to about 45-50°C. Propyl mercaptan, 1-butyl mercaptan, 2-butyl mercaptan and benzyl mercaptan were used as vapors in a closed system described by Christias (1975).

RESULTS

Effect of mercaptoethanol on mycelial growth

Figs. 1-4 represent typical growth curves of representative fungi and show the response of mycelial growth to one of the chemicals, namely, mercaptoethanol. Considerable variations in the response of the mycelial growth of the test fungi to this inhibitor were observed. _S. cepivorum_ exhibited the highest sensitivity (Fig. 1). There was practically complete inhibition of growth at 3mM conc. There was no effect on growth at 0.3, 0.6 and 1.2mM. At 2.4mM there was an initial lag in mycelial growth of about 4 days and then the rate of growth was the same as that of the control. _S. minor_ was

489

also quite sensitive to the inhibitor. At 3mM there was a considerable decrease in the rate of growth (Fig. 2).At 6mM there was no growth for 14 days. Once growth started, however, it proceeded at a fast rate and nearly approached the growth rate of the control. There was no growth at 12mM. B. cinerea (fig. 3) and R. solani (Fig. 4) exhibited very similar response. The rate of mycelial growth was slightly affected at 3mM. At 6mM there was a lag in growth of about 3 to 4 days, but once it started it proceeded quite rapidly. There was no growth at 12mM. S. sclerotiorum was similar in response to the above two fungi. Mycelial growth of S. rolfsii was not affected at 3mM. Above this, the growth decreased directly with increasing concentrations of the inhibitor.

Effect of mercaptoethanol on sclerotium formation

The formation of sclerotia occured in the following characteristic manner: First the mycelium grew and covered the entire plate. Following completion of mycelial growth, sclerotial

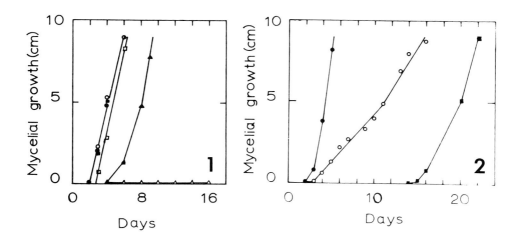

Mycelial growth of: Fig. 1. S. cepivorum: ●- control; O- 0.3mM; ■- 0.6mM; □- 1.2mM; ▲- 2.4mM; △- 3.0mM. Fig. 2. S. minor. ●- control; O- 3mM; ■- 6mM;

initials appeared over the entire plate which became mature scleroria 2-3 days later. S. minor was the only fungus which formed sclerotial initials before completion of the mycelial growth.

Sclerotium formation in S. cepivorum was completely inhibited by

490

mercaptoethanol at 2.4mM or higher (Fig. 5). Concentrations below
0.6mM had no effect on growth and sclerotium formation whereas
above 2.4mM both mycelial growth and sclerotium formation were
inhibited. Sclerotium formation in R. solani was greatly inhibited
at 3mM (Fig. 6). However, very few small initials appeared in
cultures grown at this concentration late in the growth period,
after the 20th day from inoculation, which developed into normal
mature sclerotia three days later. S. rolfsii was similar in
response to R. solani (Fig. 7). There was a complete inhibition of
sclerotium formation at 3mM or higher. Concentrations lower than 2
mM had no effect on sclerotium formation. In the fungus S. minor
there was only partial inhibition of sclerotium formation (Fig. 8).
There was no inhibition at 3mM and only partial inhibition at 6mM.
The inhibition of sclerotium formation was never complete in this
fungus, even at concentrations greatly inhibitory to mycelial
growth. S. sclerotiorum was intermediate in response. At 3mM there
was considerable inhibition of sclerotium formation but it was
never complete. Complete inhibition was obtained at 6mM. B. cinerea
was very sensitive to the inhibitor. Concentrations of 3mM or
higher were completely inhibitory to sclerotium formation (Fig. 9).
Mercaptoethanol inhibited the formation of sclerotia of all fungi

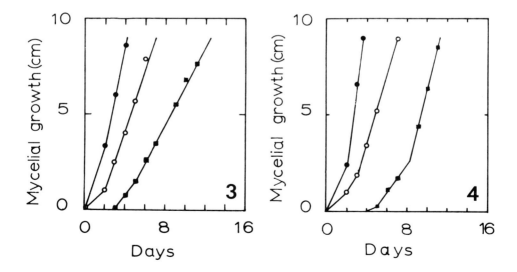

Mycelial growth of: Fig. 3. B. cinerea. Fig. 4. R. solani. ●-
control; O- 3mM; □- 6mM;

tested either completely or partially. Cultures grown in the
presence of the inhibitor remained purely mycelial for as long as
the experiments lasted (over 28 days). The mycelium was very thick

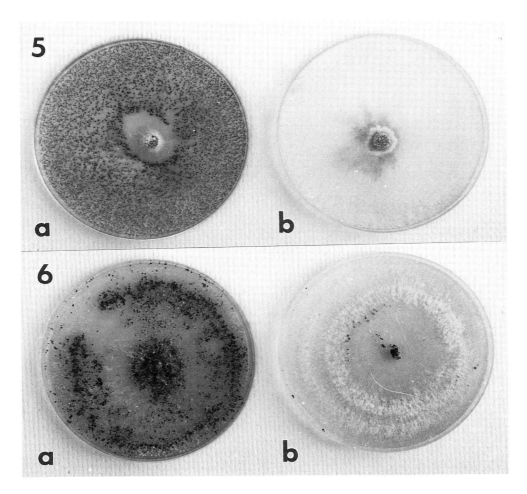

Complete inhibition of sclerotium formation in: Fig. 5. S. cepivorum. Fig. 6. R. solani. a) controls. b) 3mM mercaptoethanol.

and shiny in appearance, was thicker than that of the controls and
had a golden-yellowish hue. This was true for all fungi tested.
Effect of other sulfhydryl compounds on the mycelial growth and
sclerotium formation

Thioglycolic acid had an identical effect on mycelial growth and
sclerotium formation as that of mercaptoethanol on all fungi.

Mercaptoethylamine inhibited the formation of sclerotia but at relatively higher concentrations. So, a concentration of 6mM was necessary for complete inhibition of sclerotium formation. At this concentration inhibition of sclerotium formation was only partial in S. sclerotiorum. At 12mM the inhibition was complete but the mycelial growth was also inhibited. S. minor was the least sensitive fungus. Partial inhibition was observed at 12mM, while the mycelial growth was also inhibited. Propyl mercaptan, 1-butyl

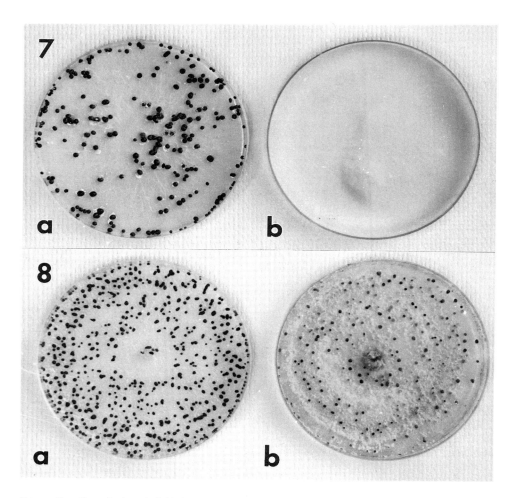

Fig. 7. Complete inhibition of sclerotium formation in S. rolfsii. a) control. b) 3mM mercaptoethanl. Fig. 8. Partial inhibition of sclerotium formation in S. minor. a) control. b) 6mM mercapto-ethanol.

mercaptan, 2- butyl mercaptan and benzyl mercaptan, all inhibited the formation of sclerotia in S. rolfsii, R. solani, B. cinerea and S. cepivorum completely at concentration of 0.15mM. At this same concentration inhibition was only partial in S. sclerotiorum. There was no effect on sclerotium formation in S. minor. Higher concentrations (0.3mM) inhibited the formation of sclerotia in S. sclerotiorum completely but the mycelial growth was also inhibited. Inhibition of sclerotium formation was never complete in S. minor, even at these high concentrations at which the mycelium growth was severely inhibited.

DISCUSSION

The inhibitors affected both the mycelial growth and the formation of sclerotia. However, there were some differences in sensitivity among the fungi tested. Regarding mycelial growth, S. cepivorum appeared to be the most sensitive organism. There was an initial lag in mycelial growth in cultures grown in the presence of inhibitors. This lag period was much longer in the higher concentrations. Once growth started, however, it proceeded at a high rate. So, in S. minor i.e. grown at 6mM mercaptoethanol, there was no growth at all for 14 days after inoculation but when it started it increased rapidly (Fig.2). This initial lag in mycelial growth observed in the presence of all inhibitors could possibly be due to either loss as a result of evaporation or adaptation. The considerable variation in the duration of this lag period observed among the species tested may be an indication of adaptation, at least partly. On the other hand the appearance of a few sclerotia in R. solani and B. cinerea, grown at 3mM mercaptoethanol, late in growth may be due to loss through evaporation which caused a decrease in the effective concentration below a certain threshold for complete inhibition of sclerotium formation.

When complete or partial inhibition occured the mycelium was much thicker in appearance. This was probably due to the concentration and storage of cell constituents in the mycelium since there was apparently no utilization of such contituents for the formation of sclerotia.

All compounds used inhibited the formation of sclerotia in the test fungi. Within each species the extent of inhibition depended on the concentration of the inhibitor. Among the test fungi the

494

response varied from complete inhibition to almost complete inhibition to partial inhibition. This response pattern with a tendensy towards inhibition may indicate that probably the control mechanism of sclerotium formation is the same in all sclerotium-forming fungi tested and that perhaps the same physiological control mechanism is operative in sclerotium formation in these fungi. This mechanism is still quite obscure in spite of the fact that extensive research work has been done (1,2,3,11,13,14,15). Some of the inhibitors used in this study could be ideal research tools to use for the study of the mechanism of sclerotium formation.

It is well known that fungi survive in nature mainly as resting

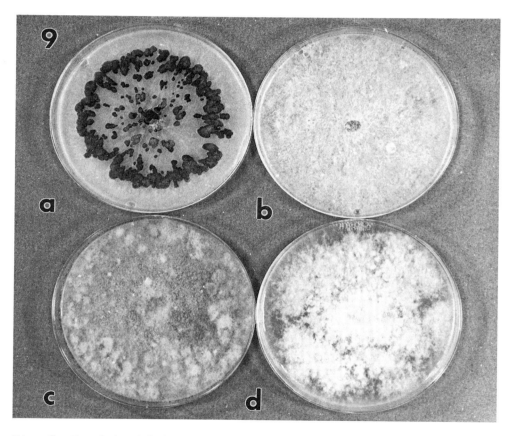

Fig. 9. Complete inhibition of sclerotium formation in B. cinerea. a) control. b), c) and d), 2,4 and 6mM mercaptoethanol respectively.

structures and that sclerotia are the propagules through which these fungi survive in the soil for long periods of time (7,12,16). In nature the inhibition of the formation of sclerotia could place such fungi in a great disadvantage. It could greatly reduce their ability to survive and, if this situation lasts for some period of time, it may be conceivable that such organisms could be eradicated from the field under the presence of continuous competition and the inability to overcome adverse environmental conditions. This could be more serious for species which do not form any kind of spores, i.e. R. solani, or species in which the sexual stage is very rare, i.e. S. rolfsii.

Inhibition of sclerotium formation can be obtained not only in pure calture but also in the diseased plants. Recently it was possible to inhibit the formation of microsclerotia of Verticillium dahliae in infected cotton stems (6). When these infected stems were incubated with thioglycolic acid no microsclerotia were formed and at the end of the incubation period (5 months) the wood was clean and healthy. In control stems the wood developed a brown discoloration and it was completely covered with microsclerotia.

Effectiveness of inhibition is highly desirable but is not the sole characteristic required of a compound to make it a good inhibitor. Other characteristics of the molecules are important, too. Some of these are, extent of volatilization, ease of use, solubility. In view of the above, it appears that of all compounds tested, mercaptoethylamine can be singled out as a very good inhibitor for further tests. Besides being an extremely potent inhibitor of sclerotium formation it is easy to use, has reduced volatility, is highly soluble and the least objectionable of all.

The availability of such potent inhibitors, like mercaptoethylamine, coupled with the sensitivity of the test fungal pathogens used, make the prospects of exploiting them in especially designed control schemes promising. Such control schemes could be alternatives to the use of traditional fungicides. A control system based on the use of specific inhibitors of sclerotium formation has the following advantages: It is highly specific for sclerotium-forming fungi, as it does not seem to affect other sporulating fungi commonly occuring in the soil (Christias, unpublished data). Its application in the field would not create serious environmental pollution problems. It is unlikely that it will disturb to any appreciable extent the biological ballance since it does not abruptly and suddenly eliminate the organisms towards which it is directed. Instead, it inhibits a very vital physiological process so that this particular fungal population is reduced gradually and may be eventually eliminated. Finally, the development of resistance to these chemicals may be more difficult than it is in the case of systemic fungicides, depending upon their mode of action, an area in which research is urgently needed.

ACKNOWLEDGEMENTS

I wish to thank Mrs. Katherine Tsakiris-Paradakis for expert technical help and Dr. Flora Zarani for assistance during the preparation of the manuscript.

REFERENCES

1. Chet I, Henis Y (1968) J Gen Microbiol 54:231-236
2. Chet I, Henis Y (1972) J Gen Microbiol 73:483-486
3. Chet I, Henis Y, Mitchell R (1966) J Gen Microbiol 45:541-546
4. Christias C (1975) Can J Microbiol 21:1541-1547
5. Christias C (1987) Proc 7th Congr Medit Phytopath Union pp 80-82
6. Christias C (1989) In: Tjamos EC, Beckman C, (eds) Vascular Wilt Diseases of Plants. Springer-Verlag, Berlin, pp 521-527
7. Coley-Smith JR, Cooke RC (1971) Ann Rev Phytopath 9:65-92
8. Henis Y, Chet I (1968) Can J Bot 46:947-948
9. Henis Y, Okon Y, Chet I (1973) J Gen Microbiol 79:147-150
10. Joham HM (1947) M.Sc. Thesis A and M College of Texas. Cited in (8)
11. Okon Y, Chet I, Henis Y (1973) J Gen Microbiol 74:251-258
12. Park D (1965) In: Baker KF, Snyder WC (eds) Ecology of Soil-Borne Plant Pathogens. Univ Calif Press pp 82-97
13. Trevethick J, Cooke RC (1971) Trans Br Mycol Soc 57:340-342
14. Trevethick J, Cooke RC (1973) Trans Br Mycol Soc 60:559-566
15. Weeler BEJ, Waller JM (1965) Trans Br Mycol Soc 48:303-314
16. Willetts HJ (1871) Biol Reviews (Camb) 46:387-407

© 1990 Elsevier Science Publishers B.V. (Biomedical Division)
Pesticides and alternatives, editor J.E. Casida

NATURAL RESISTANCE AND SUSCEPTIBILITY OF PLANT HOSTS TO FUNGAL ATTACK: THE CHEMICAL BASE

Leslie Crombie

Department of Chemistry, University of Nottingham, Nottingham, NG7 2RD, UK.

The general toxicity of certain microbiological products towards plants is well recognised, but host-specific (or better, host-selective) toxins (H-S toxins) differ not only in being highly selective in action but in being the actual initiators of disease.[1-4] Such H-S toxins are pathogenic only to their hosts, being essentially non-toxic to non-hosts which may be closely related cultivars. Spores of the pathogen release chemically identifiable H-S toxin on germination and it is possible to turn a morphologically identical, but benign, microbial strain into a virulent pathogen merely by providing it with external H-S toxin: there is complete correspondence between disease susceptibility and toxin sensitivity in the host plant.

The activities of H-S toxins in agriculture can be devastating. The introduction in 1927 of the S. American oat cultivar Victoria into plant breeding led, by the early 1940's, to new cultivars containing genetic resistance to most races of crown rust disease (Puccinia coronata) and smut (Ustilago avenae). By the mid 1940's some 80% of the U.S. oat acreage was planted with such cultivars. During 1944 a new oat disease, 'Victoria blight' appeared. It was caused by Helminthosporium victoriae and was confined to cultivars containing the Victoria gene: within 3-4 years the disease was so widespread and devastating that all such cultivars were abandoned. A similar major disaster caused by Helminthosporium maydis race T, specific for Texas male sterile (Tms) corn lines, occurred in the maize crop in 1970 - 71.

Over the years the list of fungi producing H-S toxins has grown (Table. 1), and they affect specific genotypes in a wide range of cultivated crop plants. Recently the list of hosts has been extended to include plants which may be classified as weeds, although weeds present much more genetically heterogenous types than cultivated plants. Some of the compounds proposed as H-S toxins are shown in Figure 1 and their diverse structures provide excellent opportunities for an organic chemist to participate in this fascinating area of interdisciplinary study. The isolation and synthesis of H-S toxins enables the plant breeder and cell culture worker to screen easily for resistance to the fungus involved. From the point of view of gene manipulation an advantage of the system is that a chemically characterised molecule is the final product from fungal genes for disease-inducing ability. The host plants also have single genes that control sensitivity to the toxins concerned, and it may be possible to use

Producing fungus	Species affected	Toxin
Helminthosporium carbonum race I.	Maize	HC
Helminthosporium maydis race T	Maize	HmT
Helminthosporium sacchari	Sugar cane	HS
Helminthosporium victoriae	Oats	HV
Helminthosporium oryzae	Rice	–
Helminthosporium (Drechslera) maydis	Costus speciosus	Drechslerol B
Periconia circinata	Sorghum	PC
Phyllosticta maydis	Maize	PM
Alternaria alternata	Japanese pear	AK
Alternaria alternata	Strawberry	AF
Alternaria citri (lemon race)	Rough lemon	ACL
" " (tangerine race)	Dancy tangerine	ACT
Alternaria mali	Apple	AM
Alternaria alternata f. lycopersica	Tomato	AL
Alternaria alternata	Spotted knapweed (Centaurea maculosa)	Maculosin
Bipolaris cynodontis	Bermuda grass	Bipolaroxin

Table 1. Host-Selective (H-S) Toxins, Fungus and Host.

such knowledge in designing highly selective herbicides.

The H-S toxins we have been particularly interested in recently have been those concerning the Japanese pear and strawberries. At the beginning of the century black-spot disease of Japanese pear had become prevalent in the orchards of Japan following the widespread introduction of a new cultivar 'Nijisseiki'. The fungus causing the disease, Alternaria kikuchiani Tanaka (later renamed Alternaria alternata, Japanese pear pathotype), affected Nijisseiki varieties but not other cultivars, which were resistant. In 1933 Tanaka reported that A. alternata Jpp produced

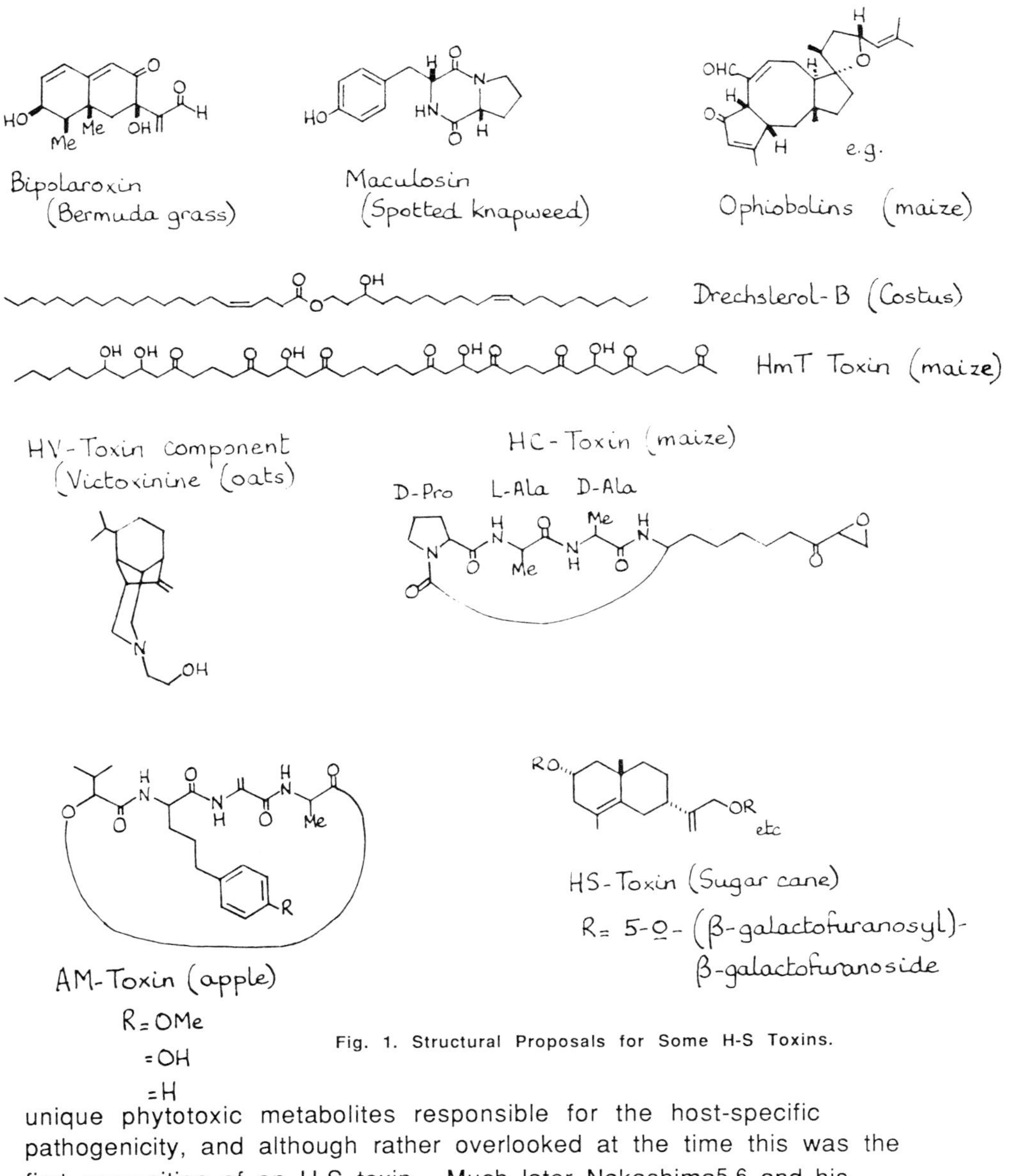

Bipolaroxin
(Bermuda grass)

Maculosin
(Spotted knapweed)

Ophiobolins (maize) e.g.

Drechslerol-B (Costus)

HmT Toxin (maize)

HV-Toxin component
(Victoxinine) (oats)

HC-Toxin (maize)

D-Pro   L-Ala   D-Ala

AM-Toxin (apple)

R = OMe
  = OH
  = H

HS-Toxin (Sugar cane)

R = 5-O-(β-galactofuranosyl)-
         β-galactofuranoside

Fig. 1. Structural Proposals for Some H-S Toxins.

unique phytotoxic metabolites responsible for the host-specific
pathogenicity, and although rather overlooked at the time this was the
first recognition of an H-S toxin. Much later Nakashima[5,6] and his
colleagues studied H-S toxin and characterised two components, AK
-toxin I and AK-toxin II (Figure 2): they were obtained from bulk
culturing of the mould, purification being followed by bioassay using
Nijisseiki pear leaves along with a resistant cultivar. AK-toxin I is
effective on a susceptible host at 5 X10-9M, toxin-II at 10-7M. The
effect of the toxins is to induce rapid lossof K+ from the host cell along

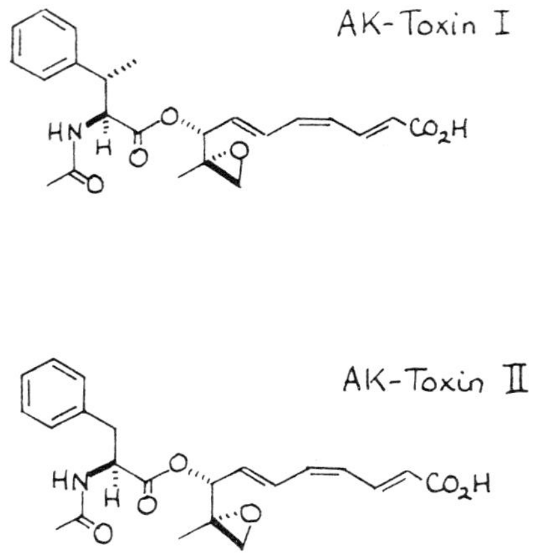

500

AK-Toxin I

AK-Toxin II

Alternaria alternata (kikuchiana) Japanese pear pathotype

Fig. 2. Structures for H-S Toxins AK-I and AK-II.

with microscopically visible effects such as cell wall invagination and damage.[7] Veinal necrosis also occurs. When added to avirulent A.alternata spores the toxins enable them to invade susceptible tissue in the same way as virulent spores do. Some thirty six Japanese pear cultivars, when challenged with H-S toxins, and then with virulent spores, showed the same type of reaction or non-reaction.[7]

Around 1975 a new black-spot disease of strawberry occurred in Japan, shortly after the widespread introduction of a newly bred cultivar Morioka-16. This black-spot disease was also attributed to a pathogenic strain of A. alternata (strawberry pathotype) and interestingly this

	Strawberry (cv Morioka-16)	Japanese pear (cv Nijisseiki)
AF-Toxin I	+	+
AF- Toxin II[†]	−*	+
AF-Toxin III	+	±

* induces K⁺ leakage but not necrosis

[†] separated into AF-Toxin IIa (9), IIb (1) and IIc (1)

Table 2. Host Selectivities for AF-Toxins.

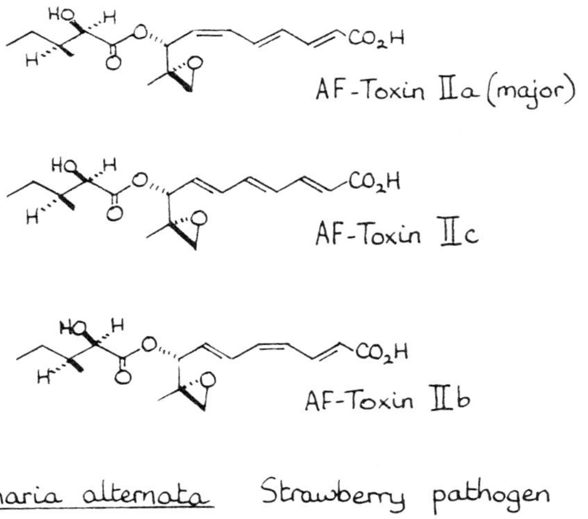

Fig. 3. Structures for AF-Toxins.

strain is pathogenic to Japanese pear cultivars of the Nijisseiki type as well.[8,9] From large volumes of the culture filtrate, three toxins were reported with host selectivities as in Table 2 (AF-I and-II are the major ones).[10] AF-II toxin has been chemically characterised and separated into three toxins AF-IIa, IIb and IIc (ratio 9:1:1) (Figure 3). It is with these, and AK-toxin II, that our synthetic work has been concerned.

Figure 4 shows our retrosynthetic plan, the salient objective being initially the synthesis of three geometrical isomers of the same hydroxytetraene structure (1) - (3). Initially this was attempted by the use of hydrozirconation, the coupling components being made as in Figure 5. Yields from the catalysed coupling (Figure 6) were poor and protection/deprotection, necessary in these reactions, caused

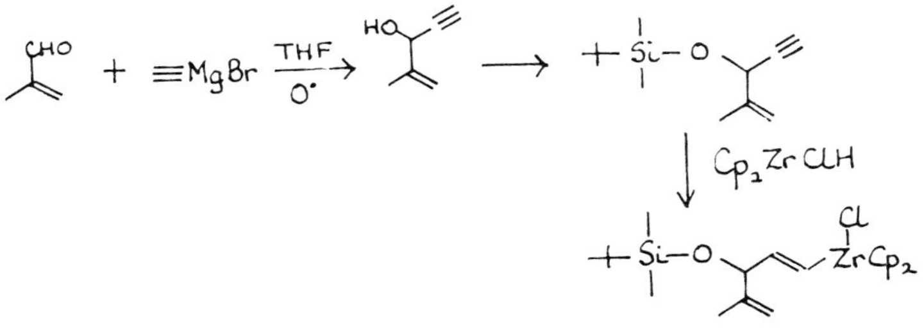

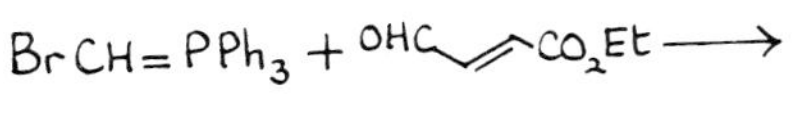

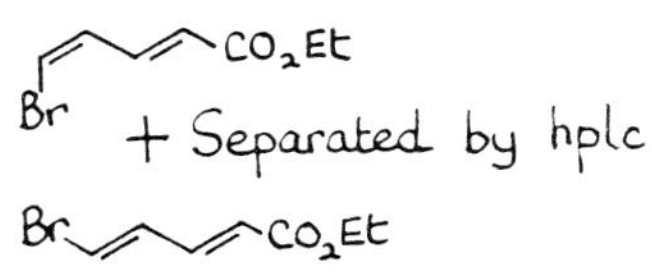

Fig. 5. Intermediates for Hydrozirconation Approach.

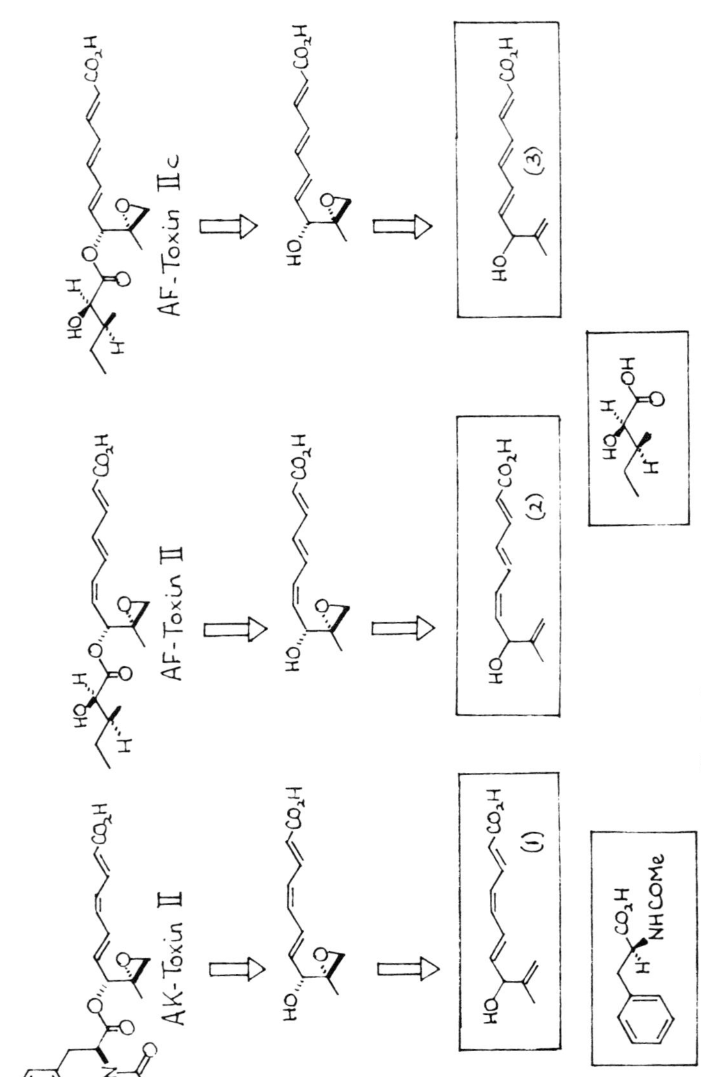

502

Fig. 4. Retrosynthetic Plan for AK- and AF-Toxins.

difficulties. Attention was therefore turned to the use of hydrostannation and both the (E)- and the (Z)-stannanes were readily obtained (Figure 7): an advantage of this procedure is that no protection of the hydroxyl is required. As Figure 8 shows, palladium catalysed coupling between the appropriate stannane and vinyl bromoester gave the three isomeric hydroxytetraenes (1) - (3) in good yields.[11]

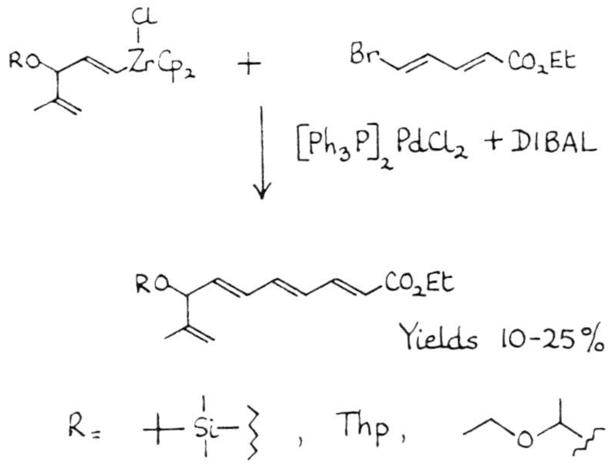

Fig. 6. Hydrozirconation Approach.

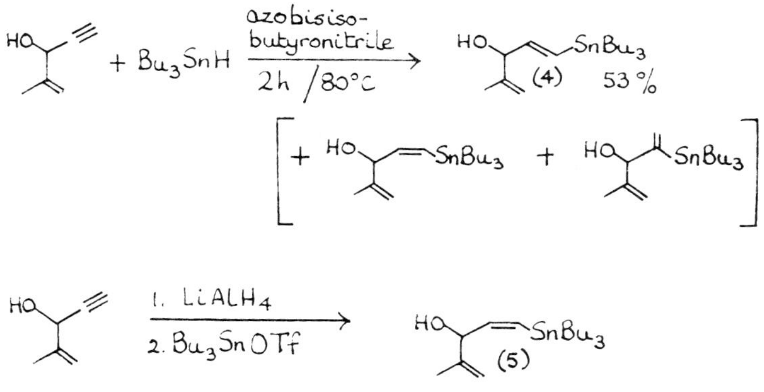

Fig. 7. Intermediates for Hydrostannation Approach.

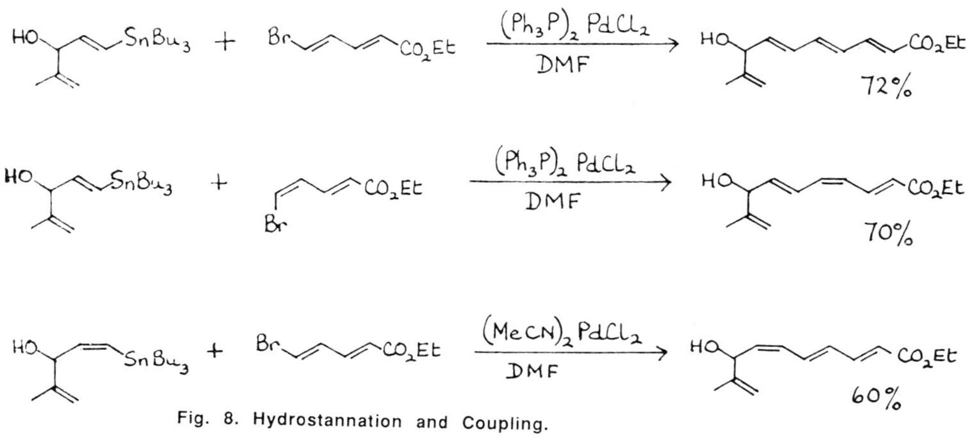

Fig. 8. Hydrostannation and Coupling.

To continue the syntheses we now have the problem of introducing into each tetraene a 9-(S)-epoxide together with an optically resolved 8-(R)-hydroxyl. A solution was made possible through the outstanding advances in chiral epoxidation by Sharpless and his colleages.[12] The D-(-)-diisopropyltartrate catalyst has high stereofacial selectivity, and one can predict that at equilibrium a predomonant mixture of (5) and (7) should result from (4) (Figure 9). The results of Sharpless[12] and others however indicate that if the epoxidation is carried out under kinetic control (5) will be the major product, being formed in a fast reaction, considerably less of (7) being produced in a slow reaction if epoxidation is allowed to proceed only to 50% completion (Figure 9). Table 3 shows the results of Sharpless epoxidation taken to 50% completion. Optically active epoxy-alcohols are obtained in satisfactory yield and these products, (A) - (C), must now be separated and identified as far as possible.

For such purposes the chiral 2-(R)-3(S)-esterifying acid (9) (Figure 10) was required in connection with the AF-toxins and it was prepared from L-isoleucine essentially by a method briefly outlined by Irie et al.,[13] though with slightly differing hydroxyl protection . Esterification of the epoxidation product A with (9) was followed by chromatography. Isolation of the main optically active diastereomer (10) (66%) was then followed by desilylation to give AF-toxin IIa ethyl ester (11)

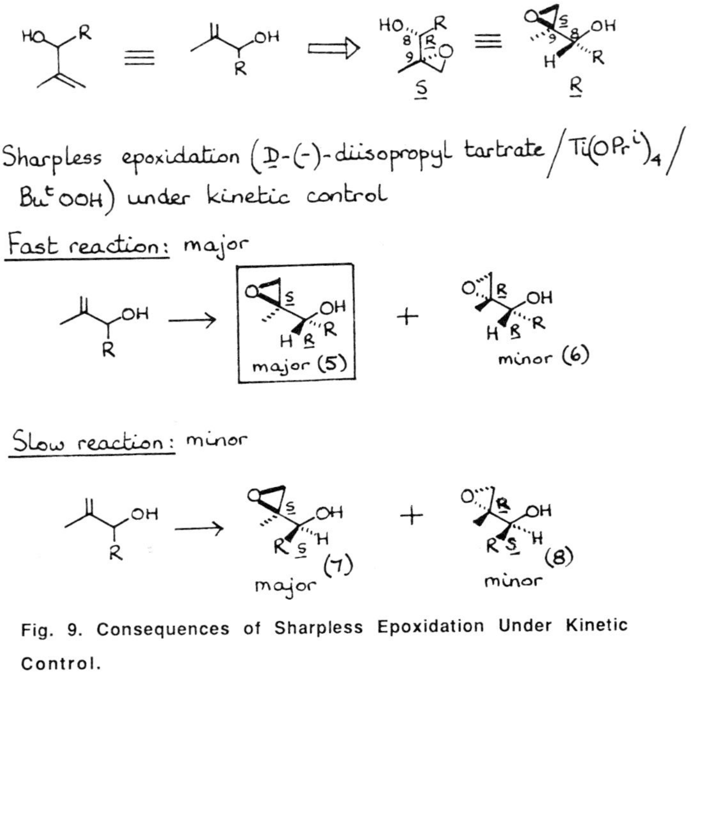

Fig. 9. Consequences of Sharpless Epoxidation Under Kinetic Control.

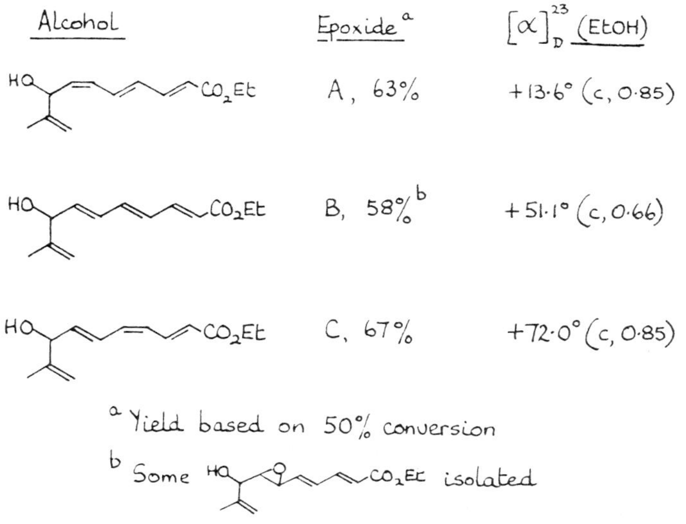

505

Alcohol   Epoxide^a $[\alpha]_D^{23}$ (EtOH)

HO─CH... (structure) CO₂Et   A, 63%   +13·6° (c, 0·85)

HO─... CO₂Et   B, 58%^{b} +51·1° (c, 0·66)

HO─... CO₂Et   C, 67%   +72·0° (c, 0·85)

^{a} Yield based on 50% conversion

^{b} Some HO─...─CO₂Et isolated

Table 3. Chiral Products (A-C) from Sharpless Epoxidation of Stereoisomeric Tetraene-Hydroxyesters.

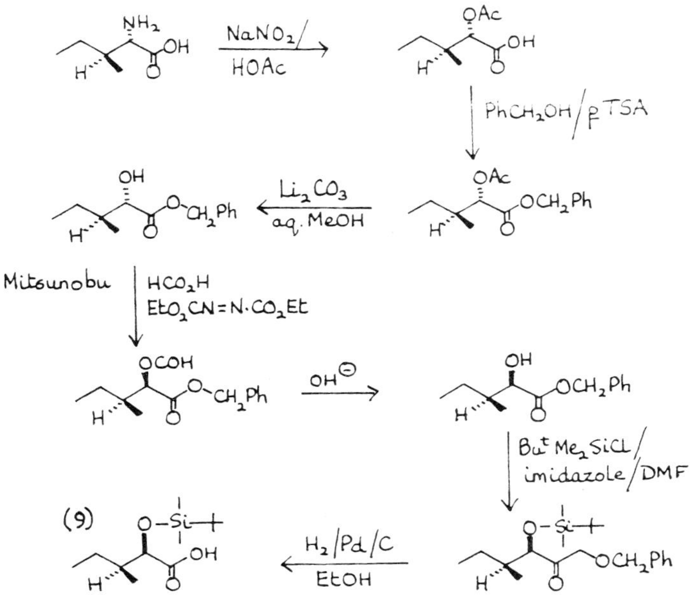

(reaction scheme)

NH₂ ... OH →[NaNO₂/ HOAc] OAc ... OH

│ PhCH₂OH/ pTSA

OAc ... OCH₂Ph

OH ... O-CH₂Ph ←[Li₂CO₃ / aq. MeOH]

Mitsunobu │ HCO₂H
          │ EtO₂CN=N·CO₂Et

OCOH ... O-CH₂Ph →[OH⊖] OH ... OCH₂Ph

│ Bu^{t}Me₂SiCl/ imidazole/DMF

(9) O-Si─+ ... OH ←[H₂/Pd/C EtOH] O-Si─+ ... OCH₂Ph

Fig. 10. Synthesis of Esterifying-Acid for AF-Toxins (Irie et al.[13]).

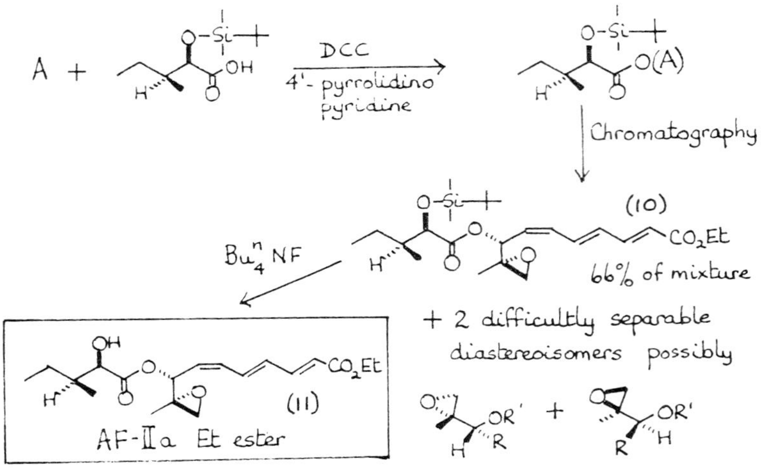

506

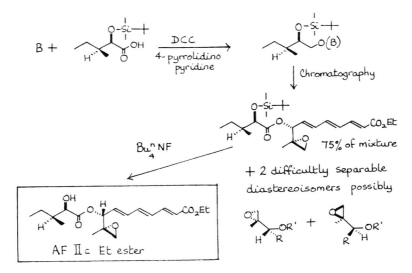

Fig. 11. Synthesis of AF-Toxin IIa (as Ethyl Ester).

spectroscopically identical (except for ester resonances) with the authentic 8-(R),9-(S),2'-(R),3'-(S),2-E,4-E,6-Z-methyl ester (Figure 11).[14] The remainder of the material consisted of two difficultly separable diastereomers, thought to be those shown in Figure 11, corresponding to (6) and (7) of Figure 9. Operating in a similar way (Figure 12), AF-toxin IIc ethyl ester [8-(R),9-(S),2'-(R),3'-(S),2-E,4-E,6-E-] was obtained.[14]

Fig. 12. Synthesis of AF-Toxin IIc (as Ethyl Ester).

For the synthesis of AK-toxin II ethyl ester the epoxidation mixture C was esterified with N-acetyl-L-phenylalanine. Unfortunately the latter racemises easily under the conditions used and chromatography gave two large bands, each accompanied by two small bands. Nmr examination shows clearly that the two large components differ in Nmr resonances only in the vicinity of the amino carbon, one diastereomer having resonances (except for esters) identical with those recorded for the methyl ester of natural AK-toxin II [8-(R),9-(S),2'-(S),2-E,4-Z,6-E-].[14] The other is the 2'-(R)- epimer. The possible configurations of the minor components are indicated in Figure 13. A

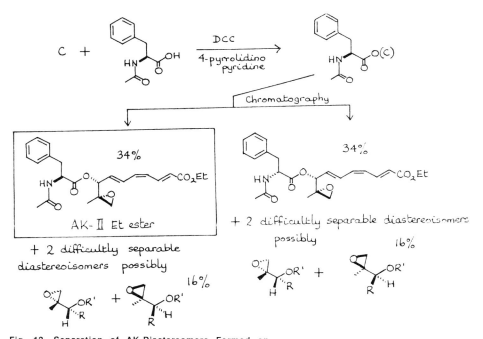

Fig. 13. Separation of AK-Diastereomers Formed on
Esterification (and Amino-acid Racemisation); Isolation of AK-Toxin II (as Ethyl Ester).

Fig. 14. The Irie Chiral Intermediate.

AF Toxin IIc Me ester
AK Toxin II Me ester

Table 4. Avenacins Isolated from Oat Roots

	m.p.	Mol. formula (M)	λmax (EtOH)
Avenacin A-1	228–233°	$C_{55}H_{83}O_{21}N$ (1093)	223 (ϵ 25,250), 255 (7,900), 357 nm (5,500)
Avenacin A-2	237–239°	$C_{54}H_{80}O_{21}$ (1064)	230 (14,700), 274 (1,200), 281 (1,100)
Avenacin B-1	glass	$C_{55}H_{83}O_{20}N$ (1077)	223 (23,300), 255 (7,900), 356 (5,300)
Avenacin B-2	glass	$C_{54}H_{80}O_{20}$ (1048)	228 (14,600), 274 (1,300), 281 (1,250)

Table 5. Avenestergenins, Aglycones of the Avenacins

	m.p.	Mol. formula (M)	λmax (EtOH)
Avenamine A-1	210–211°C	$C_{38}H_{55}O_7N$ (637.3960)	224 (ϵ 23,100), 255 (6,500), 359 nm (4,600)
Avenamine A-2	189–190°	$C_{37}H_{52}O_7$ (608.3740)	228 (12,300), 254 inf. (1,700), 274 (820), 281 (700)
Avenamine B-1	186–187°	$C_{38}H_{55}O_6N$ (621.4016)	225 (23,400), 255 (6,900), 357 (4,700)
Avenamine B-2	177–178°	$C_{37}H_{52}O_6$ (592.3764)	229 (12,200), 257 inf (850), 273 (530), 281 (360)

synthesis of AF-toxin IIc and AK-toxin II has lately been reported by the Irie group.[15] It extracts the initial chiral centre from vitamin C using a lengthy degradation sequence (Figure 14),[16] followed by building of the trienes by Wittig methods.

In the evolutionary struggle between fungus and higher plant, the plant has defensive chemicals, just as the fungus has aggressive chemicals. One of our studies has lately concerned the chemical defences of oat roots against the fungus <u>Gaeumannomyces graminis</u>, the causative fungus of 'take-all' disease. 'Take-all' is a most destructive and widespread disease, attacking the stem bases of susceptible cereals - wheat, barley and rye - and being difficult to control by synthetic fungicides. Oats however are not attacked by <u>G. graminis</u> (var. tritici) (Ggt), the strain which usually attacks wheat, and infected wheat-land may be cleansed of infection by planting with oats for a year or two. Earlier investigators showed that a fluorescent defensive material was present in oat roots, especially the root tips,[17] and though thought to be triterpenoid in type, the chemical nature of this material, named avenacin, has remained ill-defined.

Our investigation involved hydroponically-grown oats, the roots from which were freeze-dried, ground, and extracted with aqueous methanol. Reversed-phase hplc led ultimately to the isolation of four pure avenacins (Table 4), A-1 and B-1 showing an intense blue fluorescence in methanol. All four compounds were trisaccharides of identical type, formed from 1 mol of arabinose and 2 mol of glucose. The aglycones remaining after acid hydrolysis were four avenestergenins (Table 5), two containing <u>N</u>-methylanthranilic acid, and two benzoic acid (Figure 15). Structural work, mainly nmr studies, were later confirmed by X-ray single crystal analysis, and led to complete structures for the four avenestergenins as in Figure16.[18] An interesting feature of the acid hydrolysis leading to avenestergenins was the formation of material that persistently blocked hplc columns and turned out to be a series of crystalline anhydrodimers, most of which were isolated (Scheme17).

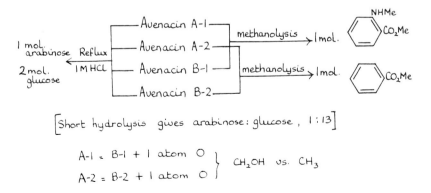

Fig. 15. Hydrolysis Products of the Avenacins.

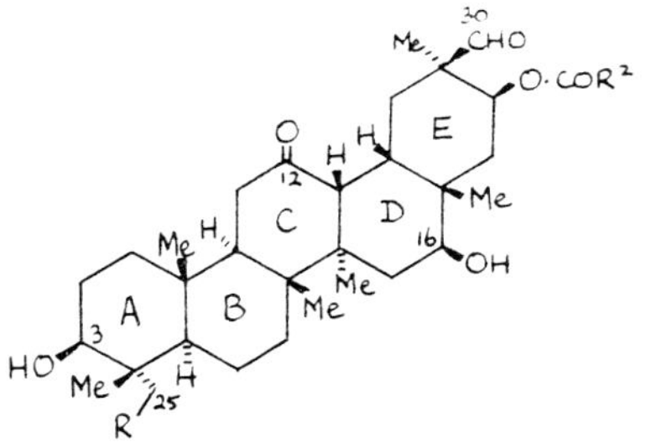

Avenestergenin A-1 R' = OH; R^2 = o-MeHNC_6H_4-

Avenestergenin A-2 R' = OH; R^2 = C_6H_5-

Avenestergenin B-1 R' = H; R^2 = o-MeHNC_6H_4-

Avenestergenin B-2 R' = H; R^2 = C_6H_5-

Fig. 16. The Avenestergenins.

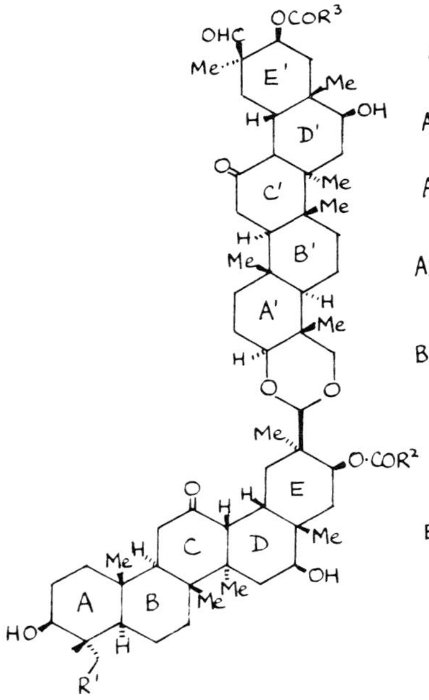

A1/A1 R' = OH, R^2 = R^3 = o-MeHNC_6H_4-

A2/A2 R' = OH, R^2 = R^3 = C_6H_5-

A1/A2 R' = OH, R^2 = o-MeHNC_6H_4-, R^3 = C_6H_5-

A2/A1 R' = OH, R^2 = C_6H_5- R^3 = o-MeHNC_6H_4-

B2/A2 R' = H, R^2 = R^3 = C_6H_5-

B1/A1 R' = H, R^2 = R^3 = o-MeHNC_6H_4-

B1/A2 R' = H, R^2 = o-MeHNC_6H_4-, R^3 = C_6H_5

Fig. 17. Anhydrodimers of the Avenestergenins.

However, analysis of spectroscopic data showed that the avenestergenins are apparent rather than true aglycones. During acid hydrolysis an epoxide - ketone rearrangement has clearly occurred (Figure18). The carbohydrate section was structurally elucidated using

	Avenestergenin A-1	Avenacin A-1
C-30 aldehyde	$1721\ cm^{-1}$	✓
C-21 ester	$1677\ cm^{-1}$	✓
C-12 ketone	$1695\ cm^{-1}$ $^{13}C\ \delta\ 211{\cdot}4s$	missing missing
H-C-12	missing	$^{13}C\ \delta\ 54{\cdot}2d$

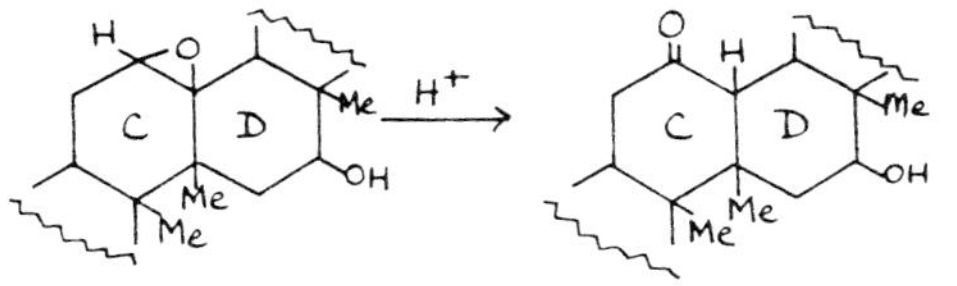

Avenacin A-1 Avenestergenin A-1

Fig. 18. The Epoxide-Ketone Rearrangement.

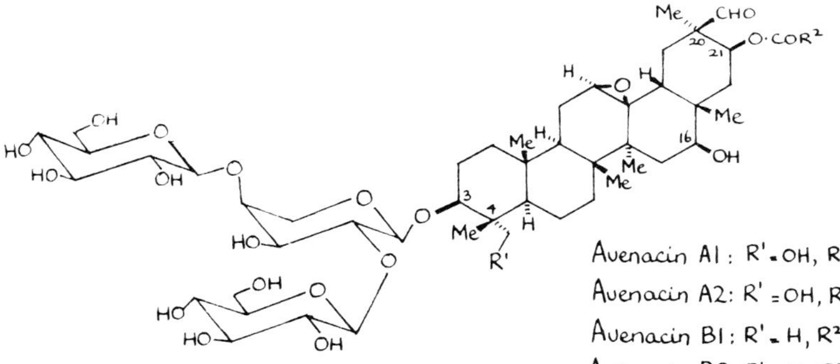

Avenacin A1: R' = OH, R² = o-MeHNC$_6$H$_4$-
Avenacin A2: R' = OH, R² = C$_6$H$_5$-
Avenacin B1: R' = H, R² = o-MeHNC$_6$H$_4$-
Avenacin B2: R' = H, R² = C$_6$H$_5$-

Fig. 19. Complete Structures for the Avenacins.

mass-spectrometry, ^{1}H nmr, ^{13}C nmr and chemical methylation techniques, leading to the complete structures for the four avenacins shown in Figure 19.[19]

The four avenacins are very inhibitory to the growth in culture of the wheat 'take-all' fungus (Ggt), with the N-methylanthranilate-containing A-1 and B-1 being more toxic than A-2 and B-2. However there is a virulent strain of G. graminis (var. avenae) (Gga) which is capable of attacking oats as well as other cereals. We have shown that one of the reasons for the success of this variant is its ability to hydrolyse first one, and then the second, glucose residue attached to the arabinose. This is clearly a detoxification process, our tests showing that the mono- and bis-deglucosyl avenacins are considerably less inhibitory to the growth of Gga.[20,21]

512

ACKNOWLEDGEMENTS
    The synthetic work on the AF- and AK-toxins was carried out by
Sandra R.M. Jarrett and, in its earlier stages, Mark A. Horsham. The
experimental work on 'take-all' fungus was undertaken by Dr. W. Mary L.
Crombie in collaboration with Dr. D.A. Whiting. I express my gratitude
to my colleagues for their enthusiasm and hard work. We thank the AFRC
and SERC for partial support.

REFERENCES
1. R.P. Scheffer and R.S. Livingstone, Science,1984, 223,17.
2 S. Nishimura, Ann. Rev. Phytopathol., 1983, 21, 87 .
3. G.A. Strobel, Ann. Rev. Biochem., 1982, 51, 309.
4. J.M. Daly and H.W. Knoche, Advances in Plant Pathology, Vol. 1,(1982),
p.83, Ed. D.S. Ingram and P.H. Williams, Academic Press, London and
New York.
5. T. Nakashima, T. Ueno and H. Fukami, Tetrahedron Lett., 1982, 4469.
6. T. Nakashima, T. Ueno, H. Fukami, T. Taga, H. Masuda, K. Osaki, H. Otani,
K.Khomoto and S. Nishimura, Agric. Biol. Chem., 1985, 49, 807.
7. H. Otani, K. Kohmoto, S. Nishimura, T. Nakashima, T. Ueno and H.
Fukami, Ann. Phytopath. Japan, 1985, 51, 285.
8. N. Maekawa, M. Yamamoto, S. Nishimura, K. Kohmoto, M. Kuwada and Y.
Watanabe, Ann. Phytopath. Japan, 1984, 50, 600.
9. M. Yamamoto, S. Nishimura, K. Kohmoto and H. Otani, Ann. Phytopath.
Soc., 1984, 50, 610.
10. S. Nakatsuka, K. Ueda, T. Goto, M. Yamamoto, S. Nishimura and K.
Khomoto, Tetrahedron Lett., 1986, 27, 2753.
11. L. Crombie, M.A. Horsham and S.R.M. Jarrett, Tetrahedron Lett.,1989,
in the press.
12. Y. Gao, R.M. Hanson, J.M. Klunder, S.Y. Ko, H. Masamune and K.B.
Sharpless, J. Am. Chem. Soc., 1987, 109, 5765.
13. H. Irie, K. Matsumoto and Y. Zhang, Chem. Pharm. Bull., 1986, 34,
2668.
14. L. Crombie and S.R.M. Jarrett, Tetrahedron Lett., 1989, in the press.
15. H. Irie, K. Matsumoto, T. Kitagawa, Y. Zhang, T. Ueno, T.Nakashima and
H. Fukami, Chem. Pharm. Bull.,1987, 35, 2598.
16. H. Irie, J. Igarashi, K. Matsumoto, Y. Yanagawa, T. Nakashima, T. Ueno
and H. Fukami, Chem. Pharm.Bull.,1985, 33,1313.
17. E.M. Turner, J. Exp. Bot., 1961, 12, 169; 1960, 11, 403.
18. M.J. Begley, L. Crombie, W.M.L. Crombie and D.A. Whiting, J. Chem.
Soc., Perkin Trans. 1, 1986, 1905.
19. L. Crombie, W.M.L. Crombie and D.A. Whiting, J. Chem. Soc., Perkin
Trans. 1, 1986, 1917.
20. W.M.L. Crombie and L. Crombie, Phytochemistry, 1986, 25, 2069.
21. W.M.L. Crombie, L. Crombie, J.B. Green and J.A. Lucas,
Phytochemistry, 1986, 25, 2075.

© 1990 Elsevier Science Publishers B.V. (Biomedical Division)
Pesticides and alternatives, editor J.E. Casida

515

RESEARCH AND SERVICE PROGRAMS OF THE USDA BIOLOGICAL CONTROL OF WEEDS
LABORATORY - EUROPE

LUCA FORNASARI AND LLOYD KNUTSON
United States Department of Agriculture, Agricultural Research Service,
Biological Control of Weeds Laboratory - Europe, Rome, Italy *

ABSTRACT

   The Biological Control of Weeds Laboratory - Europe in Rome, Italy and
Thessaloniki, Greece, conducts research on new biological control agents
(arthropods and pathogens), of weeds for release in the United States (U.S.).
The Laboratory also provides living material for research and release by other
Federal, state, and university scientists in the U.S. Many important weeds in
the U.S. came from Europe or Asia. Most were accidentally introduced without
their natural enemies and thus have been able to increase in numbers unchecked,
invading large territories, and inflicting serious losses to American
agricultural and natural ecosystems. The biology and host specificity of the
complex of natural enemies of weeds are studied to evaluate effectiveness and
safety of these organisms for introduction into the U.S. The laboratory has
worked on 26 species of U.S. weeds and over 60 candidate biological control
agents (mainly insects but also mites and pathogens), of which 27 have been
released in the U.S, resulting in establishment of 17 species attacking 12 weeds.

INTRODUCTION

   Forty-seven per cent of the weed species in the United States (U.S.) are of
European or Asian origin (1), and most were accidentally introduced free of
the natural enemies that control them in their native areas. Many have become
weeds of national or regional importance. They infest millions of hectares of
rangeland, pastures, cropland, wasteland, and natural areas, causing millions
of dollars of losses annually as well as having significant impact on
undisturbed areas. In general, the rate of establishment of new weeds is
increasing and the ranges of established weeds are expanding.
   The United States Department of Agriculture (USDA), Agricultural Research
Service (ARS) established a laboratory in Rome, Italy, in 1958 (with a
substation at the University of Thessaloniki, Greece in 1981), to conduct
research on biological control of weeds and to provide living material to
cooperators in the U.S. The Biological Control of Weeds Laboratory - Europe
(BCWL-E) is one of four overseas biological control laboratories of the
International Activities Office of ARS, other laboratories being in Paris,

*Mail address: Biological Control of Weeds Laboratory-Europe,
 American Embassy-AGRIC, APO NY 09794

516

Buenos Aires, and Seoul. The ARS is a mission-oriented agency responsible for developing new knowledge and technology to solve problems of American agriculture. Research in biological control as an economical, effective, energy-conservant, and environmentally sound pest management approach is a high priority of the Agency. Biological control offers a permanent solution for certain weed problems, while the positive effects of chemical control are limited in time and space. Concern about groundwater quality, increasing costs and use of herbicides (Fig. 1, from (2)), and the need for more productivity and profitability in agriculture are leading to increased emphasis on biological control of weeds. Also, herbicide resistance is a major problem; 20 years ago there was no herbicide resistance in weeds, but now there are more than 200 cases, and in virtually every major crop.

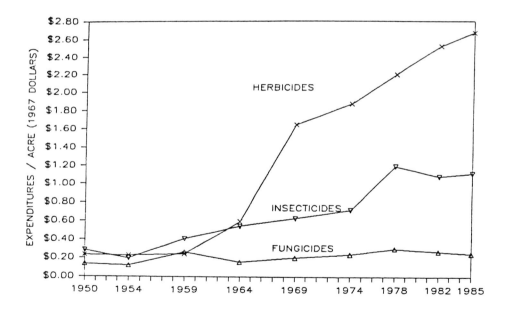

Fig. 1. U.S. pesticide expenditures per acre of cropland harvested (2).

The statistics on biological control introductions show increasing and diversifying activities (3). Up to 1980, biological control of weeds worldwide involved 174 projects against 101 species in 70 countries. Of these, 68 were successful against 48 weeds. There were 525 introductions of exotic natural

enemies, worldwide, up to 1980. From 1980 to 1985 there were an additional 120
introductions, or an increase of over 20 %. Several biological control of weeds
programs were initiated in the U.S. following the successful biological control
of Lantana ragweed in Hawaii initiated in 1902 and Klamath weed in northern
California started in 1944. Partial to complete control has been achieved using
Agasicles beetles against alligator weed, scales and coreid bugs against prickly
pear, Microlarinus beetles against puncturevine, the cinnabar moth against tansy
ragwort, weevils and a stem-boring moth against water hyacinth, and a seed weevil
and a crown weevil against musk thistle.

ACTIVITIES OF THE BIOLOGICAL CONTROL OF WEEDS LABORATORY-EUROPE

   The Rome location was chosen in 1953 because it is a convenient area for the
conduct of this kind of research in Europe, with facilities and support
resources, and because many U.S. weeds are of Mediterranean origin. The
laboratory, currently with five researchers, works closely, both in the research
and implementation phases, with other ARS laboratories, the Animal and Plant
Health Inspection Service-Plant Protection and Quarantine (APHIS-PPQ), and
biological control of weeds specialists in universities and state agencies
throughout the U. S. Close communication is maintained with the CAB
International Institute of Biological Control (CIBC) in Delémont, Switzerland;
the Commonwealth Scientific and Industrial Research Organization (CSIRO) in
Montpellier, France; and other biological control workers throughout the world.

   The mission of the Rome laboratory is to discover, conduct research on, and
provide material of insects, mites, nematodes, and pathogens for introduction
into the U.S. to abate major weeds. Basic research on how natural enemies fit
into ecosystems is conducted to develop more efficient approaches to biological
control. Applied projects involve locating records of natural enemies which
reproduce on high priority weeds, exploring for populations of these and
searching for new natural enemies, studying their biology, and conducting
host-specificity tests. Potential biological control agents are tested on as
many as 60 species to be sure they do not reproduce on plants used as food,
fiber, or ornamentals, or on other plants of value such as native endangered
species. Results of the studies are reviewed by a Technical Advisory Group,
composed of members from APHIS-PPQ, universities, and state agencies. If the
natural enemy is judged to be safe in North America, it is introduced into the
U.S., usually first into a quarantine facility for further host specificity
testing before its release. Specific guidelines are followed in carrying out the
introduction activities (4). The laboratory is also responsible for developing
new bioassays for testing potential biological control agents in the laboratory
and in the field. Dunn (5) reviewed the Laboratory's early programs.

RESEARCH APPROACHES

After study of a weed problem and a literature search on associated organisms
(insects, mites, and pathogens), surveys are conducted in the area of origin of
the target weed. The material collected is identified by taxonomic specialists,
and candidate biological control agents are selected from the resultant inventory
of species. Often, detailed taxonomic studies of the host plants and biological
control agents are essential (6, 7). The laboratory maintains a voucher
(reference) collection of weeds and natural enemies to document its studies and
aid taxonomic research, supplying specimens, as appropriate, to cooperating
laboratories. Preliminary host specificity tests are conducted. At the same
time the biology of these organisms is investigated. Basic research on
ecological aspects of natural enemies and host plants, including their
inter-relationships, is also conducted. In particular, the microhabitats and
climatic requirements of the organisms involved are studied, to evaluate their
potential action in the new environment. Biotypes (populations) of candidate
agents are characterized. After the first screening, which includes host
suitability testing against forms of the target weed from the U.S., in-depth
host-specificity testing is carried out, using methodologies appropriate to the
plant's phenology and the natural enemies' behavior. Experiments are conducted
under no-choice and choice conditions, using adult and larval stages, to evaluate
the susceptibility of selected test plants. Oogenesis, oviposition, feeding
damage, and the capacity to complete development on test plants are especially
analyzed (Table 1).

TABLE 1.
TESTS TO DETERMINE HOST SPECIFICITY OF CANDIDATE BIOLOGICAL CONTROL AGENTS.

Oogenesis -- no choice
Oviposition -- no choice, choice
Larval survival -- no choice
Larval feeding -- no choice, two choice, and multiple choice
Adult feeding -- no choice, two choice, and multiple choice
Host suitability -- no choice and multiple choice
Host suitability field test -- free choice

These tests are carried out in the laboratory or in the field. When
studies in Europe and in U.S. quarantine have been completed and release of
the biological control agent has been approved, further studies are conducted
in the release areas to determine the impact of the natural enemy on the

target weed in the new environment, especially with regard to population
dynamics and level of infestation. A management procedure for the
introduction of biological agents for control of weeds has been described by
Grabau and Spencer (8).

TARGET WEEDS AND BIOLOGICAL CONTROL AGENTS STUDIED

The BCWL-E has worked on 26 weeds occurring in the Mediterranean and nearby
regions over the past 30 years. Many studies have been conducted individually by
BCWL-E, and others have been carried out jointly or concurrently with CIBC and
other units. More than 60 insects and mites and several pathogens have been
studied by BCWL-E or, based on the studies of others, have been shipped to the
U.S. This work has resulted in the establishment of 17 species of insects,
mites, and pathogens attacking the following 12 weeds:

EUPHORBIACEAE

leafy spurge (Euphorbia esula L. complex)

COMPOSITAE

musk (nodding) thistle complex (Carduus macrocephalus Desfontaine),

C. nutans L.,

C. thoermeri Weinmann

plumeless thistle   (Carduus acanthoides L.)

Italian thistle   (Carduus pycnocephalus L.)

spotted knapweed   (Centaurea maculosa De Lamarck)

diffuse knapweed   (Centaurea diffusa De Lamarck)

yellow starthistle   (Centaurea solstitialis L.)

tansy ragwort   (Senecio jacobaea L.)

rush skeleton weed   (Chondrilla juncea L.)

LABIATAE

Mediterranean sage (Salvia aethiopis L.)

LEGUMINOSAE

scotch broom (Cytisus scoparius (L.) Link)

ZYGOPHYLLACAEAE

puncturevine (Tribulus terrestris L.)

RESEARCH AND INTRODUCTION PROJECTS LARGELY COMPLETED

In the following discussion of weeds and natural enemies, we refer mainly to
natural enemies studied by the Rome Laboratory and CIBC and subsequently released
in the U.S. Only the more recent or comprehensive papers documenting research in
Europe or release and establishment in North America are cited.

1. Musk thistle complex. This serious weed in pastures throughout the U.S.
thrives in a wide geographical range of climate and soil conditions, and was

introduced from Europe into North America in the early 1900's. In a survey of insects attacking Carduus macrocephalus in Italy, 109 species were studied (9). Batra (10) reviewed the insects and fungi associated with Carduus thistles.

The thistle-head weevil Rhinocyllus conicus Froelich from France, studied in Europe primarily by CIBC, was first released in 1969 in Montana and Virginia. It is now well established in 20 states. It is very effective, reducing musk thistle density up to 99% at some sites in Montana and Virginia (11, 12, 13, 14).

The rosette weevil Trichosirocalus horridus (Panzer) from Italy (9, 15, 16) was released between 1974 and 1976 and established in Kansas, Maryland, Missouri, Virginia, and Wyoming. It is widespread in these states, causing up to 90% reduction in musk thistle density at some sites in Virginia (17, 18).

The fly Cheilosia corydon (Harris) was studied in Italy (19, 20). Its larvae seriously damage the stems of musk thistle and move down to the root, killing the plant. Material for release in Montana, Maryland, and New Jersey was first shipped in 1989, and released in Maryland (21).

2. Plumeless thistle. This biennial herb has become widespread in North America and is a serious problem in pastures. The weevils R. conicus and T. horridus were studied in Italy and released in the U.S. in 1969 and 1974, respectively, and are showing substantial impact in Virginia (17).

3. Italian thistle. This is a common annual or biennial weed in grazing land, open woodlands, fallow cropland, and wastelands in California and Oregon. The weevil R. conicus, studied primarily by CIBC, was released in 1973 in both states, and readily became established (22, 23). Studies are being conducted to characterize different biotypes of R. conicus among populations feeding on Carduus pycnocephalus, C. nutans, and Silybum marianum Gaertner (24).

The weevil Trichosirocalus horridus Panzer was studied in Italy and released in 1974. It established in Virginia, Missouri, Maryland, Kansas, and Wyoming and is very effective in controlling the weed (18).

4. Scotch broom. This woody perennial is native to southwestern Europe and western Asia. Its seed may lie dormant in the soil for over a century (25).

The weevil Apion fuscirostre F. was studied in Italy, released in 1964 in California (26), and its establishment has been confirmed (3).

5. Mediterranean sage. This is a biennial or perennial herb native of south central Europe, western Asia, and northern Africa.

The weevils Phrydiuchus spilmani Warner and P. tau Warner (as P. topiarius (Germar)) were studied in Italy (27, 28) and released in California, Idaho, and Oregon in 1969 and 1971, respectively (3). Phrydiuchus tau established in California, Idaho, and Oregon (3); P. spilmani did not establish (3).

6. Tansy ragwort. This biennial or perennial herb native to western Europe, Asia, and northern Africa, is a problem in pastures in the northwestern states.

Three insects have been studied, primarily by CIBC.

Pegohylemyia seneciella Meade was studied in France, released in 1966, and has become established in Oregon and Washington (29, 30). This fly also established in California, but the release area was subsequently destroyed (3).

Longitarsus jacobaeae (Waterhouse) was collected in Italy and released in 1969 in California, Oregon, and Washington, where it became established and is providing substantial control (3, 30, 31, 32).

Tyria jacobaeae (L.) was collected in France and released in 1959 in California, Oregon, and Washington (30, 31).

7. Puncturevine. This annual herb from Europe has spread throughout all of the U.S. except some states along the northern border; it is particularly a problem in pastures and sometimes occurs in cultivated fields in the southwest.

Microlarinus lareynii (Jacquelin du Val) was studied in Italy (33) and released in 1961 in the U.S. It became established in Arizona, California, Florida, Kansas, Nevada, Oklahoma, Oregon, Texas, and Utah (3, 14, 30, 34). In 1962, it was released in Hawaii, where it established and has complemented puncturevine control by M. lypriformis (Wollaston) (35), which was released later.

In 1961 M. lypriformis from Italy was released in North America and established in Arizona, California, Nevada, Oklahoma, Texas, Utah, and Kansas. It has been more effective in warmer areas of the southwestern States (3, 14, 30, 34). In 1963, M. lypriformis from Italy was released and established in Hawaii.

8. Leafy spurge. Leafy spurge, of Eurasian origin, is a noxious weed in the northcentral and northwestern United States and in Canada, infesting over three million hectares of land, mainly rangeland; it is toxic to livestock.

Oberea erythrocephala (Schrank) was studied primarily by CIBC in Switzerland, Austria and Hungary, and was released in Canada in 1979 and in the U.S. in 1980 and 1983. It has established in Montana (3, 14, 36, 37).

The gall midge Bayeria n. sp. nr. capitigena Bremi was studied in Italy and released in 1985 in Montana. Its establishment has not been confirmed (38). Another gall midge, Dasineura n. sp. nr. capsulae Kieffer (Diptera: Cecidomyiidae) was studied in Italy (39) and released in 1989 in Texas and Montana. It is not known to be established.

Chamaesphecia tenthrediniformis (Denis & Schiffermüller) was studied by CIBC in Austria, released in Canada in 1971, and released in 1975 in Idaho, Montana and Oregon. It did not establish, apparently because U.S. plants are not a suitable host for its larvae (3, 14, 36).

The flea beetle Aphthona flava Guillebeau was studied in Hungary and Italy and first released in 1982 in Canada and in 1985 in Montana. Subsequent releases were made in the U.S. from material collected in Yugoslavia. It is established in Canada but its establishment in the U.S. has not been confirmed (38). Aphthona *cyparissiae* (Koch) was shipped to the U.S. from Yugoslavia in 1988 and 1989 but it is not known to be established. *Aphthona czwalinae* (Weise) from Austria and Hungary were shipped to the U.S. in 1986, 1987, and 1988, but it is not known to be established.

9. Yellow starthistle. Yellow starthistle entered North America from Eurasia, and is particularly noxious in the western states, infesting mainly rangelands, but also infests fields of alfalfa, wheat, oats, barley, etc.

The weevil *Bangasternus orientalis* Capiomont from Greece was released in Idaho, Washington, California, and Oregon 1985 (40). Its establishment has been confirmed in California, Idaho, and Washington (3).

The tephritid fly, *Urophora sirunaseva* (Hering) from Greece was released in California in 1984 and found to be established there and in southern Oregon in 1989 (41).

Another fly, *Chaetorellia australis* Hering, from Greece was released in 1988 in California (42), but could not establish because it was released too late in the fall, and additional releases are needed (41). An additional release was made in 1989; establishment is not confirmed.

10. Diffuse knapweed. This is a biennial herb, native to southeastern Europe and western Asia.

A tephritid fly, *Urophora affinis* Frauenfeld from Central Europe was studied by CIBC, released in Idaho, Montana, Oregon, and Washington in 1973 and 1979 (43, 44) and became established (30). Another tephritid fly, *Urophora quadrifasciata* (Meigen), from the USSR was studied by CIBC and released in Canada in 1972, whence it entered the U.S., becoming established by 1989 (45).

Sphenoptera jugoslavica Obenberger from Greece has been studied primarily by CIBC, was released in 1980, and became established in Idaho, Oregon, and Washington. It is also being recolonized in other states (14, 30).

Pterolonche inspersa Staudinger from eastern Europe and Greece was released in Idaho, Oregon, and Washington in 1986 (46). It has not established in Idaho and Oregon, and its establishment in Washington is uncertain.

Pelochrista medullana Staudinger, studied primarily by CIBC, was released in British Columbia, Canada and became established. It was first released in the U.S. in 1984 (collections from Austria and Hungary) but is not known to be established.

11. Spotted knapweed. This is a biennial or perennial herb native to Eurasia. There are large infestations in the northwestern states and in California, where it is a serious weed. It also occurs in the eastern half of the U.S., except in the southern states.

Agapeta zoegana L. from Hungary and Austria was studied primarily by CIBC and released in Canada in 1982, in Montana during 1984, and in Idaho in 1989. It appeared to become established in Montana, Oregon, and Washington by 1988 but was not found during 1989 in Oregon and Washington.

12. Skeleton weed. This is a perennial herb. A mite and a gall midge have been studied, primarily by CSIRO. Eriophyes chondrillae (Canestrini) from Italy was released in 1977 and is established in California, Idaho, and Washington. It has been extremely effective in Washington (30, 47).

The gall midge, Cystiphora schmidti (Rübsamen), imported from Greece via Australia, was released in California (47).

The rust, Puccinia chondrillina Bubak & Sydenham from Italy, was released in 1976 and established in California, Idaho, Oregon, and Washington (30, 48, 49, 50, 51).

CURRENT RESEARCH AND INTRODUCTION PROJECTS

The primary target weeds for which natural enemies are currently being discovered, studied, and collected for release are leafy spurge, yellow starthistle, diffuse and spotted knapweeds, Russian knapweed (Centaurea repens L.), musk thistle, and field bindweed (Convolvulus arvensis L.)

1. Leafy spurge.

Oxicesta geographica Fabricius was collected in Romania in 1984, and screening tests started in 1988. Its larvae feed on aerial parts of the weed, exhibiting gregarious behavior, and completely defoliating the plants. It has four generations per year under laboratory conditions. After observations and host-specificity testing, a petition for further study of this moth in U.S. quarantine was submitted to the T. A. G. and approval was recommended to APHIS-PPQ in 1989.

Another moth, Simyra dentinosa Freyer was collected in Greece and studied in Greece and Italy from 1981 to 1989. Its behavior is similar to the previous species, but it is univoltine. A petition for study in U.S. quarantine was submitted and approved in 1989.

Studies on the life history and host specificity of the multivoltine flea beetle Aphthona abdominalis Duftschmid are being conducted under field and laboratory conditions in Italy, where it occurs naturally. The larvae produce major damage, feeding on roots, root buds, and shoots; adults feed on leaves.

Chamaesphecia crassicornis Bartel was collected in Romania, Czechoslovakia, and Austria. A Romanian population of C. crassicornis was selected as a candidate, and studies have been conducted in Italy. Its larvae tunnel in roots, causing serious damage. It has a 1- or 2-year life cycle. A petition to introduce this moth into U.S. quarantine was submitted in 1989; actual field release was approved.

Dasineura n. sp. nr. capsulae Kieffer was studied in Italy (39). The larvae of this gall midge cause flower bud galls and prevent seed production. A petition for field release in the U.S. was submitted in 1989, and material was sent to ARS, Bozeman, Montana, and APHIS-PPQ, Mission, Texas for quarantine study.

2. Yellow starthistle.

The weevil Eustenopus villosus (Boheman) was collected in Greece and studied in Greece and Italy, and at the ARS quarantine laboratory in Albany, California (52). The larvae of this univoltine weevil feed inside buds and flowerheads, destroying the developing seeds. A petition for field release in the U.S. of this weevil was submitted in 1989.

A tephritid fly, Chaetorellia australis Hering, whose larvae feed in the flowerheads of yellow starthistle, was studied in Greece (53, 54) and released in 1988 and 1989 in California.

Larinus curtus Hochhut is another univoltine weevil collected in Greece, and studies on the biology and host specificity are underway in Greece and Italy, and at the ARS quarantine laboratory in Albany, California. Its life history is similar to E. villosus, except that it attacks the plant in later stages, and larvae develop on seeds. One larva is able to destroy almost all the contents of a seedhead. Studies on the biology and host specificity are underway.

3. Diffuse knapweed.

The weevil Bangasternus fausti Reitter was collected in Greece and approved for limited field release in Montana and Oregon in 1989. The seed-feeding larvae of this univoltine weevil are able to destroy the entire content of a seedhead.

A joint study with CIBC was undertaken on Larinus minutus Gyllenhall (Coleoptera: Curculionidae) collected in Greece and Romania. The larvae of this univoltine weevil are seed feeders and one larva is able to destroy 100 % of the seeds in a seedhead.

The mite Aceria centaureae Nalepa was collected in Greece in 1982 and is still under study. It causes severe leaf galling and sometimes death of plants in the rosette stage. A second mite from Greece, referred to as Aceria sp., attacks meristematic tissue and is under study in cooperation with M. Castagnoli, Florence, Italy. It was shipped to the U.S. for study in quarantine in 1988.

4. Musk thistle. The flea beetle Psylliodes chalcomera Illiger was studied in Italy (55, 56). The larvae destroy the shoots, flower buds, and peduncles. It has one generation per year. A petition is being submitted in 1989 for release of P. chalcomera in the U.S.

5. Field bindweed. This perennial herb from Eurasia infests cereal fields,

gardens, and uncultivated areas throughout the U.S.

Tyta luctuosa (Denis & Schiffermüller) was studied in Italy (57, 58, 59) and released in Texas and Oklahoma in 1988 and 1989. It is not known to be established.

The mite Aceria malherbae Nuzzaci from Italy and Greece was released in 1988 and 1989 in Texas and Oklahoma, and in New Jersey in 1989 (60, 61). Establishment has not been confirmed.

FUTURE PROJECTS - PROCEDURES AND TOPICS

New research and service projects for BCWL-E may be suggested by ARS research units, other U.S. Federal agencies, state agencies, and universities. Research proposals are submitted according to a standard procedure that includes a brief pre-proposal for review by the ARS National Program Staff to determine whether the proposed project meets the criteria of ARS missions and for project prioritization, and by the ARS Classical Biological Control Working Group for recommendation on technical feasibility. If approved, a work plan is prepared for further review. The T.A.G. reviews work plans for potential conflicts of interest and safety. Currently, proposals and plans for the following new projects are in various stages of development: Tamarix, gorse, Geranium dissectum as an alternate host for Heliothis, weedy species of grasses, and post-emergence application of myco-herbicides in minimum-till situations.

SUMMARY OF INTRODUCTION ACTIVITIES, 1980-1989

Although the primary responsibility of BCWL-E, as most ARS units, is to conduct research to solve agricultural problems, the laboratory also has a major responsibility to provide living material of natural enemies to ARS scientists for study in quarantine and to ARS, APHIS-PPQ, and state units for field release. A considerable amount of the laboratory resources are utilized for such "collect and ship" activities. To date, the laboratory has not been extensively involved in the establishment phase in the U.S.

Detailed records of shipment activities are included in the laboratory's annual reports. As an example of this activity, during 1989 BCWL-E shipped 64,581 individuals of 17 species of natural enemies of eight target weeds to six locations in the U.S., and two species to Canada.

COOPERATION

The BCWL-E cooperates in the research, introduction, and implementation phases with scientific collaborators in ARS, state, and university laboratories; with its clientele in federal agencies such as APHIS-PPQ and many state agencies; and with the international weed research community. Close coordination with biological control of weeds activities in Canada are especially important. The laboratory meets annually with CIBC, CSIRO, and the Zagreb Institute of Plant Protection. The BCWL-E and the Istituto Sperimentale per la Patologia Vegetale of the Italian Ministry of Agriculture and Forestry, Rome, co-sponsored the 7th International Symposium on Biological Control of Weeds (62). The laboratory also participates actively in the bi-national cooperative programs established by ARS and the Biological Control Laboratory, Beijing, and the Zoological Institute, Leningrad, in 1988.

The nature of biocontrol of weeds research requires an interdisciplinary, international, continuing, and cooperative approach. This is partly because effective research, development, and implementation in biological control requires information from various fields -- from taxonomy to biology, behavior, genetics, population ecology, and others. Also, because of the strict requirements for information on the host specificity of weed biological control agents as a result of U.S. state and national plant pest laws, there has, historically, been considerable rigor in this area of research. However, we need to make our research even more productive and to be better able to predict the likelihood of the success of biological control agents. To achieve a more comprehensive and deeper understanding of the role and mode of action of weed biological control agents, we are interested in cooperating with colleagues in various disciplines, in both basic and applied research areas.

ACKNOWLEDGMENTS

We thank the following for reviewing the manuscript and providing information: D. R. Kincaid, International Activities, ARS; A. L. Christy, R. S. Soper, and R. Villet, National Program Staff, ARS; R. Bennett, Plant Disease Research Unit, ARS; N. Rees and S. Rosenthal, Rangeland Insect Laboratory, ARS; J. R. Coulson, Biological Control Documentation Center, ARS; G. Campobasso, M. Cristofaro, and R. Sobhian, BCWL-E; D. Schroeder, CABI International Institute of Biological Control; and P. H. Dunn, former Director, BCWL-E. We thank L.A. Andres, formerly Biological Control of Weeds Laboratory, Albany, California, for historical information.

REFERENCES

1. Reed CF, RO Hughes (1970) Selected Weeds of the United States. USDA-ARS Agriculture Handbook No. 366 Washington D.C.

2. Carlson GA (1988) Economics of biological control of pests. Amer J Alt Agric 3(2,3):110-116

3. Julien MH (1987) Biological control of weeds: a world catalogue of agents and their target weeds. Second Edit CAB Int Inst Biol Control, Wallingford, U.K. 145 pp

4. Klingman DL, JR Coulson (1982) Guidelines for introducing foreign organisms into the United States for biological control of weeds. Weed Sci 30:661-667

5. Dunn PH (1970) Current projects at the Rome Entomology Laboratory of the USDA. In: Simmonds FJ (ed) Proc 1st Int Symp Biol Contr Weeds, CIBC Misc Publ 1:33-38

6. Knutson L (1981) Symbiosis of biosystematics and biological control. In: Papavizas GC (ed) Beltsville Symposia in Agricultural Research 5. Biological Control in Crop Production. Allanheld, Osmun, Totowa, NJ, pp 61-78

7. Knutson L, RS Soper (in press) The role of systematics in biological control. In: Luck R (ed) Proc Int Vedalia Symp Biol Contr

8. Grabau WE, NR Spencer (1976, 1978) A management procedure for the introduction of biological control agents for control of weeds. In: Freeman TE (ed) Proc 4th Int Symp Biol Contr Weeds, pp 13-34

9. Boldt PE, G Campobasso, E Colonnelli (1980) Paleartic distribution and host plants of Ceutorrhynchus trimaculatus (F.) and Trichosirocalus horridus (Panzer) (Coleoptera: Curculionidae). Ann Entomol Soc Amer 73(6):694-698

10. Batra, SWT, JR Coulson, PH Dunn, PE Boldt (1981) Insects and fungi associated with Carduus thistles (Compositae). USDA Bull 1616

11. Kok LT, RL Pienkowski (1985) Biological control of musk thistle by Rhinocyllus conicus (Coleoptera: Curculionidae) in Virginia from 1969 to 1980. In: Delfosse ES (ed) Proc 6th Int Symp Biol Contr Weeds, pp 433-438

12. Puttler B, SH Long, EJ Peters (1978) Establishment in Missouri of Rhinocyllus conicus for the biological control of musk thistle. Weed Sci 26:188-190

13. Rees NE (1977) Impact of Rhinocyllus conicus on thistles in southwestern Montana. Environ Entomol 6:839-842

14. Story JM (1985) Status of biological weed control in Montana. In: Delfosse ES (ed) Proc 6th Int Symp Biol Contr Weeds, pp 837-842

15. Boldt PE, and G Campobasso (1981) Biology of two weevils, Ceutorrhynchus trimaculatus and Trichosirocalus horridus, on Carduus spp. in Europe. Environ Entomol 10(5):691-696

16. Rizza A, NR Spencer (1981) Field tests with the musk thistle insects, Trichosirocalus (Ceuthorrhynchidius) horridus and Ceutorrhynchus trimaculatus to determine their impact on artichoke. Environ Entomol 10:332-334

17. Cartwright B, LT Kok (1985) Growth responses of the musk and plumeless thistles (Carduus nutans and C. acanthoides) to damage by Trichosirocalus horridus (Coleoptera: Curculionidae). Weed Sci 33:57-62

18. Kok LT (1986) Impact of Trichosirocalus horridus (Coleoptera: Curculionidae) on Carduus thistles in pastures. Crop Prot 5:214-217

19. Boldt PE ((1976), 1978) Foreign exploration for the biological control of Carduus spp. pp. 11-17, In: Frick KE (ed), Biological control of thistles in the genus Carduus in the United States. Proc. Entomol Soc Am Symp, Washington D.C. (1977), USDA/SEA. 50 pp

20. Rizza A, G Campobasso, PH Dunn, M Stazi (1989) Cheilosia corydon (Diptera: Syrphidae), a candidate for the biological control of musk thistle in North America. Ann Entomol Soc Amer 81(2):225-232

21. Tipping PW (personal communication, 1989)

22. Goeden RD, DW Ricker (1978) Establishment of Rhinocyllus conicus (Col.: Curculionidae) on Italian thistle in southern California. Environ Entomol 7:787-789

528

23. Goeden RD; DW Ricker (1985) Seasonal asynchrony of Italian thistle, Carduus pycnocephalus, and the weevil Rhinocyllus conicus (Coleoptera: Curculionidae), introduced for biological control in southern California. Environ Entomol 14:433-436

24. Goeden RD, DW Ricker, BA Hawkins (1985) Ethological and genetic differences among three biotypes of Rhinocyllus conicus (Coleoptera: Curculionidae), introduced into North America for biological control of asteraceous thistles. In: Delfosse ES (ed) Proc 6th Int Symp Biol Contr Weeds, pp 181-189

25. Haussmann G, and J Scurti (1985) Piante infestanti. Vol. I Edagricole, Bologna.

26. Andres LA, RB Hawkes, and A Rizza (1967) Apion seed weevil introduced for biological control of Scotch broom. Calif Agric 21:13

27. Andres LA, A Rizza (1965) Life history of Phrydiuchus topiarius on Salvia verbenacea (Labiatae). J Econ Entomol 58(3):314-319

28. Andres LA (1966) Host specificity studies of Phrydiuchus topiarius and Phrydiuchus sp. J Econ Entomol 59(1):69-76

29. Frick KE (1969) Tansy ragwort control, aided by the establishment of seedfly from Paris. Calif Agric 23:10-11

30. Piper GL (1985) Biological control of weeds in Washington: status report. In: Delfosse ES (ed) Proc 6th Int Symp Biol Contr Weeds, pp 817-826

31. Hawkes RB (1981) Biological control of tansy ragwort in the State of Oregon, U.S.A. In: Delfosse TE (ed) Proc 5th Int Symp Biol Contr Weeds, pp 623-626

32. Hawkes RB, GR Johnson (1978) Longitarsus jacobaeae aids moth in biological control of tansy ragwort. In: Freeman TE (ed) Proc 4th Int Symp Biol Contr Weeds, pp 193-196

33. Andres LA, GW Angalet (1963) Notes on the ecology and host specificity of Microlarinus lareynii and M. laypriformis (Coleoptera: Curculionidae) and the biological control of puncture vine, Tribulus terrestris. J Econ Entomol 56(3):333-340

34. Huffaker CB, J Hamai, RM Nowierski (1983) Biological control of puncturevine, Tribulus terristris in California after twenty years of activity of introduced weevils. Entomophaga 28:387-400

35. Maddox DM (1976) History of weevils on puncturevine in and near the United States. Weed Sci 24:414-419

36. Pemberton RW (1985) Native plant considerations in the biological control of leafy spurge. In: Delfosse ES (ed) Proc 6th Int Symp Biol Contr Weeds, pp 365-390

37. Rees NE, RW Pemberton, A Rizza, P Pecora (1986) First recovery of Oberea erythrocephala on the leafy spurge complex in the United States. Weed Sci. 34:395-397

38. Pemberton RW, G Johnson (1985) Two new insects (Dasineura capitigena and Aphthona flava) for leafy spurge control in the United States. Proc 1985 Leafy Spurge Symp, Bozeman, pp 29-32

39. Pecora P, M Cristofaro, M Stazi (1989) Dasineura sp. near capsulae (Diptera: Cecidomyiidae), a candidate for biological control of Euphorbia esula complex in North America. Ann Entomol Soc Amer 82(6):693-700

40. Maddox DM, R Sobhian (1987) Field experiment to determine host specificity and oviposition behavior of Bangasternus orientalis and Bangasternus fausti (Coleoptera: Curculionidae), biological control candidate for yellow starthistle and diffuse knapweed. Environ Entomol 16(3):645-648

529

41. Turner CE (personal communication, 1989) United States Department of Agriculture, Agricultural Research Service, Biological Control of Weeds Unit, 800 Buchanan Street, Albany, California 94710, USA

42. Turner CE, R Sobhian, DM Maddox (in press) Host specificity studies of Chaetorellia australis (Diptera: Tephritidae), a prospective biological control agent for yellow starthistle, Centaurea solstitialis (Asteraceae). In: Delfosse ES (ed) Proc 7th Int Symp Biol Contr Weeds

43. Maddox DM (1982) Biological control of diffuse knapweed (Centaurea diffusa) and spotted knapweed (Centaurea maculosa). Weed Sci 30:76-82

44. Story JM (1979) Biological weed control in Montana. Bull Montana Agric Exp Sta 717, 15 pp

45. Myers J, P Harris (1980) Distribution of Urophora galls in flower heads of diffuse and spotted knapweed in British Columbia. J Appl Ecol 17:359-367

46. Dunn PH, SS Rosenthal, G Campobasso, and SM Tait (in press) Host specificity of Pterolonche inspersa (Lep.: Pterolonchidae) and its potential as a biological control agent for Centaurea maculosa, spotted knapweed. Entomophaga

47. Sobhian R, LA Andres (1978) The response of the skeletonweed gall midge. Cystiphora schmidti (Diptera: Cecidomyiidae), and gall mite, Aceria chondrillae (Eriophyidae) to North American strains of rush skeletonweed (Chondrilla juncea). Environ Entomol 7:506-508

48. Adams EB, RF Line (1984) Biology of Puccinia chondrillina in Washington. Phytopathol 74:742-745

49. Adams EB, RF Line (1984) Epidemiology and host morphology in the parasitism of rush skeletonweed by Puccinia chondrillina. Phytopathol 74:745-748

50. Emge RG, JS Melching, CH Kingsolver (1981) Epidemiology of Puccinia chondrillina, a rust pathogen for the biological control of rush skeleton weed in the United States. Phytopathol 71:839-843

51. Supkoff DM, DB Joley, JM Marois (1985) Effect of Puccinia chondrillina on the population density of Chondrilla juncea (rush skeletonweed) in California. Phytopathol 75:1328 (abstract)

52. Clement SL, T Mimmocchi, R Sobhian, PH Dunn (1988) Host specificity of adult Eustenopus hirtus (Waltl) (Coleoptera: Curculionidae), a potential biological control agent of yellow starthistle, Centaurea solstitialis L. (Asteraceae, Cardueae). Proc Entomol Soc Wash 90(4):501-507

53. Sobhian R, H Zwölfer (1985) Phytophagous insect species associated with flowerheads of yellow starthistle (Centaurea solstitialis L.). Zeit Ang Entomol 99:301-321

54. Sobhian R, IS Pittara (1988) A contribution to the biology, phenology and host specificity of Chaetorellia hexachaeta Loew (Diptera: Tephritidae), a possible candidate for the biological control of yellow starthistle (Centaurea solstitialis L.). J Appl Entomol 106:444-450

55. Dunn PH, A Rizza (1976) Bionomics of Psylliodes chalcomera, a candidate for biological control of musk thistle. Ann Entomol Soc Amer 69(3):395-398

56. Dunn PH, A Rizza (1977) Host specificity of Psylliodes chalcomera, a candidate for biological control of musk thistle. Environ Entomol 6(3):449-454

57. Rosenthal SS (1978) Host specificity of Tyta luctuosa (Lep.: Noctuidae), an insect associated with Convolvulus arvensis (Convolvulaceae). Entomophaga 23(4):367-370

58. Rosenthal SS and GR Buckingham (1982) Natural enemies of Convolvulus arvensis in western Mediterranean Europe. Hilgardia 50(2):1-19

59. Rosenthal SS, SL Clement, N Hostettler, T Mimmocchi (1988) Biology of _Tyta luctuosa_ (Lep.: Noctuidae) and its potential value as a biological control agent for the weed _Convolvulus arvensis_. Entomophaga 33(2):185-192

60. Rosenthal SS (1983) Current status and potential for biological control of field bindweed with _Aceria convolvuli_. In: Hoy MA, Knutson L, Cunningham (eds) Biological control of pests by mites. Proc of a Conference, April 1982, Berkeley, California. Univ Calif Agric Exper Sta Spec Publ 3304, pp 57-60

61. Nuzzaci G, T Mimmocchi, SL Clement (1985) A new species of _Aceria_ (Acari: Eriophyidae) from _Convolvulus arvensis_ L. (Convolvulaceae) with notes on other eriophyid associates of convolvulaceous plants. Entomologica 20: 81-89

62. Delfosse ES (ed) (in press) Proc 7th Int Symp Biol Contr Weeds

© 1990 Elsevier Science Publishers B.V. (Biomedical Division)
Pesticides and alternatives, editor J.E. Casida

A EUROPEAN CLEARWING MOTH, CHAMAESPHECIA CRASSICORNIS BARTEL (LEPIDOPTERA: SESIIDAE), CANDIDATE FOR BIOLOGICAL CONTROL OF LEAFY SPURGE (EUPHORBIA ESULA L. "COMPLEX") IN THE UNITED STATES

P. PECORA, M. CRISTOFARO, and M. STAZI

USDA, ARS, Biological Control of Weeds Laboratory - Europe
American Embassy/AGRIC, APO NY 09794

ABSTRACT

Leafy spurge is a complex of species in the genus Euphorbia that has become a major weed in rangelands and pastures in North America. Among the root-borer moths in the genus Chamaesphecia Spüler (Lepidoptera: Sesiidae), C. empiformis (Esper) and C. tenthrediniformis (Denis & Schiffermüller) were introduced during the 1960's by the CAB International Institute for Biological Control against E. cyparissias L. and E. esula L. in North America, but neither is known have established. To find an effective agent for biological control of E. pseudovirgata Schultz (Soo), the most common leafy spurge in the U.S., C. crassicornis Bartel from Romania was selected as a candidate by the U.S. Department of Agriculture. From 1984 to 1988, biological studies and host suitability tests were carried out at the USDA Biological Control of Weeds Laboratory, Rome, Italy. Tests were conducted on 12 plant species of the family Euphorbiaceae (four were U.S. populations of E. pseudovirgata), plus the plant control. The promising results showed that C. crassicornis is restricted to plants of the subgenus Esula, and is able to develop on North American populations of leafy spurge. These results led us to submit a petition in 1989 for introduction of C. crassicornis into quarantine in the U.S. for further studies.

Key words: insect, weed, herbivory.

INTRODUCTION

The weed problem

    Leafy spurge, Euphorbia esula L. "complex" (Euphorbiaceae), is a plant of Eurasian origin that started to become a serious problem at the beginning of this century in North America. This weed is an irreversibly dominant species on rangelands and pastures, displacing useful forage plants. Leafy spurge occurs in 25 states (1), and infests almost 2.5 million acres in North America (2).

    The most common weedy type of Euphorbia in the U.S. appears to be E. pseudovirgata Schultz (Soo) (Fig. 1), which is a hybrid between E. esula and E. waldsteinii (= E. virgata Waldstein and Kitaibel) (3). Euphorbia waldsteinii

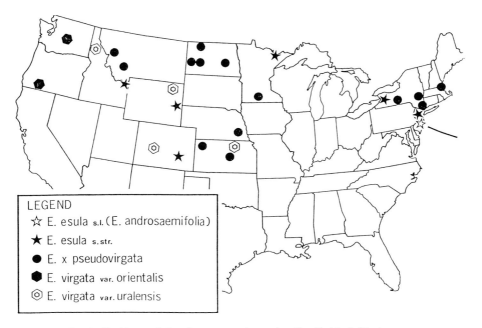

LEGEND
☆ E. esula s.l. (E. androsaemifolia)
★ E. esula s.str.
● E. x pseudovirgata
⬡ E. virgata var. orientalis
◎ E. virgata var. uralensis

Fig. 1. Distribution of leafy spurge taxa in the United States.

is native to central and eastern Europe.

Biological control programs

　　Because of its foreign origin and the large number of natural enemies
associated with it in Eurasia, leafy spurge is considered to be an excellent
candidate weed for biological control. Programs for the biological control of
leafy spurge were started by the CAB International Institute of Biological
Control, Delemont, Switzerland and Agriculture Canada in 1963, and by the
Agricultural Research Service, U.S. Department of Agriculture in 1970 (1, 4).

　　Several insects associated with Euphorbia spp. have been evaluated and
introduced as biological control agents in North America (4; 5; 6): the
hawkmoth Hyles euphorbiae (L.), Lepidoptera: Sphingidae (released in 1966 and
first known to be established in 1983); the longhorn beetle Oberea
erythrocephala Schrank, Coleoptera: Cerambycidae (released in 1980 and first
known to be established in 1983); the flea beetles Aphthona flava Guillebaume,
A. cyparissiae (Koch), A. nigriscutis Foudras, and A. czwalinae Weise,
Coleoptera: Chrysomelidae (released respectively in 1982, 1982, 1983, and 1985;
of these A. cyparissiae was first known to be established in 1986, and the
status of the others is unknown); the leaf tying tortricid moth Lobesia
euphorbiana (Freyer), Lepidoptera: Tortricidae; and the gall fly Pegomya

curticornis (Stein); Diptera: Anthomyiidae (both released in 1988 and not yet known to be established).

The potential of root borers of the genus Chamaesphecia Spüler (Lepidoptera: Sesiidae) also has been studied. Chamaesphecia empiformis (Esper), reared from Euphorbia cypariassias L. and the closely related C. tenthrediniformis (Denis and Schiffermüller), reared from E. esula , were released respectively in 1969 and 1972 in Canada. Despite repeated release attempts, neither species became established on leafy spurge in North America.

Neonate larvae of these insects were tested with some North American leafy spurge species, but complete development occurred only on the control plant (biotypes of E. cyparissias and E. esula from Austria, Hungary, and Yugoslavia). These results confirmed the impression of the high degree of specialization of Chamaesphecia spp. associated with Euphorbia spp.

With regard to the host range of Chamaesphecia spp., Schroeder (7) pointed out that

"there are 21 European species of Chamaesphecia. Three species are of central and north-western European origin, and 12 species are in southern Europe and south-eastern Europe and Asia Minor. Host plants are known for 17 of the 21 species. Three species are associated with Polygonaceae (Rumex spp.), one with Scrophulariaceae (Verbascum spp.), four with Labiate (Ballota nigra L., Satureja calamintha nepeta (Scheele), Lavandula vera De Candolle A. Pyramus and Origanum vulgare L.), one with Plumbaginaceae (Armeria vulgaris Willdenow and A. plantaginea Willdenow), one with Cistaceae (Helianthemum vulgare Gaertner Joseph and H. chamaecistus Miller Philip) and seven species with Euphorbiaceae (Euphorbia spp.). Four of the seven species of Chamaesphecia are recorded from E. cyparissias, and one species each has been found on E. palustris, E. gerardiana, and E. polychroma, respectively. Two undescribed species have recently been reared, one from E. myrsinites and another from E. virgata. Host records for individual species of Chamaesphecia strongly support the hypothesis that most, if not all, of the species are specialized on a single host plant species or on closely related species of the same genus. This holds true for the seven species of Chamaesphecia mining the stems and/or roots of Euphorbia spp.; none of these species has been found to mine a plant outside this genus."

Chamaesphecia crassicornis is a univoltine species, associated with E. virgata (8). It was described by Bartel in 1912 from adults collected near Uralski (Kazakhstan) (9). There is scattered information in the literature on the distribution of C. crassicornis in Europe; it has been found in eastern Austria (10), and southern Czechoslovakia (8).

534

Fig. 2. Adult of Chamaesphecia crassicornis on leafy spurge.

In 1984, we (Pecora and Cristofaro) found a population of Chamaesphecia crassicornis (Bartel) (Fig. 2) on individuals of the E. virgata "group" in the Danube delta area of Romania. The population that we found in Romania is probably the first record of C. crassicornis for that country (Popescu-Gorj et al. (11) reported 19 species in the genus Chamaesphecia in Romania, but not C. crassicornis).

To determine the potential host range of C. crassicornis, bionomical and host specificity studies were conducted at the USDA Laboratory in Rome from 1984 to 1988.

MATERIALS AND METHODS

Life history

Roots of the E. virgata "group", infested with larvae of various instars of C. crassicornis, were collected at two localities near the Danube Delta, Romania, at the end of October during 1984, 1985, 1986, and 1987. At both sites the habitat is typical of situations where leafy spurge grows in eastern Europe: narrow patches on the sides of country roads, and along cultivated fields (corn, sugar beet, or wheat). The roots were brought to the Rome laboratory, placed in terracotta pots (diameter 22 cm), and kept outdoors in the laboratory garden until mid April, when they were enclosed in a cage (2 x 2 x 2 m) covered with organdy cloth, and checked daily for adult emergence.

To obtain biological data such as pre-oviposition period, egg production per female, percent of egg hatching, pre-eclosion period, and adult longevity, newly emerged adults were caged during the summer of 1985 on potted plants of the E. virgata "group" in transparent plastic cylinders (diameter 20 cm, height 60 cm) with cloth covers. Eleven cages were established in 1985 with one or two females and one to three males per cage, and five cages were established in 1986. The cages were kept outdoors in a shaded area, where the temperature ranged from 11 C to 35 C and the relative humidity from 20 % to 90 %.

Adults that emerged during the summers of 1987 and 1988 were kept in eight large plastic pots (diameter 55 cm) covered with a cylinder of nylon screen (diameter 60 cm, height 80 cm) and kept outdoors. When oviposition occurred, the eggs were collected and kept in hatching containers (plastic caps with a layer of plaster of Paris). The collected eggs were used in the host specificity studies. Investigation of the duration of the life of the larvae was made by dissecting all of the infested plants 4 to 5 months after the adults emerged.

Host specificity tests

Selection of test plants. Considering the high degree of specialization of species of Chamaesphecia, the host range of C. crassicornis was investigated by testing 12 plant species of the family Euphorbiaceae, plus the plant control (E. virgata from Romania). Eleven of these test plants are in the genus Euphorbia (seven in the subgenus Esula, two in the subgenus Agaloma, one in the subgenus Poinsettia, and one in the subgenus Euphorbium), and one is in the genus Ricinus.

Larval survival test. The potential host range of C. crassicornis was determined by exposing neonate larvae or mature eggs to the various test plants. Four populations of leafy spurge (E. pseudovirgata) of North American origin (Nebraska (22 plants), Montana (35), Wyoming (6), and Oregon (6)) were tested during 1985. The test plants plus the plant control were transplanted to a cement basin (length 6 m, width 2 m, height 1 m). Three neonate larvae or three mature eggs were placed between the stem and the basal part of the leaves of each plant, using a fine brush. The first plant was infested on July 10, and the last one on August 17, 1985. During the following October, several test and control plants were dissected and the number of larvae found were recorded. The rest of the infested plants were placed in a nylon organdy screen cage and the number of adults that emerged was recorded. The other test plants (E. esula L. from Italy; E. lucida Waldstein and Kitaibel, E. lathyris L., E. tirucalli L., E. antysiphilitica Zuccar, E. pulcherrima Willdenow, E. corollata L., and Ricinus communis L.) were tested during 1988. Five replications per test plant were made, each replication received 3 neonate larvae or 3 mature eggs. The plants were infested from June 14 to July 4, 1988.

TABLE I

EMERGENCE DATA OF CHAMAESPHECIA CRASSICORNIS

Year of collection and no. infested plants of E. virgata "group"	No. adults emerged during first year and emergence period	No. plants dissected, no. larvae found, and dissection data	No. adults emerged during 2nd year and emergence period
1984	1985	1986	1986
108	13 ♀♀ 18 ♂♂ June 12-July 27	52 plants 35 mature larvae January 27, 1986	12 ♀♀ 10 ♂♂ June 10-July 20
1985	1986	1987	1987
85	5 ♀♀ 8 ♂♂ June 3-July 10	18 plants 10 mature larvae January 10, 1987	2 ♀♀ 1 ♂ June 15-20
1986	1987	1988	1988
102	12 ♀♀ 6 ♂♂ June 16-July 20	25 plants 10 larvae February 5, 1988	No adults emerged
1987	1988	1989	1989
130	22 ♀♀ 19 ♂♂ May 26-July 8	17 plants 15 larvae September 15, 1989	No adults emerged

RESULTS

Life history

Adult. Adults originating from larvae collected on leafy spurge in Romania, emerged at the Rome Laboratory from the end of May until the end of July (Table I). The mature larvae moved from the root to the lower part of the stem, where they made an exit hole, covered it with frass, and pupated. During emergence, the pupa protruded outside the stem for 3/4 of its length and was held in place by anal hooks while the moth freed itself. About 80 % of the C. crassicornis kept under study emerged during the first year, whereas the remainder emerged during the second year (Table I). Females (n = 13) had a pre-oviposition period of 1-3 days and an oviposition period of 1-5 days. Females lived 5.15 ± 2.12 days (n = 12, range = 2-9), while males lived 7.05 ± 1.96 days (n = 19, range = 4-11).

Oviposition. Eggs of C. crassicornis were found on plants of the E. virgata "group" in Romania during mid June, 1986. Fifteen plants, of a sample of 50 randomly selected plants, were found to be infested with eggs. On each infested plant, 2-4 eggs were found (laid singly or in clusters of 2 or 3 eggs), mostly along the stems.

Adults of C. crassicornis kept in cages laid eggs in clusters (5-10 eggs per cluster) along the stems or on the underside of leaves of the host plant; some were also laid on the walls of the cages. The mean number of eggs per female was 29-33 ± 27.85 (n = 9, range = 3-68). The incubation period was 11-16 days; of a sample of 357 eggs, 61.7 percent were fertile. The average length and width of the eggs was 0.68 ± 0.007 mm and 0.43 ± 0.004 mm, respectively. Eggs are oval in shape and flattened, dark brown when laid and generally light brown after emergence of the larvae. The external surface is provided with a network of slightly raised veins forming pentagonal and hexagonal shapes.

Development of larvae. Neonate larvae were observed either crawling down along the stem or dropping to the ground before penetrating the plants. The number of instars was not determined in the laboratory. However, for the closely related C. empiformis five instars have been determined (6).

Young-instar larvae of C. crassicornis were found under the cortex, just below the crown of the plant. Third instar larvae generally started to penetrate the central part of the root. Until the last instar they made tunnels 10-20 cm long in the root, which were tightly filled with larval excrement. From the repeated collections made in Romania during the second half of October, 50-60 % of the larvae were mature, while the others were in earlier stages. By the time the larvae reached maturity, the part of the root in which the tunnel was made is almost completely destroyed. The damage by larvae of C. crassicornis should contribute to reduction, in the long term, of the vigor of

TABLE II

DEVELOPMENT OF CHAMAESPHECIA CRASSICORNIS ON NON-HOST PLANTS

Test plants	Subgenus	No. plants tested	No. plants dissected (Oct.2, 1985)	No. plants infested	No. larvae found	No. adults emerged (June- July 1986)	
PLANTS TESTED DURING 1985						o	o
Euphorbia virgata (Esula) "group" (Control) - Romania		22	10	3	3	2	2
E. virgata "group" (Esula) Nebraska		22	10	3	3	2	1
E. virgata "group" (Esula) Montana		35	20	6	6	3	
E. virgata "group" (Esula) Wyoming		6	6	2	2		
E. virgata "group" (Esula) Oregon		6	6	2	2		
PLANTS TESTED DURING 1988							
E. virgata "group" (Esula) (Control) - Romania		5	5	3	4		
E. esula (Esula) Italy		5	5	3	2		
E. lucida (Esula) Italy		5	5	1	1		
E. lathyris (Esula) California		5	5	3	3		
E. tirucalli (Euphorbium)		5	5	-	-		
E. antisyphilitica (Euphorbium)		5	5	-	-		
E. pulcherrima (Poinsettia)		5	5	-	-		
E. corollata (Agaloma)		5	5	-	-		
Ricinus communis		5	5	-	-		

the root system of leafy spurge and the number of root buds.

Host specificity tests

Larval survival test. Among the species of Euphorbia tested, larvae of C. crassicornis were able to develop only on those of the subgenus Esula (Table II). The test conducted during 1985 demonstrated the ability of C. crassicornis to develop on different populations of leafy spurge of North American origin. The experiment made during 1988 indicated that the larvae are able to develop on species of the subgenus Esula.

Discussion

The density of the populations of C. crassicornis studied was concentrated in a few localities. During four years (1984 to 1988) we were able to find C. crassicornis only at two localities in the Danube delta area. The reasons for this restricted distribution could be explained by the fact that (a) C. crassicornis may require a particular microclimate and therefore it is adapted to a narrow ecological niche; (b) southeastern Europe may represent the limit of its distribution; or (c) establishment in Romania took place only recently and some years may be needed for it to expand into new areas. Lastuvka (pers. comm.) observed that C. crassicornis is also extremely localized in southern Czechoslovakia.

The host range of C. crassicornis is restricted to plant species of the subgenus Esula (genus Euphorbia), which contains 21 of the 112 Euphorbia species native to America north of Mexico (12). This indicates that the host range of C. crassicornis is broad enough for it to attack the various forms of leafy spurge and yet narrow enough to exclude the majority of native Euphorbia species. Chamaesphecia crassicornis is generally univoltine, but, in our studies, some individuals (about 20%) required two years to complete their development.

On the basis of the results obtained at the USDA Rome Laboratory, we concluded that this moth is a narrow specialist and thus we petitioned for its study in quarantine in the United States to the Technical Advisory Group on Biological Control of Weeds (TAGBCW) in April, 1989. A recommendation for release was made by the TAGBCW to Animal and Plant Health Inspection Service, Plant Protection and Quarantine (APHIS-PPQ), USDA in September 1989.

ACKNOWLEDGEMENTS

Special acknowledgement is due to Dr. D. Schroeder, CAB International Institute for Biological Control, Delemont, Switzerland for information about the distribution of Chamaesphecia; to Dr. K. Spatenka, Institute of Industry for Agriculture, Peckg, Czechoslovakia, Dr. C. M. Naumann, Institute of Biology, University of Bielefeld, West Germany, and Dr. Z. Lastuvka,

Department of Agriculture, Brno, Czechoslovakia, for identification of the insects; to Dr. N. Rees, Dr. R. Sobhian, and Dr. A. Kirk, USDA-ARS Research Entomologists, for reviewing the manuscript; and Dr. L. A. Andres for preparing an early draft of the petition.

REFERENCES

1. Dunn PH (1979) The distribution of leafy spurge (Euphorbia esula) and other weedy Euphorbia spp. in the United States. Weed Sci. 27:509-516

2. Lacey CA, et al. (1985) The distribution, biology and control of leafy spurge. Montana State Univ. Coop. Ext. Serv. Circular 309

3. Harvey SJ, Nowierski RM, and Mahlberg PG (1986) Leafy spurge taxonomy: a re-evaluation. Leafy Spurge Annual Meeting, July 9-10, 1986, Riverton, Wyoming, pp 31-38

4. Harris P, Dunn PH, Schroeder D, and Vonmoos R (1985) Biological control of leafy spurge in North America. Mono. Ser., Weed Sci. Soc. Amer. 3:79-92

5. Pecora P, Dunn PH (in press) Insect associations on leafy spurge in Europe: implications for strategies for release of biological control agents in North America. Proc. VII Int. Symp. Biol. Contr. Weeds, 6-11 March 1988, Rome, Italy

6. Rees A, Pemberton RW (1986) First recovery of Oberea erythrocephala on leafy spurge complex in the Unityed States. Weed Sci. 34: 395-397

7. Schroeder D (1968) Studies on phytophagous insects of Euphorbia spp. - Chamaesphecia empiformis (Esp.). CIBC Report No. XXI

8. Lastuvka Z (1980) Chamaesphecia crassicornis Bartel, 1912 in der CSSR (Lepidoptera, Sesiidae) Scripta Fac. Sci Nat. Purk., Brun., (Biologia) 10 (9-10):457-462

9. Seitz A (1913) Die Gross-Schmetterlinge der Erde. Die Gross-Schmetterlinge des Palearktischen Faunengebietes, I, 2. Stuttgart

10. Sterzel O (1967) Prodromus der Lepidopteranfaune von Niederösterreich. Verh. Zool. Bot. Ges. Wien

11. Popescu-Gorj A, Niculescu EV, Alexinischi AL (1958) Fauna Republicii Romine, Insecta 11, 1: Lepidoptera, Familia Aegeriidae. Bukarest

12. Pemberton RW (1985) Native plant consideration in the biological control of leafy spurge. In: Delfosse ES (ed) Proc. VI Intl. Symp. Biol. Contr. Weeds, 19-25 August 1984, Vancouver, Canada, pp. 365-390

© 1990 Elsevier Science Publishers B.V. (Biomedical Division)
Pesticides and alternatives, editor J.E. Casida

EFFECTIVE REDUCTION AND EXTRACTION OF MIMOSINE FROM LEUCAENA AND THE POTENTIAL FOR ITS USE AS A LEAD COMPOUND OF HERBICIDES

SHINKICHI TAWATA

Department of Agricultural Chemistry, University of the Ryukyus, Okinawa
903-01, Japan

INTRODUCTION

Because of its high protein content and high annual yield, leucaena (*Leucaena leucocephala* de Wit) has great potential as animal feed in the tropics, but its use is limited owing to the presence of mimosine (β-[N-(3-hydroxypyridone-4)-α-amino-propionic acid), the ingestion of which causes alopecia, growth retardation, cataract and infertility in animals. Removal, reduction, or inactivation of the mimosine before or during the preparation of leucaena as feed would enhance use of the legume as livestock feed. Mimosine can be degraded to DHP (3-hydroxy-4(1H)-pyridone) by microorganisms in the rumen, by endogenous enzymes in the leucaena plant, or by HCl hydrolysis. Although DHP has been reported to be goitrogenic in animals, it is less toxic than mimosine.

The author has confirmed that mimosine and DHP are responsible for the allelopathy of leucaena (1, 2). The present paper describes the effective extraction of mimosine from leucaena and evaluates the herbicidal activity of mimosine and its related compounds.

MATERIALS AND METHODS
Analysis of mimosine

50ml of 0.1N HCl was added to 2g of freeze-dried leucaena leaves which were made into impalpable powder by Wiley's mill, and the mixture was then homogenized for 10 min by polytron with ice cooling. The obtained mixture of leucaena was centrifuged at 12.000 rpm by Hitachi 20 PR, and the supernatant was filtered by suction through Toyo filterpaper No.52. The filtrate was brought to a volume of 100ml by the addition of 0.1N HCl, and then the solution was passed through the diskpaper for high performance liquid chromatography (HPLC). 2μl of the solution was injected to HPLC (Shimadzu LC-6A) for analysis. The column used was Shim-pack CLC-ODS (15cm x 6mm i.d.), and the column temperature was 50℃. Mobile phase employed was the mixture solution of 10mM potassium-di-hydrogen phosphate : 10mM phosphoric acid : acetonitrile (45 : 45 : 10), and finally 0.1% sodium 1-octanesulfonate was added to the mixture as the surface active agent. At the flow rate 1.5 ml/min, mimosine and DHP were detected at 280nm.

Reduction of mimosine by leaching

100g of leucaena leaves packed in a nylon bag were leached for 24 hrs at room temperature in 1 ℓ each of 0.1N solution of salts. The eluted mimosine and DHP in the medium, and the remaining mimosine and DHP in the leaves, were simultaneously determined by HPLC. The general compositions were compared before and after the leaching and also the level of protein loss was examined.

Extraction of mimosine from leucaena leaves

6Kg of freshly harvested leucaena leaves was immersed in 30 ℓ of boiling water for 10 min. The water extract was cooled to room temperature and filtered with 300 mesh sieve. Ultrafiltration was carried out at 4atm, 30℃ and 700rpm by using a Filtron Miniset Omega equipped with the cassette system membrane (molecular weight cut-off, 10.000). The filtrate was passed through a column packed with acid form Amberlite IRA (technical grade). The resin was washed with 1 ℓ of 2N NH₄OH. About 30g of relatively pure mimosine was obtained after adjusting the pH to 4.5～5.0.

Herbicidal activity

Mimosine and 29 pyridine analogues were used at concentrations of 0, 125, 250, 500, and 1.000 ppm as inhibition agents against *Raphanus sativus* var. hortensis Baker, *Brassica rapa* var. amplexicaulis, and *Bidens pilosa* L. var. radiata Scherte. Concentration values (ppm) resulting in 50% inhibition were determined by calculation.

RESULTS

Degradation or removal of mimosine is an indispensable condition for feeding leucaena to livestock. At present, it is known that there are some methods for detoxifying leucaena, as by the addition of iron salts or the heating of leucaena leaves, but such methods have the negative result of causing formation of DHP, which is also toxic. The author and coworkers have reported that mimosine can also be degraded to DHP by heating with various organic acids or by silage treatment (3-7). As reported here, leaching into various salt solutions provided the favorable results of high mimosine extraction into no significant loss of the nutrients important for livestock feed, such as crude fat, crude fiber, and crude protein. The total weight of leucaena after leaching decreased about 3%.

Residual mimosine is shown in Tables I and II. Table I shows the results of HPLC analysis of the residual mimosine content in leucaena which was leached for 24 hrs at 25℃ in water and in various 0.1N solutions of salts. Metal salts such as CuCl₂, ZnCl₂, FeCl₃, and FeSO₄, however, inhibited the elution of mimosine. Table II shows the amount of residual mimosine and DHP in the treated leucaena, and the amount of the eluted mimosine and DHP in the medium

TABLE I

PERCENTAGE OF MIMOSINE REMAINING AFTER 0.1N SOLUTION LEACHING

H_2O	7.2
NaCl	12.0
KCl	13.2
$CaCl_2$	13.2
$CuCl_2$	31.5
$ZnCl_2$	39.4
$MgCl_2$	10.7
$FeCl_3$	36.1
$FeSO_4$	27.4
Untreated leucaena	100 %

TABLE II

MIMOSINE AND DHP CONTENT IN THE EXTRACTS AND IN TREATED LEUCAENA LEAVES

	EXTRACTS		TREATED LEUCAENA	
	Mimosine	DHP	Mimosine	DHP
0.01N CH_3COONa	36.36	56.81	9.09	18.18
0.05N	36.36	84.09	4.54	13.63
0.1N	34.09	43.18	9.09	20.45
0.5N	43.18	18.18	9.09	18.18
1.0N	47.72	20.45	11.36	13.63

Untreated leucaena: Mimosine 100 %   DHP 0 %

which was leached in 0.01~1.0N CH_3COONa solutions. A comparison of the nutritional composition of 0.05N CH_3COONa treated leucaena and untreated leucaena is shown in Table III.

Recovery of the mimosine from the leachate was accomplished by the combined use of ultrafiltration membrane and ion exchange chromatography, in large-scale treatment. HOMO, LUMO and electron density of hydroxy and amino groups of mimosine and related molecules were calculated by the HMO method. Among mimosine-related compounds, the highest electron density was shown by the

TABLE III

COMPARATIVE NUTRITIONAL COMPOSITION OF UNTREATED AND TREATED LEUCAENA

	Untreated	Treated leucaena
Crude protein	21.7	20.8
Crude fat	6.2	8.3
Crude fiber	13.1	17.8
Crude ash	9.5	5.4
Water soluble carbohydrate	49.5	47.7
	100 %	100 %
Mimosine content	100 %	5.6 %

3-hydroxy-group. By using Job's continuation variation method, it was found that the maximum formation rate for the complex between mimosine and $FeSO_4$ was at the ratio of 6 : 4, with 3 : 7 for $FeCl_3$.

Inhibition concentrations (ppm) are shown in Table IV, which lists concentrations inducing 50% inhibition of stem and root of Raphanus, Brassica, and Bidens. Among the chlorinated compounds, 4-chloropyridine showed the strongest activity. Bromo, cyano and hydroxy derivatives showed relatively weak or no activity except 2,3-dihydroxypyridine. The inhibition activity of carboxylic acid derivatives was relatively high; most showed 50% inhibition of root growth with less than 100ppm. Among the tested compounds, excluding mimosine, 2,6-pyridine dicarboxylic acid showed the strongest activity; the activity occurred at less than 60ppm against Brassica and Bidens. For the monocarboxylic acids, the compound substituted at position 4 showed stronger activity than the compounds substituted at positions 2 and 3.

Efficient and economic removal of mimosine from leucaena results in two products of high potential value: (1) the protein-rich detoxified leucaena feed, and (2) substantial quantities of pure mimosine. The unique chemical structure of mimosine and its high inhibition of plant growth suggest its use as a novel lead compound of herbicides.

TABLE IV
HERBICIDAL ACTIVITY
Calculated Concentrations (ppm) Resulting in 50% Inhibition

No.	Pyridines	Raphanus		Brassica		Bidens	
		Stem	Root	Stem	Root	Stem	Root
1	2-CH₃	> 1,000	453	183	691	470	365
2	4-CH₃	583	597	775	805	667	194
3	3-C₂H₅	421	383	421	284	115	99
4	2-Cl	> 1,000	762	> 1,000	494	929	188
5	3-Cl	> 1,000	765	> 1,000	916	978	175
6	4-Cl	219	129	141	81	101	75
7	2,3-Cl	196	139	186	156	346	149
8	2,5-Cl	344	232	612	109	> 1,000	> 1,000
9	2,6-Cl	354	222	> 1,000	473	950	299
10	3,5-Cl	> 1,000	> 1,000	> 1,000	> 1,000	> 1,000	> 1,000
11	2-Br	730	675	440	277	619	612
12	3-Br	883	844	693	223	566	450
13	2-CN	635	602	159	81	624	250
14	4-CN	> 1,000	> 1,000	> 1,000	> 1,000	> 1,000	250
15	2-OH	> 1,000	420	> 1,000	> 1,000	> 1,000	> 1,000
16	3-OH	> 1,000	> 1,000	> 1,000	927	918	250
17	4-OH	> 1,000	> 1,000	> 1,000	986	> 1,000	428
18	2,3-OH	285	207	305	236	241	104
19	2,4-OH	941	777	> 1,000	> 1,000	> 1,000	750
20	3-CHO	228	123	181	91	454	104
21	4-CHO	121	105	186	109	202	117
22	2-COOH	104	79	158	87	163	75
23	3-COOH	106	85	112	81	153	78
24	4-COOH	73	65	65	64	88	72
25	2,3-COOH	100	83	92	64	100	69
26	2,5-COOH	89	69	94	66	98	75
27	2,6-COOH	86	66	< 60	< 60	< 60	< 60
28	3,4-COOH	199	89	102	66	106	72
29	3,5-COOH	242	99	123	84	101	72
	Mimosine	74	70	< 60	< 60	106	72

546

REFERENCES

1. Tawata S, Hongo F (1987) Leucaena Res Rep 8:40-41

2. Tawata S, Hongo F, Hirata K, Toma K (1987) Abstracts of the 1987 Annual Meeting of the Agricultural Chemical Society of Japan, p 725

3. Tawata S, Yaga S (1986) Report of the appropriate technology for processing and utilization of ipil-ipil for leaf meal forage, Japan International Cooperation Agency, pp 7-57

4. Hongo F, Tawata S (1986) Leucaena Res Rep 7:85

5. Hongo F, Tawata S, Watanabe Y, Shiroma S (1986) Jpn J Zootech Sci 57:223-230

6. Hongo F, Tanaka A, Kawashima Y, Tawata S, Sunagawa K (1988) Jpn J Zootech Sci 59:688-700

7. Sunagawa K, Hongo F, Kawashima Y, Tawata S (1989) jpn J Zootech Sci 60:133-140

© 1990 Elsevier Science Publishers B.V. (Biomedical Division)
Pesticides and alternatives, editor J.E. Casida

LIGHT REQUIREMENT FOR HERBICIDAL ACTIONS: ACTIVE OXYGEN PRODUCING
SYSTEMS

SHOOICHI MATSUNAKA
Faculty of Agriculture, Kobe University, Nada-ku, Kobe 657, Japan

INTRODUCTION

The author's fundamental concept of this paper is that the higher
plants, weeds and crops, are always exposed to higher concentration
of oxygen and to solar radiation in daytime. These conditions seem
to be good ones for the environmentalists, however actually are very
dangerous from the standpoint of generation of active oxygens.

As shown in Fig.1, during the process of the reduction of oxygen
to water, from the top to the bottom, we can find three active oxygen species, namely superoxide radical O_2^- , hydrogen peroxide H_2O_2,
and hydroxyl radical $OH^{\cdot}$, and finally water will be produced. Also
as shown on the top of Fig.1, usual triplet oxygen will be activated into singlet oxygen, one of active oxygen species, by some photodynamic reactions or others. These four oxygen species, superoxide,
hydrogen peroxide, hydroxyl radical and singlet oxygen, are called
active oxygens. They all have very drastic activities against living cells and may show oxygen toxicity to organisms.

Superoxide anion is found in chloroplasts in the course of usual
photosynthesis, but its scavengers, for instance superoxide dis-
mutase (SOD), will decrease its level to non-toxic one. However,
when the concentration of active oxygens will be increased by a

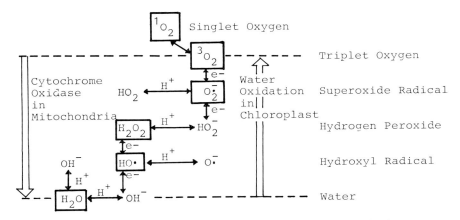

Fig. 1. Mutual relationships among oxygens and their
reduced products.

mediation of herbicides, the treated weeds will be killed by this
active agent.

In this review, two typical oxygen generating systems by herbicides will be discussed. One is paraquat or diquat group, bipyridi-
liums, which produce superoxide radical. The other is the production of singlet oxygen by diphenyl ether herbicides and the related
compounds which were previously introduced by Casida in this book.

These two examples are producing active oxygens by the help of
light, which means that they are not active under the darkness.
Later the two will be compared each other from the standpoint of
animal toxicity.

GENERATION OF SUPEROXIDE RADICAL BY PARAQUAT

Photosynthesis is biochemically explained as the production of
energy ATP and reducing power NADPH through electron transport
system as shown in Fig.2, in which the action site of the Hill
reaction inhibitors are also shown. This electron transport system
is always producing electron flow under the illuminated condition.

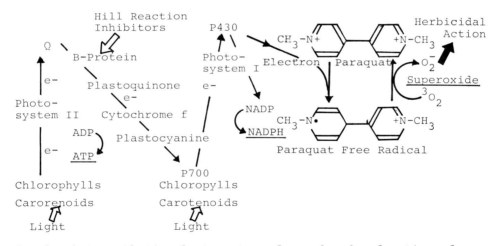

Fig. 2. Photosynthetic electron transfer and mode of action of
        paraquat

From such electron transfer system, paraquat will receive one
electron and be reduced into its free radical as shown on the right
side of Fig. 2. The formed paraquat free radical is oxidized and
changed back to the original paraquat itself by the usual triplet
oxygen. At the same time, the oxygen is reduced into the superoxide radical getting one electron. Superoxide or other active

oxygen species formed from it will destroy the cell membrane,
followed by chlorophyll breaching and browning of the weed tissues.

These succesive herbicidal reactions are inhibited by the addition
of the Hill reaction inhibitors, e.g. simazine or diuron, stopping
the electron flow shown on the left side of Fig. 2. And also in
darkness or in the absence of oxygen, no herbicidal action is observed depending upon this scheme.

Paraquat reduction into its free radical can be observed even in
animal tissues, under so reduced condition, then it shows very slow
but strong acute toxicity also to animals, especially in their lung.

SINGLET OXYGEN PRODUCTION BY DIPHENYL ETHERS AND OTHERS

Another example of active oxygen producing herbicides is the case
of diphenyl ether herbicides, which produce singlet oxygen as the
herbicidal action. This group, including nitrofen, chlornitrofen,
chlomethoxynil, bifenox, oxyfluorfen and acifluorfen methyl, has
been contributing in the practical weeding over twenty years both
in paddy field and upland.

Twenty year ago, the author (1) reported that diphenyl ethers required light for their herbicidal action and yellow mutant and green
plant are susceptible to nitrofen, while white mutant is tolerant
the the herbicide, assuming that the yellow pigment, xanthophyll,
will be the light receptor for such photodynamic action as photo-
sensitizer. These results were reported at ACS meeting in San Fran-
sisco in 1968, and after then many researchers have been studying
the mode of action of this herbicide group. And the kinds of herbicides having the same mode of action; requirement of light, browning
of plant tissues, and low toxicity to animals, were expanded to the
compounds without any diphenyl ether structure, such as oxadiazon
(2,3), phenopylate(4), chlorophthalim(5) , S-23142(Sumitomo,6),
TNPP-ethyl(Otsuka,7), 080-2216(Shionogi,8),   DDL- 1777(9), Rhone
Poulenc LS-82-556(10), and MB-39279(20)shown in Fig. 3. And the
practical dosage is also reaching to the small amount as like as
sulfornylurea herbicides. It can say that these chemicals having
different structures are sharing one of the finite action points
which indicated by Casida in the previous section in this book.

As to the mode of action of this group, there proposed many ideas
by many researchers as like as Böger(11), Dodge(12), Orr and Hess
(13), Duke (14) and others.

Two years ago in Brighton, Matringe and Scalla (15) reported that

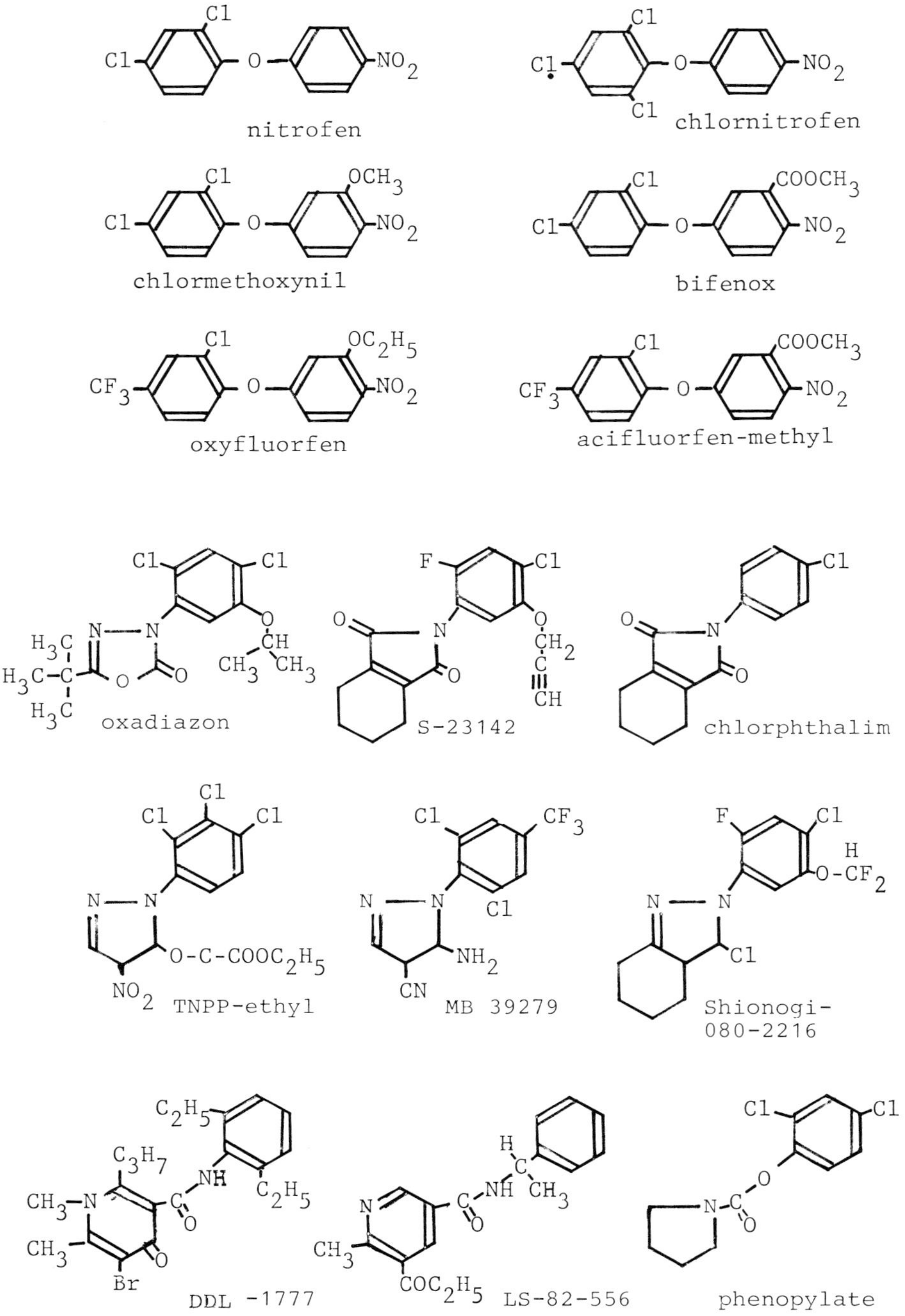

Fig. 3. Diphenyl ethers and related herbicides

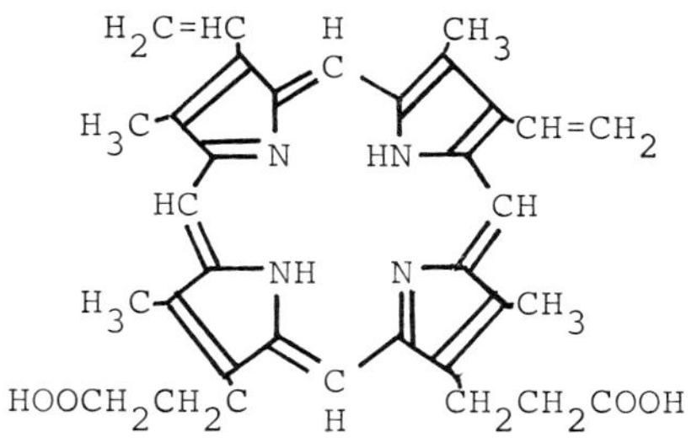

"The phytotoxicity of diphenyl
ether herbicides should be explained by their ability to cause
accumulations of tetrapyrroles,
mainly protoporphyrin IX, which
in turn induce lethal photooxi-
dative reactions producing
singlet oxygen."[15]. Protoporphyrin IX is a key metabolite
sitting at the branching point
to chlorophylls and heme bio-
synthesis(Fig. 4.) If iron atom

Fig. 4. Protoporphyrin IX

will be put in, it will proceed to form heme compounds, while
magnesium atom will make chlorophylls.

  Also recently, Haworth and Hess (16) reported that a diphenyl
ether herbicide, oxyfluorfen, caused a light induced consumption
of oxygen which resembled the electron acceptor reaction of paraquat. However this reaction is not linked to the electron transport system through photosystem I. And using the bleaching of N,N-
dimethyl p-nitrosoaniline (RNO) as a specific detector of singlet
oxygen, they demonstrated that oxyfluorfen is a potent generator of
this toxic compound, singlet oxygen. Such bleaching time course
resembles to the case of cercosporin, a photodynamic plant pathogenic compound.

TABLE I

EFFECTS OF DIPHENY ETHER HERBICIDES ON LIGHT-DEPENDENT
O_2 CONSUMPTION IN TOBACCO CELL HOMOGENATE

Chemicals	Concent-ration(uM)	O_2 Consump-tion Rate (nM/ml/min)	Growth Inhi-bition (pI_{50})	Herbicidal Activity (pI_{50})
Control	–	0.24	–	–
Acifluorfen-methyl	1	6.50	7.38	7.00
Oxyfluorfen	1	6.33	6.64	–
Nitrofluorfen	10	3.62	5.83	5.67
Nitrofluorfen Isomer*	10	0.10	4.00	4.00

 * 2-Chloro-4-trifluoromethylphenyl 2'-nitrophenyl ether.

552

Also in our laboratory, following results were reported(17).
Homogenate of nonchlorophyllous tobacco cells treated with diphenyl
ether herbicides, acifluorfen-methyl(AFM), still kept high light-
dependent oxygen consumption activity. It had been induced during
the dark incubation with such herbicides. Another experiment showed
that the lipid peroxide content was increased in the homogenate during such illumination after the dark incubation of the herbicide.
And as shown in Table 1, we found the parallel corelation between
such light-dependent O_2consumption, after dark incubation with such
herbicides, and growth inhibition or herbicidal activity of them.

After several attempts to clarify the reason of the light-de-
pendnet O_2 consumption, inducing enzymatic tests or use of inhibitors, we concluded that the O_2 consumption was done by non-enzymatic
mechanism. And in the chloroform extract we aslo found protoporphyrin IX, one of the tetrapyrroles. Along with other experimental
results, the following scheme
is assumed as shown in Fig. 5.

The diphenyl ether stimulates
5-aminolevulinic acid (ALA) synthesizing system and causes the
accumulation of tetrapyrroles,
as like as protoporphyrin IX,
in plant cells, and the tetra-
pyrroles-sensitized photooxida-
tion produces singlet oxygen to
make the membrane lipid peroxi-
dation.

As to the stimulation of ALA-
synthesizing system, we are
assuming that diphenyl ethers
show the decrease of heme
content, and the negative feed-
back regulation by heme will
accelerated the ALA-synthesiz-
ing system. Our eperiments(17,18)
showed the stimulation of ALA-
synthesis in vivo by diphenyl
ethers, inhibition of ALA-synthe-
sis by heme, and the decrease of
heme content by diphenyl ethers.

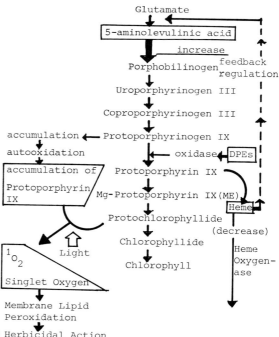

Fig. 5. Scheme of tetrapyrrole biosynthesis and possible mechanism
of action of diphenyl ethers and
related herbicides.

As described later Matringe and others(19,20) showed a very clear
result of the inhibition of protoporphyrinogen oxidase for the
accumulation of protoporphyrin IX, which was autooxidaized product
of protoporphyrinogen accumulated by the inhibition of oxidase. This
inhibition causes heme deficiency, which accelerates ALA synthesis
increasing tetrapyrroles through above-descrived chain reaction.

As to the contribution of the yellow pigment, the author re-examin-
ed his old experiment(1) and found that the white mutant of rice
was also injured by stronger herbicides such as AFM or under stronger light intencity. And the accumulated amount of tetrapyrroles was
found very small in the white mutant. Then it seems that in such
white mutant the tetrapyrrol accumulating activity is very low and
the absence of xanthophylls does not relate to the lower susceptibility to such herbicides.

ANIMAL TOXICITY

Here we should be bcak to the age of thirty years ago. Following
to the practical introduction of 2,4-D or MCPA in Japanese paddy
fields, pentachlorophenol (PCP) were used widely to control mainly
barnyardgrass. However because of PCP's mode of action, the uncoupling of oxidative phosphorylation, the herbicide showed very severe
toxic action to fish or shell-fish when heavy rain brought out the
PCP-adsorved soil particles into river, lake or shallow sea area.
Then the use of PCP was prohibited in the water-area as like as
flooded paddy field. Then at that time the decrease in shipment of
PCP was so dramatic.

However Japanese farmers were so accustomed to use herbicide in
place of severe and hard works of hand-weeding in humid , hot and
muddy paddy field. Then we should prepare new herbicide without any
fish toxicity. Cooperative works among industries and governmental
researchers began to find out new one. As a result of such efforts,
in a short period, nitrofen, chlornitrofen, dichlobenil and propanil
were registered in transplanted rice culture. Among them nitrofen
at first, secondarily chlornitrofen and at the third chlomethoxynil
became to be widely used. And oxadiazon having the same mode of
action, although its chemical structure is quite different from
diphenyl ethers, followed to the formers for the same practical
purpose, as an emulsifiable concentrate formulation which applied
directly onto the muddy flooded field without any dilution.

As shown in Table II. the acute toxicities of these compounds are

554

TABLE II

ACUTE TOXICITIES OF DIPHENYL ETHER HERBICIDES AND RELATED ONES.

Herbicides	Acute Toxicity (LD_{50} mg/kg)	Herbicides	Acute Toxicity (LD_{50} mg/kg)
Nitrofen	3,050	Oxadiazon	1,800
Chlornitrofen	10,800	Phenopylate	2,200
Chlomethoxynil	33,000*	Chlorphthalim	24,000
Oxyfluorfen	5,000		
Acifluorfen	1,300		

* Data in mouse. Others all in rat.

very low. Those are really true to all herbicides or candidates belong to this group which has the same mode of action.

Simply it was assumed that, different from the case of paraquat, the active oxygen generating system in diphenyl ether group were special to higher plants. That seems to be the reason of the low animal toxicity.

However recently Matringe and others (19) reported that the protoporphyrinogen oxidase, which catalyzes the oxidation of protoporphyrinogen to protoporphyrin IX, isolated from corn, potato and yeast, and even from mouse was strongly inhibited by diphenyl ether herbicides. It means that there is a possibility of an adverse effects by these herbicides on the heme biosynthesis of animals. We are now testing the animal toxocty by injection and other methods, and still severe acute toxicity has not been found. Then, the author hopes that the active oxygen generating system of this herbicide group is special one in higher plants and it shows low toxicity to animals. The mechanism should be clarified as soon as possible.

EPILOGUE

Here the author explained two generation systems of active oxygen. Both are utilizing a fact that weeds are being exposed to solar radiation and higher concentration of oxygen, different from animal's situation. However paraquat has high acute toxicity to animal too, while diphenyl ether group has low one. The biochemical difference should be surveyed more from this viewpoint.

Also how to utilize the photosensitizing system to pesticide development should be studied more as shown in newly published book (21).

REFERENCES

1. Matsunaka S (1969) J Agric Food Chem 17:171-175

2. Matsunaka S (1970) Weed Research Japan 10:40-42

3. Duke S O, Lydon J, Paul R N (1989) Weed Sci 37:152-160

4. Yanai I, Matsunaka S (1972) Abstract 11th Ann Meeting Weed Sci Soc Japan 75-77

5. Teraoka T, Sandmann G, Böger P, Wakabayashi K (1987) J Pestic Sci 12:499-504

6. Sato R, Nagano H, Oshio H, Kamoshita K (1987) Pestic Biochem Physiol 28:194-200

7. Yanase D, Andoh A (1989) Pestic Biochem Physiol 34:(in press)

8. Ando I (1989) Researches on synthesis, herbicidal efficacy, mode of action and formulation of tetrahydroindazole compounds, Doctorial Thesis, Kobe University, pp. 113

9. Morishima Y, Osabe H, Goto Y (1989) Abstract 14th Ann Meeting Pestic Sci Soc Japan p 27

10. Matringe M, Dufour J L, Lherminger J, Scalla R (1986) Pestic Biochem Physiol 26:150-159

11. Böger P (1984) Z Naturforsch 39c:468-475

12. Dodge A D (1983) In: Matsunaka S, Hutson S D, Murphy (eds) Pesticide Chemistry, Human Welfare and the Environment, Vol 3, Mode of Action, Metabolism and Toxicology. Pergamon Press, New York, pp 59-66

13. Orr G L, Hess F D (1982) Plant Physiol 69:502-507

14. Duke S O, Kenyon W H (1987) Z Naturforsch 42c:813-818

15. Matringe M, Scalla R (1987) Proc 1987 British Crop Protection Conf - Weeds 981-988

    Matringe M, Scalla R (1988) Plant Physiol 86:619-622

16. Haworth P, Hess F D (1988) Plant Physiol 86:672-676

17. Kouji H, Masuda T, Matsunaka S (1988) J Pestic Sci 13:495-499

18. Kouji H, Masuda T, Matsunaka S (1989) Pestic Biochem Physiol 33: 230-238

19. Matringe M, Camadro J M, Labbe P, Scalla S (1989) Biochem J 260: 231-235

20. Matringe M, Camadro J M, Labbe P, Scalla S (1989) FEBS Letter 245:35-40

21. Heitz J R, Downum K R (1987)(eds) Light-Activated Pesticides. American Chemical Society, Washington D C, pp.339

© 1990 Elsevier Science Publishers B.V. (Biomedical Division)
Pesticides and alternatives, editor J.E. Casida

THE MULTIPLICITY OF HERBICIDE BINDING SITES WITHIN THE PS_{11} REACTION CENTRE :
RESEARCH AND DEVELOPMENT IMPLICATIONS

JOHN N. PHILLIPS
CSIRO Division of Plant Industry, G.P.O. Box 1600, Canberra ACT 2601 (Australia)

INTRODUCTION

This contribution is concerned with demonstrating the presence of many
inhibitor binding sites within the domain of a single herbicide target viz: the
photosystem$_{11}$ (PS_{11}) reaction centre (RC). The extent to which this phenomenon
occurs with other herbicide targets and some of its implications with respect to
herbicide research and development will be discussed.

The photosynthetic process involves the use of light energy absorbed by
chlorophyll-protein (light harvesting) complexes in plant chloroplasts to split
water molecules into oxygen, protons and electrons, the reaction being carried
out in the $PS_{11}RC$ of the thylakoid membrane. The electrons, so generated, are
first transferred to a one electron acceptor plastoquinone (Q_A) and then on to a
two electron acceptor plastoquinone (Q_B). Subsequently, the reduced
plastoquinone (Q_{BH2}) dissociates from its binding site on the D_1 peptide and
becomes involved in a series of redox reactions ultimately leading to the
reduction of carbon dioxide to carbohydrate.

Many compounds, some of them commercial herbicides, are known to block
electron transport between Q_A and Q_B by displacing Q_B from its binding niche on
the D_1 peptide. Accordingly, the Q_B binding site in the PS_{11} reaction centre
has become an important herbicide target and compounds affecting that site have
been termed PS_{11} photosynthetic electron transport (PET) inhibitors. $PS_{11}PET$
inhibitors are not only capable of displacing the endogeneous plastoquinone from
its binding niche on the thylakoid membrane but also of competitively displacing
other PS_{11} inhibitors from their interaction sites. Such behaviour is
consistent with either all the different inhibitors interacting reversibly at a
single target site or each inhibitor interacting at specific but overlapping
sites within the target zone.

INHIBITOR INTERACTION SITES IN THE Q_B BINDING DOMAIN

There are a variety of data suggesting the presence of many overlapping
interaction sites within the plastoquinone (Q_B) binding domain. Some of this
evidence, based on the structural diversity of PS_{11} inhibitors, discontinuities
in structure-activity relationships, variable discrimination between thylakoids
isolated from wild type and mutant species and different binding kinetics, is
outlined below.

Structural diversity of PS_{11} inhibitors

Compounds known to inhibit photosynthetic electron transport at the PS_{11} level include phenyl-amides and -ureas, uracils, triazines, triazinones, pyrrolones, cyanoacrylates and nitrophenols. Such compounds range from being hydrophobic neutral molecules to hydrophilic salts, yet they bind reversibly and competitively in the same biochemical domain. The diversity of structural types involved and their different physico-chemical properties make it improbable that they could all interact in the same way with the one site - hence the likelihood of overlapping inhibitor interaction sites.

Discontinuities in structure-activity relationships

Discontinuities have been observed in a variety of structure-activity relationships involving cyanoacrylate PS_{11} inhibitors e.g. the stepwise pattern of the relationship between pI_{50} and the number of methylene groups separating the phenyl moiety from the amino group in ethoxyethyl-3-araalkyl-2-cyano-3-ethyl cyanoacrylates [1] reflects discontinuities between compounds with even and odd numbers of methylene groups. Such discontinuities suggest that, within a series of closely related structures, different inhibitor molecules can interact with different sites in the Q_B binding domain. Alternatively, it is possible that each inhibitor interacts with more than one site, so that its overall affinity for the target is determined by a combination of interaction energies. In such circumstances, a single structural modification e.g. adding a methylene group could influence the relative contribution of the various interaction energies to the overall binding affinity and lead to an apparent discontinuity in the structure-activity relationship.

Wild type/mutant discrimination

The ability of various PS_{11} inhibitors to discriminate differentially between thylakoids isolated from atrazine susceptible (wild type) and atrazine resistant (mutant) plant species provided some of the first direct evidence of overlapping binding sites within a common binding domain [2,3,]. Table 1 records the activities, expressed in terms of pI_{50} values, for atrazine, diuron, picric acid and three cyanoacrylate inhibitors with wild type and mutant *Brassica napus* thylakoids. The data indicate a high level of discrimination in favour of the wild type being the more sensitive for atrazine ($\Delta pI_{50}=+3.0$) and cyanoacrylates 1 ($\Delta pI_{50}=+1.4$) and 11 ($\Delta pI_{50}=+2.2$), a low level of discrimination in favour of the mutant for picric acid ($\Delta pI_{50}=-0.6$) and no discrimination for cyanoacrylate 111. Moreover, in a series of methoxyethyl-3-alkyl-3-pchlorobenzylamino-2-cyano acrylates, the level of discrimination has been shown to vary from nearly one hundred fold ($\Delta pI_{50}=+1.8$) in favour of the wild type brassica thylakoids to more than ten fold ($\Delta pI_{50}=-1.1$) in favour of the mutant [4]. Such variable discrimination implies that different molecules, even in the same related series, occupy different sites in the wild type and or the mutant thylakoids.

Binding kinetics

Most inhibitors of photosynthetic electron transport equilibrate rapidly (within seconds) with thylakoid membranes and as Table 1 shows these include diuron, atrazine, picric acid and cyanoacrylate 1. Some, however, equilibrate only slowly (within minutes), possibly because there needs to be a conformational change in a peptide for the inhibitor either to reach or fit the binding site. Such compounds include cyanoacrylate 11, which binds slowly with the wild type but rapidly with the mutant thylakoids, and cyanoacrylate 111, which binds slowly with both wild type and mutant thylakoids. Whilst both fast and slow binding inhibitors interact reversibly, are competitive with each other and affect the same target, their different binding kinetics make it unlikely that they interact with the same site.

TABLE 1

BINDING RATES AND PI_{50} VALUES[*] FOR PS_{11} INHIBITORS WITH WILD TYPE AND MUTANT *BRASSICA NAPUS* THYLAKOIDS

	Wild type		Mutant		
Compound	Binding rate	pI_{50}	Binding rate	pI_{50}	ΔpI_{50}
1[**]	Fast	8.4	Fast	7.0	+1.4
11[***]	Slow	6.6	Fast	4.4	+2.2
111[****]	Slow	7.4	Slow	7.4	0
Atrazine	Fast	6.5	Fast	3.5	+3.0
Diuron	Fast	7.4	Fast	7.2	+0.2
Picric acid	Fast	6.0	Fast	6.6	-0.6

[*]   see reference [5]

[**]   Ethoxyethyl-3-pchlorobenzylamino-2-cyano-3-methylmercapto acrylate

[***]   Isopropyl-2-cyano-3-methylphenylamino acrylate

[****] Ethoxyethyl-3-pchlorobenzylthio-2-cyano-3-mercapto acrylate-sodium salt.

OVERLAPPING BINDING SITES IN NON-PHOTOSYNTHETIC HERBICIDE TARGETS

Evidence of overlapping binding sites in non-photosynthetic targets is largely indirect and based on the structural diversity of inhibitors known to affect some of these targets. Acetohydroxy acid synthase (AHAS), an enzyme concerned with branched chain amino acid biosynthesis, is inhibited by compounds as

structurally different as sulphonyl ureas, imidazalones and simple amino acid
derivatives [6] whilst acetyl coenzyme A carboxylase, which is involved in lipid
biosynthesis, is inhibited by the structurally unrelated phenoxyphenoxy
propionic acids and cyclohexanedione derivatives [7]. Likewise, compounds as
different as nitrodiphenyl ethers and oxadiazoles act as bleaching herbicides by
inhibiting protoporphrinogen oxidase [8], whilst, carotenoid inhibiting
herbicides affecting phytoene desaturase, include phenylpyridazinone and phenoxy
nicotinamide derivatives [9].

It would appear from the structural variety of herbicides having a similar
mode of action that the presence of many inhibitor binding sites is a common
feature of herbicide targets. An exception is provided by the enzyme 5-enol
pyruvyl shikimic acid-3-phosphate synthase associated with aromatic amino acid
biosynthesis. This enzyme is the target of the herbicide glyphosate which is
the only herbicide known to affect it.

DISCUSSION

In many of the situations where herbicides of different structure have similar
modes of action, the endogeneous molecules involved in the biological process
being affected are relatively large compared to the size of the inhibiting
herbicides. Thus, plastoquinone is concerned with the mode of action of the
PS_{11} photosynthetic herbicides, protoporphrinogen with the bleaching herbicides
and phytoene with the carotenoid inhibiting herbicides, whilst in the case of
the AHAS inhibiting herbicides it has been suggested that the site of action is
an evolutionary relic of an ubiquinone binding site [10]. The structural
diversity of inhibitors able to interact with a target is likely to be related
to the size of the endogeneous molecule, since the larger the molecule the
larger the binding domain and the greater the number of potential interaction
sites within the target zone. Consequently, the discovery of new herbicides
will tend to be biased in favour of those affecting targets with large binding
domains and many potential interacting sites, at the expense of targets with
small binding domains and few interacting sites. This is consistent with the
situation that, although a large number of herbicides are known, relatively few
herbicide targets have been identified.

The many potential inhibitor interaction sites present within the binding
domains of herbicide targets have significant implications with respect to
herbicide research and development.

Most importantly, the lack of a constant binding site for the different
inhibitors would tend to impede a rational approach to the design of new
herbicides, by undermining the usefulness of computer modelling techniques and
complicating the interpretation of QSAR data. In addition, targets with many

interaction sites are more likely to develop resistance to herbicides than those with fewer sites, since the larger the binding domain the greater the opportunity for viable mutants to occur by variations in peripheral amino acid residues. Such changes could significantly affect the affinity of a particular inhibitor for its interaction site without greatly disturbing the binding of the endogeneous molecule. This effect is reflected in the large number of mutants showing site-based resistance to PS_{11} inhibitors which have been isolated from plants, algae and photosynthetic bacteria.

A useful consequence of the multiple binding site phenomenon is the ability to inhibit a particular herbicide target with a variety of compounds. This favours product diversification, stimulates competition and improves the chance of discovering an environmentally acceptable herbicide of appropriate selectivity.

To summarize: The multiplicity of inhibitor binding sites occurring within the PS_{11} reaction centre and other herbicide targets has been shown to account for the relatively small number of useful targets so far identified, the lack of progress in the rational design of new herbicides and the development of site-based herbicide resistance.

REFERENCES

1.   Huppatz JL, Phillips JN (1987) Z Naturforsch 42c: 674
2.   Pfister K, Arntzen CJ (1979) Z Naturforsch 34c: 996
3.   Trebst A, Draber W (1979) In: Geissbuhler H, (ed) Advances in Pesticide Science, Pergamon, Oxford, pp 223-234
4.   Phillips JN, Huppatz JL (1986) Z Naturforsch 42c: 670
5.   Phillips JN (1989) Proc VIII Int Congr Photosynthesis, Stockholm, In press
6.   Huppatz JL, Casida JE (1985) Z Naturforsch 40c: 652
7.   Burton JD, Gronwald JW, Somers DA, Connelly JA, Gegenbach BG, Wyse DL (1987) Biochem Biophys Res Comm 148: 1039
8.   Matringe M, Camadro JM, Labbe P, Scalla R (1989) Biochem J 260: 231
9.   Sandmann G (1987) In: Greenhalgh R, Roberts TR (eds) Pesticide Science and Technology. Proceedings 6 IUPAC Congress of Pesticide Chemistry, pp 43-48
10.   Schloss J, Ciskanik L, Van Dyk D (1988) Nature 331: 360

© 1990 Elsevier Science Publishers B.V. (Biomedical Division)
Pesticides and alternatives, editor J.E. Casida

ESSENTIAL AMINO ACID BIOSYNTHESIS PROVIDES MULTIPLE TARGETS FOR SELECTIVE HERBICIDES

JOHN L. HUPPATZ

CSIRO Division of Plant Industry, GPO Box 1600, Canberra, A.C.T. 2601. Australia

INTRODUCTION

The judicious application of herbicides has become an integral part of contemporary agricultural practice in the developed countries. Despite the emergence in recent years of compounds of greatly increased efficacy and safety, the agrochemical industry is facing continuing and growing criticism over the toxicity and residue problems associated with the use of pesticides, including herbicides. The strategies traditionally used for herbicide discovery involving the synthesis and evaluation of large numbers of candidate compounds are being questioned. Rapidly escalating costs and increasingly stringent regulatory requirements have led to the consideration of alternative approaches to exploit target sites specific to the plant kingdom. The possibility of designing molecules to interfere with a critical step in plant metabolism, thereby causing plant death, requires a detailed knowledge of a particular biological site or process at the molecular level. Such information has recently begun to emerge with the identification of specific targets for herbicide action in key metabolic pathways. Since they have no counterpart in mammalian physiology, photosynthesis and essential amino acid biosynthesis are obvious plant processes to be considered in seeking to design toxic molecules specific to plants.

Photosynthesis has been the most studied and best characterised of the possible plant specific metabolic pathways. In particular, those herbicides which operate by obstructing electron flow in the photosynthetic electron transport pathway at the photosystem II (PSII) level are characterised by low mammalian toxicity and few toxicological problems. However, the persistence of some of these compounds, notably atrazine, has led to the introduction of restrictions on their use. The molecular target of PSII herbicides is the D1 polypeptide, a well-characterised protein of molecular weight 32 kD, which is a component of the photosynthetic reaction centre in higher plants. The reaction centre from photosynthetic bacteria has been crystallised and the precise location of the herbicide binding site has been identified from X-ray crystallographic studies (1).

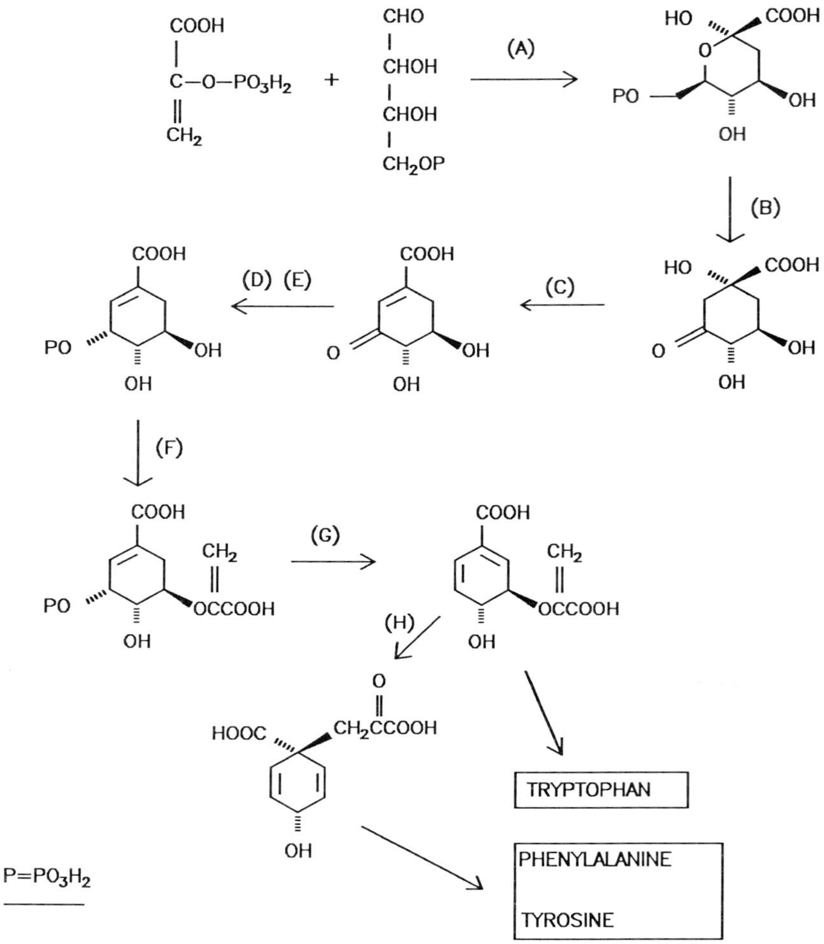

Scheme 1. Biosynthetic pathway to aromatic amino acids. (A): phospho-2-keto-3-deoxyheptonate aldolase; (B): dehydroquinate synthase; (C): 5-dehydroquinate dehydratase; (D): shikimate dehydrogenase; (E): shikimate kinase; (F): EPSP synthase; (G): chorismate synthetase; (H): chorismate mutase.

The possibility of tailoring molecules to fit this site has assumed feasibility, particularly with the increasing sophistication of computer-based molecular modelling techniques.

Whereas mammals and other higher organisms acquire essential amino acids from their diet, plants and microorganisms must synthesise them *de novo*. Accordingly, any interference with the biosynthesis of essential amino acids should lead to the cessation of plant growth but have little potential for mammalian toxicity. Interest in this general area of plant metabolism intensified with the identification of particular enzymes in the biochemical pathways to aromatic amino acids and branched chain amino acids as particularly effective targets for herbicide action. Efforts to maximise activity of known classes of compounds affecting essential amino acid biosynthesis, to identify new types of molecules affecting these pathways and to design inhibitors of the particular enzymes involved have dominated herbicide research in recent years. This paper will briefly review progress in this dynamic field and indicate the possible scope for the development of new herbicides flowing from the increased knowledge of the biochemistry and molecular biology of the enzyme reactions in these key metabolic pathways.

AROMATIC AMINO ACID BIOSYNTHESIS

The commercially important broad spectrum herbicide, glyphosate (I), inhibits 5-enolpyruvyl-shikimate-3-phosphate (EPSP) synthase (2), the sixth enzyme in the shikimic acid pathway to the aromatic amino acids, tryptophan, tryrosine and phenylalanine (F; Scheme 1). This enzyme catalyses the unusual transfer of a carboxyvinyl moiety from phosphoenol-pyruvate (PEP) to the 5-hydroxyl group of shikimate-3-phosphate. The herbicide acts by competing with PEP for binding at the active site (3). The mechanism of the enzyme reaction and its inhibition by glyphosate has been studied extensively but despite a voluminous literature, which includes DNA sequence determinations from numerous plant and microbial sources and details of the isolation of glyphosate-resistant mutants, the design of new inhibitors as potential herbicides has proved extraordinarily difficult. Indeed, glyphosate remains the only established compound exerting a herbicidal effect at this site.

However, a clearer understanding of the enzyme reaction is beginning to emerge, suggesting a more directed approach to inhibitor design. The recent work of Anderson and her colleagues provided elegant confirmation of the mechanism of the EPSP synthase transformation (4). They were able to isolate and identify a tetrahedral intermediate (II) formed by nucleophilic attack by the 5-OH of shikimate-3-phosphate on the 2-position of PEP. The two diastereoisomers of the phosphonate (III), a stable analogue of the tetrahedral intermediate (II), were synthesised by Bartlett and his coworkers (5). The R-isomer (III) is the most potent inhibitor of EPSP synthase yet reported, binding nearly 300 times more tightly than glyphosate. Significantly, the R-isomer binds two orders of magnitude more tightly than the S-isomer, suggesting that the side-chain of the intermediate (II) has the R configuration. No report has yet appeared concerning herbicidal properties associated with (II) or its derivatives. However, the success in designing highly potent inhibitors of a known herbicide target will undoubtedly give further impetus to research in this

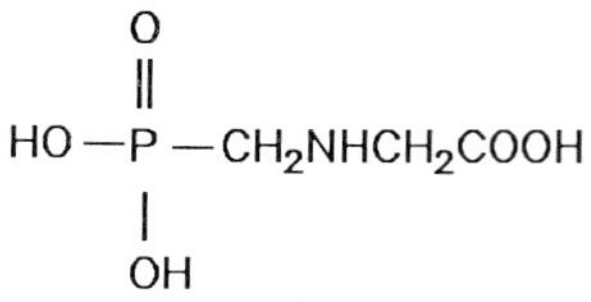

$$\text{HO}-\overset{\overset{\displaystyle O}{\|}}{\underset{\underset{\displaystyle OH}{|}}{P}}-CH_2NHCH_2COOH$$

I

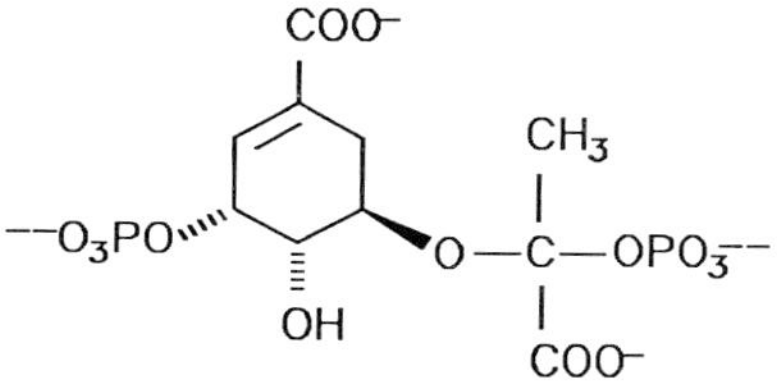

II

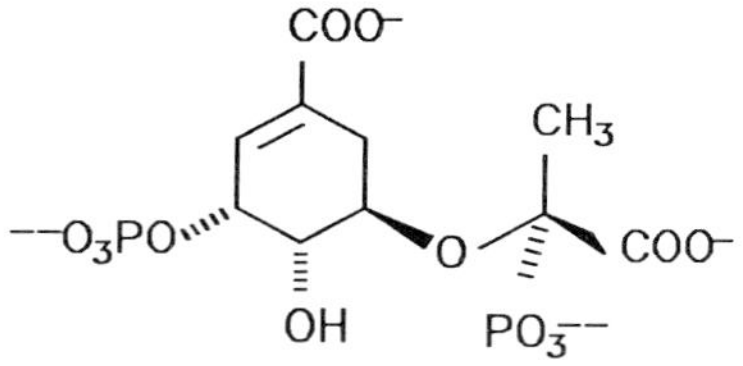

III

area. EPSP synthase has now been obtained crystalline (6) and X-ray crystallographic data should add a further dimension to the understanding of the nature and topography of the active site.

No other enzymes in the shikimic acid pathway to aromatic amino acids have been identified as specific herbicide targets. However, it has long been recognised that blocking a key enzyme in this pathway might produce a herbicidal effect. The first attempts by Baillie, Corbett and coworkers in 1972 to design inhibitors of shikimate dehydrogenase (D; Scheme 1) failed to produce compounds with significant herbicidal activity (7).

More recently, two further enzymes in the biosynthetic pathway have been investigated as possible herbicide targets. Dehydroquinate (DHQ) synthase, the second common enzyme in the sequence (B; Scheme 1), has been studied by Frost and his colleagues (8). They sought to design inhibitors of DHQ synthase isolated from both microbial and plant sources. The best inhibitor

(IV; Ki 0.8 M) was found to be competitive with the substrate *in vitro* and it was possible to demonstrate a buildup of substrate following a post-emergent application to whole plants (peas).

The design of a molecule which effectively mimics the structure of the transition state or a high-energy intermediate in an enzyme-catalysed transformation is considered a realistic approach to inhibitor design. Enzymatic rate acceleration is assumed to be due to enhanced binding of the transition state relative to the ground state. In this context, chorismate mutase (H; Scheme 1), which catalyses the rearrangement of chorismic acid to prephenic acid presents an attractive target. The reaction is unimolecular and is analogous to a Claisen rearrangement, a well understood transformation in solution chemistry. Indeed, detailed studies of the stereochemical course of the thermal rearrangement and the enzymic reaction suggested that similar transition state geometry was involved in each case (9). Bartlett and his colleagues (10) designed and synthesised potential inhibitors of chorismate mutase based on the assumption that the transition state resembles the bicyclic species (V). The endo epimer of the bicyclic diacid (VI) is the most potent inhibitor of chorismate mutase so far reported (Ki 0.12 M). This isomer is nearly three orders of magnitude more potent than the corresponding exo isomer, indicating a highly specific orientation of the bridge carboxyl function is demanded by the active site.

Finally, a recent report (11) describes the use of trypophan synthase, the final enzyme in the biosynthetic sequence leading to tryptophan, as a screening technique to identify leads to candidate herbicides. Some moderate *in vitro* activity was discovered but this did not necessarily translate to activity on whole plant systems.

BRANCHED CHAIN AMINO ACID BIOSYNTHESIS

The introduction of the sulfonylurea herbicides by DuPont in the early 1980s caused a changed perspective in the agrochemical industry. For the first time it was possible to consider weed control at levels of grams rather than kilograms per hectare. Although not without problems, particularly persistence causing toxicity to following crops, the sulfonylureas have become the industry standard for the low dose, low toxicity compounds demanded by current regulatory pressures.

The realisation that the sulfonylureas exerted their potent herbicidal effect by inhibiting aceto-hydroxy acid synthase (AHAS; also known as acetolactate synthase, ALS) led to an intensive investigation of the function and properties of this enzyme (12,13). AHAS is the first common enzyme in the biosynthesis of the branched chain amino acids, valine, leucine and isoleucine, and catalyses the condensation of two moles of pyruvate to form acetolactate or of pyruvate and 2-ketobutyrate to form acetohydroxybutyrate (A; Scheme 2). The enzyme is subject to feed-back inhibition by the amino acid end-products, probably at a site(s) remote from the functional active site.

This enzyme is now recognised as the primary target in plants and microorganisms of a number of chemically different herbicide classes, including the sulfonylureas (e.g.sulfometuron methyl VII), imidazolinones (e.g. imazapyr VIII) and triazolopyrimidine sulphonanilides (IX). Certain valine derivatives (X, XI) are also potent inhibitors of the enzyme, though the former compound is not herbicidal.

Sulfometuron methyl (VII) appears to be active site directed as the inhibitor competes for the second pyruvate binding site (14). However, the imidazolinones (VIII) and phthalyl valine anilide (X) are uncompetitive with respect to pyruvate (15,16). All three inhibitor classes are slow, tight binding inhibitors although the sulfonylureas are generally two orders of magnitude more active. Available evidence suggests that the different inhibitor classes do not share an identical binding site and it is possible that at least one inhibitor type (X) interacts with the site of natural feed-back regulation (17).

The enzyme itself is dependent on the cofactors magnesium ion, thiamine pyrophosphate and FAD. The absolute requirement of the enzyme for FAD has attracted considerable interest since there is no redox reaction involved in the enzymic transformation. Schloss and his coworkers (18) have speculated that the sulfonylurea binding site on AHAS is an evolutionary vestige of the ubiquinone binding site on pyruvate oxidase, which uses FAD for normal redox chemistry. This theory of a common evolutionary origin of the two enzymes is based on the close DNA sequence homology between the genes coding for pyruvate oxidase and AHAS from either bacterial or plant sources. Certainly, there is a striking parallel between the diversity of structures which inhibit AHAS and the many structurally dissimilar herbicides that inhibit PSII by binding to a plasto-quinone binding site. The apparent susceptibility of quinone binding sites to molecules of diverse chemical type has obvious implications for herbicide discovery. Both AHAS and PS II are particularly attractive targets for inclusion in any herbicide screening program.

The second enzyme in the pathway to branched chain amino acids, acetolactate reduc-toisomerase (B; Scheme 2) has also become an established herbicide target. The experimental compound, HOE 704 (XII), was found to have the same symtomology on intact plants as did herbicidal AHAS inhibitors (19). Lack of activity against AHAS and the observation that acetoin and acetolactate accumulated in plant tissue treated with (XII) led to the identification of acetolactate reductoisomerase as the primary target. HOE704 (XII) was found to be a slow binding inhibitor competitive with the substrate. Meanwhile, this enzyme was undergoing scrutiny as a possible candidate for inhibition by rationally designed site-directed inhibitors. Schloss and his coworkers (20) designed and synthesised molecules as analogues of a possible intermediate in the enzyme-catalysed reaction. The simple pyruvate derivative (XIII) was found to be a potent competitive inhibitor of the enzyme, more than two orders of magnitude more active than (XII).

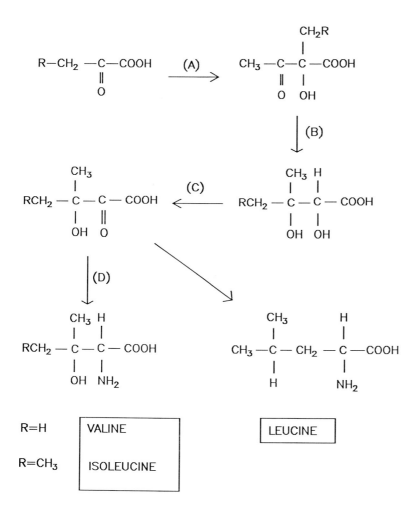

Scheme 2. Biosynthetic pathway to branched chain amino acids. (A): acetohydroxyacid synthase (AHAS); (B): acetolactate reductoisomerase; (C): dihydroxyacid dehydatase; (D): valine trans-aminase.

Compound (XIII) was also reported to be herbicidal, again with the same toxic symptoms as observed with the sulfonylureas.

The third enzyme in the branched chain amino acid biosynthetic pathway, dihydroxy acid dehydratase (C; Scheme 2) has been isolated and purified from bacteria and green plants (21). The purified enzyme was found to contain a Fe-S cluster, a structural feature probably directly involved in the catalytic functions of the enzyme. Attempts to design mechanism-based inhibitors of this enzyme have been made (22), though it has been suggested, on the basis of genetic evidence, that this enzyme may not be a potential herbicidal target (20).

CONCLUSION

Numerous enzymes in the biosynthetic pathways to essential amino acids have been studied as potential herbicide targets. Of these, only three have been established as leading to plant death when targetted by specific inhibitors. Moreover, AHAS is blocked by a range of diverse chemical types, discovered for the most part by extensive screening programs. What, then, are the prospects for the emergence of further specific inhibitors of enzymes in these pathways?

Certainly, the potential for new AHAS inhibitors is great, though the majority of such compounds will continue to arise from screening programs and analogue synthesis rather than approaches based on biochemical logic. The demonstration that inhibition of AHAS may lead to herbicides of remarkably low dose rates and hence minimal environmental intrusiveness will ensure that this enzyme will remain a principal focus of attention in the agrochemical industry. The possibility of a biorational approach to the design of AHAS inhibitors remains attractive, though an attempt to discover a herbicide by interfering with a specific biochemical feature of AHAS (feed-back regulation) resulted in potent inhibitors that were not herbicidal (17).

The concept of inhibitor design based on biochemical reasoning has yet to lead to a significant commercial product in the herbicide field. However, herbicidal activity has been demonstrated in a compound synthesised as a transition state analogue of the acetolactate reductoisomerase reaction (20). Potent inhibitors of enzymes in the aromatic amino acid biosynthetic pathway, particularly of EPSP synthase and chorismate mutase, have recently been reported (5,10), indicating an increasing sophistication in the understanding of the mechanisms of plant enzymes and in the design of specific inhibitors. It seems that these examples are only the beginning, as the enzymes involved in essential amino acid biosynthesis present some intriguing and stimulating challenges to those seeking to understand and exploit them as potential herbicide targets.

REFERENCES

1. Deisenhofer J, Epp O, Miki K, Huber R, and Michel H, (1985) Nature 318: 618

2. Steinrücken H, Amrhein N, (1980) Biochem. Biophys. Res. Comm. 94: 1207

3. Boocock M, Coggins J, (1983) FEBS Lett. 154: 127

4. Anderson K, Sikorski J, Benesi A, Johnson J, (1988) J. Am. Chem. Soc. 110: 6577

5. Alberg D, Bartlett P, (1989) J. Am. Chem. Soc. 111: 2337

6. Anderson K, Johnson K, Benesi A, Sikorski J, (1989) National Meeting, Dallas, Texas, April 9-14

7. Baillie A, Corbett J, Dowsett J, McCloskey P, (1972) Pestic. Sci. 3: 113

8. Myrvold S, Reimer L, Pompliano D, Frost J, (1989) ACS National Meeting, Dallas, Texas, April 9-14

9. Copley S, Knowles J, (1985) J. Am. Chem. Soc. 107: 5306

10. Bartlett P, Nakagawa Y, Johnson C, Reich S, Luis, A, (1988) J. Org. Chem. 53: 3195

11. Shuto A, Ohgai M, Eto M, (1989) J. Pesticide Sci. 14: 69

12. Ray T, (1984) Plant Physiol. 75: 827

13. LaRossa R, Schloss J, (1984) J. Biol. Chem. 259: 8753

14. Schloss J (1984): In Flavins and Flavoproteins (Bray, R., Engel, P. and Mayhew, S., Eds) de Gruyter, Berlin, p767.

15. Shaner D, Anderson P, Stidham M (1984) Plant Physiol. 76: 545

16. Huppatz J, Jenkins C, Hateley J, unpublished observations.

17. Huppatz J, Casida J, (1985) Z. Naturforsch. 40C: 652

18. Schloss J, Ciskanik L, and Van Dyk D, Nature (1988) 331: 360

19. Schulz A, Sponemann P, Kocher H, Wengenmayer F (1988) FEBS Lett. 238: 375

20. Schloss J, Aulabaugh A (1989) ACS National Meeting, Dallas, Texas, April 9-14

21. Flint D, Emptage M, (1988) J. Biol. Chem. 263: 3558

22. Pirrung M, Holmes C, Ha H, Nunn D, Horowitz D (1989) ACS National Meeting, Dallas, Texas, April 9-14

© 1990 Elsevier Science Publishers B.V. (Biomedical Division)
Pesticides and alternatives, editor J.E. Casida

USES AND MECHANISMS OF ACTION OF HERBICIDE SAFENERS: PROGRESS AND PROSPECTS

KRITON K. HATZIOS

Laboratory for Molecular Biology of Plant Stress, Department of Plant Pathology, Physiology and Weed Science, Virginia Polytechnic Institute and State University, Blacksburg, VA 24061-0330 (USA)

INTRODUCTION

Crop safety, circumvention of weed resistance, control of problem weeds, and adaptation to changing agronomic practices including crop rotations or double cropping systems, narrow crop row widths, and conservation tillage represent continuing challenges which must be addressed by weed scientists in the 1990s. Technological approaches allowing the improvement or expansion of the useful life of currently used, reliable herbicides serve as viable alternatives to the costly process of discovering, developing, and registering new herbicides. The development and commercialization of the concept of chemical crop safening against herbicide injury provides us with an attractive approach for achieving this goal.

Herbicide safeners are chemical substances that selectively protect crop plants against herbicide injury, without protecting any weeds. The benefits realized by the use of safeners are many (1). Safeners allow the use of increased rates of specific herbicides to obtain a wider spectrum and longer duration of weed control, including weeds that are closely related to the crop. In addition, safeners provide the farmer with greater flexibility in rotating his crops and allow the safe production of crops which are normally susceptible to soil-applied, persistent herbicides used in the previous growing season. At the manufacturer's level, safeners extend the life of reliable proprietary herbicides or expand their use into new markets. Effective combinations of safeners and cheap, reliable herbicides offer attractive alternatives to expensive new herbicides designed for the control of the same weed problems. At the researcher's level, safeners serve as useful probes for studying the regulation of plant metabolic processes involved in the action or detoxication of selected herbicides.

General and specific aspects of the chemistry, development, applications, and modes of action of herbicide safeners have been reviewed previously by a number of investigators in varying levels of detail (2-7). The purpose of this chapter is to review briefly the current progress and future prospects of the uses and mechanisms of action of herbicide safeners.

CHEMICAL MANIPULATION OF CROP TOLERANCE TO HERBICIDES: EVOLUTION OF APPROACHES

The initial phase in the exploitation of the concept of chemical safening against herbicide injury revolved around the use of activated charcoal or other adsorbents, which act as physical barriers minimizing the contact of crops with nonselective herbicides (8). The difficulty in maintaining the adsorbent barrier around the growing plant and the high cost of this type of protection have been cited as major reasons for the limited practical success of activated charcoal as a crop protectant for herbicides (9).

Structural modification of the basic chemistry of a herbicidal class may be considered as a second approach in the evolution of chemical concepts for manipulating the tolerance of crop plants to herbicides. Modification of the chemistry of a parent herbicide may influence the mobility, absorption, and selective properties of the original compound without major alterations in the spectrum of its herbicidal activity. An example of this approach is provided by the continuous optimization of the chemistry of the sulfonylurea herbicides which has resulted in the development of compounds with good selectivity for several major crops such as winter cereals (chlorsulfuron), corn (MX6316), soybeans (chlorimuron), and rice (bensulfuron) (10).

Differences in the ability of crop and weed plants in biotransforming "proherbicides" to active compounds has also been used for improving the crop selectivity of certain herbicides. Successful proherbicides such as 2,4-DB and isomethiozin are used selectively because they are metabolized to their respective active herbicides, 2,4-D and metribuzin, only in susceptible plants (11). Rubin and Kirino[12] demonstrated that this concept can be also exploited for the development of selective "prosafeners." N-phenylmaleimides and N-isomaleimides behaved as prosafeners being hydrolyzed rapidly to their respective N-phenylmaleamic acids, which are the actual safeners protecting grain sorghum against the herbicide alachlor.

The next phase in the development of chemical approaches for enhancing the crop tolerance to herbicides was marked by the discovery of auxiliary chemicals which act inside the protected plant and regulate selected biochemical functions involved either in the action or the detoxication of given herbicides. Although this concept appeared simple its evolution to an acceptable agricultural practice entailed a time span of 21 years and was mainly due to the vision and pioneering efforts of Otto Hoffman[13]. Herbicide safeners discovered and developed during this period enjoyed greater success than activated charcoal because they act selectively protecting only the desired crop and not any target weeds and offer protection for the desired length of time. Almost all of the currently marketed crop safeners for herbicides were developed by random screening and subsequent chemical optimization (3, 9, 13).

COMMERCIAL USES OF HERBICIDE SAFENERS

By necessity, search for safeners has concentrated on the most significant crop/weed/herbicide combinations (9, 13, 14). As of today, the range of crops protected by chemical safeners against herbicide injury is rather limited. Practical success has been achieved primarily with large-seeded grass crops such as maize (Zea mays L.), grain sorghum [Sorghum bicolor (L.) Moench] and rice (Oryza sativa L.) and soil-applied, shoot-absorbed herbicides such as the carbamothioates and chloroacetanilides (3, 6). The interactions of broad-leaved crops with chemical safeners against herbicide injury have not been very promising (1). In addition, attempts to develop chemical safeners for the protection of any crop from injury caused by photosynthesis-inhibiting herbicides or broad spectrum weed killers such as paraquat and glyphosate have been mainly unsuccessful.

Commercialized safeners are members of diverse chemical groups including naphthopyranones such as naphtahlic anhydride (NA, naphthalene-1,8-dicarboxylic acid anhydride); dichloroacetamides such as dichlormid (2,2-dichloro-N,N-dipropenylacetamide), BAS 145138 {1-dichloroacetyl-hexahydro-3,3-8α-trimethyl-pyrrolo-[1,2-α]-pyrimidin-6-(2H)-one}, and CGA-154281 [4-(dichloroacetyl)-3,4-dihydro-3-methyl-2H-1,4-benzoxazine]; dichloromethyldioxolans such as MG-191 (2-dichloromethyl-2-methyl-1,3-dioxolane); oxime ether derivatives such as cyometrinil {(Z)-α[(cyanomethoxy)imino]-benzeneacetonitrile}, oxabetrinil [α-(1,3-dioxolan-2-yl-methoxy)-imino-benzeneacetonitrile], and CGA-133205 {O-[1,3-dioxolan-2-yl-methyl]-2,2,2-trifluoro-4"-chloroacetophenone-oxime}; substituted thiazole carboxylates such as flurazole [phenylmethyl 2-chloro-4-trifluoromethyl)-5-thiazole-carboxylate]; and substituted phenylpyrimidines such as fenclorim (4,6-dichloro-2-phenyl-pyrimidine).

Safeners are applied either to the crop seed prior to planting ("seed safeners") or to the soil when used as additives in the formulation of the respective herbicide. Dressing of crop seeds with safeners is conducted at the manufacturer's or distributor's level and provides the ultimate in safener selectivity. Safeners formulated as prepackaged mixtures with the herbicide exhibit a high degree of specificity for the desirable crop and they do not protect any target weeds. The safener-to-herbicide ratio in such formulations ranges from 1:6 to 1:30 (1).

Dichlormid and other dichloroacetamides (BAS-145138, CGA-154281, and MG-191) have been the most successful commercialized safeners of maize against injury caused by carbamothioate (EPTC, butylate, vernolate) and chloroacetanilide (metolachlor, metazachlor) herbicides (1). Naphthalic anhydride (NA), the first commercially developed safener of maize against carbamothioate herbicides is not marketed today. However, NA is still quite useful for identifying potential

crop-herbicide-safener combinations (1, 6). Oxime ethers and flurazole are currently marketed as successful safeners of grain sorghum against injury caused by
the chloroacetanilide herbicides alachlor and metolachlor (1). Fenclorim pro-
tects rice against injury caused by the chloroacetanilide herbicide pretilach-
lor. The dichloroacetamide safeners of maize and fenclorim are applied primarily as prepackaged formulated mixtures with the respective herbicides. The
safeners of grain sorghum, however, are applied exclusively as seed dressings
(1).

More recently, acceptable protection of maize and other grass crops against
injury caused by several diverse groups of herbicides including the sulfonylureas, imidazolinones, aryloxyphenoxypropionates, cyclohexanediones, and isoxazolidinones has been demonstrated (1, 15). Other grass crops such as oats (Avena
sativa L.), wheat (Triticum aestivum L.) and barley (Hordeum vulgare L.) can be
also safened against injury caused by soil-applied herbicides. Nevertheless,
none of these successful combinations has been exploited commercially.

MECHANISMS OF ACTION OF HERBICIDE SAFENERS

Published information on the potential mechanisms of action of herbicide
safeners is getting more and more voluminous each year (4). In spite of that,
total agreement on how safeners work to protect crops against herbicide injury
has not been accomplished (16).

At the biochemical level, the two most prevalent of the proposed mechanisms
suggest that safeners act either by enhancing herbicide detoxication in protected plants (17) or by counteracting herbicide effects on a common target site
(18). The view that safeners may act by more than one mechanism has also been
proposed (19). The "gene activation" theory, which has been implicated in the
action of natural or synthetic plant hormones (20), appears promising for
explaining the protective action of safeners at the molecular level (21).

Enhancement of Herbicide Detoxication by Safeners

As mentioned earlier, commercialized safeners exhibit a high degree of botanical specificity by protecting only large-seeded grass crops. In addition, it has long been known that protected grass crops are moderately tolerant to the antagonized herbicides and capable of detoxifying them by specific metabolic reactions (16). Therefore, it is not surprising that the great majority of the accumulated evidence favors the view that most, if not all, of the currently used safeners act mainly by enhancing the rate of the metabolic detoxication of selected herbicides. A safener-induced enhancement of herbicide detoxication in protected plants is the major mechanism by which safeners may exclude the herbicide from reaching its target site in an active form (16).

Safeners may enhance herbicide metabolism in protected plants by inducing either the levels of specific co-factors such as reduced glutathione (GSH) or the activity of key metabolic enzymes involved in herbicide biotransformations such as glutathione-S-transferases (GSTs) or oxidative enzymes such as mixed-function oxidases (MFOs) (16). A safener-induced enhancement of GSH levels correlates rather poorly with their ability to ameliorate herbicidal effects on grass crops (22). In contrast, the ability of safeners to enhance GST activity seems to correlate rather strongly with the degree of protection they offer to grass crops against chloroacetanilide and carbamothioate herbicide injury (22, 23). Maize and other plants contain multiple forms of GST enzymes which exhibit a high degree of substrate specificity (24). Apart from enhancing the activity of constitutively present GST isozymes (GST I and GST III), the safener flurazole has been shown also to induce the de novo synthesis of a novel GST isozyme (GST II) which is more active in conjugating chloroacetanilide herbicides with GSH (23). At the molecular level, flurazole increased by 3- to 4-fold the levels of mRNA coding for the GST I gene of maize (21). In addition, some safeners have been shown to react with reduced glutathione and form GS-safener conjugates (25). The effects of selected safeners on GSH levels and glutathione-dependent enzymes are summarized in Table I.

TABLE I

EFFECTS OF HERBICIDE SAFENERS ON GLUTATHIONE LEVELS AND THE ACTIVITY OF

GLUTATHIONE-DEPENDENT ENZYMES*

Safener	Plant	GSH	GR	GST
NA	Maize	No effect	N.D.	Increased
	Sorghum	No effect	N.D.	Increased
Dichlormid	Maize	Increased	Increased	Increased
	Sorghum	Increased	N.D.	Increased
Oxabetrinil	Sorghum	Increased	Increased	Increased
Flurazole	Maize	Increased	N.D.	Increased
	Sorghum	Increased	N.D.	Increased
Fenclorim	Rice	N.D.	N.D.	Increased

* Compiled from information presented by Komives and Dutka[26] and Yenne and Hatzios[28].

Indirect studies employing the use of selected inhibitors of MFO enzymes have shown that a safener-induced enhancement of oxidative enzymes is very possible (2). However, detailed information on the interactions of safeners with plant MFO enzymes is limited because of the inherent difficulty in isolating, characterizing and assaying such enzymes extracted from plants (26).

Many safeners resemble structurally their respective herbicides (27, 28). Currently it is believed that the chemically similar and less phytotoxic molecules of safeners induce the levels of substrates as well as the activity of metabolic enzymes needed for the metabolism of safeners and antidoted herbicides in safened plants (7).

Interactions of Herbicides and Safeners at a Target Site

When it is not possible to exclude the herbicide from reaching its site of action, safeners could act by competing with the herbicide at its target site

(16). The lack of evidence for a specific mode of action or the involvement of a single target site affected by carbamothioate and chloroacetanilide herbicides has been greatly responsible for our poor understanding of the interactions of herbicides and safeners at a common site. Since many of the metabolic processes affected by carbamothioate and chloroacetanilide herbicides are dependent on acetyl-CoA intermediates, it has been proposed that the action of these herbicides is related to some aspect of acetyl-CoA metabolism (29). The results of recent studies by Wilkinson[30] and Yenne and Hatzios[31] indicate that chloroacetanilide herbicides and their safeners may be affecting the formation of acetyl-CoA rather than the incorporation of acetyl-CoA into fatty acids or other lipids of grain sorghum seedlings.

The safening of grass crops from the phytotoxic effects of chemically diverse groups of herbicides such as the carbamothioates, chloroacetanildies, sulfonylureas, imidazolinones, isoxazolidinones, aryloxyphenoxypropionates, and cyclohexanediones does not favor the "antagonist" theory of safener action. Many of the currently available safeners did not antagonize sufficiently the effects of specific herbicides on important target enzymes such as acetohydroacid synthase (AHAS, EC 4.1.3.18) and acetyl-CoA carboxylase (ACCase, EC 6.4.1.2) (15, 32). In addition, the "antagonist" theory for the action of safeners is disputed by the low safener-to-herbicide ratios used in many of the successful safener/herbicide combinations. Such ratios range from 1:6 to 1:30 and show that it will be unlikely for a safener to reach a target site at high enough concentrations to effectively antagonize the action of the herbicide.

FUTURE PROSPECTS

Future crop safeners for herbicides are likely to be developed by a rational design driven by a combination of biotechnology and chemistry principles rather than by the current dominant process of empirical chemical synthesis coupled with biological screening. Molecular modeling of substrates, analogs, antagonists, and metabolites of current herbicides as well as compounds of novel structure coupled with continuous advances in our understanding of the biochemical and molecular aspects of safener and herbicide action is expected to be very useful for discovering and developing the safeners of the future. Chemical alteration of the target site of action of specific herbicides may also become more feasible.

Genetically engineered microorganisms could be also used as safeners for specific herbicides in the future. Microbial safeners may result from the exploitation of the herbicide degradative potential of soil bacteria and fungi which colonize the roots of desirable crops (33).

A better understanding of the mechanisms of action of current safeners and herbicides should enable more positive attempts toward increasing the number of situations in which crop safeners for herbicides could be used. Future investigations on the mechanisms of safener action should be extended to the molecular level. Specific questions that need to be answered by future research in this area included: Do all safeners act by the same mechanism? If safeners act by more than one mechanism what determines the sequence of steps or events involved in the safener action and what triggers the function of a particular mechanism? Do all safeners affect gene expression in plants? Do some safeners act by mimicking the effects of endogenous plant hormones in protecting grass crops from herbicides? Do all safeners conjugate with GSH in the protected grass crops? How stable are the safener-GS conjugates? What is the sensitivity of GST enzymes to stimulation, inhibition, or feedback regulation by the safener-GS-conjugates? Are oxidative enzymes such as MFOs induced by safeners?

The scientific interest in the concept of chemical manipulation of crop tolerance to herbicides coupled with its practical and economic importance is expected to continue providing the needed impetus for future research and developments in the field of herbicide safeners. It is hoped that other substances or approaches will be developed to provide protection to a broader range of crops against a wider spectrum of herbicides including the photosynthetic inhibitors.

582

REFERENCES

1. Hatzios KK (1989). In: Hatzios KK, Hoagland RE (eds) Crop Safeners for Herbicides: Development, Uses, and Mechanisms of Action. Academic Press,
   San Diego, pp 3-45

2. Fedtke C, Trebst A (1987) In: Greenhalgh R., Roberts TR (eds) Pesticide
   Science and Biotechnology. Blackwell, Oxford, pp 161-168

3. Hatzios KK (1983) Adv Agron 36:265-316

4. Hatzios KK, Hoagland RE (1989) Crop Safeners for Herbicides: Development,
   Uses, and Mechanisms of Action. Academic Press, San Diego.

5. Pallos FM, Casida JE (1978) Chemistry and Action of Herbicide Antidotes.
   Academic Press, New York.

6. Parker C (1983) Pest Sci 14:40-48

7. Stephenson GR, Ezra G (1987) Weed Sci 35(Suppl. 1):24-27

8. Hoagland RE (1989) In: Hatzios KK, Hoagland RE (eds) Crop Safeners for Herbicides: Development, Uses, and Mechanisms of Action. Academic Press, San
   Diego, pp 243-281

9. Gray RA, Green LL, Hoch PE, Pallos FM (1982) Proc Brit Crop Prot Conf-
   Weeds 2:431-437

10. Beyer EM, Duffy MJ, Hay JV, Schlueter DD (1988) In: Kearny PC, Kaufman DD
    (eds) Herbicides: Chemistry, Degradation, and Mode of Action. Dekker, New
    York, pp 117-189

11. Fedtke C (1982) Biochemistry and Physiology of Herbicide Action. Sprin-
    ger-Verlag, Berlin and New York

12. Rubin B, Kirino O (1989) In: Hatzios KK, Hoagland RE (eds) Crop Safeners
    for Herbicides: Development, Uses, and Mechanisms of Action. Academic
    Press, San Diego, pp 317-336

13. Hoffman OL (1978) In: Pallos FM, Casida JE (eds) Chemistry and Action of
    Herbicide Antidotes. Academic Press, New York, pp 1-13

14. Peek JW, Dill TR, Turner WE (1981) Proc. Annu. Corn Sorghum Res. Conf
    29:31-47

15. Barrett M (1989) In: Hatzios KK, Hoagland RE (eds) Crop Safeners for Herbicides: Development, Uses, and Mechanisms of Action. Academic Press, San Diego, pp 195-220

16. Hatzios KK (1989) In: Hatzios KK, Hoagland RE (eds) Crop Safeners for Herbicides: Development, Uses, and Mechanisms of Action. Academic Press, San Diego, pp 65-102

17. Lay MM, Casida JE (1978) In: Pallos FM, Casida JE (eds) Chemistry and Action of Herbicide Antidotes. Academic Press, New York, pp 151-160

18. Stephenson GR, Chang FY (1978) In: Pallos FM, Casida JE (eds) Chemistry and Action of Herbicide Antidotes. Academic Press, New York, pp 35-61

19. Ezra G, Flowers HM, Gressel J (1983) In: Miyamoto J, Keraney PC (eds) Pesticide Chemistry: Human Welfare and the Environment. Pergamon Press, Oxford, Vol. 3, pp 225-231

20. Theologis A (1986) Annu Rev Plant Physiol 37:407-438

21. Wiegand RC, Shah DM, Mozer TJ, Harding EI, Diaz-Collier J, Sounders C, Jaworski EG, Tiemeier DC (1986) Plant Mol Biol 7:235-243

22. Gronwald JW (1989) In: Hatzios KK, Hoagland RE (eds) Crop Safeners for Herbicides: Development, Uses, and Mechanisms of Action. Academic Press, San Diego, pp 103-128

23. Mozer TJ, Tiemeier DC, Jaworski EG (1983) Biochemistry 22:1068-1072

24. Timmerman KP (1989) Physiol Plant (In press).

25. Breaux EJ, Hoobler MA, Patanella JE, Leyes GA (1989) In: Hatzios KK, Hoagland RE (eds) Crop Safeners for Herbicides: Development, Uses, and Mechanisms of Action. Academic Press, San Diego, pp 163-175

26. Komives T, Dutka F (1989) In: Hatzios KK, Hoagland RE (eds) Crop Safeners for Herbicides: Development, Uses, and Mechanisms of Action. Academic Press, San Diego, pp 129-145

27. Stephenson GR, Bunce JJ, Makowski RI, Curry JC (1978) J Agric Food Chem 26:137-140

28. Yenne SP, Hatzios KK (1989) Z Naturforsch (submitted)

584

29. Fuerst EP (1987) Weed Technol 1:270-277

30. Wilkinson RE (1988) Pestic Biochem Physiol 32:25-37

31. Yenne SP, Hatzios KK, Meredith SA (1989) J Agric Food Chem (Submitted)

32. Yenne SP, Hatzios KK (1989) Pestic Biochem Physiol (In press).

33. Karns JS (1989) In: Hatzios KK, Hoagland RE (eds) Crop Safeners for Herbicides: Development, Uses, and Mechanisms of Action. Academic Press, San Diego, pp 337-351

Index of Authors

586